TEXAS

To Magdalena Hernández de la Teja and Paula Eyrich Tyler, for their love and support
and
To Anna Beth Mitchell, always ready for an historical adventure and a proofreading job.

TEXAS
Crossroads of North America

Jesús F. de la Teja
Texas State University–San Marcos

Paula Marks
St. Edward's University

Ron Tyler
The University of Texas at Austin

WADSWORTH
CENGAGE Learning™

Australia • Brazil • Japan • Korea • Mexico • Singapore • Spain • United Kingdom • United States

WADSWORTH
CENGAGE Learning

Texas: Crossroads of North America

Jesús F. de la Teja, Paula Marks, and Ron Tyler

Editor-in-Chief: Jean L. Woy

Sponsoring Editor: Jeffrey Greene

Associate Project Editor: Shelley Dickerson

Senior Marketing Manager: Sandra McGuire

Senior Manufacturing Coordinator: Priscilla J. Bailey

Cover image: Florence E. McClung, Squaw Creek Valley, 1937, oil on canvas, 24 1/8 x 30 1/8in. (61.29 x 76.53 cm), Dallas Museum of Art, gift of Florence E. McClung.

Acknowledgment Poem on pages 54–55: Robert S. Weddle, *Wilderness Manhunt: The Spanish Search for La Salle* (Austin: University of Texas Press, 1974; Revised Edition, College Station, TX, 1999). Reprinted by permission of the author.

For product information and technology assistance, contact us at **Cengage Learning Customer & Sales Support, 1-800-354-9706**

For permission to use material from this text or product, submit all requests online at **www.cengage.com/permissions**
Further permissions questions can be emailed to **permissionrequest@cengage.com**

Library of Congress Control Number: 2001133306

ISBN-13: 978-0-618-07361-0

ISBN-10: 0-618-07361-2

Wadsworth
10 Davis Drive
Belmont, CA 94002
USA

Cengage Learning is a leading provider of customized learning solutions with office locations around the globe, including Singapore, the United Kingdom, Australia, Mexico, Brazil, and Japan. Locate your local office at **www.cengage.com/global**

Cengage Learning products are represented in Canada by Nelson Education, Ltd.

To learn more about Wadsworth, visit **www.cengage.com/wadsworth**

Purchase any of our products at your local college store or at our preferred online store **www.ichapters.com**

Printed in the United States of America
3 4 5 6 7   16 15 14 13 12

FD020

Contents

9 | Secession, War, and Their Aftermath, 1860–1876   253

PART III TEXAS REDEFINED   287

10 | Toward Modernization, 1876–1898   290

11 | The Early Twentieth Century: One Party, Half a Dozen Fights, 1900–1929   323

Preface

The idea for this textbook arose out of the authors' experience as consultants for the Bob Bullock Texas State History Museum in Austin. In struggling to present the entire scope of the Texas experience within the limited confines of three floors of approximately 34,000 square feet of exhibit space, we were forced to hone the messages we wanted visitors to gain during their visit. The more we thought about the contexts that could only be hinted at in the museum, the more attractive the idea of a Texas history survey became to us. We wanted to tell a balanced story that would appeal to an increasingly diverse twenty-first-century Texas audience.

Themes

In *Texas: Crossroads of North America,* we tell the story of this region as a dynamic process, beginning with the ways in which people—natives, adventurers, government representatives, immigrants, and residents—perceived the opportunities offered on this Indian, Spanish, Mexican, and Anglo frontier, in this republic and state. That suggests one of our first major themes—that Texas was a crossroads of intersecting geographies and cultures. People pursued these opportunities both as individuals and groups, first in the land itself, then through more complex ways of achieving social, economic, and political independence and power, which reflects our second major theme of opportunity. They found often formidable challenges, in part by coming into contact with representatives of other cultural and ethnic groups with different perspectives and agendas. As certain groups gained power—including the power to define "Texas" and "Texans" in their way—their definitions were repeatedly challenged by the vastness and energetic diversity of the state and its population, which suggests our third major theme of Texas as a "cultural centrifuge." In this geographic and cultural mix, myth and reality have combined to make and keep Texas a distinctive place.

Approach

This is a distinctly modern history of Texas. We tell the story that constitutes one of the most dramatic and colorful histories of any state in the nation, but we try to make sense of that legacy and show how it relates to present-day Texans and those to come. We haven't lost the focus on our Hispanic, African American, or German heritage, or on the brave soldiers who participated in the Texas Revolution, the war with Mexico, the Civil War, World Wars I and II, and more recent conflicts, but we also show the many contributions of Mexican Americans, African Americans, and women to the struggle for civil rights that continues as society becomes ever more mindful of inequities in opportunity. We haven't forgotten the accomplishments of Cabeza de Vaca, Stephen F. Austin, Sam Houston, James Stephen Hogg, Lyndon B. Johnson, or the presidents Bush, but we have also told the stories of Fray Isidro Espinosa, Rosa María Hinojosa de Ballí, Ignacio Pérez, Oveta Culp Hobby, Barbara Jordan, and Michael Dell. We recognize the enduring contributions of the Texas Rangers, one of the most storied law enforcement organizations in the country, but we also tell the story of the brave citizens who helped reform the Rangers and restore them as a useful state agency when others would have disbanded them.

Texas: Crossroads of North America tells the story of the people who lived within the state's borders before there was any idea of Texas or when Texas was defined in very different terms than it is today. Our text recognizes that the building blocks of today's Lone Star State have been in the making for not hundreds, but for thousands and even millions of years. Instead of a static presentation of the state's geography, this book offers a dynamic introduction to Texas as a place by emphasizing the interrelationship between people and nature as soon as people arrived. It makes clear for students how the American Indians who settled the land adapted to it and, when possible, altered it to better suit their needs. The extensive survey of the cultural diversity of the native peoples of Texas, relying on recent archeological findings and newer interpretations of the ethnographic evidence, constitutes one of the stronger features of our text.

Just as *Texas: Crossroads of North America* pays greater attention to the native American background, it also gives greater emphasis to the story of Spain in Texas. The recent discovery and recovery of one of La Salle's ships, the *Belle,* from the bottom of Matagorda Bay has rekindled interest in the formative period of the state's history. Yet, La Salle's misadventure and the attendant efforts by Spain to retain control of this back door to its silver colony to the south cannot be understood without consideration of why Spain had neglected the lands north of the Rio Grande for so long. By examining the expeditions of Cabeza de Vaca, Coronado, and De Soto in greater detail, and by stressing the settlement of far West Texas in the seventeenth century, this text lays a strong foundation for understanding Spanish actions in the eighteenth and early nineteenth centuries.

Past historiographical trends have dwelt on judging the Spanish Texas experience in terms of success or failure and in isolation from events elsewhere. This book takes a different approach. By emphasizing how Spanish colonials made lives for themselves on a harsh and remote frontier, it stresses that even under such adverse conditions, early Tejanos found opportunities and a sense of belonging. The diversity of the Spanish colonial experience in what is now Texas takes us from El Paso to Padre Island and from Nacogdoches to Laredo, a sweep of space and time that the authors believe can only be done justice by devoting three complete chapters to it.

The authors feel strongly that in laying this more complete foundation of early Texas history students will better understand and appreciate the advent and process of Anglo American colonization. We strive to show more fully how this colonization occurred within the context of the new Mexican nation and of local Mexican frontier governing structures, and what opportunities and challenges it posed for the existing Mexican population of Texas. This foundation helps us make more sense of the cultural context in which our Mexican American population is more fully appreciated as part of the Texas experience.

We devote a full chapter to the Texas Revolution. In part because of its strength as a "creation myth" for Texas, it remains the most dramatically engaging point of entry into the state's modern history and a cornerstone of a distinctly Texan identity for many readers. We think it important to illuminate the confusion and complexity of the struggle, to get beyond simplistic and ethnocentric understandings, to see the revolution as an event within Mexico itself, with a varied and sometimes conflicted cast of characters.

In the Republic era, we point up the political and economic fragility of the fledgling nation, and the uncertainty of opportunity, particularly for increasingly marginalized groups. In the early statehood era, we trace Texas's increasing identification as a southern state, and therefore one willing to throw away its hardwon annexation to join the Confederacy.

We try to provide a broad and varied picture of Texas and Texans during the Civil War, including those Texans who resisted identification with the Southern cause. Our emphasis in Reconstruction is on laying out clearly the various policies and requirements of the federal government, how Texans responded, and how and why the state reverted to conservative Democratic policies as soon as possible, undercutting any hoped-for gains by African Americans.

While Texas was still largely an agricultural state in 1900, we point out in Chapter 10 that in addition to being among the most productive agriculturally, these years also witnessed the beginnings of industrialization. The huge growth in population, the spread of railroads throughout the state, the fluctuations of the cotton market, and the discovery of oil at Spindletop in 1901, particularly as the state was coming increasingly under one-party rule, as described in Chapter 11, stressed its abilities to deal with economic and cultural problems. The economic structure, based on one-crop agriculture, began to falter in the aftermath of World War I and would have collapsed under the weight of the Great Depression of the 1930s, had not the federal government come to the rescue, as described in Chapter 12. And the cultural superstructure did collapse in the face of civil rights challenges by women, Mexican Americans, and African Americans, and we have not yet finished its reconstruction.

The increasingly significant role that the federal government played in the state's development is also an issue that began as soon as federal troops replaced the Texas Rangers as the region's major defenders and has only grown more important today. World War II, in particular, spurred development in Texas, with the completion of the "Big Inch" and "Little Inch" pipelines and the construction of the world's largest petrochemical complex along the Gulf coast. Federal government expenditures in

Texas, which today dwarf the state's own budget, suggest its huge role in the state, and the state's significant role in the federal government. The impact of all these factors is seen in Chapter 13, as the Democratic Party, for decades the only relevant forum for discussion of the state's problems and goals, begins to split between its liberal and conservative branches in the face of increasing problems of taxation, civil rights, education, water, and the many other problems associated with continued growth—not to mention the growing, highly successful Republican challenge.

Recent history can easily descend into a general recitation of diverse events and developments. In dealing with the end of the twentieth century, we have identified three significant themes: the ways in which Texas exhibits old identities and new in both politics and economics; the challenges of governing a state experiencing uneven growth and opportunity; and awareness of environmental issues, particularly in regard to water needs and availability.

Throughout this work, we have tried to engage where possible with individual stories, with the ways in which people have responded to the opportunities and challenges they found in Texas, and how these responses have led to the geographic, cultural, political, and economic landscape we have today. As a result, *Texas: Crossroads of North America* is as much a history of Texans as it is of Texas.

Teaching Aids

A printed test bank prepared by James Wilson contains multiple-choice and essay questions. These questions are also available in a computerized test bank for both Windows and Macintosh computers.

Acknowledgments

For *Texas: Crossroads of North America* to become more than rumination we needed to find a sympathetic ear. Jeff Greene at Houghton Mifflin was kind enough to hear us out. For his encouragement and patience our deep thanks. Originally, there were four of us, and we owe thanks to Doug Barnett who, although he could not collaborate on the textbook, was generous with his time, ideas, and perspective.

In writing this book the authors benefited from discussing subject matter or having chapters read by a number of knowledgeable individuals. Among those with whom we consulted are William H. Goetzmann, Creekmore Fath, and Will Wilson, Sr., and we also wish to thank Robert Utley, Randolph B. Campbell, Patrick Cox, and William H. Goetzmann for reading portions of the text. In addition, we thank the following colleagues for their invaluable suggestions: Dallas Cothrum, University of Texas at Tyler; David Cullen, Collin County Community College; Ricky Floyd Dobbs, Texas A&M University; Juanita E. Garza, The University of Texas–Pan American; L. Patrick Hughes, Austin Community College;

Jorge Iber, Texas Tech University; Charles H. Martin, University of Texas at El Paso; Kent McGaughey, Houston Community College; Nora E. McMillan, San Antonio College; Ray Stephens, University of North Texas; Brenda Taylor, Texas Wesleyan University; and Marcus S. Turner, San Jacinto College.

Jesús F. de la Teja
Paula Marks
Ron Tyler

I

UNDEFINED TEXAS

It was not a destination for the European adventurers who traipsed across the southern half of North America in the early sixteenth century. It was not a final destination for hunter-gatherer bands who followed the buffalo, the seasons, and the spirits throughout central North America in the same era. It was not a recognizable political unit, even for the widely dispersed and varied native peoples who made it their home then. It would be hundreds of years before Texas resembled the place we recognize today as the second largest state in the Union. For three centuries conflict, competition, and cooperation among Euro-Americans and Indians continually reshaped and redefined Texas.

The history of Texas—that is, the story that can be told from documents—begins during the age of the conquistadors. What brought the first Spaniards to Texas from the 1520s to the 1540s were the same motives that led them to explore from the Oregon coast to Tierra del Fuego: the search for fabulous treasures to plunder and civilizations to conquer and put to work. A century later other Spaniards, religious missionaries, began to explore the region with a much different purpose: the search for souls to save. These early settlers faced many obstacles: great distances between settlements, a difficult climate, and Indian resistance. Only at the turn of the eighteenth century did a motive strong enough to overcome these obstacles arise: stopping the encroachment into the region of French rivals.

Geopolitical motives rarely stir the movement of large numbers of people. And so it was that throughout the eighteenth century Mexico's far northeastern frontier, from the Rio Grande to the Red River, inspired the imaginations of very few colonial settlers. Ranching proved marginally lucrative to some, but military service or subsistence farming fed the majority of people. Missionaries worked with a variety of Indian groups, sometimes with success, sometimes with disastrous consequences, to create a Hispanic population that could hold Texas for Spain. Such was the Spanish way. The Indian was not an enemy of civilization, but rather a potential subject of both majesties (God and king). In the end, the population of Spanish Texas resembled that of much of the rest of the empire—Catholic, mixed-blood, agricultural and pastoral, poor, self-reliant—but in this case, small and isolated.

Relatively few thought of themselves as "Tejanos" (Hispanic residents of Texas). For all practical purposes Texas began at the San Antonio River (where San Antonio anchored settlement to the west and La Bahía anchored settlement to the east) and stretched all the way beyond the Sabine River into what is today western Louisiana. The ranching communities that occupied the lower Rio Grande valley were part of Nuevo Santander. The people who lived in these settlements traded with Texas, but typically thought of themselves in terms of the community in which they had citizenship: Camargo, Mier, Reynosa, Revilla, or Laredo. Least Texan of all were the residents of the Paso del Norte area, what is today El Paso-Juárez. Living on both sides of the river, these people descended from the sixteenth-century settlers of New Mexico, from some of the Pueblo groups that had allied themselves with the Spanish, and from other Spanish colonials who found the area perfect for cultivating the vine and raising livestock. There is no record of Paso del Norte ever having direct contact with Texas during the colonial period.

It took events far beyond the control of the people living north of the Rio Grande at the start of the nineteenth century to alter and expand the definition of Texas. The Louisiana Purchase, the Mexican War of Independence, and the consequent political upheavals and new migration patterns brought new and very different people into the region: Euro-Americans, African Americans, and Indians. Texas became contested ground as the newcomers saw opportunities west of the Sabine—rich cotton bottomlands, vast and fecund hunting grounds, proximity to Mexico's silver mining centers. That Texas had no large and prosperous cities, no grand cathedrals or imposing public monuments, no well-developed roads or ports, helped foster the impression that it was a wilderness ready to be tamed. Neither the millennia of Indian habitation nor a century of Spanish settlement could be easily wiped away, however. And, without understanding that history—the contest over what Texas should be and to whom it should belong—we cannot understand who Texans are today.   ■ ■ ■

1

Land and Life

In the opening scene of the 1963 movie "The Wheeler Deal-ers," wildcatter Henry Tyroon and his crew stand in a dusty valley by a drilling rig on the verge of blowing in. As his accountant reminds him of unpaid debts and vanishing lines of credit, the wildcatter crosses his fingers and gives the signal for the crew to clear the borehole. The earth groans and snorts and finally, with a mighty heave, coughs up a dust ball. Played for comedic effect, the scene depicts the true-life experiences of countless prospectors for black gold who have traipsed across Texas for more than a century. Many struck water or dust, but some struck vast pools of oil, eons in the making. The state's first people—the Indians—were familiar with naturally occurring petroleum deposits, which they used to waterproof and decorate pottery, as in colonial times Spanish sailors used beach tar to caulk their ships. It was not until the early twentieth century that the true potential of "Texas tea" was recognized, however. Today the search for oil and natural gas is a much more scientific endeavor, reflected in the petroleum engineering programs of Texas's premier universities. Yet, it remains a cat-and-mouse game between Earth and its most ambitious parasite—humanity. Petroleum prospecting is an activity rooted in the study of the state's natural history—a history going back countless ages, to times in which dense fern forests teeming with reptilian life and vast shallow seas nursing expanses of reefs planted the biological seeds for the mineral riches that have become such an important part of the Texas identity today.

CHAPTER 1	Land and Life
1 BILLION YEARS AGO	Granite domes of Hill Country form
570–245 MILLION YEARS AGO	Oil, coal, and gas fields of West Texas form
245–66 MILLION YEARS AGO	Salt domes, oil and gas fields of East Texas form
65–2 MILLION YEARS AGO	Gulf of Mexico begins to emerge; West Texas mountain ranges form; oil and gas fields of southeast and lower gulf coast form
2.4 MILLION–15,000 YEARS AGO	Palo Duro canyon cut, Padre Island and other barrier islands begin to form
9,200–6,000 B.C.E.	Arrival and spread of Paleo-Indian hunter-gatherers
6,000 B.C.E.–500 C.E.	Archaic period cultures—increased cultural specialization by region
500–700 C.E.	Agriculture, pottery making, bow and arrow spread
800–1800 C.E.	Caddos are dominant East Texas culture; Karankawa and Coahuiltecan cultures dominant in coastal and South Texas
1200–1500 C.E.	Antelope Creek people flourish on plains; Jornada Mogollón culture flourishes in Trans-Pecos
CA. 1500 C.E.	Arrival of Proto-Apaches on southern plains

When humans first set foot on what is now Texas soil, the natural history of the region was already hundreds of millions of years in the making. Understanding the processes that shaped the landscapes and environments of Texas seems the best place to begin the story of the Lone Star State. As large as a continent, Texas contains all of the major land forms and most climatic environments to be found in the western hemisphere, making it a natural crossroads of North America.

Humans adapted to life in these varied ecological zones, from the semitropical riverine environment of South Texas to the humid pine forests of East Texas to the short grass plains of the Panhandle. For 10,000 years the first Texans hunted, fished, farmed, and made war in what became a crossroads of native cultures. When Europeans finally arrived on the scene, what they perceived as a wilderness was in reality the home of well-adapted and widely diverse cultures. They brought with them, however, the seeds of radical change, physical and cultural, that eventually would make Texas a crossroads of empires.

Before the First Humans in Texas

A little over a billion years ago, give or take a hundred million years, in the last quarter of the Precambrian era, what is now North America collided with another continental plate. As in an automobile accident, some parts went flying, others crumpled, and still others were completely consumed by the collision. Mother Nature cleared the wreckage over the next few hundred million years— mountains flattened out through erosion, sediment covered depressions—but today we can still see the effects of that earth-shattering event. In Llano County, at Enchanted Rock State Park, for example, a granite dome sticks up out of the countryside, a beautiful reminder of the intense heat and pressures created by that long-ago collision that also brought granite near the surface as far east as Marble Falls. Texas underwent numerous cycles of uplifting and submergence, cooling and heating, wetness and drying out, and countless species of animals and plants arose and vanished before humans arrived to claim the land for themselves a mere 12,000 years ago.

The Early Natural History of Texas

Plate tectonics separated North America from that other continent beginning about 600 million years go, only to smash all the continents together into the supercontinent of Pangaea about 300 million years later. Not surprisingly, another mountain range, the Ouachita Range, rose along the arc of the collision. Today this range lies buried in Texas, except near Marathon, but remains exposed in Oklahoma and Arkansas. Once again erosion began wearing down the newly created peaks and the waters, streams, and seas began filling in the low places. An important difference this time, however, was that now the surface of the earth teemed with life. Among the materials that filled in the cracks and smoothed out the rough places were the remains of primitive trees, ferns, and, later on, a wide variety of simple sea creatures whose shells made up the first reefs.

These and many similar events, which geologists group into a large block of time called the Paleozoic era, transpired between 570 and 245 million years ago. Compressed and left to stew under mounting layers of sediment, the organic remains of these long-lost worlds eventually decayed into the vast oil, coal, and gas fields of West Texas. The shells of sea creatures became limestone deposits, and the evaporation of shallow seas deposited gypsum and salt beds. Along with granite and other hard stones of the Precambrian era, which adorn the state capitol and other public buildings in Texas and around the world, the mineral wealth of the Paleozoic era constitutes a significant bounty to the state.

If the earlier two eras left Texas an ample store of natural resources, the next two would be even more generous. The Mesozoic era, which began about 245 million years ago and ended about 66 million years ago, is often referred to as the Age of Dinosaurs. A wide variety of ecosystems flourished during this long period of time. As Pangaea broke up, creating the Atlantic Ocean and Gulf of Mexico, a great inland sea stretching from Canada to Mexico advanced and then retreated through Texas, splitting the region in two for millions of years. The geological changes took place during the period in which North America drifted north, moving the Texas region from the equator at the beginning of the Mesozoic era past 30° north latitude by the end of the era.

Dense conifer and fern forests covered the uplands in the Triassic period, the first part of the Mesozoic era, when evolution brought forth the first dinosaurs and the first mammals. It was a reptilian world, however. Along the banks of streams crocodile-like giants waited for prey to come within easy reach, while lizards and turtles hunted insects. Sharks and bony fish crowded the waters, both fresh and salt. Lost in this busy world were the earliest Texas dinosaurs, relatively small creatures that represented the two main branches of the dinosaur family and first appeared about 220 million years ago.

Texas in the Age of Dinosaurs

Texas has proven to be no Jurassic Park, however. When this second part of the Mesozoic era began about 208 million years ago the dinosaurs were on the rise and the breakup of Pangaea was underway. By the end of the period, about 144 million years ago, most of Texas was submerged in a shallow sea that covered everything east of a line from Big Bend to Wichita Falls. The shallow Gulf of Mexico often evaporated, laying down huge blankets of salt that would eventually play a major role in creating pockets of oil and gas throughout coastal Texas. Unfortunately, the rock layers that chronicle the Jurassic period are so deeply buried beneath younger rocks in Texas that it has been impossible to understand the fauna and flora of the region during those exciting times.

Texas continued its northward movement during the Cretaceous period, at the end of the Mesozoic era, as the sea that covered the eastern two-thirds of the

At Dinosaur Valley State Park, southwest of the Dallas-Fort Worth metroplex, visitors can follow the footprints of king lizards across streambeds and take in exhibits of fossil bones that have kept paleontologists busy for centuries. *(Photo courtesy Texas Parks & Wildlife © 2003, Glen Mills)*

state began to recede. New layers of sediment buried the reefs to create layers of limestone, sandstone, and shale formations. These heavy rock formations put pressure on the underlying salt layer, squeezing and compacting it until salt bubbles formed—what we refer to today as *salt domes.* The weight of the sediment layers also pressed the vegetable and animal matter within them to extract new concentrations of oil and gas that collected in pockets adjoining the salt domes. Millions of years later, the most famous of these, at Spindletop, hurled Texas headlong into the twentieth century.

During the late Cretaceous period, between about 80 and 66 million years ago, as Texas slowly resurfaced from yet another round of submergence, the great Age of Dinosaurs neared its end. Texas was a land of giants at that time, however, home to the Alamosaurus, the last of the giant herbivores. In the Trans-Pecos region roamed the fearsome Tyrannosaurus rex and the largest of all flying reptiles, *Quetzalcoatlus northropi,* which had a wingspan of over forty feet. Mammals, including the ancestral horse, remained tiny creatures forced to live on the margins of Cretaceous life. And by this time the air no longer belonged to tiny insects and giant pteradons alone, as birds had put in an appearance.

Yet ominous changes were underway. The fossil record shows that the ecosystems of ancient Texas were under stress. Then, one day, between the Mesozoic and Cenozoic eras, about 65 million years ago, the last of the major collisions that shaped our environment occurred. Hurtling out of deep space at 50,000 miles per hour and measuring six to seven miles in diameter, a meteorite smashed into the northern part of what is today the Yucatán peninsula in Mexico. The first shock of the impact caused an earthquake of worldwide proportions and the dispersion of a huge volume of water that tore up the sea floor, leveled hills, and killed everything in its path for thousands of miles in the direction of Texas. Then the long-term effects set in. The sky, already filled with dust and chemicals from hundreds of active volcanoes around the globe, darkened even more with the vaporized remains of the meteorite and the soils and rocks of the impact crater. Species perished as the plants they fed on died, or the animals on which they depended ceased to exist.

The Physical Development of Modern Texas

The impact of the meteor may not have been the single cause of the extinction of the dinosaurs, but it is a convenient reference point to mark their passing. It is also a convenient reference point to mark the rise of mammals and the birth of modern geological Texas. No more would the state be swamped by ocean waters. Instead, the rivers that would come to be known as the Trinity, Brazos, and Colorado, along with a number of smaller streams, would deposit sediment to fill in more and more of the Gulf of Mexico. It would be many more millions of years before Texas would take on its modern form, but the process was underway.

The Cenozoic era, the geological era that began about 66 million years ago, is still in progress, for in geological terms the modern age is part of this most recent period of Earth's history. To the east Texas continued its expansion into the Gulf

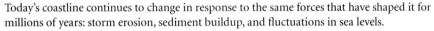

Today's coastline continues to change in response to the same forces that have shaped it for millions of years: storm erosion, sediment buildup, and fluctuations in sea levels.

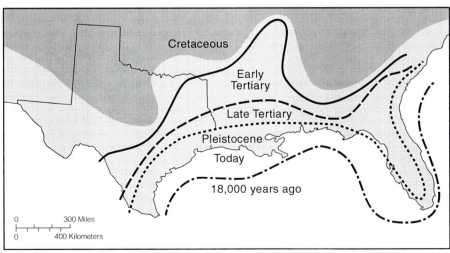

of Mexico for 64 million years, especially late in this period, which is known as the Tertiary period, when the expanding polar ice caps trapped tremendous amounts of water, causing sea levels to drop by hundreds of feet.

While the foundations of the modern gulf coast were being laid down, much was also happening in the western parts of the state. In what is now the Trans-Pecos, tensions from the last period of Rocky Mountains uplifting led to extensive volcanic activity that created the Davis and Chisos mountain ranges and other Big Bend peaks, while to the northeast the Rockies deposited sediments in the Panhandle to form the rock formations now known as the Ogallala Aquifer. Faulting between the coastal and inland formations helped produce the picturesque Balcones Escarpment.

The earth's progressive cooling during the Tertiary period contributed to change in North America's flora and fauna, with a significant impact on Texas. Evergreen tropical forests gave way to deciduous woods, which were better able to tolerate the seasonal climate that settled over North America at this time. Among the successor species were members of the walnut family, which includes the pecan tree, the state tree of Texas. Grasses also arrived on the scene during this period, contributing to the transformation of the Texas landscape. Wetter conditions in the eastern parts of the state produced lush vegetation that, in the recurring cycle of life, death, burial, and compression, produced the sandstone oil and gas fields of southeast Texas and the lower gulf coast.

Hard as it is to imagine, the exotic wildlife parks that now dot the state offer a glimpse into the variety of animal life present during the Miocene period of the Cenozoic era, between 24 and 5 million years ago. There were mastodons, rhinoceroses, camels, cheetahs, and sabre-tooth cats. Instead of zebra, there were pronghorn and as many as twelve species of horses. But most of these species died out during a great drying-out period between 5 and 2.4 million years ago. The drying of the land turned lush grasslands into the prairies known today as the Great Plains, and the western alpine forests and eastern deciduous forests were permanently separated.

The Ice Age, which lasted from about 2.4 million to 10,000 years ago, brought about the final major changes to the North American landscape, both topographical and biological, that created present-day Texas. Erosion did its job on West Texas, producing the magnificent Palo Duro Canyon and the impressive Caprock Escarpment. The state's major streams moved the eroded sediments eastward from the western formations down to the gulf coast, where they continued to add to the Texas landmass—that is, until the glaciers began to melt about 15,000 years ago. Then, sea levels began to rise rapidly, flooding the lower courses of most Texas streams to create the distinctive shallow bays and estuaries of the Texas coast. The silt and sand that continued to flow southeastward now formed barrier islands such as Galveston and Padre Island, which have proven so valuable to students seeking a respite from the arduousness of college coursework each spring.

Life in Texas was also seriously affected by the Ice Age. Mastodons and mammoths, camels, and horses all died out completely, although the latter two species, having crossed westward along the Beringian land bridge, successfully adapted to the Eurasian environment. The long-horned bison (ancestor of the American buffalo), which had crossed the land bridge eastward some 400,000 years ago, also died out by the end of the Pleistocene epoch, as this period is known to geologists. Most species of cat predators also disappeared, the mountain lion and jaguar remaining as the dominant representatives of the group in the Lone Star State. Modern bears also survived.

By the time the first Texans arrived, approximately 11,000 years ago, the land looked very much as it does today, as nature had rearranged the flora. The warming climate sent the conifer and juniper forests of West Texas back up the mountain slopes from which they had descended during the Ice Age, and grasslands returned with a vengeance to the West Texas plains. Piñon pines and junipers (Texas cedar) disappeared from the canyons of the Rio Grande and Pecos River and tributaries as this part of the state became increasingly arid. They were replaced with desert plants such as cacti and sotol. In the central Texas Hill Country, scrub oaks took the place of piñon pines next to junipers, while east of the Balcones Escarpment the older deciduous species of the Ice Age were replaced with warmer weather varieties, such as walnuts and pecans, oaks and elms. Also on the scene were loblolly pines, which although not yet dominant, made up an increasing proportion of East Texas woods. The drying of the climate also played a major hand in the retreat of South Texas scrub oaks to protected and moist areas, allowing for the spread of cacti and mesquite throughout the flat and under-watered region.

Although no Garden of Eden, the land that we call Texas today had much to offer: abundant woods and water, fertile soils and mineral wealth, and ample herds and flocks. Not surprisingly, the first Texans quickly moved to occupy just about every ecological niche the land had to offer. The human story of Texas was about to begin.

The First Texans

Armed with spears tipped with artfully crafted stone points and traveling in extended family groups, the first people to call what is now Texas home walked into the state about 11,000 years ago, toward the end of what scientists refer to as the Pleistocene epoch. These earliest arrivals, descendants of the great game hunters who had crossed Beringia from Asia to North America at least a thousand years earlier, soon spread out through the state. They became the base population for some (but not all) of the cultures found in Texas when Europeans first arrived in the early sixteenth century. The story of the first Texans is shrouded in the mysteries of stone tools, scarred animal bones, geometrically decorated rocks, the remains of cooking pits, and several human burial grounds. Yet archeologists, with the assistance of other scientists, have begun putting more and more clues together, allowing us to understand the dawn of Texas history in ever greater detail.

Big Game Hunters Populate the Land

There is disagreement among archeologists regarding the prehistory of Texas. Radiocarbon dating, site and artifact interpretation, and differences in methodological approaches all conspire to prevent the development of a single narrative framework for the story. Where the divisions between the Paleo-Indian, Archaic, and Late Prehistoric periods should come remains unsettled. When did the first humans arrive in Texas? Did early cultures succeed each other or did they overlap? Are the Archaic-period Indians the direct descendants of the Paleo-Indians, or were they new arrivals who occupied a land from which the earliest peoples had disappeared? Did Paleo-Indians hunt in groups or as individuals? How much and exactly what plants did they gather compared to their Archaic successors? We do know enough to tell the basic story of the original settlement of Texas, a story as full of danger, adventure, and adaptation as any from the days of Spanish explorers or Anglo American frontiersmen.

Having retreated northward during a long dry spell that broke about 12,000 years ago, the grasslands of the southern plains spread southward as far as the Rio Grande country below the Pecos River and into central Texas. Herds of mammoths, grazers stressed by the previous drought conditions, followed the expanding grasslands to find a last refuge from extinction in the well-watered meadows of southwest Texas. In their wake came the Clovis people. Not any specific tribe or clan that we can identify, for the archeological record has not clearly revealed the community size of these large-game hunters, the Clovis people made use of a lethal projectile point known by the place it was first discovered: Clovis, New Mexico.

Soon the Clovis hunters spread throughout the region, as far away as East Texas. Although they preferred to use rock shelters near springs and permanent streams, they also camped at convenient locations to carry out hunting and gathering activities that constituted a more than adequate subsistence economy. Most important, they adapted to the varieties of Texas environments that they found. Where mammoths were scarce they turned to the last remaining populations of elephant, camel, horse, and giant bison for meat. Their gathering techniques were amply rewarded by an environment rich in plant foods and smaller game.

Hunting was the principal livelihood for these first Texans, and they were efficient and resourceful killers. Given the size of their prey, Clovis hunters took special care to select the finest flints from which to make their lethal projectile points. Around cooking pits and campfires in the days and weeks preceding a communal hunt, a group's hunters sat exchanging stories and ideas and meticulously working flint cobbles collected at sites such as what is now Alibates Flint Quarries National Monument in the Texas Panhandle. Also prepared at this time were the *atlatls,* or spear throwers, hinged wooden launchers which held the stone-tipped spear and which lent both accuracy and velocity to a throw. Finally, when all was ready, the group would venture near the herd, where the Clovis hunters' strategy was to go after the matriarch or the weakened or wounded peripheral animals. When the object of the hunt was a large mammal such as a bison or camel, they scraped and dressed the hide for use as clothing, packaging, or sometimes even tent material.

The extinction of the mammoth, a gradual drying of the climate, and the spread of a new projectile form found at bison kill sites, marks the transition to the Folsom culture about 10,800 years ago. Facing a somewhat smaller, although equally dangerous prey, Folsom hunters relied on smaller, fluted projectile points, even more graceful and delicate in design than those of the Clovis, although just as deadly. At Bonfire Shelter near Langtry in Val Verde County—a butchering site since Clovis days—a particularly resourceful group of Folsom hunters drove groups of giant bison over the edge of a bluff to their deaths, dragging selected carcasses into the shelter for butchering. In other parts of the state, where no bison were to be found, or where other game animals made easier targets, campsites have been found containing stone tools and bones of some of the last remaining camels, horses, and sloths.

Just how long the good life lasted for these and other Paleo-Indian groups in Texas is not clear. A younger hunting culture, called Plainview, also relied on the longhorn bison. Their plain-sided projectile points, however, indicate a crisis in the large-game-hunting way of life. Also at this time the other remaining megafauna died out, bringing the Pleistocene epoch to an end about 10,000 years ago, and with it the Folsom and Plainview cultures that had relied on them.

The Paleo-Indian descendants of the Clovis, Folsom, and Plainview peoples of Texas had to rely on smaller game animals and, increasingly, on gathering practices that made greater use of plants. Between about 10,000 and 8,000 years ago communities of early Texans experimented with new projectile forms, none as artful and complex as the Clovis and Folsom points of the past, but all capable of bringing down the large game animals of that time: bison, deer, and antelope. A community of Golondrina culture hunter-gatherers of about 9,000 years ago hunted rabbits, rodents, and snake, and gathered walnuts, pecans, and other edible plants. Other Paleo-Indian communities also made use of fish and shellfish.

For centuries Texas provided well for Paleo-Indians. Hunting was good, water was plentiful, and bountiful crops of useful plants provided whatever they might need, even as the climate became drier and warmer. Around the campfires there was leisure time, evidenced by the production of stones with geometric designs and the presence of shells, ochre, and decorative stones, canine tooth necklaces, and bone needles. The careful burials of a young female at Leander, near Austin, and two males near Lake Whitney, along the banks of the Brazos River, suggest that Paleo-Indians also gave thought to the vastness of the universe and the possibility of a hereafter.

Diversifying Ways of Life

Greater experimentation with tool forms, particularly projectile points, and increasing reliance on more varied foodstuffs denote the arrival of a new age in

Texas, one marked by greater cultural diversity in response to environmental changes. By 8,000 years ago the environment of Texas had assumed its modern form: hot and dry summers and cool-to-moderate winters, depending on the region. The eastern forests had retreated beyond the Trinity River, where the loblolly pine established itself as a dominant species. Elsewhere, along the state's major rivers and creeks, walnuts and pecans continued to flourish, while the western conifers, which had descended the West Texas mountain slopes during the last centuries of the Pleistocene epoch, again retreated to their alpine homes. Water became a somewhat scarce and less reliable resource, particularly in South Texas, where mesquite and other brush plants proliferated, and in the western Rio Grande country, where agave, sotol, and other desert plants began to flourish. The migratory buffalo herds of the Great Plains dominated much of western Texas, while antelope and mule deer were the only other remaining large herbivores. Bears, wolves, mountain lions, ocelots, and jaguars competed with humans as predatory mammals, while eagles and hawks did so from the air. With the disappearance of the North American ice sheet, migratory birds proliferated, making Texas the winter home of ever greater numbers of geese, ducks, and cranes.

Following these environmental changes, by 8,000 years ago the human landscape of Texas had also changed. For the next 7,000 years Texas was home to an increasing number of more regionalized hunting and gathering cultures; this period was known as the Archaic period. Population growth fostered both trade and territoriality, evidence for both of which can be found in Archaic period cemeteries such as the Ernest Witte site near the Brazos River in Austin County. At Ernest Witte, archeologists found stone artifacts from as far away as the Ouachita Mountains of Arkansas and projectile points embedded in the bones of five skeletons. Other sites contain additional evidence of the increased use of plant foods and fish and shellfish.

As the small bands of hunters who had previously roamed over large areas of Texas in pursuit of large game began to rely more on locally available resources, they made the transition from Paleo-Indian to Early Archaic ways of life. They still launched their darts, generally small points made from locally available stone, from atlatls, but now they aimed them at smaller mammals. They probably worked on developing new methods of catching animals to eat, such as traps and nets. These early Texans also probably spent a substantial amount of time experimenting with new ways of preparing the plant foods that now made up a greater share of their diet.

Successful adaptation to the Texas environment created a population boom beginning about 4,500 years ago. Over the next 1,500 years Texas hunter-gatherers became so adept at exploiting the environment that territoriality emerged as a cultural characteristic. Some groups occupied coastal bays and estuaries; other groups claimed more arid, but still fertile, environmental niches in western and southwestern Texas. From the Panhandle to central Texas some cultures maintained an ancestral connection to the bison, whereas farther south, along the middle stretches of the Rio Grande, resourceful desert dwellers relied on smaller game and a wide variety of plants. Fish and shellfish furnished a plentiful food supply to coastal groups for a large part of the year. For the remainder of the year, these groups also lived off the small game and various plants available on the coastal prairies.

These hunter-gatherer groups adapted so successfully to their local environments that the temporary rock shelters and stream-side camps they had established in the past became more permanent camps. A sense of home is evident among Archaic peoples in their treatment of the dead, their evolving aesthetic, and the diversity of their material goods. Well-defined cemeteries were established in which men, women, and children found a final resting place close to their band's favorite site. These sites cannot be considered villages in the modern sense, for the hunter-gatherer bands needed to move, at least seasonally, to ensure adequate food sources. Within their well-established ranges, which would also have included mineral and flint deposits, campsites were used over numerous generations and provided the groups with a sense of identity.

Seasonally occupied village sites at rock shelters became canvases for the group's imagination. Archaic artists decorated their dwellings with imaginative representations of the natural and supernatural world around them. Much as modern graffiti artists express their relationship to a place by elaborate decoration

Rock shelters such as Fate Bell at Seminole Canyon State Historical Park, near the confluence of the Rio Grande and Pecos River, served as housing for early Texans. Paintings on the shelters' walls have survived thousands of years of weathering to remind us of our kinship with the Paleo-Indians, who dreamed of great hunts and spiritual journeys. *(Photo courtesy Texas Parks & Wildlife © 2003, TPWD)*

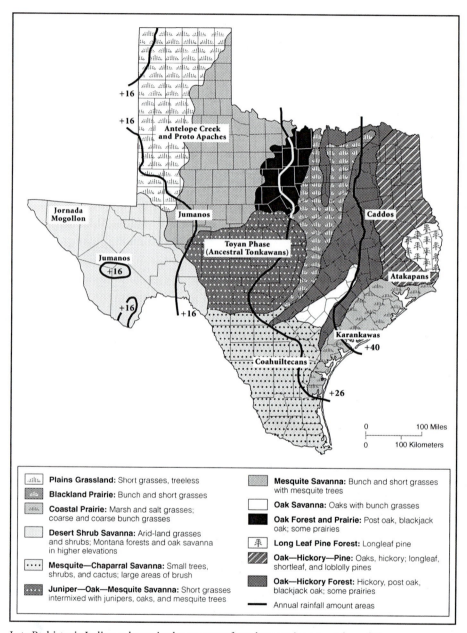

Late Prehistoric Indian cultures in the context of modern environmental conditions.

with spray paint, or urban gangs "tag" the boundaries of their turfs, Archaic rock artists transformed anonymous caves and megaliths into a band's possessions. Each succeeding generation reinforced the group's association with a place by adding to the earlier artwork, creating a historical record the meaning of which is lost to us today.

Elaborate burials attest to the increasing value placed on status and material possessions. The presence of stones from as far away as the Ouachita Mountains of Arkansas is evidence that territoriality had fostered the development of long-distance trade, another sign of increased materialism. Shell ornaments, chert knives, and even deer skulls in some graves may have been intended to introduce the departed as an important individual in the afterlife. Dart points embedded in the bones of some corpses bespeak the darker side of increased contact between groups—violent competition for land and resources.

The last centuries of the Archaic period also mark the end of a purely hunter-gatherer Texas. Far to the south, in today's central and southern Mexico, human cultural evolution had followed a similar track until about 6,000 years ago, when people started planting the seeds of various plants whose wild relatives they had been gathering for generations. By about 5,500 years ago, early gardeners had transformed the wild *teosinte* into domesticated corn, and soon this most versatile grain had begun to spread in all directions. Farming eventually produced sedentary populations of considerable size, with increasingly sophisticated cultures. In time their technologies spread northward into the American Southwest, where they had an impact on the cultural development of Texas. Between 1,500 and 1,300 years ago, three important technologies—agriculture, pottery making, and the bow and arrow—all arrived in the Lone Star State, contributing to the cultural landscape that Europeans discovered when they arrived in the early sixteenth century.

The Agricultural Revolution Arrives

The colonization of Texas by frontier agriculturalists was neither an Anglo-American accomplishment of the early nineteenth century, nor a Spanish colonial achievement of the early eighteenth century. By the time the Spanish arrived in Texas, farmers had been raising corn, squash, beans, and sunflowers for about 1,000 years. Representing two very different cultural traditions, the Desert and Mississippian agriculturalists of far West and East Texas tie the state to cultural developments in adjoining parts of North America. They are important elements in the ever diversifying cultural landscape of Late Prehistoric Texas.

Desert Farmers of West Texas

Along the course of the Rio Grande, from El Paso to Presidio, and northeastward as far as Midland, the native people of West Texas began combining some gardening with their hunting and gathering ways at the latest by 500 C.E. For hundreds of years various hunter-gatherer groups experimented with gardens of corn, squash, beans, and local plants, while still relying on foraging and hunting for their basic subsistence needs. Influenced by the Mogollón culture of southern Arizona and New Mexico, these part-time farmers built pit houses next to their fields of corn and beans. As soon as the harvest was in, however, it was off to hunt and gather in order to meet the rest of the year's subsistence needs. Seasonally occupied villages thus became a common settlement pattern for hundreds of years.

Even in the best of times, farming was a challenge in this perennially arid region. There is no evidence that the Jornada Mogollón people ever attempted irrigation agriculture on a sizable scale, as the Hohokam did in Arizona, but they did divert runoff. By placing their fields at the foot of a mountain, the Jornada Mogollón could tap spring rain runoff to give their crops a chance. Nevertheless, this was a hit-and-miss proposition, and many farming and village sites had to be abandoned after a year or two, when they were unable to support group needs.

At a select few sites, conditions were right for long-term settlement. As the pit-house dwellers succeeded in raising surpluses of corn and beans, they began to construct simple adobe pueblos, usually consisting of a number of apartments arranged in a row and containing a large room thought to be a ceremonial or communal space. Builders often plastered the floors of their pueblos and built a variety of outbuildings and cooking pits. Even in pueblo times the Jornada Mogollón did not entirely abandon their traveling ways. In some villages, including Firecracker Pueblo (so named for an abandoned fireworks stand across the road from the site north of El Paso), they scooped out storage pits in which to keep corn and other food supplies during their absences.

Increasing dependence on corn made the Jornada Mogollón people focus increasingly on agriculture and support activities. They had to make *manos* and *metates* (hand stones and grinding slabs) and transport them to the village from wherever the stone deposits were, sometimes a considerable distance away. They had to make pottery on a regular basis, given its fragility, for storage, cooking, and eating purposes. Utilitarian as the pots, bowls, pitchers, and ladles they made were, the human need for artistic expression found its way into animal motifs and geometric designs that have acquired the designation "El Paso polychrome style."

The Jornada Mogollón people were more gatherers than hunters, even in their pre-pueblo days, but animal protein, leather, bone, and sinew were essential products that could only be obtained through the hunt. Whereas rabbits, rodents, birds, and snakes provided everyday meals, deer, antelope, and bison supplied not only the village table, but its workshops as well. Killed, skinned, and butchered in the field, the animals' hide, meat, and useful bones were brought back to the village for processing. Because the Jornada Mogollón people used stone tools, they were forced to spend a considerable amount of time preparing arrow tips, dart points, scrapers, knives, and hammers from stones that sometimes came from hundreds of miles away.

And travel, whether to hunt, gather, or procure stone for tools, brought the Jornada Mogollón into contact with neighboring groups and cultures. Sometimes they brought back a pot or bowl from one of the western Mogollón or Hohokam villages, or from an Anasazi pueblo. From exchanges with other hunting parties, they obtained obsidian, turquoise, and even seashell beads. Although more important symbolically than economically, these interactions provided the

Jornada Mogollón with vital links to the technological and cultural trends of the region.

By the early fourteenth century, the peoples of the Trans-Pecos were entering a period of crisis. So successful during earlier (and wetter) times in establishing a corn-farming subsistence base for themselves, they had outstripped their capacity to survive prolonged drought and underproduction. This was not unique to the Jornada Mogollón, for the Hohokam, Anasazi, and western Mogollón were suffering from the same combination of environmental and demographic factors. Drought conditions emptied reservoirs and meant that not enough runoff came down mountain slopes to allow the large pueblos to survive. Dispersing in their efforts to survive, some of the Jornada Mogollón moved north into the Rio Grande valley of central New Mexico to join Anasazi migrants from the northwest. Other Jornada Mogollón groups entirely abandoned agriculture and returned to a hunter-gatherer way of life, especially the easternmost groups, which had easy access to migratory buffalo herds on the southern Plains.

By the time they arrived in the region, sixteenth-century Spaniards identified various Indian groups inhabiting the lower parts of the southern Plains and parts of the Trans-Pecos as Jumanos. Although they described some of these groups as purely bison-hunting societies, they described others as floodplain agriculturalists. At least some of these groups were undoubtedly the descendants of the Jornada Mogollón culture, some of whom had clung to their semisedentary agricultural ways and others of whom had become important traders across Texas. Slowly over the next two centuries, the Jumanos disappeared from the scene, some incorporated into other regional culture groups and others absorbed into northern Mexican colonial society.

Mound-Building Farmers of Southeast Texas

As late as the last decades of the seventeenth century Jumano traders were crossing the great expanse of Texas to trade with agricultural peoples, the Caddoans, who inhabited the eastern fringes of the Great Plains and the river valleys of the Mississippi basin. Some of these Caddoans lived as far west as the Trinity River and represented an even more successful Texas agricultural tradition than the Jornada Mogollón. By the time the Spanish arrived, their colonization of East Texas extended back about a thousand years, and they would continue to be an important factor in Spanish colonial Texas history up to the eve of Mexican independence.

About 500 C.E., when Caddoan groups began their southwestward migration into what is today East Texas, that part of the state was home to descendants of Paleo-Indian and Archaic-period cultures. Some of these groups, having traded with both Plains hunters to the west and agriculturalists to the east, had established substantial societies in which gardening had become a minor element of their subsistence strategy. Their settlements consisted of seasonally occupied villages of modest numbers of people. These Late Archaic people were certainly in no position to stop the Caddoan migration that swept westward over the next few centuries.

The Caddoans who moved into Texas were themselves descendants of a series of increasingly sophisticated cultures that had flourished in the Mississippi basin for hundreds of years before the Caddo emerged as a distinct society about 800 C.E. The Adena and Hopewell cultures, which flourished in the Midwest between 2,800 and 1,600 years ago were ancestors of all of the later "mound builder" societies of North America. These societies were characterized by sophisticated agricultural practices, the development of copper working, and the burial of prominent people in increasingly larger mounds. During Hopewell times, long-distance trade and a population boom led to the establishment of a hierarchical society and tribute system that extended for hundreds of miles along the basins of the Mississippi and its eastern tributaries.

Competition for resources and other undetermined factors contributed to the decline of Hopewell culture by about 400 C.E., yet its accomplishments were not forgotten. Even as Hopewell was in decline, however, a similar culture was emerging in the same area of the central Mississippi Valley. Some 1,700 years ago the Mississippian culture, with strong roots in Adena and Hopewell, but better adapted to changed conditions, had established itself in several locations. This new culture carried on the mound-building tradition of Hopewell but built its subsistence strategy on corn agriculture.

Among the regional variants of Mississippian culture was one that developed in what is today western Louisiana. This distinctive culture, which has come to be known as Caddoan, emerged by about 500 C.E., and in the course of the next three centuries spread through the area along the Red, Sabine, Angelina, Neches, and Trinity rivers of Texas. The people who brought it to Texas spoke one of a number of related languages called Caddoan today, of which Wichita, Pawnee, and Osage are other examples. In time the Caddos became the dominant society of the region, spreading elements of their culture to neighboring non-Caddo speakers.

That process took place over hundreds of years during which Caddoan culture developed into a sophisticated system of interrelated kinship-based political entities that late seventeenth-century Europeans described as confederacies. In fact, the three confederacies of historic times—the Kadohadacho, Hasinais, and Natchitoches—were the product of successful adaptation to environmental conditions in East Texas, western Louisiana, southwestern Arkansas, and southeastern Oklahoma. In this well-watered and heavily forested region, early Caddoan pioneers found abundant natural resources that enabled them to establish scattered communities which by 1,000 years ago had become completely dependent on corn as the principal staple. Squash, beans, sunflowers, and a variety of other annuals rounded out the agricultural base of Caddo society. Caddoans also hunted deer and rabbit to meet the balance of their dietary requirements and, along with the occasional bear and buffalo, to provide leather and furs for other needs.

Like Mississippian cultures to the east, the Caddoans were prolific mound builders. As their culture became more sophisticated, they developed a settlement

At Caddoan Mounds State Historical Park, the agricultural way of life of early Texas farmers has been unearthed through years of archeological excavation. Mural paintings at the visitors center colorfully illustrate their long-vanished way of life. Although Caddos no longer reside in Texas as a tribe, a group from Oklahoma returns to the park each year for commemorative ceremonies. *(Photo courtesy Texas Parks & Wildlife © 2003, Nola Davis)*

pattern based on scattered agricultural villages of conical-shaped thatch dwellings, a few important towns, and specialized ceremonial centers. Mounds near villages continued to serve the basic purpose of containing the remains of high-status individuals, and mounds at ceremonial centers served to elevate small temples in which Caddo priests and leaders could commune with the spirit world.

The prosperity indicated by widespread mound building is also evidenced by extensive interregional trade and sophisticated crafts activities. Through Plains intermediaries, the Caddo exchanged their hardwood bows, ceramics, tanned goods, and perhaps even corn, for turquoise from New Mexico, copper from the Great Lakes region, seashells from the Gulf of Mexico, and buffalo hides from Plains. They produced sophisticated agricultural and woodworking tool kits of stone and shell that included digging tools, hoes, and axes for clearing timber. In the stone-scarce environment in which they lived, the Caddo even relied on wood to make the large mortars and long wooden pestles they used to grind corn into meal. Caddo pottery and basketry from the centuries immediately preceding the arrival of Europeans was among the finest in North America. French and Spanish descriptions of their tanned and decorated animal-skin apparel indicate a long tradition of craftsmanship.

Due to extensive observation by Europeans in the late seventeenth and early eighteenth centuries, a great deal can be inferred about Caddo society on the eve of the arrival of Europeans. Overall, the Caddos were largely peaceful tribes before the eighteenth century, although defensive warfare was part of life. At the most basic level of society—the family—organization was matrilineal, meaning that descent was traced on the mother's side. Marriage took place between members of different clans, and families were grouped in clans, usually named for animals, which were hierarchically ranked. Commoner families typically lived in individual homesteads surrounded by the agricultural field assigned to them.

Political organization outside the home combined egalitarian and hierarchical practices and was partly theocratic in nature. Chiefdoms composed of groups of these scattered homesteads, one or more central villages, and a ceremonial center, were under the leadership of a hereditary *caddi,* or community chief. He governed with the support of elders called *canahas,* but in times of war, villages would select war chiefs from among proven warriors. Religious leadership in each Caddo tribal group was in the hands of the *Xinesi,* also a hereditary position in the male line, who conducted ceremonies to communicate with the spirit world. His mediation with the supreme being, and his leadership during important annual feasts to celebrate planting, harvesting, and the hunt, were indispensable to the continuation of Caddo society.

By the early fifteenth century Caddo society faced the same period of crisis that confronted the other agricultural societies of North America. Overpopulation may have combined with changing environmental conditions to create violent competition. Corn, a soil-depleting crop, may not have been planted in the proper balance with beans and other soil-enriching plants to maintain adequate production levels. Whatever the case, a reduction in the number of long-distance trade items found in Caddo archeological sites, the discontinuation of mound building, and the abandonment of many sites throughout East Texas, indicate that by the time Europeans arrived Caddoan culture was well past its prime.

The decline of Caddo fortunes, which continued throughout the colonial period, was intensified by a number of factors. Warfare with neighboring Indian groups such as the Choctaws, Osages, Wichitas, and Tonkawas became more violent as the region's animal resources became a source of contention in trade relations with the French. Epidemic diseases, which probably struck even before the first European set foot in East Texas, decimated whole villages, forcing survivors to consolidate into fewer and fewer groups. Attempting to adapt to the changing conditions of the eighteenth century, the Texas Caddos began to hunt bison on horseback, an adaptation that brought them into the realm of people for whom the buffalo had always been at the core of life and culture.

Buffalo Peoples and Fishermen

While people in eastern Texas experimented with becoming agricultural societies, from central Texas to the Panhandle the American bison and other large mammals remained basic to human subsistence. Along the Texas coast in the southernmost prairies, Indian cultures relied on seasonal migration to exploit locally available resources. All of these native groups were active in the east-west and north-south trade system that made Texas a crossroads of cultural and technological exchange long before the Spanish, the French or Anglo Americans ever set foot in the state.

Buffalo Hunters of Western Texas

In the case of central and Panhandle Texas, the lack of archeological evidence makes it difficult to tie Archaic and Late Prehistoric populations to those groups encountered by Spaniards in the sixteenth, seventeenth, and eighteenth centuries. The case of the Panhandle-Llano Estacado region appears to be the easier of the two to piece together. Late Archaic hunter-gatherers either were absorbed by eastward-moving Pueblos and Mogollón peoples, or were pushed farther east to the Hill Country of central Texas. The result was that between 800 and 500 years ago, during a period called the Antelope Creek phase, the broad expanse of northwestern Texas was home to a culture that combined bison hunting with horticulture and the construction of permanent dwellings.

Antelope Creek people may well have been Pueblo colonizers expanding eastward in pursuit of permanent water sources at the beginning of the great drought age that eventually transformed the Anasazi and Mogollón into the modern Pueblo tribes. Settling near permanent springs fed by the Ogallala Aquifer, these groups adapted to local conditions by taking up buffalo hunting as an important subsistence strategy, coming back to their villages at spring planting and fall harvest times. Besides hunting, Antelope Creek people became important traders with surrounding cultures. With buffalo hides and, perhaps, dried meat as trade items, they acquired ceramics from both the Pueblos to the west and the Caddos to the east. They also traded turquoise, obsidian, and seashells, making it clear that their exchange system functioned beyond the utilitarian level.

Successful as they were in adapting to conditions on the southern Plains, the Antelope Creek people were incapable of meeting the challenge of a new intruder group that arrived in the Panhandle region about 500 years ago. For hundreds, if not over a thousand years, Athabaskan-speaking bands of hunter-gatherers had been moving down the eastern slopes of the Rocky Mountains, adapting to conditions on the fringes of the Great Plains on the way to becoming the most formidable pre-horse buffalo people of Texas. In historic times these people came to be known as Apaches. Some groups of Apaches settled east and others west of the Rockies. Highly adaptive, the eastern Apaches not only became the most proficient bison hunters of West Texas, but they also took up gardening, mimicking the subsistence strategy of the Antelope Creek people they replaced. Arriving on the eve of the arrival of the Spaniards to the interior of North America, the ancestral Plains Apaches were among the earliest people to be described by Spanish explorers.

Unfortunately, the same cannot be said for the people inhabiting central Texas. Because European penetration of this region came rather late—in the last decades of the seventeenth century—the prehistory of the area is not definitive. For a long time informed opinion was that the Tonkawas, the people thought to have inhabited the area west of the Caddoan home territory in the early eighteenth century, were the descendants of the region's Archaic Indians. It may well be, however, that the Tonkawas represent the coming together of late-arriving southern Plains hunters and the remaining central Texas hunter-gatherer bands that were no longer independently viable.

Regardless, for a thousand years before the arrival of Europeans, central Texas was home to a succession of Archaic-period hunter-gatherer cultures that relied extensively on the buffalo for subsistence. Highly mobile, and continuing to make use of rock shelters, by 1,300 years ago these Indians had adopted the bow and arrow and made use of pottery. Within the next few centuries, the central Texas Indians joined in the interregional trade system that had developed across the expanse of Texas. Ceramics imported from Caddoan lands to the east, seashells, and stone from hundreds of miles away survive to point out the extent of this trade. But the life of these Toyah-phase people (the name given to the central Texas culture dated to 1300–1600 C.E.) was not an entirely idyllic life of following the buffalo and gathering berries and nuts. They were, it seems, basically territorial, as the presence of cemeteries associated with them attests. Numerous burials, with arrowheads found among the skeletal remains, indicate that the deceased suffered violent deaths.

Hunter-Gatherers and Fishermen of South Texas and the Gulf Coast

The violence experienced by the Toyah-phase people may have been the result of conflict with their southeastern neighbors. To the Spaniards the various hunter-gatherer groups that inhabited most of southern Texas and neighboring northern Coahuila came to be known as Coahuiltecos, a name that has remained popular with scholars of early Texas. Yet the Coahuiltecans consisted of a number of distinct cultures and language groups that had evolved in the South Texas environment over hundreds of years since Archaic times.

Generally, Coahuiltecan cultures shared a number of characteristics that distinguish them from other Texas hunter-gatherers. Very mobile, they normally occupied open campsites, relying on temporary brush or hide shelters to protect them from the elements. About 1,000 years ago the bow and arrow and a simple form of pottery made an appearance among them, although the absence of *manos* and *metates* at their sites suggests that they did not experiment with corn.

As hunter-gatherers, the ancestral Coahuiltecans had relied mostly on small mammals such as rabbits and rodents, snakes, and freshwater fish and shellfish for the meat portion of their diet. As the bison moved south in the centuries immediately preceding the arrival of Europeans, the Coahuiltecans increasingly hunted buffalo, an adaptation that may well have brought them into conflict with buffalo hunters to the north as their hunting ranges overlapped.

The territoriality of Coahuiltecans varied greatly, with some groups being more attached to specific locations than others. In the interior of South Texas, between San Antonio and the Rio Grande, the preference for isolated burials indicates that even at the end of the prehistoric period these band peoples remained not only extremely mobile, but also unattached to specific sites. Coahuiltecans in the lower Rio Grande valley, on the other hand, were attached to specific sites, and cemeteries are much more numerous in that area.

The Brownsville Complex people, as the Late Prehistoric Coahuiltecan culture of the lower Rio Grande region is known, are distinct from other Coahuiltecans in other respects. Most important, they developed a material culture that made extensive use of marine resources. They employed seashells for a wide variety of purposes: whelks became hammers, sunray clams became scrapers, and conch and clam shells were turned into projectile points. They used shells to create jewelry and other ornamentation for exchange purposes. In time the Brownsville Complex people sought to trade their shell creations with other hunter-gatherer cultures of the interior and with the Mesoamerican cultures of central Mexico, from whom they received ceramics, obsidian, and jadeite.

Up the coast from the Rio Grande delta Coahuiltecans lived another coastal culture with distinct characteristics and a long history of interaction with Euro-Americans in historic times. Collectively known as the Karankawas, these people of the bays and barrier islands from Corpus Christi to the lower Brazos River can be traced through the archeological evidence to about 1,200 years ago. With access to substantial marine as well as upland animal and plant resources, the Karankawa Indians developed an annual cycle of migration based on the seasonal availability of specific species. In the fall and winter of each year extended family groups and small bands gathered together at traditional coastal sites, where through early spring they could exploit the ample supply of drum- and redfish that spawned in the shallow bays and estuaries. Shellfish, particularly clams and mussels, made up a significant portion of their diet, but mammals, mostly white-tailed deer, only a fractional amount.

Arriving at their winter campsite in the fall, the Karankawa families erected simple brush and hide huts intended to keep out only the worst of the elements. They repaired or constructed canoes, which were of dugout design and shaped with shell adzes and scrapers. Some members of the group prepared fishing nets and traps. Others chipped away at flint cobbles to make the arrowheads and other stone tools necessary to process the catch of fish and shellfish on which the group would feed until early spring.

Each member of the camp had duties to perform, but also considerable leisure time. Although drum- and redfish were the principal meat resource for the group until early spring, an occasional white-tailed deer or rabbit not only added variety, but provided hide and bones for the group's clothing, tools, and ornaments. Some group members did not go fishing or hunting, but went out to gather roots, nuts, and leaves for food, basketry, and dyes. Some returned to camp at the end of the day with supplies of clay for pottery and asphaltum (naturally occurring marine tar) with which to coat or decorate pottery and to waterproof baskets.

The Karankawas were as concerned with the hereafter as any of their neighbors and, indeed, as just about all human cultures. A simple people with little social stratification and few measures of status and wealth, the group's members shared in both times of bounty and scarcity. If the practices described by Spanish observers in the eighteenth century stretch back to prehistoric times, then Karankawa celebrations were truly joyful affairs of group dancing ceremonies that lasted for days and wrestling and other skills competitions among the adolescent and adult males.

In late spring the camp broke up into extended family hunting and gathering groups. Moving inland to occupy sites along the coastal prairie's many streams, these smaller groups set up hunting camps to take advantage of the substantial population of bison and white-tailed deer present during Late Prehistoric times. Consistent archeological evidence indicates that this upland movement went no farther than about twenty-five miles, a boundary at which Coahuiltecan sites begin. Also evident in the remains of the camps of both Rockport-Karankawas and Coahuiltecans is shared use of this boundary area, for the sites of the former indicate spring-summer use while the camps of the latter indicate fall-winter use.

Access to a rich and varied diet made the Karankawas a strong and healthy people. Spanish observers remarked on their tall stature and robust builds, evidence of which extends into prehistoric times in the archeological record. One interesting example of their adaptation to coastal conditions that proved repellent to Spanish and Anglo American observers because of the odor was their habit of rubbing themselves in alligator grease to protect themselves from mosquitoes, a practice shared with their coastal neighbors. There is no evidence in the archeological record, however, to support the common Euro-American misconception that the Karankawas were cannibals. In fact, there is little evidence that they were significantly more bellicose than other Texas Indians in prehistoric times. It seems clear that on the eve of European contact the Karankawas were enjoying the simple prosperity of a bountiful natural environment.

So too were their neighbors to the north. Along the coast from Galveston Bay eastward and inland into the coastal prairie lived hunter-gatherers with many of the same characteristics as the Karankawa people. Known as the Galveston Bay Focus, they appear to have practiced the same kind of seasonal migration and balanced reliance on marine and upland resources as their southern neighbors. They may have been ancestors of some of the Atakapans (Akokisas, Deadoses, and Atakapans proper) that Europeans would encounter in the eighteenth century.

Conclusion

It took millions of years for Texas, as we now know it, to form. Texas is a land of geological marvels: the product of continental collisions, meteor impacts, glacial expansions and contractions, and erosion due to wind, temperature, and precipitation. It is a land of extinct volcanoes and submerged mountain ranges, of granite hills and mud flats. It contains hundreds of miles of coast, as well as hundreds of thousands of square miles of underground rivers and lakes. Also below its surface are the relics of those eons of change: dead forests and animal matter compressed into coal, gas, and oil fields that have fed the engines of industry for the last century; limestone and shale that were once an unfathomable number of sea creatures forming reefs in the shallow seas that once covered much of the state.

The diversity of Texas's geology is more than matched by the variety of its environments. The sub-humid forests of East Texas for centuries sheltered the most successful agricultural society to emerge within the state. The Plains and prairies stretching from northwestern Texas to the southern coast provided such a rich animal subsistence base in the form of bison, deer, and antelope, that full-time agriculture, or any agriculture at all in some cases, proved an unnecessary adaptation. Even in the harshest environment Texas had to offer—the desert far west—there were enough water, animal, and plant resources to meet the needs of a particularly hardy group of early Texans.

Consequently, at the beginning of the sixteenth century the land we now call Texas had already been a cultural crossroads for thousands of years. It was the meeting place of Woodlands, Plains, and Southwestern cultures. It was home to both simple hunter-gatherers and sophisticated agriculturalists. Its people spoke a number of unrelated languages and maintained widely varying traditions, although their cultures all made pottery and used stone tools and bows and arrows. Almost all Texas Indians had something else in common: To one degree or another they all made use of the buffalo, a grazing animal that due to changing environmental conditions in the Late Prehistoric period was extending its range southward and eastward across almost the entire breadth of Texas.

Not a single Indian living within the state's present boundaries would have understood the concept of Texas, however. With the exception of the complex, hierarchical, socially-stratified Caddos, no prehistoric Texas Indian group appears to have had much use for any kind of political organization beyond the local chief or head man and his group of trusted advisors. And, although most cultures had become territorial by Late Prehistoric times, that territoriality was at most a simple defense of hunting grounds or a finely tuned subsistence strategy based, as in the case of the Karankawas, on seasonal exploitation of locally available resources.

In other words, the land that the Spaniards encountered in the first half of the sixteenth century was not a wilderness or a land of savages. Crisscrossed by trade networks that tied the Rockies to the Mississippi and the Great Lakes to the Gulf of Mexico, its people were exposed to and influenced by, to one degree or another, the major technological changes of pre-Columbian North America. Occupying every possible ecological niche the state had to offer, its people had adapted to conditions with amazing dexterity.

Most of these adaptations, which relied on extensive rather than intensive exploitation of the land, seemed odd and primitive to the technologically advanced and socially complex Europeans who encountered them. Certainly, the early cultures of Texas paled in comparison to the technological and social complexity of some Mesoamerican and Old World civilizations. And so they were unprepared to meet the challenge of the new world. In the course of the next 500 years, this new world would leave no room for the descendants of the first Texans to call the state home.

SUGGESTED READINGS

The study of early Texas requires a little ingenuity, given the existing nature of the literature. Entries in the *New Handbook of Texas* (*NHOT*) covering most of the subjects treated in this chapter (except dinosaurs) will prove extremely useful as a basic introduction. The essay "Geology" in the *NHOT* gives a clear overview that complements the information in *Roadside Geology of Texas* by Darwin Spearing (1991). Dividing the state into sections, focusing on the geological features encountered on or near the state's byways, and profusely illustrated, *Roadside Geology of Texas* is a great companion for weekend excursions. Terry G. Jordan et al., *Texas: A Geography* (1984), remains the best survey on the subject.

Prelude to Human Texas

Massive amounts of technical information are available on the evolution of life in Texas and North America, most of it of such scientific rigor as to be inaccessible to the general reader. Fortunately, there are some writers who are able to make the work of scientists intelligible to the rest of us. One fascinating view of how the interaction between land and life has shaped North America, including Texas, is Tim Flannery's *The Eternal Frontier: An Ecological History of North America and Its People* (2001). Both readable and informative, it surveys the natural history of the northern part of the western hemisphere during the last 65 million years, since the meteor crashed into the northern Yucatán, helped kill off the dinosaurs, and set mammals on the road to world domination. Taking the story backwards for Texas, specifically, is Louis Jacobs's *Lone Star Dinosaurs* (1995), a nicely illustrated and easy-to-read overview of the state's paleontologic record by a practitioner.

The First Texans

The archeological literature on Texas largely consists of highly technical reports of fieldwork and efforts to reconcile findings in different parts of the state from approximately the same time frame. Although no single-author, single-volume synthesis of Texas during prehistoric times exists, the story can be pieced together from a few select sources written for students and the general public. The reader is forewarned that archeologists do not all agree on the boundaries between prehistoric periods, or on the precise taxonomy to apply to their findings, although they do tend to agree broadly on Paleo-Indian, Archaic, and Late Prehistoric as the major periods. These issues, along with many others, are presented by Linda Cordell in *Archaeology of the Southwest* (2nd ed., 1997). Although concerned only with western Texas as part of her definition of "Southwest," the text is very useful in understanding the general currents of development during Paleo-Indian times in Texas. A brief but extremely useful summary of Texas prehistory is Thomas Hester's article on the subject in the *NHOT,* as well as the appropriate parts of his *Digging into South Texas Prehistory: A Guide for Amateur Archaeologists* (1980). Now out of date with regard to the vast amount of archeological work done in Texas over the last forty years, but still useful for explaining basic lines of development in early Texas, is W. W. Newcomb, Jr.'s *The Indians of Texas: From Prehistoric to Modern Times* (1961). Newcomb also provided the text to a marvelously illustrated volume on *The Rock Art of Texas Indians* (1967), the paintings for which were done by Forrest Kirkland from original sketches and photographs.

The Agricultural Revolution Arrives

Texas Indians during Late Prehistoric to historic times have received unequal attention from scholars. Articles in the *NHOT* on individual tribes are uneven in how up-to-date they are, but generally serve as a good introduction to the background of each group. The evidence for the mysterious Jumanos, their possible origins, and what might have happened to them is presented by Nancy Parrott Hickerson in *The Jumanos: Hunters and Traders of the South Plains* (1994). As for the advanced agricultural Caddos, most of the writing about them for prehistoric times, as with all Indian groups, is highly technical. The opening parts of three works provide a useful introduction: *Caddo Indians: Where We Come From,* by Cecile Elkins Carter (1995); an overview of Caddo history down to the present, *"The Caddo Nation": Archaeological and Ethnohistoric Perspectives,* by Timothy K. Perttula (1992); and *The Caddo Chiefdoms: Caddo Economics and Politics, 700–1835* (1998) by David LaVere.

Buffalo Peoples and Fishermen

Aside from the material on them in Cordell's *Archaeology of the Southwest,* there is little available to the general reader on the pre-Apache peoples of the Texas Plains. The story of the Tonkawas and their status as "ancient" Texas Indians remains an archeological tug-of-war largely inaccessible to the general public. The story is better with regard to the Coahuiltecans, as Hester's *Digging into South Texas Prehistory* gives a clear picture of the variety of Coahuiltecan cultures. The work of Robert A. Ricklis—in particular *The Karankawa Indians of Texas: An Ecological Study of Cultural Traditions and Change* (1996)—has revolutionized our understanding of these long-maligned people. The Atakapans and other East Texas Indians are the subjects of Lawrence E. Aten, *Indians of the Upper Texas Coast* (1983).

Finally, for those readers who wish to dig into Texas Indian prehistory themselves, there are a number of out-of-print works that can serve as invaluable guides: Parker Nunley, *A Field Guide to Archeological Sites in Texas* (1989); Ellen Sue Turner and Thomas R. Hester, *A Field Guide to Stone Artifacts of Texas Indians* (1985); and, of course, Hester's *Digging into South Texas Prehistory.*

2

First Meetings, First Conflicts, 1492–1693

ooking out from behind the dune vegetation of what is now Follets Island on a crisp November morning in 1528, the island's inhabitants beheld a strange sight. In the wreckage of a large makeshift boat, a group of strangely dressed men sat close together, shivering and muttering in an incomprehensible language. In the days that followed, the scene was repeated three more times on other Texas barrier islands. In all, over two hundred members of Pánfilo de Narváez's Florida expedition had by happenstance become the first Europeans to arrive in Texas. This first recorded meeting between Texas Indians and Europeans took place on peaceful terms. The Indians offered fish, roots, and nuts, while the Spaniards reciprocated with hawkbells and beads. The chronicler of this meeting, Alvar Núñez Cabeza de Vaca records that when he and his men were unable to relaunch their boat and lost all their possessions in the heavy surf, "the Indians, at sight of what had befallen us, and our state of suffering and melancholy destitution, sat down among us, and from the sorrow and pity they felt, they all began to lament so earnestly that they might have been heard at a distance, and continued so doing more than half an hour." In the months to come the shrinking number of survivors, undernourished, suffering from exposure, and increasingly at odds with the local inhabitants, would transfer some of their negative feelings to the island, naming it *Mal Hado*, or "Misfortune." Eventually, only four men, Cabeza de Vaca and two other Spaniards along with the North African slave of one of them, returned to Christendom. Their adventures inspired others to venture into the interior of North America and take part in the initial chapter of Texas history.

1492	Columbus's voyage opens Western Hemisphere to European exploitation
1519	Álvarez de Pineda becomes first European to explore Texas coast
1521	Cortés completes Spain's conquest of the Aztec Empire
1528	Narváez's expedition to Florida marooned on Texas coast; survivors Alvar Núñez Cabeza de Vaca and companions provide earliest information on Texas Indians
1541	Coronado visits the Texas Panhandle during his 1540–42 expedition to Arizona, New Mexico, and the Plains
1542	Moscoso leads the remains of the Soto expedition (1539–43) into East Texas before returning to the Mississippi River
1554	Hurricane wrecks Spanish treasure fleet off Padre Island, confirming accounts of hostile Indians
1573	Philip II issues new colonization laws aimed at making expansion of Spanish rule more orderly
1598	Oñate's expedition crosses the Rio Grande at Paso del Norte
1659	Fray García de San Francisco establishes Mission Nuestra Señora de Guadalupe, first Spanish settlement at Paso del Norte
1680	Pueblo Revolt leads to founding of Ysleta for friendly Tigua Indians, and other settlements at Paso del Norte
1685	La Salle expedition lands at Matagorda Bay, builds Fort St. Louis
1690	San Francisco de los Tejas becomes first Spanish settlement in the province of Texas
1693	Spaniards abandon Texas

When Europeans first set foot on what is now Texas soil, they claimed by right of discovery land that for thousands of years had been the home of native peoples. The first encounters between Europeans and Texas Indians, which took place during the Age of the Conquistadors in the first half of the sixteenth century, had very different outcomes for both sides. The diseases that the Spaniards brought with them quickly began to take their toll on the native population, setting off a chain reaction of events that would last for centuries. For the Spaniards, disappointment marked their contacts with Texas. The vast expanses of the land, the dearth of precious metals, and, to their view, backward Indian cultures argued against devoting many resources to the settlement of the region. Having claimed the land and foreseeing no European challengers to the claim, Spaniards quickly forgot about Texas as they turned their attention to the more immediate task of establishing a successful colony among the civilizations of Mesoamerica.

It was not until the mighty struggles for empire that enveloped Spain, France, and England from the end of the sixteenth century onward that Spaniards began to pay attention to their long-neglected far northern frontier. Only reluctantly did Spaniards return to Texas, and when they did they were indecisive and ill equipped to meet the challenges posed by the country. And only in the El Paso area was a secure Spanish presence established before the end of the seventeenth century.

Dawn of Texas History

The first Spaniards to explore Texas lived during that restless period of frenzied searching for precious metals and great civilizations known as the Age of the Conquistadors. From their experiences in the Caribbean and Mesoamerica (Mexico and Central America), Spaniards looked upon the conquest of Indian peoples and the plunder of their wealth as legitimate goals of exploration. In fact, it was Hernán Cortés's triumph over the Aztec empire that created high expectations for what might be found in the rest of North America. From the 1520s through the 1540s numerous expeditions made their way north from Cuba and the land of the Aztecs seeking other Mexicos. Eventually, members of three of these expeditions came into contact with most of Texas's geographic regions and many of its culture groups.

Spain and America

When Pánfilo de Narváez presented his petition to King Charles I of Spain (better known as Charles V, Holy Roman Emperor) to conquer Florida in 1526, he was hoping to surpass the accomplishments of his rival and personal enemy, Cortés. From various slaving expeditions and explorations in the 1510s, including one by

Álvarez de Pineda in 1519 that mapped the entire gulf coast from Florida to Tampico, Spaniards became curious about the vast land north of Mexico that came to be known as Florida. Narváez, who had sided with the governor of Cuba against Cortés during the conquest of Mexico, had lost an eye in battle attempting to arrest Cortés. Captured, humiliated, and abandoned, he had returned to Spain intent on getting his due; this, he believed, could be accomplished in Florida.

The broad sweep of the royal *capitulación,* or charter, Narváez received in 1526 granted him all the lands between the Soto la Marina River in Mexico and the Atlantic seaboard, a vague expanse known as Florida from the time of Juan Ponce de León. This territory, he firmly believed, held within it rich and populous kingdoms capable of compensating him and his followers for their considerable expenses. For, like the other conquistadors, the members of Narváez's *entrada* (conquest, colonization, or settlement expedition) had signed up for service without any compensation except a share in the spoils and rights to land. If truly fortunate, the conquistadors might also receive an *encomienda,* a grant of a certain number of Indian tributaries as reward for their services in the expedition, but only under obligation to Christianize and protect the Indians—an obligation more often honored in the breach than in the performance. If the members of this *entrada* were like the men who followed Cortés, they had gone into debt to equip themselves. A successful venture would not only make them rich, but lords of the land. For, although some conquistadors were members of the Spanish nobility, most were not, and the prospects of becoming *hidalgos* (literally sons of something, the lowest rung of Spanish nobility), served as a powerful motive.

To be sure, daring and resourceful as the conquistadors were, they were not without their critics. One of these was the prominent Dominican clergyman Bartolomé de Las Casas. For fifty years, from the conquest of Cuba until his death in 1566, Las Casas worked tirelessly for the welfare of the native populations of the New World. He opposed everything conquistadors like Narváez represented. Indian slavery was not only unjustified, but reprehensible. The sole purpose of the Spanish enterprise in the New World should be to convert its peoples to the one true faith; to do anything else was to exploit naturally free and rational beings.

The defender of the Indians struggled mightily against a society steeped in the martial spirit, ruled by a monarch wrapped in the mantel of divine right, and equipped with the technological tools to construct a modern empire. Having expelled the last of the Muslim feudal lords in 1492, after seven centuries of religious warfare known as the *Reconquista,* King Fernando and Queen Isabel united much of the Iberian peninsula through a series of centralizing measures that gave the crown more control at the expense of free cities and the nobility. Fernando, in particular, carried the war to northern Africa, where he sought to expand the power of the Kingdom of Aragón, which had previously played second fiddle to Isabel's Kingdom of Castile. For most Spaniards, the distinction that Las Casas attempted to draw between Muslims and pagans was mere hair-splitting. War against non-Christians was justified, and there was no better proof of God's approval than the riches with which he had rewarded Spanish arms.

To further unify the country, the Catholic Kings (a title granted to Fernando and Isabel by the papacy in recognition of their religious zeal) issued ultimatums to the Jews and Muslims of Spain: convert to Christianity or leave the country. This effort at religious unification had negative consequences for Spain, however, as a large proportion of the learned and skilled population abandoned the Iberian peninsula for other parts of the Mediterranean, and those who chose conversion lived under the taint of their past religious convictions. The large population of "new Christians" also strengthened the power of the Holy Office of the Inquisition, a branch of the Catholic Church dedicated to rooting out heresy and Judaizing (continuing to practice Jewish customs after conversion). The Spanish monarchy also used the Inquisition to eliminate political enemies. Not surprisingly, the Protestant Reformation stood no chance of gaining a foothold in Spain. With the election of Fernando and Isabel's grandson Charles I as Holy Roman Emperor, a Spanish king became the successor to the Holy Roman Empire. Charles's son, Philip II, would carry his religious zealotry to the extreme, bankrupting Spain in his efforts to destroy Protestant England and defeat his rebellious and heretical Dutch subjects.

That the Spain of Las Casas was able to juggle so many balls at the same time was in large part due to its having embraced and combined a number of technologies, most of which were of foreign origin. By the late fifteenth century, Portuguese ship-building techniques had produced vessels large enough to successfully negotiate deep-ocean crossings. Improvements in instrumentation made dead-reckoning navigation a more standard practice. With these sailing technologies, the Spaniards followed their Iberian neighbors into the Atlantic Ocean in an effort to discover new sources of riches. The printing press abetted these efforts, making possible the speedy and widespread distribution of star charts and travel guides that gave sailors more confidence in challenging the unknown waters to the west. By the early sixteenth century, the crown had established the *Casa de Contratación* (House of Trade), a clearing-house for navigational information that gave Spaniards an early lead in establishing a New World presence.

Columbus's failure to reach Asia had, nevertheless, opened up a whole new hemisphere to this confident and zealous nation. The oft-quoted motto of the conquistadors, "God, gold, and glory," really did capture the ethos of the times. Steel blades, gunpowder, and horses certainly were advantages in the Spaniards' conquest of the New World, but so was their attitude and worldview. Convinced of the superiority of their God and their civilization, the conquistadors paid little heed to the pleadings of a clergyman who did not have the stomach for the job of empire building.

The Narváez Expedition: First Contact

For Charles I, granting Narváez a charter to such a vast territory represented great potential and no risk, even as it demonstrated Spanish ignorance of the true geographic dimensions of North America. As king of Castile and León, the largest and most powerful of the Iberian kingdoms that made up late medieval Spain, Charles exercised jurisdiction over the New World under the terms of Pope Alexander VI's *Inter Caetera,* a 1493 bull (papal decree) that granted the Catholic kings dominion over the western hemisphere in return for a commitment to Christianize all lands conquered in their name. Narváez's charter legitimized the undertaking without exposing the crown to financial risks. In case of success, the crown stood to gain the *quinto real* (royal fifth), a percentage of all acquired wealth to which it was entitled by virtue of its jurisdiction over the land.

Although the papacy had legitimized Spanish claims in the New World, some of the clergy, particularly Las Casas and his fellow Dominicans, vehemently protested the methods employed by the conquistadors. Largely due to their efforts, the crown had decreed use of the *Requerimiento* in every Spanish New World expedition. This document, drawn up in Spain in 1511 as a result of a debate over whether or not Indians, as pagans, were subject to enslavement, attempted to deal with the problem in a typically medieval and scholastic manner. The document consisted of a brief history of the world from the Judeo-Christian perspective, including an explanation of how the pope as successor to St. Peter had given the Spanish monarchs sovereignty over the New World, followed by the admonition that refusal to accept Spanish rule would bring forced conversion and the possibility of slavery. In other words, slavery was the Indians' fault for not willingly accepting their conquest by Christians. This document, although unacceptable to Las Casas and his colleagues, was just the pretext the crown needed to soothe its conscience while continuing to follow an expansionist colonial policy.

There would be no *quinto real* from this venture, however, and no spoils for Narváez and his men, either. Misfortune arrived shortly after the expedition's five small ships reached the Caribbean. One hundred forty men deserted at Santo Domingo, then a hurricane off the Cuban coast sank two ships and killed the sixty men on board. After wintering in Cuba, the expedition again set sail in February, encountering other storms that threatened disaster. Finally, in April 1528, the Spaniards reached the gulf coast of Florida, where they entered a large bay, probably Tampa Bay. Their luck did not improve, however. Despite the warnings of his treasurer, Alvar Núñez Cabeza de Vaca, that the land forces should not separate from the fleet, Narváez marched his men inland in a futile attempt to reach the supposedly gold-rich Kingdom of Apalachen. After four months of hostilities with Indians, and forced marches through swamps and jungles, the men had found no gold or other tangible wealth, and there was no sight of the expedition's fleet. The *entrada's* morale was broken. In September the men constructed crude boats at St. Mark's Bay, Florida, and toward the end of the month the five small craft, overcrowded with almost 250 survivors, set sail for Mexico.

Sailing westward across the northern gulf, the unfortunate expeditionaries drifted toward what they thought was the safe haven of Mexico. Soon after passing the mouth of the Mississippi, however, a storm battered the boats toward the Texas coast. Exhausted, with no water, and forced to survive on handfuls of raw corn, the survivors were in desperate straits. When Cabeza de Vaca requested orders from Narváez, the disheartened *adelantado* (governor with broad powers) replied that "it was no longer a time in which one should command another; but that each should do what he thought best to save his own life." Narváez was never heard from again.

In the first days of November, one after another of the three remaining craft beached just south of Galveston Island. Suffering from exposure, starvation, and dehydration, the would-be conquistadors were at the mercy of the Indians who inhabited the area. The initially friendly meeting between Indians and Spaniards soon took a turn for the worse as misunderstandings between the two cultures developed. Some Spaniards died of exposure and others disappeared in attempts to reach civilization; a fortunate few found "employment" among the Indian groups that took them in. Of the dwindling number of expeditionaries, only four would live to tell the tale. One of these four was Cabeza de Vaca.

For six years the survivors dwelt among the Atakapan, Karankawan, and Coahuiltecan Indians of coastal and south Texas, sometimes as "slaves," sometimes as merchants, but also as healers. In 1532 Cabeza de Vaca finally abandoned his single remaining companion, Lope de Oviedo, and made his way inland. Captured by another group of Indians, he soon discovered the presence in the region of three other expeditionaries, Captains Alonzo del Castillo and Andrés Dorantes and the latter's North African slave, Estebanico. Two years of planning resulted in a successful escape from their captors, and the beginning of an odyssey that took the four Christians across parts of present-day Texas, New Mexico, and northern Mexico, from the Gulf of Mexico to the Gulf of California between 1534 and 1536.

The First Texas Literature

Cabeza de Vaca and his companions told stories that combined personal experience with rumor. Living hand to mouth, they soon came to understand the Indians' hunting and gathering practices and how they could adapt to them. The humbled conquistador recalled: "I bartered with these Indians in combs that I made for them and in bows, arrows, and nets. We made mats, which are their houses, that they have great necessity for; and although they know how to make them, they wished to give their full time to getting food, since when otherwise employed they are pinched with hunger."

The conquistadors' healing powers made them honored guests wherever they went. In at least one case Cabeza de Vaca practiced surgery to remove an arrowhead from an Indian's chest. Most often their practice of medicine consisted of praying over their patients, but, according to Cabeza de Vaca, in every single instance the Indians who received their ministrations claimed complete recovery.

Cabeza de Vaca's detailed descriptions of the various Indian groups the four Christians encountered are a cornerstone of Texas ethnography. Among the hunter-gatherers of Texas, he reported, "all the Indians whom we saw have the custom from the time in which their wives find themselves pregnant, of not

C La relacion y comentarios del gouerna
dor Alluar nuñez cabeça de vaca, de lo acaescido en las
dos jornadas que hizo a las Indias.

Unlike his conquistador contemporaries, Alvar Núñez Cabeza de Vaca, along with the three other survivors of the Narváez expedition, was forced to "go native" in order to survive. He was also among the few to write extensively of his experience, becoming the first author in Texas history. His report to Emperor Charles V was first printed in 1542 and was published in slightly different form in 1555 along with accounts of his adventures in South America. *(South Western Writers Collection, Alkek Library, Southwest Texas State University)*

sleeping with them until two years after they have given birth. The children are suckled until the age of twelve years, when they are old enough to get support for themselves. We asked them why they reared them in this manner; and they said because of the great poverty of the land."

Cabeza de Vaca also recorded some of the local lore. He gave one account of "Badthing," a monster in the form of a man who stalked the Indians of coastal Texas and made his home in a hole in the ground. Cabeza de Vaca was convinced that the creature was an evil spirit, who would disappear if the Indians accepted Christianity.

Cabeza de Vaca and his companions were astute observers of nature as well as of the people they encountered. Descriptions of fauna, flora, terrain, and climate abound in Cabeza de Vaca's account. His is the first report of that quintessential North American mammal, the buffalo. His first-hand description of this "cattle" in Texas is as colorful as his account of the "Badthing":

> Three times I have seen them and eaten of their meat. I think they are about the size of those in Spain. They have small horns like the cows of Morocco; the hair is very long and flocky like the merino's. Some are tawny, others black. To my judgment the flesh is finer and fatter than that of this country. Of the skins of those

not fully grown the Indians make blankets, and of the larger they make shoes and bucklers. They come as far as the sea-coast of Florida, from a northerly direction, ranging through a tract of more than four hundred leagues [approximately 1,000 miles]; and throughout the whole region over which they run, the people who inhabit near, descend and live upon them, distributing a vast many hides into the interior country.

By the time Cabeza de Vaca and his companions took up the last leg of their journey in the present-day Mexican state of Sonora, they were accompanied from village to village by hundreds of men, women, and children. They were careful to preserve the illusion that they were "sons of heaven," which allowed them to maintain their positions of power: "We possessed great influence and authority: to preserve both, we seldom talked with them. The negro was in constant conversation; he informed himself about the ways we wished to take, of the towns there were, and the matters we desired to know."

The Spaniards' reports of wealthy kingdoms to the north of where they had traveled fueled a competition for the conquest of North America among Viceroy Antonio de Mendoza and the conquistadors Hernán Cortés and Hernando de Soto. This competition would again bring Spaniards to Texas in a futile search for quick riches.

Elusive Riches—Harsh Realities

Cabeza de Vaca and his companions arrived in Mexico City, capital of the newly created viceroyalty of New Spain (a jurisdiction that encompassed what is today Mexico, Central America, and Caribbean), to a heroes' reception. Every Spaniard, from Viceroy Antonio de Mendoza to Hernán Cortés to the most threadbare recent arrival from Spain put the best possible spin on the wanderers' accounts and was excited about the possibility of untold riches to be found.

In the fifteen years since the conquest of the Aztecs, Spanish expeditions had fanned out north, south, and west from the Valley of Mexico in an unrestrained and often brutal quest to replicate Cortés's success. Kingdoms had been conquered, idols smashed, and whole villages baptized into the Christian faith at once, but in the end New Spain did not contain enough material wealth to repay European investors and creditors. Nevertheless, tales of adventure and the promise of a boundless country yet to be explored brought a growing number of would-be conquerors to the viceregal capital in the hopes that the next discovery would prove the big one.

Some Spaniards had quickly lost interest in the dreams of Amazon kingdoms and lost civilizations and instead turned to a more tangible source of wealth—slaving. A number of conquistadors led raids into Indian territory solely for the purpose of capturing slaves, under the pretext that the Indians refused to submit peacefully under the terms of the *requerimiento.* The most brutal of these slavers was Nuño de Guzmán, rival of Cortés and founder of Guadalajara and other

Spanish towns in western Mexico. It was one of his parties that had stumbled upon Cabeza de Vaca and his companions during a slave raid in Sonora.

Coronado and the Exploration of the Panhandle

Antonio de Mendoza, first viceroy of New Spain, had only recently arrived in the New World when Cabeza de Vaca came out of the northern wilderness. For Mendoza, underwriting an expedition to discover and conquer the "Seven Cities of Cíbola" that the wanderers reported hearing about would be financially rewarding, would reduce the slaving that contributed to social and economic instability in the country, and would be a way to rid central Mexico of the large number of idle Spanish "gentlemen" who were a constant source of trouble. A prudent and sensible administrator, however, Mendoza was not about to invest his limited financial resources and reputation on unsubstantiated rumor. To establish the veracity of Cabeza de Vaca's reports he sent out a scout: a Franciscan friar with considerable New World experience, Marcos de Niza. He was to be guided by none other than Estebanico, the slave whom the viceroy purchased from Dorantes because none of the three Spaniards were willing to retrace their steps into the wilderness.

The Niza-Estebanico expedition turned out to be an utter disaster, the unforeseen consequences of which again brought Spaniards into what is now Texas. In the spring of 1539 Fray Niza set out with a large contingent of Indians and the irrepressible African, who soon moved far out in front of the rest of the party. By the time Niza crossed into southern Arizona, Estebanico had already reached the Zuni country, where he alienated the local population and was put to death. Hearing this news as he approached the same pueblo, the friar settled for a view of the town from a distant bluff. He then hurried back to report on this first city of Cíbola, which he judged "bigger than Mexico City," an utterly fanciful claim.

Mendoza had the answer he wanted, however, and the man to carry out the conquest. Francisco Vázquez de Coronado, who had come to New Spain with Mendoza, was a dashing and able young man with a bright future. By 1538 he was both an alderman of Mexico City and governor of Nueva Galicia. Now his benefactor bestowed on him, at age 30, the honor of leading an expedition that would bring new glory and subjects to the crown, new souls to Christ, and great wealth to himself, the viceroy, and those sturdy enough to see the enterprise to its conclusion. A thousand Spanish men-at-arms, thousands more Indian servants and camp followers, and immense herds of horses, mules, and cattle, and flocks of sheep and goats, marching out of Culiacán, Sinaloa in April 1540 must have presented an imposing spectacle.

What the villagers of Hawikuh, a Zuni Pueblo in eastern Arizona, thought of the Spaniards in their armor, riding huge beasts, and making unintelligible demands for shiny yellow and white metals they had never seen, can only be imagined. Coronado, not to be denied, took the town by storm on July 7, 1540, and set an unfortunate pattern of employing force for the rest of the expedition.

Long considered one of Coronado's campsites, Palo Duro Canyon, now a state park, has lost favor among recent historians, who consider Tule or Blanco canyons as the more likely location for the *barranca grande* mentioned in expedition journals. From their camp Coronado marched northeastward in search of Quivira, only to return to the Texas canyon country that summer. Even had they beheld Palo Duro's magnificent vistas the Spaniards, by now dejected by their failure to find rich kingdoms, would have been unimpressed. *(Photo courtesy Texas Parks & Wildlife © 2003, Earl Nottingham)*

Disappointed with the first city of Cíbola, the Spaniards moved on to the others, then eastward to the Rio Grande and Pecos River *pueblos* (settlements), where bloodshed and disappointment mixed. Niza's enthusiasm had been proved a lie, but at the Pecos River pueblo of Cicuye the Indians gave reason for hope. Far to the east, beyond the great flat lands, they promised, was the Kingdom of Quivira, where gold and silver awaited the Spaniards in plenty.

To get to Quivira, Coronado and his men had to cross a portion of northwestern and Panhandle Texas. In the spring of 1541 they visited the Blanco and Tule canyons region, where their encounter with the now-famous Texas weather provides us with the first description of a North American hailstorm: "While the army was resting in this ravine . . . a tempest came up one afternoon with a very high wind and hail, and in a very short space of time a great quantity of hailstones, as big as bowls, or bigger, fell as thick as raindrops, so that in places they covered the ground two or three spans or more deep."

Members of the Coronado expedition also recorded their impressions of the unprecedented flatness of the land, the immense bison herds of the region, and the tipi-dwelling, buffalo-hunting Querechos and Teyas who made the southern Plains their home. Pedro de Castañeda, the best of the expedition's chroniclers, described them in very favorable terms, as more numerous than the pueblo dwellers: "They have better figures, are better warriors, and are more feared. They travel like the Arabs, with their tents and troops of dogs loaded with poles and having Moorish pack-saddles with girths. . . . These people eat raw flesh and drink blood. They do not eat human flesh. They are a kind people and not cruel. They are faithful friends. They are able to make themselves very well understood by means of signs."

Quivira turned out to be another disappointment for Coronado and his men. The Wichita villages of central Kansas were not rich in gold and silver, or anything else for that matter. Although some of his men desired to stay in the pueblo country, Coronado, broken both psychologically and physically (a fall from his horse had caused permanent injuries), brought his humbled expeditionaries back to Culiacán in the spring of 1542 with nothing to show for their efforts. Their reports on the Rio Grande country, although optimistic about future prospects for the region, did not encourage Spanish settlement. The High Plains of Texas, remote and almost totally devoid of human residents, offered even fewer attractions. One lasting legacy of Coronado's bold venture seems to have been a lingering resentment on the part of the town-dwelling Indians, who henceforth would be called Pueblos by the Spaniards, and who within fifty years would confront more determined Spanish conquerors.

The viceroy was a different man when Coronado returned with his disappointing news. So many Spaniards had participated in the expedition that Nueva Galicia had been left vulnerable to Indian rebellion. The ensuing Mixtón War (1540–42), the first great Indian insurrection after the conquest, overwhelmed Spanish frontier defenses and forced the viceroy to take the field against the rebellious Indians. The costly war intensified Mendoza's disappointment with Coronado, especially as his investment in the expedition was a total loss. Although Coronado was eventually cleared of most charges brought against him for failures in leadership, he died in 1554 under a cloud of dishonor (despite the fact that fellow Spaniards who attempted the conquest of Florida were as unsuccessful as he had been).

Conquistadors in East Texas

Cabeza de Vaca had his own ideas about how Spanish settlement of Florida might best be carried out, and he hoped to gain permission from Emperor Charles V to attempt a new colonization effort. He returned to Spain in the summer of 1537 to find that he had been preempted by one of the heroes of the conquest of the Inca Empire, Hernando de Soto. This ruthless conquistador had come away from the Peruvian adventure a rich and powerful man. For him, as for most of his contemporaries, adventure and conquest had become an addiction. God, gold, and glory, although usually not in that order, were the driving motives for these men.

In the spring of 1536 Soto arrived in Spain laden down with his share of the booty taken from the Incas. Although he made a significant loan to the crown, purchased a magnificent palace, feasted with his companions in a spendthrift manner, and married into a prominent family by the end of the year, Soto found time to work on gaining his very own *capitulación* from Charles V. Impressing the most powerful monarch of the western world was no easy matter, but Soto's stories of how he and the other 130 adventurers led by Francisco Pizarro had vanquished an empire of millions did the trick. By the end of April 1537 Soto had obtained the governorship of Cuba, a knighthood in the Order of Santiago, and a charter to colonize Florida. Wisely, Cabeza de Vaca turned down Soto's offer of a place in his expedition when the conquistadors later met.

By the spring of 1539, after almost a year of final preparations in Cuba, Soto landed his 600-man expedition somewhere in the Tampa Bay area of Florida's gulf coast. He was much better equipped than Cortés had been twenty years earlier in Mexico, or than Narváez had been a decade earlier on his Florida misadventure. His quest for the wealth that had eluded Narváez and that Cabeza de Vaca and his companions had told him about led him through much of what is now the southeastern United States between May 1539 and May 1542. Wherever he and his men traveled, the least resistance from the Indians was met with steel, lead, and war dogs. Finally, racked with fever and discouraged by his failure to find the precious metals that lured him to North America, Soto died on the banks of the Mississippi River, leaving behind only a legacy of slaughter and destruction that imperiled the expedition's survival.

Succeeding Soto in command was Luis Moscoso de Alvarado. His first act as leader of the expedition, which now became known as the Moscoso expedition, was to hold a council at which the Spaniards decided to abandon the enterprise. With the most direct course for withdrawal being an overland march to New Spain, Moscoso led his men across the Red River in the summer of 1542 and got them at least to the Trinity River before determining the effort impracticable. Only slightly less brutal now that Soto was no longer in command, expedition members fought and tortured their way through the Caddo country of northeast Texas. Despite claims to the contrary by the Gentleman of Elvas, the most eloquent of the expedition's chroniclers, the Caddos encountered by the Spaniards in Texas, known as the Hasinais, must have had word of the Spaniards ahead of time. For, according to the Portuguese chronicler, as soon as Moscoso and his men approached,

> the people were called out, who, as fast they could get together, came by fifties and hundreds on the road, to give battle. While some encountered us, others fell upon our rear; and when we followed up those, these pursued us. The attack continued during the greater part of the day, until we arrived at their town. Some men were injured, and some horses, but nothing so as to hinder travel, there being not one dangerous wound among all. The Indians suffered great slaughter.

The Indians, anxious to rid themselves of the pillaging strangers, resorted to the same tactic the Pueblos had employed with Coronado: They convinced the

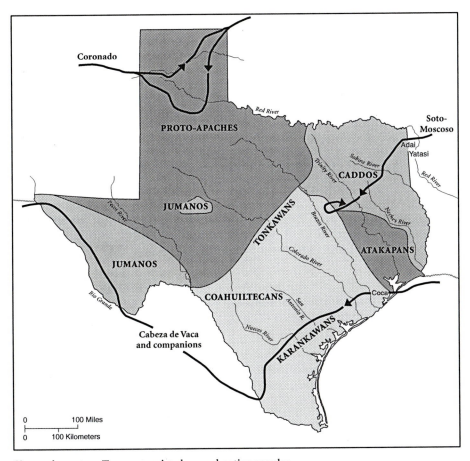

Sixteenth-century Texas conquistadors and native peoples.

Spaniards that if only they would travel on for some distance, they would arrive in a country where they could find their compatriots. The farther into Texas the conquistadors ventured, the greater their frustration with the country: "The country was very poor, and the want of maize was greatly felt. . . . For twenty days the march was through a very thinly peopled country, where great privation and toil were endured."

Despite the rumors of Christians far to the south or the west, and certain knowledge that New Spain lay to the southwest, Moscoso and the other expedition leaders based their decision to abandon the overland march on Cabeza de Vaca's experience. They recognized the country they were entering to be the one in which, according to Cabeza de Vaca, "the Indians wandered like Arabs, having no settled place of residence, living on prickly pears, and the roots of plants, and game; and that if this should be so, and they, entering upon that tract, found no provision for sustenance during winter, they must inevitably perish."

At that point, the conquistadors retraced their steps to the Mississippi, where they wintered and built boats to carry them to New Spain. In September 1543 the surviving 311 members of Soto's great expedition arrived at Pánuco. They left behind a trail of destruction from the Atlantic coast to central Texas. Most disruptive were epidemic diseases that soon wreaked havoc on the native populations of the southeastern United States, including the Hasinais of Texas.

The disheartening results of the Coronado and Soto-Moscoso expeditions convinced the Spanish to direct their attention to other parts of the New World. The absence of precious metals, the unsuitability of the native peoples for assimilation, and the difficulty of access to the region argued against a permanent Spanish presence. The absence of any foreign threat in the Gulf of Mexico further disinclined the crown from expending more resources there. Consequently, for the next four decades the little contact Spaniards did have with what is now Texas was restricted to the gulf coast, where hurricanes and other storms sometimes drove Spanish ships sailing between Veracruz and Havana.

The most famous of these incidents, the 1554 wreck off Padre Island of the *Santa María de Yciar, San Esteban,* and *Espíritu Santo,* three of four ships in a treasure fleet containing over two million pesos in gold and silver, did nothing to improve the reputation of Texas. The 250 castaways who attempted to march back to Spanish-held territory overland were attacked by Indians the whole way. The lone survivor, Fray Marcos de Mena, told stories of cannibal Indians and a waterless desert by the sea. The salvage expedition sent to recover the 1.5 million pesos on board the three ships found the shallow waters off Padre Island treacherous and lacking in adequate anchorages. If the interior of Texas offered few attractions for the fortune-seeking conquistadors, the coast of the Gulf of Mexico represented only danger for the sailing men bearing treasures from the New World to the old.

The Paso del Norte Corridor

In the years after Coronado returned from the land of the Pueblos, tensions between Spanish colonials and the Indians of northern New Spain again erupted into armed conflict. The native peoples involved, referred to collectively as *Chichimecas,* a derogatory term employed by the Aztecs for the hunter-gatherers of the region, actively resisted encroachment of their hunting grounds by Spanish ranchers intent on expanding the developing livestock industry of the colony. A series of silver strikes, beginning in 1546 at Zacatecas, brought about a new type of colonial expansion, however—the silver rush.

Development of the North Mexican Frontier

The native peoples in the mining frontier area were very different from the sedentary Aztecs and Maya. Fierce and mobile, the Chichimecas resisted Spanish encroachment in what became known as the Chichimeca War, a conflict that lasted most of the latter half of the sixteenth century. Instead of being able to exploit well-developed and sophisticated native societies, Spaniards found themselves having to build towns, start farms and ranches, open roads, establish fortifications, and settle the country. A lucky few made fortunes as miners, merchants, and *hacendados* (owners of large landed estates producing both livestock and crops for market). The vast majority, however, simply sowed the seeds of modern North Mexican society.

The northern frontier society that populated these new agricultural and mining centers was a mixed lot. At the top a relatively few European-born Spaniards, known as *peninsulares,* filled the highest administrative and commercial posts. Accompanying them from the Old World were numerous people—mostly men—of African heritage, whose status as slaves placed them at the beck and call of the dominant Spaniards. The demand for labor in the sparsely settled north also required the recruitment, both voluntary and forced, of large numbers of Indians.

In time an important new element was added to this mixed lot of Spaniards, Africans, and Indians—the *mestizo.* Because migration from the Old World in the decades following the conquest was overwhelmingly male, it was Indian women who provided the sexual companionship, both willing and unwilling, for Spaniards and Africans alike. *Mestizaje,* as the process of blending has come to be known, created an ever increasing population of mixed-blood people that collectively came to be called *castas.* The ordering of society according to a racial-ethnic hierarchy was called the *sistema de castas.* Often the product of extra-legal unions or of rape, the mestizo population found the expanding northern frontier more welcoming to them. Military service, ranching, farming, and other economic activities were more accessible on the frontier, as was the possibility to "pass" into the ranks of the *criollos,* that is, the American-born Spaniards who occupied the top level of colonial society with the *peninsulares.*

At the same time that Spaniards, Africans, mestizos, and acculturated Indians flocked to each new *bonanza* (rich mineral deposit), Spanish missionaries established new centers for the conversion of the small local Indian populations. The Catholic religious order primarily responsible for undertaking the conversion of the Chichimecas was the Franciscans. Having arrived in New Spain in the mid-1520s at the behest of Cortés, their job had at first seemed a strictly religious one—to turn the Aztec and other "civilized" Indian societies of central Mexico away from the devil and toward Christ. The farther north they expanded their efforts, however, the more complicated the problem became. Preparing hunter-gatherers and semisedentary people for life in the Spanish empire was not merely a matter of religious reeducation but of completely transforming their ways of life. Indians gathered together in communities known as missions were subjected to the regimentation of European civilization: strict and complex divisions of labor, regular work schedules, and monogamy. Although the friars were the ultimate authorities in the missions, the Indians were trained in the ways of Spanish local government and responsibilities to the greater colonial society. The search for Indians who might prove amenable to the Christian life became part of the colonization process, the goal of which was the re-creation of Spanish social, political, and economic institutions. The mass of Indians would serve as the lower strata of society, whereas European and American-born Spaniards became the lords of the land.

New Mexico and Far West Texas Explored Again

As the silver frontier expanded northward, it was only a matter of time before the Pueblos again drew the attention of the Spaniards. Following the 1567 silver strike at Santa Barbara (in present-day southern Chihuahua), Spanish prospectors, slavers, and missionaries fanned out through the far north in search of other mines, new labor supplies, and souls to save. Byproducts of this frontier activity included the founding of Saltillo in the 1570s and contact with Indians who told tales of city-dwelling peoples north of a great river. The long-forgotten reports of the Coronado expedition might have quelled new rumors of rich kingdoms, but the northward extension of the silver corridor along the Sierra Madre Occidental argued for the most optimistic view of what might lie far to the north.

By 1581 Franciscan missionaries working in the Santa Barbara area were ready to investigate the rumors of sedentary peoples to the north. On June 5, Friars Agustín Rodríguez, Francisco López, and Juan de Santa María, accompanied by Captain Francisco Sánchez Chamuscado, eight soldiers, and nineteen Indian servants, headed northward, following the Conchos River to its juncture with the Rio Grande, a site that came to be known as Junta de los Ríos. Following the great river upstream on the counsel of the various Indian groups they encountered, in August they finally arrived in the El Paso area, which came to be called Paso del Norte because of the broad valley the Rio Grande cut between mountain ranges. Continuing northward, the Rodríguez-Chamuscado expedition entered the Pueblo country. At some point in the next few months Fray Santa María left for Mexico City to report to the viceroy, but was killed by Indians along the way. During this time his companions explored the region and made plans to establish missions. When their military escort decided to return to Santa Barbara in early 1582 the Franciscans chose to remain and begin work among the Pueblos.

Fueled by the Chamuscado party's wild tales of precious metals and a rich country, Antonio de Espejo seized the opportunity to "rescue" Friars Rodríguez and López. A Spaniard who had been implicated in the murder of one his servants, he had fled to the frontier, where he saw his chance to redeem his fortunes by opening up the Pueblo country. His party left Santa Barbara in November 1582, following the same route as the Rodríguez-Chamuscado expedition. Like the earlier group, Espejo's men heard stories of wealthy cities to the north, the earlier presence of three Spaniards and a black man (the Cabeza de Vaca group), and the abundance of silver to the west. Upon arrival in the Pueblo country, they got word of the death of Friars Rodríguez and López at the hands of the Tiguex Pueblos, but Espejo was undeterred and conducted a wide-ranging exploration west and east of the Rio Grande. About thirty miles south of present-day Santa Fe, he struck eastward to the Pecos River, which he followed south to its juncture with the Rio Grande. He returned to Santa Barbara very enthusiastic about the prospects of New Mexico and was on his way to Spain in 1585 to personally lobby the king for a *capitulación* when he died in Havana.

Juan de Oñate and the Founding of New Mexico

King Philip II was quite interested in this "new" Mexico, as the Pueblo country had come to be called, not only for the reports of silver and other riches, but for its large population of sedentary peoples. Spain's European rivals had been probing the peripheries of Spanish dominions for over a decade, and there continued to be talk of a northern water passage between the Atlantic and Pacific oceans. With little sense of the true geography of North America, Spaniards were becoming increasingly alarmed that the English might find a way to approach their rich colony of New Spain from the north. Spanish occupation of New Mexico, especially if the stories of rich mines and populous cities proved true, would keep them at bay.

Having deliberated the matter carefully, the royal council on colonial affairs, the Consejo de Indias, advised the king to seek out an *adelantado* who would occupy New Mexico under the terms of the colonization laws of 1573. Concerned by continued complaints from clergy with regard to the treatment of Indians in newly conquered areas, the conflicts among rival claimants to territory, and other abuses, Philip II and his councilors devised a new set of rules for subjugation of native lands. The new code of law emphasized the religious and philosophical ideals of the monarchy and required nonviolent pacification of new territories and fair treatment of the inhabitants whenever possible. To assure that men of good character led these enterprises and to minimize conflict among potential rivals, the code also called for all exploration to be carried out only under royal license. The search for a suitable candidate, that is, one who could underwrite the cost of colonization himself, with the appropriate experience on the frontier, and willing to abide by the new rules, took more than a decade.

In 1595, twelve years after Philip II's order, the viceroy settled on an acceptable candidate for *adelantado* of New Mexico. Juan de Oñate was the son of one of the discoverers of the Zacatecas silver mines and the husband of Isabel Tolosa Cortés Moctezuma—granddaughter of the conqueror of the Aztecs and great-granddaughter of the conquered emperor. Oñate was rich, well connected, and had substantial administrative experience. Finally, late in 1597 Oñate received the king's permission to proceed.

The permanent colonization of New Mexico had begun. Oñate's expedition included about 130 Spanish soldier-settlers and their families, over two hundred other soldiers, and hundreds of Indian servants. The religious goals of the *entrada* were represented by ten Franciscans who hoped to be worthy successors of Fray Rodríguez and the other missionaries who had first attempted to convert the

Pueblos in the 1570s. Herds and flocks accompanied the colonists, who hoped to establish a successful mining colony among the sedentary Pueblo Indians. After a three-month crossing of the Chihuahuan desert, Oñate's caravan arrived at the banks of the Rio Grande at the site of present-day Juárez–El Paso. El Pasoans today claim that by virtue of the April 30, 1598, celebration of their safe arrival, Texas can claim to be the site of the first Thanksgiving. According to one of the colonists, "there was a sermon, a great ecclesiastical and secular celebration, a great salute and rejoicing, and in the afternoon, a comedy." Although a number of Indian groups lived along the banks of the river below El Paso, Oñate and the Franciscans who accompanied him had their eyes set on the Pueblos of the upper Rio Grande valley.

As Oñate took control of the upper Rio Grande valley he sent out expeditions to explore the region. In 1601 he repeated Coronado's trek across the Texas Panhandle in search of the mythical Kingdom of Quivira. As disappointed as Coronado had been before them, Oñate's group settled for establishing a modest colony among the Pueblos. A few hundred Spanish colonists lived among thousands of agricultural Indians who were under the tutelage of Franciscan missionaries. New Mexico became a land of sheep ranches and subsistence farms, hardly the prosperous and populous colony that Oñate and the crown had envisioned.

Despite the lack of development, Spanish New Mexico needed to be able to communicate with rest of New Spain; the only route by which this could occur lay along the Rio Grande and the Paso del Norte. Spanish convoys headed to and from Santa Fe regularly stopped there to rest and take on water, but for many years no one thought to establish a mission, presidio (garrison), or town at the crossing. Not until 1659 did Fray García de San Francisco gather a group of local Manso Indians in Mission Nuestra Señora de Guadalupe de los Mansos. (This was more than a century after Cabeza de Vaca had first visited them and sixty years after Oñate had claimed their land for the Spanish crown.) Within a short time a number of Spanish settlers established farms in the area and in 1665 the Franciscans started a second mission, San Francisco de los Sumas, for another of the local native groups. During this time Paso del Norte was officially incorporated into the province of New Mexico with the appointment of an *alcalde mayor,* or lieutenant governor, under the authority of the governor in Santa Fe.

The Pueblo Revolt and the Growth of Paso del Norte

Life at Paso del Norte was uneventful until the Pueblo Revolt of 1680. The rebellion resulted from continued Spanish abuse of the Pueblos: The missionaries had suppressed local beliefs and humiliated traditional leaders; Spanish settlers had exploited Indian labor; and missionaries and secular officials had fought over control of the province and Indian labor. Although their numbers had declined significantly due to epidemic diseases and dropping fertility rates, the Pueblos still numbered in the tens of thousands in 1680, whereas the Spanish population included only about 3,000 men, women, and children. In a coordinated assault on

Spanish farms, missions, and the town of Santa Fe, the Pueblos killed 21 missionaries and almost 400 settlers. The survivors fled to Paso del Norte, arriving with little more than the clothes on their backs.

When Governor Antonio de Otermín took stock of the refugees in October 1680, he found that fewer than 2,000 had made it out safely; among them were over 300 Piro and Tiwa Pueblos whose close association with the Spaniards put them at odds with other Pueblos. With no prospects of reoccupying the upper Rio Grande valley in the immediate future, Otermín set about establishing settlements for the Spanish and Indian populations. By 1684 a string of five communities lined the south bank of the river: Guadalupe, San Lorenzo, Senecú, Ysleta, and Socorro. Although the last three of these settlements were intended to serve the friendly Pueblo refugees, Spanish settlers soon moved in among the Indians. For the next 150 years these settlements, along with a small number of haciendas and smaller ranchos, flourished in New Mexico's southernmost district. The area became an important wine-producing and Indian trade center and the key way station on the Santa Fe-Chihuahua Camino Real (royal road).

With the Spaniards' expulsion from New Mexico a group of Franciscan missionaries turned their attention to Indians who had been visited in the 1580s and who periodically came to trade at Spanish outposts. East of the Mansos and Sumas, in what is today western Texas, southeastern New Mexico, and northern

The expansion of Spanish colonization in the direction of the Rio Grande in far West Texas altered Indian ways of life even in areas where the Spaniards never gained a foothold. At Meyers Springs, just east of the Big Bend, a rock shelter contains Indian artists' rendering of these contacts in the form of church towers with crosses. *(From the collections of the Texas Memorial Museum, The University of Texas at Austin)*

Chihuahua, lived various indigenous groups known collectively as Jumanos by the Spaniards. Among these groups there were both sedentary agriculturalists, some of whom had been visited by Cabeza de Vaca, and nonsedentary buffalo hunters and traders. Over the course of the seventeenth century various groups of Apaches had moved southward into the area and had begun engaging in cycles of warfare and trade with the Pueblos and other Indian groups in the interior. Also finding their way into this area were groups of Indians from Spanish frontier settlements fleeing harsh working conditions and loss of their traditional ranges. Thus, by the late seventeenth century there were thousands of Indians in the area with enough knowledge of the Spanish and enough interest in European trade goods to foster trade and missionary contacts.

In 1681 the Jumano chief Juan de Sabeata arrived in Paso del Norte asking for missionaries to visit his country. Sabeata spoke Spanish, claimed to have been baptized at the mining town of Parral, and had conducted many trade expeditions to the Hasinai country of eastern Texas, where he exchanged Spanish wares and horses for dressed hides and other Indian trade goods. In response, Governor Domingo de Cruzate, responding to the opportunity to gain additional Indian allies, sent his lieutenant, Juan Domínguez de Mendoza, and Fray Nicolás López to investigate the possibility of establishing a Spanish presence among the Jumanos in the vicinity of the Conchos-Rio Grande junction, an area that came to be called La Junta de los Ríos. Between December 1683 and June 1684, the Mendoza-López expedition visited Jumano and other groups at La Junta and ventured as far northeast as the Edwards Plateau, somewhere along the Colorado River. There the escort hunted for buffalo hides while Fray López and his companions baptized a number of Plains Indians and made plans for establishing a permanent mission field.

When Mendoza and López returned to Paso del Norte they left behind two missions, La Navidad and Apóstol Santiago, near what is today Presidio, Texas. Fathers Juan de Zavaleta and Antonio de Acevedo, who were left in charge, were soon forced to withdraw to Parral, however, when the Julime and other tribes in the area joined a general insurrection against the Spaniards. Word of the successful rebellion of the Pueblos soon spread among other tribes under Spanish control, and the whole northern frontier was aflame in an insurrection that has come to be called the Great Northern Revolt. Missions and *haciendas* burned, missionaries became martyrs, herds were scattered, stolen, and slaughtered. Communications between outlying posts and more established settlements became erratic. It took over a decade for the Spaniards to restore a measure of control and resume the process of expansion.

Despite various efforts to reestablish the La Junta missions in the years that followed, neither La Navidad nor Apóstol Santiago proved sustainable in the long run. The Spaniards turned their attention to recovering New Mexico, where their honor and their strategic interests had been wounded by the first major successful Indian revolt against Spanish rule in New Spain. As the Franciscans returned to their burned-out churches, their torn-down friaries and abandoned fields, they poured what resources they could muster into New Mexico. Little could be spared for the marginal stations at La Junta. Nevertheless, it was at these missions that Spanish authorities in Mexico first received word of the first successful intrusion by other Europeans into the colony's territory.

La Salle and the Spanish Rediscovery of Texas

Fathers Joaquín Hinojosa and Agustín de Colina were working at La Junta late in 1687, reestablishing the missions abandoned three years earlier during the Great Northern Revolt, when Chief Juan Sabeata of the Jumanos arrived with disturbing news. He had returned from the annual Indian trade fair in Hasinai country with word that other Spaniards were actively trading with the Indians of the region. Asked to bring back proof, Sabeata returned from the next fair at the beginning of 1689 with pages torn from French books, a picture of a ship with French verse inscribed on it, and the reassuring news that other Indians had attacked and destroyed the French settlement and all its occupants. In this way the Spaniards first learned of the whereabouts and fate of the La Salle colony.

Evidence of a long-distance Indian communication network across Texas comes from this unlikely source, a drawing of a European sailing vessel on which two of the La Salle expedition members wrote a message. The parchment was carried by Jumano Indians as far as the Spanish mining center at Parral, the first conclusive proof of a French landing in Spanish territory. *(Jean L'Archeveque Items, CN 02178 a, b, The Center for American History, The University of Texas at Austin)*

The French Threat

Spanish authorities had not been unaware of the Frenchman's plan. Since the fall of 1685, when a Spanish naval squadron had captured a French pirate ship in the Caribbean, colonial officials were aware that René Robert Cavelier, Sieur de La Salle, was leading a large expedition headed for the Mississippi, with the purpose of establishing a colony on the Gulf of Mexico coast. The Spaniards, having neglected the Gulf of Mexico for over a century, found themselves ill prepared to meet the French challenge. Fortunately for them, La Salle himself was poorly equipped for his enterprise, and his expedition's misfortune proved a godsend to the Spaniards.

From the time of his arrival in the vicinity of Montreal in 1666, La Salle, a French-born Canadian, took an interest in the fur trade and in creating a commercial empire in the interior of North America. He discovered the Ohio River, opened up the Great Lakes to navigation, built a string of trading posts in the upper Midwest, and in 1682 reached the mouth of the Mississippi River, claiming the entire basin, which he named Louisiana, for France. La Salle intended the name to flatter Louis XIV, before whom in late 1683 he had laid out a plan to establish a fortified colony at the mouth of the river. From a warm water port there, the French could both control the fur trade of much of the continent and pursue the conquest of the silver mining districts of nearby New Spain.

Misfortune dogged the expedition from the beginning. Soon after the four-ship fleet sailed in July 1684, its naval escort vessel had to turn back for repairs. Later, a hurricane scattered the fleet and a Spanish pirate ship captured the fleet's smallest ship. Desertions at Saint-Domingue, where La Salle had made port to reprovision, left the expedition with considerably fewer than the 400 men, women, and children with which it had started. In January 1685 the fleet sailed past the mouth of the Mississippi, finally making landfall at Matagorda Bay, where the expedition's supply ship soon foundered. When the French naval commander decided to take his ship home, a significant number of expedition members chose to abandon the venture, including the sole engineer in the company. Finally, during the following winter La Salle lost his last ship, *Belle*, which sank in Matagorda Bay during a storm.

Nothing seemed to work in La Salle's favor. The first settlement site on the bay turned out to be unhealthy (brackish water and mosquito and snake infested) and exposed to attack. La Salle soon discovered a better location on Garcitas Creek, where a small compound, which came to be known as Fort St. Louis, began to take shape in the summer of 1685. A number of the weaker members of the party died during the first months, and the "artisans" recruited for the expedition turned out to be a rather useless lot overall. The company proved ill equipped to farm under the prevailing conditions, and the first crops were lost. In addition, the local Karankawas, whom La Salle had initially decided to treat as hostile, kept the settlement under siege.

By the time the first winter arrived, work was far enough along for La Salle to feel comfortable in undertaking his first substantial exploration of the country.

The *Belle,* one of La Salle's ships, foundered in Matagorda Bay within a year of its arrival on the Texas coast in 1685. Discovered by archeologists from the Texas Historical Commission, the ship was excavated in 1996–97. Its restoration was entrusted to Texas A&M's Marine Archeology Laboratory. *(Texas Historical Commission)*

Contradictory reports and self-serving claims make it difficult to know where he went and how he dealt with the native peoples he encountered. In April 1686 La Salle and twenty men began an unsuccessful march to the northeast in an effort to find the Mississippi and seek help for the colony in the Illinois country. They made it only as far as the Hasinai country between the Trinity and Neches rivers. Only eight men made it back to the French settlement. The others had died of illness, gotten lost, or, in one case, fallen victim to an alligator.

Desertion also took its toll on the colony. Not only did men abandon the post, but some deserted La Salle during his exploration of the country. Henri Joutel remarked that two sailors had gone native:

> They had . . . so perfectly enur'd themselves to the Customs of the Natives, that they were become meer Savages. They were naked, their Faces and Bodies with Figures wrought on them, like the rest. They had taken several Wives, been at the Wars and kill'd their Enemies with the Firelocks . . . but having no more Powder nor Ball, their Arms were grown useless, and they had been forc'd to learn to shoot with Bows and Arrows.

Another member of the expedition had done so well among the Coahuiltecans who had taken him in that by the time the Spanish found him he was the chief of a sizable village. With each desertion or death by snakebite, alligator mauling, or disease, the colony became weaker. La Salle had to act.

The last chapter of the La Salle colony began in January 1687. The settlement was down to about forty people, including some women and children, and under constant attack by the Karankawas. On January 12 La Salle and the strongest seventeen men among the colonists again set out for the Mississippi to seek help. Arrogant and abusive toward his men, he forced them to carry their own supplies so that the few horses acquired from the Indians could transport his and his brother's trade goods and personal possessions. By March 19 a number of men in the party had had enough and mutinied, killing La Salle, his brother, and two servants. Eventually, six men made it to Canada, including Henri Joutel, who wrote the best existing account of the La Salle expedition and its tragic end.

At the post, conditions worsened as food ran out and disease felled the survivors. Although a temporary truce was reached with the Karankawas, the end came during Christmas 1688, when a large war party attacked the compound. Among the dead was the first child of European parents known to have been born in Texas.

The Spanish Search for La Salle and the First Occupation of Texas

The Spaniards had no way of knowing that the Texas coast and its native peoples had taken care of their problem for them. With only a rough idea of which direction La Salle's ships had sailed, colonial authorities organized a number of maritime and land expeditions to search for the French. Although five voyages to the northern Gulf of Mexico failed to turn up evidence of a French presence, they did produce the first detailed maps of the region and became the basis for Spanish occupation of the Florida panhandle in the 1690s.

Ultimately successful in locating the site of the French colony was Alonso de León, governor of Coahuila and seasoned frontiersman. Born in Nuevo León in 1639, he had studied in Spain and served in the Spanish navy before returning to the frontier and becoming an accomplished Indian fighter. Between 1686 and 1688 he made three reconnaissance expeditions in search of the French colony, pausing in between to put down an Indian revolt. In 1689 he and the Franciscan Friar Damián de Massanet undertook a fourth land expedition during which they came upon the ruins of the French post. The sight of human remains, of loose pages torn from books, of everyday household belongings scattered within the compound moved one of León's men to compose a poem commemorating the event. The first verse, as translated by La Salle historian Robert Weddle, reads:

> Sad and fateful site
> where prevails the dark of night
> because misfortune's whim
> brought thy people death so grim,
> here alone I contemplate

thou epitome of fate,
of the inconstancy of life;
since in the fierceness of the strife
the cruel enemy pressed
his heartless hand upon thy breast,
upon thy innocence so mild,
sparing not the smallest child.

Although the smallest child had not been spared, five children had survived the final Indian attack. Karankawa women protected four of the Talón family children and one other boy, all of whom were adopted into the tribe. During their 1690 expedition León and Massanet managed to ransom three of the five. The other two children were acquired from the Karankawa by Domingo Terán de los Ríos the following year.

In the spring of 1690, when León and Massanet returned to Texas together for the last time, La Salle's colony was no longer a threat but there was no clear evidence that the French were entirely gone from the region. At the same time Massanet's contacts with the Hasinai (who the Spaniards believed called themselves Tejas) led him to believe that it would be easy to convert these sedentary peoples to Christianity and incorporate them into the colonial system without the need for a military presence. León believed the Indians, although friendly, should not be trusted and that the Spaniards would need a string of four presidios to properly hold the province.

After carrying out the viceroy's orders to burn the French post, León proceeded to the Kingdom of the Tejas, where, assured of the Hasinais' continued interest in conversion, he placed Fray Massanet in charge of Mission San Francisco de los Tejas on May 25, 1690. He also invested the village head man with the symbols of Spanish authority:

> I delivered to the governor a staff with a cross, giving him the title of governor of all his people, in order that he might rule and govern them, giving him to understand by means of an interpreter that which he should observe and do, and the respect and obedience which he and all his people ought to have for the priests, and that he should make all his families attend Christian teaching, in order that they might be instructed in the affairs of our holy Catholic faith so that later they might be baptized and become Christians. He accepted the staff with much pleasure, promising to do all that was desired of him, and the company fired three salutes.

Afterwards he gathered the remaining Talón children from the colony and returned to Coahuila, reporting to the viceroy the disturbing news that a French trader had been among the Hasinais trying to undermine their loyalty to Spain.

Henri Tonti, a trader from French Illinois, had made the journey down the Mississippi late in 1689, in a second effort to locate survivors of the La Salle colony. He had visited among the various Caddo tribes, exploring trade opportunities and the possibilities of an anti-Spanish alliance, but had no success. His exploration and the arrival of the La Salle expedition survivors in New France reinvigorated French interest in the Gulf of Mexico region, however. It would not be long before better equipped and better informed Frenchmen arrived to re-assert La Salle's claim to the area on behalf of Louis XIV.

Spain Abandons the Kingdom of the Tejas

León's report of continuing French activities among the Tejas reached Mexico City about the same time as news of France's renewed hostilities against Spain. In the face of the mounting challenge it became obvious that a single Franciscan mission so far from the settlement frontier in Coahuila was inadequate to protect Spanish interests. The question for the viceroy's council was whether to accept Fray Massanet's plan for a string of missions but no presidios or León's plan for a strong military presence. Given the limited resources at their disposal and the requirement of royal approval for the establishment of presidios, the question answered itself.

The Kingdom of the Tejas, that portion of modern Texas that extends from the Trinity River eastward, first became a Spanish province with the appointment of Domingo Terán de los Ríos as its governor in January 1691. An experienced colonial official, Terán de los Ríos accepted the assignment to found seven new missions, explore the country east of the Tejas, and determine the proximity of foreign colonies; however, he protested being subordinated in all important decisions to Fray Massanet.

The Terán de los Ríos-Massanet expedition, which lasted from May 1691 to April 1692, proved that Spain was not ready to occupy Texas. Throughout the *entrada* the governor and missionaries quarreled. Even before arriving in Hasinai country they learned of an epidemic which had swept their villages and taken Fray Miguel de Fontcuberta's life along with those of many Indians. The epidemic, drought, and exhaustion of supplies began to turn the Hasinais against the Spaniards. The winter of 1691–92, which caught Terán de los Ríos in what is now the Red River country of Texas, Louisiana, and Arkansas, proved harsh and sapped what was left of the expedition's morale. In the end Terán de los Ríos had nothing to show for his year-long wanderings through East Texas: He had not founded any missions; he had not explored the country to the degree required by his instructions; and he had not established adequate lines of communication between the Kingdom of the Tejas and the interior of New Spain.

Spain's first occupation of Texas was coming to an end in the months following Terán de los Ríos's departure. Given the change in attitude on the part of the Hasinais, six of the missionaries had chosen to return to Coahuila, leaving only Fray Massanet and two companions behind. Mission Santísimo Nombre de María, which had been founded before the arrival of Terán de los Ríos, had been washed away by a flood, its Spanish residents forced to move into San Francisco de los Tejas. Efforts to resupply the missions overland from Monclova had largely failed as a result of the weather, evidence of the logistical obstacles to occupying a far-flung outpost without intermediate way stations.

Fray Massanet had tragically miscalculated his chances of success in bringing Christianity and Spanish civilization to the Hasinais. He had persuaded the viceroy and his council that missionaries working among peaceful and sedentary Indians, without the disruptions and corruption of Spanish colonial soldiers, could secure Texas for the crown. The Indians, however, lost all respect for the Franciscans, refusing to participate in religious instruction, and came to associate the waters of baptism with death. The Franciscans had misunderstood the intentions of the Hasinais in inviting the missionaries to live among them. Their real interest in courting the Spanish had not been in religious conversion, but in obtaining gifts and trade goods previously available only in limited amounts from the Jumanos and other Indian traders. When the gifts dried up and it became obvious that these Spaniards had little interest in establishing reciprocal trade relations on their terms, the Tejas saw little incentive in supporting, or even accepting, a Spanish presence among them. Finally, in October 1693 Chief Bernardino, now sporting a French suit of clothes, warned the Spaniards to leave. By the end of the month Friars Massanet and Francisco Hidalgo and a handful of soldiers were on their way to Coahuila. Ironically, waiting for them in Monclova, the capital of Coahuila, when they arrived in February 1694 was an order from the viceroy to abandon the province of Texas.

Conclusion

Happenstance brought the first Europeans to the northwest corner of the Gulf of Mexico, to a land that had no name, no boundaries, and in no way approximated modern Texas. The accidental exploration of present-day coastal Texas and much of what is today northern Mexico by Cabeza de Vaca and his fellow survivors of the Narváez *entrada* was followed by the more purposeful exploits of the Moscoso and Coronado expeditions: Dreams and tales of treasure had brought these conquistadors into the forests of East Texas and the plains and canyons of West Texas. The great disappointment at finding no new Aztec empires to conquer dampened their enthusiasm. This vast and sparsely settled land turned out to be nothing more than the least inviting corner of Spain's North American backyard.

And that part of Texas that was eventually settled by Spaniards and their Indian allies in the course of the seventeenth century was, in fact, not part of Texas at all. The Spanish colonials, missionaries, soldiers, and Indians who made up the Paso del Norte communities, along the Rio Grande, considered themselves New Mexicans. It would not be until the middle of the nineteenth century that the descendants of some of these people began to call themselves Texas Mexicans.

Finally, with the arrival of La Salle the Spaniards were forced to explore the long-forgotten corner of their backyard. What they found was the Kingdom of the Tejas, Caddoan-speaking, agricultural villagers more correctly referred to as Hasinais, whose word for "friend" or "ally"—spelled Texas in the Spanish of the times—served as the name for their country. La Salle's own wishful thinking and exaggerated expectations met disaster in the tough and unforgiving Karankawa country.

At the end of the seventeenth century Texas remained a vague abstraction that included only a fraction of its current territory. Except for the vicinity of Paso del

Norte, which was developing as an important part of the province of New Mexico, the rest of what is now Texas was well beyond the frontier line of settlement and remained unknown territory. Although the expeditions that had found La Salle's post and established contacts with the Hasinais had stressed the apparent fertility and plentiful waters of the region, few saw any immediate opportunities in a land so far removed from established lines of communication. There were plenty of Indian souls in need of salvation who were closer to central New Spain to bother much with the fickle Caddos. The long-neglected corner of the backyard was still securely a Spanish possession—clearing it, farming it, and building on it could wait a little longer. The next chapter in the Texas story would be written when the French again appeared in Louisiana to challenge Spain's claim to the Kingdom of the Tejas.

SUGGESTED READINGS

Several works provide overviews of Spanish North America, including the area that is now Texas, from the Age of the Conquistadors through the end of the first Spanish occupation of Texas. Anyone with a deeper interest in the conquest of Mexico and the establishment of Spanish institutions in North America can begin to explore the subject in Michael C. Meyer, William L. Sherman, and Susan M. Deeds, *The Course of Mexican History* (6th ed., 1999). The first six chapters of David J. Weber's *The Spanish Frontier in North America* (1992) provide a comprehensive survey of what is now the southern half of the United States through the end of the seventeenth century. The same chronological period is covered, in a very different, but highly entertaining way, in the first eight chapters of John L. Kessell, *Spain in the Southwest: A Narrative History of Colonial New Mexico, Arizona, Texas, and California* (2002). For those interested specifically in Texas, the most complete survey of this era can be found in chapters 2–5 of Donald E. Chipman, *Spanish Texas, 1519–1821* (1992). Emphasizing the Indian side of the story are two very different works: Elizabeth A. H. John, *Storms Brewed in Other Men's Worlds: The Confrontation of Indians, Spanish, and French in the Southwest, 1540–1795* (reprint; 1996), and Gary Clayton Anderson, *The Indian Southwest, 1580–1830: Ethnogenesis and Reinvention* (1999). For an understanding of Spain in the age of exploration and the age of the conquistadors, see J. H. Elliot, *Imperial Spain, 1469–1716* (1964).

Dawn of Texas History

Of the conquistadors who traveled across Texas, none has received more scholarly attention than Alvar Núñez Cabeza de Vaca, who set down the story of his adventures in North America in a work titled *Relación*. It has been translated numerous times, including the very readable and well illustrated *Castaways: The Narrative of Alvar Núñez Cabeza de Vaca*, ed. Enrique Pupo-Walker, trans. Frances M. López-Morillas (1993). Cabeza de Vaca's experiences have also produced a cottage industry of anthropological and ethnohistorical work and literary criticism on

Indian-Spanish contact. One example of this more recent work is Nancy Hickerson, "How Cabeza De Vaca Lived With, Worked Among, and Finally Left the Indians of Texas," *Journal of Anthropological Research* (1998). A more established tradition is the effort of historians and naturalists to pin down Cabeza de Vaca's route across Texas and northern Mexico. Two recent examples of this type of work are Donald E. Chipman, "In Search of Cabeza de Vaca's Route Across Texas: An Historiographical Survey," *Southwestern Historical Quarterly* (1987), and Donald W. Olson et al., "Piñon Pines and the Route of Cabeza de Vaca," *Southwestern Historical Quarterly* (1997).

Elusive Riches—Harsh Realities

Interpretation of the Coronado and Soto-Moscoso expeditions has changed significantly over the last century. The first historian to put together the story of Soto-Moscoso was the mestizo historian Garcilaso de la Vega, whose *The Florida of the Inca,* which first appeared in 1605, has been translated and edited by John Grier Varner and Jeannette Johnson Varner (1980). Bringing up to date the state of research on Moscoso's route in Texas is James E. Bruseth and Nancy A. Kenmotsu, "From Naguatex to the River Daycao: The Route of the Hernando De Soto Expedition Through Texas," *North American Archaeologist* (1993). A very good brief summary of the expedition can be found in Robert S. Weddle, *Spanish Sea: The Gulf of Mexico in North American Discovery, 1500–1685* (1985), chapter 12. The current trend in research on the Coronado expedition can be found in Richard Flint and Shirley Cushing Flint, eds., *The Coronado Expedition to Tierra Nueva: The 1540–1542 Route Across the Southwest* (1997). The best short summary of Spanish exploration in West Texas during this period is John Miller Morris, *El Llano Estacado: Exploration and Imagination on the High Plains of Texas and New Mexico, 1536–1860* (1997), part 1.

The Paso del Norte Corridor

The various early expeditions and Juan de Oñate's conquest of New Mexico in 1598 are covered in *El Paso: A Borderlands History* by W. H. Timmons (1990), which also traces the seventeenth-century history of the area. Marc Simmons's *The Last Conquistador: Juan de Oñate and the Settling of the Far Southwest* (1991), also discusses Spanish activity in the El Paso area up to 1598. The poetically inclined might wish to look up the Oñate story in epic poem form, *Historia de la Nueva México, 1610,* by Gaspar Pérez de Villagrá (1992), originally published in 1610. A very readable account of the Pueblo Revolt and the Spanish flight to the El Paso area in 1680 is Andrew L. Knaut, *The Pueblo Revolt of 1680: Conquest and Resistance in Seventeenth-Century New Mexico* (1995).

La Salle and the Spanish Rediscovery of Texas

No one has produced more work on La Salle's expedition and its consequences than Robert S. Weddle. His most recent work, *The Wreck of the* Belle, *the Ruin of La Salle* (2001), is an exhaustive study of the explorer from his early Canadian ventures to his death in East Texas. A quarter-century older, but still the best narrative of the Spaniards' efforts to find the French colony is Weddle's *Wilderness Manhunt: The Spanish Search for La Salle* (1973). Another writer who has made significant contributions to our understanding of this period is William Foster. His edition and annotation of Juan Bautista Chapa's *Texas and Northeastern Mexico, 1630–1690* (1997), ties the history of Texas to that of Nuevo León and Coahuila. Also of value are chapters 2 through 5 of his *Spanish Expeditions into Texas, 1689–1768* (1995), in which he tries to pin down the routes of the various *entradas* of the late seventeenth century.

3

New Spain's Northeastern Frontier, 1714–1767

Tired, sick, but full of hope and enthusiasm for their work, the nine Franciscan priests who participated in the reoccupation of Texas finally sat down together on July 22, 1716, to pen a joint petition to the viceroy seeking further aid for their work. "We have conceived great expectations that this province will become a New Philippine, having, firstly, Your Excellency's protection and, on the Indians' part, the great friendliness with which they have received us. We believe that their docility and good demeanor merit that our generous and Catholic King and Lord (whom God protect) attend to them as his beloved children, and extend his powerful hand to put in ours the wherewithal for them to cover their nakedness, cultivate their lands, and raise livestock for their subsistence." With a bit of hyperbole, they hoped to flatter King Phillip V by comparing their work among the Hasinais with the efforts of earlier missionaries in the Philippine Islands under Phillip II 150 years earlier. These friars and their successors represented one of the principal tools of Spanish colonial expansion, although royal support was never as generous as they hoped it would be. Along with presidios and ranches, missions were an indispensable institution of the Spanish North American frontier until the last third of the century. Missionaries firmly believed that their work served both majesties—glorifying God and expanding the dominions of the king. In Texas both these assumptions would be tested and the reality of Spanish imperial might put to the test.

1699	French occupy central Gulf of Mexico coast
1700	Mission-presidio complex of San Juan Bautista del Río Grande established
1714	St. Denis founds Natchitoches and makes contact with Spaniards at Rio Grande
1716	Ramón expedition reoccupies East Texas for Spain
1718	Governor Alarcón founds mission-presidio complex of San Antonio de Béxar
1720	Mission San José y San Miguel de Aguayo, "Queen of the Missions," founded by Fray Antonio Margil de Jesús
1721	Marqués de Aguayo establishes Presidio de los Adaes as capital of Texas; founds mission-presidio complex of La Bahía
1727	Rivera inspection
1731	Querétaro missions from East Texas transferred to San Antonio; Canary Island immigrants establish first civil settlement at Béxar
1746	Mission-presidio complex of San Xavier begins to form
1749	Escandón orders transfer of La Bahía to present location; settlement of lower Rio Grande valley begins
1755	Laredo founded
1758	Mission San Sabá, established for Apaches, destroyed by Indians hostile to Apaches
1759	Norteño defeat of Spanish-Apache expedition at Red River marks end of Spanish ambitions to expand northward
1767	Distribution of land grants in lower Rio Grande valley begins

In the years following Spanish withdrawal from Hasinai country, Spanish officials remained concerned about the French threat to their dominion of the Gulf of Mexico region, and Franciscan missionaries remained interested in the prospect of converting the native peoples of the northeastern frontier. They all failed to see the thriving and dynamic world that the diverse Indian peoples of the region had created for themselves. The various culture groups in what is now Texas had developed a vast and sophisticated trade network based on regular exchange gatherings in the Colorado-Brazos area of central Texas. Indian trade fairs included a wide variety of products, including buffalo robes and dried meat, tools, pottery, mass-produced stone projectile points, corn, some jewelry, and, most prized of all, horses. This Indian world was only vaguely understood by the Spanish, who could not accept that an Indian political economy might complement rather than threaten the Spanish imperial system. It would take much of the eighteenth century to bring Spanish policy-makers around to accepting that Indians could be allies or trade partners rather than merely enemies or heathens awaiting salvation.

Consequently, for a half century after it was reoccupied in 1716, Texas and the rest of New Spain's northern frontier were pawns in a great geopolitical contest for empire. While policy-makers in Madrid, Paris, and London maneuvered to expand and consolidate their colonies, settlement of the frontier was driven by a combination of fear and opportunity. The native peoples were seen as the prize of this imperial contest, and the frontiersmen were expected to sacrifice and forebear.

By mid-century Spanish Bourbon policy-makers were exploring new ways of colonizing and had begun distancing themselves from the missionary approach. Texas, occupied during this period of transition, proved a largely insurmountable challenge to Spanish religious, political, and economic principles.

The French Challenge

Overextended and underpopulated, by the end of the seventeenth century the Spanish empire was a feeble power—just like its king, the sickly and often irrational Charles II, who was the last of the increasingly incompetent Spanish Hapsburgs. Convinced that Pensacola Bay in west Florida was strategically the best place from which to maintain control of the Gulf of Mexico, Spanish colonial officials moved to occupy the area in 1698. If the tactic worked, there would be no need to occupy the more hazardous and inaccessible Texas coast; Pensacola would protect the entire northern gulf at minimal cost to the crown. Such optimism quickly evaporated when in January 1699 a French squadron sailed past Pensacola on its way to the Mississippi. Totally unprepared to challenge the intruders, the Spanish could do little but watch as French Louisiana came into being, first at Biloxi, then at Mobile and along the lower Mississippi River. Further complicating the situation was the death of the childless Charles II, whose vacillation over naming a successor had created competing claims by French Bourbons and Austrian Hapsburgs.

When Philip of Anjou, grandson of Louis XIV, ascended the Spanish throne in 1700 the War of the Spanish Succession (known as Queen Anne's War in English North America) followed. France and Spain were allied against the English, Austrians, Dutch, and various German states. France took advantage of the situation to claim that its expansion in Louisiana was as much an effort to protect its Spanish ally's interests in the Gulf of Mexico as it was to defend its North American colony. By the end of the war in 1714, the French were well entrenched in a series of Indian trading posts and a handful of strategic ports. It was clear to the Spanish that their erstwhile allies were now their most serious rivals in North America.

A French Trader Helps Spain Settle Texas

The new French threat did not take long to materialize. Governor Antoine de la Mothe, Sieur de Cadillac, charged with making Louisiana profitable, soon began to probe New Spain for weaknesses. He attempted, unsuccessfully, to establish trade at Veracruz, colonial Mexico's principal port. Cadillac also ordered traders westward to establish trade relations with the western Caddo chieftanships, and entrusted a most sensitive assignment to one of the oldest and most experienced residents of Louisiana, Louis Juchereau de St. Denis. St. Denis's mission was to establish contact with the Spanish on the northern frontier as a prelude to opening direct trade with the legendary silver mining region of Nueva Vizcaya.

St. Denis was in command at Biloxi at the time Governor Cadillac chose him as emissary to the Texas Caddos and the Spanish frontier. A vigorous, Canadian-born Indian trader and royal official, the thirty-seven-year-old Frenchman already had a dozen years of experience among the lower Mississippi tribes. In September 1713 he ventured up the Mississippi to the mouth of the Red River, then westward to the site of a Caddo village, where he established his post of Natchitoches and began trading with the Indians. In the course of the next few months St. Denis slowly made his way southwestward in search of a Spanish outpost. With him were Pierre and Robert Talón, who as children had survived the La Salle expedition. Finally, in July 1714 he crossed the Rio Grande near present-day Guerrero, Coahuila (about thirty-five miles southeast of Piedras Negras-Eagle Pass), and approached Presidio San Juan Bautista del Río Grande.

The story St. Denis told the commander of the small post, Diego Ramón, reveals how religious, commercial, and political forces combined to make the frontier such a fascinating place. According to the Frenchman, Governor Cadillac had sent him on a mission to find the Franciscan missionary Fray Francisco Hidalgo, who had written the French governor of Louisiana two years previously requesting assistance in the conversion of the Hasinais. So, now he was here, ready to help Fray Hidalgo in his religious work while at the same time offering to open trade between Louisiana and New Spain.

Fray Hidalgo's request for assistance may have been an excuse for Cadillac and St. Denis's efforts to establish commercial links with northern New Spain, but it was much more. It represented yet another effort on the part of the Colegio de Propaganda Fide de la Santa Cruz de Querétaro to restore its Texas mission field so precipitously abandoned two decades earlier. By the 1680s, in an effort to recapture the missionary zeal of a century earlier the Franciscans had settled on a new system for carrying out their frontier work. Missionary colleges such as Querétaro (1683), Nuestra Señora de Guadalupe at Zacatecas (1707), and San Fernando at Mexico City (1734) sent priests and lay brothers to the northern frontier. The colleges operated as independent institutions. Each served as a base of operations as well as a training center, especially in the languages and customs of the Indians. Recruiting was done both in New Spain and in Spain, and candidates for missionary work had to display a special vocation for the rigors of frontier life. The naive zeal of the Querétaro College Franciscans in the years immediately after its establishment had contributed to the initial failure in east Texas by 1693, but that setback had not dampened the missionaries' enthusiasm for work among the Tejas.

Fray Hidalgo, in particular, had opposed abandoning the mission to the Hasinais and had returned to Querétaro determined to make another attempt with them. By the late 1690s he had been assigned to the new mission field in northern Coahuila, and in 1700 he was involved in founding missions San Juan Bautista and San Francisco Solano on the Rio Grande. There, in a model of missionary frontier expansion, the missions were clustered in the vicinity of a presidio, also called San Juan Bautista del Río Grande, whose troops had responsibility for defending the missions. Together, soldiers and friars would educate the missions' Indian occupants in Spanish colonial agricultural, architectural, and artesanal practices, and teach them to dress, eat, and speak as humble subjects of the crown.

With the arrival of St. Denis at the Rio Grande outpost, Fray Hidalgo must have believed his prayers answered. The friar knew that the appearance of a Frenchman on the Coahuila frontier would create a panic in the viceroy's palace. He also knew that circumstances on the frontier had not changed appreciably since the Spanish had abandoned Texas twenty years before: The country was still misunderstood; the Indian peoples of the region remained totally independent of Spanish sovereignty; and the colonial population of northern New Spain was not large enough to populate yet another province. The missions, with their role of converting the natives into Christian subjects of His Catholic Majesty, were the only way Spain might hold such a vast and remote region against the French.

The news that came back from Mexico City in the summer of 1715 was just what Fray Hidalgo had been waiting to hear. St. Denis's testimony before the viceregal court provided conclusive evidence of French designs, not only on Texas, but on the interior mining provinces. The viceroy issued orders for the reoccupation of Texas on terms favorable to the Franciscans as well as to the French: four missions to be protected by a garrison of twenty-five men, to be established as close as possible to the westernmost French post. Fray Hidalgo would now return to the country of the Tejas and Governor Cadillac had his point of contact with New Spain.

The vanguard of Spanish colonization in Texas consisted largely of Franciscan missionaries such as Antonio Margil de Jesús. A native of Spain with over thirty years of experience in Central America and Mexico, the Texas mission field proved to be his last great effort. Judged by modern, cultural relativistic standards, his work seems misguided and destructive to Indian society, but in his day he was seen to epitomize Christian virtues. *(The San Jacinto Museum of History, Houston)*

Spain's Return to Texas

In command of this important expedition was Captain Domingo Ramón, son of the commander of Presidio San Juan Bautista and an experienced frontiersman. Setting out from Saltillo in February 1716, he continued to collect materiel and people along the way. By the time the caravan arrived in the country of the Tejas in June, it consisted of twenty-six men, seven of them married and with their families, twelve missionaries, and a number of civilians, including St. Denis, who served as guide. The missionaries included representatives of both the Querétaro and Zacatecas colleges, one of whom was the now aged Fray Hidalgo. In his thirty years of service in New Spain, Fray Hidalgo had helped establish the college he represented as well as numerous missions, and was now given the honor of becoming the first resident priest at Nuestro Padre San Francisco de los Tejas, the first mission established by the Ramón expedition. Continuing to the northeast, Querétaro friars established a second mission, Nuestra Señora de la Purísima Concepción, on the Angelina River. Still farther east, friars from the Zacatecas College established Mission Nuestra Señora de Guadalupe at the head Nacogdoche village and future site of the town of Nacogdoches. Finally, Ramón established a third Querétaro mission, San José de los Nazonis, a few miles to the north at the village of that group. Clustered between the Neches and Angelina rivers, the four missions came under the protection of Presidio Nuestra Señora de los Dolores.

Officially the leader of the Zacatecas missionaries was Fray Antonio Margil de Jesús, the most renowned Franciscan in early eighteenth-century New Spain and cofounder of the Zacatecas College, who had been too ill to make the initial *entrada* with Ramón. Early in 1717 he directed the founding of two new missions to the east, closer to the French post of Natchitoches. At the site of present-day San Augustine he founded Nuestra Señora de los Dolores at an Ais Indian village. Still farther east, in what is today the vicinity of Robeline, Louisiana, he established San Miguel de los Adaes. The considerable distance between these two missions and the presidio-mission complex on the Neches could only mean that Fray Margil had accepted St. Denis's assurance of protection and assistance. It was a decision he and his fellow friars would soon regret.

Although they had made a good start, Ramón and the missionaries were uncomfortable with the precariousness of their outpost. The Indians, happy to receive the gifts brought by the Spaniards to establish friendly relations, proved indifferent to the friars' preaching once all the goods had been distributed. The two-dozen-man garrison was certainly not big enough to provide protection to the new settlement, carry out construction and escort duties, and keep watch for the French. Also, the immense distance between the Neches presidio-mission complex and the Rio Grande settlement, more than 400 miles, made for exceptional hardship in communicating with the interior and obtaining supplies.

The missionaries' letters, a memorial by Fray Olivares, and reports by the Ramóns (father and son) reached Mexico City about the same time as new warnings that St. Denis and the French in Louisiana were intent on the commercial penetration of northern New Spain. The viceroy was determined not to let this occupation of Texas duplicate the 1690–93 experience, and not to let the French gain the upper hand. When his war council recommended occupying strategic locations on the coast and on the San Antonio River, he moved quickly. He made Martín de Alarcón governor of Coahuila and Texas and ordered him to establish a settlement-mission complex on the upper San Antonio River and resupply the East Texas establishments.

Alarcón proved to be the wrong man for the job, however. His recruitment efforts were half-hearted; he had barely enough men to carry out the first part of his mission—establishing a settlement on the San Antonio River. Fray Olivares was so upset with the governor, especially over the quality of the recruits, that he refused to travel in his company. Trailing along with all the property and a few Indian servants from the now-closed Mission San Francisco Solano, the friar met Alarcón at the San Antonio River on May 1, 1718. There he immediately took possession of land and water in the name of the local Indians for the founding of Mission San Antonio de Valero. Four days later Alarcón founded a town that he called the Villa de Béxar, in honor of the viceroy's brother, the Duke of Béjar. Failing to attract civilian settlers, however, the town quickly faded into memory, leaving Presidio San Antonio de Béxar to serve as the core Spanish settlement in the area for the next dozen years.

Governor Alarcón, having accomplished his primary objective, moved on to inspect the rest of his far-flung province. Traveling east to Matagorda Bay with fewer than thirty men, he failed to establish an outpost on the coast. Although he did visit all of the East Texas missions later in the fall, he also failed to reinforce Presidio de los Tejas. He antagonized the missionaries and other Spanish residents, further alienated the local Indians, and provoked the nearby French by confiscating their trade goods. By the time of his Texas service, Alarcón, a Spaniard with previous service in the Spanish navy, had well over twenty years of military experience in New Spain. Well past his prime, he was ill prepared to deal with the challenges of a province that existed more on paper than in reality and was unable to prevent the province's Indians from trading with the French. When hostilities that erupted between Spain and France in 1719 reached the Texas-Louisiana frontier, the viceroy sought a more vigorous man to take charge of the situation.

In the aftermath of the War of the Spanish Succession, Spain had been an unwilling party to the Treaty of Utrecht, which parceled out various Hapsburg possessions, including the islands of Sardinia and Sicily. When Spain attempted to retake these former possessions, France joined in a general European war against Spain. Word of this conflict reached Spanish Texas in a curious way. One morning in June 1719 a small troop of French soldiers from Natchitoches surprised the missionary and guard at Mission San Miguel, and took prisoner all the occupants of the mission henhouse. While Lieutenant Philippe Blondel and his men returned to their post with their feathered booty, Captain Ramón ordered the abandonment of East Texas. The episode, known in Texas history as the "Chicken War," set off a chain of events that expanded and solidified Spain's hold on Texas.

Spanish Texas Reinforced

By the time word of the French action reached Mexico City, officials were already preparing to secure their border with Louisiana. A royal decree had arrived in May ordering construction of fortifications at Matagorda Bay, the strengthening of missionary activity at San Antonio, and military protection for all missions. Fortunately for the viceroy, the selection of a leader for this expedition proved a simple matter. The Marqués de San Miguel de Aguayo, a Spanish nobleman who had married into one of the richest families in New Spain, had had his eye on Texas for some time; the prospect of serving the king by going to the Texas missionaries' rescue might further his ambitions to expand his wealth and property. Aguayo volunteered not only to lead an expedition to expel the French, but to foot the bill as well. The offer, however, turned out to be too good to be true, and the royal treasury eventually bore the brunt of the expedition's cost.

As governor of Coahuila and Texas, Aguayo found it difficult to muster the necessary resources to march on the Louisiana frontier. Insurrections among Indian groups close to home forced him to deploy men in Texas. Drought followed by floods killed livestock by the thousands, decimating the herds he needed to support the full-scale campaign he had in mind. In the meantime, he did authorize Fray Margil to establish a mission for the Zacatecas College at San Antonio. Dedicated on February 23, 1720, Mission San José y San Miguel de Aguayo was destined to become the "Queen of the Missions." Even before setting foot in Texas, the Marqués de Aguayo had already carried out one part of his instructions—to strengthen the missionary effort at San Antonio. It was more than a year before he arrived in Texas and began carrying out the rest of his orders.

Whereas previous expeditions to Texas had been makeshift, under-prepared, and largely unsuccessful, the Aguayo expedition proved an unqualified success. By the time it set out from Monclova in mid-November it consisted of almost 600 men, about 4,000 horses, thousands of head of cattle, sheep, and goats, and hundreds of pack-mules. It was the largest and best equipped Spanish force ever to enter Texas. Delayed in crossing the Rio Grande, which was swollen beyond its banks, Aguayo ordered his second-in-command, Fernando Pérez de Almazán, forward to San Antonio with over 100 men to forestall its occupation by the French. He also dispatched Domingo Ramón with forty men to occupy Matagorda Bay at the site of La Salle's post. By the time Aguayo and St. Denis (who had returned to French service and was again in command of Natchitoches) met on August 1, 1721, Aguayo's mission was all but complete. Various Caddo chiefs had already pledged their loyalty to the Spanish king, and St. Denis was pleased at the opportunity to do business with the restored missions and the new presidio that Aguayo had been ordered to build.

For the next few months Aguayo executed his plan for strengthening and reinforcing Texas. Plans for new presidios at Los Adaes and La Bahía del Espíritu Santo and for the reconstruction of Presidio de los Tejas and Presidio de Béxar reflected the expansion of military personnel in the province from approximately 50 to over 250. Aguayo reopened all of the East Texas missions that had been abandoned in 1719 and authorized the construction of new ones, including one at La Bahía called Nuestra Señora del Espíritu Santo de Zúñiga. More important, Aguayo seems to have done a good job at Indian relations and left the Spanish at peace with all of the Indians except the Apaches, who inhabited the Edwards Plateau and remained beyond the Spanish sphere of influence.

Spanish Texas Takes Shape

Fray Hidalgo did not return to the East Texas mission field following Aguayo's restoration of Spanish settlements there in 1721. He remained in San Antonio, where he labored at Mission Valero. It was an exciting and dangerous time at the presidio-mission complex on the edge of the Edwards Plateau. The south-central Texas native peoples who entered the missions spoke a variety of Coahuiltecan dialects and were sometimes antagonistic toward each other. Their hunting and gathering ways were so at odds with Spanish notions of civilized life that misunderstanding, resistance, and, sometimes, violence colored their relations with Spanish colonials. A mission, Fray Hidalgo well understood, was a risky undertaking, and failure could come from the most unexpected source.

Early Spanish-Indian Relations

Mission San Francisco Xavier de Nájera was a good case in point. Chief Juan Rodríguez of the Sanas, one of several central Texas Indian groups collectively known as the Ranchería Grande, had quickly befriended the Spanish and offered his services and those of his people in return for a mission of their own. Early in 1722 he and fifty families of Sanas arrived in San Antonio eager to start a new life. Their eagerness was in part due to depredations from Apache Indians, whose increasing raids against them made the Sanas all the more interested in alliances with the Spanish. Months turned into years as missionaries and Indians waited for official permission to proceed. A new viceroy with orders from the king to reduce the cost of defending the frontier refused to authorize the project and the Querétaro College pleaded lack of resources.

Eventually, Chief Rodríguez and the remaining dozen warriors, fearing annihilation at the hands of the Apaches if they stayed at the unprotected Nájera site, befriended the Xarames at Mission Valero and took up residence there. As for the Sanas who had returned to the Ranchería Grande, they made their sentiments clear: "The Spaniards want us to work for them; we want to be their friends and to fight no more; but to live near them, or be placed in a mission, we do not want even to speak of it." The collapse of Mission Nájera would not be the last Spanish failure with the Ranchería Grande.

The Sanas's concerns with Apache attacks was well founded. Lipan Apache raids made life dangerous in San Antonio, both at the presidio and at the missions. Retaliatory campaigns by the Spanish only increased the level of enmity. Soon the friars of the Querétaro College came to see the Apaches not as aggressors, but as the victims of corrupt military commanders and their debauched troops. So convinced were the friars at Mission Valero of the possibility of peace with the Apaches, that in 1725 Fray Hidalgo, now in his late sixties, offered to go out and preach among them. His request denied by his superiors, Fray Hidalgo retired to San Juan Bautista del Río Grande, where he spent the last year of his life.

A chronic state of warfare between Apaches and Spaniards existed for the next twenty years. The presidio-mission complex made an inviting target for these plains hunters who were slowly migrating to the south in the early eighteenth century. As the eastern Apache tribes came under pressure from the Comanches, who cut off their access to the Pueblos and Spanish New Mexico, they raided Spanish Texas horse herds to replace mounts lost to their enemies and supply convoys for manufactured items they did not have access to. Human beings also became the objects of raiding, as both the Apaches and the Spanish took women and children as hostages and slaves. The Apaches perceived that the Spanish had allied themselves with their enemies: the Hasinais, Ranchería Grande, and other eastern Indians. Apache enmity for the Spanish was reinforced as they took into their bands other Indians who had fled Spanish control in Coahuila, Nuevo León, and Nueva Vizcaya. From these forced migrations, and the addition of captured and escaped non-Apaches and Spanish colonials emerged the Lipan Apaches, whose presence in the Edwards Plateau west of San Antonio would be at the heart of Texas's Indian problems throughout the eighteenth century.

Conflict was not confined to the Apaches, however, as the Karankawan tribes along the Texas coast also proved to be antagonistic to a Spanish presence at Matagorda Bay. Shortly after its founding, Mission Espíritu Santo attracted members of various Karankawa bands, but relations between the military and the Indians in the missions soon deteriorated. The souring of relations with most of the coastal Karankawa groups frustrated efforts to remain at the Matagorda Bay site; by 1726 the new commander at La Bahía had arranged for the presidio-mission complex to relocate at what is today called Mission Valley in Victoria County. The new location was more healthful (higher ground, better water supply) and secure, and the missionaries of Espíritu Santo were able to attract bands of Aranamas and Tamiques, Coahuiltecan-speaking residents of the coastal prairies, who helped build the mission into Texas's first important ranching center. Unfortunately, even at its new location La Bahía was an extremely isolated community and was unable to attract civilian settlement. For the next twenty years Presidio La Bahía, understaffed and undersupplied, struggled to survive, until one final move in 1749 brought it to a location where increasing contacts with the outside world allowed development to take place.

Perhaps the greatest disappointment to friars and officials alike was the lack of progress they had made with the Caddoan villagers in eastern Texas. As in the 1690s and just before the Chicken War, the Hasinais and other Caddo groups quickly lost interest in the Christian conversion program. The Indians also blamed the Spanish for the epidemics and crop failures they experienced. Within a few years of their reestablishment, the missions were almost completely devoid of Indians, who preferred to live in their own villages and tolerate the occasional visits of the friars. Consequently, neither the missionaries nor the presidios could feed their residents, and they were forced to rely increasingly on either the Indians, French Natchitoches, or far-off San Antonio. Conditions in Texas, then, did not bode well for the province's long-term survival. An infusion of new blood was needed.

A New Plan to Colonize Texas

From the perspective of Mexico City, the northern frontier, Texas in particular, seemed to be little more than a money pit, where missionaries, governors, and presidio commanders exchanged charges of corruption, incompetence, and cruelty toward the natives. The viceroy, determined to get the situation under control, appointed Colonel Pedro de Rivera to carry out a thorough inspection of the frontier defense system with the goal of saving money and instilling discipline.

Armed with broad powers not only to inspect everything he deemed proper, but to issue orders on the spot, the newly promoted brigadier left the viceregal capital in November 1724; he was not to return for three and a half years.

When Rivera arrived in Texas in August 1727, he was tired and in no mood to hear excuses. What he found was shocking and troubling. In East Texas there were no Indians at the missions, and the presidios were overstaffed, given the peaceful relations with both the Hasinais and the French. At San Antonio and La Bahía the missionaries were more gainfully employed, but the presidio companies were similarly overstaffed as they had successfully handled the Apaches. Rivera's draconian reforms called for abandonment of Presidio de los Tejas, the closing of East Texas missions, reductions in the complements of the remaining three presidios, and recruitment of colonists.

The viceroy was extremely pleased with Rivera's efforts, and as a reward made him special counsel for frontier matters. Spanish Texans were not so pleased with the penny-pinching measures that resulted from the brigadier's recommendations. Instead of four presidios and 269 men, the Texans were left with only three garrisons with a total of 144 billets, with all except the officers at reduced pay. The Franciscans were also displeased, not only because the Querétaro missionaries were forced to abandon East Texas, but because they would get less assistance from the remaining smaller garrisons.

Rivera, in his rush to please his superiors, overlooked the importance of military settlements. The symbiotic relationships between presidios and missions were crucial to what little success Texas had enjoyed. Presidios served as seed settlements in regions where it was difficult to attract civilian settlers, and Texas, indisputably, was such a region. Governor Pérez de Almazán commented in 1724 that recruiting soldiers for service in Texas was a difficult task, not only because they had to be sought outside the province, but also because "some time is needed to court them, and they must be given some assistance for their costs besides their salaries, because of the resignation with which they all come to this country." Missions, if they were to evolve into permanent communities of hispanicized Indians, needed nearby presidios to protect them as well as to serve as markets for the food crops and animals that the neophytes produced.

Because the development of Texas could not rest solely on a few soldiers and christianized Indians, Rivera agreed with Spanish officials who had recognized the need for civilian settlement since the time of the Aguayo expedition. In 1719 the Council of the Indies, the royal policy-making body on colonial affairs, had recommended bringing 2,000 families from the Canary Islands and northern Spain and 100 Tlaxcalan Indian families to help instruct neophytes at the missions. Three years later the Marqués de Aguayo and the viceroy added their support for crown-sponsored immigration, and in 1723 the king relented and issued an order for the recruitment of 200 families in the Canary Islands. Years passed, and in 1727 another order was issued without effect. In 1728, Rivera explained to the viceroy how civilian settlement at San Antonio would help reduce costs: "the location being so fertile and pleasant, . . . it is particularly suited for the settlement of twenty-five families, who would fully protect the land and induce others to imitate them in settling other sites as may seem convenient." The viceroy and officials in Madrid hoped that such settlement might eliminate the annual 17,500-peso expense that Presidio de Béxar represented.

Finally, in 1729 the first ten families of a proposed 400 set out from the Canary Islands for Texas by way of Havana and Veracruz, then overland to Mexico City and onward to the frontier. The experiment proved so costly, time-consuming, and inefficient that the viceroy did not want it repeated. The fifty-six Isleños (Canary Islanders) who arrived in San Antonio on March 9, 1731 were the only product of a decade of schemes and royal decrees, but they were a fortunate lot. Dating back to the early years of colonization in the sixteenth century, the crown had granted certain privileges to the first settlers of new communities. (Unfortunately for the soldier-settlers of San Antonio, La Bahía, and Los Adaes—between 200 and 250 at each settlement in 1730—the military status of their communities precluded similar consideration.)

Treated as *primeros pobladores* (first or original settlers) the Isleños were granted a variety of privileges by the king, which must have created considerable envy among the province's already-established residents. He granted the Canary Islanders the title of *hidalgo;* he granted them land and water rights; and he authorized them to form a town government, with those selected for office getting life appointments. Most practical of all, the king granted the Isleños a year's stipend and the necessary supplies to establish themselves as farmers.

The First Civil Government of Texas

Captain Juan Antonio Pérez de Almazán, commander of Presidio de Béxar and *justicia mayor* (district magistrate), was a busy man in 1731. It must have seemed as if all the world were descending on him as missionaries, Isleños, and military settlers lined up for a piece of the San Antonio River valley. His biggest worry was keeping the Canary Islanders alive in the face of Apache hostilities and the raw wilderness conditions in which they lived. Despite the viceroy's orders that the Isleños establish a separate community, Almazán reasoned that their survival rested on the defense the presidio could provide and the instruction the experienced frontiersmen of San Antonio could supply these Old World farmers. Consequently, the captain decided to grant the Isleños farmland and a site for a town between the presidio and Mission Valero. They named the town San Fernando in honor of the heir to the Spanish throne. (For the sake of clarity, we will use the terms Béxar or San Antonio for the settlement). The decision, although expedient, brought about considerable conflict with the already-established military settlers and nearby Mission Valero.

Just four days before the Isleños arrived, Captain Almazán had begun dealing with the other group of land claimants that had descended on the fertile and well-watered valley. He had carried out the act of possession for Mission Nuestra Señora de la Purísima Concepción de Acuña at the site of the defunct Mission Nájera. The Querétaro College friars had successfully lobbied the viceroy to allow them to move the three missions near Presidio de los Tejas after it closed in 1729;

following a brief effort at what is now Barton Springs in Austin, the missionaries decided that the San Antonio River was both a safer and more convenient location. Along with Mission Concepción, Captain Almazán assigned land and water to missions San Juan Capistrano (formerly San José de los Nazonis) and San Francisco de la Espada (formerly San Francisco de los Neches). Located downstream from Mission San José, these last two stations completed the presidio-mission complex that over the centuries would blossom into the city of San Antonio.

By the end of 1731 San Antonio de Béxar, or simply Béxar, as the district was collectively known, had evolved from a simple stopover on the trail to the Texas capital at Los Adaes to the province's most diverse settlement. The friars of its five missions, which occupied rich farmland on alternating banks of the river, were busy building sophisticated irrigation systems, laying out village compounds, and attempting to transform the region's wandering bands of hunters and gatherers into villagers. They relied on *mayordomos* (overseers), usually soldiers and former soldiers, to help train, discipline, and supervise the Indians. Missions Valero and San José, which had been in operation for over a decade by then, both produced

San Antonio's Plaza de las Islas (Main Plaza) commemorates the city's early Canary Islands settlers. What is now the French gothic San Fernando Cathedral started out as the humble San Fernando church, the construction of which began under the direction of Canary Islanders in 1738. *(The Institute of Texan Cultures at UTSA)*

surpluses that the friars could sell to the presidios, the proceeds going toward the needs of the missions and the neophytes.

Similarly, the Isleños, who at first had been housed among the military settlers, were busy putting up their first homes, expanding the *acequia* (irrigation ditch) system and agricultural land they had inherited from the military settlers, and accustoming themselves to running a town government. The king's orders provided for the Canary Islanders to be a self-governing community, with a *regimiento* (town council) of six *regidores* (aldermen), two *alcaldes ordinarios* (municipal magistrates), an *alguacil mayor* (constable or sheriff), a *procurador* (municipal attorney), and *escribano* (public scribe). As a further concession to the original colonists, all the positions except those of *alcalde* were extended to the original holders for life, thus giving the Isleños sole control of local authority for well over a decade after the town's founding.

Thus the military settlers, a number of whom had retired or were about to retire and hoped for land, water, and house lots in the community, were at first excluded from this town-building activity. The presidio, although adjacent to the new town, represented a separate jurisdiction, and its commander continued to exercise exclusive authority over soldiers, their dependents, and any settlers not considered *vecinos* (citizens) of the town. Most Isleños, concerned about competition from retired soldiers in selling their crops to the presidio, made every possible effort to exclude military settlers, whom they referred to as *agregados* (additional or secondary settlers), from access to water and agricultural land. And the Old World immigrants, now bearing noble status, considered themselves racially superior to the mixed-blood military population, many of whom were descended from the unions of Spanish men and Indian and Afro-Hispanic women.

Time and numbers were not on the Isleños' side, however. On the one hand, construction projects, supply convoys, and retirements and recruitments at the presidio all brought people to San Antonio, reinforcing the non-Isleño population. On the other hand, it soon became apparent that no more Canary Islanders would come to reinforce the initial contingent. Isleño offspring soon began looking for spouses among the military families. Lacking business ties and appropriate economic skills, some Isleños formed partnerships with military settlers. A few Isleños even abandoned civilian life for the financial security of military service. To cement these partnerships and to foster family alliances, *agregados* and Isleños established ritual kinship relations through *compadrazgo* (godparenthood) and support for selected non-Isleños to participate in town government.

Squabbling between Isleños and *agregados* was not San Antonio's most pressing problem; that honor went to the continued hostilities with the Lipan Apaches. It was a situation at least in part of the settlers' making, however, or so thought the missionaries. Fray Benito Fernández de Santa Anna complained after a major campaign in 1739 that "the expedition was profitable only to those who had horses and other goods, which they sold at excessively high prices . . . and had greater hopes of a considerable prize of horses, hides, and Indian men and women to serve them." Whether it was the Lipans who retaliated for unprovoked campaigns by the settlers, or the settlers who exacted a measure of retribution from the Apaches for their continual depredations, the result was that everyone was at constant risk: mission Indians tending herds and flocks, settlers among their crops, and muleteers carrying supplies into and out of the province. Finally, following a major campaign in which the Spaniards pursued the Apaches deep into the Edwards Plateau, the Lipans were ready to call a truce in 1745. The cease-fire lasted until August 1749, when, at a formal treaty ceremony held at San Antonio, Lipan chiefs, military officers, the missionaries, and town officials literally buried the hatchet. Into a great hole dug in the presidio plaza the participants threw a live horse, arrows, a lance, and a ceremonial hatchet. As the hole was covered, they held hands and embraced.

The Rio Grande Frontiers

The Apache peace at Béxar came just as colonial New Spain underwent its last and most successful colonization effort on the northeastern frontier. For a number of years officials in Mexico City had been increasingly concerned about Spain's weak presence along the Gulf of Mexico coast between Tampico and La Bahía. The rugged mountain chains of the Sierra Madre Oriental, the mosquito-infested lowlands of the immediate coast, and the semiarid expanses north of the Rio Grande had all contributed to discouraging Spanish interest in the area. As a result, the Seno Mexicano, as the area was commonly called, remained home to numerous hunter-gatherer groups and became a haven for Indians fleeing Spanish domination, who then turned around and launched highly destructive raids into Spanish areas. Increased foreign activity in the gulf added to government concerns, especially in view of growing tensions between England and Spain over colonial boundaries and trading privileges. English occupation of any portion of the Seno would be a strategic disaster for Spanish interests. The Seno Mexicano had to be settled.

New Times, New Methods for Settling the Frontier

Colonial officials charged with defending New Spain, crown jewel of the empire, faced a daunting problem: how to effectively gain control of the vast and isolated coastal territory between Tampico and Texas while spending as little as possible from the royal coffers. Not wanting to rely on missionaries, policy-makers searched for an individual willing to organize and underwrite a systematic colonization of the Seno. After considering a number of proposals in the 1730s and early 1740s, José Escandón y Elguera's plan emerged as the favorite.

Escandón was a Spanish-born military officer who had made a name for himself as an honest and successful Indian fighter. He received his appointment in September 1746, along with the title of lieutenant general to the viceroy, which was a high honor. Given his military background and the contradictory and incomplete information available about the vast area in question, Escandón determined that before colonization could begin he would need to mount a comprehensive exploration. Only by determining the best trails, most fertile and well-watered locations, and the territories of existing Indian groups, could the project achieve quick success. In early 1747 he organized seven expeditions that penetrated the Seno from the south, west, and north.

From the reconnaissance of the region, Escandón came up with a bold plan to gain Spain complete control of the coastal region. Colonists would enter the Seno from neighboring provinces and occupy strategic locations as far north as the Nueces River. To facilitate contacts with Texas, Escandón ordered the relocation of La Bahía from its Mission Valley site to its present location on the San Antonio River. For his part, Escandón would recruit families to settle a new town on the Nueces River, near present-day Corpus Christi, to serve as the northern limit of Nuevo Santander. Although the Nueces River settlement never materialized, La Bahía flourished at its new location. Captain Joaquín Orrobio y Basterra, who directed the transfer, liked the new location, commenting on the availability of timber and stone for construction, open prairies for farming and grazing, plentiful water in the San Antonio River, and a prominent hill on which to build the presidio. His successor, Captain Manuel Ramírez de la Piscina, who took over in early 1750, was similarly impressed and predicted a quick increase in civilian settlement.

The missionaries shared the optimism of the military community. At Mission Espíritu Santo the Indian population quickly recovered from the move, and by 1758 they had replaced the initial wooden church and friary with stone-and-mortar structures. This success prompted renewed efforts among various Karankawa groups, as Fray Juan de Dios María Camberos gathered hundreds for a new mission. Not waiting for an official reply to his request for permission, Fray Camberos established Mission Nuestra Señora del Rosario about five miles west of Espíritu Santo in 1754.

Throughout the 1750s and 1760s La Bahía made steady progress despite the advent of Apache and Comanche raiding. Until the early 1760s La Bahía had only had to contend with the minor depredations of the coastal band peoples. The Karankawas had a fierce reputation, but for the most part they did little damage to the presidio and mission. After the establishment of Mission Rosario, most Karankawa bands remained at peace with the Spanish, even though they refused to become full-time mission dwellers. As the Comanches and other northern tribes put pressure on the Lipan Apaches, the Lipans moved farther east, launching their first raids on La Bahía in 1762. Their enemies soon followed them, with devastating results on local cattle herds and considerable loss of human life.

Nevertheless, the herds grew, the mission populations remained constant, and the number of civilian settlers increased. From just a handful of civilians in 1749, the settlement's population increased to forty-six civilian households in 1767. Marriage among the presidio company added to the nonmilitary population, and by the 1760s the sons of former soldiers were themselves enlisting in the company. At the missions, although the numbers fluctuated, populations numbered in the hundreds, more than enough to perform all the essential functions at the mission compounds and at the outlying ranches.

Increased economic activity centered on livestock. Thousands of head of cattle grazed the open ranges of the coast. Mission Espíritu Santo, although it could only count a few thousand branded head, claimed over 40,000 animals between the San Antonio and Guadalupe. Captain Piscina's Rancho San José, which occupied thousands of acres on the west bank of the San Antonio, was so productive that he employed both civilians and enlisted men in its operation. Over time the community's growing prosperity encouraged the appearance of the first merchants and craftsmen.

Of importance to the history of Texas was not only the relocation of La Bahía, but Escandón's founding of a series of settlements along the Rio Grande. By the end of March 1749 he had authorized two settlements along the south bank of the lower Rio Grande: Camargo, under the leadership of Blas María de la Garza Falcón, a member of a leading stock-raising family from Coahuila; and Reynosa, under another wealthy *hacendado*, Captain Carlos Cantú of Nuevo León. As families continued to respond to Escandón's initial success, new settlements were founded over the course of the next few years. In 1750 Vicente Guerra, another Nuevo León landowner, established Revilla upstream from Camargo on the south bank of the Rio Grande, and José Vázquez Borrego, a stockman from Coahuila who had been grazing his animals in the area for some time, received permission to establish Rancho de Dolores on the north bank. Two years later José Florencio Chapa of Nuevo León received permission from Escandón to found a village on the south bank, downstream from Revilla, known as Mier. Finally, in 1755 yet another wealthy stockman, Tomás Sánchez, received permission to found the town of Laredo on the north bank of the Rio Grande.

Late in 1755 Escandón stepped back to make an account of his efforts. In the previous six years he had authorized the founding of twenty-three civilian settlements, including five along the Rio Grande, fifteen missions, and two mining camps. By his reckoning he was responsible for the settlement of 1,337 civilian and 144 military families, for a total of 6,385 persons. In the fifteen missions under the direction of the Colleges of Zacatecas and San Fernando there were 2,837 neophytes. These accomplishments had been possible even in the face of adverse conditions: three years of drought that required purchase of corn in neighboring provinces, followed by severe flooding that had brought on epidemics and malaria, and the continued hostility of some of the region's native people. The contrast with Texas, where settlement had not successfully expanded beyond the three mission-presidio complexes left behind by the Marqués de Aguayo in 1722, and which contained a Spanish population of only 1,800, could not be more stark.

The Roots of Hispanic South Texas

Escandón's reports were one thing, independent verification another. In 1757 the viceroy instructed José Tienda de Cuervo, an experienced administrator, to carry out a thorough inspection of the province. The viceroy was impressed with what he found. The population had increased to almost 9,000 settlers and 3,500 neophytes, and the number of missions had increased to eighteen. The number of mines had increased to eleven, and five salt deposits were being exploited. It was obvious that this was livestock country, especially the area north of the Rio Grande, where the largest ranches were located. In all, the province had 58,000 horses, 25,000 cattle, and 288,000 sheep and goats. The inspection went so far as to describe the residents of Revilla, Camargo, and Reynosa as rich from the livestock and salt trade.

The people of Nuevo Santander, like those of Texas and the rest of New Spain's northern region, were ethnically and socioeconomically mixed. *Criollos* made up about one-third of the population, *castas* about half, Christianized Indians approximately 15 percent, and peninsular Spaniards only 1 or 2 percent. These proportions were a source of disappointment for Escandón, who preferred *peninsulares* for important positions, but had few from whom to choose. Many of the people of Nuevo Santander, as one local official reported in 1757, were poor families that had no home of their own, but lived off the seasonal employment they could obtain from *hacendados*. Escandón was more blunt, declaring that his recruiting success, which continued long after the initial expeditions, were a result of the colonists fleeing the abuses of local officials and "the slavery in which they lived, having been made debtors to the hacienda owners, and aspiring to free themselves." Presaging the Anglo-American immigration trend of the 1820s and 1830s in Texas, many of the new arrivals were fugitives from the law fleeing prosecution for debt, theft, and even murder. Without a doubt, however, the Nuevo Santander-South Texas frontier offered opportunities for those intrepid enough to face the risks.

Although Escandón had made exceptional progress in transforming Nuevo Santander into a secure and productive province of New Spain, there were problems. The missionaries complained that rather than carrying out their primary mission of converting the Indians, they were forced to serve the civilian population. Most missionaries, therefore, had become little more than parish priests. Worse, the *reducción* (gathering of nonsedentary Indians in formal missions) of the native peoples had become the means by which prominent landowners and military men throughout the province exploited their labor. The friars accused the governor of "having not the slightest interest in the most important and proper matter of the pacification and settlement of the Indians." As a result, the most peaceful Indian groups had fallen into virtual slavery and the most aggressive ones had abandoned the missions and started preying on outlying ranches and settlements. Under these conditions, the missions quickly declined; by the 1760s many contained no neophytes at all. By the 1790s the mission system in Nuevo Santander had completely collapsed. An Indian population in the territory estimated at approximately 25,000 in 1750 stood at less than 2,000 at the end of the century.

The missionaries were not Escandón's only critics. Many settlers, especially those of substantial means, complained that although they had repeatedly been assured of land titles (one of the recommendations of the Tienda de Cuervo inspection), none had as yet been distributed. Although he could deflect or ignore the missionaries' complaints, the governor did have to account for the unsettled state of land ownership in the province. Escandón's explanation to the viceroy was that his extensive duties kept him from attending to the matter and that he had no qualified subordinate to see that the job was done properly. Moreover, because settlers continued to arrive, some of whom he considered of better quality than the original settlers, he wanted to wait longer and make sure the land went to those most capable of making the best use of it.

Determined not to allow such a promising start to descend into chaos, the viceroy appointed a royal commission to carry out a general inspection and distribution of lands to the settlers of Nuevo Santander in 1767. By the time the commission reached the Rio Grande settlements, it had worked out a very efficient system of land distribution. The commissioner named local leaders as subordinates and individuals with experience appraising land as surveyors. Thus, the locals had primary responsibility for establishing which lands were to be granted for ranching, farming, common use, and town use. Conditions along the river created unique problems: abundant water in the Rio Grande, but a scarcity of fresh water away from it, especially on the north bank; an adequate amount of good bottomland available for agriculture, but high flood banks that limited irrigation on the south side and made it impossible on the north bank. Naturally most people wanted to stay close to the river and to the settlements, especially in light of continued Indian depredations. As stockmen, they needed large parcels of land, but also access to drinking water for their herds.

What the local experts came up with was a unique solution to the complicated set of issues. After setting aside the required amount of land for each town and mission tract, all of which, except for Laredo, were located on the south bank of the river, they prioritized the limited amount of agricultural land in favor of the oldest settlers. When it came time to distribute grazing land the experts gave each family access to the Rio Grande. They laid out each tract of approximately 8,000–10,000 acres with a very narrow frontage on the river. Some families, given their status, received more than one tract and, because of the delay in distribution, others had sons who could claim tracts of their own. These long, narrow lots, which received the name *porciones,* allowed stockmen to move their herds and flocks close to the river during the dry season and graze them away from the stream during rainy periods. So efficient were the surveyors that in some settlements, such as Laredo, a considerable number of *porciones* went undistributed for a number of years.

On their departure for Mexico City in fall 1767, the commission left behind a well settled and quickly expanding ranching kingdom. The commission had issued land grants to over a thousand settlers, most for tracts intended for ranching purposes. Even the territory north of the Rio Grande, the most exposed to hostile Indians and the most arid, saw a steady advance in cattle operations that produced many *ranchos* (the root of the English term ranch) measuring in the

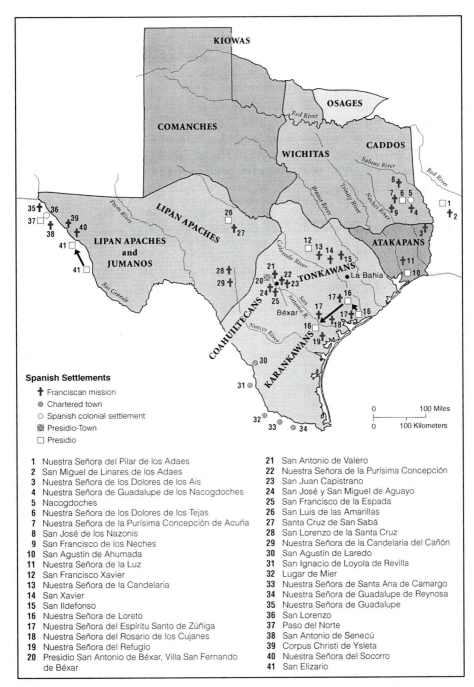

Spanish Settlements

✝ Franciscan mission
◎ Chartered town
○ Spanish colonial settlement
▨ Presidio-Town
□ Presidio

1 Nuestra Señora del Pilar de los Adaes	**21** San Antonio de Valero
2 San Miguel de Linares de los Adaes	**22** Nuestra Señora de la Purísima Concepción
3 Nuestra Señora de los Dolores de los Ais	**23** San Juan Capistrano
4 Nuestra Señora de Guadalupe de los Nacogdoches	**24** San José y San Miguel de Aguayo
5 Nacogdoches	**25** San Francisco de la Espada
6 Nuestra Señora de los Dolores de los Tejas	**26** San Luis de las Amarillas
7 Nuestra Señora de la Purísima Concepción de Acuña	**27** Santa Cruz de San Sabá
8 San José de los Nazonis	**28** San Lorenzo de la Santa Cruz
9 San Francisco de los Neches	**29** Nuestra Señora de la Candelaria del Cañón
10 San Agustín de Ahumada	**30** San Agustín de Laredo
11 Nuestra Señora de la Luz	**31** San Ignacio de Loyola de Revilla
12 San Francisco Xavier	**32** Lugar de Mier
13 Nuestra Señora de la Candelaria	**33** Nuestra Señora de Santa Ana de Camargo
14 San Xavier	**34** Nuestra Señora de Guadalupe de Reynosa
15 San Ildefonso	**35** Nuestra Señora de Guadalupe
16 Nuestra Señora de Loreto	**36** San Lorenzo
17 Nuestra Señora del Espíritu Santo de Zúñiga	**37** Paso del Norte
18 Nuestra Señora del Rosario de los Cujanes	**38** San Antonio de Senecú
19 Nuestra Señora del Refugio	**39** Corpus Christi de Ysleta
20 Presidio San Antonio de Béxar, Villa San Fernando de Béxar	**40** Nuestra Señora del Socorro
	41 San Elizario

Eighteenth-century Indian tribes and Spanish settlements.

tens of thousands of acres and some measuring hundreds of thousands of acres. These *ranchos* became the progenitors of the famous Texas ranches of later generations.

Escandón had not been perfect: He had taken advantage of the Franciscans to gain easy access to religious services for his colonists; he had allowed extensive exploitation of the local native population, despite his stated intentions to bring them the benefits of civilization; he had taken care of his personal and family interests, and those of colleagues, before the interests of the general population of colonists. Nevertheless, the settlement of Nuevo Santander had been a spectacular success, especially in contrast to the continued struggle for survival experienced by its neighboring province of Texas throughout this time.

The Desert Blooms at Paso del Norte

Hundreds of miles upstream from the developing ranching communities of the lower Rio Grande valley a very different type of settlement activity had produced a thriving set of communities at Paso del Norte. Located at a crucial juncture of the road between New Mexico and Chihuahua, the residents of Paso del Norte prospered from providing services to travelers, but the area also had products to offer. A combination of climate, soil, and the waters of the Rio Grande made the area a desert oasis and ideal viticulture country. By mid-century Paso del Norte's wines, brandies, and raisins were in great demand throughout northern New Spain. Farming extended to the cultivation of wheat in well-irrigated fields that produced substantial surpluses for export to the mining camps to the south. In fact, the use of farmland for grapes and wheat meant that in some years residents did not harvest enough corn to meet local needs.

Economic success brought population growth to the communities that made up the district. Despite increased raiding by Apaches, the population of the district grew from about 1,000 people at the turn of the century to almost 5,000 in 1765. The civil-military settlement located on the south bank of the river, El Paso del Río del Norte, was home to over 2,800 residents. The presidio company of 49 men and their families, 230 persons in all, made up less than 10 percent of the total. Indians and *genízaros* (New Mexico term for detribalized Indians incorporated into Spanish society) made up about 20 percent of the population. The remaining 70 percent consisted of *criollos* and *castas*, usually referred to as mestizos, but also including mulattoes. Some of the genízaro families had even managed to gain *vecino* status, that is, they were considered full citizens of the settlement, an indication that economic and social opportunities on the frontier conspired to downplay the social and racial labels that restricted social mobility elsewhere.

Also prospering were the three mission communities established for area Indians—Guadalupe, Senecú, and Socorro—and Ysleta, the settlement established for the Tigua Indians who fled New Mexico with the Spaniards at the time of the Pueblo revolt of 1680. Although all three communities had substantial numbers of non-Indians living in them by the middle of the eighteenth century, each retained its distinctive Indian character. Franciscan missionaries supervised these communities, in addition to providing spiritual services to the non-Indian population of the area.

As successful as the Paso del Norte district was, it shared a major problem with Texas, Coahuila, and the other northern frontier provinces: Apache Indian raids. As in Texas, the most important factor contributing to the increase in hostilities was the pressure from the north being put on the eastern Apache tribes (those located east of the Rio Grande) by advancing Comanches. The problem had been at its worst in the first decades of the eighteenth century, until reorganization of the presidio led the raiders, mostly Gileños, Mescaleros, and Natagés, to choose targets farther south. Nevertheless, sporadic depredations took their toll, mostly in lost horses and mules, which the Apaches used both for transportation and for food, but also in the occasional killing of a field hand. Given the strategic and developing economic importance of the Paso del Norte district, however, the problem was manageable.

The Failure of Missionary Expansion in Texas

Unlike Nuevo Santander, where José de Escandón directed an essentially civilian colonization effort, or Paso del Norte, which occupied a significant economic niche, much of what is today Texas remained fundamentally a religious-military frontier. Efforts at expansion in Texas during the 1740s and 1750s were tied to the twin objectives of bringing more Indians into the fold of the Catholic church and preventing French penetration of Spanish territory.

Missionary Expansion into Central Texas

For Fray Mariano Francisco de los Dolores y Viana, missionary at San Antonio de Valero since the mid-1730s, the appearance at Béxar of a delegation from the Ranchería Grande tribes on June 2, 1745, was an answer to his prayers and years of patience and hard work. For over a decade while out in search of runaway neophytes, he had taken the opportunity to preach the benefits of mission life to independent Indian groups he encountered. Now representatives of Tonkawan, Atakapan, and Ervipiame that made up the Ranchería Grande requested that a mission be established in their territory—a large area of central Texas between the Colorado and Trinity rivers. They insisted, however, that the friars come to them, as San Antonio was too far from allies and hunting grounds.

Not waiting for authorization from his superiors, Fray Mariano obtained the services of five presidio soldiers and with a group of trusted neophytes headed for the Ranchería Grande. He caught up with the Indians in January 1746 near the junction of the San Gabriel River and Brushy Creek (present-day Milam County). He soon had a makeshift mission in operation, describing the land as "much better than that found in San Antonio, and there is an abundance of *cíbolos* (buffalo), deer, turkeys, fish, persimmons, prickly pears, and other fruits used by the Indians." Although other reports were less optimistic, the viceroy ultimately consented to the project, creating a garrison out of detachments of soldiers from Los Adaes and La Bahía.

Despite the enthusiasm of Fray Mariano and the other friars, the San Xavier settlement was short-lived and marked by tragedy. The missionaries accused the soldiers of debauchery and corrupting the Indians. Supplies at the missions were inadequate; a smallpox epidemic killed more than forty Indians, and there were mass desertions. Matters only got worse when Captain Felipe de Rábago y Terán, the new garrison commander, arrived with his fifty-man company in December 1751. He found only 100 neophytes at Mission San Xavier, none at San Ildefonso and just twenty-five at Candelaria. Disappointed in the missionaries and the remote location, he recommended abandonment of San Xavier in favor of a site on the San Marcos River, which he considered much more favorable. Having been sharply rebuked by the friars for his affair with the wife of one of his men, Rábago refused to discipline his men, whom the friars accused of adultery and rape. The situation deteriorated until May 1752, when one of the missionaries and the man whose wife Rábago y Terán had been living with were murdered. In the aftermath of the crime (which the captain blamed on Indians, but which the missionaries blamed on him), most of the neophytes fled the missions.

A Mission for the Apaches

Would it be possible to salvage something from the failure of the San Xavier project? The Spanish had lost the trust of the Indians; a severe drought had shown the area to be unsuitable for a presidio-mission complex, and disease had decimated both the remaining Indian population and the garrison. Even Fray Mariano surrendered to the inevitable and in September 1753 added his voice to those of the presidio officers and other missionaries calling for the removal of the missions and presidio to a more promising location.

A number of friars had dreamed for many years of converting the Lipan Apaches. Periodically, individual Apache chiefs approached the missionaries claiming to want the benefits of Spanish civilization; accordingly, the Franciscans blamed the Spanish colonists for the hostilities. Fray Mariano's insistence on the potential for peace with the Lipans if a mission were established for them in their own territory led to expeditions into the hill country northwest of San Antonio. Expeditionaries returned with a favorable impression of the area, particularly at the indications of silver deposits and the friendliness of the Indians.

In 1756 the Franciscans got their wish. When Fray Alonso Giraldo de Terreros's rich cousin stepped forward to help underwrite the project, the viceroy issued orders for a new mission-presidio complex for the Lipan Apaches. He placed Colonel Diego Ortiz Parrilla, a former frontier governor and veteran soldier, in charge of the military component of the expedition, but gave Fray Terreros independent authority to negotiate with the Indians. The colonel, cynical about the Indians' intentions, soon quarreled with the missionaries. He complained to the viceroy that "the state in which we have found the Apaches is so different from

No greater gift could a man give God than to sacrifice himself in the cause of the faith. So thought the Franciscans who achieved the "crown of martyrdom" at Mission San Sabá, when they became victims of an Apache-Norteño struggle for control of western Texas. *(Destruction of Mission San Sabá in the Province of Texas and the Martyrdom of the Fathers Alonso Giraldo de Terreros, Joseph Santiesteban, by José de Páez [attrib.], ca. 1763. Oil on canvas. 83" × 115". Courtesy Instituto National de Anthropología e Historia, Mexico City)*

what I expected that I assure you the method of their pacification is a major concern to me."

Indeed, when the *entrada* arrived at the site of present-day Menard and pitched camp, the Lipans were nowhere in sight. Construction soon began on a mission and presidio, but each passing day gave another indication that the San Sabá complex was not to flourish. Three thousand Apaches appeared near the mission in June, but soon departed to hunt buffalo and raid their enemies, the Norteños. With the Apaches unwilling to settle down and no prospects for attracting other groups, some of the missionaries gave up on the project, leaving Mission San Sabá in the hands of Fray Alonso and two colleagues from the San Fernando College. During the fall and winter of 1757–58 various Apache bands made rest stops at the mission, but all refused to stay. They did bring rumors, however, that the Norteños, including the Comanches, were massing to attack the Apaches and their allies at San Sabá.

The end came in March 1758. At the beginning of the month a war party attacked the presidio's horse herd and made off with sixty-two mounts. On March 16 a large group of warriors, including Caddos, Tonkawas, Atakapans, Wichitas, and Comanches encircled the mission compound, many of them bearing French muskets and swords. After ransacking the buildings, the warriors turned on the mission's residents, killing friars Alonso and José Santiesteban along with a few of the assistants and soldiers. Fray Miguel Molina and a few others took refuge in an office and survived the burning of the compound. Unwilling to challenge the military directly, the Indians approached but did not attack the presidio.

Unable to pursue the attackers, Colonel Parrilla sought revenge in a more deliberate way. Parrilla offered to lead a campaign not only to avenge the deaths of two friars and eight other Spanish subjects, but also to demonstrate to the Norteños that they could not act with impunity. In a January 1759 meeting between Parrilla, the governors of Texas and Coahuila, and the region's presidio commanders, it was decided that they would mount a 500-man expedition against the Wichitas and Tonkawas that summer.

Although it achieved a minor victory against a Tonkawa camp near the Clear Fork of the Brazos, the expedition's encounter with the Wichitas was a disaster. The Wichita village, at present-day Spanish Fort on the Red River, was not only fortified but was also flying a French flag. The Wichitas, armed with French muskets, were every bit a match for the ragtag force under Col. Parrilla. The engagement turned into a rout: The Wichitas repulsed the Spanish assault and the Lipan

Today the ruins of the Spanish Empire's last effort to expand into western Texas rest next to a golf course in Menard. Photographs and captions chronicle a failed reconstruction effort in the 1930s, documenting how for many years the locals continued to believe the stone presidio was the remains of the wooden mission destroyed by the Norteños in 1758. *(Photo by Frank de la Teja)*

Apache allies fled. Although the Spanish suffered only fifty-two casualties, the humiliating defeat spelled the end of Spain's hopes of expanding into the southern plains from Texas.

The San Sabá episode illustrated two major problems with Spain's frontier system in Texas: the inadequacy of the presidio-mission system for expanding Spain's territory and the inability to prevent foreign access to Indians. At San Sabá, as at San Xavier earlier, the Spanish came into contact with Indians bearing French muskets, wearing French clothing, and boasting of their ties to Louisiana. Spanish security along the Louisiana frontier proved so lax that by the early 1750s a small party of Frenchmen under the direction of Joseph Blancpain was able to establish a trading post on the lower Trinity River.

Discovery and arrest of the Frenchmen probably reflected the governor's effort to protect his own pocketbook (he was involved in contraband himself) rather than to defend imperial interests, but it did set off another abortive attempt to expand Spanish control over Texas. In 1756 Viceroy Marqués de las Amarillas authorized a presidio-mission complex for the lower Trinity River. By the end of the year a thirty-man post had been established, named Presidio San Agustín de Ahumada in honor of the viceroy. (Agustín de Ahumada y Villalón, Marqués de las Amarillas holds the distinction of being the only viceroy to have two presidios named for him.) A mission named Nuestra Señora de la Luz had also taken shape near present-day Anahuac in Chambers County.

El Orcoquizac, as the complex was commonly referred to, proved a complete disaster from the beginning. The Akokisa and Bidai Indians, for whom Mission Nuestra Señora de la Luz was built, showed as little interest in settling down permanently at this location as they had at the San Xavier missions a few years earlier. The thirty-man garrison at the presidio suffered great privation as flooding and the stifling heat and humidity made it difficult to keep the presidio store stocked and the crops growing well. About the only thing that made life bearable for the garrison was trading in contraband—the very thing they were there to prevent.

Conclusion

By the early 1760s there was a marked contrast between Texas and the neighboring provinces of Nuevo Santander and Coahuila. José de Escandón had fired the imaginations of thousands of Spanish frontiersmen with his offers of generous land grants and effective measures against the Indians of the region. Towns, ranches, and mining camps soon dotted the Nuevo Santander countryside from the area just north of Tampico to the Rio Grande valley. Even the least settled part of the new province, the semiarid prairies of what is now south Texas began to see the expansion of a ranching culture that played a significant role in New Spain's economy. Similarly, in Coahuila, although the progress was slower, the subjugation of the province's Indians led to the founding of new towns and great haciendas. The Apaches remained a constant menace, but the province showed signs of flourishing, especially in the realm of livestock production.

In Texas, however, Spanish civilization was stalemated by Indian cultures capable of successfully fending off both its military might and its religious blandishments. Of the early settlements, only San Antonio de Béxar seemed to have the necessary natural resources and diversity of population to sustain itself. Béxar did not offer many attractions for migrants from the interior of New Spain; La Bahía and Los Adaes offered even fewer. With royal resources insufficient to meet frontier needs, officials played a shell game with the few soldiers and missionaries at their disposal. The successive failures at San Xavier, San Sabá, and El Orcoquisac largely discredited the presidio-mission system of frontier expansion. (California, however, founded in 1769, seems to have been the great exception that proved the rule.)

Fortunately for the Spanish, events that took place far away from the prairies and forests of Texas brought about a radical change of circumstances in 1763. Spain had allied itself with France in a European conflict known as the Seven Years' War (called the French and Indian War in America) and lost. Forced to give up Florida to England in return for recovering Havana, France made it up to Spain and prevented England from gaining most of North America by ceding Louisiana to the Spanish Crown. With Louisiana no longer a foreign colony, Texas ceased to be a border province. French traders would no longer undermine Spanish authority among the province's Indians, and the Spanish could move the line of defense against foreign aggression eastward to the Mississippi River. The last third of the eighteenth century offered Spain a new opportunity to make something of Texas, if it could simply overcome the other great barrier to development: the objections of the Norteños, the Comanches, and the Apaches to becoming part of the Spanish Empire.

SUGGESTED READINGS

The first half of the eighteenth century coincides with the arrival of the Bourbon dynasty on the Spanish throne. David Weber's overview of the imperial rivalries and realignments that brought Spanish Texas into being in chapters 6 and 7 of *The Spanish Frontier in North America* makes very interesting reading, as do chapters 8 and 9 of John Kessell's *Spain in the Southwest*. Those interested in the social history of northern Mexico and the American Southwest at that time can turn to the very readable *Los Paisanos: Spanish Settlers on the Northern Frontier of New Spain* by Oakah L. Jones, Jr. (1979, 1996). Understanding the Spanish frontier military system is vital to an appreciation of colonial Texas history, and the work that does the best job of explaining that system is Max L. Moorhead's *The Presidio: Bastion of the Spanish Borderlands* (1975). The most controversial of Spanish frontier institutions is the mission. Missions were traditionally viewed as the great civilizing force through which the Spanish brought both salvation and enlightenment to the native peoples; see, for example, the introductory chapter in Marion A. Habig, *The Alamo Chain of Missions: A History of San Antonio's Five*

Old Missions (1968). A newer generation of scholars has come to focus on the negative effects of the missionary project on the target populations; see, for example, David Sweet, "The Ibero-American Frontier Mission in Native American History," in Erick Langer and Robert H. Jackson, eds., *The New Latin American Mission History* (1995).

The French Challenge

When Louis Juchereau de St. Denis arrived at San Juan Bautista del Río Grande in 1714 the first Spanish missions of Texas had already been abandoned for twenty years. Texas remained a mostly unknown land, despite a few *entradas* north of the Rio Grande by missionaries and military men. In chapters 6–9 of *Spanish Expeditions into Texas*, William Foster discusses the expeditions that brought the Spanish back to Texas permanently. Louis Juchereau de St. Denis not only instigated the permanent occupation of Texas by Spaniards, but founded Natchitoches and a French colonial dynasty there, a story well told in "Tios and Tantes: Familial and Political Relationships of Natchitoches and the Spanish Colonial Frontier," by Patricia R. Lemée, *Southwestern Historical Quarterly* (1998). Ross Phares, *Cavalier in the Wilderness: The Story of the Explorer and Trader Louis Juchereau de St. Denis* (1952) is a full-scale biography of St. Denis. Essays on "Francisco Hidalgo/Louis Juchereau de St. Denis," "Antonio Margil de Jesús," and "Marques de San Miguel de Aguayo/Pedro de Rivera y Villalón" in *Notable Men and Women of Spanish Texas* by Donald Chipman and Harriett Denise Joseph (1999) provide a good understanding of the backgrounds of the military and religious leaders of early Texas.

Spanish Texas Takes Shape

Rivera's record of his inspection of Texas in 1727 provides a good description of the province ten years after its founding. His diary and report, along with an assessment, are included in *Imaginary Kingdom: Texas as Seen by the Rivera and Rubí Military Expeditions, 1727 and 1767*, ed. Jack Jackson, annot. William C. Foster (1995). Updating our understanding of Spanish-French rivalry in Texas is David LaVere, "Between Kinship and Capitalism: French and Spanish Rivalry in the Colonial Louisiana-Texas Indian Trade," *Journal of Southern History* (1998). Historical work on colonial Texas has overwhelmingly centered on San Antonio, the province's largest and most diverse community. The story of its founding and early development appears in *Tejano Origins in Eighteenth-Century San Antonio*, ed. Gerald E. Poyo and Gilberto M. Hinojosa (1991) and Jesús F. de la Teja, *San Antonio de Béxar: A Community on New Spain's Northern Frontier* (1995).

The Great Colonizer

What is now South Texas, from Corpus Christi to Laredo to Brownsville and South Padre, was the northern half of Nuevo Santander during the colonial period. Most of the historical work on this region has been done by Mexican scholars, and remains untranslated although there is a handful of very useful recent works on the subject in English. The colonization and early development of this vast region that became the home to huge ranching estates is told by Armando Alonzo in the early chapters of *Tejano Legacy: Rancheros and Settlers in South Texas, 1734–1900* (1998) and in "José de Escandón y Elguera," chapter 7 in *Notable Men and Women of Spanish Texas*. A useful synthesis of what is known of the aboriginal peoples of that area is found in *Indians of the Rio Grande Delta: Their Role in the History of Southern Texas and Northeastern Mexico*, by Martín Salinas (1990). The story of La Bahía has yet to receive comprehensive scholarly treatment, but two works, along with the article "La Bahía" in *The New Handbook of Texas*, provide basic information: Kathryn Stoner O'Connor, *Presidio La Bahia, 1721–1846* (1966), and Craig H. Roell, *Remember Goliad! A History of La Bahía* (1994). For developments at Paso del Norte, W. H. Timmons offers a good overview in chapter 2 of *El Paso: A Borderlands History* (1990).

The Failure of Missionary Expansion in Texas

The collapse of Spanish expansion efforts in Texas centers on two pivotal events: the disintegration of the San Xavier mission-presidio complex and the successful Norteño and Comanche resistance to a Spanish punitive expedition following their destruction of Mission San Sabá. Herbert E. Bolton's *Texas in the Middle Eighteenth Century: Studies in Spanish Colonial History and Administration* (1915, 1970) remains the best survey of Spanish activities in the region, except the San Sabá story. That tale, and the followup Spanish effort to punish the Indians responsible, is told by Robert S. Weddle in *The San Sabá Mission: Spanish Pivot in Texas* (1964, 1988). The Norteño-Comanche destruction of the San Sabá mission, which the Spanish built for the Lipan Apaches, is also notable for having produced the first artwork with a Texas theme, a large allegorical painting executed in Mexico City in the early 1760s. The painting itself has an interesting story, nicely summarized by Sam D. Ratcliffe in "'Escenas de Martirio': Notes on *The Destruction of Mission San Sabá*," *Southwestern Historical Quarterly* (1991).

4

The Age of Reform, 1767–1800

In October 1770 Athanase de Mézières, the French-born lieutenant governor for the Natchitoches district of Louisiana, traveled to the Kadohadacho village of San Luis on the Red River to meet with various groups of Caddo and Wichita-related Indians. He brought word to the skeptical chiefs and elders of the new colonial order in Louisiana and the wishes of His Catholic Majesty to forget the unpleasantries of San Sabá and to establish a lasting peace:

> Do not forget that there are now no Frenchmen in these lands, and that we are all Spaniards. I have and will keep in mind your promises in order to report them to my chief, to whom they will undoubtedly be pleasing, and he will receive you into the number of his children and of the happy subjects of our monarch. But meanwhile it is fitting, since you have committed so many insults, robberies, and homicides in San Antonio de Vexar and vicinity, that without loss of time you should journey to that city. . . . There you will humble yourselves in the presence of a chief of greatest power who resides there, and whose part it is to ratify the treaty which you seek, since you have established yourselves within his jurisdiction, and to name the light and easy conditions to which you must conform in order not to incur the misfortune of being deprived of so desirable a boon.

Mézières's words reflected both the challenges and opportunities that the acquisition of Louisiana represented for Spain. On the one hand, Spanish officials had to gain the respect and loyalty of a large number of tribes that until recently had been incited by the French to hostility against Spaniards. On the other hand, without a European rival on the doorstep of New Spain, colonial officials could look for ways to reorganize the frontier in more efficient and thriftier ways.

1766	Marqués de Rubí begins inspection tour of Texas region at Paso del Norte
1772	*Reglamento de 1772*, intended to reorganize frontier defense system, issued
1773	Presidio Los Adaes and East Texas missions suppressed; San Antonio de Béxar becomes capital of Texas
1774	Refugees from Los Adaes found settlement of Nuestra Señora del Pilar de Bucareli at Trinity River crossing of Camino Real
1777	Comandancia General de las Provincias Internas organized
1778	Commandant General Croix holds war council in Béxar, establishes Mesteña tax on unbranded livestock
1779	Nacogdoches established when Bucareli abandoned following Comanche raids and flooding
1785	Governor Cabello makes peace with Comanches and Norteños
1790	Commandant General Ugalde defeats the Apaches at Sabinal Canyon
1793	Secularization of Texas missions begins with San Antonio de Valero (the Alamo)
1797	La Bahía missions exempted from secularization
1800	First permanent bridge across the Rio Grande in operation at Paso del Norte; Rosa María Hinojosa de Ballí controls ranching empire of 1 million acres

For Charles III, his ministers, and their subordinates throughout the Spanish Empire there was much work to do in the aftermath of the Seven Years' War. The defeat of the Spanish military in the Old World and the New revealed superficiality and inadequacy of the military reforms and rebuilding programs of Philip V and Ferdinand VI, Charles's father and brother. Charles III, determined to recover Spain's fortunes as a world power, committed himself to bold action. Only a radical shakeup in colonial policies and institutions could overcome the inertia of colonial officials and the inadequacy of military preparedness. Charles thought that only peninsular Spaniards had the necessary detachment and training to carry out the reforms. In the long run, this policy shift away from American-born Spaniards alienated many *criollos* who came to resent their lack of opportunities, but in the short term, it seemed to bear good results.

Charles was a son of the Enlightenment, a movement born in the France of Louis XIV, his great-grandfather, and brought to Spain by his father, Philip V. True to Enlightenment ideals, Charles believed in the progressive and absolute power of the monarchy and the value of scientific knowledge and rational thought. Like his fellow Enlightenment monarchs throughout Europe, he was determined to curb the power of the Catholic church, which remained a useful instrument of government, but represented the old, less rational, less modern way of doing things. Although his immediate predecessors had focused on reforming the political, economic, and social institutions of peninsular Spain, Charles turned his attention to the empire by sending out like-minded officials with broad powers to shake up a colonial system over 250 years in the making.

The most prominent of this new breed of enlightened administrators was José de Gálvez. An accomplished judge with a no-nonsense attitude, in 1765 Gálvez became *visitador* (inspector general) for New Spain, with power to implement immediate reforms to increase revenue, foster government efficiency, and strengthen the colony's defenses. When he did not get along with the viceroy, the king replaced the viceroy with the more collegial Marqués de Croix. Between them, Gálvez and Croix initiated a series of measures intended to strengthen Spanish control in North America. During his six years in New Spain, Gálvez established a tobacco monopoly and other royal monopolies, overhauled the tax structure, and began designing a new administrative system which, although not implemented until 1786, divided New Spain into eleven large districts called *intendencias*. He also ordered the occupation of Alta California (what is today the state of California) in order to forestall Russian moves in that direction. With regard to the Catholic church, he removed the Jesuit order from New Spain in response to the king's decree expelling the Jesuits from the empire on charges of disloyalty. The Spanish Enlightenment legacy of Charles and his ministers would extend even to far off and neglected Texas.

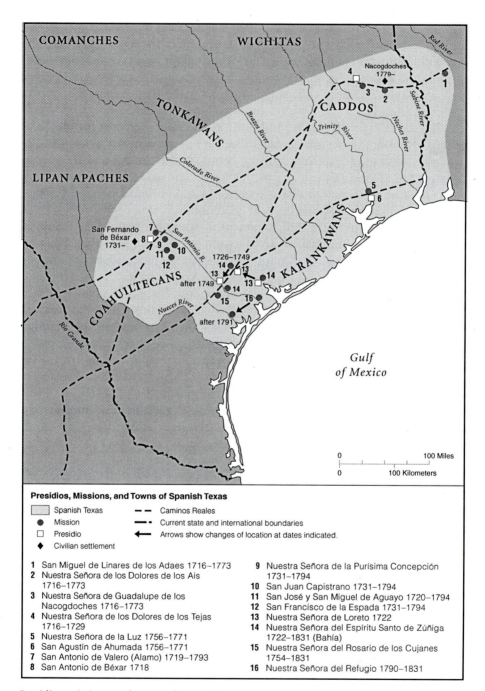

Presidios, Missions, and Towns of Spanish Texas

- ░ Spanish Texas
- ● Mission
- ☐ Presidio
- ◆ Civilian settlement
- – – Caminos Reales
- –·– Current state and international boundaries
- ⟵ Arrows show changes of location at dates indicated.

1 San Miguel de Linares de los Adaes 1716–1773
2 Nuestra Señora de los Dolores de los Ais 1716–1773
3 Nuestra Señora de Guadalupe de los Nacogdoches 1716–1773
4 Nuestra Señora de los Dolores de los Tejas 1716–1729
5 Nuestra Señora de la Luz 1756–1771
6 San Agustín de Ahumada 1756–1771
7 San Antonio de Valero (Alamo) 1719–1793
8 San Antonio de Béxar 1718

9 Nuestra Señora de la Purísima Concepción 1731–1794
10 San Juan Capistrano 1731–1794
11 San José y San Miguel de Aguayo 1720–1794
12 San Francisco de la Espada 1731–1794
13 Nuestra Señora de Loreto 1722
14 Nuestra Señora del Espíritu Santo de Zúñiga 1722–1831 (Bahía)
15 Nuestra Señora del Rosario de los Cujanes 1754–1831
16 Nuestra Señora del Refugio 1790–1831

Presidios, missions, and towns of Spanish Texas.

Reorganization of the Frontier

Maximizing royal revenues and streamlining colonial government were not Charles III's only concerns in New Spain: There was the critical matter of the military. The weaknesses of the colonial army and navy had come to light during the Seven Years' War, when the English captured Havana and other Caribbean ports, forcing Spain to give up Florida to the English in order to recover Cuba. New Spain's military establishment was small, consisting of only a couple of garrisons protecting the major ports; its militias were disorganized and poorly trained, and the navy was outdated and in disrepair. On the northern frontier, the presidio system, despite the reforms implemented following Brigadier Pedro de Rivera's inspection tour of the 1720s, was in disarray. There was little standardization in anything: uniforms, equipment, or training. Chains of command were mixed, with some commanders reporting to the local governor and others to the viceroy, and there was little cooperation among units. Furthermore, the acquisition of Louisiana required a rethinking of frontier military strategy, particularly with regard to Texas.

Texas Comes Under Inspection

The job of reforming frontier defenses in response to the new international situation fell on Cayetano María Pignatelli Rubí Corbera y Saint Climent, Barón de Llinas, Marqués de Rubí, a career military officer holding the rank of field marshal and a knight in the Order of Alcántara. Rubí had come to New Spain in 1764 and had already undertaken a number of reform projects when he received his orders in August 1765. The king wanted him to inspect "all the presidios of this Kingdom, examine their condition, their location, inspect their troops, review the old price regulations under which they subsist, and, having assessed things time has changed since their establishment . . . propose changes appropriate to the present situation and spell out everything else that for their better government and defense you consider necessary." To assist him, the viceroy appointed two engineers, Nicolás de Lafora and Joseph de Urrutia, who eventually produced a series of detailed maps and plats of the region including Texas.

Rubí's inspection tour left Mexico City in March 1766 and visited the western frontier for over a year. In August 1766 he visited the Paso del Norte area, which at the time consisted of a presidio, a civilian settlement, and various haciendas and missions. Rubí found the Paso del Norte district to be flourishing, which prompted him to recommend moving the presidio to Carrizal, about seventy miles to the southwest. A detachment from the presidio had already been assigned to that location. A militia company could easily protect the area's settlers and peaceful Indians.

It was not until spring 1767 that Rubí's entourage headed for the eastern frontier provinces of Coahuila, Texas, and Nuevo León, reaching the Rio Grande at what is today Eagle Pass on July 14, 1767. His first inspection stop in what is now Texas occurred at Mission San Lorenzo, where a detachment of thirty-one men from Presidio San Sabá was stationed. Mission San Lorenzo (near present-day Camp Wood, Real County) and another mission, Candelaria (near present-day Montell, Uvalde County), had opened in 1762 and in a followup attempt to convert the Lipan Apaches after the disaster at Mission San Sabá. Located along the upper Nueces River, the missions were collectively known as El Cañon. Conditions at the sites were dismal: Mission Candelaria was completely abandoned, there were no Indians at San Lorenzo, and the detachment was totally destitute.

Moving on to San Sabá, which remained under the direct authority of the viceroy, Rubí's immediate assessment was that the presidio there was about as useful "as a ship anchored in mid-Atlantic would [be] in preventing foreign trade with America." He found the presidio's walls badly constructed, its horse herd under constant assault from the Comanches and Norteños, and the men poorly equipped and prone to desertion. Captain Felipe Rábago y Terán, who had been exonerated of all charges in the San Xavier murders of a decade earlier, had taken command in 1760 and tried to make San Sabá an efficient and vital post. He had sent detachments to explore a possible route to New Mexico, accommodated the Franciscans in establishing their missions at El Cañon, and spent lavishly on presents for Indians and supplies for his command (although much of what was requested never made it to the missions or the presidio). As the years wore on and Mexico City continued to ignore the plight of San Sabá and El Cañon, conditions deteriorated and Captain Rábago turned to profiteering. Isolated and unable to attract civilian settlers because of constant assaults by the Indians, the soldiers and their families, numbering approximately 300 individuals, lived in constant terror. Rubí rode out of Presidio San Sabá on August 4, 1767, already formulating his final recommendation—abandonment of the site and transfer of the handful of civilian families to Béxar.

Nothing could have prepared Rubí for conditions at San Antonio when he arrived on August 8. In the forty years since Rivera's inspection San Antonio de Béxar had undergone considerable change. To the two missions Rivera had found in 1727 another three had been added, and the presidio now shared the space between the San Antonio River and San Pedro Creek with the municipality of San Fernando de Béxar. The combined civilian and military population of Béxar had grown to over 700 individuals, representing a diverse ethnic mix of *criollos, castas,* and acculturated Indians. At each of the missions the friars led 200–350 neophytes, for a total population of over 1,200 men, women, and children from a dozen or more Coahuiltecan, Karankawa, and Apache tribes. General farming and a limited amount of ranching supported the majority of the population, and textile manufacturing was beginning at some of the missions. Unlike Paso del Norte, Béxar was still in no position to defend itself, especially as the mission Indians remained prone to flight, but the location showed promise in its fertile and irrigated fields, its vast grazing lands, and its healthy climate.

For all the development over the course of its first fifty years of existence, Béxar remained a decidedly backward place. This was due to decisions years earlier to deprive the presidio of its fighting strength: Rivera's recommendation to reduce the garrison from fifty-four to forty-four in 1729 and the viceroy's decision to take twenty-two men from Presidio de Béxar for service at San Sabá in 1757. A decade later Rubí found a garrison that was ill equipped, undisciplined, and overextended. The presidio was in disrepair in part because only seven men were available to the captain at any one time; the other fifteen were assigned to mission guard duty. Captain Luis Antonio Menchaca was more businessman than officer: he had his men uniformed in a colorful mix of lace, silk, and silver, which kept his pockets full and the men in want of basic necessities. The shortcomings of the garrison went beyond the men's uniforms, however, as the horse herd was depleted and many of the animals unfit for service. Although the soldiers were armed, their weapons were of many different calibers and a number of them were unserviceable.

Never a successful settlement despite being the capital of Texas from 1720 to 1773, Los Adaes remained an isolated military outpost that was often dependent on nearby French Natchitoches. José de Urrutia's map and elevation of the presidio accentuates both its isolation and its architectural distinctiveness from other Spanish colonial settlements. *(By permission of the British Library)*

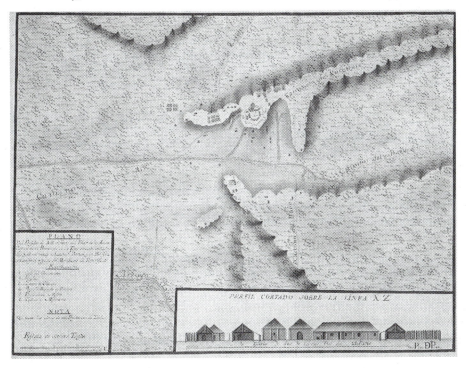

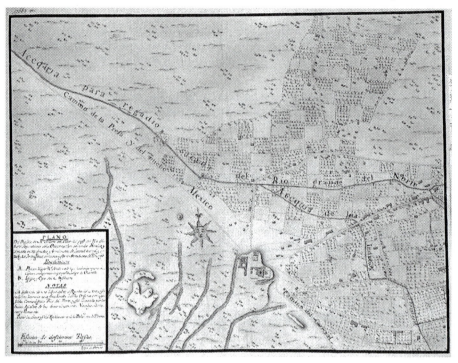

Compare Urrutia's map of Los Adaes (p. 97) and this one of Paso del Norte. Note the number of structures along roads, the agricultural fields, and extensive irrigation system. By the time the Marqués de Rubí and Urrutia visited what is now the El Paso-Juárez area, the missions, presidio, and civilian settlement had a flourishing economy combining ranching, viticulture, and subsistence crop production. *(By permission of the British Library)*

On receiving Rubí at his headquarters at Los Adaes on September 11, interim Governor Hugo Oconor must have been terribly embarrassed by conditions at the "capital" of Texas. He had assumed command of the province just a month earlier from Ángel Martos y Navarrete, whose tenure had been marked by disaster (the destruction of Mission San Sabá), scandal (his arrest order for the presidio commander at Orcoquisac had resulted in the death of a soldier and the burning of the presidio), and dishonesty (he had made huge profits on the sale of goods to his men). The goods he had sold to his men were goods he had purchased illegally at French Natchitoches. Presidio Los Adaes exhibited the scars of Martos's neglect: Serviceable weaponry among the company of sixty-one soldiers consisted of two muskets, seven swords, and six shields; instead of the regulation 500–600 horses, the company herd contained just 117, only twenty-five of which were fit for service; a number of soldiers lacked basic items of dress, including shirts, shoes, and hats. The former governor had illegally employed the men in his command as cowboys and farmers on his private ranch and had sold back to them part of the crop that they had grown in the company's communal farm. Oconor's memories of the poor conditions at Los Adaes would lead him to strongly support Rubí's recommendations.

Spanish East Texas, the marqués found, did not meet expectations for a Spanish provincial capital. The settlement lacked a substantial civilian population beyond the soldiers' families, although there may have been as many as 100 families living on ranches in the forest clearings and at former Hasinai Indian village sites in the countryside. In general, the approximately 500 people who lived in East Texas lived off subsistence farming, trapping, Indian trade, and contraband commerce with Louisiana. The steadily declining Caddo population, having experienced a series of epidemics as well as the adverse climatic conditions of much of the eighteenth century, had never been converted; the area's three missions contained not a single neophyte.

If Los Adaes had proven to be a viable settlement, Rubí's judgment might not have been so harsh. As matters stood, however, the Texas capital was a drain on the viceroyalty's overextended resources. As was the case throughout Texas, in Paso del Norte, and the rest of the northern frontier, each missionary received a yearly stipend of 450 pesos from the government. This sum might have been justifiable in the case of San Antonio, where the missions had healthy neophyte populations, but was unjustified where the friars had no Indians to instruct and only a few civilian settlers for whom to provide spiritual care. Keeping soldiers at government expense when they did little more than work on their commander's private estate was equally unacceptable. With Natchitoches in Spanish hands, and with its French residents on good terms with the area Indians, what need was there to maintain Los Adaes? As the inspector's entourage departed for Orcoquisac, Rubí must already have arrived at the solution to reinforcing San Antonio: close down the presidio and transfer the local population to Béxar, where plentiful lands awaited the civilians and genuine military service awaited at least some of the soldiers.

Following a circuitous and tortuous route through woods and swamps, it took the Marqués de Rubí from September 28 to October 15 to reach Presidio San Agustín de Ahumada and Mission Nuestra Señora de la Luz del Orcoquisac. Since its founding in 1756 near present-day Wallisville, Chambers County, to counter French penetration of southeast Texas by way of Galveston Bay, El Orcoquisac had failed by every measure. The garrison itself had turned to contraband and Indian trade in the absence of any opportunity to raise its own food or meet its other needs. The presidio suffered from constant desertions; the mission had failed to attract the local Atakapa-speaking Indians; and no civilian population had established itself in the vicinity. Best for all concerned—the royal treasury, missionaries, and beleaguered soldiers and their families—was the complete abandonment of the site.

In November 1767, when Rubí reached La Bahía (his last stop in Texas) he was in sore need of some good news. Although conditions were not perfect at Presidio La Bahía, they were better than conditions anywhere else in the province. This was due in large part to Captain Manuel Ramírez de la Piscina, whose seventeen-year tenure had begun when the complex had been moved to the lower San Antonio River. Although the old captain, who had died the previous July, had some of the same faults as his contemporaries at the other Texas posts—he overcharged for the goods he sold to his soldiers and had soldiers work at his ranch—he had kept his command disciplined and relatively well supplied. Most of the horses and firearms were in good condition, and all fifty soldiers were properly uniformed, if somewhat dirty, threadbare, and lacking in shields and lances.

Unlike the situations at San Sabá, Los Adaes, and El Orcoquisac, settlement at La Bahía seemed to be moving in the right direction. The number of families was increasing, from under ten in 1762 to about twenty-five at the time the marqués made his inspection. Although there was no formal town as yet, the more than 300 inhabitants of the presidio settlement seemed to be flourishing. Captain Ramírez had successfully dealt with the Karankawas and Coahuiltecans of the area, and the missionaries had learned to be patient with these hunter-gatherers who could not fully adjust to the sedentary life of Spanish colonial society. As a result, La Bahía was an oasis of peace and relative efficiency. As far as Rubí was concerned, it was worthy of serving as the eastern anchor in the presidio line he was about to recommend to the viceroy.

Rubí's Blueprint for the Reorganization of Spanish Texas

Bypassing Laredo, which did not have a presidio, Rubí and his retinue visited Presidio del Río Grande in November 1767, before arriving in Mexico City the following February. There he prepared a *dictamen* (official opinion) regarding matters on the frontier. It was not favorable in the least. The twenty-four presidios then in operation were in random, and sometimes ill-advised locations, and their commanders for the most part lacked the necessary training and abilities and seemed more interested in turning a profit than carrying out their duties. The men were poorly trained, ill equipped, alternately underutilized and overburdened, and in general taken advantage of by their commanders. To remedy this situation, Rubí proposed that the entire frontier, from the Gulf of California to the Gulf of Mexico be considered a single unit, so that officials could base their decisions on overall strategic considerations rather than immediate tactical or local interests. Further, he proposed a complete reform of the organization, command structure, and financial management of the presidios, which would produce cost savings to the crown and better conditions for the soldiery.

Rubí's recommendations were incorporated into a series of reforms carried out in the 1770s that streamlined not only military policy but political and religious administration as well. The first, known as the *Reglamento of 1772,* called for a complete overhaul of the presidio system. With the exception of Santa Fe and San Antonio (which was to become the capital of Texas) all the presidios would now line up roughly along 30° north latitude, from Altar in Sonora to La Bahía in Texas. Presidios above or below that line would be relocated or closed, according to regional needs, so that in the end a string of fifteen presidios, approximately 100 miles apart from each other, could effectively coordinate their activities. In Texas that meant closing El Orcoquisac and Los Adaes and transferring San Sabá to a site on the Rio Grande under the jurisdiction of Coahuila. In order to curb the abuses of the presidio commanders, who also controlled the purse strings of their individual garrisons, each company was to elect a commissary officer who would be held strictly accountable for his financial dealings. Soldiers' salaries would be reduced in light of reforms certain to lower their expenses, and they would receive part of it in cash. Training and duties were to be standardized, as were soldiers' uniforms, and presidio commanders were to keep regular muster rolls and enlistment papers.

The big winners in Texas were Presidios de Béxar and La Bahía. At San Antonio the *Reglamento* called for a company commanded by the governor and manned by eighty officers and men, and a chaplain. Presidio La Bahía was to be manned by its captain, fifty officers and men, and a chaplain. Not all Tejanos (Texans of Spanish-Mexican descent) were happy with the reforms, however, and the new governor assigned to the province had his hands full attempting to placate the disgruntled and dispossessed denizens of East Texas while pleasing his superiors in Mexico City and Madrid.

The Death and Rebirth of Spanish East Texas

Colonel Juan María Vicencio, Barón de Ripperdá, a Spanish-born career military man, accompanied by his Mexican-born wife, Mariana Gómez de Parada Gallo y Villavicencio, arrived in San Antonio early in 1770, marking the beginning of a new chapter in Texas history. Technically, his command was Presidio Los Adaes, but the pressing needs of reorganizing and strengthening defenses at Béxar, not to mention the perils and inconveniences of taking his new wife to East Texas, led him to take up residence in the *casas reales* (town hall). He and the baroness must have been greatly relieved when late in 1771 Viceroy Antonio María de Bucareli denied Ripperdá's half-hearted request to transfer to Los Adaes with the admonition that because Natchitoches was now in Spanish hands, he should remain where he was. Although San Antonio de Béxar was not officially to become the provincial capital until 1773, Ripperdá's presence there from 1770 signaled the complete acceptance of Rubí's recommendations for the reorganization of Texas.

Colonial Frontier Society

Although they were members of the elite, the baron and his wife's arrival in Texas was an example of a common occurrence at the time: the migration of families to the frontier. The myth of a European, male-only frontier does not stand up to close scrutiny in the Texas case. La Salle had attempted to establish a well-rounded colony by bringing a number of French women along on his tragic expedition of 1685. The Spanish Crown, always interested in establishing stable colonial communities, had encouraged married soldiers to move to Texas from the time of the Ramón and Alarcón expeditions of 1716–18. One of the viceroy's counselors commented that married soldiers were a double benefit, as "they will be able to fill their presidios with the children that their wives bear them," and they would be less likely to make advances to the neophyte females and take advantage of them. The effort to bring Canary Islanders to Texas had also been predicated on the migration of families, rather than single individuals; of the fifty-five who eventually made it to Béxar in 1731, only four were single adult males.

Of course, frontier conditions made Texas essentially a male-dominated society, and Spanish females were always in short supply. Women like the Baroness de Ripperdá, a high-born *criollo,* were rare. Most Spanish women in Texas had been born on the frontier, and their "Spanish" status was often based on social convention rather than biological grounds. Beginning with the conquests of the sixteenth century, exclusively male undertakings, many men had found companionship in Indian women, and some took women of African descent as wives. Over the course of generations, if family circumstances improved, the children of such mixed couples might "pass" into the ranks of the "Spanish"; by the late eighteenth century the term "Spaniard" was more a recognition of social status than an ethnic label, especially on the frontier. In the case of Texas, although the evidence points to considerable ethnic mixing, "Spaniards" were reported to make up a majority of the population. The continued infusion of significant numbers of acculturated Indians (and a smaller number of individuals of African descent) into the Hispanic population, kept the reported Indian population consistently at about 25 percent and the mixed-blood population at about 20 percent.

For all women, Texas was a harsh environment. Aside from her relative wealth, the Baroness de Ripperdá was fortunate in a number of respects. Her husband, despite his military career, lived out his stay in Texas, whereas many other Tejanas could expect to be widowed once or twice if they did not die in childbirth, in one of the periodic epidemics that swept through the province, or during an Indian attack. The baroness delivered six children during her husband's tenure in Texas, at least two of whom died in infancy. Her experience was not uncommon: Most women in Texas, indeed throughout New Spain, could expect to lose half of their children in infancy (from birth to two years).

Although the baroness did not have to worry about food or shelter (despite her husband's repeated complaints about their quarters' poor state of repair), the overwhelming majority of her contemporaries faced lives of unremitting toil. With the exception of a few families who had one or more servants—sometimes a hired hand, sometimes a captured Apache or Comanche child who was brought up in the household as a *criado* (someone having servant status)—women worked long hours to maintain their households. The large number of widows meant that many women had to take on the role of sole provider for their families. As heads of households, they engaged in a variety of occupations outside the home such as seamstress, midwife, and shopkeeper. A few women acquired property through inheritance and marriage and became leading ranchers and farmers in their communities. For some, economic reversals and lack of other opportunities prescribed a life of prostitution, an activity which seems to have been grudgingly accepted in colonial Texas.

Active public participation in the economic life of Texas required women to have legal rights that afforded them considerable protection in what was a man's world. Thus the Baroness de Ripperdá and all women, from the best-positioned Spanish matriarch to the lowliest Indian maid, benefited from a legal system that recognized them as individuals. Women had the right to their own separate property, including those goods and real estate they had acquired before marriage or that had been bequeathed to them. Moreover, after marriage they were entitled to half the property that husband and wife acquired as a couple. The right to defend one's property and honor required that women play a role in legal proceedings, so they could initiate legal actions and give testimony. These rights extended even to slaves, who on a number of occasions successfully petitioned to be removed from the homes of abusive masters. And, as theirs was a Roman Catholic society, women could file for divorce from abusive or runaway husbands, although neither party could remarry before the death of his or her former spouse.

The First Capital of Texas Abandoned

Los Adaes, despite the Marqués de Rubí's dismissive assessment of East Texas, was the second largest settlement in the province of Texas, and the most ethnically diverse. Over 500 Spanish subjects lived among the remaining aboriginal inhabitants, members of various Hasinai and Atakapan groups, and a growing number of Louisianians, white and black. The death warrant for the fifty-year-old capital of the Province of the Tejas and Nuevas Philipinas had long since been signed, however, and it fell to the Baron de Ripperdá to execute it. In the process he and the policy-makers in Mexico City came to discover just how deep-rooted the local Tejanos' attachment was to their homes in the woods and swamps of East Texas.

In January 1773 Viceroy Bucareli informed Ripperdá that it would be his responsibility to carry out Spain's withdrawal from the Texas side of the Louisiana border. His instructions were draconian: Not only were the existing missions to close, but the governor was to see that the two presidios were destroyed and the entire Hispanic population of the area relocated to San Antonio. Ripperdá arrived in Los Adaes in early June 1773 and made the bad news official. Resentment and resistance emerged on all sides. Some families fled to Natchitoches and others into the isolated woods where they had cleared fields and built their cabins. The various Hasinai groups in the vicinity took the withdrawal as evidence that the Spanish had allied with the Apaches, and were preparing to make war on them. After the governor failed to adequately reassure them, the refugees had to leave two families behind at Nacogdoches in a sign of goodwill.

The overwhelming majority of refugees from Los Adaes arrived in Béxar on September 26 to a less than enthusiastic welcome. They were instructed to look for house lots and farmlands in the vicinity, but without disturbing the property of Bexareños or missions. This was impossible without moving so far away from the settlement that they would be exposed to Indian attack and have no access to irrigation water. Some families did find places for themselves, either as share-croppers at the missions, hired hands for some of the better-off residents, or in military service at the presidio. At least half of the refugees, however, were deter-mined to return to East Texas, and soon after their arrival they petitioned for per-mission to establish a new settlement at the site of the former Mission Nuestra Señora de los Ais (at present-day San Augustine).

The Adaesanos' petition had Governor Ripperdá's support. He was not only sympathetic to the plight of the dispossessed Tejanos, but their return to East Texas would buttress the Indian policy he favored: forming alliances with area Indians through trade. Of particular importance was establishing friendly rela-tions with the Wichita groups that had moved into north central Texas. The Wi-chitas seemed well disposed toward the Spanish, but were actively trading with Louisiana. Ripperdá believed that removing the Hispanic East Texas population would not solve the illegal Indian trade problem, but would only serve to under-mine the authority and respect officials in San Antonio commanded among the Indians of the region. His opinions were not shared by Oconor or the viceroy, both of whom wished to tow the line in regard to closing Texas off from Louisiana, prohibiting trade in firearms with the Indians, and sticking to Rubí's presidio line of defense. Eventually, the baron's refusal to carry out instructions he regarded as counterproductive cost him his office.

As for the Adaesanos, although he could not grant their request, Ripperdá gave them permission to carry their petition to the viceroy. When the viceroy re-sponded that he would not allow them to settle so close to Louisiana, but that they could select an intermediate location, the governor had the necessary ap-proval to authorize settlement at the Camino Real crossing on the Trinity River. More than 120 families made the decision to move while about sixty or seventy families remained behind.

As for the new settlement, Nuestra Señora del Pilar de Bucareli required gov-ernment and protection. No presidio or army detachment had been authorized for Bucareli so the governor organized a militia, pending the viceroy's approval. Ripperdá named Antonio Gil Ybarbo captain of the militia and *justicia mayor*, ef-fectively making him lieutenant governor for the district. It is difficult to imagine anyone better suited to the job of running what was essentially a renegade settle-ment of smugglers and Indian traders. A native of Los Adaes, Ybarbo was schooled in various Indian languages and French, adept at contraband trade, and skilled in the arts of political survival. His rather loose interpretation of property

On the campus of Stephen F. Austin University in Nacogdoches sits a reconstruction of the "Old Stone Fort." Antonio Gil Ybarbo built his *casa de piedra* shortly after founding Nacogdoches in 1779. For more than a century the building served as home, store, government headquarters, and saloon, until it was demolished in 1902. In 1936, the stones from the original structure were used to construct the replica, which today serves as a museum of early East Texas history. *(East Texas Research Center at Stephen F. Austin State University)*

rights had landed him in jail in New Orleans by order of Governor Oconor in the late 1760s, when he was caught with horses alleged to have been stolen by Indians from various Texas settlements. Any enemy of Oconor's was a friend of Ripperdá, and the Texas governor soon obtained Ybarbo's release from jail. The two men saw eye-to-eye on a variety of issues: the need for a continued Spanish presence in East Texas; the need for broad and sympathetic trade relations with the northern tribes; and the need to maintain commercial ties with Natchitoches.

Indian Relations Transformed

Under Ybarbo's guidance Spanish East Texas was reborn, even as the settlers were forced to abandon Bucareli for the site of Mission Nacogdoches in early 1779 because of hostilities with the Comanches and flooding on the Trinity River. The abandonment of Bucareli and the settlement of Nacogdoches coincided with administrative changes both at the local and the viceregal level. In late October 1778 Colonel Domingo Cabello y Robles, Governor Ripperdá's replacement, arrived in Béxar. A career army officer like his predecessor, the fifty-three year old had considerable experience in colonial matters, but none in frontier Indian affairs. He had served in Cuba twice, displaying conspicuous valor during the English capture of Havana in the Seven Years' War. His gallantry earned him the governorship of Nicaragua, a position he held for almost twelve years before receiving the Texas post.

Cabello must have wondered what he had done to deserve such a posting. Texas had such a bad reputation in the viceregal capital that his cook, "a very good one that I employed at Cádiz in 1763, when I went to serve in the government of Nicaragua, was told so many things about this place as soon as we arrived in Mexico City last year, that he came to believe that the Indians would eat him, for which reason he resigned from my service. And the same thing happened with my manservant and a secretary. . . . Although I recognize that they did right, because this [place] is worse than Siberia and Lapland." There were, of course, no cannibals in Texas, but Cabello's comments reflect the general perception of the Texas frontier as a savage land.

By the time Cabello assumed office the most revolutionary of the frontier reforms was underway: the creation of an independent administrative and military jurisdiction for the frontier provinces. The Comandancia General de las Provincias Internas, as the new entity was called, represented José de Gálvez's attempt to make government in northern New Spain more responsive and efficient. The region, including the provinces of Sonora, Sinaloa, Nueva Vizcaya, New Mexico, Coahuila, and Texas, would be administered by a commandant general, a military official holding both military and political authority, and independent from the viceroy.

On January 1, 1777, Caballero Teodoro de Croix became the first commandant general of the Interior Provinces. Croix was an experienced army officer who had served in various political capacities under his uncle, a former viceroy. He was acquainted with the situation on the northern frontier and in Texas, and did not agree with the policies of either the current viceroy or Inspector General Oconor. He soon replaced Oconor, and began to carry out an inspection tour of his jurisdiction that included holding a war council at San Antonio de Béxar.

As far as Texas was concerned, Croix was in accord with Ripperdá and Athanase de Mézières: make peace with the Nations of the North and the Comanches, and make war on the Apaches. Athanase de Mézières, a native of Paris and former French army officer and Indian trader, had served at Natchitoches beginning in the 1740s. Louisiana governor Alejandro O'Reilly appointed De Mézières, who had readily accepted Spanish rule, lieutenant governor for the Natchitoches district, a post in which the Frenchman could help the Spanish maintain good relations with the frontier tribes. De Mézières quickly won over Governor Ripperdá to his ideas on Indian relations, particularly regarding whom should be considered friend versus foe. Beginning in 1770 he had undertaken a series of missions to various East Texas tribes on behalf of the Spanish Crown.

Not surprisingly, the war council held by Croix at San Antonio in January 1778 placed blame of Texas's Indian problems squarely on the shoulders of the Apaches, especially the Lipans, and called for all-out war against them. The Nations of the North and the Comanches had not been hostile to Spanish interests until the Spanish had made peace overtures to the Apaches and built missions and a presidio for them. Even worse, because the Apaches refused to keep their word, Spanish Texas had ended up at war against all these groups. The council also approved Ripperdá's agreements with the Nations of the North negotiated through De Mézières. "Although some have groundlessly regarded these treaties as deceitful, all the nations except the Comanches have scrupulously kept them." Only all-out war against the Apaches, combined with concerted diplomacy toward the Nations of the North and the Comanches, could bring peace and prosperity to the province. And only Athanase de Mézières had the necessary diplomatic skills to bring the province's Indians into an alliance against the Apaches. De Mézières's declining health did not permit him to accept Commandant General Croix's offer of the Texas governorship, however. He died in San Antonio in November 1779, having made peace between the Nations of the North and the Spanish and still advocating diplomacy toward the Comanches and war against the Apaches.

The situation was not so clear to Governor Cabello, however. On his arrival he was confronted by Comanche raids on Bucareli and friendly visits from Lipan and other Apache chiefs. From Cabello's brief survey of the situation, De Mézières's insistence that the Comanches were not the problem made little sense. Consequently, Cabello decided not to take sides. Unfortunately, De Mézières's death left Cabello with no one to help him keep the peace with the Nations of the North, and during the early 1780s Spanish Texas was exposed to increased raiding. Only in 1785, after implementing a new policy of gift-giving and diplomacy and after experienced translators became available to him, was Cabello able to work out new agreements with various Texas tribes, including the Comanches. The program, also known as "peace by purchase," required Spanish officials to make regular gifts to the Indians and allow trade with settlers, including, ultimately, muskets and ammunition. Until well after the turn of the century only the various Apache tribes and occasional groups of young independent warriors troubled Spanish Texas. It was the longest period of relative peace that the province would enjoy for decades to come.

Sunset for the Missions

Reform and change marked the religious realm as well as the military and political spheres of life in late eighteenth-century Texas. The mission system, backbone of Spanish policy on the frontier, had given way to a more secular and economic perspective of Spanish-Indian affairs. In Texas the East Texas missions had failed to produce tangible results among the Hasinais in over fifty years of existence, and the mid-century experiments at San Sabá and El Cañon with the Lipans, San Xavier with the Ranchería Grande, and El Orcoquisac with the Akokisas had been disastrous. Even the active missions at Béxar and La Bahía faced new challenges that would prove insurmountable in the long run.

The Missions in Decline

For all intents and purposes the only active missions in Texas were located at Béxar and La Bahía. These missions had made such remarkable progress in physical terms through the early 1770s, that there was considerable animosity between Hispanic settlers and the friars over livestock, land, and water rights. The missions controlled some of the best grazing land in the San Antonio River basin, having established their ranching operations long before the civilian population had begun to venture into the countryside. The Béxar missions, having claimed their land before the arrival of the Canary Islanders, had gained control of the best agricultural land in the region, on which they had built extensive and sophisticated acequia systems. The mission compounds included large stone churches, workshops, granaries, and living quarters. In effect, the missions were independent communities that competed with civilian settlements for both resources and markets.

Despite all these physical advantages the missions had always faced one important hurdle in becoming the ideal Christian Spanish communities the friars wanted them to be: maintaining adequate Indian populations. The Ranchería Grande, Coahuiltecans, and Karankawas on whom the Franciscans of Béxar and La Bahía had depended to populate their missions had never been numerous peoples to begin with. Life at the missions often proved detrimental to the health of these hunter-gatherers. Dietary changes combined with different hygiene regimens weakened immune systems already under assault from a variety of pathogens alien to the region. Periodic epidemics of smallpox, measles, and other Old World diseases took a great toll on all residents of Texas, but particularly on the Indians. In addition, the missionaries' efforts to impose European values, particularly in the areas of division of labor, work routines, and sexual relations, contributed to the Indians' frequent flight.

In time the mission system faced a population crisis that the Spaniards were unable to overcome. Although the Béxar missions had averaged more than 200 neophytes each during the 1750s and 1760s, by the mid-1770s there were fewer than 200. At La Bahía, there had been a large number of Indians at Espíritu Santo and a new station, Nuestra Señora del Rosario, had been constructed for local groups in the 1750s. Neither establishment contained more than fifty families by the 1770s. The collapse or flight of neophyte populations forced friars to undertake frequent forays into the countryside to round up runaway neophytes or recruit new ones, but these were increasingly unproductive. The Coahuiltecans were becoming scarce. Coastal Indian groups, which proved particularly well insulated from Spanish encroachment, found that they could incorporate the missions into their annual cycle of seasonal migration without having to accept unwanted aspects of Spanish civilization. The Lipan and other Apaches might flirt with the missions, but as groups they proved unwilling to abandon their independent way of life, even in the face of increasing pressures from their Norteño and Comanche enemies. Missions were never able to attract the most populous tribes of Texas Indians, the Comanche and Wichita of northern and western Texas. As a result missions came to depend on a small core of acculturated Indians and increasingly larger numbers of non-Indian residents to maintain operations.

Presidio-mission complexes had operated fairly amicably with the community in East Texas and at La Bahía, because for the most part, in East Texas the missions never developed substantial resources and at La Bahía the civilian community remained small. Such was not the case at Béxar, however. From the time of the Canary Islanders' arrival, there had been considerable tension between the civilian and mission communities. There was competition over land, water, cattle, and the sale of agricultural products to the presidio market; the settlers attempted to gain access to the labor of neophytes; and the friars felt that the settlers were corrupting their Indians. These were the complaints that royal officials regularly received from both sides.

These circumstances combined to increase pressure on the Texas mission system to scale down its operations. The first missions to close were the remaining East Texas stations, those among the Hasinais as far east as Los Adaes and the one for the Akokisas on the lower Trinity River. This was a result of Rubí's claim that East Texas was not worth the investment in money and resources. These closures released Zacatecas College friars for duty at the four Béxar missions operated by

For Spanish colonial administrators, including Teodoro de Croix, first commandant general of the Provincias Internas, Texas posed a series of frustrating and seemingly insurmountable problems. Arriving in San Antonio in January 1778 for a council of war, Croix experienced firsthand the penury of the Tejanos, the struggles of the missions, and the neglect of the presidio system in the province. Later he would comment that Texas "did not deserve the name of the Province of Texas . . . nor the concern entailed in its preservation." *(Teodoro de Croix and the Northern Frontier of New Spain, 1776–1783, Alfred B. Thomas, University of Oklahoma Press)*

the Querétaro College, which abandoned Texas to concentrate on its more successful operations in Sonora and Arizona.

The pressure mounted with the arrival of Commandant General Croix for his 1778 war council in San Antonio. Croix listened to the complaints of settlers and missionaries about each other. He certainly understood the problems, and as a member of the new breed of more secular and regalist officials that the Spanish Bourbons were employing to modernize the empire, his actions favored settler and government interests. As far as the province's livestock was concerned, he strictly enforced the property rights of all parties, including the crown. As for the dispute over resources between Mission Valero and the townspeople of San Antonio, he ordered the suppression of the mission. Each Indian family would gain agricultural land and a house lot from the distribution of mission property, after which the Adaes settlers and other civilians would have access to the remaining farmland and lots. It was not until the early 1790s that both of these decisions were implemented, however, as lawsuits and reprieves wound their way through the imperial bureaucracy.

Secularization Begins

When the president of the Texas Franciscans, Fray José Francisco López, sat down to make his report on the state of the missions in 1789 there was little positive to say. Nine friars attended to the needs of the province, one at each of the six operating mission communities, another two at the Nacogdoches settlement, and one as a substitute wherever he was needed. Only San José and Espíritu Santo counted more than 100 Indian residents, most of whom spoke imperfect Spanish even after such a long time in residence. In fact, the missions had become multiethnic communities, "the Indians," as Fray López wrote about Valero, "having married mulattoes and mestizoes." The physical plants of the missions varied widely in quality and state of repair, with Valero and the abandoned Rosario in the worst shape, and Espíritu Santo and San José in good condition. Various construction projects had had to be abandoned for lack of Indian labor, including larger churches at Valero (the main part of today's "Alamo chapel") and at Capistrano.

Although the Texas missionary enterprise seemed to have some life left to it in the coastal environs of La Bahía, conditions at Béxar were such that the Zacatecas College could no longer justify operating five stations there. Fray Manuel Julio de Silva had proposed a plan for converting all the coastal Indians from Nuevo Santander to the Mississippi, which required a redistribution of the college's resources. Although the plan ultimately foundered and only the Copano Bay mission, Nuestra Señora del Refugio, was built, the project did set in motion the suppression process for the Texas missions.

Governor Manuel Muñoz received the viceroy's order for the suppression of San Antonio de Valero in February 1793. Suppression, or secularization, was the final stage in the life cycle of a mission, and marked the successful transition of a new Christian community to parish status. Secularization was not a mark of failure, therefore, but of success for the religious, as it marked the formation of a permanent Catholic community. The goods and property of the mission were divided among the Indians, who had farmed communally and, except for a limited amount of self-governance, followed the directives of the friars. They were now considered adult Christians and full citizens in Spanish colonial society. Leftover land and water could be used by the community to attract additional settlers, in this case, the Adaesanos and other worthy San Antonio families, or held in reserve for the children of current families. In the spring of 1793, therefore, San Antonio de Valero became a separate civilian community (although, as far as religion was concerned, it became part of San Fernando parish).

On April 10, 1794, a year to the day from when secularization of Mission Valero began, Commandant General Pedro Nava issued a decree for the secularization of all missions more than ten years old in the Provincias Internas. The order had two principal objectives. First, it was meant to address the complaints of ranchers, farmers, and mine owners throughout the region that the missions only served the interests of the friars, who had sole access to Indian labor. Suppression of missions would free up valuable and scarce water and land for the expanding civilian population. Second, a reduction in the number of missions would mean a real savings to the crown, which had to provide each friar with an annual stipend. In addition, with the reduction in the cost of guards, escorts, and incidental expenses, the savings to the royal treasury would be substantial.

In Texas the decree meant closure, not only of the remaining four Béxar stations, but also of Espíritu Santo and Rosario. Typical of the confused and contradictory "enlightened" reform effort of the Spanish Bourbons, the decree gave the mission Indians their freedom, granting them all the rights and privileges enjoyed by *gente de razón* (people of reason, that is, full members of Spanish society), while at the same time ordering governors to appoint local officials as *justicias* (magistrates) to oversee the activities and property of Indians, so that they would not be victimized and they would not become lazy and debauched. The Indians were no longer under the supervision of the missionaries, who were now limited to looking after their spiritual welfare, yet they were not completely independent either.

Governor Muñoz was skeptical about whether secularization would be successful, particularly in the case of the La Bahía missions, where populations consisted of Indians only recently brought under instruction. Consequently, he decided to start with the four Béxar missions, where he carried out the distribution of property during July 1794. Beginning at Espada, and moving northward to Capistrano, San José, and Concepción, he took inventory of all property, made surveys of agricultural land, and distributed it to the resident Indians, with most of the land set aside for future use. Concerned that there were still a few Indians under instruction, he divided responsibility for the mission residents between the *justicias,* who had authority over those Indians deemed civilized enough to participate in the new order, and the friars, who remained in charge of neophytes.

Nevertheless, it seems clear that the four missions continued much as they had in the past. The friars continued to exert considerable influence over the activities of the Indian residents. The residents continued to elect a governor and *alcalde* annually. The farming and animal husbandry that went on was mostly on a subsistence basis. Every once in a while a small group of Indians would appear at the gates of the mission compounds and come in for instruction. The one significant change was the steady growth in the number of settlers who occupied farm and ranch land in the vicinity of each mission. By the turn of the century, Concepción, Capistrano, and Espada all had a majority of non-Indian residents.

Having completed his work in Béxar, Governor Muñoz traveled to La Bahía early in the fall of 1794 to inspect the missions there. He found too few of the Indians at Espíritu Santo and Rosario ready for "civilized" life and so petitioned the commandant general for an exemption. It took until May 1797 for the commandant general to decide to grant the two La Bahía missions a five-year exemption from the secularization decree. In that time Mission Nuestra Señora del Refugio, which had first been founded in 1793 as part of Fray Silva's project for the conversion of coastal Indians, had found a permanent home at the site of present-day Refugio. At the end of the eighteenth century the three La Bahía missions represented the only fully authorized Franciscan missions in the province.

The Birth of the Texas Cattle Kingdom

By the time secularization of the San Antonio missions began in 1793, all of the Franciscan establishments in the San Antonio River basin had long ceased to play an important role in the province's economy. In fact, because they controlled valuable irrigable farmland near Béxar and vast expanses of grazing land as far away as the coast, the missions stood in the way of progress. Although they had been instrumental in establishing the first successful livestock concerns in Texas, by the 1780s the missions could no longer train or employ enough Indian herders to maintain themselves or challenge the increasingly aggressive civilian ranchers who were encroaching on mission ranch land.

The First Texas Ranches

Stock raising had been an important economic activity from the very beginning in Texas. The early expeditions introduced herds of horses and cattle, and sometimes sheep and goats. The Marqués de Aguayo brought thousands of head of stock, not only to supply his army, but also to help seed the presidios and missions he left in the wake of his expedition. One of the wealthiest ranchers in northern New Spain, he might have been using his visit to Texas to scout out the country for potential expansion of his haciendas. In the end, neither he nor any of the other great stockmen—sheep- and cattlemen known as *hacendados*—established operations as far north as Texas.

A few of the early military settlers managed to build up small herds. Mateo

Pérez, an early soldier who died in 1748, left over 200 head of cattle and 50 horses in his will. Early soldiers Bernabé Carbajal and Francisco Hernández had herds large enough by the 1730s that they obtained grants of grazing land, but their operations were limited by the threat of Indian attacks and their own meager economic means. In fact, it was the very limitations of livestock raising in Texas that influenced use of the term *rancho* (small ranch) rather than *hacienda* (large estate) for Texas livestock properties.

It was the missions, particularly those at La Bahía and Béxar, that first developed herds and flocks large enough to require construction of ranch compounds. At first the mission herders, specially trained neophytes with civilians or soldiers acting as overseers, maintained their animals in the vicinity of the missions. As the herds grew, however, it became necessary to move them farther away. Except for Mission San José, which headquartered its operations south of Béxar on the Atascosa River, the other San Antonio missions established their ranches southeast of the settlement. East of these ranches, between the San Antonio and Guadalupe rivers, Mission Espíritu Santo claimed land in what are today Victoria, Goliad, DeWitt, Gonzales, and Karnes counties.

Of all the mission ranches established in Texas, the one with the best story to tell is Rancho de las Cabras (Goat Ranch), the livestock enterprise of Mission San Francisco de la Espada, and today a state historical park. By the 1740s the southernmost of the Béxar missions had established its pastures along the south bank of the San Antonio River opposite present-day Floresville. The ranch was more than a goat ranch, however, as flocks of sheep and herds of cattle and horses also required the attention of a growing number of neophyte ranch hands (making these Indians among the first Texas cowboys). In time the operation grew to comprise an impressive complex of structures that were the envy of the area's civilian ranchers. From the extensive archeological remains, we know that red sandstone walls enclosed a large compound that contained a sturdy stone chapel, dwellings for the ranch families, and utility buildings and corrals. For defensive purposes two *torreones* (towers) served as bastions at the northwest and southeast corners of the compound.

Although its stonewalls could protect the residents of Rancho de las Cabras, nothing could protect the open range claimed by the mission from the assaults of both settlers and Indians. Following the 1749 treaty with the Apaches, a number of families with livestock interests moved into the countryside in force, claiming what pastures and watering places the missions had not reserved for themselves, and conflict soon arose. The missionaries charged that the so-called ranchers were moving next to the mission ranches in order to efficiently despoil the neophytes of their livestock. They argued that all the cattle in the countryside, branded and unbranded, belonged to their Indians because the missions had brought the first cattle to the area.

The ranchers responded that their parents and grandparents too had brought cattle and horses into the province. As one San Antonio *alcalde* reported to a Mexico City judge hearing a complaint from the missionaries: "this so distant

Province could be no less populous than that of Saltillo, because its land is pleasingly fertile, with abundant places to take water, and fields and plains sufficient to receive and maintain large populations; but as these waters and lands are only diverted in order for the missions to make ranches, the nonholding *vecinos* do not benefit nor does His Majesty in that his dominions are not settled."

While the ownership issue slowly made its way through the courts and various layers of bureaucracy, Indian warfare had created a crisis situation. By 1772 only Ignacio de la Peña's ranch and Rancho de las Cabras had withstood the Indian assaults that had resulted in the destruction or abandonment of all the other ranches in the area. Construction of a military post, Fuerte de Santa Cruz del Cíbolo, halfway between Béxar and La Bahía on Cíbolo Creek, was ineffective. The fort was conceived by the Marqués de Rubí as a way to repopulate the area by offering immediate protection against Indian assaults. Governor Cabello, never happy with the location of the understaffed and overextended fort, eventually prevailed upon the commandant general to destroy and abandon it in 1782.

Governor Ripperdá had attempted to mediate the complaints of both camps, only to find himself the subject of complaints. When Commandant General Croix arrived in Béxar in January 1778 to hold his war council, he was forced to listen to days of grievances from governor, missionaries, and ranchers alike. Although the positions of friars and stockmen were similar—the unbranded stock belonged to them—the governor had a larger agenda. Ripperdá pointed out to Croix that the uncontrolled and indiscriminate slaughter and export of cattle from the province was bound to lead to its extinction. Also, here was a public source of wealth being exploited by people who paid no direct taxes to the crown.

The commandant general responded by issuing what can be considered Texas's first environmental regulation. His ordinance of January 11, 1778, declared all unbranded stock property of the crown, required licensing of all cattle exports from Texas, established a tax on all unbranded stock captured either for export or slaughter, and imposed heavy fines for the unlicensed slaughter of unbranded cattle. Through this measure Croix hoped to raise revenue from a province that had always been a drain on the royal coffers while protecting the cattle population and ending the ownership dispute. The *mesteña* (unbranded stock) fund, as the livestock tax was commonly known, proved extremely controversial, and was challenged by all stock raisers in the province. Efforts by succeeding governors to control the consumption of breeding cows, a particularly detrimental practice, only served to increase animosities. Only in 1795 did one of Croix's successors, Pedro de Nava, reaffirm the measure, forgiving back taxes owed, but granting all legitimate stockmen just one year to gather *mesteño* cattle and horses before taxes were assessed again.

The governmental regulations putting the missions on a par with the ranchers in regard to unbranded stock contributed greatly to the demise of the Texas mission system. Continued Indian depredations and an inability to recruit neophytes took their toll on Rancho de las Cabras, which, although it still had twenty-six residents when Croix and Fray Morfi passed through on their way to

La Bahía early in 1778, was already in decline. The murder of six to eight Espada herdsmen by raiding Indians in 1780–81 was an almost insurmountable loss, especially when hiring civilian cowboys cost one peso a day, the highest wage for any skilled work in colonial Texas. When Governor Cabello ordered a branding roundup at the end of 1780, Rancho de las Cabras was unable to participate. In fact, Valero was the only Béxar mission able to field a roundup and branding crew; the rest of the participants were private ranchers.

Triumph of the Ranchers

By the time Governor Cabello managed to negotiate a general peace with the Comanches and Norteños in 1785, the end of the mission ranches was in sight. Cabello's successor, Rafael Martínez Pacheco, who was sympathetic to the plight of all Texas stockmen, crafted a series of roundup agreements in 1787 that allowed the missions and ranchers to round up as many animals as they could within assigned territories. Fray Pedro Noreña, representing Espada, was optimistic that somehow he could field a crew and revive the fortunes of Rancho de las Cabras. Such was not the case, however. When Martínez Pacheco issued his final report on the roundups, neither Espada nor any of the other Béxar missions had managed to capture a single animal. Only Mission Espíritu Santo had branded cattle: 1,418 head, compared to 6,231 cattle and 183 horses branded by the ranchers.

Without neophyte *vaqueros* (cowboys) to maintain the mission's ranching interests, Espada's missionaries, along with the friars at the other missions, had long since begun to make compromises with encroaching stockmen, which led to the eventual transfer of Rancho de las Cabras to civilian ownership. Ignacio Calvillo had occupied land in the vicinity of Rancho de las Cabras as early as 1774, and had gained the mission's approval by 1778. Within three years he was the recognized owner of Rancho Paso de las Mugeres. Similarly, Juan Barrera, a native of Coahuila and tithe collector for Texas, moved into the area during the 1780s. He operated a ranch he called Santa Gertrudis, possibly only renting the land so he could pasture the stock he collected as *diezmero* (tithe collector). Soon after secularization the two men moved to complete their takeover of Rancho de las Cabras, Calvillo taking the upper portion of the mission ranch, including the site of the headquarters compound, and Barrera taking the lower portion, which came to be called Las Cabras Viejas. This process was repeated at the other San Antonio missions.

The return of mission grazing lands to the royal domain that accompanied suppression was the ultimate victory for the civilian stockmen of Béxar who had vied with the missions for control of this valuable asset for more than half a century. Ranchers won in two ways. First, they acquired large numbers of unbranded cattle that roamed the prairies of south-central Texas. Second, in the three decades following secularization, civilian stockmen moved onto the former mission ranches and claimed them for themselves.

By the turn of the century, ranching had become the principal economic activity of Texas, despite adverse climatic conditions, severe financial constraints, persistent though greatly diminished Indian raids on herds, and continued reliance on natural reproduction of the semi-wild stock on the open range. At Béxar, where there were fourteen recognized ranch owners in 1791, there were thirty-five in 1810. Nacogdoches too saw a boom in ranching, particularly in horse breeding, during the 1790s, as the final collapse of the area's Caddo population left a number of clearings open for the taking. By 1810 there were more than twenty registered ranch owners in East Texas, including a number of Anglo and French Americans who had made their way into the area as authorized Indian traders, government agents, and squatters.

Ranching Empires of the Lower Rio Grande Valley

By the time secularization of the Texas missions began in the 1790s Nuevo Santander had become an even more successful ranching region than its neighbor to the north, Texas. No one knew this better than Rosa María Hinojosa de Ballí, matriarch of its most powerful ranching clan. From the various explorations of the region, José de Escandón had come to believe that this part of Nuevo Santander, which is sometimes referred to as the trans-Nueces, was best suited to a stock farming way of life, and he had encouraged *hacendados* from Coahuila and Nuevo León to establish sheep and cattle operations in the region. With no missions to stand in the way of occupation, one of these hacendados, Captain Juan José Hinojosa, with his relatives, friends, and a select group of other families, fanned out from the Rio Grande settlements in the last three decades of the eighteenth century to establish ranches as far north as today's Nueces County.

Among these stockmen was militia captain José María Ballí, whose father had brought his family to Reynosa in the earliest days. Like other prominent heads of family, Ballí served as a militia officer as well as *alcalde.* By the late 1750s, the Hinojosas and Ballís were two of six families, all interrelated, that controlled the economic and social life of Reynosa. The alliance between the two clans was further cemented through the marriage of Hinojosa's daughter Rosa María to Ballí, and during the 1770s and 1780s father-in-law and son-in-law worked as business partners to build up a ranching empire. The partnership included making joint application for a 37-*sitio* (166,500-acre) grant along the Rio Grande east of Hinojosa's *porciones* in the Reynosa jurisdiction.

Hinojosa must have seen something special in his daughter from early on. Unlike the vast majority of women in the Spanish world, including many elite women, Rosa María received an education under the direction of a local priest. Later, she received business training from her father and husband. As a result, upon their deaths in the late 1780s she was more than ready to handle the family's affairs. By age 38 she had become matriarch of the Ballí family and was known to many area residents as *la patrona* (the mistress).

Not only did she inherit property from her husband and her father, but she inherited their debts and obligations. Between 1790 and 1803, the year of her

Wealth entailed social responsibility, even on the frontiers of Texas and Nuevo Santander. Doña Rosa María Hinojosa de Ballí, matriarch of the wealthiest ranching family of the lower Rio Grande valley, was an important contributor to worthy causes, including the construction of Nuestra Señora de la Purísima Concepción Church in Mier. The church, construction of which began in 1780, is part of a binational heritage corridor that includes numerous sites on both sides of the river from Laredo to Brownsville-Matamoros. *(Photo by Frank de la Teja)*

death, she not only reversed the family's financial fortunes but more than doubled its land holdings. In the process she became a pillar of the community, serving as witness to legal proceedings, becoming godmother for dozens of children born to friends and employees, and serving as lender to fellow ranchers and benefactor to the churches in Reynosa, Camargo, and Matamoros.

The Hinojosa-Ballí land empire was Doña Rosa's greatest accomplishment. A shrewd businessperson, she spent much of her time during the 1790s expanding upon the 12 sitios (54,000 acres) she inherited from her husband, and her 3-sitio inheritance from her father. On behalf of one son she applied for 72 sitios (324,000 acres) to the northeast of other family holdings, a grant known as San Salvador del Tule. As financier for her brother Vicente she obtained 12 sitios out of the 35-sitio Las Mesteñas grant she helped him obtain. In partnership with another son, Nicolás, a diocesan priest by calling, she acquired an interest in the lower portion of Isla de Santiago (now Padre Island). Purchases and other transactions brought tens of thousands of additional acres under her control, so that at the beginning of the nineteenth century the Ballís controlled about 1,000,000 acres of grazing lands in what are now Cameron, Hidalgo, Willacy, Kenedy, Kleberg, and Nueces counties.

These vast holdings were managed principally from Doña Rosa's headquarters on the La Feria estate. Like the other few major ranch owners in the region, she maintained one residence in town (in her case, Reynosa) and another at the ranch headquarters. Although some subsistence farming took place, the primary sources of income came from grazing horses, cattle, and sheep and leasing out pastures to landless or land-poor ranchers.

Despite her impressive accomplishments Doña Rosa was representative of a society and an economic system that was land-rich, but money-poor. Many ranchers of the trans-Nueces owned little, if any, land at all, and grazed their small herds and flocks on the more marginal and isolated, as yet unclaimed, land in the area. Others leased land from the better-off stockmen who were able to establish legal title to large tracts that often contained what little permanent water was available in an area. The marginal quality of most unimproved land meant that even the major stockmen, such as the Ballís, ran only a few thousand head of all types of stock combined. With the relatively low prices the ranchers received for the animals and byproducts they produced, few ranchers had the means to improve their production capabilities. For example, the obstacles to effectively fencing the trans-Nueces range meant that selective improvement of stock was impossible. Animals mated in the field, to be rounded up only for branding, slaughter, or sale.

Nevertheless, Doña Rosa and the other leading ranchers were the *patrones* (masters) in a social system in which hierarchical relationships were all-important. *Patrones* met the needs of their employees (sometimes referred to as *peones*), and employees were expected to have unconditional loyalty to their *patrones*. Especially at Reynosa, the large ranchers held the local political and military posts, so their interests and concerns had a better chance of being addressed than those of the majority of the settlers, the rancheros, and the mestizos, mulattoes, and Indians that made up the majority of the population.

Conclusion

In the last third of the eighteenth century Texas and neighboring Mexican provinces made considerable strides toward development. Rubí's reforms and the creation of the Comandancia General de las Provincias Internas had reinforced Béxar and La Bahía and even presented an opportunity for Tejano frontiersmen to establish a civilian community in East Texas. All three communities experienced significant population and economic growth—none more so than Béxar, where the increasing number of merchants and artisans attested to expanding market opportunities.

The new policy of making war on the Apaches and pacifying the other independent tribes eventually bore fruit. From the Spanish perspective, the most spectacular demonstration of the efficacy of the new policy was the defeat that Commandant General Juan de Ugalde and his troops and Indian auxiliaries inflicted on over 300 Lipans, Lipiyans, and Mescaleros at Sabinal River canyon in 1790.

The increasing security of the countryside allowed Tejanos to expand the boundaries of settlement beyond their rather small and marginal communities, especially with the decline of the missions. The markets for colonial beef, hide, tallow, and other beef byproducts provided an incentive for civilian ranchers to challenge missionaries for control of the countryside in Texas and to meet the challenge of the semiarid prairies of the trans-Nueces. In the last third of the eighteenth century Texas became a cattle empire, establishing a legacy for centuries to come.

At Paso del Norte, too, the reduction in Indian hostilities was noticeable in a number of ways. Rapid population growth brought the number of residents in the district to almost 6,000 by the end of the century. Paso del Norte had become the only part of New Mexico connected to the rest of the Provincias Internas by a regular mail system. Economic activity along the road between the rest of the province and the interior of New Spain had increased to such a degree that the first permanent bridge across the Rio Grande—500 feet long and 17 feet wide—was in operation by 1800.

The birth of new ways to foster the development of the frontier brought the death of old ways. The missions, which had played such an important role in the permanent occupation of Texas, no longer had anything to offer. The remaining Indians of Texas were either friendly to the Spaniards, had been co-opted through better trade relations and ritualized gift-giving, or were sorely weakened enemies. Although young Apache, Comanche, and Norteño warriors sometimes tested their mettle by launching minor raids on cattle and horse herds, mechanisms were in place for resolving conflict without the terror of generations past.

Texas and surrounding areas were headed in the right direction, an observer at the end of the eighteenth century might have concluded. Population and economic growth were evident, peace with all of the native peoples was in sight, and Louisiana now served as a buffer to foreign threats. Then it happened: The nineteenth century blew in like a blue norther.

SUGGESTED READINGS

In the last third of the eighteenth century, Texas and all of northeastern New Spain again came under the scrutiny of royal officials eager to make the empire more efficient and defendable. The broad outline of this story, and Texas's place in it, is presented in chapters 8 and 9 of David Weber's *The Spanish Frontier in North America*, and in chapters 10 and 11 of John Kessell's *Spain in the Southwest*. Works from the first half of the twentieth century remain our best English-language sources for the two most important figures in frontier reform efforts: *José de Gálvez, Visitor General of New Spain, 1765–1771* by Herbert I. Priestly (1916, 1980) and *Teodoro de Croix and the Northern Frontier of New Spain, 1776–1783* by Alfred B. Thomas (1941). The economic expansion of New Spain, from which Texas benefited only marginally, is well covered by David A. Brading in *Miners and Merchants in Bourbon Mexico, 1763–1810* (1971). Donald Chipman continues the story of Texas during this time frame in chapters 9 and 10 of *Spanish Texas, 1519–1821.*

Reorganization of the Frontier

Reform had to be based on firsthand knowledge, and so the Marqués de Rubí, on instructions from José de Gálvez, set out in 1766 on an inspection tour of the Indian frontier from the Gulf of California to the Gulf of Mexico. The Texas portion of his travels is covered in Jackson and Foster, *Imaginary Kingdom.* A second opinion on Texas appears in *The Frontiers of New Spain: Nicolas de Lafora's Description, 1766–1768,* ed. Lawrence Kinnaird (1958). V. A. Vincent discusses the consequences of the Rubí inspired regulations of 1772 in "The Frontier Soldier: Life in the *Provincias Internas* and the Royal Regulations of 1772, 1766–1787," *Military History of the Southwest* (1992).

The Death and Rebirth of Spanish East Texas

The reorganization of Texas and the restructuring of Spanish-Indian relations fell to a high-born Spanish governor and two frontiersmen, one a native of East Texas and the other a long-time resident of French Louisiana. Although the Spaniard, Governor Barón de Ripperdá, has yet to receive the separate attention he deserves, his role in the abandonment of Los Adaes and establishment of Bucareli is covered well in the chapters on "Athanase de Mézières" and "Marqués de Rubí/ Antonio Gil Ibarbo" in Chipman and Joseph, *Notable Men and Women of Spanish Texas.* Ripperdá's successor, Governor Domingo Cabello, does get his own chapter in *Notable Men and Women of Spanish Texas.* On the development of Nacogdoches as the heterogenous center of Spanish East Texas, see Patrick J. Walsh, "Living on the Edge of the Neutral Zone: Varieties of Identity in Nacogdoches, Texas 1773–1810," *East Texas Historical Journal* (1999).

Sunset for the Missions

The secularization of the Texas missions was a drawn-out process that only began in the 1790s. As with other subjects in Spanish Texas history, most work has focused on the San Antonio area. The process of secularization in the context of rivalry between mission communities and the civilian population of Texas is treated in Félix D. Almaráz, Jr., "San Antonio's Old Franciscan Missions: Material Decline and Secular Avarice in the Transition from Hispanic to Mexican Control," *Americas* (1987). A missionary's view of the need for secularization at San Antonio is presented in "Report on the San Antonio Missions in 1792," ed. Benedict Leutenegger and Marion A. Habig, *Southwestern Historical Quarterly* (1974). Although secularized, the San Antonio missions survived as living communities with their own folklore, essential portions of which were gathered by Adina de

Zavala early in the twentieth century and published under the title *History and Legends of the Alamo and Other Missions in and around San Antonio* (reprint, 1996).

The Birth of the Cattle Kingdom

Given the state's heritage of cattle raising, it is not surprising that a number of authors have addressed the Hispanic elements of the Texas livestock industry. An exhaustive narrative history, focusing on political struggles among civilians, missionaries, and royal officials is Jack Jackson, *Los Mesteños: Spanish Ranching in Texas, 1721–1821* (1986). Much shorter, and focusing on the practices and institutions is *The Ranch in Spanish Texas, 1691–1800* by Sandra L. Myres (1969). A useful short essay on the subject, somewhat dated in light of more recent research, is Odie B. Faulk's "Ranching in Spanish Texas," *Hispanic American Historical Review* (1965). The difficulties of creating a safe environment for cattle operations in Spanish Texas is one of the principal subjects of *El Fuerte del Cíbolo: Sentinel of the Béxar-La Bahía Ranches,* by Robert H. Thonhoff (1992). For South Texas, in addition to the appropriate parts of Armando Alonzo's *Tejano Legacy,* Jesús F. de la Teja looks at the interrelationship between environment, economics, and legal practices in "'Only Fit for Raising Stock': Spanish and Mexican Land and Water Rights in the Tamaulipan Cession," in *Fluid Arguments: Five Centuries of Western Water Conflict,* edited by Char Miller (2001).

5

New Rivals, New Challenges, 1800–1821

Benito de Armiñán, interim governor of Texas in the spring of 1814, had an impossible task to perform. In the aftermath of the royalist victory over the latest rebellion in the province families had been broken up by the death or flight of husbands, fathers, and sons; crops had been destroyed or consumed by the contending forces; and the little commerce the province enjoyed had been subject to disruption by Indian attack. Ill and depressed Armiñán sat down to write his superior, Commandant General Joaquín Arredondo, to explain why he might have to resort to force to keep his men fed if higher authorities did not see fit to send relief immediately. "They are hopelessly lost in their misery. They have been weakened by their past misfortunes. They are complaining most pitiously over the lack of sustenance for themselves and their families. They are lamenting over the crisis and weeping bitterly over their fate—especially when they remember the terrible misery which lies before them." Relief did not come for Armiñán and it did not come for his successors. What did come were adventurers, pirates, and Indian raiders who made life as precarious as it had been at the height of the Indian wars of the 1770s and 1780s. The news that Spain and the United States had agreed on a border that respected Spanish claims to Texas was of little consolation to frontier officials or the surviving Tejano population. A decade of destruction and terror had left them so "hopelessly lost in their misery" that they greeted Mexican independence with no great jubilation. Rather, they began to heal the wounds that had divided families; they began to think about hoping again.

1800	Napoleon forces Spain to return Louisiana to French control
1801	Philip Nolan killed during his fourth trip to Texas since 1791 when he resists Spanish efforts to arrest him for spying
1803	Louisiana Purchase
1805	Baron of Bastrop proposes to colonize Texas with Louisiana families
1806	Neutral Ground Agreement between Col. Herrera and Gen. Wilkinson averts war between Spain and the United States over Texas; town of Santísima Trinidad de Salcedo founded
1808	Town of San Marcos de Neve founded
1810	Father Hidalgo launches revolt against Spanish rule
1811	Casas revolt in Texas fails; Father Hidalgo executed
1812	Gutiérrez-Magee expedition begins invasion of Texas
1813	Republic of Texas proclaimed; Gen. Arredondo defeats Republican Army of the North at battle of Medina
1815	Rebels under Father Morelos declare Mexican independence; filibusters and pirates occupy Galveston Island
1818	French settlement Champ d'Asile fails
1819	Adams-Onís Treaty recognizes Spanish title to Texas; James Long launches first expedition to liberate Texas for the United States
1820	Moses Austin proposes to colonize Texas with Catholic families from the United States
1821	Mexico gains independence; second Long expedition fails

The last two decades of Spanish rule in Texas found the province battered by political storms that its few Spanish residents were ill equipped to weather. First, Louisiana changed hands from Spain to France to the United States. Napoleon Bonaparte had had dreams of reconstructing a great French empire in America and in 1800 had forced the weak Charles IV of Spain to return Louisiana to the French. In 1803, when the cost of his empire became too great, Napoleon sold the territory to a very willing Thomas Jefferson. But what, exactly, was Louisiana? The Americans thought it should include all the territory to the Rio Grande. Thus Texas became a bone of contention between the oldest empire of the New World and its first republic. Its population boomed as Spanish troops, Louisiana exiles, and displaced Indian groups from east of the Mississippi sought the protection of Spanish territory.

Second, a whirlwind of revolution brought insurgents, filibusters, and royalist armies into Texas in destructive waves of violence. The destruction caused by warfare was compounded by the depredations of Comanche, Norteño, and Apache bands determined to take from Tejanos what they could no longer obtain in trade and gift exchanges. At the end of this tumultuous era Texas lay in ruins, its ranches largely abandoned, its fields largely untilled, its remaining people largely destitute. The future would belong to those who were the first to take hold of the shattered remains and build a new Texas.

Louisiana

In 1800 no one in Texas or Mexico City, or even in Madrid, could have foreseen the chain of events that left the Spanish empire in ruins and Texas as part of an independent Mexico. For more than a decade New Spain had fought against United States expansionism along the Mississippi River and its eastern tributaries. Although the situation was precarious, it was not out of control.

Spanish officials recognized U.S. expansionism as a dangerous successor to British imperialism and moved to counter the threat with the meager resources at their disposal. Forced to be flexible, beginning in the 1780s local officials took matters into their own hands and allowed Protestant families to settle in Louisiana. These settlers, often English or Anglo American royalists who no longer had a home on the U.S. side of the Mississippi River, in time were joined by other Anglo Americans more interested in the economic opportunities available in Spanish Missouri, Natchez, and Louisiana. Spanish officials in Florida and Louisiana also took advantage of Indian dissatisfaction with Anglo American pioneers to keep the United States at bay. A number of southeastern tribes took refuge on the Spanish side of the border or conducted raids against intruding Anglo American settlers with the support of local Spanish authorities. Slavery was legal in the Spanish world, but slaves from U.S. territory were granted their freedom in Spanish Florida and Louisiana: another method of fending off Anglo American encroachment of Spanish territory.

After Spain was drawn into the French Revolution and the Napoleonic wars, it proved impossible to maintain adequate commercial contacts with its American empire or to properly defend it against outside threats. As tensions over trade, Indian relations, and slave flight mounted, Madrid forestalled a direct confrontation with Washington by entering into the Treaty of San Lorenzo in 1795. By the terms of the treaty, U.S. citizens enjoyed navigation rights on the Mississippi River and the right to use New Orleans as a trans-shipment port for their products. In addition, both countries would restrain the Indians on their side of the border from conducting depredations on the other side.

Philip Nolan: Horse Trader or Spy?

It was in these circumstances that adventurers like Philip Nolan and the self-styled Baron of Bastrop, made their way to the Louisiana-Texas frontier. The two men could not have been more different. As a young man Philip Nolan had immigrated from Ireland to the western frontier of the new United States, where he became a protégé of General James Wilkinson. The American military man, who maintained very friendly relations with the Spaniards (at one point in his career he was actually employed by the Spanish Crown), soon had Nolan acting as his business agent in New Orleans.

While in the Louisiana capital the twenty-year-old Irish American learned about the Indian trade opportunities in Texas, which led in 1791 to the first of a number of trips there for him. Officially, commercial contacts between Texas and Louisiana were forbidden under Spain's tightly regulated mercantile system. Despite a series of reforms intended to expand trading opportunities among its various American colonies, Spain's mercantilist policies remained the most restrictive of the European empires—that is, on paper. In reality, an inefficient and corrupt customs and administrative system meant that contraband, graft, and incompetence were rife. At the time of the American Revolution the Spanish Crown had consented to a limited livestock trade between Texas and Louisiana, and it was this authorization that adventurers like Nolan took advantage of in order to trade with Texas Indians. The governor of Spanish Louisiana did not think twice about giving Nolan a passport to gather livestock in Texas.

To Texas authorities Nolan's trading license was not valid. They suspected the Irish American tradesman of being a spy, a contrabandist, or both, and officials in Nacogdoches confiscated his merchandise. Financially ruined and in no hurry to return to Louisiana, Nolan chose to spend some time living with various Texas Indian tribes, among them the Comanches. Although Nolan claimed that "the freedom, the independence of the savage life was always congenial to my nature," he also admitted that he could not completely "indianify."

Between 1794 and 1799 Nolan made two more successful trading expeditions to Texas. It was not just the province's Indians who welcomed the opportunity to trade for higher-quality manufactured goods that Nolan's company brought with him: Tejanos also did business—illegally—with the American. Nolan eventually sold the horses, hides, and furs he collected in Texas as far east as Frankfort, Kentucky, attracting even more interest among American frontiersmen in the Texas trade.

Nolan had caught Texas fever, but he had also caught the attention of Spanish authorities. Their suspicions were confirmed by his decision to return to Texas in the fall of 1800 leading a large body of men in the face of Spanish disapproval. In fact, a deserter from the expedition, Mordecai Richards, later declared that Nolan "had maps of all the rivers, marked all the distances, and explored everything more attentively than a man would do who had not other ends in view than that of catching horses—that he had told him many times that there were mines in this country, and moreover that he had assured his men that if the Spaniards killed a single one of them he would take a commission as an English general . . . and would take possession of all this country."

It was not one of his men, but Nolan himself who died at the hands of the Spaniards. He had built corrals and begun catching horses and trading with Wichita and Comanche bands in what is now Hill County, but a Spanish patrol caught up with him in March 1801. After Nolan was killed by a cannonball his men quickly surrendered, claiming that their only goal had been to capture mustangs. Authories remained unconvinced, however.

The Baron of Bastrop: Would-be Colonizer

Another adventurer who eventually turned to Texas for new opportunities was the Baron of Bastrop. A native of Dutch Guiana, Philip Hendrik Nering Bögel had moved to Holland as a child and had grown up to become a tax collector. Accused of embezzlement in 1793, he fled the country, adopting the title by which he would henceforth be known. After arriving in Louisiana in 1795 he undertook a variety of business ventures, including real estate development, all with only minor success.

As a would-be colonizer Bastrop joined a number of Anglo American and European entrepreneurs who saw great opportunities in Spain's desperate effort to reinforce Louisiana and Texas in the face of the United States challenge. Some had big schemes, like Pennsylvania Dutch innkeeper Pedro Paulus, who offered to settle 3,000 families as long as they had freedom of worship, local self-government, and generous land allotments. (His plan never amounted to anything.) Some had more modest ambitions, like William Barr, another Irish immigrant who became a Spanish subject in Louisiana before moving to Nacogdoches in 1793. Barr established himself as an Indian trader and entered into partnership with Natchitoches merchant Peter Samuel Davenport. Having gained a monopoly on Indian trade in northern Texas, the House of Barr and Davenport had made Barr a wealthy man by the time he died in 1810.

Bastrop fell somewhere in between. Shortly after his arrival in Louisiana he received permission to settle families along the Ouachita River. During a recruiting trip to the United States in 1797, a new governor arrived in Louisiana who opposed settlement by Protestant Anglo Americans and suspended Bastrop's project. With this turn of events Bastrop saw his land schemes evaporate and he turned to the Indian trade as a means of recovering his fortunes. Although he obtained a contract to supply the Indians along the Ouachita River with merchandise, the sale of Louisiana to the United States in 1803 brought an end to his monopoly and to his profits.

Bastrop, like a number of other Louisiana land promoters, now turned his attention to Texas. Bearing a letter of recommendation from his friend, the former governor of Louisiana, in the fall of 1805 he arrived in San Antonio, where he proposed to establish a colony between Béxar and the Trinity River. The settlers would be some of the families he had previously brought to Louisiana along with friendly and agricultural Choctaws. Having learned his lesson from the Ouachita project, he pledged to introduce only Catholic families.

Both Texas Governor Antonio Cordero and Commandant General Nemecio Salcedo thought the project worth pursuing, as it fit with their plans to expand settlement in Texas in the face of U.S. occupation of Louisiana. Immediately after the territory's transfer to the United States, President Thomas Jefferson, basing his position on French documents, had claimed that all the lands as far as the Rio Grande were included in the purchase. Spanish colonial authorities, facing what the baron called the "daring land-hunger of the infamous class of Americans" along with Jefferson's claims, naturally grasped at the colonization proposals of Bastrop and other Louisianians in order to create a first line of defense in Texas. Although none of the plans ever took shape, the baron soon settled in San Antonio, where he became a leading member of the community. A decade later he would become involved in a colonization project beyond his wildest dreams.

Neutral Ground

Whatever disappointment Governor Cordero felt about the results of Bastrop's mission could not have measurably added to the distress he already suffered. In 1805 United States troops had arrived in the vicinity of Natchitoches and asserted U.S. claims to the area. By early 1806 both sides were convinced that the other was preparing for war. In March President Jefferson reported to the United States Congress: "Some time since, however, we learnt that the Spanish authorities were advancing into the disputed country to occupy new posts and make new settlements."

Jefferson responded by ordering U.S. troops to chase out the Spanish detachment that Governor Cordero had ordered to occupy the Los Adaes district, in response to which the Texas governor ordered the militia to reinforce Nacogdoches. To defuse the situation Commandant General Nemecio Salcedo proposed establishing a neutral ground between Natchitoches and the Sabine River while the boundary between United States and Spanish territory was negotiated.

To these developments were added the complications of the Aaron Burr conspiracy and U.S. reconnaissance of the Red River country. Dissatisfied with his

Los Adaes State Historic Site, outside Robeline, Louisiana, preserves a piece of Spanish Texas. Although Spanish forces briefly reoccupied the long-abandoned first capital of Texas following the Louisiana Purchase, it, along with the rest of the territory west to the Sabine River soon became part of the Neutral Ground, and then part of the United States under the Adams-Onís Treaty of 1819. *(© Alex Demyan/Fineart Photography)*

prospects in the United States, Burr, the volatile former vice president, developed a scheme with a number of associates to separate the trans-Appalachian states from the Union and combine them with the Louisiana Purchase and the silver mining region of northern New Spain into a great empire. As soon as rumors of Burr's scheme reached Salcedo, he advised Cordero "it is a very grave matter . . . that some 10,000 men, subjects of the United States, are being prepared in Kentucky with the object of overpowering the uninhabited provinces of this kingdom and our Indian allies, with no respect for the boundaries of Louisiana. You will, therefore, take extraordinary precautions toward putting the country in a good state of defense by bringing up all the auxiliaries."

The commandant general's response to another incident was even more confrontational. In the spring of 1806 an exploratory expedition under Major Thomas Freeman began to ascend the Red River. When he received news of this obvious violation of Spanish territory, Commandant General Salcedo issued orders to stop the expedition from continuing westward. Freeman had managed to travel 600 miles up the Red River before he was confronted by a large Spanish detachment and decided to turn back.

Throughout these months the Spanish had been reinforcing the small Texas garrisons with auxiliary units from other provinces. First to arrive was a light cavalry unit from Coahuila known as the Second Flying Company of San Carlos del Alamo de Parras. The unit arrived in Béxar in 1803 and occupied the abandoned buildings of Mission San Antonio de Valero, lending its name to the site, which would ever after be known as the Alamo. Militia units from Nuevo Santander and Nuevo León brought total troop strength in the province to over 1,000 by early summer.

Despite growing war hysteria along the U.S. frontier and the troop buildup on the Texas side, cooler heads prevailed. Wilkinson arrived unopposed at the Sabine River on October 29 and immediately sent a message to the Texas governor proposing an agreement by which the Spaniards would not recross the Sabine and the Americans would retreat to Natchitoches and not recross the Arroyo Hondo until the boundary had finally been negotiated. While Cordero hesitated, Lieutenant Colonel Simón Herrera seized the moment and on his own authority accepted Wilkinson's terms. On November 5, 1806, at the U.S. Army camp on the Sabine, General Wilkinson and Inspector Francisco Viana signed what came to be called the Neutral Ground Agreement. Cordero could now turn his attention to preparing the rest of Texas for what he was sure would be an inevitable onslaught of Anglo Americans.

Fortress Texas

Governor Cordero and his superiors knew that troops alone could not hold the province. Defending the Texas frontier of New Spain from the land-hungry Anglo Americans would depend on increasing the population. The times seemed propitious for a concerted population drive as Spanish subjects in Louisiana deserted what was now U.S. territory and relative peace reigned between Texas's remaining native peoples and their Spanish colonial neighbors. It would not be easy to overcome the obstacles of distance and climate, but there was reason for hope among the long-suffering Tejanos that this might be their day in the sun.

Still a Country of Indians

Antonio Cordero y Bustamante had been thrown into a difficult situation, but this was not the first time in his long and successful career as a frontier officer. Born in Cadiz, Spain, in 1753, he had come to New Spain as a cadet and soon found himself fighting Indians on the northern frontier. He distinguished himself in campaigns against various western Apache tribes before being assigned to the Coahuila theater of action in 1795. Throughout this time he strengthened presidio defenses and organized new settlements, activities that he continued after becoming governor of Coahuila in 1798. Commandant General Nemecio Salcedo turned to the popular Cordero in the summer 1805 to assume the reins of command in Texas when the health of the incumbent took a turn for the worse. About a month after Cordero's arrival, Juan Bautista Elguézabal, the incumbent who himself had been serving in an interim capacity since 1799, died. It would be up to Cordero to make sense of the increasingly chaotic situation.

The interim governor could see that there was much work to do in Texas. Formal settlement remained confined to San Antonio de Béxar, the capital of the province, the presidio-mission complex of La Bahía del Espíritu Santo, and the village of Nacogdoches. Of these population centers Béxar was by far the largest, containing over 2,000 men, women, and children, the other two having roughly 900 Tejanos each. Also during the 1790s an informal settlement of 100 to 200 persons called Bayou Pierre had begun to form in the old Los Adaes district. In addition, in 1803 the Alamo company added considerably to the military population of the province and put Cordero's available fighting strength at about 350 soldiers when he arrived in Texas.

Cordero also inherited the difficult problem of Louisiana émigrés. The Baron of Bastrop was not the only Louisiana subject of His Catholic Majesty who sought to start a new life in Spanish Texas. A number of individuals and families petitioned for Texas land. Commandant General Salcedo, suspicious of the situation, especially as the United States was claiming Texas as part of the Louisiana Territory, allowed the settlement of people who could prove their loyalty to the crown, while absolutely forbidding the admission of Anglo Americans. The latter were particularly suspect, because they seemed intent on undermining Spanish-Indian relations on the frontier.

As for the Indian peoples of Texas, some groups were in decline and facing extinction, others were expanding, and there were opportunities for new arrivals. By the early nineteenth century many Coahuiltecan bands had died out completely as separate culture groups. A similar trend was evident among the elusive Tonkawas of central Texas, who at several hundred tribe members, were at least holding out better than the Bidai and Akokisa, who numbered no more than 100 or 200. The Caddoan speakers of East Texas had also experienced drastic drops in number, most tribes consisting of no more than a few hundred individuals. Many villages had been abandoned and their surviving members had moved in with Caddo relatives on the Louisiana side of the frontier.

For Cordero the Indians requiring serious attention were the various Apache, Wichita, and Comanche tribes that still ranged freely on the western peripheries of Spanish Texas. The combined pressure of Comanches and Norteños on the Apaches, especially the Lipans, had forced the Lipans southward until, by the end of the eighteenth century, they inhabited a territory southwest of San Antonio and stretching into northern Coahuila. There Mescaleros and Lipans had made peace with each other and, in relative terms, with Spanish colonials, whose main complaints continued to be loss of livestock to young warriors.

Cutchatés.

Among the Indian tribes from east of the Mississippi River that sought the protection of Spanish authorities in Texas at the beginning of the nineteenth century were the Alabamas and Coushattas. In time the two small bands joined together on a single reservation in Polk County, where they remain today. This watercolor of Coushatta warriors by Lino Sanchéz y Tapia captures the degree to which southeastern Indians had adopted Western dress and technologies. *(Lino Sánchez y Tapia,* Cutchatés, *plate xviiii, from the collection of Gilcrease Museum, Tulsa, Oklahoma)*

More formidable were the Comanches and Wichitas. Their commercial contacts with Louisiana and New Mexico and their large numbers gave them an independence that required Spanish officials to deal with them as equals. Governor Cordero continued the successful policy of peace by purchase, but faced a new challenge in Anglo American tradesmen who moved onto the southern plains in an effort to gain the friendship—economic and political—of these peoples. Numbering in the thousands, mobile and aggressive, they posed the most serious threat to Spanish Texas in the first decade of the nineteenth century.

Another type of Indian challenge developed at this time in the form of immigrant tribes from U.S. territory. Spain's rivalry with the United States made Texas an attractive destination for groups seeking to escape Anglo American control. Small bands of Indians from a number of tribes began making their way into Spanish territory during the 1790s, particularly into the eastern part of the province, where the decline of the Caddos had left a considerable amount of land suitable for settlement. Among the immigrant tribes that Cordero had to deal with during his service in Texas were Alabamas, Apalaches, Cherokees, Chickasaws, Chocktaws, Coushattas, Pascagoulas, and Shawnees.

Defensive Colonization

Cordero concluded that settlement should concentrate on the Camino Real between Nacogdoches and San Antonio. Occupation of strategic sites along the road would expedite communications within the province and make it easier for the new settlers to transport their goods. By the end of September 1805 Governor Cordero was requesting permission to found towns on the Trinity and Brazos rivers with a mix of native Tejanos and Louisiana émigrés. In December 1805 five families from Béxar that had been recruited for the project were on their way to the Trinity, where they discovered a group of Louisiana émigrés waiting for them. Early in 1806 they founded the town of Santísima Trinidad de Salcedo, most often referred to as Salcedo, under the supervision of a military officer from Béxar. By late January, titles to house lots and agricultural land were being issued, and construction began on a number of buildings. So successful was this first settlement effort under Cordero that families from Nacogdoches petitioned for permission to relocate to the new town.

Despite Salcedo's approval of Cordero's initial settlement plan, the two men did not see eye to eye on how best to utilize the growing pool of immigrants. In particular, Cordero saw the Louisianians, many of whom wished to remain in the Nacogdoches area, as the only means to populate East Texas in the absence of any significant migration from the interior of New Spain. This was especially important as the Tejano population of that part of the province was unable to supply provisions to the growing number of troops. Salcedo, concerned about the ever-present contraband problem and suspicious of the loyalties of many of the new arrivals, refused to allow them to locate permanently east of the Trinity.

His superior having made clear his hard line on settlement in the Nacogdoches region, Governor Cordero turned his attention to promoting new settlements farther west. He now requested permission to found towns on the Colorado, Guadalupe, and San Marcos crossings of the Camino Real, a request that was granted by the commandant general. The first and only one of the three towns that was actually established was San Marcos de Neve. Cordero worked out a deal with Felipe Roque de la Portilla, a fellow army officer from Spain who had seen service in Nuevo Santander. In return for a sizable land grant and a sizable subvention to the families he recruited, Portilla gathered a group of followers and a substantial number of animals and brought them to San Marcos in April 1808.

Of the five authorized settlements in Texas only Salcedo and San Marcos were established. Unlike Salcedo, which was made up of Bexareños and Louisianians, San Marcos was settled mostly by families from below the Rio Grande. Whereas Salcedo enjoyed military protection from the beginning, San Marcos had no garrison and was therefore exposed to Indian depredations. Salcedo enjoyed modest growth until its abandonment, but San Marcos attracted no new settlers after the first few months. Both ultimately suffered the same fate, however, falling victim to the warfare that engulfed Texas during the Mexican War of Independence.

Last Efforts at Reform

In the summer of 1808, much to Cordero's relief, his replacement arrived. The new governor turned out to be none other than Nemecio Salcedo's thirty-two-year-old nephew, Manuel María de la Concepción Josef Agustín Eloy de Salcedo y Quiroga. Despite his young age, Manuel came with considerable experience: he had assisted his father, who had served as the last Spanish governor of Louisiana. To assume his post Manuel Salcedo and his family had traveled by way of the United States, landing at New Bedford, Massachusetts, going on to New York City, then to Philadelphia and Pittsburgh, Pennsylvania. Riverboat travel down the Ohio and Mississippi rivers brought them to Natchez. From there they traveled by coach to Natchitoches. In Natchitoches Salcedo met with U.S. government officials before proceeding to Nacogdoches, where he arrived in early October 1808. By the time he reached the Texas capital at Béxar at the end of the month, Salcedo must have been fully aware of the challenges that confronted him.

Manuel Salcedo took over the most exposed province of a colony under assault. Not only had Texas territory been compromised through establishment of the Neutral Ground Agreement in 1806, but the United States continued to claim the Rio Grande as the true boundary of the Louisiana Purchase. Also, various foreign agents had penetrated the province before his arrival. One of these, Zebulon Montgomery Pike, had succeeded in crossing the southern plains to arrive in New Mexico early in 1807. Treated well by the Spaniards, he collected considerable information on the state of Spanish defenses on the northern frontier, including conditions in Texas, through which he passed on his return to Louisiana. A year later another foreign adventurer, the Napoleonic agent Octaviano D'Alvimar, crossed from Louisiana into Texas with instructions to sow insurrection in New Spain. Captured by Texas troops, he was brought before Governor Cordero, who shipped him off to the interior before he could cause much harm to Spanish interests. The presence of runaway slaves and U.S. Army deserters also added to tensions.

The aggressive moves of the United States along the border were only one concern for Salcedo, who also had to consider recent events in Spain and Mexico City. Napoleon had forced the abdication of the Spanish Bourbon King Charles IV and his son Ferdinand VII in favor of his brother Joseph Bonaparte. That move had met with resistance both in Spain and throughout the colonies. From Mexico City had come news of an abortive move by the colonial capital's criollo elite to take over the government, an effort that had been frustrated by the powerful resident peninsulares. The peninsulares replaced a pro-criollo viceroy with one of their own. Eventually word arrived that a revolutionary Cortes (parliament) in Spain had declared the empire a constitutional monarchy. Traditional lines of authority were being disrupted, the legitimacy of the crown was being questioned, and misinformation and disinformation were rife.

Conditions, therefore, were ripe for an Anglo American move against Texas, and Salcedo pleaded for reinforcements and extensive economic investment in the province. His request was grounded in what he perceived to be essentially a problem of political economy. Like his predecessor, Salcedo considered the government responsible for existing conditions because it had failed to provide the necessary resources with which Tejanos could develop the province.

> The industry of these inhabitants is nonexistent, because neither have they had nor do they have elements for it. And one even marvels at how most of them cultivate their lands without the necessary farming tools by substituting for them as best they can, how some have built houses without artisans and how others suffer the rigorous cold and hot weather in those homes that they have made with sticks and shed-roofs of straw, and lastly at how in this poverty they have been able to dress themselves and their families, since this province has no other port of entry than that of Veracruz distant more than five hundred leagues.

Certainly there was some exaggeration in the governor's description of the situation, but not much. A few families at San Antonio and a few at La Bahía and Nacogdoches were living above a subsistence level, enjoying the meager profits of the livestock trade, an occasional sale of provisions to the local military, or participation in contraband activities. The province's few artisans could not practice their crafts on a regular basis, but relied on subsistence agriculture to make ends meet. If not for the military payrolls, there would have been practically no business for the few legitimate merchants, who themselves combined a variety of economic pursuits and credit schemes to keep their doors open and feed their families.

Governor Salcedo's plans required money and more communication between Texas and the outside world, of course, and Commandant General Salcedo was not in a position to grant the former or allow the latter. A port at Matagorda Bay would only create increased opportunities for smuggling and illegal immigration from Louisiana. The expense of raising, equipping, and maintaining the kind of force Governor Salcedo proposed was impossible. No, Texas would have to get by on what it already had.

Short of resources (his uncle would not even permit him to hire a secretary), Governor Salcedo took up the task of reforming the frontier province in every imaginable way. He issued orders on the proper preparation and filing of legal documents and he attempted to increase the efficiency of the mail system. He reorganized troop deployments, hoping to put soldiers lacking weapons to work on military construction projects for which no labor funds were available. Officials at La Bahía and Nacogdoches were snowed under by Governor Salcedo's constant requests for information and detailed instructions on just about every issue. In particular, they had to adjust to the commandant general's change of heart regarding immigrants, as the governor ordered that former Spanish subjects from Louisiana were to be received openly and warmly in Texas.

At San Antonio de Béxar, capital of Texas since 1773, Governor Salcedo took a personal hand in bringing order to a people that previous governors had considered unruly and untrustworthy. He issued ordinances on everything from the licensing of midwives to the licensing of ox carts (in effect, the first vehicle registration law in Texas history). He restructured local government and organized the countryside into police jurisdictions. He established a curfew, instituted a noise ordinance, and required owners to keep their properties clean and well maintained. Unfortunately for Manuel Salcedo and the other representatives of the Spanish monarchy, these last efforts at enlightened government could not hold back the tide of rebellion that began to sweep New Spain toward independence.

Insurrection on the Frontier

The urgency of Governor Salcedo's appeals to the loyalty and patriotism of Tejanos intensified as rebellion broke out in the central parts of the viceroyalty. At the beginning of the nineteenth century New Spain was rife with the social and economic contradictions that have often made for revolution. A tiny percentage of the population lived in opulence in Mexico City, Guadalajara, and a handful of other major urban centers, whereas the overwhelming majority of colonial Mexicans lived in abject poverty. Although the silver mines of the colony remained the driving engine of the economy, most people relied on subsistence agriculture for a living. In the very small manufacturing sector, consisting mostly of second-class textiles and ceramics, as well as on the large agricultural estates, abusive labor practices predominated.

The Causes of the Mexican War of Independence

Spanish colonial institutions were antiquated and corrupt. The church represented the largest and richest property owner in the colony, recipient of a tithe that the government collected for it and beneficiary of innumerable bequests. The church, consequently, served as the colony's principal landlord and lender. Yet, in the countryside many parish priests lived a poor, hand-to-mouth existence that led many to become disaffected. Exploitation of the rural Indian and *castas* population also came at the hands of an underpaid and, therefore, extremely corrupt local officialdom. Bourbon reform efforts ultimately failed to solve any of these problems, as they only replaced one group of corrupt petty officials with another. Although the *intendentes,* the regional administrative heads who exercised considerable economic and political power, were themselves well educated and well paid, their local subordinates, known as *subdelegados,* were not, and they came to rely on graft and extortion just as the *alcades mayores* and *corregidores* they replaced had.

Compounding these problems, which to one degree or another were endemic to most polities of the time, was the complex and oppressive ethnic ordering of society inherent in the *sistema de castas.* Spanish colonial society, which consisted of about 6 million people at the turn of the century, was divided into two large groups, the *república de indios* and the *república de españoles,* with separate codes of law governing each. Mexico's 3.5 million Indians remained perpetual wards of the crown, with a protective legal structure governing their economic and political dealings. The overwhelming majority lived in ancestral villages, spoke their native languages, and practiced syncretic forms of Catholicism. Local representatives of the crown took advantage of their authority over the Indians to exploit their labor and monopolize business dealings with them.

The rest of the population, about 15,000 *peninsulares,* 1 million *criollos,* and 1.5 million *castas*—the *república de españoles*—was governed by a legal code that operated on the assumption that all men were not created equal. Punishment for criminal offenses was based on ethnicity: Spaniards often received fines whereas the *castas* were subject to corporal punishment of varying degrees. The legal code, which was intended to preserve the position of Spaniards, dictated who could ride a horse, carry different types of weapons, and wear certain types of clothing. "Purity of blood" did matter, even to the point of restricting the access of *castas* to membership in some of the religious orders.

The legal distinctions among the various social groups extended to opportunities for advancement in both the public and private sectors. The late Bourbon push to entrust positions of higher authority such as *intendente,* bishop, and high court judge to *gachupines* (a derogatory term for European Spaniards) troubled the considerable number of well-educated *criollos* who saw their prospects limited. In the many guilds and associations that governed New Spain's economy *castas* could not hope to rise to the top ranks of the organization or fully participate in the government. Although *criollos* made up the overwhelming number of hacienda and mine owners and occupied the vast majority of local government posts, they did not run the viceroyalty. Although blacks, mulattos, and mestizos made up the bulk of the non-Indian population, they were denied full opportunities for personal advancement.

At the same time that the crown and its advisers were consolidating power and "modernizing" the empire in Madrid, they were ignoring the needs and wishes of their colonial subjects. In America, meanwhile, *criollos* were developing a sense of nationalism. American-born Spanairds began to resent the superior attitude and privileged status of *gachupines* and advocated a new relationship to mother Spain. *Criollo* intellectuals began to feel pride in their early civilizations and to regard their accomplishments as no less worthy than those of ancient European societies. They challenged the idea that the New World environment was intrinsically inferior to that of the Old World. The American provinces were no different from, and certainly not inferior to, the European possessions of the crown, and the American colonies should be governed by Americans.

Added to this long-simmering disaffection, economic and political upheavals in the first decade of the nineteenth century precipitated insurrection. First, cut off from its American possessions by whichever enemy—England or France—it happened to be fighting at the time, Spain's normal commerce was disrupted; European imports flooded colonial markets, disrupting domestic manufacturing.

Second, in 1804, desperate for revenues with which to fund its war effort, the crown confiscated church assets, eliminating the single largest source of available capital in the viceroyalty. Third, drought late in the decade produced famine and widespread rural unemployment, especially in the Bajío, the colony's most productive economic region. Fourth, although New Spain's elites unanimously rejected Joseph Bonaparte as their sovereign in 1808, a power struggle between the *criollo* and *peninsular* elites of the capital left the latter in control of the viceregal government.

The Struggle Begins

In this atmosphere of political and economic turmoil, groups of discontented *criollos* and mestizos began to conspire to overthrow the government. One such group, centered at Querétaro, a major agricultural center in the Bajío, included the man who would come to be known as the father of Mexican independence, Miguel Hidalgo y Costilla, parish priest of the small agricultural town of Dolores. Hidalgo, along with the lower-rank military and political officials who made up the conspiracy, was a *criollo* of rather liberal bent and broad interests. The conspirators had read the writings of French Enlightenment thinkers and were informed about the political thought behind American constitutionalism. They did not entirely reject their ties to Spain, indeed Hidalgo never declared the outright independence of Mexico from the mother country, but they did believe that Mexico should be governed by Mexicans rather than *peninsulares*. Unlike the majority of their fellow *criollos,* whose fear of the masses kept them allied to the *gachupines,* they were willing to gamble on their ability to control the Indians and mixed-bloods who would bear the burden of fighting.

Unfortunately for the conspirators, their plans were discovered and Hidalgo had no choice but to launch his revolt before preparations were complete. In the early morning hours of September 16, 1810, the bells of his church signaled to townspeople and nearby peasants that something was wrong. He stepped out on the front steps of his church and made an impassioned speech to the gathering crowd. He said, in part, "my friends and compatriots, for us there no longer exist either king or tributes; this shameful burden fit only for slaves, we have borne for three centuries as a sign of tyranny and servitude, a terrible stain that we shall wash away with our own efforts." In contradiction to this first line of the speech, he is said to have ended it by uttering his famous *grito* (cry): "Long live Religion! Long live our Blessed Mother Guadalupe! Long live Ferdinand VII and death to bad government!"

News of the revolt made its way northward within days, where at first there seemed to be little support for expanding the insurrection. The north did not have large numbers of disgruntled and hungry Indians and had only a few *peninsulares,* so discontent in the region appeared to be under control. In fact, however, the same class of disaffected *criollos* and *castas* that existed in the more central portions of the colony also existed in the northeastern provinces. In addition, the large number of frontier troops, overwhelmingly locals serving either in the frontier presidio companies or in militia units, had conflicted loyalties. Unlike regular army troops these men had been recruited from the frontier population to serve as a sort of home guard. They were accustomed to fighting Indians to protect their homes. How would they respond to their Spanish officers' efforts to employ them against insurgents?

The answer to that question was alarming to royal authorities, as they discovered in December 1810. The military units in Nuevo Santander revolted against the royalist government when told to prepare to march on the rebels farther south. Early in January, the entire command of the well-liked but royalist Antonio Cordero defected when confronted by a rebel force of 7,000–8,000. When insurgent envoys arrived in Nuevo León soon thereafter, that province too allied itself with the insurrection. Of the northeastern Interior Provinces only Texas remained under royal control.

Texas Joins the Revolt

In Texas Governor Salcedo desperately attempted to retain the loyalty of the inhabitants of the province. Arrests of suspected instigators (both Tejanos and outsiders), speeches on the need for loyalty to king and God, and assurances of the safety of the population from Indian attack did little to quell a growing unrest. From Natchitoches, American agents reported to the U.S. government that substantial numbers of Tejanos, including members of leading San Antonio families, were preparing to overthrow the royalist authorities. The troops stationed in Béxar were uneasy about the possibility of being marched south to confront the insurgents, in the process leaving their families exposed to Indian attack. This unease only increased with news of the revolt's spread through neighboring provinces.

Texas, however, was awash in disaffection. Some Tejanos were upset with the crown's lack of responsiveness to the needs of the province. For all of Governor Salcedo's efforts, there were few signs that the necessary investment in money and people were coming any time soon. At San Antonio, where the reforms of Governors Cordero and Salcedo had most affected traditional patterns of leadership, there was resentment. There was also resentment among those whose economic interests had been hurt by the military's efforts to curtail contraband. Even more critical was the anxiety that Salcedo had created among the troops when he announced that the entire garrison at San Antonio might have to march south against the insurgents.

The man who led Texas's first revolt against Spanish rule, Juan Bautista de las Casas, was himself a retired *criollo* militia officer. He later claimed he was a loyal subject of Ferdinand VII and that his sole purpose in deposing Governor Salcedo had been to prevent the province from falling into anarchy, but his actions indicated otherwise. Although his motives may never be known, much weighed against him: the participation of a number of known Hidalgo sympathizers and disgruntled citizens of San Antonio in his coup, his constant communications with the insurgency's leadership in the interior of Mexico, and his orders for the

Texas presidial troops at the beginning of the nineteenth century were poorly equipped to handle a well-armed adversary. Smooth-bore carbines and pistols, often in disrepair, were considered less reliable than the lance, short sword, and shield. Leather jackets with cotton padding provided added protection from arrows. (© *Ministerio de Educación, Cultura y Deporte. Archivo General de Indias, MP-UNIFORMES. Diseño de uniforme de las fuerzas de Caballeria que guarnecen la línea de frontera de las nueve Provincias Internas de Nueva España, Soldado de Cuera, 1804*)

arrest of all *gachupines* in the province as well as anyone who did not recognize him as governor.

The Casas revolt, which took place on January 21, 1811, was on shaky ground almost from the very beginning, however. Many among the province's leading families had stayed on the sidelines, unwilling to risk alienating a government that, although it might not be as responsive as they wanted, still paid for the defense of Texas against hostile Indians. News of Hidalgo's defeat at Guadalajara on January 17 and the flight of the insurgent leadership toward the frontier contributed to the sense of unease among prominent Tejanos. Casas's own arbitrary rule antagonized members of San Antonio's elite families who rallied instead around Father Juan Manuel Zambrano, a native of Béxar with aspirations of his own.

On March 17, not three months after his assumption of power, Casas was overthrown by Zambrano and his supporters. Most of his followers quickly switched allegiance and royalist officials throughout the province soon took up their posts again. Restored to the governorship, Manuel Salcedo now governed a province that was very different from the one he had lost the previous January. The Comanches and Norteños resumed large-scale raiding, dissatisfied that Spanish officials no longer had the gifts and merchandise that had been the basis of the peace that had existed for a quarter century. Salcedo considered the 1,136 men who formed the province's military defense largely untrustworthy. They had already mutinied once, and they continued to be exposed to the revolutionary rhetoric of disloyal kinsmen and ever-present foreigners. Every day shortages mounted: Paper, clothing, candles, even horses, were all in short supply. But, most troubling of all were reports filtering in from Louisiana of preparations for an invasion of Texas by a force of insurgents and Anglo American mercenaries.

The Struggle Takes a New Twist

The reports were not rumors. Mexican revolutionaries had fled to the United States at the time of Hidalgo's debacle and were attempting to enlist U.S. support for their cause. In the aftermath of the royalist capture and execution of Hidalgo on March 21, 1811, leadership of the war against Spanish rule devolved upon another cleric, Father José María Morelos, a mestizo whose more realistic grasp of the situation and better organizational skills brought him considerable initial success. Under his leadership a revolutionary congress finally declared independence from Spain, abolished slavery, and drafted a constitution for Mexico. Still, Morelos proved unable to convince enough *criollos* to back the cause. In November 1815 Father Morelos was captured and executed in southern Mexico. By that time Texas had experienced a second failed insurrection and was teetering on the brink of utter devastation.

José Bernardo Gutiérrez de Lara was a *criollo* and a native frontiersman. He had been born in the Rio Grande valley town of Revilla (now Guerrero Viejo, Tamaulipas) in 1774, the son of pioneer settlers in Escandón's colony. By 1810 he was a family man, a petty merchant, blacksmith, and, like many settlers of the area, a landowner. He was also disaffected. When the Hidalgo revolt erupted he immediately embraced the cause. As a result he played a prominent role in helping the insurgents achieve early success in Nuevo Santander.

The defeat of the rebellion in the early months of 1811 did not discourage Gutiérrez de Lara. Claiming to have been assigned to seek assistance in the United States, he traveled to Washington, D.C., in July. Although he failed to obtain overt assistance from the U.S. administration, it is obvious that Gutiérrez de Lara received tacit approval for his plans. Back in Louisiana by the spring of 1812, he met with local authorities and began recruiting for what eventually became the Republican Army of the North. His most important collaborator in organizing the invasion was a U.S. Army officer, Augustus Magee. The West Point graduate resigned his commission to take up military leadership of the Anglo American volunteers in the army, which came to consist of about equal numbers of Anglo Americans and Mexicans.

When the Gutiérrez-Magee expedition crossed the Sabine River in August 1812 it encountered little resistance and had quick success. It arrived in Nacogdoches to find the local troops unwilling to fight. In September, now grown to 300 effectives, the Republican Army of the North took Santísima Trinidad de Salcedo. Discovering that Governor Salcedo had marched to the Guadalupe River to obstruct their advance on Béxar, Gutiérrez and Magee turned southeast to La Bahía, where they occupied the presidio in early November. Between November 1812 and February 1813 the royalists besieged La Bahía, but were unable to dislodge the insurgents, who finally went after Salcedo's army as it retreated to Béxar. The royalists made one last stand about nine miles southeast of San Antonio on March 29. At the battle of Rosillo about 1,200 men under Colonel Simón Herrera met the approximately 800-man Republican Army of the North. Having lost hundreds of men, more than a thousand horses, all of his field artillery and most other equipment, Salcedo had no choice but to surrender. On April 1, 1813, the Republican Army of the North, under the command of Gutiérrez de Lara and Samuel Kemper, Magee's successor, took San Antonio. The first Texas republic was born.

The First Republic of Texas

The process of nation building began with bloodshed. On the evening of April 3, Salcedo and his subordinates, a total of fourteen *gachupines,* were assassinated a few miles outside of Béxar as they were being "escorted" out of the province. Kemper and a number of other Anglo Americans were outraged by the brutal action. A declaration of independence adopted on April 6 and a constitution that the Mexican insurgents drew up in the following days completed the alienation of many Anglo officers, who took their leave and returned to Louisiana. According to the Constitution, the state of Texas was to be governed by a "president-protector," whose power would be shared only with a *junta* of five men that enjoyed a merely advisory role. Catholicism remained the established religion. If anything served to partially appease some of the filibusters, it was the constitutional provision for land grants of approximately 4,500 acres to each volunteer.

In short order factionalism overwhelmed the republicans. Gutiérrez de Lara and his supporters, mostly Mexican insurgents and sympathizers, faced off with the Anglo American volunteers and U.S. government agents, who perceived Gutiérrez de Lara as an arbitrary and divisive leader. Pressing for the removal of Gutiérrez de Lara was William Shaler, a U.S. State Department official who championed José Alvarez de Toledo as the solution for the problems of the republic of Texas. In the days following his arrival in Béxar on August 1, 1813, Toledo and Gutiérrez de Lara fought over control of the government. In the end, Toledo won and Gutiérrez de Lara withdrew to Louisiana.

By this time it was clear that Viceroy Calleja was determined not to allow the murders of Salcedo and the other Spaniards to go unavenged or to have Texas remain in the hands of filibusters. The man he charged with recovering control of the errant province was General Joaquín Arredondo, who had recently been promoted to commandant general for the eastern Interior Provinces. Arredondo had considerable experience fighting insurgents in the north, having served as military governor of Nuevo Santander and having put down the rebellion in that province in 1812. With an army of over 1,800 men, Arredondo moved north toward San Antonio in early August for a final showdown with the Texas insurgency.

On August 18, 1813, Arredondo's royalist army fought Toledo's 1,400-man Republican Army of the North a few miles south of the Medina River, near the Laredo-San Antonio road. The daylong battle was a complete disaster for Toledo's army of Mexicans, Anglo Americans, and Indians. Colonel Ignacio Elizondo, the man who had captured Hidalgo, was now turned loose on the fleeing insurgents. With a 200-man force he pursued what remained of the Republican Army of the North northward and by September had reached Nacogdoches. He reported having executed 71 rebels and taken over 100 people captive, mostly women and children. Arredondo, meanwhile, had executed hundreds more and imposed martial law in San Antonio. He began his final, and rather inflated, report on the campaign: "The ever victorious and invincible arms of our Sovereign, aided by the powerful hand of the god of war, have gained the most complete and decisive victory over the base and perfidious rabble commanded by certain vile assassins ridiculously styled a general and commanders." Texas was again in the royalist fold.

A Howling Wilderness

Spanish Texas in the fall of 1813 was a land devoid of hope. From across the border in western Louisiana, Juan Martín Veramendi, Francisco Arocha, Vicente Travieso, and Francisco Ruiz, all Tejanos who had participated as local leaders in Gutiérrez de Lara's republican experiment, heard the news that they were not included in the general amnesty granted to contrite rebels. Yet others, such as Erasmo Seguín, were caught between loyalties. The one-time Béxar postmaster and leading member of Zambrano's revolt against Casas had been accused of providing letters of introduction for insurgents, for which crime all of his property had been confiscated. It took years for him to clear his name. Some unrepentant Tejano insurgents continued to work actively against Spanish rule. One such insurgent was Vicente Tarín, a former officer in the Alamo Company who had joined the Gutiérrez-Magee expedition. He organized a small company of like-minded men and roamed throughout northern Texas, bartering with the Indians and inciting them against the Spaniards. For the general population of Texas, even those who had remained steadfastly in the royalist camp, the abandonment of crops, the sequestration of property, impressment into military or other public service, and the constant menace of Indian attack meant a precarious existence.

Indians, Filibusters, and Pirates

One Tejano who saw his fortunes rise was Ignacio Pérez. Descended from original military settlers and Canary Islanders, he had become a prominent rancher and militia officer at Béxar. He was also a staunch loyalist (his daughter was married to former governor Cordero). Among his services to the crown would be an eight-month stint as interim governor of Texas between 1816 and 1817. Pro-

Presidio La Bahía, which by the early nineteenth century consisted of a stone enclosure with battlements, was the scene of repeated attacks by insurgents and filibusters. The fortification has been rebuilt by the diocese of Victoria and today serves not only as a museum, but as a favorite living-history location for reenactors of the Texas War of Independence. (© *Cathi M. Bunn*)

moted to lieutenant colonel for his service against the Gutiérrez-Magee expedition, he became a trusted field commander in the Indian war that followed the insurgency.

Hostilities with Comanches, Wichitas, and other Norteños had already been going on for years by then, brought on by a combination of factors over which Spanish authorities had little control. With the onset of Hidalgo's revolt, crown resources for placating Indian demands completely dried up. Wichitas and Comanches, formerly enemies of the Lipan Apaches, now joined together with them to raid Spanish settlements from San Antonio to the lower Rio Grande valley, causing settlers to abandon San Marcos de Neve, Santísima Trinidad de Salcedo, and many of the ranches south of the Nueces River.

By the time Antonio Martínez arrived in Texas to take over as governor in May 1817, things had reached the breaking point. Agriculture in the province had completely broken down and grain shipments from Coahuila were unreliable and inadequate to meet Texas's needs. With Ignacio Pérez and most of the other able-bodied men in the province impressed into active militia service, cultivation of even subsistence crops proved extremely difficult.

The situation was not new, but it had become critical as Texas faced a new wave of invasions from the United States and beyond. In late 1815 a former U.S. military officer and member of the Gutiérrez-Magee expedition, Henry Perry, organized a successful though minor invasion of Galveston Bay and occupied the mouth of the Trinity River. He was joined in the area in September 1816 by Louis Michele Aury, a pirate who had sold his services to a group of New Orleans conspirators intent on turning the Mexican War of Independence to their own advantage. Setting up headquarters on Galveston Island under the authority of Mexican rebel agent Manuel de Herrera, Aury was soon joined by other pirates, the brothers Jean and Pierre Lafitte. Spanish authorities, aware of these activities, could do little but stay informed and bide their time.

An abortive invasion of Mexico agreed upon by Perry, Aury, and the newly arrived insurgent Francisco Xavier Mina in April 1818 became the basis of the first filibustering expedition since Gutiérrez-Magee. After a fallout among the three leaders, Perry decided to lead his men to La Bahía. When Governor Martínez received word of Perry's arrival at Matagorda Bay, he transmitted the information to Commandant General Arredondo, along with a general assessment of how things stood:

> The pitiful condition of [La Bahía commander] Castañeda's few forces—in addition to his lack of supplies for subsistence, they are unmounted and barefooted—does not permit him even to select parties to go out on observation duty and those whom he does send in this condition go at full risk, and I am almost in the same situation. Now I cannot furnish him any kind of assistance. In regard to the forces, I have fifty men at Río Grande to transport corn, as I have already told you, and 100 men commanded by Lieutenant Colonel *Don* Ygnacio Pérez have had to go out to punish large bands of Indians who raid us quite frequently. I am alone in this capital with thirty or forty men, most of whom are ill, and I cannot count on those who are not because they are on foot and the arms they have are useless. My sole protection depends on the few citizens who without exception are in exactly the same condition I have said the troops are in.

Fortunately for the royalists, on June 18 one of Martínez's subordinates caught up with Perry and his forty-three men north of La Bahía and defeated the filibusters.

Despite the problems, and his limited ability to carry out any consistent reconnaissance beyond the vicinity of Béxar and La Bahía, Martínez was resourceful enough to confront the major challenges that presented themselves in the last three years of Spanish rule. Certainly the presence of the Lafitte brothers, who had usurped Aury's position in Galveston, was not a critical issue for the Texas governor. The pirates were interested in maritime conquests and Texas was receiving no seaborne traffic that might be affected. The Indians too were an intractable problem, but they had been so for a century. No, the challenge that concerned Martínez was the one posed by foreign invaders who might seize Texas.

One such challenge arose in 1818, when a large group of Napoleonic exiles attempted to establish a French outpost on the Trinity River. Charles Lallemand, a general in Napoleon's armies, led more than 150 men and a few women and children to a spot near the present town of Liberty, where they built a fort called Champ d'Asile. Although Lallemand claimed that his followers were peaceful agricultural colonists, the military nature of the encampment—with 600 muskets and 12,000 cartridges—and the failure of the colonists to clear land and plant crops points to other purposes. From the Spanish ambassador to the United States came word that Lallemand's intention was to occupy part of New Spain in order to proclaim Joseph Bonaparte king of Mexico.

Martínez could do little but send out scouting parties during the months following initial word of the arrival of the French. It was only in mid-September that Captain Juan de Castañeda, former commander at La Bahía and now in charge of the Alamo company, set out for the Trinity with 240 men. His orders, beyond expelling the French intruders, included driving out squatters and Indian traders, punishing the local Indians who had sided with the filibusters, and destroying the abandoned settlement of Nacogdoches. Fortunately for Castañeda, when he arrived at Champ d'Asile he found that the French had already abandoned the fort and taken refuge on Galveston Island. Although he sent an ultimatum ordering them to immediately depart or surrender, he had no boats to cross the bay and was in no position to attack. Neither was he in a position to carry out a punitive campaign against East Texas Indians or even to drive out squatters and illegal Indian traders. Castañeda had to be content to tear down the French fortifications and cabins and head back to Béxar.

From the Adams-Onís Treaty to Mexican Independence

The good news that Captain Castañeda brought back from Galveston Bay marked a temporary improvement in Spanish fortunes in Texas. U.S. interests in the last remaining vestige of the Spanish empire in eastern North America brought more good fortune to Spanish authorities in New Spain the following spring. Although the United States had continued to claim Texas as part of the Louisiana Purchase, General Wilkinson's acceptance of the neutral ground in 1806 had weakened the U.S. position. During and after the War of 1812, Spanish Florida had become a haven for Creek and other Indians hostile to the United States, leading to two invasions of the province by Andrew Jackson's army. Expediency demanded that U.S. Secretary of State John Quincy Adams and Spanish ambassador Luis de Onís reach an agreement. In February 1819 they reached a compromise: Spain would keep Texas but give up Florida.

Perhaps Adams and President James Monroe concluded that Spain would not long be in control of Mexico and that Texas would naturally fall to the United States soon thereafter. Whatever the case, the Adams-Onís Treaty (also known as the Transcontinental Treaty) did not win the approval of western political interests, who had long been advocating Anglo American expansion in that direction. Certainly the speculators who had backed Perry, Aury, and Mina would not sit still for the Yankee secretary of state giving away American rights to Texas. Meeting in New Orleans in May, the group began organizing a filibustering expedition

Texas at the end of the Spanish Empire in North America.

to "liberate" Texas from Spain. At Natchez too, irate citizens of the West organized to bring about a proper resolution to the situation. The conspirators found the man to lead the liberation of Texas in James Long, a Natchez merchant and veteran of the War of 1812.

What has come to be known as the first Long expedition began in June 1819, when an advance party of 120 men crossed the Sabine and occupied Nacogdoches. Long arrived later in the month and immediately organized a government that declared the independence of Texas on June 23, 1819. The document, drafted by Long and a group of Anglo American supporters, presumed to declare, "The citizens of Texas have long indulged the hope, that in the adjustment of the boundaries of the Spanish possessions in America, and of the territories of the United States, that they should be included within the limits of the latter." One of the new government's first acts was to grant each soldier in the army 6,400 acres as compensation for service. Within a month Long had more than 300 men at his service, including Mexican insurgent Bernardo Gutiérrez de Lara, Tejano rebel Vicente Tarín, the Anglo American Indian agent John Sibley, and former Spanish Indian agent Samuel Davenport.

To counter this new threat to Spanish sovereignty in Texas, Governor Martínez turned to Ignacio Pérez. The governor was unsure of the size of the threat—reports filtering in ranged from several hundred to several thousand invaders—but no better man could be entrusted with the mission than Lieutenant Colonel Pérez. Mustering 550 men, two cannons, 425 pack mules, and enough horses to provide each man with two or three remounts, the small army left Béxar on September 27,

1819. Pérez's instructions were not only to drive out all foreigners from East Texas, but to punish any Indians in the area who had supported the filibusters.

By the time Pérez and his now reinforced command of 650 men reached Nacogdoches, Long and most of his men had withdrawn to Louisiana. A few stragglers were captured, but the danger seemed to have passed. Pérez pardoned some of the remaining residents of Nacogdoches on the grounds that they had joined the rebels only because they could not resist.

The expedition returned to San Antonio by February 1820, a resounding though not total success. Pérez had captured forty-four Anglo American filibusters and Mexican rebels, not including a large group of squatters he had allowed to cross over into the Neutral Ground and the residents of Nacogdoches he had pardoned. Just as important, he had managed to free ten residents of Béxar, Laredo, and Camargo being held by the Comanches. He had also managed to take a large amount of booty, including valuable tools and dry goods. Pérez had not destroyed another squatter settlement at Pecan Point as he had wished to do, however, and he had not been able to establish a military post at Nacogdoches from which the Spanish could watch the border.

After fleeing to Natchitoches, the president of the Supreme Council of the republic of Texas proceeded to New Orleans. There he met with another Mexican insurgent, José Félix Trespalacios, a native of Chihuahua who had recently escaped a royalist dungeon in Mexico and was now preparing his own invasion of Texas. The two men decided to join forces and by early 1820 Long had established new headquarters at Point Bolivar. There he remained until September 1821, when, not having heard or not being interested in the news of Mexican independence, Long marched for La Bahía. He captured the presidio on October 4, but was forced to surrender to Ignacio Pérez, who was now in the service of the new Mexican nation.

The writing on the wall that Long had failed to see or chosen to ignore had been clearly visible for some time. A revolt by a Spanish army waiting to sail for Spanish America to put down independence movements had forced Ferdinand VII to restore the liberal Constitution of 1812. For *criollos,* many of whom had lost faith in the legitimacy of the Spanish government, the changes merely symbolized the continued instability of royal authority. One of these *criollos* was a royalist officer named Agustín de Iturbide. Sent into the field to crush the leading rebel, Vicente Guerrero, Iturbide instead reached an agreement with him for the separation of Mexico from Spain. The Plan of Iguala, signed by the two men on February 24, 1821, consisted of three important clauses: 1) the continued special status of the Catholic church in Mexican society, 2) the independence of Mexico as a constitutional monarchy, and 3) equality between *peninsulares* and *criollos.*

Curiously, many staunch royalists in northern New Spain, who until the beginning of the year had still been fighting the insurgents, accepted the inevitable with great aplomb. At his headquarters in Monterrey, Commandant General Arredondo took the oath pledging support of the Plan of Iguala in June and sent word to all his subordinates to do likewise. He soon resigned his position and withdrew to Cuba. In Coahuila Governor Cordero took the oath and continued in service to Mexico as commandant general of the western Interior Provinces until his death in 1823.

Hesitant to appear rebellious after carefully cultivating their royalist connections since August 1813, Béxar's leaders waited until the very last moment to endorse independence. On July 19, two months before Iturbide's triumphant Army of the Three Guarantees entered Mexico City, with a large part of the community drawn together in the main plaza, civilian and military officials, including Lt. Col. Ignacio Pérez, took the oath to the new nation. A few days later word arrived from La Bahía that its officials had also taken the oath. Spanish Texas was no more.

Conclusion

In the second decade of the nineteenth century the progress of the previous century had been almost totally undone. The extent of the damage done by filibusters, insurgents, royal armies, and hostile Indians made Texas appear to be a "wild, howling, interminable solitude," to Stephen F. Austin as he traveled from the Sabine toward San Antonio in the summer of 1821. Austin's father, Moses, one of the Anglo Americans who had settled in Spanish Louisiana, had lost everything during the panic of 1819 and had looked to the green pastures and rich bottom lands of Texas to restore his fortunes. He had come to Béxar in December 1820 with a proposal to settle 300 Anglo American Catholic families on the Brazos or Colorado River. And Governor Martínez and Commandant General Arredondo had been so desperate to do something for the forlorn province that they had agreed to the plan.

A survey of what was left of Texas gives an idea of why Austin might have had big dreams for Texas and why Spanish officials would accept his offer. Salcedo and San Marcos, two towns established by Antonio Cordero in the first decade of the century, had been totally wiped out by the end of August 1813. Nacogdoches was a virtual ghost town, although a few buildings remained standing and a handful of families remained in the vicinity.

Texas, then, consisted of little more than the San Antonio River valley settlements of San Antonio de Béxar and La Bahía del Espíritu Santo, with a population of about 3,000. Ranches throughout the area were largely abandoned and most crop land lay fallow. The settlers of La Bahía were able to reap only a meager harvest that could not possibly meet even subsistence needs. The presidio company had no horses and remained barefoot. Conditions at San Antonio were equally bad. A major flood in July 1819 had added to the local misery, as had field fires intentionally set by hostile Indians. As a result, harvests were poor or nonexistent and the towns found themselves at the mercy of whatever convoys of corn and flour could make it up the road from Río Grande and Laredo.

Men who had not seen their homes for the better part of a decade, some with families, returned to Béxar, Nacogdoches, and La Bahía under such conditions.

Former royalists and former republicans were now all Mexicans. Surprisingly, it appeared to work. Ignacio Pérez continued to serve in the military as if there had been no change in sovereignty. Erasmo Seguín, who had been suspected of collaborating with insurgents but who had vehemently protested his loyalty to the crown, eventually represented Texas at the congress in Mexico City that framed the country's first republican constitution. Juan Martín Veramendi, who had been pardoned and had returned to San Antonio, soon reentered public life, first as a customs agent and later as chief executive of the state. Vicente Tarín and Francisco Ruiz, who had stayed on the run, were commissioned by the new government to negotiate with the Indians who had helped bring Spanish Texas to its knees.

Could this partnership between former enemies be successful and could it extend to the Anglo Americans so eager to make Texas their home? With the odds stacked against them, old-stock Tejanos and newly-minted Texians got to work on answering that question.

SUGGESTED READINGS

Texas was no longer an isolated and backward Indian frontier province after 1800. Events over which colonial officials and Tejanos had no control thrust the poor and underpopulated colony into the thick of international politics and revolution. The literature on the major international events of this period—the Louisiana Purchase, the Aaron Burr conspiracy, the War of 1812, and the Napoleonic Wars—is too voluminous to discuss adequately here. Some understanding of the processes by which the Spanish empire collapsed, particularly in Mexico, can be gained from *The Independence of Latin America*, ed. Leslie Bethell (1987). In chapter 10 of *The Spanish Frontier in North America*, however, Weber provides a useful summary of events along the Spanish borderlands, as does John Kessell in chapter 13 of *Spain in the Southwest*. Don Chipman surveys the era from the Texas perspective in the aptly titled chapter 11 of *Spanish Texas*, "The Twilight of Spanish Texas, 1803–1821."

Louisiana

Just as Spanish Texas had its beginnings in the French occupation of what eventually came to be known as Louisiana, so too is the end of Spanish Texas tied to its eastern neighbor. For the story of the most representative of the early intruders, see Maurine T. Wilson and Jack Jackson's *Philip Nolan and Texas: Expeditions to the Unknown Land, 1791–1801* (1987). Although Charles A. Bacarisse's doctoral dissertation on the Baron of Bastrop was never published, he did prepare an article summarizing his research: "Baron de Bastrop," *Southwestern Historical Quarterly* (1955). Extensive accounts of Spanish efforts to stop Anglo American penetration of Texas appear in *Jefferson & Southwestern Exploration: The Freeman & Custis Accounts of the Red River Expedition of 1806,* by Dan L. Flores (1984), and Jack D. L. Holmes, "Showdown on the Sabine: General James Wilkinson vs. Lieutenant Colonel Simon de Herrera," *Louisiana Studies* (1964).

Fortress Texas

The Opening of Texas to Foreign Settlement, 1801–1821, by Mattie Austin Hatcher (1927; reprint 1976) remains unsurpassed in telling the story of Spain's desperate efforts to hold back the tide of Anglo American westward expansion. Spanish policy in Louisiana, which helped shape attitudes in Texas, is the subject of Gilbert C. Din's "Spain's Immigration Policy in Louisiana and the American Penetration, 1792–1803," *Southwestern Historical Quarterly* (1973). The colorful and competent Governor Antonio Cordero still awaits a biographer, but his successor has received much closer scrutiny in *Tragic Cavalier: Governor Manuel Salcedo of Texas, 1808–1813* by Félix D. Almaráz (1971). The problems these officials had in keeping undesirable people and ideologies from taking hold in Texas is the subject of Odie Faulk's "The Penetration of Foreigners and Foreign Ideas into Spanish East Texas, 1793–1810," *East Texas Historical Journal* (1964). Chapter 6 of F. Todd Smith's *The Wichita Indians: Traders of Texas and the Southern Plains, 1540–1845* (2000) gives considerable attention to the Indian side of Spanish troubles during this period.

Insurrection on the Frontier

No period of Texas colonial history has received more attention than that of 1811–13, when the province was caught up in the whirlwind of the Mexican War of Independence. Julia Kathryn Garrett's *Green Flag Over Texas: A Story of the Last Years of Spain in Texas* (1939) remains a very readable narrative of the entire period. A number of more specialized studies add to or provide a different perspective on events. An essay appearing in *Tejano Journey, 1770–1850*, edited by Gerald E. Poyo (1996), "Rebellion on the Frontier," by Jesús F. de la Teja, discusses local political conditions, especially in San Antonio, and how these contributed to partisanship during the war of independence. A very interesting collection of documents related to the first revolutionary episode was translated by Frederick C. Chabot in *Texas in 1811; the Las Casas and Sambrano Revolutions* (1941). The story of how San Antonio's elites restored royal government is told by J. Villasana Haggard in "The Counter-Revolution of Béxar, 1811," *Southwestern Historical Quarterly* (1939). A good summary of the Gutiérrez-Magee expedition that is also a detective story about the author's efforts to pin down the site of the battle of Medina is Ted Schwartz, *Forgotten Battlefield of the First Texas Revolution: The Battle of Medina, August 18, 1813*, edited and annotated by Robert H. Thonhoff (1985).

A Howling Wilderness

The history of the last years of Spanish Texas has been given over to stories of pirates and filibusters. The classic study in the field is Harris G. Warren, *The Sword Was Their Passport: A History of American Filibustering in the Mexican Revolution* (1943). Other useful readings include Fane Downs, "Governor Antonio Martínez and the Defense of Texas from Foreign Invasion, 1817–1822," *Texas Military History* (1968), and Ed Bradley, "Fighting for Texas: Filibuster James Long, the

Adams-Onís Treaty, and the Monroe Administration," *Southwestern Historical Quarterly* (1999). The story of French exiles who made a brief, unsuccessful attempt to establish themselves on the lower Trinity River is told by Kent Gardien in "Take Pity on Our Glory: Men of Champ d'Asile," *Southwestern Historical Quarterly* (1984). On the ever-popular Jean Laffite story, Jack C. Ramsay, Jr.'s *Jean Laffite, Prince of Pirates* (1996) makes entertaining reading. The anticlimactic change of sovereignty is the topic of Félix D. Almaráz's *Governor Antonio Martínez and Mexican Independence in Texas: An Orderly Transition* (1979).

II

DEFINING TEXAS

In 1821 the Mexican government, newly independent from Spain and seeking ways to populate its northern frontier, permitted a colony of families from the United States to settle on the coastal and blackland prairie lands of southeastern Texas. This officially sanctioned effort led to other colonization attempts by and for immigrants from the United States and Europe, and to independent immigration. As a result, Texas developed along new political, social, and economic trajectories. The present-day state took shape, and a distinctive Texas identity was forged, but not without tremendous struggles or significant costs.

Initially, the newcomers agreed, at least nominally, to abide by the rules and regulations of the Mexican government and the Catholic faith. Most had been propelled westward by the prospect of cheap and fertile farmlands, but increasingly they were joined by adventurers looking for diverse political and economic opportunities. Arriving primarily from the southern states, the immigrants adopted some Mexican practices and policies but held allegiances to the U.S. form of government and to the southern agricultural system in which cotton was central and slave labor was promoted.

The settlers' view of the government's role in their lives clashed with the realities of their status as remote residents of a vast Mexican state, Coahuila y Texas, and with the government's turn away from republican reforms included in the 1824 Mexican Constitution. In the quest for increased political recognition and autonomy that ensued, new Texans—together with disaffected Tejanos—acted from a mix of idealistic, practical, and self-serving motives. At first calling for recognition of Texas as a separate Mexican state, they soon called for—and won—independence from Mexico.

Most voting Texans were in favor of annexation to the United States as the next step, but in this desire they were rebuffed by a U.S. government wary of Mexico's reaction and of bringing another slave state into the Union.

So, rather haphazardly, Texas not only became a nation but remained one for almost a decade. Rejected by the United States, still threatened by a Mexico that refused to recognize Texas independence, harassed by Comanche raids, and struggling economically, Texans developed a strong sense of their separate identity and even entertained dreams of empire. They sought to claim most of present-day New Mexico as part of the Republic, and some contemplated extending Texas's rule into Mexico or to the Pacific.

Such grand imperialistic vision and pride in "going it alone" did not disappear when Texas was eventually annexed as a state in a changed U.S. political climate. Although Texans voted decisively for statehood, knowing the stability and development possibilities it would confer, they continued to nurture a sense of their own exceptionalism. The U.S. government reinforced this feeling by allowing the state to control its own land sales, for example, and paying the Texas government to relinquish its New Mexican land claims.

At the same time, however, Texans were firmly developing their state's southern identity. Statehood increased the flow of immigrants from the American South. Gins overflowed with "King Cotton." A planter class wielded political, social, and economic power. African Americans were held as slave labor, and Tejanos were pushed to the periphery of public life and cut off from economic opportunity. By the eve of the Civil War, the majority of Texas citizens were Anglo Americans who identified with the systems and philosophies of the antebellum South.

Thus, in 1861 Texas voters overwhelmingly favored secession from the Union that they had entered in 1846. Although a few flirted with the idea of independent nationhood once more, most were ready to join the Confederate States of America in its assertion of states' rights and its defense of the southern slave system.

There were dissenters, and the war years brought not only privation and loss of Texas soldiers but severe tensions among Texans themselves. Many Unionists were killed for their beliefs. The war years also exposed other serious problems within the state, such as lack of adequate frontier defense along the western border of settlement and lack of industrial development to sustain a war effort.

The defeat of the Confederacy was felt as bitterly in Texas as in other southern states. An Anglo majority had defined the state based on an agricultural system that was no longer politically or morally acceptable. Cotton remained Texas's premier cash crop, but it could no longer be the fulcrum of political, social, and economic power. The plantation system had been broken, and new forms of economic enterprise were developing, born along on the burgeoning tracks of the railroads that not only connected the settled regions but helped open up West Texas for settlement and development.

Reconstructionists sought to dismantle the old political structure in favor of one in which Unionists and African Americans participated freely. Although the plantation system had been broken, however, old political structures and beliefs were harder to erase, and in the gubernatorial election of 1874, antebellum southern forces regained much of the power they had lost. Theirs was still essentially an agrarian vision, and one strongly favoring Anglo hegemony. But new social and economic forces coalescing would force new definitions for Texas, including new political ones. ■ ■ ■

6

The Americanization of Texas, 1821–1835

He had been unsure of the venture at first, so much so that his father had written, "I hope and pray you will Discharge your Doubts, as to the Enterprise." But trusted friends had been enthusiastic, and all the arrangements had been made. In Natchitoches, Louisiana, a delegation headed by Erasmo Seguín met twenty-seven-year-old Stephen Fuller Austin and in July 1821 escorted him across the Sabine into Spanish Texas, where he was to meet his father Moses and commence their colonizing work. Barely had the traveling party started, though, when word came of Moses's death in Missouri. Now it would be up to Stephen F. Austin himself to start the Anglo colony that had been his father's dream. As the party moved deep into the interior of Texas, to the Brazos River and beyond, he encountered few settlers; aside from the reduced settlement of Nacogdoches through which he had passed, most of the Mexican population was concentrated at San Antonio de Béxar and far off along the Rio Grande. He saw no Indians. Austin noted with enthusiasm the abundant wildlife, the fertile soil, the clear-running rivers, the pleasing way in which woodland alternated with prairie. He was bound for San Antonio, hoping and trusting that the Mexican officials there would allow him to carry out his father's deathbed wish that his son replace him in the Texas enterprise. Outside the town, an advance party returned with the news that Mexico had declared its independence and Texas was no longer under Spanish rule. This news posed another complication for Austin, but by now he was fully committed to the vision of a U.S. colony flourishing in Texas. His work toward that end would prove crucial to the reshaping and redefining of nineteenth-century Texas.

1821	Stephen F. Austin arrives in Texas and proceeds with his father's colonization plans
1824	Federalists create a republican constitution for independent Mexico; Mexican Congress passes National Colonization Law; Texas becomes part of Mexican state of Coahuila y Texas
1826	Empresario Haden Edwards and his supporters stage the Fredonian rebellion
1828–29	Gen. Manual Mier y Terán travels in Texas and reports back to Mexican government
1830	Law of April 6 seeks to greatly restrict U.S. immigration into Texas
1832	First Anahuac disturbance erupts in conflict between garrison commander and colonists; Texas colonists, including a Tejano delegation from Goliad, hold convention to take concerns to Mexican government
1833	Santa Anna is elected president of Mexico as federalist but moves quickly toward centralist rule; second colonist convention convenes and prepares a provisional state constitution
1834	Stephen F. Austin is arrested in Saltillo, returning from Mexico City to Texas
1835	Second Anahuac disturbance reflects, helps stimulate political unrest in Mexican Texas

Colonization Efforts, 1821–1829

In San Antonio, Spanish governor Antonio María Martínez continued to oversee the political affairs of Texas in the wake of Mexican independence. Mexico's independence both followed upon and fed the country's severe economic distress and political divisiveness, ensuring that the new nation would be unable to mount colonization efforts from within to protect its northern frontier. Having originally accepted Moses Austin's settlement project as a necessary means of building and reinforcing Mexico's Texas frontier, Martínez now approved of Stephen Austin's moving forward with it. Other Tejano leaders, too, welcomed Austin's efforts, as evidenced by the guidance and counsel of Erasmo Seguín, Juan Martín de Veramendi, and other political and cultural leaders who wished to build on mutual interests: the economic development and political stability of Texas.

Austin's Colony

Governor Martínez asked the younger Austin to devise a plan for land grants to the colonists. Austin complied, specifying that families would receive 320 acres of farming land and 640 acres of grazing land, with extra allotments provided to the head of the household for each family member and each slave. From the beginning, then, the extension of antebellum slavery from the American South characterized the Americanization of Texas, despite Mexican objections to the practice.

Austin found that the region his father and Mexican officials had been considering for colonization would indeed sustain agricultural settlers. It stretched southward from the Nacogdoches–San Antonio trail he had just traveled, encompassing a sweep of present-day Southeast Texas. In surveying the region after his initial visit to San Antonio, Austin observed not only pleasing pastoral vistas but plenty of timber, water, and good river-bottom soil. His first colony would be bordered on the east by the San Jacinto River, on the west by the Lavaca, with long, fine stretches of the Brazos and the Colorado between them. This constituted the best farming land in Texas. Initially, Austin would obtain an empresario grant for the land all the way to the coast, where these rivers emptied into the gulf and where ports could be established.

Austin's contract specified that he could settle 300 families, and he had begun recruiting efforts before leaving New Orleans. In December 1821, his colonists began arriving and locating along both the Colorado and the Brazos. Overwhelmingly, the newcomers were American farm families of English origin migrating from nearby U.S. states, especially Louisiana and Alabama.

Barely had the settlement begun when Austin made his way to Mexico City to get his grant confirmed by the government there. He spent almost a year in the Mexican capital, witnessing a dizzying array of political reversals: Augustín de Iturbide was crowned emperor; one congress dissolved to be replaced by a junta

Stephen F. Austin led the colonization of Texas from the United States. This watercolor, done by British artist William Howard in 1833, highlights Austin as a pioneer leader even as empresario Austin faced some of his most intense challenges in the role. *(Prints & Photographs Collection, CN 01436, The Center for American History, The University of Texas at Austin)*

charged with congressional duties; a rebellion spread; the federal cabinet was pressured into resigning; another congress convened; and Iturbide abdicated.

Out of all of this turmoil, however, came a generous colonization law for Mexico's Texas frontier and specific approval for Austin's effort. The Imperial Colonization Law of 1823 set up an empresario system that surpassed Austin's initial allotments, offering a square league, or *sitio*, of about 4,428 acres to each family involved in stock raising and a *labor* (Spanish colonial unit of cropland), or 177 acres, for a family's farming operation. It provided further inducements as well, such as a six-year moratorium on taxes. Austin would not receive payment for his colonization efforts from the government until he had settled at least two hundred families, at which point he would receive choice lands of his own. Until then, he had to rely on the moderate fee he charged settlers to offset his surveying and administrative costs, although he offered to accept whatever items of value the colonists might have to offer, from beeswax and deerskins to livestock.

During the period from 1821 to 1824, Austin would exceed the 200-family requirement for his own land, and by 1827 he would approach the projected number of settlers, with 297 families, later referred to as the "Old Three Hundred," receiving land titles. By the terms of settlement laid out in 1823, they were to be "of unblemished character, good Morals, Sobriety, and industrious habits," each man "also hav[ing] sufficient property to begin with either as a farmer or mechanic besides paying for his land." They were also supposed to be Catholics; for the overwhelmingly Protestant settlers, this was a conversion in name only. Austin would have to remind them repeatedly that "the Roman Catholic is the religion of this nation."

As a group, Austin's colonists had high literacy rates for the era and were people of some means. Of those who had settled by the fall of 1825, sixty-nine families possessed slaves. Jared Groce of Alabama, the wealthiest colonist, brought with him ninety slaves whose labor quickly helped him consolidate his wealth and position in their new location beside the Brazos.

The Mexican government and Mexican public in general did not favor slavery, but the government allowed concessions to enhance the colonization efforts. Austin won the first such concession on that initial trip to Mexico City. He felt that the colony's success would depend in large part on its ability to attract slaveholders such as Groce—and would-be slaveholders—from the American South. The colonization law allowed slaves to enter Texas but did not allow slave trading, and it specified that the children of slaves should be freed at age fourteen. Austin won his colony's exemption from such measures. By 1825, slaves made up almost 25 percent of the population of 1,800 in Austin's colony. From the earliest years, then, the institution of slavery was a significant part of the economic development of Anglo Texas.

Other Colonizing Efforts

As word of Austin's enterprise spread, other empresarios responded to the opportunities that Texas offered for colonization. And in its 1824 immigration law, the Mexican government declared itself "desirous of augmenting by all possible means the population of its territory; of encouraging the cultivation of its fertile lands, the raising of stock, and the progress of arts and commerce." The government sought to refine colonization laws, so that subsequent empresario contracts were somewhat different from that of Austin's first colony. But with a grant from the government and six years to settle a requisite number of families, these empresarios—primarily Anglo, but also Mexican, German, Scottish, and Irish—could promise families more land at a lower rate than what they could obtain in the United States and the opportunity to make their own fortunes in the bargain.

Martín De León, member of an aristocratic Mexican family, had petitioned the Spanish government as early as 1807 to establish a colony south of the land Austin claimed. De León had come to Texas in 1805 and developed a ranching empire. In 1824, he won a contract to locate forty-one Mexican families on the lower Guadalupe River. Although Mexican authorities had questioned De León's loyalties, he would be the only colonizer to bring predominantly Mexican families in to Texas.

Just to the north of De León, in 1825 Green DeWitt, a former Missouri sheriff, with the help of Austin and the Baron de Bastrop, was awarded a grant bordering Austin's on the west and was authorized to locate 400 families further inland on the Guadalupe. As with the other colonizers, his contract with the government

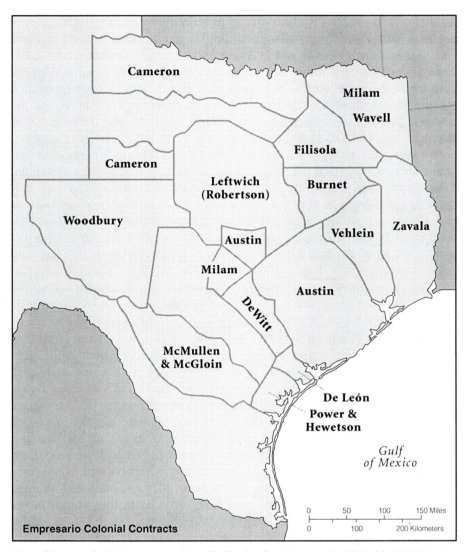

Map of Texas and adjoining states. Compiled by Stephen F. Austin. Published by H. S. Tanner, Philadelphia, 1836. Shows the boundaries of the empresario "grants."

specified that they were to be Catholic families of "good moral character"; DeWitt was not to admit "criminals, vagrants, or persons of bad morals," and should they enter the colony, he was to "cause them to leave the republic, by force of arms if necessary."

In each colony, a core settlement came into being. For Austin's, it was San Felipe de Austin, set on a bluff on the west bank of the Brazos River. San Felipe was never very prepossessing; adventurer and blacksmith Noah Smithwick would remember it in 1827 as "[t]wenty-five or perhaps thirty log cabins strung along the [river] bank," with "every fellow buil[ding] to suit himself." Yet San Felipe was vital to the colony's identity and to Americanization in general; it proved a fulcrum for political, economic, and social activity for colonists and newcomers from the United States. As San Felipe began to thrive, in 1824 De León established Nuestra Señora Guadalupe de Jesús Victoria on the lower Guadalupe, and the next year DeWitt's surveyor, James Kerr, founded Gonzales near the point where the Guadalupe and San Marcos rivers met.

Between 1825 and 1829, various empresarios and empresario companies won grants to most of present-day Texas, as well as parts of New Mexico, Colorado, Kansas, and Oklahoma, which Texas later tried to claim as its own. As a result of the Mexican Congress's National Colonization Law of 1824, they were not allowed to colonize within ten leagues of the gulf coast without federal approval, although Austin and De León successfully made cases for their own original grants to the coast. Mexican officials had hoped in vain for more Mexican colonizers and colonists to strengthen Texas's Mexican identity. On a map, entrepreneurs like Scotsman John Cameron were given permission to settle colonists on vast swaths of West Texas that would not be home to anyone but Native Americans until after the Civil War. Others received grants of land in Texas's eastern and southern regions, in closer proximity to the United States, the gulf, and the rest of Mexico. Arthur Wavell, an Englishman who had served as a brigadier general in the Mexican army and had assisted Austin in his colonization, in 1826 won a grant in northeast Texas, primarily consisting of what is now Red River, Lamar, and Bowie counties. Other Europeans with Mexican ties also secured grants. Irishmen James Power and James Hewetson had both located in Coahuila, engaging in mining and other enterprises, and in 1828 received a grant to settle both Mexican and Irish families in the coastal area between the Lavaca and Guadalupe rivers. John McMullen and James McGloin, also Irish merchants in Mexico, took over an empresario contract from two Anglo entrepreneurs in 1828 and brought Irish men, women, and children recently arrived in New York City to their colony in the brush country of South Texas.

By 1834, about 150 Irish families would be settled in the colonies of Refugio and San Patricio. Most of the colonizers, however, had little success in attracting a significant number of settlers: Only one-third would manage even to bring colonists to Texas. Even in East and Central Texas, empresarios experienced major difficulties.

The Fredonian Rebellion

One difficulty the would-be colonizers had was encountering people who already occupied the land. These people included both Native Americans and earlier immigrants of European and Mexican extraction. On his initial surveying expedition, Austin had encountered a band of Cocos Indians, a branch of the Karankawas. Their meeting was peaceful, and Austin hoped to avoid conflict, but he anticipated that "there will be no way of subduing them but extermination." The dwindling Karankawas did not have a strong enough presence to challenge the part of Austin's colony that infringed on their traditional grounds. Instead, they moved in and out of the colony boundaries, quickly coming to be considered a nuisance and a threat because of occasional attacks they made on solitary colonists or small parties. The Tonkawas and other small tribes further inland had been weakened by the Spanish presence, wars with other Indian groups, and disease and cultural change. The Wacos and Tawakonis retained strength in their solid agricultural communities and intermittent alliances with the Comanches to the west and north, but these two groups, like the Tonkawas, became known primarily as horse stealers to Austin's colonists.

There were also immigrant Indian groups pressed westward by Anglo migration: Alabamas, Coushattas, Shawnees, Choctaws, Chickasaws, and Cherokees. The Cherokees figured in a major land dispute in the Nacogdoches area in 1825 and 1826. Empresario Haden Edwards, a wealthy former U.S. senator from Kentucky and Mississippi plantation owner, had lobbied with Austin for the colonization laws in Mexico City; for his efforts he had gained authorization to locate 800 families in Nacogdoches and to the west and south of the decimated far East Texas community. There were other groups, however, already established not only in the town but in the outlying areas. "Old settlers"—both Mexican and Anglo—had held on to their homesteads through the political intrigues and official neglect of the region and possessed their own land grants from the government. Shortly before Stephen F. Austin entered Texas, approximately sixty Cherokee families forced westward by Anglo settlement in Arkansas had crossed the Sabine and begun attempts to gain title to land in the Nacogdoches area. And various "squatters" had settled in the area, gambling on gaining title to land at some point.

Edwards antagonized the "old settlers" and even the squatters, some of whom had lived in the area for a number of years, by posting notices stating that they would have to document their land claims or their lands would be given to his colonists. When residents complied, Edwards questioned the validity of some of their titles. With those he judged legitimate, he attempted to extract payments, claiming that he was now empresario over the lands and charged more per grant than the government did, so the settlers would have to make up the difference.

The antagonism Edwards engendered only intensified after an election for *alcalde* in January 1826. Edwards's Irish son-in-law Chichester Chaplin, a lawyer recently arrived from Louisiana, garnered more votes than "old settler" Samuel Norris, a Maryland native. Norris's supporters claimed vote fraud, and in March 1826 political chief José Antonio Saucedo in San Antonio ordered that Norris be installed as *alcalde.*

In another blow for Edwards, the Mexican government soon judged that he was not abiding by the terms of his colonization contract and voided it. Edwards had already poured considerable money into the enterprise and had gathered around him colonists who shared his dissatisfaction with the turn of events. In

November, a group led by Edwards supporter Martin Parmer simply took captive a number of the key players in the political struggle, including Norris and Edwards himself. Edwards was quickly released, but members of his faction tried and convicted Norris and others of "oppression and corruption in office" and installed their own *alcalde*.

This was just the kind of extralegal maneuvering that Mexican officials had hoped to avoid by controlling the issuance of colonization contracts in the first place. Now Lieutenant Colonel Mateo Ahumada was dispatched from San Antonio with a force of dragoons and infantrymen. Edwards, his brother Benjamin, and Parmer responded by declaring the institution of a separate republic in the Nacogdoches region, the republic of Fredonia.

In doing so, they enlisted the support of the Texas Cherokees. Just north of Nacogdoches, occupying lands that were partially in the northern boundaries of Edwards' colonization grant and partially in the grant of empresario Frost Thorn, these immigrant Indians had cleared land, planted crops, constructed homes, and integrated themselves into the life of the region. Mexican officials saw them as a buffer against uncontrolled Anglo settlement. But they were regarded with suspicion by native tribes, by some officials, and by other settlers. The repeated and vigorous efforts of Cherokee representative Richard Fields and John Dunn Hunter to negotiate a land title from the government in Mexico had proven futile. The Cherokees could only surmise that they would again be forced out as more United States immigrants arrived.

The Fredonians had not recruited as many men for the cause as they hoped, and Benjamin Edwards turned to the Cherokees, offering them the land they currently occupied and much more land to the west if they would fight along with the Edwards faction. The Fredonian Declaration of Independence, then, claimed to speak for "the White and Red emigrants from the United States of North America" in its resistance to "an imbecile, faithless, and despotic government, miscalled a Republic." But as soon as they heard of the Cherokees' involvement, representatives of the Mexican government in Texas began trying to dissuade the Indian leaders by holding out the promise of a land grant from the government. Stephen F. Austin joined these government representatives; as the leading empresario in Texas, he took seriously his responsibility for the orderly implementation of colonization efforts as the Mexican government required. The Cherokee peace chiefs under Chief Bowl, also known as Duwali or Chief Bowles, heeded the government's counsel and withdrew their support of Edwards, going so far as to order the execution of Fields and Hunter in an attempt to reassure Texas authorities that they had no wish to foment trouble.

With Mexican troops and a militia from Austin's colony on the way, the Fredonian rebellion fell apart, and Haden Edwards escaped temporarily to Louisiana. The conflict had demonstrated to Mexican officials some of the dangers of allowing colonization from the United States, but the Edwards faction's failure to recruit many colonists, the Austin colony's response, and the reversal of

Cheraquis.

Cherokees: *Indigenes des C.U. de L'Amerique emigrés avec autorisation au Nacogdoches.*

Cherokees who had been pushed westward preceded colonists from the United States and hoped to gain title to the East Texas lands they occupied. This watercolor of "Cheraquis" in Texas by Lino Sánchez y Tapia was based on descriptions from the 1828 Mier y Terán expedition. *(Lino Sánchez y Tapia,* Cheraquis, *plate xv, from the collection of Gilcrease Museum, Tulsa, Oklahoma)*

the Cherokees' position seemed to indicate that they could maintain peace, order, and governmental authority in the face of such threats.

Continued Colonization Difficulties

Land disputes, however, continued to contribute to uncertainty and strife in Mexican Texas. Wavell's grant overlapped a section of southwest Arkansas. De León's boundaries were unspecified, and the Mexican government wound up including his colony within DeWitt's grant, leading to boundary clashes between De León and DeWitt, followed by boundary clashes between De León and Power and Hewetson.

Boundaries were not the worst of their problems. Empresarios had difficulties attracting colonists to regions remote from Mexican and U.S. supply centers. They also had trouble transporting those who responded and then following through on promises to provide basic services. Even East Texas was still remote from U.S. cities and supply routes. Austin and his colonists fared better than the others, and Austin extended his colonization grants northward, westward, and southward in a series of five grants, gaining land from the gulf coast to the heart of Texas. Austin's success was due to several factors: He captured some of the best river bottomlands for farming; his settlements were located close to major rivers and the gulf coast; there was only a limited threat from Indians in southeastern Texas; he had selected colonists of some means, education, and experience in reestablishing themselves successfully; and, finally, he paid constant attention to myriad aspects of the colonization, including the all-important relations with the Mexican government.

This does not mean that Austin or his colonists had an easy time of it. Austin learned Spanish and worked ceaselessly to cultivate government officials in Mexico City, in Coahuila, and in Texas, adjusting to frequent changes in government and government policy regarding empresario contracts. His work—and that of other empresarios and of Mexican officials in Texas—was complicated by the fact that the fledgling Mexican government was struggling against serious odds to administer the North American empire it had won from Spain.

After the 1823 abdication of Iturbide, who had sought to establish a constitutional monarchy in independent Mexico, there was political competition between two groups throughout the rest of the decade. Centralists were regarded as conservatives: They continued to favor old imperial models of government, including an authoritarian national government. Federalists looked in part to the United States for a more liberal alternative: They espoused republican principles and the transfer of many governmental powers to the Mexican states. The federalists, including Texas representative Erasmo Seguín, managed to pass a constitution in 1824 that resembled the U.S. Constitution in its emphasis on a free republic. A president with limited powers was to be elected every four years by the legislatures in the Mexican states, and a national Congress was to convene annually. The Constitution garnered enthusiastic support from Tejano and Anglo American leaders in Texas.

A more dubious development for Texas, especially with the two groups vying for control of the Mexican government, was the designation of Texas as part of a larger state of Coahuila y Texas. In fact, all of Texas from the Sabine to the Nueces was initially designated simply the "Department of Béxar." (Distant El Paso and other western Rio Grande settlements were part of the state of Chihuahua, whereas the far southern Rio Grande, now the tip of Texas, was included in the state of Tamaulipas.) This meant that the interests of Mexican citizens in Texas, whatever their origins, were subsumed into those of their larger neighbor Coahuila. Coahuila's state government was based in Saltillo, across the Rio Grande, deep in Coahuila, and high in the Sierra Madre Occidental mountain range. This relationship took on new importance in 1825, when the new federalist legislature passed a national colonization law giving the states authority over colonization contracts. Coahuila officials would decide who received these contracts in Texas. The leaders and people of both Coahuila and Texas, however, were ill served by a shifting government in Mexico City with limited ability to address the needs of far-flung areas.

Struggling with some of these external issues, Austin also worked tirelessly on internal issues in his colonies: dealing with Indian threats, administering land grants, setting up internal colonial civil codes, addressing disputes and potential disputes among colonists, and responding to colonist complaints against his administration, particularly in the matter of land grants, which many considered inequitable. He wielded extensive judicial power within his colonies without deviating significantly from Mexican codes of law or overstepping government control. His capital, San Felipe, remained a rude collection of cabins, its often-muddy, often-dusty thoroughfares still forested with raw tree stumps. Reports of crop failures and other woes in the colony made their way to U.S. newspapers and no doubt deterred some would-be colonists.

Those who settled in Austin's colony in these early years faced frontier isolation, danger, and crude living conditions. Mary Crownover Rabb, who arrived in Austin's colony from Arkansas as a young woman with her husband John in 1823, would remember, "We come to [the Colorado River] where LaGrange now is, but there was no house there then nor nothing but a wilderness, nor even a tree cut down to mark that place." They settled with relatives in the small community of Indian Hill, further upriver, but John grew impatient with the constant Indian depredations. The couple moved from one isolated farming location to another, camping out or creating rudimentary log shelters. In the U.S. colonial tradition,

Mary Crownover Rabb and her husband John were among Austin's "Old Three Hundred" settler families; Mary left a vivid and engaging account of frontier life. *(Prints & Photographs Collection, CN 00878, The Center for American History, The University of Texas at Austin)*

they produced what they needed at home: John constructed a loom and Mary sat under a tree weaving mosquito netting—"a thing quite indispensable," another early immigrant wrote—before their cabin was constructed. Later, often left alone with her children at the cabin for long periods, Mary dealt with her loneliness and Indians ranging nearby by working late into the night and sprinkling shelled corn on the floor for the family pigs, noting "by the time I got in the bed, all them little pigs would be in the house cracking corn until I would be asleep and the Indians gone and the pigs gone."

In other colonies, conditions were even more precarious. Noah Smithwick visited DeWitt's colony two or three years after its founding and found that the inhabitants, "consisting of a dozen families, were living—if such existence could be called living—huddled together for security against the Karankawas, who, though not openly hostile, were not friendly." Smithwick provided a particularly vivid picture of the lives of the women, who lamented "old homes and friends left behind" and did not share the men's excitement about hunting and exploring:

> They had not even the solace of constant employment. . . . There was no house to keep in order; the meager fare was so simple as to require little time for its preparation. There was no poultry, no dairy, no garden, no books, or papers. . . . no schools, no churches—nothing to break the dull monotony of their lives. . . ."

Despite the struggling character of the colonies, other colonizers continued to advance their own settlement plans, fired by the opportunity to gain access to vast tracts of land, develop a vision of settlement and trade, and add to their own status and wealth. In 1822 Sterling Robertson, a Tennessee plantation owner, joined other stockholders in a "Texas Association" planning a settlement in Mexican Texas. In 1825 his colleague Robert Leftwich secured a grant to settle 800 families in what is now central Texas but was unable to follow through. Robertson continued his attempts to recruit settlers in Tennessee and Kentucky but would not be able to advance the colonization under his own name until the 1830s. David G. Burnet, a New Jersey native, Ohio lawyer, and Louisiana trader with the Comanches on the Brazos, obtained a grant in central East Texas in 1826 and spent the following years trying to raise money and colonists for the enterprise. Joseph Vehlein, a German trader in Mexico, received two 1826 grants south of Burnet's, but also lacked the resources to follow through. Lorenzo de Zavala, an accomplished political leader in Mexico, obtained an empresario grant in East Texas between Vehlein's and the Sabine in 1829. One stimulus to colonizers and colonists was an 1829 homestead exemption rule provided by the Mexican government, which secured from creditors colonists' land and the tools to work it.

In 1830, however, the picture in Mexican Texas would change considerably, the challenges for colonizers growing more difficult. Spurred by a report from Mexican Brigadier General Manuel de Mier y Terán, officials within the Mexican government were questioning the wisdom of allowing colonization efforts from the United States.

Growth of Political and Cultural Tensions, 1829–1833

In many ways, the government of Mexico had been accommodating to the colonizers and settlers from the United States. Not only had the federal government and the government of Coahuila encouraged immigration with generous land grants, but despite general Mexican opposition to slavery, exceptions were made for U.S. immigrants, and an 1828 decree declared that slaves would be considered contract labor or indentured servants. Even when President Vincente Guerrero officially abolished slavery in 1829, he issued an exemption for Texas. Yet political problems were mounting between the government and its citizens in Texas, particularly the newcomers from the United States.

Tensions and the Law of April 6, 1830

There were four contributing factors to the tensions that existed in Texas at this time: First was the general restiveness of the recent immigrants under Mexican and empresario authority. A number of colonists and other immigrants settled on land without authorization, ignored the government's other conditions of residence, and sought at the local level to replicate American political and legal customs. In other words, many continued to think of themselves as Americans. Further, many continued to think of themselves as American Southerners—and to consider slaveholding an inalienable right, even as the Mexican government continued its efforts to restrict or end the practice in Texas.

The second factor was the dissatisfaction of Tejanos and immigrants alike with Texas's status as part of Coahuila y Texas. The 1827 Constitution of Coahuila y Texas provided for a twelve-person legislature: eleven representatives from Coahuila and one from Texas. A third factor was the federalist/centralist power shifts in Mexico. Tejano and Anglo leaders continued to favor the federalists, with their republican ideals and rejection of a strong, authoritarian central government. Yet a Coahuila y Texas state government that really worked for Texans could not develop in the fluid political climate of the 1820s, a fact that affected Tejanos as well as immigrants. Béxar's population and status as a political center declined in the 1820s, and the soldiers of its garrison, deprived of pay and necessities, became a drain upon the citizens rather than a ready market for their goods. Tejanos, like the immigrants, had little influence in Mexico City, and could only observe as centralists in 1829 firmly took control of the Mexican government.

The final factor was the Mexican government's own concerns over immigration from the United States. Whether federalist or centralist, officials watched this migration with growing alarm: It was neither as orderly nor as controlled as previous officials had envisioned. Adding to their concerns was the fact that U.S. President Andrew Jackson was trying to purchase much of present-day Texas for the United States. Although Mexican officials rebuffed these overtures, they found them disquieting evidence of American designs on Mexican soil. Also disturbing was the report they received from General Terán, who traveled on government business in Texas in 1828 and 1829. On an expedition called the Comisión de Límites (Boundary Commission), Terán moved northward through the American settlements to establish the Mexican-United States boundary on the east and north but also to assess the American presence in Texas.

Terán, who had served in the first independent Mexican Congress, working specifically on how the new nation could colonize its frontier regions, was disturbed by the "smoldering fires" he found. He spoke bluntly in an 1828 letter to President Guadalupe Victoria: "I am warning you to take timely measures. Texas could throw the whole nation into revolution." In Nacogdoches in particular, he found a lack of necessary authority and order. New immigrants from the United States were streaming in and simply appropriating plots of land, many of them "fugitives from our neighbor republic and bear[ing] the unmistakable earmarks of thieves and criminals," although he noted that some of these "have reformed and settled down to an industrious life." The Mexican population in Nacogdoches he judged "comprising what in all countries is called the lowest class—the very poor and the very ignorant." Terán found the population mix to be volatile, with Anglo immigrants, Indian immigrants, and slaves naturally growing restive in a Mexican Texas less restrictive than the American South.

On one issue, however, he found most Texas residents in agreement, from Austin's colony northward: the need to separate Texas from Coahuila. Terán cited reasons such as the impracticality of having to seek recourse from a state capital in Coahuila "so distant and separated from this section by deserts infected by hostile savages" and the friction resulting from "the mixing of [Texans'] affairs with those of Coahuila."

The general's subsequent report indicated that Mexico stood in real danger of losing Texas to the United States. He recommended that the government expend more effort in recruiting Mexican and European settlers, in developing trade with the Mexican interior, and in encouraging foreign trade along the gulf coast.

Terán's report formed much of the basis of the Law of April 6, 1830, a centralist decree that attempted to restrict and control American immigration into Texas. Among other provisions, this law halted most of the empresario efforts at colonization, and thus most U.S. immigration. It was clearly aimed at U.S. empresarios and immigrants, not Mexican or European colonization. With Terán's blessing, Austin won an exception for his colony and DeWitt's; the next grant, however, in 1831, went to Vincente Filisola, a Mexican official who was allowed to settle 600 families in East Texas with the understanding that they were not to be Anglo Americans. The Mexican government installed its soldiers, forts, and officials along Texas's border with Arkansas and Louisiana and along the gulf coast to discourage independent immigration. It also closed the legal loopholes on bringing slaves into Mexican territory. It made Mier y Terán commandant general for the Eastern Interior Provinces of Mexico, including Coahuila y Texas, and charged him with enforcing the new law—which was appropriate, but also ironic, as he had not recommended or anticipated some of its stricter provisions.

From the conservative Mexican perspective, however, officials were acting prudently to stem a threat to Mexican control of Texas. And from this perspective, the threat could still be considered manageable. The empresario attempts were faltering anyway; even DeWitt, despite a reprieve, would fail to fulfill his contract in 1831 and would not ask for a renewal. True, there were thousands of colonists and independent adventurers from the United States now inhabiting Texas after a decade of immigration, many of them with continuing allegiance to their own homeland, but they were not organized or united on any broad level. The most cohesive group might be said to have been Austin's colonists, but they numbered only a few thousand and often disagreed among themselves on political allegiance and governance questions. Other potential immigrants from the United States had stayed away, uncertain about American fortunes in Mexican Texas and uneasy as early as 1822 over its reputation as a haven for American criminals.

Yet the Law of April 6 drew the first stirrings of unified protest. Among the protesters were members of Austin's colonies and federalist Tejanos who still rejected the centralists and welcomed the economic and republican promise of the American influx. The federalist Tejanos were joined by political and economic leaders in Coahuila, other federalists who continued to welcome Anglo settlement and enterprise in their state. Austin himself still professed strong loyalty to the Mexican government, rejecting the criticisms he suffered from "bawling democrats who know nothing of liberty but licentiousness," but his loyalty had limits, as he indicated to T. F. Leaming in July 1830.

> As to my colony I can say that we have been true and religiously faithful in our acts and in our views, to Mexico—and so we will remain—but I also say that Mexico cannot oppress us alive—we may be overwhelmed & anihilated—but we cannot be treated like children nor like slaves. . . .

With more Mexican soldiers at Nacogdoches, Goliad, and San Antonio and new presidios on the coast, immigration from the United States slowed but did not stall. One complication was created by empresarios De Zavala, Vehlein, and Burnet, who in 1830, having been unsuccessful, had passed their grant rights to the Galveston Bay and Texas Land Company. In violation of law, this company began selling land scrip to immigrants as if it had full authority to establish titles to the 13 million acres encompassed by the three grants.

Trouble at Anahuac

The next major event in the struggle over Texas identity occurred in 1832, in what became known as the first of two Anahuac disturbances. Anahuac, perched above the mouth of the Trinity River on Galveston Bay, had been established as a coastal fort after passage of the Law of April 6. The commander of the garrison, John (or

General Manuel de Mier y Terán worked diligently to address problems for the Mexican government as American colonization in Texas—legal and illegal—continued, but he despaired of maintaining effective control of the frontier.

Juan) Davis Bradburn, was a Virginian by birth who had become a Mexican military officer. General Terán had sent Bradburn to establish the fort at Anahuac and enforce Mexican laws. In 1831, Bradburn was joined by customs collector George Fisher. The exemption from tariffs had expired for Austin's colonists, and the government wanted to collect the monies to use to fund its Texas forts. Fisher angered Texans not only by insisting on imposing the customs duties, which was, after all, his job, but by decreeing that all ships in Texas ports had to obtain permission to sail at Anahuac. This meant that ships at Brazoria had to make a trip of more than a hundred miles to gain official government approval to operate from the Texas coast. Even Austin protested the situation at Anahuac, asking Bradburn if it was the government's goal to have Texas "totally broken up and all commerce totally annihilated?" An exasperated General Terán, who had learned of ships defiantly sailing by Anahuac, their commanders refusing to pay customs duties, replied pointedly, "You want the government to adopt a more liberal policy. You should say what liberality you long for beyond that which you already receive." Terán did, however, establish a customs house at Brazoria to address the problem.

Anahuac remained a trouble spot, for tensions had also quickly developed between Bradburn as a representative of the centralist government and the federalists as well as prickly Anglo immigrants impatient with Mexican government restraints in general.

The first problem surfaced in Bradburn's feud with Jose Francisco Madero, another Mexican official, but a member of the federalist state's-rights camp. Madero had been sent by the state of Coahuila y Texas to Anahuac to issue land titles to residents of the area who had arrived before 1828. Bradburn, citing the National Colonization Law of 1824, argued that Madero had no authority to do so within the ten-league coastal reserve.

Madero, briefly jailed by Bradburn, nonetheless issued the land titles and also formed an *ayuntamiento,* or local government, at a nearby Trinity River community which quickly became known simply as "Liberty." It was within Madero's authority to create a municipality with its own governmental structure, but this further rankled Bradburn as a representative of the centralist government.

The Anglo settlers of Liberty and the surrounding area embraced the *ayuntamiento.* They resented the garrison, whose members included former convicts and a handful of runaway slaves. Further, the settlers were increasingly annoyed by Bradburn's attempts to regulate them; under orders from Terán, Bradburn was checking land titles and the licenses of Anglo American lawyers. Meanwhile, Fisher continued to impose customs duties on ships already anchored in Galveston Bay and on the Brazos River.

Tensions escalated when Bradburn imprisoned Anglo law partners William Barret Travis and Patrick Jack. The two men had entered Texas from the American South, Jack in 1830 and Travis in 1831, clearly after the Law of April 6, 1830; however, both had obtained land grants in Austin's colony. An Alabama lawyer, Travis in a few years would become an icon of Texas history; like so many other new immigrants, he was both fleeing the past—in his case, an apparently unhappy marriage—and seeking an opportunity to distinguish himself economically, socially, and politically in the new environment. As he practiced law and learned Spanish in Anahuac, he and Jack had already organized a citizens' "militia." Ostensibly it was for defense against Indians, but their antagonism against the Mexican garrison was already obvious. The pair then tried by roundabout means to convince Bradburn that a large American force from Louisiana was coming to claim the runaway slaves in the garrison.

When an exasperated Bradburn placed Travis and Jack in jail, a group of Anglo colonists marched to within six miles of the fort, capturing the nineteen cavalrymen attached to the Anahuac garrison and stopping at Turtle Bayou. The colonists sent a delegation to Brazoria to obtain a cannon to use against the fort. When the military commander at Velasco, Domingo de Ugartechea, attempted to stop the ship carrying the cannon, the battle of Velasco ensued. An estimated 100–150 Texans fought 90–200 Mexicans under Ugartechea, and there were casualties on both sides. Ugartechea had to surrender when his troops ran out of ammunition.

Meanwhile, on Turtle Bayou, the insurgents produced the Turtle Bayou resolutions. Significantly, they represented themselves not as wishing to sever Texas from Mexico but as supporting the federalists in Mexico. Federalist forces were still battling the centralists and had just achieved a major military victory under the leadership of Antonio Lopez de Santa Anna, who nine years earlier had been instrumental in toppling Emperor Iturbide. With a somewhat hazy understanding of what was happening in Mexico, the resolution framers pledged their "lives and fortunes" in support of "the highly talented and distinguished Chieftain—General Santa Anna."

One outcome of the federalist-centralist battles and the growing troubles with Anglo settlers was the suicide of General Terán. Terán had served Mexico under both federalist and centralist regimes only to see civil war divide Mexico and daunting problems multiply in Texas. Terán had support throughout Mexico as a strong enough leader to end Santa Anna's revolt and bring federalists and centralists together. But he recognized the precariousness of his position as a representative of the centralist government, and he despaired over Texas. On July 2, he wrote presciently to another Mexican official, "How could we expect to hold Texas when we do not even agree among ourselves. . . . As it is, we are lost. . . . Texas is lost. . . . What will become of Texas? Whatever God wills." The next day, he killed himself with his sword.

The controversy at Anahuac ended—temporarily—when Bradburn's military superior, Colonel José de las Piedras, replaced the unpopular garrison commander and released the prisoners. (Bradburn's cavalry had already been released.) But Travis and Jack continued to cause trouble. The centralist government still controlled the fort at Anahuac, and the two Anglo attorneys encouraged garrison members to reject its authority. Finally, a federalist officer relocated the whole garrison to the Rio Grande.

Growth of Political Opposition

In reviewing the first Anahuac disturbance, it is important to note that not all colonists supported Travis and Jack, considering them rash troublemakers. In fact, newcomers and observers in Mexican Texas often found that many colonists cared little for political turmoil, being determinedly individualistic and concerned with building their own fortunes in the demanding but bounteous regions of eastern and southeastern Texas. And overall, despite the Law of April 6 and the furor surrounding Bradburn, the Mexican government had imposed only intermittent and limited controls on their presence.

Many Texans, however, were frustrated and impatient with the government's continued political shifts and its attempts to exercise authority even as it failed to provide for the safety and well-being of its citizens. In 1832 Béxar Tejano leaders sent a petition to the Mexican Congress in which they complained of the "inaction and apathy" of the government as Comanches scourged their area, in the absence of any sizable and effective frontier military. Texas trade was languishing, and the Law of April 6 had only ensured that "capitalists and industrious and honorable" immigrants from the States were kept out, whereas "wicked adventurers and others who constitute the dregs of society" kept arriving.

The primarily Anglo colonists—along with others who had slipped into Texas without the sanction of empresario contracts—also spoke out. In October 1832, fifty-eight representatives of the colonists met at San Felipe and petitioned the Mexican government for, among other things, a repeal of the Law of April 6 and separate statehood for Texas. Stephen F. Austin presided, walking a fine line between his responsibilities to the government and to the colonists. To the delegates, the convention was their way of democratically advancing political agendas, but to Mexican officials, it was illegal, as only the Coahuila y Texas legislature could file petitions. Further, the meeting was evidence of insurgency. The idea of a Texas separated from Coahuila also sparked Mexican fears of a Texas separated from Mexico itself.

Among the Tejano settlements, only Goliad had sent a delegation to the convention, and Austin particularly wanted to get the *ayuntamiento* of San Antonio involved as well, as Béxar leaders favored reform and would be important allies in convincing the Mexican government that the petitioners were still loyal Mexican subjects. He was working toward this end when Anglo colonists called for a second convention in April 1833 at San Felipe. In the meantime, the federalist Santa Anna won election as Mexico's president, leading to hopes in Texas that the new government would look more favorably on the idea of statehood and accept a great degree of local autonomy.

At the convention of 1833, Austin recapped why the delegates had been called together: "The political system under which Texas has heretofore been governed, tends to check the growth of the country, and to produce confusion and insecurity, rather than to extend protection to lives liberty and property."

The convention called for the repeal of the Law of April 6, for frontier defense, for tariff exemptions, and for more effective and efficient handling of criminal acts and legal disputes. It again petitioned that the union of Coahuila and Texas be "dissolved, abrogated, and perpetually cease," with Texas residents "authorized to institute and establish a separate state government, which will be in accordance with the federal constitution." This time delegates went so far as to prepare a provisional state constitution.

The convention appointed Austin, Erasmo Seguín, and physician James B. Miller to take the petition to Mexico City. Some of his own colonists did not trust Austin, given his previous attempts to placate the Mexican government. One of these, John P. Coles, wrote ominously, "[I]f for the want of proper Exertion on his part the application should fail Col. Austin will be a Ruined man in Texas." But Austin had come to the conclusion that he must press for statehood, and that if the petition failed, he and Texas would have to prepare for war.

Miller, tending victims of a cholera epidemic, was unable to make the trip. Seguín had tried to anticipate such a petition in 1824 when he served in the Mexican constitutional congress that had combined Coahuila and Texas. At that time, he had labored to insert a provision allowing Texas to petition for separate statehood. Now, however, although he continued to favor separation, he declined to make the trip.

Thus, Austin made the journey by himself in the late spring of 1833, nearing Mexico City in a countryside still ravaged by civil war, with a revolt against Santa Anna's new federalist government already in progress. Austin was ready to align himself with this government and aware that "[t]he consequence of a failure [to win statehood] will no doubt be war." He pledged, "So soon as I am convinced that there is no hope of success I shall return as quick as possible by water." Austin was right in his assessment of the seriousness of the situation, but he would be unable to follow through on his pledge. He would not see Texas again until the late summer of 1835.

The Burgeoning American Presence and the Impetus to Revolution, 1833–1835

In 1835, the number of Texas residents who had migrated from the United States reached approximately 30,000. Many were diligent settlers, others were young male adventurers who might or might not settle down. Most were drawn by the potential of Mexican Texas for farming, stock-raising, trade, town-building, and/or land ownership and speculation. Many were "pushed" from the States, not necessarily fugitives from the law but people who were trying to leave financial and other failures behind. One visitor from Louisiana noted, "[W]hen a new-commer averred that he had *ran away from his creditors* ONLY, he was regarded as a gentleman of the *first water.*" Whatever their circumstances, their participation in the definition of an American identity would have significant consequences for everyone involved with the province.

Continued Immigration and Colonization

When Austin left for Mexico City in 1833, families and adventurers from the United States continued to cross the Sabine illegally, disregarding the Law of April 6 and hoping to seize the opportunity to build homes and/or find prosperity in Mexican territory. Some were drawn by an 1833 book on Texas by Austin's widowed cousin from Connecticut, Mary Austin Holley. The cultured Holley had made an initial tour of the Texas settlements in 1831. Her travel account provided a detailed picture of life in the Anglo colonies. Among other observations, she noted the work necessary to establish one's family in the colonies, and the lack of ready and regular supplies: Mattress cases brought from the States, she advised, could be stuffed with tree moss, perhaps with "some layers of wool, well carded" on top of the moss for warmth.

Despite the constant need to create whatever one wanted or needed, Holley noted that "even privations become pleasures" as "people grow ingenious in overcoming difficulties." She characterized the Texans she met as "kind and hospitable,"

In frontier Texas, the natural environment often provided challenges to travelers. With this illustration from an 1834 book titled *A Visit to Texas*, J. T. Hammond conveys the size of the thick cane breaks through which travelers found and forged routes. *(CN 11582, The Center for American History, The University of Texas at Austin)*

like many travelers in the settlements finding them generous with what they did have. And she spoke glowingly of the natural abundance of the country.

Others were less sanguine about the privations of life in Texas. Ann Coleman, arriving in Brazoria in 1832, noted with humorous consternation the common practice of sharing a room—and even a bed—with one's hosts when visiting at isolated cabin homes. Carolyn Ernst von Roeder von Hinueber, daughter of German settlers who arrived in 1831, would write, "No one can imagine what a degree of want there was of the merest necessities of life, and it is difficult for me now to understand how we managed to live and get along under the circumstances, yet we did so in some way."

In spite of the challenges, land speculators as well as farm families continued to be undeterred by the Law of April 6, eager to claim tracts of land unsettled by Mexicans or U.S. or European immigrants, and able to devise strategies to do so. Jane McManus Storm Cazneau is an example. Daughter of a New York congressman, Cazneau arrived in Texas in December 1832 with scrip from the Galveston Bay and Texas Land Company and a recommendation from former U.S. vice president and speculator Aaron Burr stating that she could "send out one or two hundred substantial settlers in less time . . . than any man or half a Dozen men whom I this day Know." At San Felipe, she was designated a Mexican citizen and received the transfer of an eleven-league grant through the approval of the San Felipe *alcalde*. Stymied in her own efforts to settle a colony of Germans, she sought to act as an agent providing immigrants to Austin's colonies and was a speculator in Texas lands for many years.

In the meantime, Power and Hewetson moved forward with a series of empresario contracts, because they, too, were seeking to settle Europeans. In 1833, Power journeyed to Ireland and returned with more than 300 settlers, most from his home parish on Ireland's southeast coast. Most of these immigrants would die of cholera, either en route in New Orleans or shortly after reaching Texas, but the remainder would join a group of Mexican settlers enticed from Coahuila.

Another colonization effort had gotten underway in late 1832 with the blessings of the Mexican government. James Grant, a Scotsman who had established himself in the political hierarchy of Coahuila and Texas, and Englishman John Charles Beales, a Mexico City–based surgeon, obtained a land grant far to the west of the settled colonies, between the Nueces and the Rio Grande in South Texas. They were allowed to bring 800 European families. Beales traveled in late 1833 and early 1834 to the area with fifty-nine colonists—some German, some English, and some American. They settled on a creek near the head of the Nueces and surveyed their surroundings with some despair. Although their new settlement—named Dolores, after Beales's Mexican wife—was well chosen, much of the country was desert. They found little game to provide meat; crops could not thrive without irrigation in an area of so little rainfall and such intense heat; wood for building was some distance away; and the Comanches regularly passed through the area and harassed its occupants.

No one except the Comanches would contest Grant and Beales for their chunk of South Texas desert, but in the more desirable areas, by 1834 the land ownership situation was hopelessly tangled among the various empresario and other claims. Over the years since the grants had begun, settlers had located outside the perimeters originally determined or had established settlements under competing authorities. DeWitt's and De León's colonists continued to argue over boundaries. To the south and west, long-term Mexican residents and newer immigrant residents occupied a checkerboard, claiming title based on Goliad *ayuntamiento* authority or on the empresario grants of De León, McMullen and McGloin, or Power and Hewetson. Hundreds of immigrants from the United States were squatting on the lands east of Austin's colony, which Vehlein had turned over to the Galveston Bay and Texas Land Company. Sterling Clack Robertson was angrily disputing the claims of the absent Austin to the grant Robertson had failed to colonize, which had become the "upper colony" of Austin and his friend and partner Samuel May Williams. Eleven-league grants to Mexican citizens from the Mexican government had passed into the hands of speculators in Texas and the United States.

One group consistently left out was the Texas Cherokees. They had made repeated attempts to gain title to the lands north of Nacogdoches. They lived, farmed, maintained towns, raised livestock, and traded with their Mexican, Anglo, and Indian neighbors on these lands. But the government included these lands in various unfulfilled empresario grants. As commandant general, Terán had tried in 1831 to secure land title for them, and in 1833 Chief Bowles and other tribal leaders had journeyed to Monclova, then the capital of Coahuila and Texas, in an attempt to have their claims recognized. Not only did these efforts fail, but new U.S. immigrants swelled settlements to the east, west, and south of the Cherokees, pressing in upon them.

Texans of African extraction also found themselves constantly hard-pressed. Free Africans lived increasingly uncertain lives and had little hope of gaining a plot of land, while slaves continued to work land for their owners.

Many of the immigrants arriving in the early 1830s, and particularly in 1833 and after, had little patience with Indian or even Mexican land claims. Neither did they feel the necessity of allegiance to the Mexican government; whether they settled in Austin's colonies or other areas, they were more likely to align themselves with the Travises and Jacks of Texas. They were inclined to be contemptuous of slow diplomatic efforts when their freedom to locate where they pleased and do what they pleased was at issue.

Tejano Perspectives

What of the Mexican population, many of whose roots coiled deep in Spanish and Mexican Texas? Some still lived their lives far from the U.S. immigrants' influences. Along the Rio Grande far to the west, in 1833 El Paso boasted a population of 5,801 and continued, as part of the Mexican state of Chihuahua, to develop as a Mexican trading center with no "Texas" identity. Its leading citizens were more concerned with frequent Apache depredations than with the political disruptions to their south in Mexico or to their east in Texas, although they kept a wary eye on American expansion in general.

Many of the 4,000 Mexicans within the Texas portion of the state of Coahuila y Texas had become disillusioned with the Anglo presence. This was particularly true in Victoria and Goliad, where Tejanos and Anglos had been at odds since DeWitt's colony had been established. Tejanos complained that Anglos violated the law, rustling cattle and smuggling and generally being rude and disruptive. Religious differences had become painfully apparent, with few Anglo colonists even keeping up the pretense of adherence to Catholicism, and many expressing a prejudice against Catholics as "papists." The Anglo immigrants combined republican spirit with a Protestant belief in free will and an individual relationship with God, impatient or suspicious of the ritualized and hierarchical Catholic faith.

Some Tejanos continued to see a partnership with Anglo immigrants as the economic lifeblood of Texas, the only clear hope for a region that had suffered too long from the crudest frontier conditions. For this reason, liberal Tejanos continued to support the Anglos' attempts to win exceptions to Mexican laws

In 1834 Lino Sánchez y Tapia drew this view of the Goliad presidio from a late-1820s sketch, providing an early depiction of the site that would soon figure in the Texas Revolution. *(The Yale Collection of Western Americana, Beinecke Rare Book and Manuscript Library)*

against slavery. With slaves and the right techniques, they could grow enough cotton to be exported, building an economy beyond subsistence and barter. Added to this economic interest was the shared desire among many Tejanos and Anglos for an end to the vacillating political regimes in Mexico City and the triumph of a consistent liberal federalist agenda.

Tejano leaders had reason to be proud of the regional political system they had nurtured before and during the influx of U.S. immigrants. The Tejanos had developed a workable and often farsighted range of solid frontier adaptations, from water systems to livestock roundups, from educational initiatives to military response units. The more thoughtful of their Anglo colleagues were beginning to learn from and build upon these adaptations.

However, there is no denying that by late in the Mexican period, Tejano communities were beginning to feel cut off from and out of step with their Anglo neighbors. One Anglo observer noted that "[t]he Mexican population is Entirely sepperateed from the N. American people in Texas." Tejanos continued to share much of the Anglos' impatience with the Mexican government; in fact, Tejanos at Goliad had held their own meeting in January 1833 and concluded in their memoria, "[L]et's be republicans, let's be men, let's defend our rights, or let's not exist at all." But too often they found the Anglo declarations and actions to be precipitous and intemperate. As newcomers, they became political agitators without any sense of the intricacies of Texas's frontier relationship with the Saltillo and Mexico City governments.

Austin and the Developing Crisis

Stephen F. Austin continued to pursue the careful diplomatic course, working dutifully in Mexico City for Texas statehood. He spent months in the Mexican capitol, enduring a devastating cholera epidemic, fluctuating responses from Santa Anna's government, and concerns about the outcome of a cholera outbreak in his own colonies. Finally, in October 1833, deeply frustrated, he informed Vice President Valentín Gómez Farias "that Texas must be made a state by the Govt. or she would make herself one." He also wrote a fateful letter to the *ayuntamiento* of San Antonio recommending that the Texas *ayuntamientos* "unite in a measure to organize a local government independent of Coahuila, even though the general government withholds its consent."

Austin continued to meet with Mexican officials, winning such concessions as a repeal of the suspension of unfulfilled empresario contracts in the Law of April 6. The Mexican Congress agreed to officially allow U.S. immigration into Texas again, beginning in May 1834. But the officials remained cool to the idea of statehood for Texas. In December, Austin started home, feeling that he had made some progress even on the statehood question. In January of 1834, however, when he reached Saltillo, the capital of Coahuila y Texas, he was arrested by the commandant there, on orders from Mexico City. Austin's remark to Farias had caused suspicion, and officials had learned of Austin's letter to San Antonio and considered it treasonous.

Austin was held in a series of prisons in Mexico for almost a year, then waited in Mexico City through early 1835 for resolution of his case. Shortly after Austin's arrest, Farias dispatched Colonel Juan N. Almonte to inspect the various political regions of Texas. In his 1834 report, Almonte noted many of the same conditions that Terán had noted in 1828, but did not sound any significant alarms about the loyalties of the population, whom he found generally peaceful. He did note the constant influx of immigrants from the United States in the Nacogdoches area and the need for adequate troops to maintain Mexican law.

The Coahuila y Texas Congress of 1833—still largely federalist and, in general, friendly to Anglo immigration and economic activity—had actually passed a number of liberal reforms advantageous to developing Texas, including approval of English as a legal language. The next year, while Austin was held in prison, the state government passed further political reforms to benefit Texans, including some needed judicial reforms and the addition of another Texas representative in the state legislature. Such measures helped to quiet the Texas frontier while Austin was imprisoned. In the colonies, this gave a "peace party," including empresario David Burnet and various Austin supporters, the upper hand against a "war party," including Travis and Austin colonist Jared Groce's son-in-law William Wharton. The latter group consisted in general of younger, brasher, less-established immigrants (those who had entered Texas in the early 1830s), as well as more-established settlers disillusioned with controversies over land titles and the general state of the region under Mexican rule. Land speculator A. C. Allen of Nacogdoches noted, however, "The people generally appear to be satisfied with what has been done for the present [and] are willing to defer the state question. They consider their pro[s]pects truly cheering."

Ultimately, though, any hope of bringing Texans smoothly under a liberal Mexican system of state government was undermined by the government's instability and the escalating demands of Texas residents, whether newly arrived or long-term. Texans were accustomed to freedom from much government control. Hope was also undermined by Santa Anna's surprising 1834 shift to centralist policies, and his declaration that he was the sole Mexican government authority.

Centralists and Colonists

In 1835, as Santa Anna installed centralist officials and his new Congress dismissed the federal Constitution of 1824 for a set of centralist laws, the Coahuila and Texas governor, Agustin Viesca, tried unsuccessfully to rally Texas as well as Coahuila residents against the repressive measures.

Texas residents, confused and divided over the appropriate response to this latest and spectacular shift of power, were unable to see the possible dire consequences for their region. Many had considered Santa Anna a good federalist, and they had reservations about supporting the state government of Coahuila y Texas, which appeared to favor a few Texans in land speculation, in a fight with the federal government. Only Béxar sent a group of militiamen under Erasmo Seguín's son Juan to help defend the state at its new capital of Monclova; by the time they arrived, however, Viesca backed down.

Through the early summer of 1835, Texas residents had discussed what to do; some, including leaders in the Austin colony capital of San Felipe, argued that the new centralist regime posed a real and immediate threat. But even Anglo settlers considered members of the "war party" counseled "union, concert, and moderation."

Meanwhile, tensions at Anahuac had erupted again over the collection of tariffs, and William Barret Travis again emerged at the center of the resistance, in late June leading fifty men in an attack on the fort that forced the commander's surrender. This action sparked no rebellious unity among Texas colonists; in fact, many rushed to disassociate themselves from Travis's action. Mexican and Anglo settlers alike seemed to wish to adjust to the new government and go about their business. Mexican and Anglo officials either accepted the centralist agenda or vacillated between rebellious and conciliatory rhetoric.

There were disturbing—and true—rumors, however, of a Mexican military force on its way to Texas to subjugate a rebellious populace swollen and agitated by people from the United States who were not Mexican citizens. Santa Anna's brother-in-law, Brigadier General Martín Perfecto de Cos, had been troubled by reports of an increased influx of immigrants from the United States. Observers called the 1835 migration "astonishing," with reports of 250 families locating in the Nacogdoches area in one month and a thousand colonists reaching the Brazos River in January, with another thousand in February.

Cos was also angered by reports of the immigrants' continued resistance to government policies, as evidenced by the troubles at Anahuac. Reassured by the minister of war that troops would be available after they suppressed a revolt in the Mexican state of Zacatecas, Cos wrote that such an expedition would let "[t]hose ungrateful strangers know that the Govno. has sufficient power to repress them" and that they should leave Mexico "if they do not want to submit themselves to its laws."

Hints of this impending punitive action from Mexican troops sparked new talk of concerted opposition in Texas. Public meetings were held across the frontier communities, and people began to talk of a convention, or consultation, to address the governmental threat. Both those who wanted to move cautiously but purposefully and those who breathed open defiance saw a convention as a vehicle for action.

So did Stephen F. Austin, who had been released from his extended imprisonment and detention, in part through the influence of Almonte, and returned to Texas via New Orleans. In that city, he called—defiantly now—for new immigrants, asserting "I wish a great immigration this fall and winter from Kentucky, Tennessee, every where . . . any how." Austin was ready to declare with other members of the former "peace party" that "Texas shall be effectually, and fully, Americanized."

Both firebrand orators and respected leaders were warning that the centralist forces would disrupt and destroy the settlements—particularly the Anglo settlements—and deny the rights of their citizens, all in violation of the overturned federal Constitution of 1824. Instigators of rebellion argued that the centralist government, not the residents of Texas, had abrogated Mexican liberal principles, and in this way they sidestepped the question of whether it was right and moral for Anglo Americans to seize control of Texas from Mexico. But this was the implicit agenda for many as Anglo Texas communities in particular galvanized into military preparedness against the oncoming army. At the end of September 1835, Texas was teetering on the edge of revolution.

Conclusion

In 1820 and 1821, Spanish and Mexican officials saw U.S. colonization efforts as an opportunity to strengthen Mexico's devastated northern frontier and to offset the threat of U.S. expansion by controlling and limiting immigration through an empresario system. When Stephen F. Austin first entered Béxar, this had seemed a feasible course to follow in Texas: What did a new republic of 6 million have to fear from a few attempts at colonization in its remote regions? Few Mexican citizens could be drawn to these colonies. And what did Mexico have to lose? Either the colonizers would do their work well and reinforce Mexican claims by occupying and cultivating the land and building towns and trade networks or they would forfeit the grants, and the officials would devise another remedy for the problems of maintaining the northern frontier.

In Austin, Mexican authorities had found an Anglo entrepreneur initially devoted to his charge to uphold a Mexican Texas. They had also selected other empresarios, such as Martin De León, Joseph Vehlein, and Vincente Filisola, who could be expected to remain loyal to the republic of Mexico. The government had offered the colonizers generous terms in establishing settlers.

When it became clear that colonization was not working as authorities had hoped it would, the centralist government attempted to stop most immigration from the United States with the Law of April 6. Even after this, however, the Mexican Congress and the state government in Coahuila continued to establish policies favorable to settlers wishing to participate in the development of Mexican Texas.

Yet it became clear that the immigration from the United States had spiraled beyond Mexico's control. Texas residents had different perceptions of their loyalties and relationship with the government than did the officials in Mexico City and Coahuila. From Texans' vantage point, their needs had been neglected, particularly with the constant political upheaval in the Mexican capital. They had had to struggle at the local level with disputes over land titles, troubles with hostile Indians, and lack of an economy beyond a system of barter. In a way, the isolated life had suited them, for most residents demanded considerable autonomy, but this demand was constantly undercut by Texas's position as part of a larger Mexican state.

Tejanos and U.S. immigrants alike chafed under the sometimes indifferent, sometimes apparently arbitrary rule of a federal government always in flux. They also chafed under the government's retreat from the republican principles in the Mexican Constitution of 1824.

At the same time, some Anglo immigrants cared little for Mexican claims to the region, and they behaved in more exclusionary ways as their numbers grew. Such changes demonstrated that Anglo hegemony was growing. The term "manifest destiny" had not yet been coined, but the feeling it represented—that Anglo Americans had both the God-given right and the duty to claim and develop the continent to their own ends—was increasingly evident. Anglo Americans had little regard for the rights of Tejanos, Indians, and African Americans and were dissatisfied with any attempts of the Mexican government to exert its authority.

Who, then, would have the power to define Texas in the future? In the following months, that question was to be fought out from Béxar to the South Texas plains to the coastal marshes and bayous bordering the San Jacinto.

SUGGESTED READINGS

The arrival and settlement in Texas of the first significant numbers of Anglo-Americans has been heavily researched over the years. Eugene Barker led in his work on the chief Anglo colonizer, Stephen F. Austin, and his colony, *The Austin Papers* (1924–1928) and *The Life of Stephen F. Austin: Founder of Texas, 1793–1836* (1969), but Gregg Cantrell's *Stephen F. Austin: Empresario of Texas* (1999) supersedes the Barker biography. Among other works focusing on Anglo pioneers in this period, the most prominent and popular has been Noah Smithwick's *The Evolution of a State, or Recollections of Old Texas Days*, first published in 1900; despite concerns about its veracity, it is an entertaining and illuminating first-person look at early Texas life.

In addition to the focus on Anglo pioneers, there has been scholarship on the dynamics of Mexican rule in this period. In particular, Paul Lack's *The Texas Revolutionary Experience, A Political and Social History, 1835–1836* (1992) provides insight into the ways in which Mexico governed this portion of Coahuila y Texas and the challenges the government faced in the years leading up to the Revolution.

Recent scholarship has also explored Mexican self-government and experience in Texas in this period. The most prominent work is Andrés Tijerina's *Tejanos and Texas under the Mexican Flag, 1821–1836* (1994), which in part argues that Mexican Texans had already established many frontier government forms adopted by emerging Anglo leaders. Useful regional sources are Jesus F. de la Teja and John Wheat's "Béxar: Profile of a Tejano Community, 1820–1832," *Southwestern Historical Quarterly* (1983), and W. H. Timmons's "The El Paso Area in the Mexican Period, 1821–1848," *Southwestern Historical Quarterly* (1980).

For the origins of American-imported slavery in Texas, a key source is Randolph B. Campbell's *An Empire for Slavery: The Peculiar Institution in Texas, 1821–1865* (1989). For an examination of a forming Texas identity, see Mark E. Nackman, *A Nation Within a Nation: The Rise of Texas Nationalism* (1975).

Colonization Efforts, 1821–1829

Lester G. Bugbee pioneered in documenting "The Old Three Hundred," Austin's early settlers, with his article of that title in *The Quarterly of the Texas State Historical Association* (1897). For early Anglo women's experiences, part 1 of Jo Ella Powell Exley's *Texas Tears and Texas Sunshine: Voices of Frontier Women* (1985) provides three early first-person accounts, and Dianna Everett's *The Texas Cherokees: A People Between Two Fires, 1819–1840* (1990) chronicles the Cherokees' attempts to establish a home in East Texas. For information on prominent people and events of the period, the *New Handbook of Texas* (1996), edited by Ron Tyler, Douglas Barnett, and Roy Barkley, is invaluable; the reader will find clear and specific entries for such subjects as the individual empresarios and the Fredonian rebellion.

Growth of Political and Cultural Tensions, 1829–1833

With Stephen F. Austin remaining a key political figure, Cantrell's *Stephen F. Austin: Empresario of Texas* helps explain the overall political tensions and developments, as does "The Austin-Leaming Correspondence, 1828–1836," edited by Andreas Reichstein, in the *Southwestern Historical Quarterly* (1985). Much primary material for the events in this period and those immediately surrounding it can be found in Ernest Wallace, David M. Vigness, and George B. Ward, eds., *Documents of Texas History* (1994).

The Burgeoning American Presence and the Impetus to Revolution, 1833–1835

Continuing empresario attempts are chronicled in such works as Linda S. Hudson's *Mistress of Manifest Destiny: A Biography of Jane McManus Storm Cazneau 1807–1878* (2001) and Carl Coke Rister's *Comanche Bondage,* first published in 1955 and republished in the 1980s. The former deals in part with Cazneau's attempts to colonize in Texas, the latter with John Charles Beale's attempt to establish a colony between the Nueces and the Rio Grande. For a detailed look at a colonization effort, see Malcolm D. Maclean, ed., *Papers Concerning Robertson's Colony in Texas,* seventeen volumes published between 1974 and 1991.

For Tejano experience and relations with Anglos, see not only the works cited above but also Timothy M. Matovina's *Tejano Religion and Ethnicity, San Antonio, 1821–1860* (1995) and Arnoldo de León's "Early Anglo Settlers View Mexicans with Hostility" in Sam W. Haynes and Cary D. Wintz, eds., *Major Problems in Texas History* (2002).

The variety of people seeking refuge in Texas is represented by the Cherokees, with Everett's *The Texas Cherokees* the standard, and by the beginning of German migration, as chronicled in Crystal Sasse Ragsdale's *The Golden Free Land: The Reminiscences and Letters of Women on an American Frontier* (1976).

7

Revolution, 1835–1836

B y September 1835, Juan Seguín had become convinced that the time for revolution was "close at hand." The twenty-eight-year-old political chief in San Antonio had been baptized as an infant in the community, as had his father, Erasmo, and his grandfather, Santiago. The Seguíns had successfully navigated a number of Spanish and Mexican political shifts that affected their community. Juan had his father's example of befriending and partnering with the new Anglo immigrants to Texas. The Seguíns had even taken in Stephen F. Austin's younger brother, James, and introduced him to the Spanish language and Mexican culture.

Now the younger Seguín wanted to take a stand against Santa Anna. In the spring his militia had been the only one from Texas to respond to Coahuila y Texas governor Agustín Viesca's call for resistance to Santa Anna's imposition of centralist control in Mexico. When that attempt failed in Monclova, Seguín and his company returned in June, as he wrote in his memoir, "pledg[ing] to use all our influence to rouse Texas against the tyrannical government of Santa Anna." Yet both within his own native community and among the settlements made up primarily of U.S. immigrants, people either tried to avoid actions that would affect their private fortunes and daily lives, or they remained confused and divided on what actions to take in response to the centralist control and the looming threat from Mexican troops.

On September 27, Seguín traveled to Salvador Flores's ranch to convince the Mexican ranch owners along the San Antonio River that they should arm themselves against the current Mexican government. He was to play an active role in

CHAPTER 7	Revolution, 1835–1836
SEPT. 1835	Gen. Martín Perfecto de Cos reaches the Texas coast
OCT. 1835	Texians refuse to give up Mexican cannon in incident near Gonzales; Cos arrives in San Antonio de Béxar; Texian volunteers march on San Antonio and camp at nearby creek; colonists' "Permanent Council" attempts to devise a revolutionary government
NOV. 1835	"Consultation" continues work of Permanent Council; Texians remain camped outside San Antonio
DEC. 1835	The Texian volunteer siege force takes San Antonio; small volunteer force remaining in San Antonio fortifies the Alamo for siege
FEB. 1836	Provisional Texian government has fallen apart; Santa Anna begins siege of Alamo
MARCH 1836	Texian convention meets at Washington-on-the-Brazos, declares independence, and sets up new interim government; Alamo falls; Texas residents flee Santa Anna's troops in the Runaway Scrape; James Fannin and his troops are captured by Gen. José de Urrea and most are executed (Fannin Massacre)
APRIL 1836	Sam Houston's troops defeat Santa Anna's at San Jacinto and Santa Anna is captured

the upcoming struggle. The participation of Seguín and other Mexican residents with deep Texas roots reminds us that the Revolution was not a simple battle between Anglo colonists and Mexican troops. It was a complex redefining of Texas carried out—often with much tension and confusion—by people with different experiences of and expectations for the region.

The Revolution—Early Months (October–December)

In the fall of 1835, the *Telegraph and Texas Register* newspaper began publication in San Felipe de Austin. It promptly dealt with an issue of some debate, an appropriate name for the people of Texas, concluding, "We believe that, both by the Mexican and American residents of the country, the name commonly used is Texians." Among those responding to Santa Anna's political and military threat, many would soon claim the name "Texian" as an independent—and revolutionary—identity.

Come and Take It

As Juan Seguín rode to the Mexican ranches to encourage revolt, others rode out of San Antonio on a different mission: A company of 100 dragoons under Francisco de Castañeda was being sent by Domingo de Ugartechea, military commander of Texas, to retrieve a cannon provided to the citizens of Gonzales in 1831 for defense against Indians. In the charged political climate, Ugartechea felt it was dangerous for the colonists to possess the cannon, especially because they had already refused to turn it over to one squad sent to retrieve it.

The town of Gonzales, the center of Green DeWitt's colony on the Guadalupe River, had been vulnerable to raids by bands of Indians, and its citizens had gratefully accepted from the Mexican government the protection of a six-pound cannon. Further, they had refused to succumb to the revolutionary fervor circulating through the colonies since 1832. Yet a Mexican soldier had attacked a colonist in September, and there was a sense that the government might be as harsh and uncompromising as some of the revolution-minded were claiming. The cannon quickly became a symbol of potential resistance not to the Indians but to the Mexican government.

This was the situation Ugartechea sought to address by sending the dragoons, with orders to try to retrieve the cannon peaceably. Upon reaching the outskirts of Gonzales, however, the soldiers found their passage blocked: The Guadalupe was rain-swollen and the colonists had removed the ferry. On the other side of the river stood eighteen colonists led by Albert Martin, a local storekeeper. When a Mexican courier swam across the river, Martin informed him that the force must remain on the other side of the river until the local *alcalde*, Andrew Ponton, returned to Gonzales. The colonists then used the time to bury the cannon in a peach orchard and to send out a call for resistance to volunteers from neighboring settlements.

Camped on a high mound across the river, Casteñada repeatedly tried to convey that he had not come to fight and was eager to talk with the colonists' representatives. But volunteer forces were arriving from Fayette and Columbus. The militiamen elected Henry Moore of the Fayette contingent as their commander and applauded the rhetoric that linked their resistance with that of the patriots of the American Revolution. They unearthed the cannon and loaded it with metal scraps, as cannonballs were not available.

Casteñada moved to a less exposed site on the riverbank. But the Texians, now 180 strong, moved across the river during the evening of October 1 and approached the Mexican military camp in the early hours of October 2. They were discovered quickly and there was a short burst of gunfire followed by defensive scrambling on both sides. As the daylight arrived, the two sides skirmished again, the settlers falling back from a 40-man Mexican cavalry charge. Casteñada and Moore then parleyed, without result, Casteñada protesting that he, too, was a supporter of the Constitution and that he had no order, and no desire, to force the cannon issue.

With a makeshift flag flying—white with an outline of the disputed cannon and the emblem "Come and Take It"—the Texians began firing the cannon and their Kentucky rifles as well. Castañeda withdrew rather than "compromis[e] the honor of Mexican arms," for his carbines were no match for the Texians' rifles. The Mexicans had suffered only one or two casualties, the Texians none. Thus ended the first "battle" of the Revolution, significant not for its scope but for its effect: Texians were in open defiance and had shown they would fight.

An Army and Government Form

Meanwhile, the rumored military force sent to require Texas's allegiance to the current Mexican government had arrived, all too real, on Texas soil. General Cos had sailed into Copano Bay with 500 soldiers on September 20, and he scoffed at the revolutionaries' motives, writing, "[I]t is quite useless and vain to cover them with a hypocritical adherence to the federal constitution." Meanwhile, the formerly conciliatory Stephen F. Austin was writing that Cos's own motive was "to destroy and break up the foreign settlements in Texas," concluding that, in response, "WAR is our only resource."

Cos quickly moved his troops to the presidio of La Bahía at Goliad. A volunteer Texian force, made up primarily of Anglo men from Matagorda but including Mexican *vaqueros* (cowboys) and African American freedman Samuel McCulloch, hurriedly gathered to storm La Bahía, but Cos continued moving. Just eight days after the confrontation at Gonzales, these Texians took the inadequately-manned presidio and also took control of Goliad, whose Mexican officials had initially protested, despite some sentiment among the Mexican population in favor of the insurgents. Cos had already arrived with his battalions in San Antonio de Béxar, with every intention of imposing military control over Texas, including disarming colonists and arresting and banishing insurgents. To help him in this endeavor, he had a well-fortified position, a well-trained cavalry, and twenty cannons.

In Gonzales, in the wake of the successful resistance there, volunteer forces began to coalesce into an army: an army bent on winning San Antonio de Béxar away from Cos. Yet this was no well-defined, well-disciplined fighting force. With no clear governing structure to this volunteer enterprise, companies voted on their commanders. As new combinations of militias formed, however, the elected leadership often changed, and there was no commander-in-chief. Enlistment periods were unclear or unenforceable. In many cases, the volunteers—especially young, single men with little to lose—were just looking for a good fight, and almost all militiamen remained fiercely individualistic. Lorenzo de Zavala, the Mexican empresario and statesman casting his lot with the revolutionaries in Texas, warned Stephen F. Austin that although there was "individual patriotism," a "unified patriotism" did not exist: "They will defend their private rights until death; but still they do not realize the necessity for cooperation."

Nonetheless, Austin accepted the role of commander-in-chief when those present in the Gonzales volunteer camp voted on October 11. He was not a military man, and not in very good health, but Austin seemed to be the one candidate on whom the volunteers could agree. No sooner had a commander been chosen than the Texas volunteer army at Gonzales began its march on San Antonio de Béxar. Their course led them directly westward, over the oak-studded savanna and the prairies interspersed with stands of post oak, blackjack oak, and hickory. Along the way, other volunteers joined. Austin had summoned Juan Seguín and, when he arrived, promptly made him a captain. The new captain and Plácido Benavides, *alcalde* in Victoria, both brought Texas Mexican contingents to the revolutionary force. By October 19, this force drew near to San Antonio de Béxar, making camp on Salado Creek.

As the volunteers set up camp on the creek, Texians were struggling toward a rude revolutionary governing system. Almost 100 delegates had been elected to a "Consultation" scheduled for October 15, but with all the military activity and confusion, most delegates were slow in arriving. In the meantime, a "Permanent Council" made up of representatives from San Felipe and a few other communities met and dispatched supplies to Austin's army; they also directed that the land offices be shut down to reduce the tension and turmoil over land claims and took steps to raise funds in the United States for the Revolution.

The Permanent Council was anything but permanent, however, for on November 1, the Consultation took over. With only fifty-eight of the delegates ever in attendance, over the next two weeks this group wrestled to establish the ideological stand to take, whether insistence on a return to the Constitution of 1824 with Texas as a Mexican state or complete independence from Mexico. The divided delegates argued for both courses, with the result that both the principles of the Constitution and Texians' sovereignty were affirmed.

The Consultation also hammered out the structure an independent provisional government should take, devising a general council made up of representatives

Juan Seguín, like his father, Erasmus, a San Antonio native and political leader, sided with the Anglo newcomers in the fight for Texas's freedom from Santa Anna's centralist government. *(Texas State Library and Archives Commission)*

from each municipality. In theory, these representatives were to aid a new executive authority, the Texas governor, sharing in his duties and even extending his powers if and when they deemed it necessary. In reality, the plan would prove troublesome, as would the Consultation's authorization of a regular army, governed by U.S. Army regulations, in addition to the volunteer forces already in the field.

This new Council could authorize a regular army, but it couldn't produce one. It did, however, produce a commander—the popular Sam Houston, already commanding the volunteer troops from Nacogdoches—and give him the rank of major general.

Houston was about to become one of the major figures in Texas history, but he was already a figure of some renown in the United States. A native of Virginia, he had a dramatic past, which included a three-year sojourn with a Cherokee band as a teenager and notable service in the 1814 battle of Horseshoe Bend during the War of 1812. The latter brought him to the attention of General Andrew Jackson. As Jackson's political star rose in the 1820s, Houston had become a leading "Jacksonian Democrat," loyal to a war hero of the frontier who championed a vision of America as an egalitarian republic for Anglos and who seemed to represent the common man against privileged interests. Living in Tennessee after the war, Houston rose to become state governor, acting as "unofficial campaign manager" in Jackson's successful bid for the U.S. presidency in 1828.

Soon thereafter, Governor Houston married nineteen-year-old Eliza Allen, but the marriage ended quickly, mysteriously, and disastrously, with Eliza returning to her parents. Houston then left Tennessee. He had helped the Cherokee band of which he had been a part when the U.S. government "removed" them to Oklahoma Territory, and he now joined them for another three years.

Eventually, Houston again traveled back to the East Coast. In Washington, D.C. in April of 1832 he felt insulted by an Ohio congressman and beat him with a cane. Tried and reprimanded by the House of Representatives, Houston, like many Americans seeking a new start, looked to Texas. He hoped to become an agent for the Galveston Bay and Texas Land Company. When that did not work out, he determined to go anyway.

Houston did, however, have a mission, one provided by his old friend President Jackson: to parley with the Comanches as members of southeastern tribes were pushed toward their territory and to assess the Indian situation in Texas in general. Jackson was particularly interested in the tribes that might act as "buffers" between the Comanches and those tribes being pushed westward.

In Mexican Texas, Houston had set up a law practice and immediately become involved in the political unrest. He served as a delegate to both the Consultation of 1833 in San Felipe and the current Consultation that named him major general of a nonexistent regular army.

In late October Houston had visited the volunteer army camped outside Béxar, finding the men divided as to when to attack the town. Houston suggested that they wait until they had obtained more cannons and were more fully trained. Austin was still the commander, and the army's numbers ebbed and flowed as some men chose to go home and re-provision or see to business there while others arrived.

The Siege of Béxar

The siege began with the volunteer army's arrival outside Béxar, but the first engagement of any note occurred on October 28, when Austin dispatched a ninety-two-man contingent under famed frontiersman James Bowie to locate a site closer to Cos's defenses. Bowie, too, had traveled to Texas with a messy past and an eye to opportunity. Known as a scraper in his native Louisiana, he was already renowned for his use of the "Bowie knife" in a Natchez duel that ended in a violent melee. Bowie had engaged in apparently fraudulent land speculation and "slave running" (taking captured slaves from the Caribbean and selling them in Louisiana). Turning to entrepreneurial opportunities in Texas, he had applied for Mexican citizenship in 1830, won huge land grants, and married Ursula de Veramendi, member of a leading San Antonio family. Veramendi and her influential father, Juan Martín de Veramendi, died in an 1833 cholera epidemic; Bowie continued to try to build his Texas holdings while advocating for war.

Now Bowie's contingent had spent the day of October 27 searching out various sites and had found a good one, at a bend in the San Antonio River near the Mission Concepción, but by then nightfall was approaching. Bowie and his men camped at the mission for the night rather than return to the main army.

This gave Cos an opportunity to attack the small group, and he dispatched 100 infantry and 300 Mexican dragoons. The Texians dug in against the riverbank. In the battle that ensued, the Mexicans' advance with muskets and belching cannons proved ineffective against the Texians' long rifles, accurate at a greater distance than the muskets, and their "snipe-and-hide combat." Only one Texian was fatally wounded. Approximately seventy-six men in the Mexican force were killed or wounded.

Austin, anticipating a clash, had been busily moving the rest of the volunteer army forward and came upon the scene shortly after the Mexican soldiers had retreated. Heartened by the apparent ease with which the contingent had forced the Mexican troops back, Austin wanted to press forward into San Antonio itself. Cooler heads prevailed, however, reminding him of the defensive fortifications into which the soldiers had retreated. Again, the volunteer army made camp, this time at the bend in the San Antonio River.

Now the opposing forces sat and waited—Cos for reinforcements, Austin for reinforcements and for a siege gun or guns that would breach Cos's defenses. Neither could wait with any complacency. On November 2, Austin wrote Dimitt at Goliad, "Whether the army can be kept together long enough to await the arrival of reinforcements, and the necessary supply of heavy battering-cannon and ammunition, I am sorry to say is somewhat uncertain."

Indeed, some men left again, impatient with the lack of action or eager to get home and get more clothing as the weather turned cold. Those who stayed did not take well to attempts at regimentation. Many fell ill, without medication or treatment available. Enough men drank heavily to create new problems in the camp. Tied to these problems were a lack of strong, decisive leadership and a shared understanding of what they were trying to accomplish. Seguín's men and other mounted volunteers patrolled the roads into San Antonio to keep supplies from reaching the town and to alert their encampment if Cos's reinforcements showed up. Minor skirmishes ensued, but November dragged on.

A bright spot for the Texians was the acquisition of a number of pieces of artillery, which they put into use against the Mexican fortifications, although with little effect. Many were also cheered by the arrival of the Greys, a company formed in New Orleans. The Greys brought visible volunteer support from the United States, a development that galled Mexican officials and heightened their suspicions of U.S. designs on Mexican territory. (Volunteer companies to fight in Texas were formed in Kentucky, Mississippi, Georgia, and Alabama as well.) One of the Greys, Herman Ehrenberg, would remember that the camp stretched "at least half a mile wide," surrounded by dormant corn fields and prairies, the latter "overgrown in places by mesquite brush and by enormous groups of gigantic cactus."

Many volunteers were growing deeply disenchanted. Austin, who wrote dejectedly on November 8 that he had "[n]ever pretended to be a military man," still tried to rally the troops, even after receiving word on November 18 that the provisional government had made him a commissioner to the United States and had therefore given him ample reason to resign his command. In fact, on November 21 Austin ordered his troops to prepare for an attack, relying on reports that the Mexican force was demoralized and desertions were common.

Austin's officers had to tell him that no more than 100 men would obey this order; the others had become disillusioned with his command. There are hints in the record that Houston may have been behind some of the dissatisfaction, as he had made no secret of his concerns about the wisdom of the siege and of his desire to do things differently with a regular army under his own command. Reluctantly, Austin rescinded his order and, acknowledging that he could better play a diplomatic role, assembled the troops on November 24. He determined that more than 400 were ready to stay and fight under an elected leader, and they voted for Colonel Edward Burleson to fill this role. On November 25, Austin left the camp for San Felipe.

A resident of Texas since 1830, Burleson had been active in protecting the frontier against Indian raids. Under Austin, he had served as lieutenant colonel of the infantry. The provisional government would recognize his new status as commander of the volunteer army on December 1. Despite the men's vote of confidence, he inherited a fractured and debilitated fighting force, one ready to strain at any rumor. Thus, when a scout entered camp on November 26 with a report of a hundred men in a large pack train headed toward San Antonio, word quickly spread that it was a company of dragoons that had been dispatched from Béxar about two weeks earlier, and that they were returning carrying silver as payment for the garrisoned Mexican soldiers.

Burleson sent James Bowie with a hundred mounted men to survey the pack train, warning him to refrain from engagement, if possible. But on finding the train beside a creek south of town, the pugnacious Bowie immediately attacked them. Meanwhile, most of the volunteer soldiers left behind, driven to distraction by the idea that their fellows would get to the silver first, simply rushed to the scene of the fight, disregarding orders. With little bloodshed on either side, the Mexican column, at a disadvantage with their muskets, abandoned the pack train for the safety of the Béxar fortifications.

The Texian volunteers found only grass in the packs; the train had been a foraging party trying to supply the hungry horses in the garrison, evidence that the Mexican garrison was indeed in difficult straits. Burleson, who had been considering withdrawal, began to think seriously about ordering an attack.

Further confirmation of the Mexican garrison's plight came when Cos released two Anglos living in San Antonio, John Smith and Samuel Maverick, on the condition that they return to the United States. Instead, they made their way to the ranch of José Antonio Navarro, a revolution-minded Mexican citizen, and thence to the Texian camp. They brought encouraging reports of the garrison's vulnerability. Burleson gave the order to attack, but he had not reckoned with strong internal dissent. Officers responded with further arguments, and Burleson, like Austin before him, rescinded the order. Those who had finally been preparing to fight responded with anger. An estimated 250–300 men left camp, and the others sank into gloom.

Burleson decided that his only recourse was to give up the siege and retreat to Goliad to establish winter quarters. Many of the troops responded to his announcement of this decision on December 4 with palpable anger and frustration. Why had they marched to the outskirts of Béxar and lived for as long as seven weeks on short rations and rumors?

Divided Opinion

It is tempting to speculate what would have happened if the volunteer army had indeed retreated at this point. Revolutionary allegiances had built in the Texas settlements and been reinforced by the arrival of young, restless, and aggressive adventurers such as the New Orleans Greys. But opinion was still divided, both outside Texas and within it. Abolitionist Benjamin Lundy would charge that U.S. land speculators and slave interests threatened by Mexican policies against slavery stood behind the uprising. He warned, "Influential slave-holders are contributing money, equipping troops, and marching to the scene of the conflict."

There was some truth to Lundy's charges, as leading slaveholders in the American South were seeking ways to protect and expand the institution of slavery against threats from the American North and vacillation on the issue from the Upper South (states bordering the northern states). In Texas, colonists, most of whom were from the American South, continued to argue publicly against any Mexican threat to their human "property." Their fears had been heightened by a slave revolt on the Brazos River in October, an uprising that ended with one observer noting "many whipd nearly to death some hung etc."

But beleaguered revolutionary leaders could only hope for such aid as Lundy suggested, for southern slavery leaders were too involved in their own political battles in the United States. And even within Texas the revolutionaries found significant lack of interest among the citizens. Revolutionary leaders despaired when Anglo settlers—including some prominent ones—avoided aiding the war effort in any way; They did not share their food or other resources, and the men did not even serve in local militias.

The response was uneven from other groups as well. Although some Tejanos joined the war effort, those in the Nacogdoches area were already being unmercifully pressed by Anglo immigrants, who were suspicious of all Mexicans and had reason to be wary of a revolutionary effort that could leave them even more at the mercy of this group. A local Tejano militia would be formed at the instigation of revolutionary leaders, its commander a prominent area landowner, Vincente Córdova. But Córdova and his fellows carefully distanced themselves from the war against the Mexican government, instead concentrating on trying to defend Tejano rights and Tejano participation in the local power structure. In the meantime,

Irish settlers had fought alongside the Mexican military when, in a side action in late October, Goliad commander Dimitt had sent a small force to take the Mexican post of Lipantitlán on the Nueces River. The Irish of San Patricio shared allegiances with their Mexican neighbors in South Texas, who had assisted them in getting settled in and shared a Catholic church with them.

The Irish of Refugio, on the other hand, sided with the Texians. But Houston was having little luck recruiting for his regular army. Despite the work of the Permanent Council and the Consultation, efforts to resist allegiance to Santa Anna's government or to declare outright independence remained confused, piecemeal, diffuse. This sullen, ragtag volunteer army camped outside San Antonio was, for better or worse, the most united, potent force the Texas revolutionaries had. And this army was about to move the conflict to a new level, to make it indisputably a revolution.

The Revolution—Victory and Defeat (December–March)

Benjamin Rush Milam had both a deeper and more checkered past in Texas than most of his fellow volunteers at the Siege of Béxar could imagine. A veteran of the War of 1812, by 1818 he had made his way to Spanish Texas, where he traded with the Comanches. In New Orleans the following year, he had joined James Long's first filibustering expedition, traveling to Vera Cruz and Mexico City. Although he spent time in jail in the capital, after the Constitution of 1824 introduced republican government, he became a Mexican army colonel. As an unsuccessful empresario in Texas, he took his case for land titles to Agustín Viesca in 1835, just as Viesca's resistance to Santa Anna formed, and wound up captured and jailed with Viesca. Escaping, he had made his way northward to the Goliad area. Here the Texian detachment sent to take Goliad had found him, weary and alone, hidden under a tree. Then and there Milam had become a member of the volunteer army. It was Milam who refused to accept Burleson's order to retreat, thereby providing the spark for the next series of revolutionary events.

The Taking of Béxar

Returning to camp from a scouting mission to find his compatriots packing up on December 4, Milam went first to Colonel Frank W. Johnson; then both men went to Burleson. Milam prevailed on Burleson to agree that, if he could convince enough of the remaining men to storm the city, Burleson would stay with the others as a reserve force to cover a possible retreat. Milam emerged from the meeting asking the legendary question, "Who will follow old Ben Milam into San Antonio?" Three hundred of those remaining in camp—about six out of ten— said they would.

Milam and other officers devised a plan: to attack in two columns. Milam's column advanced up Acequia Street toward the Garza house, while Johnson's scurried up Soledad toward the Veramendi house. When a sentry discovered the invaders, however, the Mexican artillery released a rain of canister shot, and the Texians sought cover within the homes that lined the streets. Fighting erupted wherever the Texians and the soldiers encountered each other, on the streets and in the dwellings. The Texians climbed onto roofs, hoping to use them as vantage points, but Mexican soldiers were already positioned on other roofs and in the San Fernando Church bell tower, from which they could pick off the enemy.

What followed were four confused days of fighting within Béxar. Although many San Antonio families no doubt simply wished for the fighting to move elsewhere, Erasmo Seguín supplied the rebels with livestock and grain from his ranch. At least a few dozen Tejanos joined with other Texians in the slow infantry advance, although most of them, skilled horsemen, were more comfortable on a horse.

The Texians fought hard and well, as did many of the soldiers under Cos. When Ugartechea finally arrived with a relief column on the afternoon of December 8, most of the men he brought with him to be soldiers were recalcitrant and shackled convicts. Unshackled, the convicts proved not only resistant to taking orders but disruptive and violent.

By this time, the heavy artillery fire from both sides had created a landscape of "blackened tree-stumps, battered walls, smoldering ash heaps." Cos was running out of supplies and workable defense plans. Over the objections of some of the soldiers who had been defending their fortifications for the past four days, on the morning of December 9, Cos had one of his men unfurl the white flag of truce. Colonel José Juan Sánchez-Navarro negotiated surrender terms with volunteer army commander Burleson and Colonel Johnson. Colonel Milam did not live to witness the capitulation, having been struck down by a sniper's bullet during the fighting. He was one of only four Texians who died, with an estimated fourteen wounded. Mexican losses were estimated at 150 dead and wounded.

Burleson and Johnson granted liberal terms to Cos, among other things allowing him time to remove his wounded and supplying him with "such provisions as can be obtained" for the troops' retreat to the Rio Grande. In turn, Cos promised not to take up arms against the rebel forces again. As he directed the removal of his troops, residents of San Antonio who had been forced to flee the fighting returned. Juan Antonio Chávez remembered, "When we returned we found the house badly shattered with shot and shell. The doors were riddled with bullets and grape shot from the cannon and escopetas [muskets] and the rifle balls." Although some Béxar residents supported the Texians and some the Mexican government, a bond that transcended these differences was that of citizens subjected to war in their own community.

The men who had taken San Antonio felt that they had sent a decisive message in favor of a return to the Constitution of 1824 that would serve as a rallying signal for a general Mexican revolt against Santa Anna. At the same time, many Anglos clearly favored complete independence, either long-term or as a means of

Antonio López de Santa Anna had appeared to be a strong federalist leader for Mexico, but his switch to centralist policies and his authoritarian presidency greatly fed unrest in Mexican Texas. (*The San Jacinto Museum of History, Houston*)

transferring the region to the United States. A couple of weeks after the Texians' victory at Béxar, the Goliad garrison proclaimed its independence from Mexico. A Texas official in New Orleans collecting supplies for the Texians expressed his sense that "a very large majority of the people wish to come into the Union with Uncle Sam." Yet in general, Anglo leaders remained cautious about advocating a full break from Mexico.

Readying for War

Santa Anna sought to contain and crush the rebellion in Texas. He had already tried to send word to Cos that the rebels were to be given no quarter. He even "stepped down" as president in order to lead an army across the Rio Grande. Even as the Goliad garrison was making its declaration of independence, Santa Anna was amassing his troops at San Luis Potosi. By the end of the month, they were on the march toward San Antonio.

Santa Anna's threat to the fledgling rebellion was very real but the Mexican force had its own problems: Many of the recruits had only minimal training, and many were draftees who would welcome a chance to bolt; the officers relied on outdated tactics of warfare; there was a serious lack of basic supplies and medical treatment for the widespread illness; there were periodic Indian threats; and the cold was bone-chilling, which proved especially hard on the recruits from tropical Yucatán.

The Texian army had serious problems as well, problems of almost farcical proportions. In November the Consultation had voted an independence advocate, Henry Smith, into the provisional governorship of revolutionary Texas. He and the Council established by the same body had quickly split. The split was in part over a scheme to take Matamoros by federalist José Antonio Mexía and volunteer army leaders, including Frank Johnson and empresario James Grant. The Council supported the enterprise, one of the goals of which was to rally federalists in the other regions of Mexico. Smith stood adamantly against such a brazen gamble with limited forces even as Santa Anna responded to the rebel victory at Béxar.

The Council appointed Johnson and James Fannin as commanders of a Matamoros expedition. Fannin was another veteran of the siege of Béxar and an ardent revolutionary. He had attended West Point, which gave him an added cachet in revolutionary war circles. Immediately after the siege, Houston commissioned him a colonel in the regular army.

Governor Smith insisted that Houston take control of the Matamoros expedition, if there was to be one, and dispatched him to Goliad, the rallying point. Here Houston found James Grant claiming to be acting commander-in-chief. With Grant directing the volunteers, Houston simply joined the enterprise and bided his time.

Soon word came that the Council had rescinded Houston's appointment as commander-in-chief and directed that James Fannin command the expedition. The Council had also deposed Governor Smith after he tried to dissolve it. Houston continued taking orders from Smith, leaving the expedition (which soon fell apart) and going to East Texas to persuade the Cherokees not to align themselves with the Mexican army. A regular army was still a chimera, and the volunteer army was fragmented and confused.

Back in San Antonio, however, J. C. Neill was directing a concerted effort to resist Santa Anna's thrust into Texas. Neill was an artilleryman who had provided cannon-firing distraction as the siege of Béxar began. In the wake of the Texian victory over Cos, the Council had given him a regular army commission as lieutenant colonel of artillery and had left him in command of the volunteers remaining in San Antonio. Neill wrote to Smith and the Council on January 14, "There can exist but little doubt that the enemy is advancing on this post, from the number of families leaving town today." But the Matamoros expedition leaders stripped Neill of men and much-needed supplies; he complained that soldiers who "had not been in the army more than four days" commandeered the clothing sent by the Council for those who had "endured all the hardships of winter

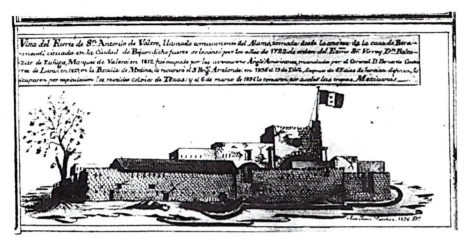

This 1836 view of the Alamo, sketched by Alamo siege participant Lieutenant Colonel José Juan Sánchez-Navarro, indicates that Texians flew the flag of Coahuila y Texas over the old mission, thereby couching the resistance as a struggle of Mexican subjects against the centralist government. *(Benson Latin American Collection, University of Texas at Austin)*

and who were not even sufficiently clad for summer." With only a hundred men, he chose to fortify the old Alamo mission.

In this effort, at least, he had plenty of weaponry—all the artillery left by Cos. Neill and his men mounted the guns on the walls and made other preparations for a siege. Even as they did so, Houston was ordering James Bowie to the Alamo and reportedly instructing him to destroy the mission and remove the troops.

When Bowie arrived on January 19, however, he found Neill's improvements compelling justification to maintain the Alamo as a Texian post, and he entered enthusiastically into preparations for a siege. He also notified Smith that he and Neill were resolved to stay and defend the position. In response, a convinced Smith ordered William Barret Travis, now a regular-army lieutenant colonel, to raise volunteer reinforcements for the post.

Travis balked. He could raise a company of only thirty men, few well-armed. "I am willing, nay anxious, to go to the defense of Béxar, but sir, I am unwilling to risk my reputation (which is ever dear to a soldier) by going off into the enemy's country with such little means, so few men, and with them so badly equipped." Nevertheless, Travis led his meager contingent into the Alamo on February 3.

They were joined on February 8 by a small volunteer force from Tennessee, including one of Tennessee's most famous sons, David, or Davy, Crockett. As a frontier character, Crockett was already the subject of popular literature. A former frontier militiaman and U.S. congressman from Tennessee, he had lost a congressional re-election campaign, and Texas had beckoned as a new avenue for his political and economic aspirations. Like other enthusiastic volunteers, he judged the region "the garden spot of the world. . . . a world of country here to settle."

Furthermore, he anticipated "being elected a member to form a constitution for the province" while "making a fortune yet for myself and family."

At the Alamo, Crockett did not press for a leadership position, which was just as well, as there was already dissension over who would be in command. J. C. Neill was called home by illness in the family on February 14. Travis, with his regular army commission, technically succeeded him, but the volunteers lobbied for Bowie, an elected colonel, to be commander. A vote split along predictable lines: the regulars for Travis, the volunteers for Bowie. Bowie promptly got drunk, then sobered up and suggested that they share the command along the lines already established. Travis agreed, and none too soon, for Santa Anna crossed the Rio Grande on February 16. The next day, General José Urrea crossed as well, his objective to "sweep . . . the coastal prairies" and reclaim Goliad. At about the same time, Jesse Badgett left the Alamo garrison as its delegate to a new convention called by the Council at Washington-on-the-Brazos for March 1; the other garrison-elected delegate, Samuel Maverick, remained.

The convention was a desperate necessity. The provisional government had dissolved in squabbling, leading one citizen to write Sam Houston, "I sincerely hope the Convention will remedy the existing evils and calm the Public since if not Texas must be lost." And squabbling had occurred over who was allowed to elect delegates. Many of the Anglo revolutionaries looked upon the Tejanos with suspicion, although it was finally decided that Tejanos who were against the Mexican government could vote. Two natives of Texas, José Antonio Navarro and José Francisco Ruiz, were elected, along with relative newcomer Lorenzo de Zavala, who had resigned his appointment as a Mexican diplomat in Paris to protest Santa Anna's shift to centralism. Brash recent arrivals including a group of Kentucky volunteers vociferously protested their exclusion from voting, forcing a place for themselves at the ballot box and influencing the election in favor of proindependence candidates unconcerned with a return to the Mexican Constitution of 1824.

When Badgett left to join the other elected delegates, the Alamo defenders still felt that Santa Anna would not be able to reach San Antonio before mid-March. They were wrong. On February 20, some of the local citizens began to depart, accompanied by some of the Tejano members of the garrison. On February 22, a messenger reported that an advance Mexican force was camped only eight miles south of town. The next morning, even more Béxar residents left hastily. By afternoon, garrison members could view from their parapets an ominous sight: Mexican troops flowing into and around the town.

Siege and Fall of the Alamo

Santa Anna began by demanding that the rebels surrender and "place themselves immediately at the disposal of the Supreme Government from whom alone they may expect clemency after some considerations are taken up." Travis responded with a defiant cannon shot. The Mexican army then began shelling the Alamo walls.

Everyone knew that the walls had to give at some point. The only advantage the Texians enjoyed in this regard was that the Mexicans' heavy siege guns had not yet arrived, and their attempts to position their small cannon close to the structure were met with withering fire from the rebels' accurate long rifles.

Nevertheless, the walls would eventually crumble. Further, supplies and ammunitions within the Alamo would dwindle quickly. The Texians' only real hope lay in the arrival of reinforcements. Bowie and Travis wrote to Fannin at Goliad urging him to bring his force.

The Texians placed their artillery at strategic points, but with only about 150 men, they couldn't hope to keep the Alamo's perimeters covered. Nor did the old mission have defensive firing ports. Even when it had served as a barracks for Mexican troops, the thick adobe walls had not been strong enough to withstand Indian attacks. Now men had to stand, "upper bodies . . . exposed," to pick off approaching soldiers. Even the cannon were exposed to enemy fire.

That fire rained unceasingly upon the compound. On February 24, Travis sent Gonzales resident Captain Albert Martin out to raise volunteer reinforcements. Martin rode to his hometown with Travis's famous "Victory or Death" letter": "*I shall never surrender or retreat.* Then, I call on you in the name of Liberty, of patriotism & everything dear to the American character, to come to our aid with all dispatch." At Gonzales, Martin recruited the Gonzales Ranging Company of Mounted Volunteers, two dozen or so men ranging in age from sixteen to forty-one. A few others joined them on the seventy-mile ride to the Alamo's defense. Nevertheless, the thirty-two reinforcements must have looked paltry indeed when the defenders opened the gates to them on February 29.

Yet these were the only reinforcements the besieged garrison would receive. Fannin had started toward Béxar, then turned around, citing as his reasons an oxcart breakdown on the road and the warnings of his officers, and arguing that he needed to defend Goliad, as Santa Anna had targeted it, too, and "Both places [Goliad and San Antonio] are importent [*sic*]."

Travis had suspected that Fannin was not coming, and a courier, James Butler Bonham, on March 4 confirmed his apprehension. In the meantime, the Mexican forces, working repeatedly under cover of darkness, extended their batteries so close to the north wall that every volley caused it to disintegrate further.

As the end drew near on March 5, Santa Anna called a meeting of his officers. Many of them listened in consternation as their commander outlined plans for an attack. In their view, the siege was wearing down the Texians garrison, which was running out of provisions. The heavy artillery should arrive in a couple of days and the walls would come down. Why attack at all?

Santa Anna was adamant, arguing that the action would improve the soldiers' morale. But it is clear that what he wanted was a violent retributive victory. Travis, too, had called a meeting of his men. (Their number was long thought to be 189, but modern-day researchers believe there may have been as many as dozens more than this.) The story of Travis's drawing a line in the sand and asking those who would fight to the death to step over the line is apparently only that—a story. But he did apparently offer all of his men the opportunity to slip away if they chose; according to legend, only one—a Frenchman named Louis Rose—did so. Couriers had managed to come and go; Samuel Maverick had finally departed for the Washington-on-the-Brazos convention on March 2; and Juan Seguín had taken Travis's appeals for aid to the settlements, remaining in Gonzales under Houston's orders. By some accounts, Travis also promised the remaining men that they would surrender or attempt to escape if help did not arrive. He even sent an intermediary to Santa Anna in an attempt to discuss surrender terms, only to be rebuffed.

Santa Anna was busy readying the final assault: four columns coming from each direction, with the commander himself overseeing the reserve troops. At the head of one column was General Cos, who had been persuaded by his brother-in-law, Santa Anna, that a promise given to rebels was not binding.

The Mexican forces began their attack at 5:30 A.M. on March 6, the soldiers who had waited through the cold night marching silently into position. The Texians were asleep, their dozing sentinels easily dispatched by an advance guard of light infantry. A few in the Mexican ranks, however, could not resist rallying cries, which woke the Alamo defenders to the sight of the columns already drawing near to the walls.

There followed a bloodbath for both sides. The Texian cannons quickly began spitting grapeshot and followed it with nine-pound iron balls. The metal shards ripped through the tight columns, the iron balls adding to the general destruc-

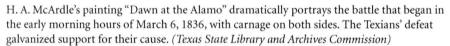

H. A. McArdle's painting "Dawn at the Alamo" dramatically portrays the battle that began in the early morning hours of March 6, 1836, with carnage on both sides. The Texians' defeat galvanized support for their cause. *(Texas State Library and Archives Commission)*

tion. At the same time, Texians were being picked off the wall at close range by the soldiers' Baker rifles, British arms with great short-distance accuracy. But even the Mexican army's muskets were hitting their marks.

Soldiers scaled the walls. Although they had only a few ladders, they found enough footholds on the north wall that some men were able to slip over and open the north gate. Ironically, the long rifles that had served the Texians so well proved a poor defense at this point, for they took too long to reload, and the troops were pouring into the breach. The invaders even turned the captured cannon on the doors through which the defenders were firing by means of loopholes.

Travis fell early in the fighting, with a bullet in the forehead. Some Texians tried to surrender by waving white cloths, but others fired on the advancing troops. Bowie was killed in his sickbed. The chapel was overrun last, James Butler Bonham and Almeron Dickenson dying beside the cannon they had manned.

Various accounts stated that a few of the defenders fought to the last and were taken prisoner, then executed upon Santa Anna's orders. Certainly the Mexican commander had made it clear that he would grant no quarter. Among those captured and executed, it was rumored, was David Crockett.

The diary of Mexican officer José de la Peña confirmed these accounts. Although the validity of the diary has been challenged, many historians agree that it is legitimate and that Peña's description of events provides an important eyewitness record. In Peña's account, fighting officers, including General Manuel Fernández Castrillón, wanted to spare the six or seven captives, but Santa Anna reacted in disgust, insisting that they be executed. Some of his staff officers, seeking to curry his favor, set upon the captives with bayonets.

San Antonio resident Eulalia Yorba and her children had gone to the home of a Spanish priest to get some food and watched from there as the shooting began. "It seemed as if there were myriads of soldiers and guns about [the Alamo,]" she recalled. "There was volley after volley fired into the barred and bolted windows," with answering volleys and "puffs of smoke from within the Alamo." She observed that "The din was indescribable."

Yorba related that a Mexican colonel came and asked those in the house to minister to the dying Mexican soldiers. When she emerged to do so, "The roadway was thronged with Mexican soldiers with smoke and dirt begrimed faces, haggard eyes and wild, insane expression," she related. In the Alamo itself, she observed doors "splintered and battered in," floors "crimson with blood," the air "dark with powder smoke" and "hot and heavy." Tending to the wounds of some of the Mexican soldiers, she saw dead Texians lying "singly and in heaps of three or four, or in irregular rows here and there all about the floor of the Alamo, just as they had fallen."

Santa Anna summoned Béxar mayor Francisco Antonio Ruiz to identify Travis, Bowie, and Crockett. He also ordered Ruiz to see to the interment of the dead Mexican soldiers, estimated at 600, or one-third of the attack force. But Ruiz did not have the resources to bury so many dead, and his workers threw many in the San Antonio River, where they jammed up in the curves. Pablo Díaz remembered that the sight of the bodies in the river and their stench made him ill, "for they lined the river's course and banks all the way from Crockett Street to more than a mile below."

The Alamo defenders met a different fate, for Santa Anna ordered two funeral pyres built for them. Díaz recalled these ten-foot-high pyres with alternating layers of corpses and firewood. "Grease of different kinds, principally tallow, was melted and poured over the two pyres," he noted. "I saw ashes, as well as the blackened chars of the different anatomical fragments. They emitted an odor even more sickening than did the corpses of those who had been thrown into the river. . . ."

The only Alamo defender to receive burial was Gregorio Esparza, who had served under Juan Seguín in the siege of Béxar and had stayed in his command afterward. Esparza's brother Francisco had served under General Cos. Francisco went to Cos and got permission to take his brother's body. "I proceeded to the Alamo," Francisco would relate, "and found the dead body of my brother in one of the rooms," with "a ball in his breast and a stab from a sword in his side."

Not everyone in the Alamo died. The old mission had also sheltered a number of noncombatants, most of whom survived the carnage. Most famous in Anglo annals are Susannah Dickenson, wife of Almeron, and the Dickensons' child Angelina. But there were also African Americans, chief among them Travis's slave Joe, and a number of members of Tejano families, including Gregorio Esparza's wife and children. One of the children, Enrique, would later relate his mother's courage and pain. The family was marched to the home of Ramón Músquiz, a merchant and political leader who had argued for Anglo American colonization but remained loyal to the Mexican government. Enrique's mother began searching for food in the house for the children and the other refugees. When Músquiz warned her that she was under guard and should not be moving about, "[s]he told him she did not care whether she was under guard or not, she was going to have something to eat for herself, her children, and her companions whom she intended to feed if Santa Anna did not feed his prisoners." Enrique noted, "[a]fter our release we went back to our home and my mother wept for many days and nights."

The Revolution—The Winning of Independence (March–April)

At the Alamo, a small contingent of men had come together—natives and immigrants, Mexicans, Anglos, and Europeans, old settlers, more recent immigrants, and newly arrived adventurers. They had all sensed opportunity—for glory, for a return to republican principles, for land, for a separate Mexican state of Texas or a Texas tied to the United States. Now their deaths would provide a rallying point for the Texian cause.

At the Independence Convention

Now delegates to the independence convention were at work at Washington-on-the-Brazos anxiously awaiting news of the Alamo defenders. On March 2, they still thought that Fannin was headed to the Alamo's aid, and they adopted a Texas declaration of independence, decisively breaking with the idea of Texas continuing as part of a federalist Mexico. "The necessity of self-preservation," they concluded, ". . . now decrees our eternal political separation. . . . the people of Texas do now constitute a FREE, SOVEREIGN, and INDEPENDENT REPUBLIC."

Fifty-nine delegates would arrive by March 11, and these members—primarily from the American South, with only one in six residing in Texas before January 1830—set about creating a constitution modeled on the U.S. Constitution and fulfilling as much as possible the functions of a government.

There was no word from or of the Alamo. Lawyer William Fairfax Gray, a land agent traveling in Texas, attended the convention and wrote on the 13th, "The anxiety begins to be intense." Houston, again named military commander-in-chief by the convention, had not tried to hurry to the Alamo's relief, even though Travis's final appeal to the Council, where Houston was a delegate, had arrived on March 5. By one account, Houston doubted the reports from Travis and from Fannin, considering them political grandstanding. Departing on March 6 for Gonzales, however, he had just begun to put together a new force composed of both volunteers and militia, and even if he had hurried, he would have been too late.

News of the Alamo's fall reached Gonzales on March 11, the same day as Houston's arrival, and was quickly followed by the arrival of noncombatant survivors. With so many of the townsmen in the Alamo and now dead, the community took on a horrified mourning. Houston resolved not to be trapped in any one place and retreated to Burnham's Crossing on the Colorado. With both Santa Anna's and Urrea's forces threatening the western settlements, he ordered that Gonzales be burned and abandoned—no doubt adding to the grief and disorientation of its residents. He had already sent word to Fannin at Goliad to join him, with plans to combine Fannin's volunteer army of about 400 with his own force of about the same size.

At Washington-on-the-Brazos, delegates worked hurriedly to define laws and the governmental structure of a new republic. They followed some Spanish and Mexican precedents, for example, in laws on homestead exemptions and debtor relief. The delegates tried to address the thorny issue of land claims through such measures as voiding some eleven-league claims and questionable titles, noting that "one of the great duties of this convention" was "the protection of the public domain from unjust and fraudulent claims, and quieting the people in the enjoyment of their lands."

Convention members used a definition of citizenship that included Tejanos but excluded "Africans, the descendants of Africans, and Indians" and affirmed the continued practice of slaveholding. The republic Congress would not "have power to emancipate slaves," although an owner who did so would either need the Congress's approval or have to "send his or her slave or slaves without the limits of the Republic," because congressional approval would be required for a freedman or -woman to reside in the state.

The governmental structure devised by the convention reflected the American system: executive, legislative, and judicial branches; a Senate and a House of Representatives; and supreme, district, county, and justice courts.

On March 17, members approved the document in an atmosphere of continued anxiety and uncertainty. They settled on an interim government that included empresarios David G. Burnet as president and Lorenzo de Zavala as vice president, with Samuel P. Carson as secretary of state, Robert Potter as secretary of the tiny Texas navy, David Thomas as attorney general, Bailey Hardeman as treasurer, and Thomas Jefferson Rusk as secretary of war.

Further Setbacks: The Runaway Scrape and the Fannin Massacre

As the independence convention ended, a general panic swept the settlements with the news of the Alamo's fall and Houston's retreat. Families began a pell-mell rush eastward and southeastward in what became known as the Runaway Scrape. "Deserters were constantly passing us on foot and on horseback," remembered Rosa von Roeder Kleberg, who had settled outside San Felipe. "The old men who were with the families laughed at them and called to them, 'Run! Run! Santa Anna is after you!'" Frances Meneffee Sutherland, mourning the loss of her son, William DePriest Sutherland, in the Alamo, reported, "We went to the Colorado, forty miles, but after some time, [Houston] thought proper to retreat farther and of course we had to go, too." At the Brazos River, they stopped for a few days, her husband leaving to join the republic army. But news came that the Mexican army was drawing near, and the settlers continued their confused flight. "I wish you could know how the people did as they kept going about trying to get somewhere," Sutherland wrote, "but no person knew where they were going to get to."

Families suffered greatly. Dilue Rose Harris, "near eleven years old" when the Alamo was under attack, would later remember her family's desperate flight: "We left home at sunset, hauling clothes, bedding and provisions on the sleigh with one yoke of oxen." At the Lynchburg ferry on the San Jacinto River, they found "fully five thousand people trying to get across," including a number of slaves. After waiting three days to cross, they proceeded onto a prairie where her uncle's wagon bogged down. At the next stage of the journey, the crossing of the Trinity River, again people were jostling to cross. One of Harris's sisters had fallen ill, and the family was allowed to cross first, but their boat flooded and Harris's little sister "was in convulsions." (The girl would later die on the five-week journey.) For some, however, the advancing Mexican troops evoked a quite different response. Some slaves, rather than aiding in the retreat, simply rushed to meet the troops, gaining protection and freedom, for Santa Anna and General Urrea no longer countenanced the practice of slavery.

As many Texians scrambled, wondering if they would ever be able to return to their frontier homes, Houston continued to fall back—and Fannin failed to appear to join forces with him. Fannin had his own escalating troubles. He had ordered a company to Refugio to evacuate settlers there, only to have them run into a detachment of Urrea's troops. Urrea had been making a successful incursion into the coastal prairies, crushing what was left of the Matamoros expedition at San Patricio. His troops now bested the Goliad company and the battalion sent to reinforce it, the Georgia battalion. Most of the latter managed to get away, but Urrea was helped by loyal Tejano residents of the Refugio-San Patricio area, some of whom had received highhanded treatment from the Texian volunteers.

The Goliad garrison consisted almost entirely of very recent newcomers to Texas, Fannin being one of the exceptions with about a year and a half residence. Fannin was also unusual because he had some formal military training, although it did not serve him well. His situation was unfortunate, but he compounded it, with fatal consequences.

Fannin had not wanted to leave his troops at Refugio, but when he received word of their defeat on the afternoon of March 17, he still failed to follow Houston's orders to retreat. This gave Urrea's scouts time to start reconnoitering the garrison. By the evening of the 18th, Fannin was trying to get the march started, but the night was deemed "too murky for a proper march." The next morning, the garrison members delayed further, failing to make use of an obscuring fog. Fannin, ignoring Houston's order to dump the nine cannons in the river, instead burdened underfed oxen with baggage and artillery. When the troops finally departed, the oxen proved agonizingly slow. Garrison member Herman Ehrenberg noted "disgust at the creeping pace of our column induced us finally to abandon all our equipment."

In perhaps his most inexplicable move, Fannin called the column to a halt for a rest break in the middle of a prairie after only six miles of travel. Some of his men protested, eyeing the relative safety of a distant tree line, but he apparently felt that the Mexican troops would not attack a 400-man contingent. Fannin's troops rested for an hour without incident, but soon after resuming the march, they looked back to see numerous Mexican cavalrymen spilling from the timberline two miles away.

Again, Fannin rejected the idea of trying to reach the tree line ahead, despite the arguments of his officers that it would be better to push toward a defensive position even if casualties were high along the way. Fannin had the men "form a hollow square, with the artillery posted at the corners." In the early afternoon, the Mexican dragoons began the attack. Fannin's men were able to direct withering rifle, musket, and artillery fire on the advancing troops, but Mexican sharpshooters picked off the Texian gunners. The Mexicans mounted charge after charge, and Fannin, to his credit, bravely led the defense. But the Texian force had run out of water, and the Mexican troops had shot the oxen, making it impossible to move the baggage and the wounded. With nightfall came a cessation in the fighting, aside from sporadic sniper fire, but also the knowledge that Urrea's troops had them surrounded.

The only possible escape seemed to be a stealthy nighttime retreat, but Fannin's men agreed that they could not do this for it would mean abandoning the wounded. They tried through the night to erect breastworks, but when the morning dawned, they were greeted with reinforcements and more artillery on the Mexican side. An injured Fannin called a truce and approached General Urrea to discuss terms. Urrea offered him only the opportunity to "surrender at discretion." Fannin interpreted this to mean their lives would be spared.

Fannin's command surrendered. On the Texian side, nine had been killed, fifty-one wounded; among the Mexican troops, fifty had been killed, 140 wounded. The prisoners would be held in Goliad, and joined by members of the Georgia battalion captured by Mexican cavalry. Urrea was one of a number of Mexican officers who disagreed with Santa Anna's edict that captured rebels should be killed; he wanted to spare the men. He even allowed Fannin to go to the coast with a German in Mexican service, Colonel Juan Holsinger, to see about gaining passage for the prisoners on a ship bound for New Orleans. But no ship was available, and Santa Anna reiterated his edict.

On Palm Sunday, March 27, the order was carried out. The Texians were divided into four groups and told they were being marched to Matamoros. Instead, after a short march, with the groups now isolated from each other, Mexican infantry opened fire on them, with lancers backing them up. Three hundred and forty-two of the prisoners died outside Goliad that day; twenty-eight would

"The March to the Massacre," by Andrew Houston, depicts James Fannin's troops leaving Goliad as prisoners. Told they were being marched to Matamoros, instead most were executed a short distance from Goliad. (*The San Jacinto Museum of History, Houston*)

manage to escape the carnage, including two doctors spared because they were desperately needed to tend the Mexican troops. A firing squad executed Fannin separately, his mortal wound a bullet through the face. Again, the Mexicans burned the Texian dead. The killings would become known to Texans as the "Fannin Massacre."

Sam Houston and San Jacinto

During this time Secretary of War Thomas Jefferson Rusk, a South Carolinian who had joined Burnet's colony in 1835, was active in moving the interim government to the relative safety of Harrisburg and in organizing militias to defend against the eastward-moving Mexican forces. He also found himself in the unenviable position of trying to coordinate with and direct General Houston. Despite grumblings from his army, Houston had retreated again on March 19, judging the Burnham's Crossing location indefensible and a poor strategic location to keep Santa Anna from striking the settlements. At his new location, Beason's Crossing, he welcomed a sizable number of new volunteers, residents of the settlements who had tried to stay out of the conflict but now had been galvanized by news of the Alamo's fall. Here, however, on March 23 he received news of Fannin's defeat and surrender. It was a terrible blow. Along with the news that Santa Anna had dispatched General Joaquín Ramírez y Sesma to Beason's Crossing with a large force, it caused Houston to retreat again, this time to San Felipe.

Houston's decision brought him further censure and even desertion among the troops, who resented the apparent weakness of such a move. Historians, however, have generally concluded that an engagement at Beason's Crossing would not have helped the Texian cause, at least not in the long run.

In the meantime, Urrea's troops had been effective, especially in the victory over Fannin and in shutting off to the Texians all coastal ports except Galveston. Yet torrential spring rains had slowed the movement of the entire Mexican army, and Santa Anna was just rousing himself to leave San Antonio. He joined Sesma and General Eugenio Tolsa, their goal an attack on San Felipe, Houston's new headquarters and the heart of the Anglo colonies.

At San Felipe, to the dismay of many of his troops, Houston ordered another retreat, to Jared Groce's plantation twenty miles away. He left two companies guarding the San Felipe and Fort Bend crossings and departed with the rest of the army, now numbering about 500.

Santa Anna's combined forces pressed toward San Felipe, arriving nine days after Houston's departure. By this time, the remaining Texians had burned the town and disappeared. But Santa Anna had discovered that the Texian government was in nearby Harrisburg, to the east of the army, whereas Houston's force was to its west. Santa Anna saw an opportunity to seize the rebel government and at the same time cut off Galveston Bay, the one remaining "rebel lifeline to the United States."

The rebel government, like many of the soldiers, chafed at Houston's inaction.

President David Burnet sent a missive to Houston: "Sir: The enemy are laughing you to scorn. You must fight them. You must retreat no further. The country expects you to fight. The salvation of the country depends on your doing so."

Houston's army had swollen again—to 900—and the two weeks at Groce's plantation had allowed them to rest and recuperate from a host of ills brought on by hard camp living and relentless rain. They had also drilled in some of the rudiments of warfare. Rusk had been told to seize command from Houston if he still refused to attack, and some of the troops clearly wanted Rusk to do so. But the secretary of war listened to Houston's justifications for his actions up to this point and responded by joining the army. On April 12, Houston started them eastward.

Santa Anna's advance troops made it to Harrisburg late on April 15, but the governor and his cabinet escaped to New Washington, a short distance to the south on the San Jacinto River. As Santa Anna's troops pursued, they moved away again, to Galveston Island. Santa Anna was still between Houston and the Texas government. Learning that Houston was moving eastward toward the Trinity River, the Mexican general prepared to block the Texian march at the Lynchburg Crossing on Buffalo Bayou near Harrisburg.

Houston's plans and motives at this point remained unclear; some of his officers later maintained that he was seriously considering taking his force across the Sabine to Louisiana to recruit more volunteers. The Texian army was coming to a crucial crossroad: If Houston ordered them to go north, they would be headed toward Nacogdoches and away from Santa Anna. If he ordered them to follow the road to Harrisburg, they would be almost sure to fight.

As it turned out, the army did not await a command, but simply surged toward Harrisburg when they reached the crossroad. Houston was simply carried along by the tide, his intentions still unknown. The army would fight.

Santa Anna was in New Washington, with about 660 of his men. Houston learned this from letters seized from a captured Mexican messenger and realized that he had a good opportunity to strike. He had had to leave almost 250 men ill at Harrisburg, but his numbers were swelling again, and he finally exhorted the troops, urging them to remember the Alamo. The troops added a cry of "Remember Goliad!" and commenced the tricky crossing of Buffalo Bayou, then marched till about midnight. The next morning, they learned that the Mexican troops were headed toward Lynch's Ferry. Whoever reached it first would gain the advantage of the best tactical position from which to fight.

The Texians arrived first and established themselves in a high oak grove, a position particularly well suited for their riflemen. Santa Anna had to take a relatively risky position, but he immediately sent men to test the Texians' defenses. They were greeted by fire from two cannons, dubbed the Twin Sisters, and responded with their own twelve-pounder, but the Texians won this initial skirmish, forcing the Mexican artillery back into a wood.

Some Texians wanted to press on immediately. Although Houston said no, he did allow the hotspur Sidney Sherman to reconnoiter with a group of mounted riflemen. Sherman immediately ignored orders and charged the Mexican cavalry.

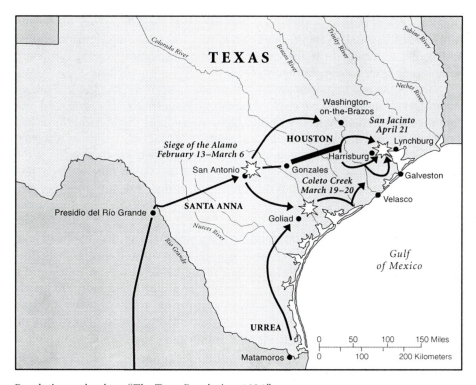

Revolutionary battles—"The Texas Revolution, 1836."

When he asked for infantry assistance, Houston refused. But again, the Texian army took the decision out of their commander's hands, a whole infantry regiment responding to Sherman's plea and deliberately ignoring Houston's order to turn around. This time the Mexicans successfully repulsed them.

Both armies settled down for the night, although the Mexicans were busy building breastworks in their relatively vulnerable position. They were also eagerly awaiting the arrival of General Cos, on his way with reinforcements. At 9 A.M. the next morning, Cos appeared with about 540 men.

This, of course, shifted the numerical advantage: Houston had 910 men, Santa Anna about 1,200. Historians have asked why Houston did not attack during the night, as he knew Cos was on his way. Houston's troops asked the same thing. Many of them were also furious when the whole morning went by with no action on Houston's part. What if further reinforcements arrived? Houston and his officers met from noon to 2 P.M., with differing accounts of the meeting. But finally, as the afternoon wore on, Houston himself ordered the men into battle positions, to advance in two lines over a rise that had separated them from the Mexicans' view. Houston had at first denied Juan Seguín's detachment a place in the battle force because many of the other soldiers had demonstrated considerable animosity toward Mexicans in general; Houston was afraid that some of the

Mexicans might be shot by their own compatriots as the battle raged. But Seguín and his men had argued for the opportunity to fight, reminding Houston of their unflagging commitment to the cause. They went into battle wearing cardboard insignias on their hats to distinguish them from Santa Anna's forces.

Santa Anna had kept a close watch through most of the day but had grown complacent, despite the worries of some of his officers. Houston had not mounted a full attack yet; why should he now, just after the Mexican force had built breastworks and received reinforcements?

Thus, the Texians' artillery unit advanced "within two hundred yards of the enemy's breastworks" and opened fire. This was immediately followed by a Texian cavalry charge. Houston had the infantry hold their fire, but once they had fired the first volley he lost command of them and they fell to skirmishing, some using their rifles as clubs.

The Mexican officers also struggled to organize their startled, confused, and frightened troops and get them to listen to orders, but without success. With Texians scaling the barricades, the eighteen-minute battle became a rout—and a bloodbath. The Texians were bent on revenge, and they killed indiscriminately and often brutally. Even the Tejano volunteers proved ruthless. Many Mexican soldiers jumped into a nearby lake, calling desperately "Me no Alamo—me no Goliad!" but they were easy targets for the Texian guns, and the lake soon ran red with their blood.

This William Huddle painting of Houston accepting Santa Anna's surrender after the battle of San Jacinto shows Houston reclining as a result of an ankle wound sustained in the battle. (*Texas State Library and Archives Commission*)

Six hundred and fifty Mexican soldiers were killed, most of them after the brief battle, and most of the rest were captured quickly. The victory for the Texians was decisive but not complete. They had subdued only a part of the Mexican army. At first, they even feared that Santa Anna had escaped them, but he was apprehended after spending the night of April 21 hiding in a marsh. Under terms of his surrender, Santa Anna ordered his second-in-command, Vincente Filisola, to retreat to Béxar. Filisola judged the campaign lost, with Santa Anna captured and Mexican supply lines stretched thin. He refused to listen to some of the other Mexican officers who counseled continued warfare, especially the able Urrea, and instead retreated not just to Béxar but all the way across the Rio Grande.

Conclusion

The volunteer army had made the independence declared at Washington-on-the-Brazos a reality. Texas was now a nation born in conflict—not only the conflict between the Mexican government and its recalcitrant Texas subjects, but conflict among those subjects as well. There had been the war and peace parties, and within the war party those fighting for recognition of a separate Mexican statehood and those fighting for separation from Mexico. There had been those who simply wanted to be left alone and were drawn unwillingly into the conflict. There had been tensions between newcomers and established Texians, with the roles constantly shifting. Newcomers did not have the perspective of residents of a year or two; residents of a year or two did not have the perspective of Austin's Old Three Hundred; and Austin's Old Three Hundred did not have the perspective of Tejano residents. There had been tensions between Anglos and Tejanos, even as some of them had worked and fought well together. There had been tensions among the Anglos dominating the new military and the new government, with pro- and anti-Houston factions, pro- and anti-Smith factions.

Somehow, in part due to Santa Anna's harsh and arrogant conduct of the war in Texas, all of this had added up to a victory for the revolutionaries. But there were still many tensions to be resolved. The Mexican government would refuse to recognize Texas independence; Mexicans were bitter about losing part of their territory so early in their own history as an independent nation, with many struggling to maintain republican principles shared with the United States. The United States would see the developments in Texas as both a blessing and a curse: With possible annexation, Texas provided an opportunity for U.S. westward expansion, but it would also be a catalyst for further problems between the slaveholding antebellum South and the North. Texas slaves themselves saw any hope of an improvement in their status and for freedom disappear. With Anglos from the American South overwhelmingly in positions of power, racial and ethnic differences would become more significant. Juan Seguín would find post-revolution Texas more difficult to endure than the sieges of Béxar and the Alamo and the battle of San Jacinto, until he became, as he said, "a foreigner in my native land."

But he was indisputably one of the most prominent revolutionary veterans, and he would continue in the service of the republic. To him was given the task of burying the remains of the Alamo defenders. Shortly before the first anniversary of the Alamo's fall, he located the heaps of ashes from the cremation and interred them after a sober procession, with "three volleys of musquetry . . . fired over the grave by the whole Battalion." Seguín did not have enough powder to fire the larger guns, "but every honor was done within the reach of my scanty means." The Alamo would ever loom large in Texians' memory, but old and new challenges awaited.

SUGGESTED READINGS

The Texas Revolution—particularly the defense of the Alamo—has generated copious scholarship and dramatic conjecture. A classic scholarly work is Amelia Williams's "A Critical Study of the Siege of the Alamo and of the Personnel of Its Defenders" in *Southwestern Historical Quarterly* (1932–33). Paul Lack's *The Texas Revolutionary Experience, A Political and Social History, 1835–1836* (1992) is a key scholarly source for understanding the events of the Revolution. Another key source is Stephen L. Hardin's clear and informative *Texian Iliad: A Military History of the Texas Revolution (1994)*. A good brief overview is provided in "Colonization and Revolution," the first chapter of Richard Bruce Winders's *Crisis in the Southwest: The United States, Mexico, and the Struggle over Texas* (2002). The *New Handbook of Texas* (1996) has a detailed "Texas Revolution" entry and helpful entries on the key events and participants.

Despite the debates as to its veracity, José Enrique de la Peña's *With Santa Anna in Texas: A Personal Narrative of the Revolution* is an important source for the period. For other primary sources, consult *Documents of Texas History* (1994), eds. Ernest Wallace, David M. Vigness, and George B. Ward; *The Papers of the Texas Revolution* (1973), compiled by John H. Jenkins; and "Revolutionary Texas, 1835–1836," in Sam Haynes and Cary D. Wintz's *Major Problems in Texas History* (2002).

The Revolution—Early Months (October–December 1835)

In addition to the works above, Gregg Cantrell's *Stephen F. Austin, Empresario of Texas* provides good secondary material on the early months of the war. Alwyn Barr focuses on the siege of Béxar in his *Texans in Revolt: the Battle for San Antonio, 1835* (1990). Interesting primary accounts are included in Noah Smithwick's *Evolution of a State* and Herman Ehrenberg's "The Fight for Freedom in Texas," included in Natalie Ornish's *Ehrenberg: Goliad Survivor, Old West Explorer* (1997). Graham Davis's "Models of Migration: The Historiography of the Irish Pioneers in South Texas" in *Southwestern Historical Quarterly* (1996) includes an analysis of how one ethnic group split in its loyalties between the Mexican government and the revolutionaries.

The Revolution—Victory and Defeat (December 1835–March 1836)

William C. Davis's *Three Roads to the Alamo: The Lives and Fortunes of David Crockett, James Bowie, and William Barret Travis* (1998) examines in detail the three men's paths to the Alamo and provides a brief account of the Alamo's fall. *A Line in the Sand: The Alamo in Blood and Memory* (2001), by Randy Roberts and James N. Olson, examines both the events at the Alamo and the myths surrounding them. Primary accounts of the period leading up to the Alamo battle and the Alamo's fall appear in Bill Groneman's *Eyewitnesses to the Alamo* (1996), Ron Jackson's *Alamo Legacy: Alamo Descendants Remember the Alamo* (1997), and Timothy M. Matovina's *The Alamo Remembered: Tejano Accounts and Perspectives* (1995).

The Revolution—The Winning of Independence (March–April 1836)

Good primary accounts are included in Jackson's *Alamo Legacy,* in editor Paul Lack's *The Diary of William Fairfax Gray from Virginia to Texas, 1835–1837* (1997), in Crystal Sasse Ragsdale's *The Golden Free Land* (1976), and in the reminiscences of Dilue Rose Harris, included in Jo Ella Powell Exley's *Texas Tears and Texas Sunshine.* Juan Seguín's story from this period is told in *A Revolution Remembered* (1991), edited by Jesús F. de la Teja.

Sam Houston comes to prominence in this portion of the Revolutionary story; there have been numerous biographies of this leading Texas figure. A good one for reference is Randolph B. Campbell's *Sam Houston and the American Southwest* (1993).

8

Texas Independent, Texas Annexed, 1836–1859

Pleasant and Margaret Fowler were bringing their young family home to their farm in Austin's colony near the gulf coast, the Runaway Scrape over, independence a fragile reality. The family arrived after dark and camped, having heard that Mexican troops had vandalized their house. When morning dawned, they found hogs exiting its front door, floorboards pulled up, and their possessions scattered. Pleasant immediately began plowing, while Margaret shocked daughter Dilue Rose by veering from religious observance and doing the family wash on a Sunday. Neighbors were filtering back, tired and threadbare. Bread was hard to come by. Across the settlements, homes had to be restored, cattle reclaimed or replaced, food provisions renewed. "Mother was very despondent," Dilue would write, "but father was hopeful. He said Texas would . . . become a great nation."

The challenges in this assessment were immense. Mexico was refusing to recognize its newly won independence, and other nations—including the United States—would be slow with official recognition. The populace lived under a continued threat of renewed attack from Mexico, as well as from the Comanches and other hostile tribes to the north and west. All of the old problems of living on a frontier had been exacerbated by the losses and disruptions of the war. Many residents now openly advocated annexation to the United States, both because most of the population had strong American roots and because of the need for stability and security. Yet annexation would be long in coming, and when it finally occurred, new struggles over identity would stress and eventually fracture the state.

1836	Sam Houston becomes first elected president of Republic of Texas
1837	U.S. recognizes Republic of Texas but rebuffs Texas attempts to win annexation
1838	Mirabeau B. Lamar succeeds Houston as republic president; Vicente Córdova leads Córdova rebellion
1839	Cherokees are forced from Texas
1842	Houston again becomes republic president; Mexican troops twice invade Texas, which Mexico refuses to recognize as independent; Somervell and Mier expeditions are mounted in retaliation
1844–46	German stock company Adelsverein transports thousands of German immigrants to Texas
1845	Mexico offers to recognize Texas if the republic will not annex itself to another country, but Texas wins annexation to the U.S.
1846	War between Mexico and the U.S. begins; Baylor University opens in Independence
1848	Treaty of Guadalupe Hidalgo cedes Mexican holdings in American Southwest and West to U.S.
1850	Compromise of 1850 limits Texas boundaries but gives the state a financial boost
1859	Indians on West Texas reservations are expelled to Indian Territory; Juan Cortina leads insurrection in South Texas
1860	Texas slave owners make up just over a quarter of the population but hold three-fourths of the wealth; Texas is strongly identified as a southern state

Dilue Rose Harris was only eleven years old when she participated in the Runaway Scrape of 1836; she would remain a Texan, watching the Houston area grow, marrying, and bearing nine children. (*The San Jacinto Museum of History, Houston*)

The Quests for Annexation and Empire, 1836–1841

The captive Santa Anna had been sent to Washington, D.C., but not before signing two treaties at Velasco: a public one in which he promised not to engage in warfare against Texas, and a private one, in which he agreed to work to get the Mexican government to recognize Texas's independence. But for many an independent Texas was simply a prelude to annexation to the United States. As interim president David G. Burnet struggled to get the government on a solid footing, setting national elections for September 1836, the ballot would include the proposition that Texas seek annexation.

Sam Houston's Administration

In the new republic, old antagonisms and factions had resurfaced, men jockeying for positions of influence and power in the new order. The situation was intensified by the volatile mix of newcomers who had arrived during the Revolution and by the lack of a strong, well-established governmental structure.

Many were concerned about the new state of affairs. Revolution veteran

Mirabeau B. Lamar lamented that Texas was "upon the verge of anarchy, with too little credit abroad, and too much of the fiery elements of discord at home." Thomas Jefferson Rusk, the popular commander-in-chief of the postwar army of Texas, wrote in August: "If we do not soon adopt some system and some rules of Law to govern the angry passions of men we shall forfeit all our claims to the benefits of that kind providence to whom we owe our success so far."

Rusk refused to run for president of the republic. Stephen F. Austin was being promoted in some quarters and agreed to serve if elected, but many—especially newcomers and those who had served or were serving in the army—saw him as too vested in the empresario system, still tied to old ways of relating to Mexico. Another candidate, strongly opposed to Austin, was the volatile former provisional governor Henry Smith. However, the enmities that had developed between him and other officials during his provisional governership were deeply troubling; Texas could ill afford another situation with such divisive leadership.

On August 20, a third candidate entered the race: Sam Houston. Houston had had strong critics throughout the Revolution, and the victory at San Jacinto had not completely silenced them. But Houston brought to the table the glory of the victory, a strong public identity and presence, and a background in both political and military affairs. He announced that he was stepping forward because "the crisis requires it."

In the election that followed, both Houston and the annexation proposal won resounding victories. Measures to approve the Constitution hammered out at Washington-on-the-Brazos and to authorize the new Texas Congress to make changes to that constitution also passed.

Thus, even as they approved the document that spelled out their independence, Texas voters favored annexation. In doing so, they were saying from shortly after the birth of the republic that they preferred to identify with the United States, that they preferred the security and definition of being part of that nation to "going it alone." Yet annexation was beyond the control of Texans and would not occur for longer than many expected or hoped. The quest for annexation would color the decade Texas spent as a republic, especially the politics of the era, even as new Texans—the term "Texian" no longer widely used—and new developments altered the social and economic landscape.

When Sam Houston took office in October 1836, Texas had already begun to press the U.S. government for annexation. Interim president Burnet had sent two representatives to Washington that summer. They had made little headway. Houston also declared a commitment to Texas's annexation to the United States, proclaiming in his inaugural address, "The appeal is made by a willing people. Will our friends disregard it? . . . We are cheered by the hope that they will receive us to a participancy of their civil, political, and religious rights, and hail us welcome into the great family of freemen."

Despite Houston's optimistic plea, the U.S. government was wary of even providing diplomatic recognition of the new republic. In December, President Andrew Jackson told the U.S. Congress that they should delay recognition, as

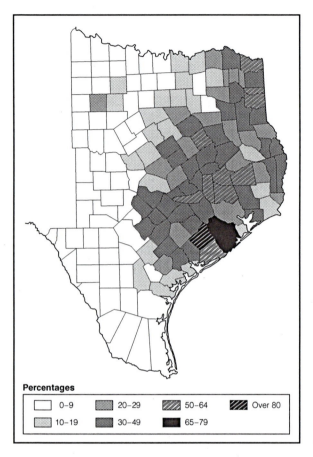

Percentages

☐ 0–9	20–29	50–64	Over 80
10–19	30–49	65–79	

Slaves as a percentage of total population, 1860.

acknowledging Texas's shaky independence would only deepen the Mexican government's anger and convince it that the United States was in league with the Texans in plotting annexation. Also, Jackson was wary of the powerful antislavery forces opposing annexation in Washington.

The North and South had been increasingly at odds on this issue since the inception of the American republic. When President Thomas Jefferson completed the Louisiana Purchase in 1803, there were no stipulations against slavery in this vast tract west of the Mississippi, stretching from Louisiana in the South all the way to present-day Montana.

Missouri was one of the first areas in the region to be settled by U.S. emigrants. When Missouri applied to be admitted to the Union as a slave state in 1819, much bitter wrangling ensued among proponents of slavery and aggressive expansion of the slave system (mostly in the Lower South), those adamantly opposed to it (mostly in the North), and those with more tentative or limited proposals in the middle (mostly in the Upper South). These different views reflected different economic and political realities and visions, pitting the North with its growing emphasis on industrialization, free labor, and republicanism against the

Lower South, burgeoning economically through the cultivation of cotton with a large, captive work force and defining itself by old paternalistic models of privilege and responsibility. The Missouri Compromise that ultimately emerged involved maintaining the balance between slave and free states in the Union, establishing a latitudinal boundary, and admitting Missouri as a slave state and Maine as a free state at about the same time.

Aside from these serious divisions over slavery, which would continue to affect Texas's fortunes, it was unclear whether Texas was even going to survive as a republic. A U.S. agent had noted in August that Texas "may still be considered a mere experiment upon independence which the loss of friends or of a single battle may disperse to the winds."

With Texas agents in Washington working feverishly, Congress recognized the Republic of Texas in the spring of 1837. Yet Texans were disappointed, having hoped for annexation. As one observer wrote, the prospect was grim for a "Texas independent, and compelled to fight her own battles and pay her own debts."

Yet this was the reality, and republic officials had begun trying to address the challenges. In the fall the first Congress had established the new town of Houston as the temporary capital and had identified twenty-three counties, based primarily on the Mexican municipalities already in existence. They had set up a Supreme Court with a chief justice and four associate justices, as well as a county court system. They had approved development of an army, a navy, a small force of mounted rangers, a militia, and frontier forts and trading posts. In December, they had also attempted to establish the southern and western boundaries of Texas: the length of the Rio Grande as it arced from its source in what is now southern Colorado and vertically bisected present-day New Mexico, then veered southeastward, forming the extended southern boundary of Texas and emptying into the Gulf of Mexico.

The Adams-Onis Treaty of 1819, which affirmed U.S. claims to Florida and Spanish claims to Texas, had established the eastern boundary of what was then Spanish Texas along the Sabine River, and the northern and northwestern boundaries along the Red River westward and northward to the Arkansas River. Texas and Louisiana would continue to quibble over the exact location of the eastern boundary. But far more problematic was the action of the First Congress regarding the southern and western borders. First, Mexican officials were not prepared to accept any borders between Mexico and an independent Texas, having rejected any treaties Santa Anna signed at Velasco. Second, the Nueces River, in some places more than 150 miles north of the Rio Grande on its west-to-east course, seemed a likelier southern border to some; there was very little Texas settlement beyond it. The same argument could be applied to Texas's grandiose claims to the Rio Grande on its vertical course through New Mexico, as republic settlement barely extended westward to what is now central Texas. These border issues would take on more and more significance.

Even as Texas leaders sought to claim an extended domain, however, most Texans continued to look toward annexation to the United States as the answer to many of their problems—in particular, defense against a Mexican invasion, protection against hostile Indians, and debt relief. The new republic had started with a debt of $1,250,000 and had little hope of doing anything but adding to it.

In the summer of 1837, Houston started diplomatic negotiations with Great Britain and France in hopes of strengthening Texas's position through further recognition and political and economic alliances. At the same time, Texas formally asked the U.S. government for annexation. The administration of Martin Van Buren argued that such a move would violate U.S. treaty agreements with Mexico. But again, there was another factor behind the government's reluctance: strong resistance in the North to the specter of another slaveholding state entering the Union. The request languished until the following summer, when Houston appointed Anson Jones minister to the United States and instructed him to withdraw it.

In the last days of the first Houston administration, officials pursued two courses simultaneously: developing Texas's ability to stand alone by establishing alliances with European nations and enticing United States officials to reconsider annexation.

Mirabeau Lamar's Administration

Major changes occurred, however, with the election of Houston's vice president, Mirabeau B. Lamar, to the presidency in November 1838. The Constitution had prohibited the first president of the republic from seeking a second consecutive term. Lamar had emerged as one of the heroes of San Jacinto. A native of Georgia, he had been a Georgia state senator before two failed attempts at a congressional seat. After arriving in Texas and participating in the Revolution, he had briefly and unsuccessfully acted as major general and commander-in-chief of the chaotic Texas army.

Lamar differed from Houston in many ways. He had an intense interest in education and the arts and was known as the "poet-president" of Texas. Early on he succeeded in passing a land act for public education that set the stage for the development of public education in Texas.

Lamar's differences from Houston were more evident, however, in his attitude regarding Texas independence. Lamar was an unabashed proponent of an empire for the Republic of Texas. In other words, he had little use for talk of annexation. Instead, he looked to strengthen and expand the republic—even as far as the Pacific Ocean. As one step in this process, Lamar moved the capital of Texas from Houston, near the gulf coast, to the ragged little settlement of Waterloo on the eastern edge of the Edwards Plateau in what was then far West Texas. Rechristened Austin in honor of Stephen F. Austin, who had died in a bout with pneumonia in December 1836, the remote settlement on the banks of the Colorado River would serve as the seat of Lamar's administration—and his projected empire.

Under Lamar, the Texas Congress ratified Jones's withdrawal of the annexation request. The diplomatic work abroad begun by Houston continued, as Texas struggled to take its place among other nations. Some European nations gradually began to realize that it would be in their best interests to acknowledge the new

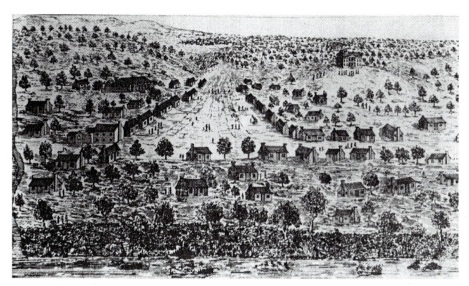

This lithograph of Austin, the new capital of Texas in 1840, appeared in an 1844 emigrants' guide. It shows a rudimentary settlement, with Congress Avenue stopping at the site of the future state capitol. *(CN 01547, The Center for American History, The University of Texas at Austin)*

republic. In September 1839, France, embroiled in a war with Mexico, recognized the independence of Texas. The government of England had also become more receptive to the republic's request for recognition. England faced a possible war with the United States and wanted to maintain a flow of cotton, which Texas could help provide. It also did not want France to gain the upper hand in trade and negotiations with Texas. In 1840, English and Texan representatives signed three treaties acknowledging Texas's independence and setting trade and navigation guidelines.

Lamar also sought to stanch the threat from Mexico, where Santa Anna had regained power. Released in Washington, D.C. less than a month after the battle of San Jacinto, Santa Anna had temporarily retired, then reemerged as a military leader in an 1838 conflict between Mexico and the French, becoming acting president of Mexico in 1839 and dictator in 1841. Not only had the Mexican Congress rejected his Velasco treaties, but the Texas government had not fulfilled all of the treaties' stipulations, and Santa Anna himself had little use for these promises made under duress.

A member of the Lamar administration, former South Carolina lawyer Bernard Bee, served as a diplomatic agent to the government of Mexico. He sailed to Veracruz in May 1839, carrying an offer of a $5 million payment if Mexico would recognize Texas's independence and accept the Rio Grande as the southern and western boundary between the two nations. Santa Anna, however, rejected a meeting, and the Mexican Council of State quickly rejected the proposal.

Lamar sent envoys to Mexico in late 1839 and in early 1841, but again without results. Meanwhile, he looked to other means of establishing Texas's claims to the plateaus, prairies, and plains to the west. He also recognized the need to bring trade dollars into Texas, as the republic treasury had never been adequate for the demands made upon it, much less for expansionist plans, and Lamar was significantly adding to Texas's debts. Thus the Santa Fe Expedition of 1841 was born.

The Santa Fe Expedition

In 1840, Lamar had enlisted three citizens of Santa Fe as commissioners for Texas. The three were to offer Santa Fe citizens the opportunity to declare their allegiance to the Texas republic. This extension of empire reflected Lamar's political plans, but it also fit well with plans for economic expansion, as there was a considerable amount of potentially lucrative trade in Santa Fe. Via a letter carried by one of the commissioners, Lamar promised Santa Fe residents that other representatives of the Texas government would arrive in Santa Fe to discuss the plan and effect a union with them.

The Texas Congress, fearing to provoke the Mexican government, refused to endorse this plan. It had appropriated money for a commercial expedition, however, so Lamar made it a volunteer venture. The subtext was still to bring the New Mexico settlements within Texas's political sphere, but the aim stated in the call for volunteers in Texas newspapers also rang true: "for the purpose of opening a commercial intercourse with the people of Santa Fe; for which purpose troops are necessary to escort the merchandise through the Comanche wilderness."

In June 1841, more than 300 men started out from a fort north of Austin. The expedition included merchants, teamsters, four civil commissioners, and a large volunteer military contingent of six companies under twenty-six-year-old Hugh McLeod, a Georgian who in 1836 had resigned his U.S. army lieutenant's commission to cast his fortunes with Texas. Here he had quickly become a leader in Indian warfare and risen to the rank of brigadier general.

The expedition headed north into unsettled territory, planning to reach the Red River and follow it westward toward Santa Fe. With "not a single map of the route among them," however, they cut their way through the dense timberlands called the Cross Timbers rather than detouring around them. Upon reaching the Wichita River, they mistook it for the Red River and began traveling along its valley. With Comanches and Kiowas threatening them and water and provisions running low, they tried to correct their course, again striking northward for the Red River. But the Caprock Escarpment that divides the rolling plains of West Texas from the High Plains proved daunting for the wagons.

With progress agonizingly slow, McLeod authorized about one-third of the expedition members to ride ahead. This group arrived in the Mexican settlements of New Mexico to find Governor Manuel Armijo had marshaled his troops to meet them, and first the advance group, then the main expedition were forced to surrender their arms and become prisoners of the Mexican government. They began a harrowing forced march to Mexico City, with summary executions along the way.

As members of the expedition staggered southward, Texans were again contemplating whom to elect as president of the republic. The failure of the expedition pointed up the unrealistic nature of Lamar's expansionist plans for the republic. Sam Houston, now in the Texas Congress, had been a steady critic of Lamar's vision, and of the fact that he was spending Texas money to achieve it even as the republic sank deeper into debt—debt that now totaled more than $8 million. In the election of fall 1841, Houston won the presidency again. And once again Houston would seek a solution for many of independent Texas's woes through the pursuit of annexation to the United States.

Challenges and Opportunities in the Republic of Texas

Because of the unsettled state of affairs and the remoteness of much of the available land, not as many people immigrated to the republic as promoters and other Texans hoped. Simply getting to Texas and traveling within it remained a challenge, transportation problems during this period judged by some "the chief obstacles to prosperity." Continuing frontier conditions and political uncertainty proved vexing, but not insurmountable to certain groups.

Challenges

Immigrants continued to haul wagons over the primary travel route, from Natchitoches in Louisiana through Nacogdoches, fighting choking dust at times, oceans of sticky mud at others. By the late 1830s those who came by sea to the coastal settlements could travel in impressive steamboats, although most couldn't afford the cabins and crammed into steerage or took deck passage. Within Texas, despite the advent of a few stagecoaches, the standard modes of transportation continued to be horseback, wagon, and ox cart.

The Texas rivers had already proven a disappointment in terms of moving people and goods. Even steamers designed for shallow rivers could not navigate the Trinity, the San Jacinto, the Colorado, the Guadalupe, the San Antonio, or the Nueces. The Brazos was barely navigable on its lower reaches, between Washington-on-the-Brazos and the gulf. And the republic was far too poor to mount railroad and canal projects. Only Buffalo Bayou between Houston and Galveston would develop into an important commercial waterway during the republic period; it, too, was difficult to navigate but had some natural canal-like qualities.

All of this meant that the settlements of the Republic of Texas were a series of remote sites, difficult to reach and particularly difficult to supply with goods, except along the gulf coast. In addition, there were uncertainties over hostilities with Mexico, the Mexican government still insisting on sovereignty over the region, and with warring Indian tribes, particularly the Comanches. Mexican troops invaded Texas twice in 1842. The first time, General Rafael Vásquez's troops sparked a second Runaway Scrape, leading President Houston to try—unsuccessfully—to move government records from Austin to Houston in what became known as the Archive War. The second time, General Adrián Woll in September took a few dozen prisoners and began marching back to the Rio Grande, in the process killing thirty-six members of a volunteer force gathered to stop him at Salado Creek. Such incidents heightened the uncertainty that Texas immigrants felt about their long-term prospects in their new home. Even two years later, many Texans were reportedly still in "a State of excitement and apprehension truly painful" regarding further Mexican invasions.

After Texas became a state and immigration increased, the first state census in 1847 counted about 142,000 Texas residents, more than a quarter of them African Americans, fewer than 1 percent of whom were free. This population total is probably low, but it reflects the fact that immigration to Texas was still limited, with the Missouri frontier and even distant Oregon beckoning many from the United States and Europe.

Stephen Pearl Andrews, a Houston lawyer, reasoned that slaveholders stayed away from the republic because of the political and economic uncertainties and others stayed away because of the slavery. Convinced that slavery was holding back economic development, he tried in the early 1840s to persuade others, but many Texans identified strongly with the American South and would not countenance talk of eliminating slavery. Andrews soon tired of the effort and left the republic.

Those who arrived in Texas and stayed had various reasons for abandoning old homes for this frontier. Many had been propelled westward in part by a spirit of adventure and wanderlust and/or by the specter of previous business, political, and personal losses. But common to virtually all was the hope for economic opportunity. In the American South, from whence most of the emigrants came, economic opportunity was tied up with the ownership of land for farming, ranching, and/or speculating and colonizing.

And Texas had plenty of it—more than 250 million acres of public domain as the Republic era began. More than 26 million acres had already been granted through a hodgepodge of Spanish, Mexican, and empresario claims. But the new government was more than ready to use much of the rest as an inducement to settlers.

The Constitution allowed for a league and a labor for every head of household in Texas at the time of independence and for one-third of a labor for every single man, although African Americans and Indians were excluded from this liberal policy. The Texas Congress followed up with a series of grants for new arrivals in the period from March 1836 through December 1841. These newcomers had to live in Texas for three years before gaining clear title to the land, but grants were still generous.

As a further inducement, on January 26, 1839, the Texas Congress passed a homestead exemption act to protect debtors from seizure of their homes. Although this act had its origins in the Mexican period, when the legislature of Coahuila y Texas had enacted a similar statute, it was a first in American jurisprudence, stipulating that a citizen was protected in retaining "fifty acres of land or one town lot, including his or her homestead, and improvements not exceeding five hundred dollars in value."

When even the homestead measure did not stimulate enough migration, in 1841 the Texas Congress authorized the president to implement another empresario contract system. The following year, a colonization law stipulated that the new empresarios would receive "ten premium sections, each to be settled by one hundred families," with the government holding on to alternate sections to sell after the original sections were settled.

As with the previous empresario efforts, the results were uneven at best. They depended in large part on European immigration. William Peters established a colony in the vicinity of present-day Dallas, with the assistance of both English and American investors, thrusting settlement far northward, close to the Red River. Henri Castro brought Catholic Alsatians from Europe and settled them deep in an expanse west of San Antonio and the Medina River, pushing the Texas frontier westward. Henry F. Fisher and Burchard Miller contracted to introduce a large number of German immigrants to Texas; although they faltered, others picked up the challenge, and the resulting colonies, like Castro's, extended the western frontier.

Nineteenth-century painter Carl G. von Iwonski titled this painting "Log Cabin, New Braunfels." It provides one picture of antebellum Texas farm and frontier life. *(Courtesy Daughters of the Republic of Texas Library)*

Visitors and immigrants continued to be excited by the agricultural potential of the lands they saw in traveling through the settlements. Cotton cultivation in particular was developing, and with it a planter class that depended heavily on slave labor. In the republic era, however, most immigrants were looking for that initial golden opportunity. In 1845, a Texan wrote, "All are land-hunting, seeking sugar, cotton and stock farm lands, but are as much at a loss in their selection as children in a toy-shop."

Merchandising offered another economic opportunity; the field was wide open for the buying and selling of goods. Merchants or traders would buy items on credit and then sell them to farmers, planters, townspeople, even to other merchants, often taking crops in place of cash. Many merchants, however, suffered in the financial instability of the republic, with its paper money worth only twelve cents in exchange with the U.S. dollar, and in the extended aftermath of the global economic Panic of 1837. Adolphus Sterne, a merchant who had been in business in Nacogdoches since 1826, would complain in May 1842, "[T]imes have never been so hard in Texas, like they are now, I have never known the want of two bits until now,—!!!!!"

Sterne was also a land agent, and many like him tried to seize the opportunities to make money in land speculation. The empresarios hoped to make a profit from their colonization efforts. Land agents and land lawyers bought and sold and took commissions, "organiz[ing] the land market in the new territories" and serving as "critical intermediaries" between the Tejano elite who still owned title to desirable lands and those who wanted them. In a well-established American tradition, speculators bought up whatever lands they could in hopes of realizing vast profits, but many bought on credit, then saw the acreage drop in value.

Some used the fledgling towns both as objects of speculation and as bases for it. A visitor to Houston in 1837 found "the spirit of speculation . . . afloat," with lots "selling at enormous prices, in some instances as high as four and five thousand dollars apiece." Few of the towns could be said to be flourishing, however, and some would even decline during the republic years: By 1844, Brazoria was looking distinctly rundown. Texas entrepreneurs, like their government, lacked a vital trade system, a stable currency, and hope of attracting outside investors.

Most Texans, whatever their location and pursuits, still could expect to have very rudimentary homes. In general, Tejanos had one-story stone or adobe homes or even simple structures with picket walls and thatched roofs; Anglo settlers lived in log cabins, known as "dog-trot" cabins because they were designed with a room on either side of a central "dog-trot" breezeway. The floors consisted of clay or dirt.

Food was usually equally simple—beef, cornbread, coffee. Wheat flour proved so scarce throughout the period that many families relied on cornmeal instead. "Raising corn," wrote one German settler, "was a matter of life and death, since upon it depended the existence of the colony." Others grew their own wheat. Many were happy to get a cow; as one young woman who arrived shortly after the republic period explained to her father: "[F]or over three months we had neither a scrap of butter or a drop of milk, but we got by nicely and oh how wonderful did the first cup of coffee with milk and the first piece of cornbread with butter taste to us!"

Anglos and Europeans

In these challenging times, those who were best able to seize opportunity were Anglo men of some means from the American South, men who had previous experience with American forms of economic and/or political power. They resembled—and in many cases were—the architects of the late revolution, men who knew their way around a cotton farm and a courtroom, a plantation and a political office. They had migrated primarily from the Lower South—Alabama, Louisiana, Mississippi—bringing with them strong proslavery views. Many had experienced failure—business reverses, lost political elections, fractured personal lives—yet they maintained a sense of unbridled optimism and entitlement. In the United States, only white males could exercise that most basic right of citizenship, the vote. These men had absorbed the concept of manifest destiny, although it still did not yet have a name: They saw themselves as representatives of a culture and a race destined for greatness and control of the American continent.

European men, too, found opportunities, although most of them were new to the continent and had to adjust to American ways as well as the presence of Mexicans and Indians. To a great extent, the immigrant European groups stayed together, setting up their own small German, Alsatian, Czech, and Norwegian enclaves; however, the men moved about freely and engaged in farming and business along with their American counterparts. The largest European immigrant group by far was the Germans, whose numbers would be estimated at more than 11,600 by 1850. Germans had migrated to Texas as early as the 1820s. By the late 1830s, numerous Germans were looking to do so. Merchants and craftsmen had been losing economic ground in Germany with the advent of industrial production and population growth. They were finding it prohibitively expensive to maintain even a small business. And land was a powerful allure. Especially after the failed German revolution of 1848, many political dissenters came looking for freedom in Texas; these new arrivals became known as the "Forty-Eighters."

The 1842 Fisher and Miller contract to bring German colonists to Texas was expanded in 1844, but the two men soon sold it to a German organization called the Adelsverein, or Society for the Protection of German Immigrants in Texas. In exchange for a flat fee, the Adelsverein, now a joint-stock company, promised to transport German colonists to America and then to Adelsverein lands in Texas. Because the Fisher-Miller grant was so remote, located between the Colorado and Llano rivers, the Adelsverein selected and purchased a site on the Guadalupe River closer to the edge of Anglo settlement.

The Adelsverein brought an estimated 5,200 German immigrants to Texas between 1844 and 1846. Many journeyed with difficulty from Indianola on the coast to the Guadalupe site, New Braunfels, established in 1845. The travelers

John O. Meusebach (center), Commissioner General of the German immigrant company the Adelsverein, led the German colonists in parleying with Comanche chiefs near the lower San Saba River in March 1847. Two months later, the chiefs signed the Meusebach-Comanche Treaty. *(Courtesy Gillespie County Historical Society)*

were already weary from the long sea voyage, and the Adelsverein had not been able to make the small coastal settlement of Indianola an adequate staging area for the long journey inland. Travelers struggled with illness, incessant rains, and oxcarts mired in mud.

The first commissioner-general, or leader, of the Adelsverein colonization was Prince Carl of Solms-Braunfels, who cut quite a swath through Texas frontier society. A tireless worker in the colonization effort, he was nonetheless best remembered for his aristocratic and eccentric ways, including the cock feathers he and members of his entourage wore in their hats. Following him in the role was Otsfried Hans von Meusebach, who in Texas became John O. Meusebach and guided the Adelsverein colonists well, establishing a second center of settlement, Fredericksburg, some sixty miles northwest of New Braunfels.

In the ideology of the era in America, women were to stay at home, to maintain the "private sphere," while Anglo and northern European men engaged in the business and politics of capitalistic empire building. This division of labor was reinforced by women's frequent pregnancies and, in Texas as on frontiers elsewhere, by the very real work of maintaining a frontier home whose residents had to rely to a large extent on their own self-sufficiency and inventiveness rather than on nonexistent or erratic supply networks.

Yet the same frontier conditions also gave Anglo and European women some autonomy. They ran farms and businesses as well as homes in the absence of their menfolk; many of these absences were frequent and prolonged. They operated boarding houses, participated in a frontier bartering economy, hunted and harvested as need dictated, and worked to establish schools and churches. These Texas women also had more rights under the Hispanic-influenced community property laws than did women in the United States, for economic gains in a marriage were considered both the woman's and the man's.

They could also expect some court protection against abusive or wayward husbands; recognizing the isolation and vulnerability of many frontier wives, republic lawmakers established standards penalizing abandonment and cruelty in their 1841 divorce act. State lawmakers would follow with anticruelty standards "among the most liberal found in the antebellum South." Nonetheless, political opportunities remained off-limits, economic opportunities meager; legally, women could not accumulate property or sell it without the permission of their husbands.

Marginalized Groups in the Republic

If women of the increasingly dominant Anglo and European American culture faced restrictions, women and men of different ethnic groups found their opportunities even more restricted. Increasingly, African Americans, Tejanos, and Native Americans found far more challenges to survival than opportunities to thrive in the Republic of Texas.

African American Experience

Of course, African American slaves lived the most circumscribed lives. Most arrived in Texas with their masters, rather than being brought to Texas to be sold. Some historians have noted that the shared pioneer enterprise with its intimate working conditions on the Texas frontier created stronger bonds for both owners and slaves. Whereas most slaves in the southern states lived on large plantations, in Texas most lived on small isolated farms, both in the republic era and in the early statehood era. Even in 1860, more than half of the slaveowners in Texas held four slaves or fewer, only 1.5 percent claiming to own more than fifty.

In a land of rough conditions, however, slaves experienced the worst. William Fairfax Gray would judge some of the slave homes he saw in the midst of a chilling norther in 1837 "more open than the log stables in Virginia." But rough living conditions were not all they faced. The Republic of Texas government meted out harsh punishments for any crimes or even perceived crimes committed by slaves. "Insulting or abusive language" directed at a white person earned twenty-five to a hundred lashes. White owners could hire out slaves at will and controlled all their transactions, as it was forbidden for anyone to buy something from a slave without written permission from his or her master. There were harsh penalties, too, for anyone harboring an escaped slave or in any way encouraging or abetting his or her escape. Marriages of African Americans and Anglos were simply outlawed.

The few liberties a slave might enjoy depended upon the kind of owner the slave had: Would the owner, for example, allow the slave to marry someone on a neighboring plantation, or even to visit him or her? Even under a relatively lenient master, slaves could not choose their own marriage partners, learn to read, or escape arbitrary punishment. And there was no guarantee that their families would remain intact if the owner needed funds and chose to sell one or more of them.

Free African Americans were restricted as well. The punitive legal codes applied to slaves also applied to them, and the Constitution of 1836 required them to receive special permission to live in the republic. In 1837 Congress qualified this requirement, allowing those in Texas at the time of independence (approximately 150 people) to reside in the republic "as long as they choose." One of those affected by these laws was Samuel McCulloch, Jr., who had fought in the Revolution as a member of the Matagorda volunteer company. After passage of the 1836 law, McCulloch had petitioned for citizenship and land grants; the 1837 law had automatically granted him citizenship but left his land grant request in limbo.

In 1840, Congress again reversed itself, passing a law barring the immigration of free blacks to Texas and stipulating that all free men and women must leave within two years or be sold into slavery. Although this draconian plan was not fully implemented—for example, McCulloch and four relatives won exemption—free African Americans faced an uncertain existence at best.

The lives of African Americans in Texas reflected the long-lasting effects of the slave system in the South. Blacks coming to Texas, usually through no choice of their own, knew all too well the ways in which their lives could and would be restricted and constricted. In the republic era, however, many Tejanos were just beginning to comprehend the full implications of the growing Anglo presence for their own future.

Tejano Experience

Immediately after the Revolution, Tejanos were pushed, prodded, and deprived of opportunity in a variety of ways. Members of the Tejano elite who had worked with Anglo leaders were increasingly excluded from or moved to the margins of the developing power structure of the republic. Tejano settlers near the Anglo colonies found themselves, their homes, and their livestock targeted by former soldiers bitter toward Mexicans. It didn't matter whether the Tejanos had actively aided the revolutionary effort, remained loyal to the Mexican government, or tried to be neutral. Many were driven from their homes, particularly those who lived near the Austin and DeWitt colonies, as immigrants spilled onto accessible lands with little or no regard for Mexican land titles. (These titles were clouded by confusion over previous land claims under earlier governments but also by Anglos having taken control of political and legal systems.)

The Rio Grande region contained relatively intact Mexican enclaves; Laredo was still considered a part of the Mexican state of Tamualipas and El Paso still a town of the state of Chihuahua. But former Texian soldiers raided south of the Nueces, in one of the territories disputed by the Texas and Mexican governments. Emboldened by a republic decree that Mexican livestock was public property, the former soldiers took cattle belonging to Mexican residents, many of whom had sought refuge in the Rio Grande towns during the war.

Far to the east in Nacogdoches, tensions between Tejanos and Anglos continued to ignite. In the wake of the Revolution, emigrants from the United States decisively outnumbered Tejano residents and showed little interest in or respect for Mexican social and political structures and history. Some Tejano residents rallied around Vicente Córdova, the Nacogdoches-area landowner and former *alcalde* and militia commander. Tired of the conspiracy rumors surrounding him and the continued intimidation of Tejanos, Córdova had been in touch with Mexican authorities intent on disrupting Republic of Texas affairs. Now he gathered supporters from among the local Tejano and Indian populations in what would come to be known as the Córdova rebellion.

In early August 1838, Thomas Jefferson Rusk, now major general of the militia, received word that Córdova and a hundred or more Mexicans had set up camp on the Angelina River. As Rusk readied the local militia, President Houston issued a proclamation aimed at Córdova banning unlawful assembly and the carrying of arms.

Córdova and eighteen companions signed a proclamation in response, asserting that they had been stripped of their rights but would die defending them. A detachment sent by Rusk and led by Major Henry W. Augustine, a veteran of the Revolution and former republic senator, tracked and set upon Córdova's band, which now had a few hundred Indians added to its numbers.

Córdova escaped and traveled to Mexico, but as a result of the incident, thirty-three men of Mexican heritage faced treason charges in the Nacogdoches and San Augustine district courts. Only one, a former Nacogdoches official, would be found guilty. Sentenced to hang, he eventually received a pardon. But the ultimate result of the troubles in the Nacogdoches area was that more than a hundred Mexican families were forced out the following year.

In San Antonio, as in Nacogdoches, the old cooperative structures were crumbling, with land and power rapidly shifting into Anglo hands. Some newcomers voiced suspicion of the Mexican population, but others acknowledged the plight of the Tejanos. Many of the elite Tejanos, in particular, were caught between economic and political ties with Anglos—even personal ties, as daughters of leading Tejano families married prominent or soon-to-be-prominent Anglo men—and their Catholic, Spanish, and Mexican identity and heritage. Despite conditions on the frontier, the Tejanos of San Antonio had preserved their heritage through attention to religious practice, nationalistic and religious celebrations, and schooling for their children. Increasingly, Anglos ignored or paid little attention to this heritage.

Juan Seguín, however, remained an influential figure—an indisputable war hero who had an ability to bridge the Mexican and Anglo communities. He was repeatedly elected to the republic Senate, where he was the only Tejano. Returning to San Antonio, he generated enough support in the Anglo community as well as the Tejano community to be elected mayor in late 1840. As mayor, he found that "[a]t every hour of the day and night my countrymen ran to me for protection against the assaults or exactions of those adventurers."

Seguín, who had connections with Mexico through his continued support of the federalists against the centralists, soon found himself suspected of collaborating with the Mexican government against the Texas republic by giving away information about the ill-fated Santa Fe expedition. Yet, denying the charge, he won reelection as mayor. More trouble awaited, however. Seguín requested from Mexican frontier commander General Rafael Vásquez a pass to travel to Mexico "for a drove of sheep," and the manner of Vásquez's reply led Seguín to surmise "that an expedition against Texas was in preparation for the following month of March." Without further credible information of an impending Mexican army invasion of San Antonio, Seguín could not get the secretary of war to send aid, and he did not think he could defend the town without help. Thus, he, his family, and other Tejano residents left town for outlying ranches as Anglos in San Antonio tried to set up a defense.

The Mexican troops arrived and occupied the town for two days in March 1842. Seguín served in a company that pursued the troops, but when he returned to San Antonio he found "reports about my implausible treason were spreading widely." Seguín heard daily threats: "All the parties of volunteers en route to San Antonio declared 'they wanted to kill Seguín.'" He resigned as mayor in April, reluctantly preparing to move to Mexico to escape the "constant wretchedness" his family was experiencing.

Cherokee and Comanche Experience

If Seguín had been caught in a cultural and political crossfire in San Antonio, the same could be said of Chief Bowles, or "Duwali," and the Cherokee Indians in East Texas. They were beset by conflicting claims on their loyalties, by factionalism within the tribe, and by possibilities of alliances with other Indians. During the war, Chief Bowles had signed the treaty pledging loyalty to the independence movement in return for clear land title, and Houston had reassured him, saying, "You will get your land as promised in our Treaty." Now, after the war, the Cherokees faced increased suspicion and hostility from Anglo neighbors, and they had no treaty for the land they had cultivated as long as Austin's early colonists had cultivated theirs. When Mexican agents continued to move around Texas, attempting to weaken the republic and reassert Texas claims by enlisting the tribes, some Cherokees were ready to listen in order to survive.

In August 1836, the republic government received a report that the Cherokees, Comanches, and a number of smaller groups were preparing to attack settlers. When Sam Houston took office in October, he attempted to defuse the tension created by the reports by enlisting some of the Cherokees as rangers against the Comanches and other hostile Indians. This did not deter some Cherokees from meeting with Mexican officials planning a spring 1837 attack on the settlements; when spring arrived, however, Chief Bowles went as an emissary from the Texas government to the Comanches and other western tribes.

Later that year, a Texas Senate committee rejected the Houston-Bowles treaty of 1836, calling the Cherokees, who had proven the most adept of the five "civilized" tribes in adopting Anglo ways, "the most savage and ruthless of our frontier enemies." This harshly worded rejection only fueled the pro-Mexican faction among the Cherokees. At the same time, new immigrants were pushing onto the lands occupied by the tribe, rendering even Chief Bowles desperate. He sent an emissary to the Cherokees already in Indian Territory asking for warriors and promising Cherokee land titles for them, but without success.

Then came the Córdova rebellion, in which a few hundred Indians, including many Cherokees, clearly aligned themselves with the Mexican plotters. Houston tried to prepare against the threat militarily while still reaching out to the Cherokees, ordering a survey of the boundaries of the land claimed by the Cherokees, even though the treaty had been rejected.

Events continued in this contradictory vein. Survivors of autumn 1838 Indian raids in the settlements implicated Cherokees, and Thomas Jefferson Rusk led the Texas militia in a show of force through the Cherokees' region. With feelings running high, tribal members, whether aligned with the Mexicans or not, had to take measures for self-defense, even as the surveyors finished marking the boundaries of their disputed land.

Mirabeau Lamar's election to the presidency effectively sealed the Cherokees' fate. If there was a second major difference between Houston and Lamar, beyond their opposing attitudes toward annexation and expansion, it was in their attitude toward Indians. Houston, with his experience among the Cherokees, had been remarkable for his era in his attempts to treat the Indians fairly. To Lamar, as to many frontiersmen, Indians were simply hostile or potentially hostile nuisances to be removed without compunction by whatever means necessary.

One of Lamar's first stated intentions in office was to remove the Cherokees. In the meantime, Vicente Córdova was still building alliances from Mexico. The group that would later be known as the Texas Rangers had been formed in 1837, largely in response to Indian threats, and in May 1839, rangers took from a Mexican agent letters addressed simply to "the various immigrant chiefs." Lamar used them as evidence of collusion by the Cherokees and ordered their removal. In July Lamar sent Rusk to begin the forced removal. The Cherokees were told they would be paid for their improvements and their crops. Many balked at the news that they would have to remove the gunlocks from their weapons and accept a militia escort. When the militia attempted to force the terms, the Indians simply left on their own, pursued by the militia.

On July 16, the militia caught up with the Cherokees, as well as with allied Delawares, Shawnees, and Kickapoos. Chief Bowles was shot and killed, and the Indians were scattered, some to Mexico, some to other tribal groups.

The Cherokees' story vividly demonstrates the limits of opportunity in Texas for those who were perceived as a threat or a nuisance by members of the dominant immigrant culture. The Comanches, who perceived the surveyor's compass as "the thing that steals the land," posed a much larger threat. They remained violently resistant to attempts to encroach upon the land they ranged and to restrict their mobility, freedom, and autonomy.

Texas had barely become independent when a sizable force of Comanches, with some Kiowa and Kichai allies, rode up to a settler enclave known as Parker's Fort near the headwaters of the Navasota River. Inhabitants fled in fear as the Indians speared and killed several and took five captives, including Rachel Plummer, who left a dramatic account of her captivity, and her cousin Cynthia Ann Parker, who would grow up among the Comanches and become the mother of the last Comanche chief, Quanah Parker.

The Comanches and their allies continued to kill settlers and to pluck captives from the settlements as companies of rangers tried to pursue and punish them in a lurching yet escalating warfare. This conflict flared on the streets of San Antonio in the Council House Fight of March 1840. A delegation of Penateka Comanche leaders had come to the town to negotiate a peace treaty with representatives of the Texas government eager to redeem Comanche prisoners. Yet the Indians had brought only a handful. The Texans demanded other prisoners; the Indians responded that they had no direct control over the others. When the Texas officials tried to take the assembled chiefs hostage in a ploy to redeem the other prisoners, a general bloody melee broke out, spreading through the Main Plaza and into the side streets. Many of the Indians were killed, others held hostage, but the incident only heightened Comanche resistance. In retaliation the Comanches raided even deeper into the settlements, in August penetrating all the way to Victoria and Linville. They were led by Buffalo Hump, a war chief of the Penateka Comanches. A volunteer army met the Indians on their return, on the banks of Plum Creek near Lockhart, and defeated them. But Buffalo Hump and other warriors escaped to fight again insisting that the republic keep settlement to the east of the Edwards Plateau.

In his second term as president, Houston negotiated a treaty with the Comanches and their allies near what is today Waco. This 1844 Treaty of Tehuacana Creek declared that "the tomahawk shall be buried, and no more blood appear in the path" between the parties, but the grievances on both sides endured. The continued incursions of adventurers and settlers onto the lands occupied by the Comanches led to further raids, both by the warriors against settlers and travelers and by Texas Rangers against Indian camps.

In response to the Indian threats, as well as the Mexican threats, the republic could mount only a limited and scattershot defense. For this and other reasons, Sam Houston and most of his fellow Texans remained convinced that they needed the protection and resources annexation would bring. But how could they obtain it?

The Annexation Quest Continues, 1841–1845

Houston's election to the presidency in 1841 again brought the issue of annexation to the fore. Lamar had declared in his inauguration speech that the "imposing considerations which at one time rendered [annexation] seemingly desirable" no longer existed, but in fact, the republic was now in even deeper economic distress. During Lamar's administration, not only had the government's debts spiraled, but the vast amounts of paper money the Texas treasury printed beginning in 1839 had become virtually worthless. Republic leaders could not develop trade and settlement with vigor or effectively protect the citizenry. Thus, Houston again quietly began trying to build support for the republic to become part of the United States.

Yet the officials of the U.S. government remained indifferent, hesitant, or even hostile to the idea. Not only did they wish to avoid further difficulties with Mexico, but many national leaders actively resisted the idea of another slave state entering the Union. Meanwhile, Houston grappled with an impoverished treasury and the unrelenting threat from Mexico.

The Mier Expedition

The Mexican incursions of 1842 stimulated the fighting spirit of many Texas volunteers, who signed up in San Antonio after Woll's departure. Houston preferred diplomatic maneuvering but sent Brigadier General Alexander Somervell to control and direct the angry, combative forces. In late November 700 men marched south under Somervell and seized Laredo, but many of the men remained undisciplined and greedy for both revenge and plunder. One hundred and eighty-five headed home after the capture of Laredo. Somervell led the rest in the capture of Guerrero, but it became apparent to him that they could not hope to further the campaign. He ordered the volunteer army disbanded.

Many of the volunteers resisted. Revolution veteran William S. Fisher, a captain in the expedition, assumed command of the more than 300 men who refused to disband, wanting at least to raid the Mexican settlements for horses and cattle. On December 23, this group crossed the Rio Grande into Mier and demanded supplies, then retreated across the river to wait for the goods that the town residents had nervously pledged. Meanwhile, however, the Mexican military arrived in Mier and stopped delivery. With no supplies forthcoming and news of the Mexican force's presence, the volunteers crossed the river again on Christmas Day and fought a battle with the soldiers. Although the Mexicans suffered heavy losses, they prevailed and took most of the Texan force prisoner. The Texans were scheduled for execution, then spared and marched toward Mexico City. They attempted an escape, but almost all were recaptured.

In "The Mier Expedition: Drawing the Black Bean," well-known late-nineteenth-century artist Frederic Remington depicted the fateful ceremony in which men of this expedition drew beans to determine who among them would be executed by Mexican troops. In this way, seventeen of the 176 prisoners received their death warrants. *(The Museum of Fine Arts, Houston; The Hogg Brothers Collection; gift of Miss Ima Hogg)*

This account provides the background for the famous "black bean" episode, in which the 176 prisoners were each required to draw a bean from an earthen jar. Those who drew the seventeen black beans were slated for execution. The Mier expedition thus came to a tragic end: The seventeen black bean holders were shot and Ewen Cameron was executed, on an order by Santa Anna, because of his leadership in the escape attempt. Other members of the expedition gradually won their freedom from a Mexican prison.

Changing Climate for Annexation

In the meantime, opportunities to further the cause of annexation to the United States presented themselves in Texas. England was eager to continue to deal with Texas as an independent nation in hopes of building a viable commercial trade, arresting U.S. westward expansion in the Southwest, and indirectly exerting some control over American slavery and tariff issues. The British were actively working against annexation. A worried President John Tyler, who shared southern attitudes on slavery, reopened communication on the subject with Houston.

Sam Houston moved cautiously—too cautiously for many in Texas. One member of the republic legislature worried that Washington didn't understand how devoutly most Texans hoped for annexation and concluded "We are obliged to leave much to [Houston], and I am sorry to leave in such suspicious keeping a thing so valuable to us all." Nonetheless, Houston had deftly played American authorities against the British, with Texas minister in Washington, James Pinckney Henderson, reporting in February 1844, "All things prove now the *very great* desire of the U.S. to annex us."

Houston, however, was worried about reactions from Mexico and wanted U.S. troops in place in Texas before any news of annexation negotiations leaked out. Negotiation attempts limped along until Tyler's negotiator, the energetically proslavery John C. Calhoun, signed a proposed treaty of annexation with Henderson and second Texas minister Isaac Van Zandt. But antislavery forces again opposed the idea of admitting another slave state; they and others also argued against the move on the grounds that it would bring on war with Mexico. The U.S. Senate in June 1844 rejected the document by more than a two-to-one margin.

Five months later, expansionist James K. Polk of Tennessee won election as U.S. president, in part through advocating annexation of Texas, and added weight to Tyler's efforts to bring Texas into the American republic. At about the same time, Houston was succeeded by Texas secretary of state and Houston supporter Anson Jones. Jones sensed that Texas now had a fair amount of bargaining power given Polk's election, American fears of a Texas-British alliance, and the potential British brokering of a Texas-Mexico peace. Jones refused to request annexation again without assurance that the U.S. Senate would now approve it.

Tyler continued to work toward this end, and on March 1, 1845 won congressional passage of an annexation agreement. The agreement was designed to please Texas leaders, allowing Texas to enter the Union as a slave state and hold onto "all the vacant and unappropriated lands lying within its limits." This was a major victory for the South, as northerners still vigorously protested admitting another slave state to the Union.

Now, however, the Texas government was also being courted seriously by England and France in an attempt to stave off annexation to the United States. The British and French representatives convinced Jones to delay an answer and pressured Mexican officials to belatedly recognize the still-shaky republic rather than confront the specter of a strong United States on their border. In late April 1845, Mexican officials tentatively recognized the independence of the Republic of Texas if Texas would not annex itself to another country.

Thus, Jones was able to offer the republic Congress, meeting in special session in June, both the annexation agreement and an alternate choice: continuation of the republic under a treaty of peace with Mexico, with the stipulation that Texas would not annex itself to the United States. The congressmen unanimously chose annexation, but their choice had to be approved by "the representatives of the people of Texas in convention assembled." On July 4, by a vote of 55 to 1, representatives led by Thomas Jefferson Rusk resolved that the territory of the republic "may be erected into a new State, to be called the State of Texas . . . in order that the same may be admitted as one of the States of [the American] Union."

In "The Republic of Texas Is No More," illustrator Norman Price envisioned the annexation ceremony of February 19, 1846, with President Anson Jones leading in the lowering of the republic flag. *(Prints & Photographs Collection—Annexation File, CN 03085a, The Center for American History, The University of Texas at Austin)*

The Convention then proceeded to create a state constitution, the Texas Constitution of 1845, providing for election of a governor, a lieutenant governor, and a legislature, as well as the appointment of other state officials. On October 13, Texas voters overwhelmingly approved both the document and annexation to the United States. In a special election they proceeded to vote for J. Pinckney Henderson as the first governor. Meanwhile, the U.S. Congress also approved the state constitution, and on December 29 President Polk signed the act making Texas a state.

On February 19, 1846, with the first meeting of the state legislature in Austin, Jones turned over the reins of government to Henderson in a ceremony at noon in front of the capitol. With the republic flag lowered and the American flag raised to fly over it, Jones proclaimed to the gathered crowd, "The lone star of Texas . . . has . . . become fixed forever in that glorious constellation . . . the American Union." According to a newspaper report, many in the crowd cried, but few of them would have wished for a different course for Texas, given the American origins of most of the citizenry and the experiences of the previous ten years. "Thank God, we are now annexed to the United States," wrote Mary Maverick, "and can hope for home and quiet."

The New State Takes Shape

With annexation, the struggles over Texas's identity seemed to recede into the past. New state officials busily worked to bring Texas into the federal system. Two prominent leaders since the Revolution, Thomas Jefferson Rusk and Sam Houston, headed to Washington, D.C., as U.S. senators. Texans looked to a more stable future, and to increased growth and development.

The Mexican War and Texas Territory

Texans could now even regard the outbreak of a U.S. war with Mexico with little trepidation. And war broke out almost immediately, in part because of the annexation treaty and continuing boundary disputes, including the one over the Rio Grande. Polk had sent General Zachary Taylor and troops to a post at the mouth of the Nueces River in the summer of 1845. Polk's representative, sent to Mexico to negotiate in November, was rebuffed by officials angry about the annexation proceedings. Shortly after the American flag was raised over the Texas state capitol, Taylor's troops were dispatched to the Rio Grande, where Mexican troops were also massing. On April 23, 1846, Mexico declared a defensive war against the United States. President Polk won a declaration of war as well, citing a late-April incident in which Mexican troops had crossed the Rio Grande near Matamoros and fought an American patrol. The first substantial conflict, the battle of Palo Alto near Brownsville on May 8, grew out of American troops' attempts to supply the Fort Texas Rio Grande border post (later Fort Brown) from Port Isabel to the east and Mexican troops' attempt to stop them.

There was serious opposition to the war in the United States, especially among prominent members of the Whig political party, which had been established in the 1830s to challenge President Jackson and the Jacksonian Democrats. Many felt that Polk, an expansionist Democrat, had provoked the conflict in a bid to seize Mexican holdings stretching to California. In Texas, public sentiment among the Anglo American majority was decidedly prowar, with resentment and even bitter hatred against the Mexican government still lingering.

Governor Henderson asked the legislature to release him to command the Second Texas Regiment, and he led this unit in the U.S. forces' taking of Monterrey in September. The Texas Mounted Rifles under Colonel John Coffee "Jack" Hays also participated in this victory. Major Benjamin McCulloch's spy company contributed to the American victory at the battle of Buena Vista in February 1847, and Hays, now leading a company of Texas rangers, aided General Winfield Scott on his march to Mexico City. With the fall of Mexico City in September 1847, the United States claimed ultimate victory. The 1848 Treaty of Guadalupe Hidalgo that followed shifted to the United States Mexican claims on a great swath of the West, including California, New Mexico, and Arizona, and portions of Utah, Nevada, and Colorado.

For Texans, the treaty secured their southern Rio Grande border for the state and the nation, and meant that they would need to negotiate with the federal government regarding their continuing claims to a large portion of New Mexico.

Within six weeks of the treaty being signed, Texans tried to further these claims by creating Santa Fe County, with boundaries extending through most of eastern New Mexico. The next year, the state redrew these boundaries and added three more counties in the disputed territory. Governor Peter Hansborough Bell sent Robert Simpson Neighbors, a former volunteer ranger and the first Indian agent for Texas, to organize the four counties. Neighbors was successful with El Paso County but met resistance from antagonistic New Mexicans intent on bidding for separate statehood.

Texans continued to cling fiercely to their claims to New Mexican territory, winning an advantageous compromise in September of 1850. Texas would relinquish most of its New Mexico claims except for the El Paso region. In exchange, the federal government offered the state $10 million. Voters approved the offer, two to one, and in November 1850 Bell signed the compromise, fixing the present boundaries of Texas and giving Texas a tremendous economic boost. The federal government retained half of the $10-million award to settle "revenue debt" owed

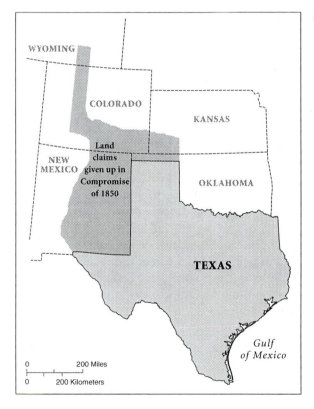

Compromise of 1850.

to those holding Republic of Texas securities. But with the other half, state officials were able to pay off all claims by participants in the Texas Revolution and suppliers of the Texas army and still have $3.75 million left. With these funds, they would set up an endowment for public schools, provide loans to railroads in hopes of developing rail lines in Texas, and remit most county taxes for a number of years, enabling the counties to use the money for development.

Although the money was a tremendous boon to a government just a few years removed from the financial ruin of the republic, Texas was not yet able to attract viable railroad projects. The lack of fast, efficient transportation remained an obstacle, within the settlements and especially beyond the lines of settlement, to the west and northwest. With annexation, immigrant numbers were swelling, with the population reaching 212,592 in 1850, including 58,161 slaves. One of the primary tasks for the state and federal government in the late 1840s and through the 1850s became the establishment of a line of forts through central, north, and west Texas, in preparation for trade routes through and immigration onto the plateaus and plains of the region.

Soldiers were dispatched to establish posts along a south-to-north frontier line running through Austin, from Fort Brown (1846) at the southern tip of Texas to Fort Worth (1849) at the junction of the Clear Fork and West Fork of the Trinity River in the north, a short distance west of the small settlement of Dallas. Fort Belknap (1851), beyond Fort Worth, was the northernmost of these posts, with Fort Bliss (1848) and Fort Quitman (1858) the westernmost, along the Rio Grande near El Paso. In between, a host of forts dotted the Texas frontier, from the Rio Grande northward to the southern reaches of the Llano Estacado, or "Staked Plains." Although settlement would not reach to most of these forts in the 1850s, it did push westward into the Texas Hill Country and northward through the Eastern Cross Timbers.

Soldiers partnered with merchants and others intent on finding the best routes through the vast and often forbidding stretches to the west. In 1848, a civilian expedition under the command of Jack C. Hays and financed in part by San Antonio merchants teamed with a small military force under Captain Samuel Highsmith to try to map out a trade route between San Antonio and El Paso. The Hays-Highsmith expedition helped spur two more the following year, a topographical engineers' expedition which established a "lower route" across West Texas and an expedition led by Neighbors. First moving northward to where the new town site of Waco was being plotted, Neighbors used his contacts with the Indians to trace a northern route to El Paso. In the meantime, Captain Randolph B. Marcy of the U.S. Army explored a wagon route across the Texas Panhandle to Santa Fe.

Pressures on Indians and Tejanos

All of this activity, of course, periodically incited Comanches and their allies on the southern plains in the late 1840s and the 1850s. Neighbors, appointed Texas Indian agent again under a new federal administration, worked to set up two western Indian reservations in 1855. (A third, established the previous year in East Texas, was for the Alabama and Coushatta Indians who had migrated from Alabama to Spanish Texas beginning in the 1780s.)

About half of the Penateka Comanches agreed to occupy the reservation on the Clear Fork River in Throckmorton County; the other western reservation, at the junction of the Brazos and Clear Fork rivers, was home to what remained of a hodgepodge of tribes, including Waco, Caddo, and Tonkawa. Neighbors labored tirelessly to get the Indians onto these reservations and to protect them once they were there. Settlers pressed unmercifully, however, contending that Indians from the reservations were responsible for depredations against them, rather than blaming nonreservation Indian bands or even Anglo outlaws. Neighbors had to employ federal troops to protect the western reservation Indians, many of whom had helped frontier volunteers and the military in campaigns against the hostile bands of Indians. The situation grew so bad that Neighbors requested and received permission from the Commissioner of Indian Affairs in Washington to remove the reservation Indians across the Red River to Indian Territory. Even removal of the western Indians, however, did not occur fast enough for armed bands of Indian hunters among the Anglo population. In late summer 1859, Neighbors accompanied his charges across the river to Indian Territory, only to be shot and killed at Fort Belknap en route home, the victim of an attack by an Anglo immigrant. At about the same time, hostile Comanches and Kiowas began mounting extremely severe raids along the Texas frontier, forcing Sam Houston, now elected governor of the state, to dispatch a large force of Texas Rangers who in turn raised militia companies.

More and more immigrants were pouring into Texas, filling up the eastern regions, swelling the population of such now-major towns as Houston, Galveston, and Marshall, venturing westward in search of opportunity along the frontiers. They were still overwhelmingly from the states of the Lower South, Arkansas, and Missouri. And the hostility many of them felt toward Indians in general was matched by hostility toward residents of Mexican heritage. There was increasingly less tolerance for the presence of Mexican Texans. Some simply left the areas of the Anglo settlements, thereby contributing to their marginalization. But some were strongly pressured into leaving. In September 1854, Seguin residents tried to ban Mexicans "of the peon class" from visiting or living in Guadalupe County, and in Austin a similar movement forced out all except "those vouched for by 'respectable citizens.'" In 1857, journalist Frederick Law Olmstead observed that most Tejanos had voting rights but few used them. If they did vote in a place such as San Antonio, where they might be able to prevail in an election, Olmstead surmised that it could result in a "revolution" among the Anglos, who "constantly distinguish[ed] themselves as 'white folks,'" superior to Tejanos as well as to African Americans and Indians.

The principle activity of the Tejano men was hauling goods between the coast and inland towns, but even this was not to be allowed. More successful than rival Anglo freighters, beginning in 1855 the Tejano haulers faced the threat of theft, destruction of their carts, and physical attacks. In the summer of 1857, "cart war" attacks became common, and by November, Governor Elisha M. Pease was announcing, "It is now very evident that there is no security for the lives of citizens of Mexican origin engaged in the business of transportation, along the road from San Antonio to the Gulf."

The state legislature approved a militia to protect the freighters, but the pattern was clear. Economic opportunity and any kind of power—economic, political, and social—were to be the provenance of the Anglos. Not only did the Mexican freight business not recover, but even the remaining Mexican elite in San Antonio were now relegated to lower-level positions.

South and west of the Nueces, in traditionally Mexican cultural territory (especially in Laredo), some families managed to hold onto their land and some of their power, but many of the greediest and most prejudiced newcomers tried to uproot the populace and lay claim to land. In El Paso, Anglos assumed control of the town while Tejanos held sway in the country. Resentments festered among the Mexican Texans; it took an incident on the streets of Brownsville for these resentments to crystallize into a challenge to Anglo hegemony.

Juan Cortina had grown up the eldest heir of the second family of José Narciso Cavazos, who owned a large grant in the area of Brownsville. Although Cortina and his family held legal title to the grant, his father's first family sold it to Charles Stillman, who with two partners established the town of Brownsville in 1848.

Cortina fought not only the appropriation of his land but that of the land holdings of other Mexican Texans in the area as well. Then, on July 13, 1859, he observed the Brownsville city marshall abusing and arresting a former Cortina employee. Cortina shot the marshall and departed with the former employee. A few months later, he returned with a force of men and took over the town. Persuaded to abandon the occupation by a Mexican official from Matamoros, he retreated, but also produced a manifesto on the wrongs done to Mexican Texans and his intention to punish the wrongdoers. He also petitioned Governor Houston to protect the rights of Mexican Texans.

Cortina's force reportedly grew to 400 men, and he engaged in repeated skirmishes with Texas rangers before retreating into Mexico. "Our object," he had insisted, ". . . has been to chastise the villainy of our enemies," who had robbed and harassed with impunity "without any cause, and for no other crime on our part than that of being of Mexican origin." He would mount a second challenge to Anglo Texas during the Civil War, a reminder of a Texas vastly different from the image upheld by many of its citizens: that of a southern state deeply and irrevocably committed to the institution of slavery.

Texas as a Slave State

In the years 1845 to 1860, the Texas economy revolved more and more around the production of cotton, with more than 58,000 bales produced in 1849–50, but more than seven times that much only ten years later. Cotton cultivation continued to expand in the older settled areas but also in central Texas. The number of slaves jumped from 30,505 in 1846 to almost 183,000 in 1860; this was one-third of the Texas population. In thirteen counties, slaves accounted for over half the population. Yet throughout this period, most Texas citizens did not own slaves; of those who did, most owned only one to four.

Nonetheless, by 1860, the 27 percent of the population that owned slaves held almost three-fourths of the wealth in Texas. The bulk of that wealth was concentrated among the elite—the approximately sixty owners of more than 100 slaves. Texas's identity—economic, political, and social—had become intricately tied to the "peculiar institution."

It is not hard to see how Texas developed an identity as a slave state, from the concessions Stephen F. Austin had won from the antislavery Mexican government to the fact that the largest group of immigrants had come from the American South with proslavery attitudes. National events had also helped shape Texas responses. Even before Texas became a republic, South Carolina had attempted to override, or "nullify," federal law, in late 1832 holding a Nullification Convention to reject high tariffs the federal government was imposing on imports. The nullification controversy, which was tied to a defense of slavery as well, had ended due to lack of support in the South for such an extreme step and President Jackson's upholding of federal power. But the stage had been set for further divisiveness, especially as the nation continued to expand. In 1854, the Kansas-Nebraska Act repealed the Missouri Compromise outlawing slavery north of a certain latitude. Now the people of Kansas and Nebraska were to determine whether they would become part of slave or free territory. The act caused great consternation in the United States and led to near-anarchy in Kansas after vote fraud gave the win to the proslavery forces. The Kansas situation remained volatile through the late 1850s, feeding national tensions and southern intransigence.

Southerners justified slavery on a number of grounds, primarily the sheer necessity of having a large labor force and their feeling that the slaves, as an inferior, childlike people destined for servitude, benefited from the benevolence of their masters and the material conditions they provided. As fanciful and morally reprehensible as this argument was, it was an accepted tenet of southern thought. Those who questioned it usually knew to keep their mouths shut; those who did not often aspired to become slaveowners themselves.

As in the Lower South, then, Texas institutions reflected the acceptance and promotion of slavery. By the late 1850s, the "Calhoun Democrats," staunchly in favor of states' rights, were in ascendance. For much of Texas's brief history as a republic and a state, politics had been a distinction between those who supported Democrat Sam Houston and those who didn't. The Whigs had made inroads in Texas in the early 1850s, as had the nativist Know-Nothing party in the mid-1850s, the latter an unabashedly anti-Catholic and antiforeign organization. Both of these parties had quickly faded from the Texas scene, leaving two primary groups: the Jacksonian, or Unionist, Democrats, and the Calhoun, or states' rights, Democrats.

Now preachers extolled the institution of slavery from their pulpits and editors from their newspaper columns, and the Texas legislature actually considered voting in favor of resuming an African slave trade. Part of the feeling directed against Mexican Texans in this era stemmed from the perception that they encouraged slaves to escape to Mexico (by 1851, an estimated 3,000 had done so).

The conditions of slavery as it developed in Texas varied. Some slaves were brutalized, forced to work incessantly, kept hungry and ragged, even whipped to death. Former Texas slave Lulu Wilson would recall that the master and mistress "nearly beat us to death," working their slaves incessantly from early childhood on and feeding them poorly: "For years all I could get was one little slice of sowbelly, a puny little piece of bread and a tater. I never had enough to stave the hongriness out'n my belly." Although Lulu was able to stay with her mother, the owner spirited other children away for sale when Lulu's mother was working in the fields.

For others, life was not as harsh. A fair number of slaves were allowed to hire themselves out, despite an 1846 law prohibiting this passed by the first state legislature. Some gained limited protection from juries against cruel treatment. But none of them were free.

To Anglo and European Texans, who overwhelmingly shared a sense of racial superiority, the slavery of African Americans was an accepted means of pursuing the best economic opportunity in the state: the growing of cotton. And most would defend that course with vehemence. The 1850s were rife with incidents that demonstrated the allegiance to the South of a sizable and vocal segment of the dominant culture. For example, in 1854, when German "Forty-Eighters" called a political convention at San Antonio and denounced slavery as an "evil," the outcry was instant and vitriolic, even though the Germans had also argued for the right of the state to decide without federal intervention whether to perpetuate slavery or not. In 1855, Galveston lawyer Lorenzo Sherwood received encouragement for his plan for economic development for the state, which involved making banking and railroad building "semipublic enterprises." Sherwood viewed slavery as a "temporary institution" incompatible with democracy, a view long held by many in the Upper South as well as the North. Sherwood was forced from office, faced censure by the House, and was denied the opportunity to speak publicly in Galveston.

This public reaction did not represent the feelings of the full voting populace, as evidenced by the fact that in 1859 Sam Houston, still an ardent Jacksonian Democrat, defeated incumbent Democrat Hardin Runnels, who had signed a bill encouraging free blacks to enslave themselves by selecting a master. In fact, antisecessionist feeling was strong in some areas; in the same year, an audience at a public debate near Paris, Texas, left after the Union speaker's talk, despite his urgings that they stay to hear the secessionist. He was told, "no damned Secessionist could speak there, or if he did, he would speak to an empty house."

But Texas in the 1850s was rapidly defining itself in opposite terms. "Vigilance committees" sought to stanch any signs of slave uprisings or attempts by others to encourage slaves toward freedom. In 1857 the *Galveston Weekly News* announced, "Those who denounce slavery as an evil, in any sense, are the enemies of the South. . . ." The architects of antebellum Texas—southerners invested culturally and emotionally, if not financially, in the slave system—were ready to take a stand.

Conclusion

Through the republic and early statehood periods, some of Texas's identity questions seemed to have been answered. The difficulties of maintaining an independent republic, much less trying to build an extended empire, had proven formidable; in the near-decade of independence, the fledgling nation had fallen more deeply into debt and remained an uncertain frontier plagued by external threats and internal divisions. Most Texans had been glad to see Texas enter into American statehood. Texas then began to develop as a state in the Union—but, significantly, as a southern state aligned with the other states that championed slavery, a state in which cotton was "king" and slavery was increasingly to be defended at all costs. In commenting on Lorenzo Sherwood's mild criticism of the "peculiar institution," the Dallas *Herald* had vehemently editorialized, "A man, a Texan, a southerner who could get up in the legislature of a southern State, of the most southern State, and deliberately outrage the feelings of the whole people . . . possesses a heart too callous to be reached by votes of censure."

"The most southern State"—it was a curious identification for a former Spanish and Mexican province, a former republic, a state with a strong Mexican heritage, a state with thousands of European immigrants, a state that was made up of people from all over the American South and all over the Union as well. That the newspaper could write so blithely of Sherwood's "outrag[ing] the feelings of the whole people" indicated not only a moral obtuseness but a dangerous blindness to Texas's heritage and diversity. The state was headed into another crisis of identity, one that would prove to be both extended and costly.

SUGGESTED READINGS

The Republic era stands as a very distinct period of almost a decade in Texas history, a period in which Texas leaders struggled to create a stable government and economy and to withstand challenges from Mexico while residents struggled to survive and thrive under continued frontier conditions. Readings that focus on this period include William Ransom Hogan's classic *The Texas Republic: A Social and Economic History,* first published in 1946, Stanley Siegel's *The Political History of the Texas Republic, 1836–1845* (1956), and John Edward Weems's *Dream of Empire: A Human History of the Republic of Texas 1836–1846* (1971). The *New Handbook of Texas* (1996) has a good "Texas Republic" entry and entries for various events of the era.

On the subject of Texas annexation, Frederick Merk's *Slavery and the Annexation of Texas* (1972) is considered a classic. Subsequent works have built on and challenged Merk, significantly William W. Freehling's *The Road to Disunion: Secessionists at Bay, 1776–1854* (1990) and Sam W. Haynes's "Anglophobia and the Annexation of Texas: The Quest for National Security" in *Manifest Destiny and Empire: American Antebellum Expansion* (1997).

Much of the scholarly research on the early statehood period, from annexation to the Civil War, as well as in the Republic period, focuses on ethnic groups or individual families; some of these are noted below under "Challenges and Opportunities in the Republic of Texas" and "Marginalized Groups in the Republic." A useful source for understanding gender and ethnicity issues is Mark M. Carroll's *Homesteads Ungovernable: Families, Sex, Race, and the Law in Frontier Texas, 1823–1860* (2001). The *New Handbook of Texas* contains many useful entries for the early statehood period—for example, on the Mexican War and the "Cart Wars."

For primary documents of the republic and the early state, see *Documents of Texas History* (1963, 1994), edited by Ernest Wallace, David M. Vigness, and George Ward. For primary accounts, see *Rip Ford's Texas* (1963, 1987), edited by Stephen B. Oates; *Texas Tears and Texas Sunshine: Voices of Frontier Women* (1985), edited by Jo Ella Powell Exley; and Crystal Sasse Ragsdale's *The Golden Free Land* (1976). An oft-quoted account of Texas in early statehood is Frederick Law Olmsted's *A Journey Through Texas, or a Saddle-Trip on the Southwestern Frontier* (1857, 1978).

To place Texas's movement toward secession at the end of this period into a national context, an excellent resource is Freehling's *Road to Disunion*.

The Quests for Annexation and Empire, 1836–1841

Randolph B. Campbell's *Sam Houston and the American Southwest* (1993) provides an accessible overview of the first Houston presidential administration. Because Sam Houston was such an important Texas figure throughout the periods covered in this chapter, the Campbell work is also more broadly useful, as is Sam W. Haynes's "Sam Houston and His Antagonists" in *Major Problems in Texas History* (2002). For a detailed account of the Santa Fe expedition, see Paul N. Spellman's *Forgotten Texas Leader: Hugh McLeod and the Texan Santa Fe Expedition* (1999).

Challenges and Opportunities in the Republic of Texas

In addition to the general works on the republic, individual family fortunes are traced in Margaret Swett Henson's and Delolece Parmalee's *The Cartwrights of San Augustine: Three Generations of Agricultural Entrepreneurs in Nineteenth-Century Texas* (1993) and Paula Mitchell Marks's *Turn Your Eyes Toward Texas: Pioneers Sam and Mary Maverick* (1989). Two good sources for German immigration and settlement are Terry Jordan's *German Seed in Texas Soil: Immigrant Farmers in Nineteenth-Century Texas* (1966) and Walter Struve's *Germans & Texans:*

Commerce, Migration, and Culture in the Days of the Lone Star Republic (1996). A good source on women is Fane Downs's "Tryles and Trubbles: Women in Early Nineteenth Century Texas," *Southwestern Historical Quarterly* (1987).

Marginalized Groups in the Republic

Sources on African Americans include Randolph B. Campbell's *An Empire for Slavery: The Peculiar Institution in Texas, 1821–1865* (1989), Elizabeth Silverthorne's *Plantation Life in Texas* (1986), and Alwyn Barr's *Black Texans: A History of African-Americans in Texas, 1528–1995* (1996). Sources on Tejanos include Timothy M. Matovina's *Tejano Religion and Ethnicity, San Antonio, 1821–1860* (1995), Jesus F. de la Teja's *A Revolution Remembered* (1991), David Montejano's *Anglos and Mexicans in the Making of Texas, 1836–1986* (1987), and Andrés Tijerina's *Tejano Empire: Life on the South Texas Ranchos* (1998). Dianna Everett's *The Texas Cherokees: A People Between Two Fires, 1819–1840* remains the best source of information on the Cherokees' tragic end in East Texas.

The Annexation Quest Continues

The annexation sources cited above prove useful for understanding the final movements toward annexation within and outside Texas as well. For the Mier expedition, the best source is Sam W. Haynes's *Soldiers of Misfortune: The Somervell and Mier Expeditions* (1990).

The New State Takes Shape

Most of the sources above also deal substantially with the early statehood period, as reflected in some of their subtitles. A good source on Texas and the Mexican War is Richard Bruce Winders's *Crisis in the Southwest: The United States, Mexico, and the Struggle Over Texas* (2002). For the Compromise of 1850, see Mark J. Stegner's *Texas, New Mexico and the Compromise of 1850: Boundary Dispute and Sectional Crisis* (1996). For Texas's development as a southern state, see Freehling's *Road to Disunion* and Walter Buenger's "The Roots of Texas Secession" in *Major Problems in Texas History* (2002), eds. Sam W. Haynes and Cary D. Wintz. For resistance to this southern definition for the state, see David Pickering and Judy Falls's *Brush Men & Vigilantes: Civil War Dissent in Texas* (2000).

9

Secession, War, and Their Aftermath, 1860–1876

Texas Congressman Sam Maverick was in a quandary. Decades earlier, he had left his home in South Carolina in part because he disagreed with the widely-held states' rights and secessionist views in that state. Now, after a quarter-century as a Texan, once again he found himself surrounded by calls for states' rights and secession. With another national presidential election approaching, in April 1860 secession advocates dominated the state Democratic convention in Galveston, some arguing for Texas to become an independent nation again. Meanwhile, at the national Democratic convention, the Democratic party split in two. Northerners nominated Stephen A. Douglas, the U.S. senator from Illinois who had argued that territories could not be compelled to pass laws protecting slavery. White southerners, on the other hand, were looking for someone who held their strong proslavery views. They held a separate convention, naming Kentuckian John C. Breckenridge as their Democratic presidential candidate.

The Republican Party had coalesced in the mid-1850s in the North, largely to battle the extension of slavery. Delegates to its convention in Chicago now nominated lawyer Abraham Lincoln, a leading Illinois Republican, for president.

Maverick had strong feelings about maintaining the Union—to the extent that, despite his own frequent criticism of Sam Houston, he had supported Houston's 1859 gubernatorial bid, concluding "Old Sam is the right man for this delicate occasion." Maverick had also judged that a curse

1860	Republican Abraham Lincoln is elected U.S. president
1861	Texas joins other southern states in seceding from the Union
1862	Federal troops make inroads on Texas gulf coast; suspected Unionists are executed in the "Great Hanging at Gainesville"
1863	Confederates retake or defend key points on Texas gulf coast
1865	War ends with South's defeat; on June 19 in Galveston Gen. Gordon Granger declares slaves in Texas to be free, providing basis for the Juneteenth holiday; President Andrew Johnson begins mild presidential Reconstruction
1866	New state constitutional convention meets as a condition of Texas's reentry into the Union
1867	First Reconstruction Act of U.S. Congress ushers in congressional Reconstruction
1868–69	Another constitutional convention meets under requirements of congressional Reconstruction
1870	Under Republican governor E. J. Davis, Texas gains readmittance to the Union and home rule
1872	State elections favor resurgent "Old South" Democrats
1873	Democrat Richard Coke is elected governor over Davis
1875	Another constitutional convention meets and produces the Texas Constitution of 1876, still in use (with multiple amendments) into the twenty-first century

seemed to hang over a slave country but had determined "to use without abusing the institution." He held a few slaves and as a lawyer and land speculator was included among the wealthy southern elite of Texas. He became "a good Breckenridge man," still hoping that secession could be averted. But this time he could not avoid a fateful decision.

Texas and the Confederacy

In the summer of 1860, much of Texas simmered with unrest and suspicion. There was a series of mysterious fires in North and East Texas during the scorching season, with temperatures hitting 114 degrees. Parts of downtown Denton and Dallas went up in flames. Proslavery agitators began attributing these fires to slaves and their northern sympathizers, and slaves were coerced into "confessions" as a panicked vigilantism mounted. Vigilantes killed at least thirty people, perhaps many more. Even in September, when the panic was subsiding, a posse chased down and hung Anthony Bewley, an antislavery Methodist minister suspected on questionable evidence of provoking the arsons.

The "Texas Troubles," as they came to be called, were both a sign and a cause of the Texas secession that was to follow. Although the fires were subsequently determined to have been the result of high temperatures and the spontaneous combustion of new phosphorus matches, the proslavery propagandizers' manipulation of racist fears showed how strongly many Texans identified with the South and made them even more combative.

Secession

In the elections of 1860, southern Democratic candidate John C. Breckenridge garnered 858,356 votes, with major support across the South and in Texas. Yet to the horror of many southerners, from South Carolina to Texas, Abraham Lincoln was elected president, garnering 1,865,593 votes, and Hannibal Hamlin vice president. Southerners felt that the northern states had prevailed in electing, in the words of Texas's subsequent declaration of secession, "two men whose chief claims to such high positions are their approval of . . . long-continued wrongs, and their pledges to continue them to the final consummation of these schemes for the ruin of the slave-holding States." In Texas, as in the rest of the South, Lincoln was viewed as an archfiend, his party as "behind the Texas Troubles."

Texas secessionists began to clamor for a state convention that would declare a complete break with the U.S. government. As governor, Houston remained adamantly opposed to furthering this cause. On December 17, in response to secessionists' call for a January convention, he reluctantly called the legislature into session for January 21, hoping that moderates in that body would prevail, forestalling such a gathering. In the meantime, South Carolina seceded from the Union. When the Texas legislature met in the new year, delegates had already been elected to a Texas secession convention a week later. The legislature simply voted to authorize the scheduled convention. As a member of the House, Maverick reluctantly cast his vote for this convention. In doing so, he had unwittingly placed himself in the middle of the latest struggle for the identity of Texas.

On January 28, the convention met, with O. M. Roberts, Texas Supreme Court judge and avid secessionist, presiding. Members moved speedily to vote in favor of breaking away from the United States. They insisted that "the governments of the various States . . . were established exclusively for the white race, for themselves and their posterity," with "the African race . . . rightfully held and regarded as an inferior and dependent race."

Houston and others favoring federal union and compromise had insisted that the people of Texas vote as well. With this vote set for February 23, both supporters and opponents of secession took their arguments into the voting districts and to the newspapers of the state, printing and distributing copies of the ordinance of secession in English, Spanish, and German. In the meantime, the convention appointed a Committee of Public Safety to authorize volunteer troops and force the U.S. military to turn over the 2,700 federal soldiers, twenty-one forts, and weapons stores in Texas. On February 16, Texas volunteer troops arrived in San Antonio and effected the surrender of military personnel, sites, and stores.

A week later, Texas voters approved secession by a vote of 46,129 to 14,697. To understand why Texas voters approved secession, it is important to remember the developing sectionalism between the North and South of the United States throughout the early nineteenth century, most of it in regard to slavery. Factors included the delay in Texas annexation, the Compromise of 1850, the Kansas-Nebraska Act, the emergence of the Republican Party, and Lincoln's election. Those Texans who could vote—overwhelmingly, white southern males—favored a southern economic system based on cotton cultivation, and, by extension, on slave labor. They also favored a caste system that valued white over black. And they valued states' rights over continuing in a Union controlled by people who opposed the continued growth of a slave system.

In eighteen counties in Northeast and Central Texas and one in East Texas, however, the vote actually went against secession. Counties with significant numbers of Germans or immigrants from the Upper South—in Texas, primarily former residents of Missouri, Arkansas, and Tennessee—and from the North were far less likely to approve secession than were those with immigrants from the Lower South, especially those with large slave populations. But despite the opposition—which would continue during the war—the convention had its mandate and made the break with the Union official on March 2. Texas quickly joined the Confederacy, requiring everyone in office to take a loyalty oath to the new confederation. When Sam Houston and his secretary of state, E. W. Cave, refused to do so, they were removed, with Lieutenant Governor Edward Clark put in Houston's place. Less than a month later, the Civil War commenced with the Confederate firing on the federals' Fort Sumter, South Carolina.

Although Samuel Maverick had long opposed secession, he finally voted in favor of a Texas secession convention and became a leading Confederate supporter in San Antonio. *(Courtesy of the Witte Museum, San Antonio, Texas)*

Where was Sam Maverick as all of this transpired? As one of the three members of the Committee of Public Safety charged with appropriating federal troops and stores, he became a leading Confederate official, taking the loyalty oath and voting that those who did not should be deposed. His wife Mary, who would join in the war effort herself by leading the Ladies Aid Society and the women's wing of the Southern Defense Aid Society in San Antonio, offered an explanation: "At last he came to believe the quarrel was forced upon us, and that there was before us an 'irressible [*sic*] conflict' which we could not escape, no matter where we turned." The decision would cost them dearly.

Texans as Part of the Confederacy

Even before the citizen vote for secession, Texas had dispatched seven delegates to a Confederate government organizing convention in Montgomery, Alabama. Once Texas entered the Confederacy, it was obliged to acquiesce to central Confederate authority in such matters as conscription laws, use of slave labor, and cotton trade with Mexico, and to recruit increasing numbers of its men of fighting age to serve the Confederacy. At the same time, it had its own representatives and influential men in the Confederate government: Texans Louis T. Wigfall and W. S. Oldman became members of the Confederate Senate, and John H. Reagan, Texas lawyer, judge, and legislator, became postmaster general of the Confederacy.

There were occasional tensions between the state and Confederate government over policy and procedure, such as when to give men exemptions to Confederate service so as to retain a defense force in Texas. And throughout the war, both governments would contend with deserters and evaders of the conscription laws. But in the recruiting of fighting men, Texas built an impressive record. Within ten months of the firing on Fort Sumter, Texas had 25,000 men in the Confederate army. Two-thirds of them were in cavalry units; eventually, almost 59,000 Texans would serve in the cavalry. Although Governor Francis Lubbock's November 1863 estimate of a total of 90,000 Texans in Confederate service has been dismissed as too high for any one time, historians say that the figure probably has validity for the whole war effort—this in a fighting-age population estimated at 100,000 to 110,000.

Texans were well represented, too, in the Confederate officer ranks, with numerous brigadier generals and colonels. The highest-ranked officer was General

Nineteenth-century Texas painter Carl G. von Iwonski created this dramatic portrait of four members of Company B, Eighth Texas Cavalry, better known as Terry's Texas Rangers. This unit participated in some of the major battles of the Civil War. *(Courtesy of the Witte Museum, San Antonio, Texas)*

Albert Sidney Johnston, a veteran of the Texas Revolution and the Mexican War, who assumed command of the Western Department of the Confederacy but died leading troops at the battle of Shiloh in 1862. John Bell Hood rose from captain to colonel to brigadier general in charge of Hood's Texas Brigade in Robert E. Lee's Army of Northern Virginia. A promotion to major general followed, then one to lieutenant general. Hood commanded the Army of Tennessee in the later months of the war.

Major generals from Texas were Tom Green, Samuel Bell Maxey, and John A. Wharton. Wharton, a wealthy planter, first served as captain of Company B, Eighth Texas Cavalry, better known—and celebrated—as Terry's Texas Rangers. After the deaths of Colonel B. F. Terry and his lieutenant colonel, Wharton led the Rangers at the battle of Shiloh, then received rapid promotions. He was killed before the end of the war in a dispute with another Confederate officer.

The highest-ranking Tejano Confederate commander was Santos Benavides, a descendant of the founder of Laredo, county judge of Webb County in 1859, and colonel of the Thirty-Third Texas Cavalry. Benavides, aided by his brothers Refugio and Cristóbal, led efforts to protect the Mexican border, pushing back both Union guerillas and Juan Cortina, who in 1861 again tried to rally supporters on the Texas side of the border. The Thirty-Third built an impressive record, but Tejanos also served throughout the Texas Confederate forces. More than 300 enlisted in the Eighth Texas Infantry, and there are estimates that at least 2,500 Tejanos were Confederate soldiers, in encounters from Virginia to New Mexico.

Not all Texans who fought or commanded did so for the Confederacy. Many who opposed Texas's stance joined Union troops. E. J. Davis, another Texas judge, had resigned rather than take the Confederate loyalty oath and traveled to New Orleans, where he organized the First Texas U.S. Cavalry to fight against the Confederacy. The Second Texas Cavalry comprised Tejanos and Mexicans from the Rio Grande, drawn by the bounty money they received for enlisting but also propelled by grievances about their treatment by Texas officials and by opposition to slavery.

Most Texas Confederate troops—about two-thirds—stayed in the western theater, or west of the Mississippi, many serving in the Louisiana and New Mexico campaigns. In fact, Texas became the base for two attempts to extend the Confederacy westward in an echo of previous Texan attempts to claim New Mexico.

In the first attempt, John Baylor, lieutenant colonel of the Second Texas Mounted Rifles, had simply been told to protect the overland route to El Paso. Upon reaching nearby Fort Bliss, however, he was determined to invade the Mesilla Valley and claim New Mexico for the Confederacy. This effort would quickly founder as Baylor antagonized even his Confederates.

Meanwhile, Brigadier General Henry Hopkins Sibley was proceeding with a similar conquest plan, having convinced Confederate President Jefferson Davis that he could take a group of Texas volunteers, arm them from the federal forts and arsenals now under Confederate control, and seize New Mexico in "the westernmost campaign of the Civil War." The Confederacy would then be in a position to move its troops onward to claim Colorado and the Southwest all the way to southern California. This would bolster the rebel economy and its chances of being taken seriously as a viable republic by nations other than the United States.

Sibley, a West Point graduate who had five years of military service on the Texas frontier, began recruiting in San Antonio in August 1861. By late October, he had more than 3,000 men in three regiments and in supply and artillery units. They marched out along the San Antonio-El Paso Road in detachments, their numbers staggered to make use of the limited water holes.

Following Baylor's steps—and incorporating some of Baylor's volunteers—in January 1862 Sibley made Mesilla his base of operations. Meanwhile, to meet the Confederate threat, Colonel Edward R. S. Canby, commander of the federal Military Department of New Mexico, was busy amassing federal troops and volunteers from Colorado and New Mexico at the Union post of Fort Craig.

In February, Sibley began moving most of his force toward Fort Craig, where twenty-one captured volunteers were being held. Canby, however, had fortified Craig to the point that the Confederates dared not try an assault. Instead, they detoured eastward around the fort and drew Canby's troops out for a battle at Valverde Ford on the Rio Grande.

This engagement was followed by a Confederate push to Albuquerque and to Santa Fe and by a series of clashes, the most significant of which is known as the battle of Glorieta, which occurred near Glorieta Pass on March 28, 1862. With Sibley still in Albuquerque, Lieutenant Colonel William R. Scurry led the main Texas force against 850 Union fighters. When these fighters destroyed the Confederate supply train, the Texas troops began a slow retreat.

The suffering on the return trip to San Antonio was intense. A San Antonio resident who had seen the brigade march out the previous October, "finely dressed, splendidly mounted and elegantly equipped" now observed fewer than half their number "come straggling back on foot, broken, disorganized in an altogether deplorable condition." Not all of the missing were accounted for, but approximately 500 had died, either from wounds or disease, and another 500 had been taken prisoner and marched to Illinois. Like previous Texas attempts to expand westward, this Confederate one had ended badly.

Particularly in the eastern theater, as battle piled upon battle, casualties soared in ways few could have anticipated. Texan W. R. Bell of Blossom wrote of the aftermath of the battle of Franklin, Tennessee, "I helped bury the dead . . . and I think I could have walked all over the battlefield on dead men." Battlefield deaths, injuries, illness, and desertion all took their toll; B. F. Carpenter of Gainesville would recall, "Our regiment went out of Texas with 1180 men and when we surrendered at Canton, Mississippi, there were 240 at roll call."

The War in Texas and Its Impact

There were few and limited Civil War battles in Texas, and Texans did not experience the invasion and destruction visited upon the Old South; one need only think of Union General William Tecumseh Sherman's burning of the city of Atlanta and punishing "March to the Sea." The war did reach Texas, however, and it affected the state and its citizens in very important ways.

Military Conflict in Texas

In the wake of the Confederates' firing on Fort Sumter, Union naval vessels began blockading southern ports, extending the blockade to Texas very quickly. Confederates tried to strengthen the Texas coastal positions, but in the fall of 1862 Union ships were shelling the sites. On the Texas coast, the bark USS *Arthur,* the yacht *Corypheus,* and the steamer *Sachem* harassed trade and Confederate positions, seizing Confederate sloops and schooners. In August the *Arthur's* commander tried to follow up by taking the town of Corpus Christi but was repulsed in two engagements by a Confederate force of 700, a combination of local volunteers and four companies of the Eighth Texas Infantry battalion.

Despite this victory, the Texas coast remained vulnerable as the war seesawed in the East. The battle of Antietam in September put an end to Robert E. Lee's attempt to press into Union territory in Maryland. That same month, a federal blockade patrol shelled the Texas coast at Fort Sabine, constructed by local residents to protect the community of Sabine Pass, near the juncture of the Sabine River and the Gulf of Mexico. Damage to the fort and an outbreak of yellow fever caused local militia and Texas infantrymen to abandon the post. In October, a squadron of Union ships sailed into Galveston harbor, with their commander demanding surrender of Galveston Island as well. Confederate Brigadier General Paul O. Hébert, in charge of the Confederate District of Texas, judged the island to be indefensible, and Confederate troops removed to the mainland.

This military abandonment of the island dealt a blow to the spirits and fortunes of many Texans. The town of Galveston on the island had been developing as a significant commercial and transportation center, with steamers taking people and goods to Houston and back through Galveston Bay and Buffalo Bayou. A railroad company had even built a bridge to the island in 1860 and constructed a short railroad line. Now this vital coastal artery was severed.

Major General John Bankhead Magruder, a Virginian and Mexican War veteran, followed Hébert as commander of the district. He assumed command on November 29 and immediately began planning to retake Galveston using two river steamers for a naval attack as well as infantry and cavalry forces.

On New Year's morning 1863, the Confederates struck, the troops crossing

Civil War activity in Texas.

over the railroad bridge and the two steamers opening fire from behind the Union ships. Twenty-six Confederates were killed and 117 wounded, whereas the Union had about 150 casualties. The federal ships departed, leaving Union infantrymen in Confederate hands. Magruder had retaken Galveston.

This victory was followed by news of Lee's December victory over the Army of the Potomac near Fredericksburg, Virginia, and by the January 21 retaking of Sabine Pass. On January 30, Mary Maverick, busy with relief efforts for soldiers and their families, wrote to her son in Confederate service, "With all our grand victories & all their losses, won't we have peace soon think you?"

But the war was far from over, the southern secession far from secured. In summer 1863, the biggest single battle of the war occurred at Gettysburg, Pennsylvania, where Lee's southern troops were pushed back and combined casualties—dead, wounded, or missing—topped 43,000. Further Union victories in the South positioned the federal forces to control the Mississippi River and freed Major General Nathan Banks to look toward a conquest of Texas.

His first attempt came at the previously contested Sabine Pass, from which Banks hoped to capture Houston, recapture Galveston, and gain entrance to the state's interior. Banks sent 4,000 troops by ship, and the U.S. Navy dispatched four gunboats to cover their landing.

At Sabine Pass, the Davis Guards, Company F of the First Texas Heavy Artillery Regiment, had been busy fortifying the site and preparing for an attack by sea. When one of the four gunboats, the *Clifton,* appeared and began shelling them from a distance on the morning of September 8, the Confederates bided their time. The other three ships joined the Clifton in the afternoon, advancing on the pass. Under Lieutenant Dick Dowling, a genial Houston saloon owner from Ireland, the forty-seven-man Confederate force made good use of its six cannons, firing more than 100 times in a thirty-five minute battle.

The small Confederate force turned back the invasion, the federal troops returning to New Orleans. The Confederates also captured two of the gunboats and more than 300 Union soldiers. General Banks, however, maintained pressure on Texas. In particular, he was eager to capture Brownsville, which had become a key import/export center for the western Confederacy, with southern cotton going to Europe through Matamoros and war supplies and other essentials coming in to Texas. In November Banks took Brazos Island, off the mouth of the Rio Grande near Brownsville, forcing Confederate troops to abandon defense of the town. Banks's occupation of Brownsville and disruption of trade there would be temporary, but federal soldiers worked their way along the Texas coastline, occupying the port of Indianola as well. Eudora Moore, a fifteen-year-old resident of the port town, would later recall the federal soldiers "digging rifle pits and building forts on the prairie back of town" and appropriating the family's cattle. Soon Galveston and Sabine Pass were the only ports remaining in Confederate hands, and as far inland as San Antonio, residents prepared to flee.

In yet a third thrust, Banks and General Frederick Steele planned a two-pronged attack into East Texas, Banks from Lousiana and Steele from Little Rock,

THE CONFEDERATES EVACUATING BROWNSVILLE, TEXAS.—[SKETCHED BY AN ENGLISH ARTIST.]

EVACUATION OF BROWNSVILLE BY THE CONFEDERATES.

Brownsville lies on the Texas side of the Rio Grande opposite Matamoras, which is two collos distant. We present above the hasty departure from this place of the Confederate garrison on November 2, 1863. The occasion of this sudden flight was the anticipated arrival of our fleet of transports off Brazos, Santiago. For two days every avenue of transit across the river was overcrowded with goods, furniture, cotton, and baggage, while upon both banks were piled, in confused heaps, bedding, cotton bales, luggage, vehicles, and merchandise of every description. The garrison buildings in the mean time were burned, and all cotton and stores that could not be removed. On the 6th the Federal troops occupied Brownsville, where once the head-quarters of General Herron. It was General Banks who originally occupied the position.

In January 1864 the *London Illustrated News* ran this wood engraving titled "The War in America: The Confederates Quitting Brownsville, Texas, on Hearing of the Approach of Federal Transports." Confederate troops under John S. (Rip) Ford reoccupied the town in summer 1864 and held it until the end of the war. *(CN 01535, The Center for American History, The University of Texas at Austin)*

Arkansas. But in spring 1864, Steele was halted by Confederate troops—including Texas brigades—at Camden, Arkansas. Banks's troops met the Confederates at the battles of Mansfield and Pleasant Hill in Louisiana but then fell back east of the Mississippi. One Texan, John Howard King of Gilmer, remembered of Pleasant Hill, "Here was the wildest shooting that I saw during the war. They shot the tops of the trees all to pieces. . . ."

As the war dragged on for another year, Texas troops retook Brownsville and other points along the coast. But the Army of the South was faring badly. In September 1864, Sherman took Atlanta in a terrible blow to the Confederacy. By the end of the year, John Bell Hood's Army of Tennessee had been devastated. In truth, southern manpower and resources had been strained to the breaking point. The greatest blow to Confederate hopes would come in the East on April 9, 1865, when Lee surrendered the army of Northern Virginia to Grant at Appomattox Courthouse, Virginia. Nine days later, Joseph E. Johnston surrendered "the last major Confederate army."

The war was essentially over, but in early May Lieutenant General Edmund Kirby Smith, commander of the Confederate Trans-Mississippi Department, announced that his western Confederate forces would continue to fight. In the meantime, the Union commander on Brazos Island was negotiating unsuccessfully for a Confederate surrender at Brownsville. This continued resistance brought to Texas soil the last engagement of the Civil War—the battle of Palmito Ranch.

Learning of the surrenders in the East, many soldiers in the Brownsville area left for home, but others continued to occupy and hold the town. They skirmished twice with Union forces before Colonel Benavides and Colonel John Salmon "Rip" Ford appeared with Confederate reinforcements. Ford was one of the more ubiquitous and colorful characters in this era of Texas history. He had arrived in Texas immediately after the Revolution and had worked as a medical doctor, Texas military officer, state senator, Texas ranger, and newspaper editor. His nickname stemmed from his dispatches reporting deaths of American troops during the Mexican War; he would use "RIP" as shorthand for "Rest in Peace." He, too, had engaged in extensive border service during the war.

At Palmito Ranch, the numbers were now nearly even. With their field artillery firing, Ford and Benavides's forces attacked the Union troops from the left, the right, and the center, forcing them into a rout. The federal troops hurried back toward Brazos Island with the Confederates in pursuit, the four-hour battle ending when the federal troops reached reinforcements near Brazos Island.

Even as the battle raged, Kirby Smith and other western Confederate officials acknowledged the futility of a continued Confederate resistance. Federal officers entered Brownsville to arrange a Confederate surrender. On June 2, Smith formally turned over the Confederate Trans-Mississippi Department to General Canby, who had stopped the early Confederate advance into New Mexico.

After four years of conflict, the loss would rankle those Texans who had embraced the identity of Texas as an extension of the American South. But whatever one's political stance, the war in Texas had had a significant impact, in spite of the fact that invasion had been confined to the coast. The war effort had both drained Texas resources and development and created division and new uncertainties about Texas's identity.

Wartime Conditions

During the war years, more and more men were conscripted into Confederate service. At first, the call was for men aged 18 to 35, but by war's end, with Confederate losses mounting, conscription acts included men from 17 to 50. Unpopular laws, the Conscription Acts of 1862 allowed those overseeing twenty slaves an exemption from Confederate service, but the great majority of Texas men either volunteered or were conscripted. Some of the youngest and oldest recruits served in the "Home Guards" in each county. Farming, ranching, and businesses naturally suffered with the absence of men of fighting age. But many women, following the American colonial tradition of women as "deputy husbands," took over the management of farms, plantations, ranches, and businesses during this period.

Union blockades and the disruptions of war meant that Texans learned to make do or do without. Texans learned to concoct coffee substitutes out of peanuts, corn, barley, and even okra. Eudora Moore would recall her mother constructing a pair of pants from a "parlor table cover." When items previously in good supply did appear, they commanded exorbitant prices. In early February 1864, Mary Maverick squeezed into the crowded Mutual Aid store in San Antonio, getting for her efforts and $180 a bolt of domestic cloth, a pair of shoes, and a dozen candles.

Homespun and handwoven clothing became a symbol of patriotic pride; Governor Francis R. Lubbock was inaugurated in a homespun suit in 1861, and the chorus of the Confederate song "Bonny Blue Flag" noted "My homespun dress is plain I know/My fan is homemade too/But then it shows what Southern girls/For Southern rights will do." Despite the severe shortages at home, girls and women also worked hard to clothe the soldiers and provide them with medicine and food, as the Confederate and state governments struggled to provide them with the most basic necessities.

Texas did enjoy an important trade advantage over other southern states in its proximity to Mexico. At Matamoros, on the Rio Grande across from Brownsville, and at Bagdad, Tamaulipas, bordering the mouth of the Rio Grande, Texas cotton was shipped out, helping shore up the Texas and western Confederate economies, and items such as medicine and tobacco intermittently made their way to inland Texas. Mexican, Tejano, and Anglo merchants operating on the Rio Grande made "small fortunes" in trade during the war years as blockade-running vessels carrying supplies and cotton evaded the Union ships in the gulf.

Nonetheless, the war greatly hurt economic and cultural development in Texas. The state was just beginning to establish the transportation arteries necessary for increased trade and growth when the conflict broke out. For example, railroad projects of the 1850s, although limited and short-lived, had already made a difference in Texas travel. A thirty-six-mile trip northwest from Houston to the Hockley area took a day and a half by stagecoach (through mud) in 1854; the same trip over the same ground took an hour and forty minutes by rail in 1857.

The war played havoc with fledgling railroad efforts. Although a few short railroad lines in Texas were actually completed and put in service during the war years, others had to shut down. In some cases, their rails were dug up and used as military fortifications or laid elsewhere as part of the military supply effort. Meanwhile, many railroad construction efforts simply stopped midway through.

By the same token, work ground to a halt on other community development efforts. For example, since her first arrival in San Antonio in 1838 Mary Maverick had longed to worship in an Episcopal church, practicing the faith in which she was raised. By 1850, a small core congregation had been formed, but despite the efforts of the Mavericks and others, attempts to build a church repeatedly faltered. Construction on St. Mark's Episcopal church finally commenced in the midst of the statewide agitation over secession, but was suspended with the advent of the war.

At its most extreme, the war pushed Texans back into uncertain frontier conditions, not only in terms of supplies and community development but in terms of safety. During the early statehood period, American and European immigrants had moved westward through the Texas Hill Country, pushing settlement onto the Edwards Plateau. To the north, they had moved onto the grand prairies and into the western cross timbers of north central Texas, pressing westward to the prairies beyond. In both cases, they were drawing near to the rolling plains still occupied by embattled Indians. Although the early months of the war were relatively quiet on Texas's western frontier, with the northern and southern states at war and men and resources being drained for the fighting, the remaining free-roaming Comanches, in particular, began to use the situation to their advantage. They mounted punishing raids on the outlying western settlements, hitting hard in Cooke, Denton, Montague, Parker, and Wise counties. Texans "forted up," as they had in earlier days, families coming together and stockading for protection.

From the outset of the war the state government had tried to address the need for frontier protection, from Indians as well as other threats. In December 1861 the Texas legislature authorized a Frontier Regiment to replace a Texas Confederate regiment briefly assigned to home-front protection. Led by Colonel James M. Norris, the new force of more than 1,000 men established a frontier defense line a short distance west of the settlements, from the Red River on the north bordering Indian Territory southward to the Rio Grande, with a string of sixteen forts bisecting the state, north to south. (In the south along the Rio Grande, a Confederate regiment patrolled the border area.)

In spring 1862, Confederate President Jefferson Davis responded to complaints about lack of protection by Texas governor Francis R. Lubbock and Missouri's governor by establishing a Trans-Mississippi Military Department with Edmund Kirby Smith commanding. But the Confederacy's military attention and resources remained directed eastward.

At first, Norris's troops patrolled regularly from fort to fort, but the Comanches and their allies from other tribes, discerning the pattern, stepped up their attacks on temporarily exposed areas. In 1863, Governor Lubbock reorganized and expanded the Frontier Regiment, which was rechristened Mounted Regiment, Texas State Troops. It abandoned the patrol system in favor of an aggressive series of scouting parties beyond the line of defense.

As the frontier force sought to quell the Indian threat, state officials and President Davis sparred over its status. State officials wanted the regiment to be a Confederate force, but to remain under state control to respond quickly and knowledgeably to Indian threats. Davis wanted the regiment to be subject to all Confederate rules and regulations, which meant that its members could be pulled from the Texas frontier and used elsewhere.

In an agreement that became official in March 1864, the regiment was switched to Confederate service and divided, some of the companies moving elsewhere in Texas. On the western frontier, those remaining were joined by more than 4,000 local militia men, like other "Home Guard" units mostly older men and teenage boys too young for service.

Indian depradations continued, the most prominent of which was the Elm Creek raid of October 1864. Comanches and Kiowas rode into the Elm Creek Valley in Young County and raided the settlements, killing eleven residents and five Confederate troopers and capturing seven women and children.

Dissent Within Texas

In the waning months of the war, the Comanches and their allies shifted their attentions away from the Texas frontier, a move that should have ensured a much-needed peace. But the frontier—and much of North Texas—remained chaotic and strife-filled, the remaining companies riding out not only after outlaws but after deserters and those who refused to serve in the Confederacy or Home Guard. In October 1864, General Edmund Kirby Smith noted, "The frontier counties . . . are . . . a grand city of refuge where thousands of able-bodied men have flocked to escape service in the Confederate Army." The conscription evaders and the deserters were called "brush men" because they hid in the brush. All attempts to corral and control them ended in failure. Henry McCulloch, commander of the Northern Sub-District, offered the deserters an amnesty in the fall

In the year this photo was taken, 1859, Sam Houston was about to mount a victorious campaign for the governorship of Texas. But when he refused to take a loyalty oath to the Confederacy in 1861, he was removed from the office. *(Sam Houston Memorial Museum, Huntsville, Texas)*

of 1863 and included those who responded in the "Brush Battalion," charged with chasing down other deserters and protecting against Indians. But the members of the battalion were so troublesome, and prone to desert, that McCulloch disbanded it in March 1864.

McCulloch's experience points up one impact of the war in Texas: increased divisiveness. Not only had some Texans chosen to fight for the Union, but some of those who stayed refused to commit to the war effort, or actively opposed it. At first, many Texans excused immigrants from Europe, in particular, from embracing the cause with fervor. But as the casualties began to mount, and as the Confederacy fought for survival, dissent or even neutrality was viewed as suspect at best, traitorous at worst. In San Antonio, as one resident noted, "It was like living in an asylum where every one was crazy on one especial subject; you never knew what dangerous paroxysms were about to begin."

Secessionists perceived opposition to the southern cause among the Germans of central Texas and the immigrants from the Upper South living in frontier north Texas. Although members of both groups enlisted and fought for the Confederacy, their numbers did include staunch antislavery contingents, people who felt that slaveholding provided an unfair advantage in an agricultural society and was at odds with the principles of democracy. Further, there were avowed Unionists in both groups; many of the North Texans were rumored to be members of a Union League formed during the war as a means of pledging continuing fidelity to the United States. The opposition of the two groups was explained in part by the fact that many Germans had left their home country disappointed by its failure to reach unification, and by the fact that the Upper Southerners, whether or not they favored slavery, felt that the issue should be resolved without secession.

Some Upper Southerners moved on to Kansas or California, and some Germans left for Mexico. One such group of German Unionists, en route to Mexico and camped beside the Nueces River in Kinney County, were set upon by Confederate troops in August 1862. Of the sixty-plus members of the traveling party, nineteen were killed in the "battle of the Nueces," along with two Confederates. Confederates executed the nine wounded Germans as well.

Many Upper Southerners in North Texas felt secure and well established in their independent views. After all, they lived in an area of the state where slavery had only a tentative foothold, and many had arrived in the 1830s and 1840s. Yet immigrants from the Lower South, especially those holding slaves and with more wealth, in general, had arrived in the 1850s. Some of these representatives of antebellum southern culture, spurred in part by stories of the Union League, in part by tales of North Texans' collaboration with Kansas abolitionists and Indians across the Red River, began to form vigilante groups to ferret out Union sympathizers.

This atmosphere led to a series of vigilante killings of suspected or known Union sympathizers in Cooke, Grayson, Wise, and Denton counties. The most notorious killings occurred in Cooke County and became known collectively as the "Great Hanging at Gainesville."

Suspicions had been provoked when a number of Cooke County citizens

This oil painting, done by C. B. Clauss in 1888, depicts the "battle of the Nueces" in August 1862, when Confederate troops set upon more than sixty German Unionists camped beside the Nueces River en route to Mexico. Two troopers and nineteen Germans were killed and nine wounded Germans were executed. *(Comfort Historical Museum, Comfort, Texas)*

signed a petition protesting the Conscription Acts of April 1862 because the acts exempted men in charge of at least twenty slaves. The acts had caused grumbling statewide, but resistance was stronger and more vocal in the northern counties, where dissenters were unhappy about being drafted or seeing their sons drafted. When rumors began to circulate of a Unionist plot to seize the militia arsenals at Sherman and Gainesville, the commander of the Gainesville-area militia district authorized the arrest of any able-bodied men who failed to respond to a call to arms. Colonel James G. Bourland, a former state senator and plantation owner, led state troops in arresting more than 150 men on October 1. They were to be tried by a "citizens' jury" organized by Bourland and Confederate colonel and fellow slaveholder William C. Young, who happened to be home on leave.

None of the accused owned slaves, but seven of the twelve jurors did. The jurors proceeded to convict seven leading Unionists of "conspiracy and insurrection" or "disloyalty and treason." These seven men were summarily hung, but the jury was exonerating others when a mob demanded more convictions. Fourteen more men were turned over to the vigilantes, escorted by Bourland's troops, and hung from a large elm tree on the banks of Pecan Creek just east of Gainesville.

In Gainesville, it appeared that the rest of the prisoners would be released, but then William Young and another man were ambushed and killed by unknown assailants. Many of the prisoners were immediately retried, and nineteen more were executed. In all, forty men were hung and two killed while trying to escape before the troubles in Gainesville came to an end. A family member of one of the executed men charged that most of the dead "were old settlers in this country, and had fought the Indians from their doorsteps. And they did not want to be crowded back on the back seat by a few newcomers that was trying to take the lead and run the country."

The war left a palpable bitterness between those who had wholeheartedly embraced the cause and those who could not and would not do so. In San Antonio, as people like the Mavericks struggled to comprehend and accept the defeat of a cause to which they had given time, energy, money, and sons, Confederate veterans raided and looted, defending their actions on the grounds that San Antonians had not fully supported the war effort.

Aftermath

Even without the internal enmities, the military and political loss festered. "Our humiliation in defeat . . . is harder to bear, than all the exposure, hunger and wounds during the war," former Confederate soldier J. L. Greer of McKinney would write. "It rankles me in my heart still. . . ."

The war, then, left many Texans exhausted, disheartened, and divided, with not only the plantation system but their towns and farms in disorder and decay. Galveston's population had declined, and a local newspaper reported that even Confederate troops had "torn [fine residences] to pieces merely for fuel during the whole war, and that too while there has been an abundance of wood at the head of the bay." Beaumont had been growing in promise and prominence before the war as a sawmill and ranching town and a railroad transportation hub, but after the war the sawmills sat deteriorating, the railroad bridges and roadbeds untended and unused. In the countryside, much farming land lay uncultivated, its cash value diminished, and farms had deteriorated.

If any group had reason to rejoice at the South's capitulation, it was African Americans, most of them slaves. Texas had more slaves than ever at war's end— an estimated 250,000—because of the southern practice of sending them beyond the reach of the Union army. The feeling of freedom was sweet to people who had lived so long without it; Annie Hawkins would remember, "We was the happiest folks in the world when we knowed we was free."

Nevertheless, former slaves had reason to be uneasy. General Gordon Granger had arrived in Galveston on June 19 and proclaimed enforcement of the Emancipation Proclamation in Texas, an event that would later spark the creation and observance of "Juneteenth" celebrations among African Americans. But even the wording of the proclamation seemed to send mixed messages. It demanded "an absolute equality of rights and rights of property between former masters and slaves," yet also suggested that the slaves "remain at their present homes and work for wages" and warned that "they will not be allowed to collect at military posts" or be "supported in idleness, either there or elsewhere." Some even had to overcome the deception of their owners; Lulu Wilson's owner told her stepfather that adults had been freed, but children had to remain with masters until they reached adulthood.

Many of Texas's leaders and voting citizens had defined Texas as part of a southern Confederacy built on cotton culture; its most powerful citizens were those who managed large-scale cotton cultivation with slaves. They had separated Texas from the very Union it had sought to enter in the 1830s and 1840s. Now Texans were going to have to redefine themselves and their relation to that Union, including expanding definitions of citizenship—or accept definitions imposed from outside.

Reconstruction in Texas

With the defeat of Texas and other seceded states, the federal government faced the problem of bringing them back into the Union and ensuring their adherence to federal law, including the emancipation of former slaves. President Lincoln considered this an executive branch responsibility and in December 1863 had issued the Proclamation of Amnesty and Reconstruction by which southern voters were to pledge their loyalty to the U.S. Constitution and the Union.

By the time Edmund Kirby Smith surrendered the western Confederate forces, President Lincoln had been assassinated, and his vice president and successor, Andrew Johnson, had already offered amnesty to most Confederates if they would take a loyalty oath to the United States. Like Lincoln, Johnson saw the southern states' attempt to withdraw from the Union as an illegal action that the executive branch should handle through a program of "reconstruction." But powerful Republicans in national government had a different interpretation: The southern states had given up their statehood in the Union. Because it was the responsibility of the U.S. Congress to admit new states, Congress should direct the "reconstruction," and do so in such a way as to ensure the rights of the former slaves and advance Republican principles. At first Johnson prevailed, allowing the old southern power order to begin reasserting itself. Then Congress took over, trying to force the old southern electorate to accept enhanced federal control and rights for African Americans. In Texas, as elsewhere in the South, some sought to construct a new order as others sought to reclaim the old one.

Presidential Reconstruction

A former Democratic senator from Tennessee who had become vice president in 1864, Johnson proceeded with his mild restructuring plan. He ordered a constitutional convention "to restore [Texas] to its constitutional relations to the federal government." Delegates would have to take the loyalty oath, but again, all but the most prominent Texas Confederate leaders would be allowed to participate in the new political order.

John H. Reagan, the Texan who had served as postmaster general in Jefferson Davis's cabinet, wrote from prison in Boston to "the People of Texas" in August 1865 urging that they "accept the present condition of things, as the result of war, and of inevitable necessity," accepting "the supreme authority of the Government of the United States" and the abolition of slavery as conditions for regaining "the blessings of local self-government" and banishing military rule.

Johnson had appointed Andrew J. Hamilton provisional governor of Texas. The controversial Hamilton embodied many of the political dilemmas of the era. An Austin lawyer and former Democratic state representative, Hamilton had been among those moderate Democrats who tried to fight the secessionist tide in the 1850s. His popularity was such that he won a U.S. congressional seat in 1859 and a special election to the Texas Senate early in the war. But by mid-1862, he felt harassed for his views and left Texas. In the U.S. cities of the Northeast, he lectured on the evils of slavery and slave owners' power. With the North anticipating the occupation of Texas, Hamilton was actually appointed military governor of the state and participated in the Union troops' foray into South Texas in the fall of 1863. But he waited out the later stages of the war in New Orleans.

Despite Reagan's admonishments to Texans to accept federal measures, Hamilton and other Unionists encountered intense enmity. Many Texans remained bitter in defeat and unwilling to tolerate newly freed slaves as anything but a controlled labor force whose conditions were not that different from their previous conditions. Nor did the disaffected Texans have much to fear from military enforcement, as few federal troops were stationed in Texas or remained in the South. The Unionists had their own record of wrongs to settle from the war years. Hamilton tried to place only staunch Unionists in high-level state positions as well as in positions at every other level—district, county, and precinct; even the most nominal Confederates, people who had served in minor governmental roles during the war years, were denied positions. Even under Johnson's mild version of Reconstruction, former Confederates often felt the wrath of those the secessionists had silenced and marginalized. Minyard H. Harris of Kirvin, whose Confederate duties had included chasing down deserters and forcing them back to their units, reported himself after the war "in constant danger of being caught and shot or hanged."

Overall, however, in most parts of the state, the old southern order managed to reassert itself fairly quickly, in part thanks to Johnson's lenient pardoning policy. Many Confederate leaders were elected to serve, along with Unionists, in the federally required constitutional convention of early 1866. For readmission to the Union, members were expected to repudiate the right of secession, to ratify the Thirteenth Amendment to the U.S. Constitution outlawing slavery, to determine fairly and objectively the "social and political status of freedmen," and to repudiate the state's war debt.

Members agreed to nullify Texas's act of secession, but not to do so *ab initio* (from the beginning) as this would mean that they had had no right to secede in the first place and would also nullify all laws and transactions made in Texas since 1861. They skated around ratification of the Thirteenth Amendment; because it had already become national law the previous year, they argued, in agreeing to support the Constitution, they were also supporting the amendment. They repudiated the war debt and acknowledged certain freedman rights, including protection of person and property, but they rejected any idea of freedmen voting or holding public office. None of this was likely to satisfy Reconstructionists in Congress, and it did not.

In June, Texas voters approved the resulting constitution and chose their first elected postwar governor in a contest between two moderates: the constitutional convention's chair, J. W. Throckmorton, and former Texas governor E. M. Pease. Throckmorton, a member of the Texas legislature before the war, had held out against secession until it was accomplished. He had endeared himself to supporters of the war, however, by enlisting quickly in frontier defense, then in the Sixth Texas Cavalry. A former surgeon and soldier in the Mexican War, Throckmorton had fought in various Civil War engagements, eventually serving as Edmund Kirby Smith's Confederate commissioner to the Indians.

Elisha Pease possessed exceptionally strong Texas credentials as well, having participated in the writing of the Republic constitution in 1836 and having served in a variety of government roles since that time, including two terms as an able governor of the state in the 1850s. Like Throckmorton, he had resisted secession; unlike Throckmorton, he had chosen not to participate in the Confederacy but had quietly continued to adhere to Union principles.

In the election, Throckmorton emerged the victor, in part because Pease's support of even limited African American voting was perceived as "radical" by "unreconstructed" Texans. With the power structure of the Old South reasserting itself, even many southern moderates refused to support some of the most basic citizenship rights for African Americans. When the Eleventh Legislature convened in August 1866, it not only appointed leading secessionist O. M. Roberts to the U.S. Senate but set "black codes" limiting African Americans' movements in Texas—for example, specifying labor contracts that required them to get permission to leave the home workplace.

In truth, African Americans found precious little freedom or independence after the war and much hostility to their assuming any role but a variation of the slave role. Because they remained landless, they had few choices but to labor for whites as tenants. The best hope for many became an agency established in March 1865 to be administered by the U.S. Army; the Freedman's Bureau came to Texas in September of that year.

Agents of the bureau—including military men, northerners, and some Texans—were charged with helping former slaves make the transition into citizenship. This included ensuring that blacks had the same protections under the law as whites, helping them set up schools and providing teachers, monitoring the freedmen's labor contracts for fair terms, and helping former slaves unite with scattered family members. One of the most active agents, George T. Ruby, soon established himself in Texas politics. A freeborn native of New York who had traveled extensively, Ruby moved to Galveston from Louisiana after the war. Here he served as a *New Orleans Tribune* correspondent, started his own Galveston newspaper, and taught school. Soon he was administering the Bureau's schools in a number of counties.

At its peak, the bureau had fifty-nine agents in fifty-nine districts in Texas. The difficulties of travel and communication, as well as resistance to the bureau's efforts by many white Texans, made the agents' job a hard and dangerous one. Even though Andrew Johnson in late August 1866 declared "the insurrection which heretofore existed in the State of Texas is at an end," violence—especially violence directed against African Americans and representatives of the national government—was all too prevalent.

Nationally, the picture was equally dismal. Only Tennessee among the Confederate states had been induced to ratify the Fourteenth Amendment, granting citizenship rights to former slaves. In the eyes of Republican leaders, presidential Reconstruction had failed miserably, allowing the old southern hierarchy to begin to reassert itself, and members of the U.S. Congress refused to seat Roberts and other members of the Texas delegation when they arrived in Washington.

Congressional Reconstruction

Republican leaders wrested control of Reconstruction from the executive branch. They began passing Reconstruction legislation over Johnson's veto and in 1868 the House of Representatives impeached him over his attempt to remove a secretary of war. Although Johnson would barely survive the impeachment in a close Senate vote, by 1867, he had lost almost all support. Congress now assumed military control of the southern states and forced them to do what most had failed to do under presidential Reconstruction: involve African American men in the reconstruction of state government and grant freedmen voting rights.

The First Reconstruction Act, signed on March 2, 1867, essentially reestablished and reasserted military rule in the South. Two more acts followed, specifying who was disqualified from voting and authorizing military commanders to "suspend or remove" and replace any officeholders in their districts. Congress also stipulated that the southern states must have new constitutional conventions that would support the Fourteenth Amendment, which penalized states for denying adult male citizens the right to vote ("except for participation in rebellion, or other crime") and made it more difficult for former Confederates to gain a pardon. General Charles Griffin, who had risen to major general as a Union commander during the war, now had federal authority over the Department of Texas and pursued an ambitious agenda of new voter registrations, black and white. He repeatedly clashed with Governor Throckmorton, the governor charging that the military was taking on too much civil authority and Griffin charging that the governor was being obstructionist and allowing violence against blacks and Unionists. Griffin complained to his superior, General Philip H. Sheridan, and got Throckmorton removed. Although Sheridan appointed the seasoned and respected E. M. Pease in Throckmorton's stead, this blatant use of military power only hardened many Texans against the occupation.

Like former provisional governor Hamilton, Griffin also replaced other former

Confederates holding office with Union men. He enforced the congressional voting restriction by which officials, candidates, potential jury members, and even voters had to swear that they had never taken an oath to uphold the U.S. Constitution, then participated in rebellion. Radical Reconstructionists reasoned that these exclusions were necessary, at least temporarily, in order to carry out congressional Reconstruction. After Griffin died suddenly in the summer of 1867 in a yellow fever epidemic, his successor, Joseph J. Reynolds, stepped up the removals of state, county, and local officials who had any ties to the Confederacy.

Given the major restructuring going on, it was no surprise when the elections for a new constitutional convention in Texas yielded a distinctly different set of delegates from previous conventions. In addition to supporting the Fourteenth Amendment, Congress expected the delegates to revisit the *ab initio* question and nullify the original secession decision and any laws in the state that followed from it. Congress also expected them to support the Thirteenth and Fifteenth Amendments, the latter a flat statement that voting rights would not be denied "on account of race, color, or previous condition of servitude."

Many Democrats were adamantly opposed to the new convention and a new constitution, and many of them simply stayed away from the polls or were barred from them by the loyalty voting restriction. For the first time, African American men voted, and voted in large numbers, spurred on by the voter registration campaign administered by the military. Ten of the ninety delegates elected were African Americans, the most prominent of whom was probably George T. Ruby. Ruby had not only administered schools for the Freedman's Bureau in their most successful Texas program but had served as president of the Union League, a Unionist organization effective in involving African Americans in politics. Although there were a few Democrats, most of the delegates were Republicans who had opposed the old southern leadership in one way or another. A. J. Hamilton, in something of a shift, now led the moderate Republicans loyal to Pease. One contingent consisted of the "radical" Republicans intent on forcing Texans into line with federal mandates and keeping all former Confederates out of power. This group was led by A. J. Hamilton's brother, Morgan C. Hamilton, and Edmund J. Davis. Davis had first been appointed a district judge by Pease in the 1850s but had won the undying hatred of many Civil War Texans by joining the federal forces as a cavalry colonel and participating in the Union's attempted invasions of Texas.

The delegates, with Davis presiding, argued interminably, with the *ab initio* issue again receiving much attention: Should nullification extend to the initial act of secession? Another primary issue at this convention was whether to divide Texas into two states, east and west. Delegates from both East Texas and West Texas favored this move as a means of addressing the fact that East Texas remained in many ways an extension of the American South, whereas West Texas— represented most vocally by the radical Republicans—had a more independent population less tied to the cotton culture of the South.

After three months, the money set aside for convention expenses ran out, and the delegates adjourned without even getting to the wording of a constitution, although they did call for ratification of the Thirteenth and Fourteenth Amendments by the first legislature to assemble under the new constitution. Everyone waited to see what shifts the national presidential election would bring. When Union General Ulysses S. Grant won the presidency, the radical Republicans felt affirmed in their vision of a reconstructed Texas, which not only included a state of West Texas but delayed statehood for East Texas because of the continuing hostility against Reconstruction manifested there.

The convention met again in December 1868 and again delayed producing a constitution, breaking up in early February. Its members had done some visionary work, particularly in the area of education, setting aside monies from the sale of public lands for a permanent school fund to be used to educate Texas children "irrespective of race and color." But they had drawn up only a partial constitution for the state, one signed by only half the delegates. Subsequently, a committee appointed by General Reynolds completed the work, using records from the convention.

The document that went before voters in November 1869 both softened the restrictions against former Confederates' political participation and finally affirmed voting rights irrespective of "race, color, or former condition." It contained the far-reaching public education plan under a state superintendent of public instruction. Perhaps the most important aspect of the constitution in the short run was its centralized vision of government. This vision was at odds with the Jacksonian democracy that had underpinned Texas politics in the decades before the Civil War, when many Texans had taken as a tenet of faith the idea that the "common man" in the Anglo population played a part in governmental decision making and compromise agreements. The constitution gave great powers to the governor, who would have a longer term—four years—and would appoint district judges and some key state officials who had previously been chosen in elections. As part of the consolidation of control, elections were to be held at the county seats, not at precincts, and county commissioners were eliminated, with justices of the peace taking over county court functions.

At the same time voters were asked to weigh in on the new constitution, they were also asked to vote for new state and county officials. For the first time, black candidates appeared on a number of ballots. The race for the governorship was key to the next stage of Reconstruction. As a candidate, former provisional governor Hamilton continued to adopt a more conservative course than he had in the early days of Reconstruction, opposing the radicals' attempt to form a state of West Texas and even backing off from support for black suffrage. His opponent, E. J. Davis, continued to represent radical Republicanism—and was supported and assisted by military commander Joseph Reynolds, whose cavalry Davis had commanded in the later stages of the war. Reynolds, continuing to exercise his power over even local appointments, saw to it that supporters of Davis filled the voter registration boards and so angered Governor Pease that Pease resigned in protest in September.

With leading Democrats disenfranchised or disaffected and divided on how to combat the new Republican-driven constitution, the constitution was approved in the November election. Two African Americans were also elected to the Texas Senate—Ruby and Matthew Gaines, a Baptist preacher who had been born a slave in Louisiana—and twelve African Americans were elected to the Texas House. In the gubernatorial race, charges and countercharges of vote fraud flew during and after the elections, and there may well have been fraud on both sides. Davis emerged the victor by a narrow margin, helped along by the heavy turnout of African Americans. They recognized in him a champion of new definitions for Texas in which blacks could play roles previously denied them.

Conditions in Texas

Davis took office in 1870 in a state still scarred, battered, and divided. Land values had dropped, cotton prices had been cut almost in half just since 1866, and sharecropping—the farming of someone else's land in exchange for a place to live and a third to a half of the money earned—was becoming a way of life for many whites and blacks alike. A young Englishman who had immigrated to Texas the previous year wrote, "Times are awful hard now in Texas. Money is scarce, land is worth almost nothing . . .things generally are in a state of stagnation."

There were signs of economic health, however: The rate of population growth was higher in Texas than in the nation as a whole; industry was developing; key towns were growing again, with Galveston and San Antonio leading the way; and the 1870 census showed that 60 percent of employed Texans were "property-holding farmers, businessmen, members of professions, or skilled tradesmen." The ranks of the wealthiest Texans were shifting, with merchants and bankers replacing plantation owners and farmers. Yet most of the wealthy Texans had deep roots in the state, and none more so than Sam Maverick, the only member of the Independence Convention of 1836 to be listed among the wealthiest Texans in the 1870 census.

Despite his continued holdings, Maverick's experience demonstrates the difficulties encountered by many former Confederates in this period. After passage of the First Reconstruction Act, he and fellow secession commissioner Thomas Devine were "summoned to appear before the Federal Court to answer for the three million dollars worth of U.S. property they receipted for as Rebel commissioners." The case was suspended indefinitely, but it left the accused in limbo. In 1869 he wrote to his sons in college that they would have to come home or teach school, as the U.S. government was refusing to pay rent on some of his lands, the Reconstruction San Antonio mayor was threatening to sue him, and "several conspiracies [have been] got up here against me financially." A beleaguered Maverick would die of a "wasting illness" early in the Davis administration.

Whatever one's social, political, and economic standing and fortunes, Texans through the Reconstruction period found violence continuing and intensifying. Local and regional feuds erupted, the most extended and violent the Sutton-Taylor Feud in DeWitt County. Indians had continued to scourge and push back the Texas frontier, Kiowa leader Satanta arguing vehemently that the Kiowas and Comanches owned West Texas. The U.S. government had provided a limited, ineffective force for frontier Texas forts, and Congress had tried unsuccessfully to stop the raiding and get all of the Indians onto reservations in Indian Territory with an 1867 parley between a commission and southern Plains Indian leaders at Medicine Lodge Creek, Kansas. But by 1870, the attacks were worsening.

There were also outlaw gangs to contend with, such as that of Cullen Baker, a resident of northeast Texas whose murderous tendencies were already documented before the war. After the conflict, in which he served intermittently as a Confederate soldier, he turned his ire against African Americans and Reconstruction representatives, he and his band killing a number of people, including Freedman's Bureau agents.

Meanwhile, the Ku Klux Klan, first formed by Confederate veterans in Tennessee in 1866, had spread to Texas by spring 1868. This secret organization, loosely organized in Texas, had among its goals resistance to Reconstruction and restoration of white supremacy. Members throughout eastern Texas—particularly the northeastern region—targeted African Americans, "carpetbaggers" (northerners representing federal control and privilege), and even Republicans in general. They destroyed crops, stole horses, burned houses, beat and murdered victims, and intimidated local authorities. Some forced former slaves into registering to vote as Democrats. Similar secret organizations arose, promoting a rhetoric of white superiority, the Knights of the Golden Circle pledging to "maintain and defend the social and political superiority of the White race on this Continent; always and in all places to observe a marked distinction between the White and African races. . . ."

A committee for the 1868–69 constitutional convention had determined that of the 939 murders reported by county officials between 1865 and 1868, almost half were committed by whites against other whites and 40 percent were committed by whites against blacks. Many other murders and other crimes remained unreported. Military commander Reynolds had been at least partially effective in prosecuting some of the more flagrant lawless acts, but many problems remained.

Home Rule

When Davis and radical Republican legislators took office, they acted quickly to pull Texas out of Congressional Reconstruction, in part by adopting the Fourteenth and Fifteenth Amendments. With a constitution acceptable to Congressional Reconstructionists in place and adoption of these amendments, on March 30, 1870, Texas gained official readmittance to the Union. It now had home rule, although "unreconstructed" Confederates considered it as far from their own rule as possible.

Davis and the Republican-dominated Twelfth Legislature moved to create some far-sighted policies. Most significantly, they passed laws in 1870 and 1871 that made public schooling free and compulsory, to be supported with an adequate tax base. They also tried to address the continuing violence and chaos by creating a state police force. The Police Act of July 1870 was only one of what came to be known by resistant white Texans as the "obnoxious acts," but it was probably the most hated. The force would answer to Davis as governor and be able to move at will about the state, having local law officers who failed to cooperate removed from their positions. This force, which reached a size of about 200, contained African American and Tejano men as well as Anglos and both former Union soldiers and former Confederate ones. The majority, not surprisingly, were Republicans. Some abused their authority, yet much of the ill-feeling against the state police grew from its oversight by Davis and the fact that 40 percent of the troopers were African American.

Other controversial measures which Davis and the legislature enacted included a militia bill which authorized him to declare martial law and enroll and command any able-bodied males in Texas, ages 18 to 45, if he deemed local or state policing too weak. The legislature gave him even more power to select state, district, and county officials previously elected by citizens. It also delayed the regular election until November 1872, advocates citing the need to bring state and congressional elections in line. To Democrats and dissatisfied Republicans, however, this simply looked like another power play, for Davis and the Republican legislators now had another year on their terms.

To add further fuel to the fires of resentment, Davis did not hesitate to use martial law in various counties. His calling out the militia was often to protect African Americans against some very real threats, but at other times it smacked of intimidation against Democrats. And the Democrats, with many of their number no longer excluded from voting and holding office, were gaining in power. They continued to resist citizenship rights for African Americans, and they saw Davis's presence in the governor's mansion as yet another feature of federal Reconstruction. In the elections of 1872, they would be ready.

The "Redeemers" in Control

Democrats and conservative Republicans demonstrated their active resistance to Governor Davis's administration in September 1871, with a Taxpayers' Convention in Austin. Former governor Pease presided as they protested not only Davis's expenditures but his "despotic power." The demands of congressional Reconstruction had brought a concentration of power which most Texas citizens would not have accepted in other circumstances. Now delegates charged Davis with a "violation of nearly every private right of the citizen" in the Police Bill. In sum, the delegates concluded, "The . . . people of the State no longer govern themselves, but are governed by E. J. Davis, as completely as if there were no Constitutions, State or Federal." The next month, Democratic candidates won all four Congressional seats. The editor of the *Neches Valley News* crowed, "[T]he people of Southeast Texas have done handling political issues with gloves and intend to do their share in tearing down and uprooting the government policy implemented by Eastern fanatics."

Democrats continued to seek to "redeem" Texas from the hands of the radical Republicans. In the fall elections of 1872, they won a majority in the House and decisive election victories throughout the state. In part, this shift reflected the intimidation of freedmen in exercising their voting rights. In part, it reflected the disenchantment of former Davis supporters, some of whom had participated in the Taxpayers' Convention. In large part, it reflected the continuing southern sentiment among Anglos, especially with the steady influx of southerners into Texas; in 1873, an estimated 80 percent of the 125,000 immigrants would be from southern states.

When the Thirteenth Legislature convened in January 1873, even many of the Republican members jumped into a dismantling of the previous legislature's acts. The state police force was eliminated, some of the governor's appointments were changed to elective office, and the governor's power to declare martial law was erased. Voting could be moved back to precincts, and the school system was broken up, with much authority shifting to local school boards. By the elections of November 1873, the radical Republicans in office were the remnants of radical home rule serving out their terms.

It was no surprise, then, when Davis was decisively voted out of office in favor of Democratic candidate Richard Coke, a Waco lawyer, Confederate veteran, and district and state judge under Presidential Reconstruction. But what followed only added to the abundant partisan ill-feeling and left Davis in an impossible position.

The governor still had supporters, and they identified two issues that made the transfer of executive power problematic. First, the state constitution gave two dates for the transition: "the first Thursday after the organization of the legislature"—in this case the second Thursday in January 1874—and the end of the four-year term, which would be April 28, 1874. Second, the constitution said one thing about the length of time the polls should be open, while the statute passed by the Thirteenth Legislature to govern the 1873 elections specified another. Davis supporters challenged the constitutionality of the statute, and thus of the election results.

In December, the state attorney general ruled that the governor's term should run a full four years. Further, on January 5, 1874, the state Supreme Court agreed with the Davis supporters in judging the election unconstitutional, thereby voiding results not only in the governor's race but in all other categories—and opening the door to legal challenges to anything the new slate of state and county officers would do governmentally.

Davis had stayed removed from the court challenges. Now, however, he felt obliged to uphold the rulings of the attorney general and the Supreme Court even as the Democrats proceeded with plans to convene the legislature and inaugurate Coke in January. Davis sent President Grant a request for federal troops to delay the seating of the Fourteenth Legislature. He also wanted Grant to address

Douglas Jerrold's sketch of the inauguration of Richard Coke as governor in January 1874 illustrates a turning point in Texas political history, as Democratic "redeemers" replaced the Reconstruction government of E. J. Davis. *(PICA 26678 Austin History Center, Austin Public Library)*

the issue of the body's legitimacy: Would Grant recognize the election results as valid, essentially overruling the state Supreme Court?

Grant refused to send troops and failed to respond to Davis's repeated requests for an authoritative response on whether the election could or would be considered valid by the president. Meanwhile, the Democrats convened the legislature on January 13. Davis finally disbanded his supporters and stepped down after the president again rebuffed his request for troops and a ruling.

As a political player and as governor, Davis had been punitive and controlling, but he had also been genuinely concerned with the law, with the problems post-Civil War Texas faced, and with the rights of freed African Americans. In the other camp, even his moderate detractors had acquiesced to a condemnation of "the unseemly advances of the Negro" under Davis. Their racist rhetoric and their desire to overturn progressive Reconstruction policies were apparent, yet they had also championed a theoretically more balanced and less centralized government.

Coke and his supporters lost no time in consolidating their power, placing Democrats in district judge positions and seeing to it that Democrats filled all five positions on a new state Supreme Court. Another matter would take more time: the revision or replacement of the Constitution of 1869.

In particular, Democrats wanted to dismantle the centralized powers born of Reconstruction and spelled out in this constitution; they wanted to limit the governor's and legislature's authority and to do away with the voter registration provisions that had kept many of them from the ballot box.

At first, a legislative commission tried simply to revise the 1869 constitution, but this method still smacked of centralized government. So in August 1875 the new legislature asked voters to approve yet another constitutional convention. Among the representatives elected, there were five Democrats for every Republican, but the fifteen Republican delegates included six African Americans. A number of the delegates had served as officers in the Confederate army; there were also a few U.S. Army veterans. Significantly, more than 40 percent of the delegates belonged to a newly formed farmers' organization, the Patrons of Husbandry, or the "Grange," a cooperative to protect and improve the lives of farm families who were feeling threatened in their livelihoods and increasingly marginalized after the economic Panic of 1873.

The document that resulted called for economy and limited power in state government, especially in the governor's office. Government salaries and expenditures were to be kept low, and terms of office were shortened even as the framers shifted many of the offices from appointed to elected. The governor would not be able to call out the militia or fill vacancies by appointment without approval of the Senate, nor did he have any constitutional control over the other state executive officers. The legislature was to meet regularly only every other year, its members receiving a modest sum. To support such fiscally conservative measures, delegates built in lower tax rates. They also included a homestead exemption protecting family homes and limited acreage from forced sale, reflecting both Mexican precedent and the "pro-debtor, anti-bank" attitudes long held by Texans. This distrust of corporate power was also reflected in a ban on state-chartered banks and in attempts to regulate the railroads by declaring them "common carriers" and having the legislature set limits on freight and passenger rates. In education, the convention followed the Thirteenth Legislature by gutting the Davis administration's centralized public school system, rejecting compulsory attendance and essentially creating segregated schools administered locally. They provided for some taxation and continued the idea of a permanent school fund, establishing one that would grow substantially, first through land sales and leases and later through off-shore oil leases and fuel taxes. But by cutting the local tax base for schools at the same time it mandated local control, the new constitution left Texas schools in an untenable position.

The delegates made no provisions for another constitutional convention, and their involved, detailed document, approved by voters on February 15, 1876, would remain the law of the land in Texas, with increasingly frequent amendments. It was a document that reflected the interests and priorities of most of the delegates, and of most of the voters in 1876, their definitions of what Texas should be and how its government should function. But ultimately, it also reflected an old agrarian outlook, with vestiges of the old plantation South but depending for its definitions on a rather homogenous population engaged primarily in independent farming. In this sense, it was a poor document for a Texas which contained thousands of tenant farmers and people engaged in nonfarming pursuits as well as an ethnically diverse population which included free African Americans, approximately 24,000 Tejanos, and another increasing immigration of Europeans. And the constitution was a poor document for a Texas that was beginning to develop industrially and geographically far beyond the old antebellum definitions.

Conclusion

As a state—as a southern state—Texas had chosen to define itself apart from the American Union it had sought during the republic years. The resulting war had temporarily drained the state of most of its manpower and, despite the trade at Brownsville, had retarded growth and development, extending or renewing frontier conditions. It had also fed serious divisions, both between the American North and South and among Texans. The extent of these divisions became abundantly clear in the troubled Reconstruction period. As the federal government sought to "reconstruct" the southern states, first with fairly mild measures, then with more stringent ones, Texans struggled to determine who they were going to be outside the familiar dimensions of antebellum southern life. For the first time, African Americans as a group were able to seek opportunity, but found little, as proponents of a racial caste system reasserted it with a vengeance. Many Texans became concerned about their agricultural prospects, what they had considered their livelihood. Although farming—especially the farming of cotton—remained the chief economic activity, it was growing difficult to make a living in this way, especially as cotton prices slid downward. Some Texans were beginning to move into the drier areas of the state, areas that initially seemed less suited to agriculture. The movement called for a different identity, a western one.

Meanwhile, modernizing influences were beginning to alter old understandings, offer new ways of living and connecting. As Texas came out of Congressional Reconstruction, railroad construction took off, linking Texas markets and culture with other parts of the nation, especially the powerful Northeast. Manufacturing began to develop in the state, most of it initially connected to farming, but sawmills, textile mills, and iron smelters and foundries signaling steps toward industrialization. Towns were becoming cities, the largest, Galveston, boasting not only colleges, banks, theaters, and concert halls, but such modern amenities as street cars and gas lights. More and more, Texas would become firmly linked culturally and economically to the rest of the nation. But it would carry its southern legacy as well, in attitudes toward government, political parties, and race.

SUGGESTED READINGS

Good primary sources for the Civil War and Reconstruction periods can be found in Ernest Wallace, David M. Vigness, and George B. Ward, *Documents of Texas History* (1994) and in chapters 8 and 9 in Sam W. Haynes and Cary D. Wintz, *Major Problems in Texas History* (2002). Because these are two very distinct crisis-ridden periods, the sources for each are specified below.

Texas and the Confederacy

The *New Handbook of Texas* has a number of useful Civil War–related entries, including one on the "Texas Troubles" and entries on various military units, battles, and campaigns. A good source for understanding Texas's decision to secede from the Union is Walter L. Buenger's "The Roots of Texas Secession" in Haynes and Wintz, *Major Problems in Texas History*, pp. 230–237. For general Civil War information, readers are encouraged to look at the work of Ralph A. Wooster: *Texas and Texans in the Civil War* (1996) and *Lone Star Generals in Gray* (2000). For the story of the Confederacy's thrust into the Southwest, see Donald S. Frazier, *Blood and Treasure: Confederate Empire in the Southwest* (1995) and Jerry Thompson's *Civil War in the Southwest: Recollections of the Sibley Brigade* (2001). Thompson has also written about Mexican Texans in the war: *Mexican Texans in the Union Army* (1986) and *Vaqueros in Blue and Gray* (1976). Evault Boswell's *Texas Boys in Gray* (2000) offers reminiscences by Confederate soldiers.

The War in Texas and Its Impact

For African Americans' experience in the war, see the accounts in Haynes and Wintz and Randolph B. Campbell's *An Empire for Slavery* (1989). Jo Ella Powell Exley's *Texas Tears and Texas Sunshine* (1985) contains some women's accounts of the period; Paula Mitchell Marks in *Turn Your Eyes Toward Texas* (1989) charts the Maverick family fortunes during the war. David Montejano's *Anglos and Mexicans in the Making of Texas, 1836–1986* (1987) deals briefly with the war years. For dissent in Texas, see L. D. Clark, ed., *Civil War Recollections of James Lemuel Clark and the Great Hanging at Gainesville, Texas in October 1862* (1997) and David Pickering and Judy Falls, *Brush Men & Vigilantes: Civil War Dissent in Texas* (2000).

Reconstruction

General works on Reconstruction in Texas include the Charles W. Ramsdell classic, *Reconstruction in Texas* (1910), but there are various late-twentieth-century reassessments, including Edgar Sneed's "A Historiography of Reconstruction in Texas: Some Myths and Problems" in Ralph A. Wooster and Robert Calvert, *Texas Vistas: Selections from the Southwestern Historical Quarterly* (1980), Carl Moneyhon's *Republicanism in Reconstruction Texas* (1980), and Barry Crouch's "'Unmanacling' Texas Reconstruction: A Twenty Year Perspective" in the *Southwestern Historical Quarterly* (1995). More recent general Reconstruction studies include Randolph B. Campbell's *Grass-Roots Reconstruction in Texas, 1865–1880* (1997).

The *New Handbook of Texas* has an excellent entry on Reconstruction and useful entries on the constitutional conventions and constitutions produced in this period.

For information on African American leaders in Reconstruction, see Alwyn Barr and Robert A. Calvert, *Black Leaders: Texans for Their Times* (1981), James M. Smallwood, *Time of Hope, Time of Despair: Black Texans During Reconstruction* (1981), and Carl Moneyhon, "George T. Ruby and African American Politics During Reconstruction" in Haynes and Wintz, pp. 260–269.

An interesting view of Texas life in this period is provided by Robert J. Robertson, *Her Majesty's Texans: Two English Immigrants in Reconstruction Texas* (1998). The endemic violence is discussed in Barry A. Crouch's "White Violence in Reconstruction Texas" in Haynes and Wintz, pp. 252–260. Also see Crouch's work on the Freedmen's Bureau: *The Freedmen's Bureau and Black Texans* (1992). Ralph A. Wooster's "Wealthy Texans, 1870" examines economic, political, and social power in Wooster and Calvert's *Texas Vistas,* pp. 75–186.

A good study of the end of Radical Reconstruction is Carl H. Moneyhon's "Edmund J. Davis in the Coke-Davis Election Dispute of 1874: A Reassessment of Character" in *Southwestern Historical Quarterly* (1996).

III

TEXAS
REDEFINED

In 1936, in the middle of the Great Depression, Texans threw themselves a big six-month-long party in Dallas, ostensibly to celebrate the centennial of Texas's independence from Mexico. The live show "Cavalcade of Texas" described four centuries of Texas history in documents and maps and artifacts, recalling the halcyon days of the Texas Revolution and republic, Stephen F. Austin's "Old Three Hundred," and Sam Houston. University of Texas historian Walter Prescott Webb published his still-popular *The Texas Rangers,* and historical museums were established throughout the state—in Austin, Huntsville, Gonzales, Lubbock, and El Paso.

The real theme of the Centennial, however, was the modernization of the state. A lot had happened to Texas since its reentry into the Union following the Civil War, and the Centennial organizers wanted the people of Texas as well as the larger public to know the story. The cotton planter, represented by Dallas *Morning News* cartoonist John Knott's "Old Man Texas," might still have been the state's most widely recognized symbol, but oil production had eclipsed cotton as the most important product in the state's economy in 1929. Railroads crisscrossed the state, giving Texas more miles of railroad track than any other state by 1911. By 1940 there were 19,000 miles of road. In addition, the Texas population had increased significantly in every decade following 1870, and the growth did not slacken until the depression year of 1930. From a state that was 93.3 percent rural in 1870, Texas had become a state with the majority of its population in cities by 1950; that same year, Houston, with a population of 596,163, ranked fourteenth in the nation. By 1990 Texas contained three of the largest ten cities in the nation—Houston, Dallas, and San Antonio—and was the third most populous state.

With futuristic glimpses of automobiles, television, and air conditioning, the Centennial organizers suggested that opportunity awaited in Texas. They hoped to attract tourists by marketing the state in a different way—as part of the new West rather than the Old South—and adopted the cowboy and a more western look as the theme for the celebration. In addition to the palm trees of the Lower Rio Grande valley and the Spanish missions of old San Antonio, the Centennial publicists used the stunning mountain scenery of the Big Bend, in the Trans-Pecos region, soon to become Texas's first national park. Helping to deliver the message of the new, modern Texas, but one nourished by its historical roots, was the celluloid cowboy from Tioga, Texas, Gene Autry.

In 1939, Texas was on the threshold of a new, modern, industrial age. How did the state transform itself from a rural, slaveholding member of the

Confederacy with a one-crop economy to the diverse, multiracial economic juggernaut that we know today, third only to California and New York in population and with a gross national product (GNP) greater than that of most European nations? Here is that story.   ■ ■ ■

10

Toward Modernization, 1876–1898

As Texas began to recover from the economic impact of the Civil War and Reconstruction, the cattle drives up the Chisholm Trail brought thousands of Longhorns through Fort Worth, a former army post on the Clear Fork of the Trinity River, and the "cow town" began to grow. The North Texas *Epitomist* published what became known as the "tarantula map," which showed Fort Worth as a regional center with rail lines (spider legs) extending in every direction; cattle buyers, professional people, and merchants moved to the city with the understanding that it would soon become a railhead. In the spring of 1873, 116 new buildings were erected, and forty new stores opened within one week.

Then came the Panic of 1873, one of the worst economic depressions that the country had seen. It began when one of the most respected firms on Wall Street, Jay Cooke and Company, failed. The New York stock market closed for ten days in September; a month later trail drivers arriving in Kansas either found no market for their herds or had to sell at a considerable loss. As the shock waves spread, the Texas & Pacific (T&P) Railroad, which had expected to reach Fort Worth that year, stopped construction at Eagle Ford, six miles west of Dallas, and Fort Worth's overnight boom turned just as quickly into a bust. Dozens of businesses closed and hundreds of economic refugees flooded the wagon road east to Dallas as the city's population dropped from an estimated 4,000 to approximately 1,000. One of the defectors, newly

1870s	Windmills in widespread use in West Texas
1874	Invention of barbed wire
1874–75	Indian wars end
1875	Scott Joplin moves to Texarkana with his family
1876	State adopts present constitution; the Agricultural and Mechanical College (now Texas A&M University) opens
1877	The Compromise of 1877 ends Reconstruction; Texas Farmers Alliance established
1883	Cowboy Strike in the Panhandle; University of Texas opens in Austin
1885	Open range trail drives decline
1888	New Texas state capitol inaugurated
1891	Texas Railroad Commission established
1898	Spanish-American War; Texas public domain exhausted

arrived in Dallas, published a letter in the newspaper saying that Fort Worth was so desolate that he had seen a panther "sleeping undisturbed in the business district which was as quiet as a cemetery."

Refusing to accept defeat, Fort Worth citizens took matters into their own hands. In 1875 they formed the Tarrant County Construction Company to grade the railroad bed so that the T&P could lay the track, and the city gradually began to recover its confidence. The T&P had to reach Fort Worth by the time the legislature adjourned the following spring in order to receive the 15-million-acre land grant that the state had promised. As the deadline drew near, Tarrant County employed 100 laborers to prepare the roadbed and called for volunteers to assist in the effort; the T&P sent 300 mule teams and 1,000 men to lay the track. And, according to legend, as the road approached Fort Worth, Tarrant County's representative, Nicholas H. Darnell, who was seriously ill, had to be carried on a cot into the House chamber each day for fifteen days to cast his vote against adjournment. Finally, the track was completed on July 18, and the first train arrived the next day.

As businesses returned—many boasting the word *Panther* in their names as a proud response to the newspaper article—Fort Worth became a shipping center for cattle, buffalo hides and bones, lumber, cotton, and groceries and a supply depot for the cattle trade as well as expansion into West Texas. As the railroad grew during the last quarter of the nineteenth century, it brought similar economic benefits to every region of the state.

Although the last quarter of the nineteenth century was dominated by agrarians, who constituted the large majority of the state's population and controlled the writing of the 1876 Constitution, it also saw the beginnings of industrialization and the birth of the modern state. During these years, most people in Texas still earned their living from the land, and many joined organizations such as the Patrons of Husbandry, or the Grange, and the Farmers' Alliance. But these years also witnessed a tripling of the state's population, a huge increase in industrial output, the birth of labor unions, and unprecedented growth in railroads, pushing the state from twenty-eighth in miles of track in 1870 to first in 1904. This was what economic historian Walt Rostow called the "take-off" phase of industrialization that occurred between 1843 and 1900 in the United States but occurred several decades later in Texas.

In 1870 there were more Texans than ever—818,579, according to the census—with more than 93 percent of the population living in rural areas. The state's continuing need for population spurred the establishment in 1871 of the Texas Bureau of Immigration, abolished in 1876, but only after its generous land grant policies had had significant impact. The state continued that official effort with the publication of the "forgotten census of 1887," an attempt to "call attention of the overcrowded population of the East . . . to our millions of acres of rich virgin soil, which can be had almost for the asking." Preemption and homestead grants and cheap land policies made acquisition of land relatively easy until 1898, when the Texas Supreme Court declared the public domain to be exhausted.

Aside from the natural population increase, immigrants—blacks as well as whites—came mostly from the Southern states, such as Arkansas, Alabama, Mississippi, and Tennessee, that had been devastated by the Civil War. Despite the immigration, the state's established cultural patterns remained largely intact. By 1900 the population had grown to 3,048,710, with almost 83 percent still living in rural areas.

At the same time, however, the value of the state's manufactured items increased from one-fourth of the gross farm income in 1870 to one-half in 1900. But more people probably were involved in non-farm sectors of the economy than the raw census data would suggest. In 1860, for example, although 89 percent of the people lived in rural areas, only 59 percent of all Texans considered themselves to be involved in agricultural pursuits. Ten percent claimed to be involved in manufacturing, and 11 percent pursued one of the professions, owned or worked for a business, or worked in transportation. By 1870 all but thirty of the state's 324 sawmills, the largest industry, had converted from waterpower, which was sometimes undependable, to steam. The average mill was larger, and a number of them had begun to specialize, for example, in planing lumber.

Economic Recovery

Three major changes occurred in the 1870s that greatly influenced the economic development of the state. The first was the adoption of an agrarian-dominated constitution in 1876, which enabled Texans to nurture the political will and organization to permit industrialization to occur. But the fact that most of the capital for this development came from eastern investors and banks, and that the changes wrought by the industrial revolution initially took capital out of the state at a time of depression, created significant opposition. Reeling from what they considered an abusive and dictatorial Republican government under Reconstruction, the agrarian Democrats and ex-Confederates did all they could to ensure that taxes would be low and the government would remain weak. The delegates took advantage of the only asset that the state possessed—land—and continued the cheap land policy that the state had been following. The two other major changes that occurred in the 1870s were expansion into West Texas and the accumulation of enough capital to accommodate huge projects such as the construction of railroad tracks, the improvement of port facilities, and the growth of large businesses, including the state's first multimillion-dollar corporation. These three changes helped fuel the state's rapid growth.

Texas Industries Develop

The leading industries in the state in 1870 were what economic historian John S. Spratt called "migratory," meaning that the owners had little capital invested and they could easily move from one community, source of raw materials, or market

Joseph Landa built a complex of water-powered mills at Comal Springs in New Braunfels and established Landa Mills during the 1890s. Photograph by Henry Stark. *(Courtesy Dallas Historical Society)*

to another. Flour and grist mills were the leading industry, and virtually every community was home to a mill of some kind. But only about 1 percent of the population—fewer than 8,000 wage earners—was employed in all of the 2,400 manufacturing shops in the state. The total value of the capital invested in the more than 500 mills was little more than $1 million, and the value of all manufactured goods produced in the state was less than $12 million, less than 25 percent of the value of agricultural products. By 1900 the value of manufactured items had jumped to more than $92 million, which was one-half the value of the state's agricultural products.

The first big change came in the timber industry. East Texas was a veritable woodland of yellow pine, extending westward from the Louisiana border across perhaps 20 million acres of heavily timbered terrain but concentrated in what is known as the Big Thicket, now a national preserve. By 1870 only about 100 million board feet of lumber were being cut annually in Texas, and that primarily by commercial mills in Orange, Beaumont, and Houston. More of the early settlers undoubtedly would have cut timber, had their routes to mills and markets not been limited to the Neches and Sabine rivers and to rough wagon roads.

Another initially limiting factor was the wood itself, for most lumbermen considered the Upper Midwestern white pine superior to the Texas yellow pine. But as supplies of white pine began to run short, entrepreneurs looked again at East Texas, encouraging the construction of railroad lines into timbered areas. The *Galveston News* noted in 1880 that there were twenty sawmill towns located on the Texas & Pacific Railroad east of Dallas with a combined capacity of 595,000 board feet of lumber daily. Indeed, as railroad expansion increased in the 1880s, the subsequent demand for wooden rail ties further stimulated the industry, with the T&P ordering 500,000 crossties in 1880 alone. The railroads provided the inexpensive transportation needed to propel lumbering into the forefront of Texas industry by the end of the century, and Texas into one of the top ten lumbering states in the nation.

Lack of capital was also a problem, but the arrival of entrepreneurs like Henry J. Lutcher and G. Bedell Moore from Pennsylvania in 1877 marked a change in the East Texas industry. Lutcher and Moore built sawmills near Orange, and established both a domestic and an international trade. John Henry Kirby and Nathan D. Silsbee, who acquired more than a quarter of a million acres of pine forests, built large corporations that brought order to the industry. They constructed company towns that often included churches, schools, stores, and homes and virtually controlled the life of their employees, one-third of whom were African Americans. By the turn of the century, although individuals still owned half of the lumbering plants, corporations so dominated the industry that they employed three-quarters of the workforce, produced three-quarters of the industry's total value, and were growing at an accelerated rate. The total value of lumber and other timber products produced in the state was $16,296,473, with a capital investment of $19,161,265 (another characteristic of the take-off phase is reinvestment of capital), and the Kirby Lumber Company, chartered the following year, became the state's first multimillion-dollar company.

The same kind of concentration occurred in the flouring and gristmill industry. Although the industry had slipped to third in the state in overall value by 1900, and the number of mills had decreased by almost 50 percent, total capital investment had increased significantly, and total output had increased almost 600 percent, to $12,333,730. In 1877 mills in Dallas County alone produced $2.75 million worth of flour for a market that ranged from Shreveport and Jefferson on the east to Austin and San Antonio in the southwest. This total exceeded the entire 1870 output of the state by more than $300,000. No longer was every town required to have its own mill; larger mills ground grain more cheaply than the small mills and shipped it inexpensively by rail.

The largest and most productive industrial city in the state in 1870 was Galveston, with a population of 13,818 and more than $1.2 million in total value of manufactured products. Second was Jefferson, the state's leading river port, at the head of Big Cypress Bayou in Marion County. But the city that benefited most from the developing East Texas lumber industry was Houston, by virtue of its location at the southwestern edge of the thick forests to the east and north. Timber fueled the industrial revolution nationwide, providing power for railroads, steamboats, and city-based factories, and Texas was no exception. As the nearby supplies were depleted, Houston's business leaders organized and built a narrow-gauge railroad into the Big Thicket to ensure a continuing supply of wood. The city's population grew from 9,382 in 1870 to 27,557 in 1890, despite the fact that it lacked a reliable source of coal—even poor-grade coal, which had to be shipped in at almost prohibitive expense. (By the 1880s, coal had become the fuel of choice in the industrial East and Midwest.) Still, the growth continued, with Houston's population reaching 44,633 in 1900 and the total value of manufactured products $13 million, making Houston the top producer in the state.

Dallas was the state's second largest manufacturing city in 1900, followed by El Paso, San Antonio, and Fort Worth. Galveston, focusing its efforts on obtaining a deepwater port and solidifying its position as the major Texas trade center, had fallen to sixth in manufacturing value. The completion of the railroad lines to Marshall, Longview, Texarkana, and other cities in Jefferson's economic sphere ended the city's dominance of Northeast Texas because rail transportation was more reliable than the untimely steamboats. East Texas cotton began to flow toward St. Louis, an important rail center, rather than the gulf port of New Orleans. While Galveston struggled to recover from the devastating hurricane of 1900, the discovery of oil at nearby Spindletop in 1901 would stimulate Houston's growth even further in the twentieth century.

As Texas cities grew, citizens expressed their civic pride in public architectural monuments. The new state capitol in Austin, designed by Michigan architect Elijah E. Myers and completed in 1888, was the most important new public building. Inspired by the nation's capitol, the new Texas state capitol is some 562 feet long by 287 feet deep. The star that the Goddess of Liberty holds in her hand is 311 feet above the ground. Restored and greatly enlarged with an underground expansion during the 1990s, the structure still serves as the seat of the state's government. The capitol, in turn, inspired several county courthouses, for example, those in Fort Worth and Marshall. County seats in Anglo American communities sited the courthouse in a public square, whereas communities of European origin, such as San Antonio, Castroville, and New Braunfels, reserved open spaces for public activities and located the courthouse prominently nearby. Both plans provided residents the opportunity to make a symbolic statement, and dozens of counties built impressive courthouses during these years, including Austin, Galveston, Houston, Dallas, Fort Worth, El Paso, and San Antonio. Many of these turn-of-the-century palaces of justice still serve today as centers of government (in Fort Worth, Albany, San Antonio, Lockhart, and New Braunfels, to name only a few), whereas others have been converted for use as public libraries (in Brazoria and Fredericksburg), museums (in Marshall and Tascosa), and community centers (in Blanco and Clairemont) or some kind of private use (in Brownsville).

One of the most prominent architects working in the state at this time was J. Reilly Gordon of San Antonio, who designed a number of the most distinctive courthouses. His buildings in Decatur, Giddings, Gonzales, La Grange, Lockhart,

New Braunfels, San Antonio, Sulphur Springs, Stephenville, Waxahachie, and Victoria still serve as government centers. Frederick E. Ruffini of Austin designed the old main building at the University of Texas as well as courthouses in Blanco, Paint Rock, and Franklin, and Nicholas J. Clayton of Galveston, who is perhaps better known for his many commercial buildings on The Strand and residential structures in Galveston, also designed the main building for the University of Texas Medical Department in Galveston, the Galveston County Courthouse, and St. Edwards University in Austin. County governments, working in many cases with the Texas Historical Commission, have restored many of these distinctive courthouses in communities such as Albany, Belton, Cameron, Brazoria, Canton, Cuero, Del Rio, and Gatesville, which are still in use as governmental seats.

At the same time, a lesser-known manifestation of civic pride and promotion was the publication of dozens of lithographic bird's-eye views of Texas cities sold by itinerant salesmen and produced by out-of-state printing firms. Although part of a national fad that included the publication of almost 5,000 views of American cities during the century, the Texas images ranged from the largest cities in the state—Houston, Galveston, San Antonio, Dallas, Fort Worth, and El Paso—to some of the smallest, such as Wolfe City, Sunset, and Clarendon. Chauvinistic residents apparently constituted a ready market for the handsome pictures, which depicted the cities from an imaginary point high in the air—sort of a combination of a panoramic view and a map—and merchants and city fathers used them to advertise the communities as well as individual businesses. In truth, one can tell a great deal about a community from these images, just as modern satellite photography provides information about landforms, patterns of settlement, and the growth of a community—all the way down to individual blocks and residences. And the fact that almost sixty-five different views of Texas cities were produced between 1871 and 1900, along with dozens of guides to the state, suggests the enthusiasm with which Texans promoted their communities.

The Impact of Railroads

The most important element of industrialization—and the catalyst for so much of the economy—was the expansion of railroads into almost every part of the state by 1900. As the nation slowly recovered from the Panic of 1873, Texas entered its greatest era of railroad building, and one of the greatest in the nation. The state had only 1,650 miles of track in 1875, all in East Texas, but more than half of the total railroad construction in Texas occurred during the next decade. In part, this was because the Constitution of 1876 authorized land grants to railroads to encourage their construction. The state awarded sixteen sections of land for every mile of track laid, and Texas rail companies collected 32,153,878 acres of land in return for 2,928 miles of track. The era of land bonuses came to an end in 1882, when state officials were embarrassed to discover that the supply of public land had been exhausted and that they had commitments for 8 million acres more than they could supply. In 1877 Texas led the nation in miles of track built

Grand Central Depot on Washington Street in Houston, 1894, with rail cars loaded with bales of cotton. *(Houston, 1880–1910, CN 02747, The Center for American History, The University of Texas at Austin)*

and in the following year more track was laid in Texas than in all the other states and territories combined.

Although such a vast state had a genuine need for economical transportation, and construction of the railroad lines clearly spurred the industrial revolution along, the spurt in railroad building also resulted from outside factors, including competition between two of the most powerful and storied railroad moguls of the Gilded Age: Jay Gould, who acquired the Texas & Pacific Railroad in 1879, and Collis P. Huntington, who owned the Southern Pacific. Together, they owned or controlled more than half the track mileage in Texas. The T&P began construction westward from Fort Worth in April 1881, and the Southern Pacific reached El Paso in May of that year.

This competition is reflected in the track mileage built in Texas during those years: 1,527 miles of track were laid in 1881 and 1,349 miles in 1882. By 1900 Texas had almost 10,000 miles of track, approximately 5 percent of the total railroad mileage in the United States, and every city of significant size had service, with cities such as Denison, Greenville, Dallas, Fort Worth, San Antonio, and Houston being served by multiple lines.

The Growth of Labor Unions

One response to the growing industrialization of the state was the establishment of labor unions. Before the Civil War, for the most part Texas unions were limited to typographers and carpenters, because most of the workers lived in widely separated rural areas, which was not conducive to the organization of unions. Public sentiment initially seemed to be neutral or sympathetic toward unions, but that changed as the unions began to engage in what many regarded as bothersome if not "revolutionary" activities. The flashpoint was an 1886 strike, called by the Knights of Labor against the T&P and Jay Gould. Thousands of men, many of whom had hoped to improve their lot by moving west with the railroad, became disappointed when they got caught in the squeeze of economic depression and declining wages and walked off the job, seriously affecting service in North and West Texas. Gould himself was caught in a similar squeeze, as he attempted to negotiate the fine line between tough competitors and expansion, made more problematic by the same depression that bedeviled the workers. When he refused to compromise with the workers, an armed clash occurred in Fort Worth, and Governor Ireland sent the Texas Rangers and the state militia to restore peace. The affair was settled when the T&P passed into the hands of a federal receiver, and the court held the strikers in contempt. The Knights' power declined rapidly thereafter; however, they played a role in the successful boycott of the contractors building the new capitol in Austin because they had imported Scottish granite cutters, a violation of the Alien Contract Labor Law.

African Americans were usually barred from white unions, although some were members of the Knights of Labor, including David Black, who served on the union's state executive board. Concentrated in East Texas and in the coastal cities, they were able to establish their own unions, such as Negro Longshoremen's Association in Galveston. Most Mexican Americans, by virtue of their residence in South Texas, were not involved in unionization activities, although two dozen Hispanic laborers worked for the Texas and Pacific Coal Company in Thurber by 1900. Because the state was largely rural and the electorate increasingly suspicious, Texas labor unions remained weak as the nineteenth century drew to a close.

Expansion into West Texas

Because the state had no navigable rivers, Texans any distance from the coast were for all practical purposes landlocked. The extension of railroads into the western portions of the state offered a solution to this problem, but, first, the hostile Indians on the northwestern and western frontiers had to be subdued. The U.S. Army reoccupied the frontier forts of Texas and resumed the frontier defense following the Civil War, and the slaughter of the great southern buffalo herd, undertaken to supply Eastern factories, became an integral part of that process.

The transcontinental railroad, completed in 1869, had divided American bison into two huge herds, one in the north and the other in the south. The southern herd ranged deep into Texas, coming into contact with the advancing cattle and farming frontier and with the deadliest killers that the bison had yet encountered—white hunters. J. Wright Mooar, a Kansas buffalo hunter, glimpsed the potential of the buffalo trade in 1871 when he sent fifty-seven hides to relatives in New York with instructions to try to sell them. A Philadelphia tanner purchased the lot for $200. When the hides proved to make fine leather, he gave the Mooar brothers an order for 2,000 more, and by the mid-1870s there were, perhaps, 3,000 buffalo hunters roaming the Texas Panhandle in search of what was left of the once great Southern herd. The slaughter that would bring the American bison almost to extinction had begun.

The Slaughter of the Buffalo

Whereas the Plains Indians depended upon the bison for every aspect of their lives, white men had previously killed them for sport and food, primarily for the crews building the transcontinental railroads. Now they slaughtered them for their hides, which could be quickly converted into cash, and left the carcasses on the ground to rot. "No mercy was shown the buffalo," plainsman and Indian fighter Billy Dixon recalled of his 1874 hunt. "I killed as many as my three men [skinners] could handle, working them as hard as they were willing to work. This was deadly business, without sentiment; it was dollars against tenderheartedness, and dollars won."

The buffalo hunters were engaged in an unprecedented slaughter of what General Philip H. Sheridan had called the "Indians' commissary," and he concluded that they had "done more in the last two years and will do more in the next year to settle the vexed Indian question than the entire regular army has done in the last 30 years." Within five years, the last hostile tribe had been defeated and settled on a reservation, ending the conflict that had raged along the Texas frontier for more than half a century and opening West Texas to ranchers and farmers, which set the state on a course different from that of the other Southern states.

After the hunters came the "bone pickers." Northern industries had been using buffalo bones for buttons, combs, and knife handles for some time, but they soon realized that bones could be ground into meal or charred and used to remove the color from sugar. Fresh bones also provided calcium phosphate ash for bone china furnaces. By the mid-1870s, bone pickers got from $7 to $9 per ton for bones and $12 to $15 for hooves and horns. And the prairie was littered with the bleached bones of the millions of animals that the hunters had killed and left to rot. Pickers hauled wagonloads of bones to the railroad right of way and stacked them by the tracks, some of the mounds reaching a height of sixteen feet and stretching for half a mile. Texas led the world in bone production for a brief period during the early 1880s, and prices got as high as $22 to $23 per ton. Within a few years, however, the bone pickers had gathered virtually all of the bison skeletons and by the turn of the century industries were using cow bones instead.

Displacement of the Indians

At the same time, even though they were issued government rations and provisions on the Fort Sill Reservation in the Indian Territory, the Kiowas and Comanches continued to raid the Texas frontier and into Mexico. The much-acclaimed "peace policy" of President Ulysses S. Grant afforded Texans little relief, for it barred the army from pursuing raiding Indians onto the reservation. When the Salt Creek massacre of 1871 resulted in the deaths of seven teamsters and almost snared General William T. Sherman himself, however, the army obtained permission to operate against marauders, even in their Fort Sill "city of refuge." The conflict approached its climax when Comanches, Kiowas, and Cheyennes attacked a camp of buffalo hunters at Adobe Walls, northeast of what is today Borger, in June 1874. Indians of all three tribes fled their reservations and took refuge on the Staked Plains of the Texas Panhandle. Army columns advanced from five directions but fought few battles. The most notable was Colonel Ranald S. Mackenzie's surprise attack on a camp in Palo Duro Canyon. Because the Indians were elusive and would fight only under favorable conditions, the army resorted to brutal tactics such as slaughtering their horses, ravaging villages, and confiscating food, weapons, and anything the Indians needed to survive. So relentlessly did the army harass the Indians through the winter of 1874–75 that most returned to their reservations and surrendered. The Red River War ended Indian hostilities on the southern Plains and brought to a close more than fifty years of bloodshed and plunder on the Texas frontier.

The final defeat of Indians in Texas occurred in the summer of 1880, when units of "buffalo soldiers" of the Tenth Cavalry stationed at Fort Davis confronted the wily Apache Chief Victorio and his band. The Indians called the black troops, who served in both the Ninth and Tenth Cavalry and the Twenty-fourth and Twenty-fifth Infantry, buffalo soldiers, probably because the texture of their hair reminded the Indians of the buffalo. The black troops realized that the Indians regarded the buffalo as sacred and accepted the term as a compliment. One of the ablest Apache leaders, Victorio had rejected the intolerable life on Arizona's barren San Carlos Reservation and for several years had tried to get along on the Fort Stanton Reservation in New Mexico. When that proved impossible, he and his band raided ranches on both sides of the border as well as stagecoaches and travelers on the San Antonio-El Paso Road. They led military columns on a wild chase across New Mexico, Mexico, and Texas. Rather than pursue them further, in August 1880, Colonel Benjamin H. Grierson and his buffalo soldiers established impregnable positions commanding seasonal water holes at Tinaja de las Palmas, fifteen miles southeast of Sierra Blanca, and Ratttlesnake Springs, forty miles north of present-day Van Horn. Grierson knew that the Apaches could not make it through the dry desert country without water. Unable to displace the soldiers,

Victorio and his band fell back into Mexico. There, in October, Mexican troops assaulted him on the rocky slopes of Tres Castillos, wiped out nearly all of his followers, and killed the dynamic chief himself.

The human suffering and drama on both sides of the Indian wars was deplorable and poignant. "The Indian loves to live as well as the white men," Buffalo Good, a Wichita, had said in 1871, "and [we] can't help being there." But, as anthropologist W. W. Newcomb observed, "the obliteration of Texas Indians was but a small part, a footnote really, to the nineteenth-century development and emergence of a new, and in technological terms, a tremendously powerful nation-state."

The Impact of Barbed Wire

About the time of the defeat of the Plains Indians, the introduction of a new type of fencing encouraged the settlement of West Texas. Fences had always been a problem. In East Texas, where timber was plentiful, most fences were made of board, split rail, or, in some cases, rock. On the plains, lacking timber or rock, ranchers used hedges, with bois d'arc being the favorite because, planted along a line, the scrubby trees could be bent and shaped into an almost impenetrable barrier.

That changed when J. F. Glidden of Illinois invented barbed wire in 1874. Meeting with only limited success in Illinois, Glidden's agents, Henry B. Sanborn and Judson P. Warner, moved to Texas. Barbed wire was controversial when it was first introduced: People thought that it would not restrain wild cattle or horses, and, if it did, that the animals would be severely injured when they threw themselves against it. Sanborn and Warner made their first sale in Gainesville in the fall of 1875, and barbed wire soon proved to be a huge success. It was cheap and effective in fencing livestock, and in only a few years it changed the nature of western agriculture. Now ranchers could keep livestock out of farmlands and selectively breed their animals by controlling access. With all these conditions in place, the stage was set for accelerated growth in the Texas economy.

The Cotton Culture Expands

Farmers, as unlikely as it may seem, were also among the first to feel the effects of modernization. Just as in industry, the trend in agriculture was toward concentration and efficiency, and in Texas that meant cotton. Cotton had been the major cash crop in Texas prior to the Civil War, and the move into West Texas did nothing to lessen its dominance. In West Texas, farmers had to dig deeper to find water, there were few springs, and gypsum rendered most of the stream water undrinkable. But, by 1875, windmills offered a solution to the problem of deep wells by harnessing the power of the ever-present West Texas wind to pump ground water, and in the late 1880s and early 1890s farmers developed several techniques

The eclipse windmill was the most popular one on the plains and made settlement of the plains possible. This one was located on the XIT Ranch. *(Courtesy Panhandle-Plains Historical Museum)*

that enabled them to make the dry but fertile land productive, and the number of acres devoted to cotton climbed steadily throughout the last quarter of the century.

Another factor contributing to the increase in cotton production was the proliferation of tenant farmers. Tenant farming—whether the farmers are renters or sharecroppers—although often perceived in a negative way, can enable people with no savings to get a start; however, in Texas at this time the conditions under which credit was extended, the owners' pressure on tenants to produce the most profitable crops, and the economic depression of the 1890s combined to leave most tenants little hope of improvement. As long as inexpensive or free public

Plowing the field on a farm near Bonham. Photograph by Henry Stark, 1895–96. *(Courtesy Dallas Historical Society)*

lands were available in West Texas, renters had the option of settling a homestead there, but sharecroppers, mostly African Americans, were usually so indebted that they could not move. And, at about the same time that the public land was exhausted, in 1898, population had increased significantly, depression drove some families from the cities back to the farms, and cotton prices declined precipitously—to 5.7 cents per pound.

As farmers adapted to this new environment, the line of settlement moved rapidly westward. It reached the northern Panhandle, the South Plains, and the Trans-Pecos region in the 1880s. The number of acres under cultivation skyrocketed—from 36,292,000 in 1880 to 51,407,000 in 1890, and 125,807,000 in 1900. It would be thirty-five years before that total was exceeded. Additional counties were organized until, by 1900, all but twenty-four of Texas's 254 counties had been established. The "almost unprecedented tide of immigration," according to an Agricultural Commission report, had brought the Texas frontier to a close. And, at the same time, immigrants to East Texas—in many cases, African Americans from other Southern states—had more than replaced the population that had moved west.

The expansion of cotton farmers onto ranch lands was not always harmonious. The newcomers always sought land near streams and rivers and often

Acreage in Texas Farms, 1850–1960

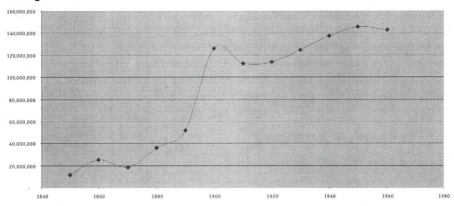

Taken from *Historical Statistics of the United States, Colonial Times to 1970*

fenced the water off from the cattlemen, who had in some instances been grazing their livestock on public land for years. J. L. Driskell of Austin, for example, began with a herd of only 800 cattle in 1873 and by 1884, courtesy of the state's free grass, was worth an estimated $800,000. The ranchers' practice was to buy the land with the water and use the rest. Most ranchers felt they were entitled to free use of the state's land because they had suffered the risks and hardships of settling the frontier. But the increased use of barbed wire—by 1883 almost $1 million worth was sold in Texas annually—resulted in extensive fencing, even in West Texas. This precipitated such widespread fence cutting that the Texas Rangers had to be called in. The farmers were not always the catalyst in these cases, nor the rancher always the perpetrator, for competition between ranches sometimes produced a similar result.

Following a heated debate, the legislature passed a law in 1884 declaring that fence cutting and setting grass fires were felonies punishable by one to five years in prison. Knowingly fencing public lands, or lands belonging to others, without permission became a misdemeanor. And, if a fence blocked access to a public road, the builder was required to place a gate every three miles and to keep the gates in repair.

Production of all the major crops—wheat, corn, oats, and cotton—increased during these decades, but, abetted by tenant farming, cotton far outpaced the others with a more than fourfold increase, from 805,284 bales produced on 2,178,435 acres in 1879 to approximately 3,500,000 bales produced on 7,178,915 acres in 1900. The expansion of railroads into the cotton-producing areas helped to make this possible. Farmers, who had lived in a barter economy and maintained subsistence farms that supplied virtually all of their family's needs, now turned almost wholly to cotton. They could ship their crop to market and obtain consumer goods via the new railroads.

Despite these innovations, there were those who warned against dependence upon a single crop. "Plant cotton," the editor of the *Albany News* counseled, "not all cotton, but some cotton." The logic of the warning became apparent when the price of cotton declined in the 1890s, and all farmers were hurt, especially the tenant farmers and sharecroppers, who found themselves deeply in debt. As farmers continued the move toward commercialized agriculture, organizations like the Patrons of Husbandry and the Farmers' Alliance proposed solutions for their problems, and many farmers were ready to join.

The Growth of Ranching

The open range of South Texas seemed made for cattle, and they bred and multiplied in the wild as well as under the care of the mission priests and *rancheros*. It was here that the Spanish *vaqueros* developed the techniques and costume that later spread throughout the American West. Anglo Americans and African Americans contributed their own sets of skills to the handling of cattle when they began to arrive in large numbers in the 1820s. The cattle industry of South Texas, the home of the Ballí, King, Kenedy, O'Connor, and other large ranches, grew rapidly during the postwar period. Led by Gail Borden's invention of the meat biscuit (made of dehydrated meat and flour) in 1849, Texas boasted fifteen factory-size meatpacking plants in 1870. After the Civil War, as the U.S. Army moved the line of defensive forts farther westward, the cattlemen resumed their westward march. By 1876 ranchers like Charles Goodnight had passed the 100th meridian all the way from Kimble County in the Edwards Plateau to Childress County in the eastern Panhandle. By the mid-1880s, enterprising salesmen and drillers had solved one of the most difficult problems for plains ranchers: how to get adequate water in a land of little rain. Goodnight installed his first windmill in 1886 to pump water from the Ogallala Aquifer, a huge, natural underground reservoir that stretched from the High Plains of Texas to South Dakota.

Ranchers had already begun to address another serious concern—how to get their cattle to market. Because it was cheaper to walk the beef to market, feeding it on free grass and water, than to slaughter and pack it in Texas, by 1880 the number of packing plants declined to three; throughout the heyday of the trail drives (1867–85) the second most lucrative part of the business, after raising and selling the cattle, was the service that the drovers provided in getting them from ranch to market. Men like Goodnight, Thomas S. Bugbee, and C. C. Slaughter pushed into West Texas, New Mexico, and Colorado to occupy the newly cleared land. By the mid-1880s, Texas-style ranchers had extended their operations as far north as Alberta and Saskatchewan to take advantage of the free grasslands.

The American Cowboy

Out of these trail drives came the most popular folk character in American history: the cowboy. The real Texas cowboy was usually a young, small, wiry character with a knack for herding animals, hardly a hero in the normal sense.

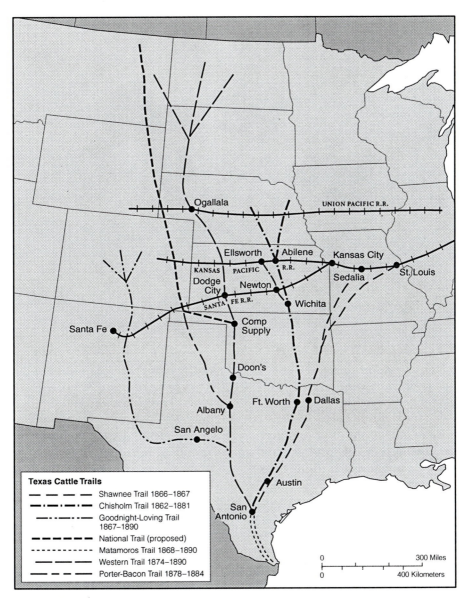

Texas cattle trails.

The highlight of his year was the spring and summer cattle roundup and drive to one of the Kansas railheads. Except in the way the Texas cowboy practiced it—cowboys usually were hired specifically for the trail drive, as opposed to ranch hands who remained at home and worked year-round—the trail drive itself was not unique. His cow-handling predecessors in Europe and colonial America had driven cattle to market, but the cowboy lived with the cattle, camped out for the

A Texas cowboy. Photograph by William Henry Jackson. *(Courtesy Colorado Historical Society, CHS-J1005)*

three months of the drive, and slept on the ground nightly. He got up before the sun rose to begin his work and did not turn in until it had set. In between he stood his turn at watch, losing two or three hours of sleep. Throughout the drive the cowboy ate only the chuck that the cook had on his wagon. The day was filled with hard, difficult work, for a herd of 3,000 cattle did not maintain itself.

The cowboy is personified by Charles A. Siringo, who was born to an Italian father and an Irish mother in Matagorda County in 1855, became a cowboy at the tender age of fifteen, and thirty years later wrote the first cowboy autobiography, *A Texas Cowboy; or, Fifteen Years on the Hurricane Deck of a Spanish Pony—Taken from Real Life,* which proved to be immensely popular, particularly among cowboys themselves. But there are many other representative types; one historian has estimated that perhaps as many as one-third of the drovers were Hispanic or black.

Sometimes the experience was more than hard work, because the trail drive was often dangerous. In *Lonesome Dove,* a fictional treatment of Goodnight and Loving's stories, among others, Texas novelist Larry McMurtry has enshrined the water moccasin attack in the river as one of the dreaded events of the trail. But becoming unhorsed in midstream was equally perilous, for few of these dry land laborers could swim. One of the main advantages of the Chisholm Trail was the absence of large rivers. Of course, one stood a good chance of getting caught in a lightning- or hailstorm or stampede, and had to endure blistering sun that dried up the streams and turned the cattle into thirst-crazed creatures that might stampede at the slightest incentive. Rain and bone-chilling cold wind were equally certain to make the trip north as miserable as possible.

Despite the demanding hours and even more demanding work, countless youngsters who read about cowboys in Siringo's book or in dime novels tried to imitate them. They hit the trail inspired to challenge "Texas Jack" Omohundro's or "Buffalo Bill" Cody's greatest feats. The trail drive was not just a character-building experience for ambitious wanderers, but also an original piece of Americana. In many ways it resembled a military expedition, as the boss gathered his crew, rounded up the cattle, and set out for Dodge City, Abilene, Sheridan, or one of the other small cattle towns that dotted the Kansas Pacific and Union Pacific railroad lines.

The storied camaraderie of the campfire helped to combat the loneliness of a three-month trip, but, as E. C. "Teddy Blue" Abbott (a young Englishman turned cowboy) said, they had "told each other everything we knew in a week." But even the trail drives, supposedly the epitome of freedom and independence, fell victim to the changes wrought by the industrial revolution. By the time he quit the range in 1884 and located in Caldwell, Kansas, where he became a merchant, Siringo was aware of the changes going on around him. The first trail drives were for the purpose of getting mature cattle to market for slaughter. But when the Missouri, Kansas and Texas Railroad reached Denison, near the Red River, and the Texas & Pacific reached Dallas, it became easier and less expensive for ranchers to ship their mature cattle by rail. Yearling steers made up most of the drives by 1880, driven north for the purpose of stocking the northern ranges, and the Kansas railheads became clearinghouses where northern ranchers purchased stock rather than shipping points.

One of the reasons that the Texas cowboy is such a folk hero today may be that he stands as a symbol of all the workers whose lives changed under the pressure of industrialization. But specialization, one of the byproducts of barbed wire and the industrial revolution, affected the freedom-loving cowboy every bit as much as it did the sodbuster.

Perhaps the most famous illustration of the changing management-worker relationship is the Cowboy Strike of 1883. With the end of open-range cattle ranching came stock farming and the improvement of herds, which encouraged many eastern and European investment companies to get into the business and brought about innovations that many cowboys considered a threat to their livelihood. In earlier years ranch hands could take part of their pay in calves, brand mavericks for themselves, and graze their small herds on their employers' land. But the new managers often represented absentee owners who wanted hands to work for wages only and who provided none of the opportunities of the past. To the cowboys it seemed that the more conventional roles of owner/manager and worker were replacing the traditional, more fraternal relationships that they had enjoyed.

In 1883 Tom Harris of the LS Ranch led a small group of cowboys in drafting an ultimatum demanding higher pay and threatening a strike against several ranches, which they believed to be controlled by corporations or individuals who were involved in ranching only for quick profit. Twenty-four men signed the document, which set March 31, 1883, as the strike date and promised limited assistance to strikers who needed money. Harris and others attempted to recruit all the cowboys in the area, but no one knows for sure how many actually participated; it might have been anywhere from thirty to 325. With a combination of temporarily higher wages for those who defied the strike, immediate firing of those who participated, and rumors of violence on the part of the strikers, the stockmen defeated the fledgling union within two and a half months, and the spring roundup occurred without incident. But the failed strike was a clear indication that modernization and industrialization had changed ranching. Many of the old-timers like Siringo had gone into ranching themselves or into some other line of work, and the new breed of ranch hand represented the working class more than the undisciplined, freedom-loving character of popular culture.

Historians disagree as to whether this strike was part of the larger labor movement in Texas, but the fact that it seemed to share some of the same causes as other labor unrest—growing anonymity on the job, changing worker-employer relationships—has invited such speculation, especially because it occurred at the same time as the Knights of Labor's greatest successes.

The Political Will, 1876–1898

Politics reflected the economic realities that Texans faced during the last quarter of the century. Supporters of the new governor, Richard Coke, elected in 1874, represented what they called the New South and proposed to industrialize Texas by enticing railroads, lowering taxes, holding down government expenses, and creating an inexpensive labor supply. Largely ex-Confederates, these men felt that Republican misrule during the years after the Civil War had destroyed Southern prosperity by upsetting the traditional relationship between the races. Although they represented the party of slavery, secession, and defeat, they now cast themselves as the redeemers of the Democratic Party of their forebears and the true South, and the 1876 Constitution, still in effect today, was an effort to erase all traces of the Republican regime.

Texas Uses Its Land

Just as before the Civil War, the state was dependent upon one crop—cotton—and was in debt, and its only asset of any consequence was the land itself. Because per capita income in Texas was only 63.2 percent of the national average at the end of the decade, more than 5.5 percent lower than the average personal income in the adjacent states of Louisiana and Arkansas, and because of a nationwide depression in 1873, Democrats felt that their only option was retrenchment. Coke resigned the struggle in 1876 to accept appointment to a seat in the U.S. Senate, and Richard B. Hubbard replaced him. Hubbard was denied the 1878 nomination, however, because critics claimed that he had not done enough to reduce the state's debt. Instead, the Democratic convention nominated ex-Confederate Oran M. Roberts, of Tyler, who had served as chairman of the secession convention of 1861 and was now chief justice of the state supreme court. With Roberts leading the way, the Democrats began to decrease taxes and instituted what many considered draconian measures to restore the state's financial stability.

Roberts also wanted the state to "get out of the land business" and led efforts to dispose of public land as quickly as possible. Such policies hurt the big landowners, the railroads, and the Capitol Syndicate, a group that had accepted land in return for building additional railroad tracks and the new state capitol. Under the law, the railroads had to dispose of their land within eight years of receipt, but when they tried to sell it, they found that the state, with its cheap land, was their main competitor. The Syndicate, which had ultimately received more than 3 million acres of Panhandle lands that had been set aside for the construction of the new capitol building, had initially hoped to subdivide its land and sell it to settlers at a profit. But the state's land policies kept prices so low that the Syndicate established a ranch instead: the famous XIT Ranch, which was at one time the largest piece of fenced property in the world, with 6,000 miles of single-strand wire fence ringing its ninety-four pastures and outer perimeter. The imposing, new red granite capitol building opened in the spring of 1888 with a gala party, marred only by the huge leak in the roof that drenched the celebrants during a typical Texas thunderstorm.

Roberts's land policies engendered widespread opposition. The ferocity of the conflict may well have been the reason that he did not seek a third term. But he had compiled a formidable fiscal record. By the time he left office, he had balanced the state's budget, reduced the debt by $500,000, and gathered a treasury surplus of $300,000.

New Political Issues

Issues that would dominate the state's politics for decades gradually emerged over the next few years. Roberts's successor, Governor "Oxcart John" Ireland (1883–87), had earned his nickname by opposing land grants to the railroads when he was a member of the legislature, but he continued the probusiness policies that had prevailed, and the railroads continued to build.

Consumption of alcoholic beverages became a growing concern during the administration of Lawrence Sullivan Ross (1887–91), one of the state's most popular Texas Rangers and military heroes. He was the person who had brought Cynthia Ann Parker back (albeit unwillingly) from Comanche captivity in 1860. The Women's Christian Temperance Union, United Friends of Temperance (the first statewide prohibition organization), and other groups had been preaching prohibition for decades; now the message began to resonate, especially among the fundamentalist Protestants, and found supporters among such capable politicians as Senator John H. Reagan. The state constitution authorized local option elections, but prohibitionists now called for a statewide ban on the sale of alcoholic beverages and convinced the legislature to put a constitutional amendment on prohibition before the electorate in 1887. Even though it carried only thirty-two counties and failed by a vote of 220,627 to 129,270, the prohibitionists vowed to continue the fight.

A third reality of the political scene was the decreasing importance of the Republican Party. Known as the party of African Americans ever since its organization in 1867, the Texas Republican Party suffered a devastating blow when the Democrats returned to office in 1873 and 1874. With the percentage of African Americans in the state's population decreasing from 31 percent in 1870 to 20 percent in 1900, the Republicans realized further losses when whites began to split from the party (the "lily-whites") and to disenfranchise African Americans through the organization of white men's political clubs, the legal process, and intimidation (it is likely that as many as 300 to 500 African Americans were lynched during the last quarter of the century). Norris Wright Cuney, an able African American politician from Galveston, became head of the party when former governor Davis died in 1883. As sergeant-at-arms during the Twelfth Legislature (1870–71), Cuny was skilled in the use of political patronage, especially after President Benjamin Harrison appointed him collector of customs in Galveston in 1889. He even survived various modifications in the election code, such as the elimination of the use of colored paper ballots to aid illiterate voters, and was resourceful enough to continue to get Republicans elected to office in a few counties in East Texas and along the gulf coast. But he could not prevent the passage of such Jim Crow segregation laws as the one offered in 1889 by the state senator from Marshall, William H. Pope, requiring railroads to provide separate coaches for African Americans and whites. As the Republican Party became increasingly marginalized, Cuney tried to maintain his power by allying with a Democratic Party faction or with a third-party movement.

Populism Challenges the Status Quo

The status of farmers in the newly evolving economy led them to search for new solutions too. The state's reliance on one crop became all too apparent when farmers received 22 percent less income between 1887 and 1890 despite harvesting 25 percent more cotton. Feeling the brunt of extensive societal changes as well, they expressed their concern through the Grange, or the Patrons of Husbandry, Greenback clubs, and the Farmers' Alliance.

The Grange began in 1867 as a secret social and educational society, but soon began to advocate political and cooperative solutions to agrarian problems. The primary allure of the Greenback Party to farmers was its campaign for an inflated currency through issuance of paper money (greenbacks) not backed by coin (gold). By the 1880s, the Texas Farmers' Alliance had become the dominant agrarian

Reformer James Stephen Hogg served as attorney general from 1886 to 1891, then as the first native son to be elected governor, 1891–95. *(James Stephen Hogg Photographs, 1836–1969, CN 05612, The Center for American History, The University of Texas at Austin)*

group in the state. From its beginning in Lampasas in 1877, it had been more political than the Grange and demanded wholesale economic changes rather than modest reforms. The Alliance shared many goals with the Greenback Party, advocating the establishment of a subtreasury system, the abolition of the national banking system, abandonment of the deflationary gold standard in favor of free coinage of silver, adoption of an income tax, an eight-hour workday, direct election of senators, the Australian (secret) ballot, and referendum and recall, but it made fewer and less radical demands than its counterparts in other states with regard to issues such as government ownership of the railroads and the establishment of a new political party. The group took no stand on the sale of alcoholic beverages, perhaps because the farmers saw it as too divisive an issue. Seeing no place for themselves in the evolving economy, many of the have-nots of society would later rally first under the People's Party and then the Populist Party banners.

Although these agrarian movements attracted many voters, the person who most effectively voiced these concerns in Texas was Democrat James Stephen Hogg, a crusading East Texan, who had served as attorney general under Governor Ross and in 1891 became the first native-born Texan to be elected governor. As attorney general, Hogg had zealously defended the public lands, regaining over 1.5 million acres for the state. He demanded that out-of-state insurance companies comply with Texas law and drove from the state those who did not. He sought to regulate railroads under the Constitution of 1876, breaking up the Texas Traffic Association, and helped to write the second state antitrust law in the nation. But he soon realized that neither the legislature nor his small office could deal effectively with the railroads and campaigned for governor in 1890 on a platform that included passage of a constitutional amendment that would enable the establishment of a railroad commission.

A tall man who weighed more than 250 pounds, Hogg was an energetic campaigner with a common touch, a love of the vernacular, and a native understanding of people. He easily ingratiated himself with rural audiences, who seemed immediately to identify with a man named Hogg. It is difficult to imagine the task that campaigners faced in addressing the huge outdoor crowds in those days. When Hogg opened his campaign for the governorship at Rusk in April 1890, for example, perhaps 3,000 people gathered in a shady grove outside of town for the event. Without the benefit of the public address systems we have today, Hogg's strong and intelligible voice gave him a big advantage over his opponents in such situations; even the men and boys in the trees near the edge of the crowd could hear him. Once he tore into the railroads and others who took advantage of farmers, he could hold an audience for hours. As the temperature rose on a hot summer afternoon, he would fling off his coat, loosen his suspenders, and gulp water to refresh his throat and maintain his strength. At times his plain speech may have offended the ladies, but still they came even though they could not vote. His zeal and personality earned him a long list of enemies by the time he decided to run for governor, but, fortunately for Hogg, he also had a much longer list of friends.

Hogg's Reforms

Hogg called for a number of policies in the 1890 campaign, such as reform of the state's land policy, longer school terms, an endowment for the University of Texas and the Agricultural and Mechanical College, a home for disabled Confederate veterans, and, regrettably, separate railroad coaches for African American and white passengers, but he focused on the need for a constitutional amendment to enable the state to regulate railroads. In doing so, he appropriated one of the main tenets of the Farmers' Alliance, or the Populist Party, as they became known, and appealed to them to join his campaign. Five Democrats announced against him at one time or another, and the railroads favored each of them in turn, but only Lieutenant Governor Thomas Benton Wheeler stayed in the fight until the convention. The railroads helped finance Hogg's opponents and resorted to such practices as laying off engineers and canceling planned new construction in certain areas "until the commission question was settled." But the agrarians remained with Hogg, whom they saw as their defender even though he did not endorse a subtreasury, and he had only token opposition. He swept into office, and the constitutional amendment permitting a railroad commission also passed handily.

Hogg quickly established the Railroad Commission as an appointive body and convinced John H. Reagan, who as a member of the U.S. House of Representatives had shepherded the Interstate Commerce Act through Congress in 1887, to resign his new seat in the U.S. Senate to become chairperson. Reagan's appointment drew widespread praise, but the Alliance had wanted an elective commission, and Hogg added fuel to the flickering fire by declining to appoint any of their supporters to it. The People's Party, or the Populists, formally organized into a third national political party in St. Louis in April 1892, leading conservative Democrats, who had opposed the establishment of the commission, to believe that their more liberal colleagues might desert the party, enabling them to unseat Hogg in the next election.

Hogg's election represented a rebuke to the Bourbon, or conservative, wing of the Democratic Party, leading them to bolt in the 1892 election. Hogg might not have survived had his campaign not been masterminded by one of his close friends, who later became one of the most unusual, mysterious, and influential figures in American politics. Edward Mandell House of Austin had enjoyed a privileged youth as the son of a wealthy Houston merchant, banker, and landowner and had moved to Austin in 1885 to escape the heat of Houston and to be closer to his cotton plantations. There he befriended a number of political leaders, including Governor Hogg. He admired Hogg, especially his reform efforts, and learned politics from him. "When I found out that the railroads and the entire corporate interests of Texas were combined to defeat Hogg," House later wrote, "I enlisted actively on his behalf." It would be largely through House's guidance and organizing skills, both at the state and national levels, that Hogg would gain reelection and that Texas would later become a major influence in the federal government before the other states of the old Confederacy.

As the Democrats gathered in Houston in August 1892 for what would become known as the "street car barn" convention, the Hogg forces were in control. More or less according to plan, the conservatives bolted, held their own convention, and nominated Waco attorney George W. Clark, a staunch supporter of the railroads, to oppose Hogg. The race for the governorship soon became a three-way contest with the entry of Thomas L. Nugent, the Populist candidate. Able African American leaders such as John B. Rayner of Calvert hoped that they could bring Republican Party chair Cuney and other African Americans into the Populist fold, but Cuney had other plans. Thinking that the liberal votes would be split between the Democrats and the Populists, he formed a coalition with Clark in an effort to gain some of the spoils that he believed the Republicans and the conservative Democrats would be able to win. In fact, the coalition abetted a split that was already under way in the Republican Party itself. Objecting to continued African American domination of the party, the small white faction known as the lily-whites held their own convention and nominated A. J. Houston, Sam Houston's youngest son.

Hogg also made a serious appeal to African American voters. He campaigned vigorously on the issues, including his opposition to lynching, which he eloquently expressed in a Brenham speech in June. He pardoned several African American prisoners in an obvious attempt to influence the electorate, and African American speakers volunteered to campaign for him and organized

"Hogg clubs" throughout the state. This was the first election in which large numbers of African American voters deserted Cuney and the Republicans to vote for the Democratic candidate.

The Populist campaign, meanwhile, took on the aura of a religious crusade. Men like former Methodist minister H. S. P. "Stump" Ashby, labor leader W. R. Lamb, and Ben Terrell, a well-known Southern Alliance orator, fanned out across the state, holding camp-meeting style rallies on Nugent's behalf. They used Biblical rhetoric to tell familiar stories and substituted political slogans for the words of well-known hymns. Hoping to challenge the Democrats with a biracial coalition, they promised equal protection under the law as well as guaranteed suffrage, regardless of race.

Ultimately, Hogg won the bitter race, but only by a plurality—190,486 votes to Clark's 133,395 and Nugent's 108,483. Populist candidates drew even more support at the congressional level, finishing second in ten of thirteen races. The election served notice to the Democrats that a Populist alliance with the Republicans could be a real threat, especially if they were unable to heal the breach in their own party.

Now wary of the Populists, Hogg continued his reform program. He had already begun to incorporate many of their issues into his own platform—making the railroad commission elective rather than appointive, for example—but he refused to go so far as to endorse a subtreasury system. He signed the Perpetuities and Corporations Land Law with the intention of keeping companies "whose main purpose of business is the acquisition or ownership . . . of lands" from owning lands, but it missed its main targets, the great land and cattle companies, because they defined their primary activity as cattle raising. He signed the Stock and Bond Law of 1893 in an effort to keep railroads from issuing "watered," or overvalued, stock and another law restricting the amount of indebtedness that counties or municipalities could incur. He established the Board of Pardon Advisors to review the hundreds of clemency pleas and make recommendations to the governor, extended the public school term from four to six months, and increased the appropriation for the new University of Texas.

House became Hogg's closest advisor. He visited with the governor virtually every day and was the man to see if one wanted a political appointment or to petition the governor on any subject. He also continued his correspondence with his far-flung network of friends and confidants that he began to refer to as "our crowd." Although Hogg offered him several political positions, House refused them all, finally accepting the honorary title of Lieutenant Colonel, which the press quickly shortened to Colonel. House had begun to perfect the behind-the-scenes political machinations that would ultimately take him to Washington as a personal advisor to President Woodrow Wilson in 1912.

Women and Minority Rights

Hogg was also more active than any other governor in trying to bring an end to lynchings in Texas, which one authority has estimated might have resulted in the deaths of 300 to 500 African Americans between 1870 and 1900. Hogg called those who would lynch a fellow citizen "bands of murderers" who had "no respect for constitutional guarantees or the stability of government or the lives of human beings." When a mob seemed about to threaten the life of an African American man arrested for murder in Bastrop County, Hogg notified the sheriff that he had posted a $1,000 reward for the arrest and conviction of each member of the mob if a lynching occurred; the mob dissipated. Then, responding to the horrible torture and burning death of Henry Smith at Paris in 1893, Hogg called the affair a disgrace to Texas and unsuccessfully petitioned the legislature to pass an anti-lynching bill.

One issue that neither Hogg nor the Populists would touch was women's suffrage. It had been an issue for a number of years, but both constitutional conventions, in 1868–69 and 1875, had refused to take any action. Rebecca Henry Hayes of Galveston led in the establishment of the Texas Equal Rights Association at a Dallas meeting in May 1893, but the effort to get the three major political parties to include a suffrage plank in their platforms failed the following year. She and others were successful in arousing interest in the cause as auxiliaries spread to a number of cities, and newspapers began to take notice of their efforts. But the organization split after it failed to get the state House of Representatives to recommend a constitutional amendment in 1895.

Another trend became apparent while Hogg was in office. The state census of 1887 counted only about 83,000 Hispanics, about 4 percent of the population, and they lived mostly along the border. But Mexican immigration had begun to increase before the American Civil War and continued to grow into the 1890s. Mexicans were not so much attracted to Texas as they were driven from Mexico by the developing social chaos, the increased population, the collapsing economy, and the spread of entrepreneurs, who drove the village farmers from their *ejidos* (common lands) in the name of government-approved development. The newcomers were generally limited to hard labor such as grubbing and picking cotton, sheepherding, and ranch work, but because they constituted a large majority of the population in the counties along the Rio Grande, they were generally able to keep their culture intact, including language, religion, holidays, foods, folk medicine, and family structures. The 1900 census showed that there were perhaps as many as 165,000 Mexican Americans in Texas, some 71,000 of them born in Mexico. There was similar growth in the Anglo population, it is true, but with far fewer foreign-born.

Although he could easily have won a U.S. Senate seat, Jim Hogg, who had no means of support except his job, announced at a "harmony meeting" in Dallas in January 1894 that he would not be a candidate for political office. In debt and feeling that he should tend to his family's needs, he entered into what became a lucrative legal practice in Austin, serving the same corporations and railroads that he had attacked while in public office. After the discovery of oil at Spindletop in 1901, he moved his practice to Houston and became involved in the oil business, helping to organize the Texas Company, which ultimately became Texaco, with Joseph S. Cullinan and others. Some ten years after his death, oil was discovered on property that he had purchased near West Columbia, making his three children "oil rich."

Business-Oriented Democrats

Hogg's 1892 reelection was only the beginning for Colonel House, who controlled the state Democratic Party machinery for the next decade, orchestrating the elections of a series of business-oriented Democrats to the governorship. Each of the Democratic factions fielded candidates again in 1894, the most reputable of whom was former U.S. Senator and railroad commissioner John H. Reagan, the "old Roman," whom Hogg favored. But Charles Allen Culberson, a reformer who had supported Hogg's platform and as attorney general had enforced the laws that he passed, entered the race with House's assistance. Culberson stood with Hogg on most state issues, but not on many national issues, such as the free coinage of silver. The House organization went into action, blanketing the state with hundreds of letters to "our crowd" as well as to influential Democrats in every section, arranging for speakers at local meetings, and making sure that Culberson's views made it into the press and into thousands of brochures. While Culberson was on the stump, House remained in Austin, handling the arrangements for his appearances—from publicizing events and making sure that the right people would be there to meet him to deciding upon the refreshments. Culberson's headquarters sent out bales of campaign literature and copies of his speeches. The turning point proved to be Reagan's withdrawal, when the convention produced a platform document that he could not support, and his votes went to Culberson.

In the general election, Culberson had to contend with an invigorated People's Party that had increased its influence by taking over most of the Farmers' Alliance structure in the state and made its best showing to date in Texas with 35 percent of the vote. Realizing that he had lost a number of voters both to the Populists and to Hogg in 1892, Cuney and the Republicans fielded their own candidate in this election, as did the "reform" Republicans (lily-whites) and the Prohibitionists. Culberson won by a plurality, 216,373 votes to 159,676 for Nugent, again the Populist candidate, and 57,147 for the "regular" Republican, W. K. Makemson. The growing Populist totals did not bode well for the Democrats.

Unfortunately, no one will ever know what the actual vote might have been, for both the Democrats and the Populists had honed a number of techniques to sway the African American vote. White sheriffs intimidated African Americans with guns or courted them with whiskey. In some counties, the parties paid influential African American men to pressure their friends and neighbors. In others, they sponsored all-night parties with lots of food and drink; the next morning mounted and armed white men escorted the African Americans to the poll, supplied them with ballots, and paid them twenty-five or fifty cents. Such practices gave credence to the Greenback and Farmers' Alliance charges of vote fraud and their campaigns for the Australian (secret) ballot and an honest count.

House's organizing genius was needed even more in Culberson's reelection bid two years later, because the feared union between the Populists and the Republicans became a reality. In the midst of a national depression, Culberson was an easy target. "Almost every working man is idle," former Confederate colonel and Democratic state senator John S. "Rip" Ford wrote from San Antonio that summer. "If these things increase how can common people procure the means of livelihood?" Many shared his view and joined the Populist crusade. Populist candidate Jerome C. Kearby campaigned hard on issues such as the free coinage of silver, direct election of U. S. senators, and an income tax and made a genuine effort to attract African American voters, at one point serving with two African Americans on the state executive committee and using talented spokesmen such as Rayner. But Kearby was greatly disenchanted when the great Populist orator and champion of free silver, William Jennings Bryan of Nebraska, accepted the nomination of the Democratic Party as well as that of the Populists.

House's political instincts were still good. He relied upon the proven formula of thousands of personal letters to local and regional leaders, tons of brochures and leaflets, and large rallies with talented speakers, including the African American Republican William M. "Gooseneck Bill" McDonald, who refused to go along with his party because he opposed many of the planks in the Populist platform. House even had one of Culberson's speeches translated into Swedish. Kearby polled 44 percent of the vote, the largest total that the Populists would ever receive in Texas, but he still lost to Culberson by an official count of 298,528 to 238,692. The Populists elected twenty-two state representatives and two senators. The Democrats claimed that 47 percent of the African Americans voted for them, but the election is generally considered one of the most corrupt in the state's history, with the widespread use of "influence" men on both sides, and historians generally doubt the claim. The coercion that occurred in Franklin, the county seat of Robertson County, is representative of what occurred, as armed white Democrats patrolled the streets all day, turning away African American would-be Populist voters. In Hearne, white men stood in front of the polls and fired pistol shots into the air to break up a crowd of African Americans who were attempting to vote. Some historians think that an honest election might have resulted in a Populist victory.

Following the 1896 election, the Populist coalition in Texas broke up. Part of the reason was that the national Democratic Party had adopted some of the Populist positions after Bryan became its candidate for president. Race was an issue in some precincts, particularly in East Texas, and a genuine conflict with Republican ideology left others no choice but to return to the Democratic Party, the Socialist Party, the Farmers' Alliance, and other organizations. The impact of the People's Party on the state was the same as its impact on the nation, because the Democrats adopted a number of its proposals, but it ultimately had little direct influence on Texas because the party elected only a few members of the legislature and never gained control of the executive office. At the same time, it attracted so many agrarians that the Democratic Party became more urban and conservative, reducing the number of farmers and farmer sympathizers serving in the legislature. It is possible that their absence from the Democratic Party made possible Culberson's 1894 nomination.

Colonel House, meanwhile, continued his influence over the state's politics by allying himself with a long-haired, smooth-talking Southern orator named Joseph Weldon Bailey. Originally from Mississippi, Bailey had come to Texas in 1885 and settled in Gainesville, where he practiced law. His outgoing personality and flair for spinning yarns in the Jim Hogg style soon won him many friends, who urged him to run for Congress. Elected in 1890, he became a spokesperson for the silver Democrats and by 1897 had become the House minority leader. With Texas Senator Roger Q. Mill's seat becoming vacant in 1899, Bailey lent his support to Culberson, who cinched the nomination when House convinced his main opponent to quit the race. With his reputation as a political kingmaker enhanced, House turned his attention once again to the statehouse.

Several able candidates, including Attorney General Martin M. Crane, had announced for the 1898 race. Crane was a well-known politician who, as attorney general, had won some of the most impressive legal victories in support of Hogg's reforms. He did not ask for House's support because he was not particularly close to the colonel and probably thought he would face only token opposition. So, when Congressman Joseph D. Sayers of Bastrop, whom House had assisted in his 1896 race, asked for help, House agreed and quietly began lining up newspaper support throughout the state. House's accomplishment in this race was that he convinced "our crowd," the Hogg-Culberson network that he had helped create, to support Sayers, rather than Crane, who appeared to be the natural heir to the mantle.

House's strategy of tight organizational control paid off in an unexpected way. He had learned the value of organizing early conventions in counties favorable to his candidate to create a bandwagon effect. As county after county declared for Sayers in the weeks before the convention, the ploy worked, and, in a fit of depression, Crane withdrew from the race. The night of his withdrawal a reporter for the *Dallas Morning News* called House at midnight to inform him of it and to ask for a statement. House recalled that he "lay awake for nearly an hour, enjoying" the fact that he had taken a mediocre candidate and beaten the obvious choice. This incident suggests that, rather than pushing a political agenda, House enjoyed the feeling of power that he gained by manipulating other men, and he extended his influence over the Texas Democratic Party.

Conclusion

Some of the men who served in office during these years are among the most popular and capable Texans in the state's history. Oran M. Roberts, although generally faulted for viewing government in narrow, legalistic terms, returned the state to financial solvency. After leaving office, the "Old Alcalde" served for ten years as professor of law at the University of Texas and became the founding president of the Texas State Historical Association in 1897. Lawrence Sullivan Ross's two terms were so peaceful and prosperous that historians have often referred to his tenure as an "era of good feeling." The people so revered the "Old Roman," John H. Reagan, that Jim Hogg felt that only he could bring to the new railroad commission the credibility it needed to succeed. Colonel House will forever be regarded as the cagey Texas kingmaker who would go on to succeed in the same low-key and personal manner at the national level. And most historians still consider Jim Hogg, who personified the reform movement in Texas, one of the best chief executives the state has ever had.

Nevertheless, these men left unresolved some of the most troubling and complex issues of the day, including prohibition, segregation, civil rights, and women's suffrage. An issue ever since the days of the republic, support for prohibition was particularly strong in most rural areas of the state and gradually increased as the decades passed. Prohibition would recover from its resounding defeat at the polls in 1887 to become a virulent political issue as the twentieth century dawned. Although legally prevented from voting during this time, women used voluntary organizations to address legal and social problems; when supporters of these two issues—prohibition and women's suffrage—merged, beginning with the state branch of the Woman's Christian Temperance Union in 1883, the issues become even more compelling to Texas voters. The abolition of segregation and the expansion of civil rights would require more time.

The last quarter of the nineteenth century brought tremendous change to Texas. Although the population was still largely rural in 1900, it had increased by more than 370 percent, and many citizens felt that Texas had fulfilled its vision as a land of promise. Railroads had spread throughout the state, encouraging immigration, urban growth, and labor unions, exhausting the public domain through land grants, helping to close the hostile frontier of more than half a century, and engaging in excesses that required governmental regulation. Although industry now accounted for half as much production as agriculture, farmers had greatly increased their output through commercialization, used the expanded railroad network to ship their produce greater distances, and responded to national and even international markets. Although one may credit the state's successes to the indomitable spirit and resilience of the early settlers, it is also important to remember that these two and a half decades also witnessed the virtual extinction of the buffalo, the overgrazing of West Texas rangelands, and the first large-scale exploitation of the East Texas timberlands. Indeed, many of the coming twentieth-century political battles would revolve around the state's use of and/or protection of the environment as Texas became even more populous and urban.

SUGGESTED READINGS

The best overviews for the latter part of the nineteenth-century are Billy Mac Jones, *The Search for Maturity* (1965), and Alwyn Barr, *Reconstruction to Reform: Texas Politics, 1876–1906* (1971).

Economic Recovery

For the beginnings of industrialization, see John S. Spratt, *The Road to Spindletop: Economic Change in Texas, 1875–1901* (1955), and Robert S. Maxwell, *Sawdust Empire: The Texas Lumber Industry, 1830–1940* (1983); Thomas L. Miller, *The Public Lands of Texas, 1519–1970* (1972); and S. G. Reed, *A History of the Texas Railroads* (1941).

Expansion into West Texas

There are literally hundreds of studies on the ranching industry and the cowboy, but the most helpful are Ernest S. Osgood, *The Day of the Cattleman* (reprint, 1957); William C. Holden, *Alkali Trails, or, Social and Economic Movements of the Texas Frontier, 1846–1900* (1930); Jimmy M. Skaggs, *The Cattle-Trailing Industry: Between Supply and Demand, 1866–1890* (1973); and Joe B. Frantz and Julian Ernest Choate, *The American Cowboy: The Myth and the Reality* (1955).

Information on the Indian wars may be found in Rupert Norval Richardson, *The Comanche Barrier to South Plains Settlement: A Century and a Half of Savage Resistance to the Advancing White Frontier* (1933); William H. Leckie, *Military Conquest of the Southern Plains* (1963); and Robert Wooster, *Soldiers, Sutlers, and Settlers: Garrison Life on the Texas Frontier* (1987). For the settlement of West Texas, see Frederick W. Rathjen, *The Texas Panhandle Frontier* (1975). For information on the agrarian movement, see Roscoe C. Martin, *The People's Party in Texas* (reprint, 1970).

The Political Will

Useful biographies for the period include Robert Cotner, *James Stephen Hogg* (1951); Ben H. Procter, *Not Without Honor: The Life of John H. Reagan* (1962); Gregg Cantrell, *Kenneth and John B. Rayner and the Limits of Southern Dissent* (1993); John Anthony Moretta, *William Pitt Ballinger: Texas Lawyer, Southern Statesman, 1825–1888* (2000); and Rupert Norval Richardson, *Colonel House: The Texas Years* (1964).

For information on minorities and women, see Alwyn Barr's *Black Texans: A History of African Americans in Texas, 1528–1995* (reprint, 1996); Arnoldo De León, *Mexican Americans in Texas: A Brief History*, 2nd ed. (1999); and Ann Patton Malone, *Women on the Texas Frontier: A Cross-cultural Perspective* (1983).

The *Southwestern Historical Quarterly* and the *New Handbook of Texas,* both published by the Texas State Historical Association, contain dozens of useful articles relating to the period. The *New Handbook* is available free of charge on the Internet at www.tsha.utexas.edu.

11

The Early Twentieth Century: One Party, Half a Dozen Fights, 1900–1929

Jim Ferguson was a virtual unknown when he stepped up to the makeshift outdoor podium on the main street of the small Central Texas town of Blum, northwest of Hillsboro. Almost 600 men and perhaps a dozen women stood for two hours in the "penetrating cold and raw, damp chill" on March 21, 1914, to hear the first speech of his campaign for governor. Backed by fluttering American flags and red, white, and blue bunting draped from a storefront awning, Ferguson told the rural audience that "I am the thirteenth candidate for governor of Texas, announcing in the year 1913, on the thirteenth day of the month in the thirteenth year of my married life, and my platform was completed on Friday. . . . I have caught the black cat tail of superstition and I intend to twist and pinch it until I am inaugurated Governor of this great State on or about the thirteenth day of next January."

Ferguson was a handsome forty-three-year-old banker from Temple, looking like "the substantial business man of farm origin that every town in Texas knows well." He was a political neophyte but not an innocent. He had some formal education, including a working knowledge of the classics, which he revealed from time to time, quoting Adam Smith in his Blum talk, but he also reverted to "country talk" to emphasize his points. Prohibition was the overriding social and political concern of the day, but Ferguson rejected it, telling the farmers, "If I am elected Governor, and the Legislature puts any liquor legislation up to me, pro or anti, I will strike it where the chicken got the ax."

1900	Galveston hurricane
1901	Oil discovered at Spindletop
1902	Poll tax enacted
1903	Terrell election law disfranchises blacks
1904	Texas ranks first in railroad track mileage
1913	Sixteenth (income tax) and Seventeenth (direct election of U.S. senators) Amendments to the U.S. Constitution ratified
1914	Houston Ship Channel opens
1915	*Plan de San Diego* discovered
1917	U.S. enters World War I
1918	Legislature ratifies Eighteenth Amendment (prohibition) to the U.S. Constitution
1919	Legislature grants women the right to vote in Texas primaries
1929	Value of crude oil production in Texas exceeds the value of the cotton crop, and Texas is the world's leading supplier of crude oil

Instead, he addressed a greater evil, one that kept the majority of farmers economically prostrate and threatened our political system. The amount of rent that many landlords were now charging tenants, Ferguson shouted, amounted to usury, which was against God's law and man's. It had led to statewide poverty and the rise of the Socialist Party. "As long as the tenant was treated fairly and equitably," he reasoned, "the claims of the Socialist were a matter of fine spun theory. Take away the abuses of the present rent system, and the Socialist would not have a leg to stand on." No other politician in the Democratic Party proposed such a radical measure. To the *Dallas Morning News* reporter at the scene, he was "frank and outspoken," but a neighbor recalled that Ferguson could "electrify and sway audiences to the near frenzy of a wild mob." The Socialists would claim that he had stolen their thunder, and the farmers had found their champion.

The first two decades of the twentieth century, give or take a few years, are generally known as the Progressive Era in American history. Although this is an unsatisfactory, and in many ways misleading, term, it has been used historically to embrace the social and political reforms that a rising middle class and agrarian and social reformers proposed during the early years of the twentieth century.

Texans, nevertheless, shared many of the reformers' concerns, some of which are evident in the four primary factors that facilitated the state's drive toward modernism during these opening decades of the twentieth century. The first was a good economy, rooted in ranching and cotton production and greatly bolstered in January 1901 by the discovery of what was, at that time, the world's largest oil deposit at Spindletop. Second was the political and cultural climate—one-party control—that permitted and at times even encouraged the reforms; indeed, one historian of the era even refers to the state as a "bastion of reform" during these years. Third were the reforms themselves, which originated from societal needs and pressure to modernize as well as to maintain Democratic Party control. And the fourth factor, but by no means the least important, was the role of the federal government, the role that Texans played in it, and the fact that Texans were willing to look to it for assistance when other Southern states had not yet overcome the divisive effect of the Civil War.

It is difficult to categorize these reformers as a movement because of the increasing political, economic, cultural, and racial diversity of Texas society during these years. Almost 200,000 Mexicans probably immigrated to Texas between 1890 and 1910, for example, producing a more than 300 percent increase in the number of Mexicans in Texas, whereas the state's overall population grew by only 75 percent. This represented the largest increase in the Mexican population in Texas since the Texas Revolution in 1836 and meant that in Texas those who called themselves Progressives, whose social and political goals were largely based on a homogeneous society, sometimes could not agree on social and political agendas. And it meant that, from the perspective of a Hispanic, African American, or poor white, there were many events during these years that would not have been considered "progressive" at all.

The Texas Economy in 1900

Agriculture—farming and ranching—still fueled the state's economy in 1900. Since the mid-1870s, Texas farmers had led the South in the production of cotton. By the turn of the century, the state produced more than 3.5 million bales on 7,178,915 acres of land, and there was still arable land yet to bring under the plow.

Cotton production dipped when the boll weevil, a native Mexican insect, began to make its way northward from South Texas, where it was discovered in 1894. The weevil flourished in the semitropical warmth of much of South and East Texas and proved resistant or immune to most known insecticides and poisons. In 1904, the small weevil destroyed more than 700,000 bales of cotton, in 1910 6 percent of the entire cotton crop, and in 1921 34 percent, costing farmers millions of dollars.

The pest's susceptibility to freezing temperatures spurred the migration of farmers to West Texas and the High Plains, which had begun with the aid of barbed wire and the construction of railroads. Despite the boll weevil infestation, even as late as 1927 the value of the state's cotton crop was still more than three times the value of its oil production.

The fact that agriculture was flourishing did not mean that Texas farmers earned as much as their counterparts in other regions of the country. Texas led the South in farm income per family during these years by a wide margin, but it trailed the Midwest and much of the rest of the nation.

Tenant Farmers

Despite the fact that state law declared that every Texan was entitled to a homestead of 160 acres, little tillable land remained to be distributed by 1880, and tenants operated about 37 percent of Texas farms. After the state Supreme Court declared in 1898 that unappropriated public lands were exhausted, that figure jumped to more than 49 percent in 1900, a direct result of the continuing population increase and the devastating depression of the 1890s, and to nearly 52 percent by 1911.

Some were "share tenants," who furnished their own tools, plows, work animals, seed, and food, and bargained over the percentage of the crops that they paid the landowner. In a common arrangement, a tenant farmer would provide the landlord with one-third of the cotton crop and one-fourth of the corn crop ("third and fourth" renters). But others—"halfers" or "croppers"—simply worked for the landlord, providing nothing but their labor in return for the proceeds from one-half of the crop, less any debts they might have accumulated during the year. As one would have expected in a segregated state, most of the share tenants were white, whereas most of the "halfers" were African Americans and Mexicans.

Number and Value of Cotton Bales, 1900–1932

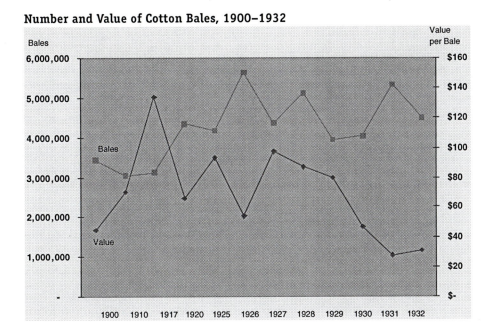

As agricultural prices dropped, farmers and their supporters attempted to organize to improve their conditions. The Renters' Union of North America established more than 200 chapters throughout the state and tried to set rules for tenancy and improve the marketing of agricultural products. Originating in Emory, Texas, in 1902, the Farmers' Union became the 140,000-member Farmers' Educational and Cooperative Union of America (ECUA) by 1914, with a Colored Farmers' Union providing services for African Americans. The ECUA constructed some 1,300 cotton warehouses and marketing cooperatives throughout the state and operated more than 100 cotton gins, but it is best known for the "plowup campaign of 1908," in which it tried to create a shortage of cotton by destroying one-third of the crop. Another result of the increasing number of tenant farmers was the rise of the Socialist Party in Texas. The most successful of all the organizations was the Farm Bureau, more conservative than its forebears and focused on landowners rather than tenants or sharecroppers, but also dedicated to getting more credit for the farmer and helping to sell the crops at the highest prices possible. Ultimately, in terms of the average farmer of the 1920s, they all failed.

The Lumbering Bonanza

With the huge East Texas forest at its disposal, the state's lumbering industry reached its zenith in 1907, cutting 2.25 billion board feet (a board foot is a square foot of lumber one-inch thick), the third highest production rate in the United

States. Entrepreneurs such as Henry J. Lutcher, G. Bedell Moore, Thomas L. L. Temple, and John Henry Kirby had changed the industry by establishing complete plants and company towns in remote parts of East Texas—Camden, Fostoria, Kirbyville, Diboll—that received the logs from the forest and delivered finished lumber to the railhead. The work was long, difficult, dangerous, and low-paying. The workers averaged about ten hours a day on the job between 1900 and World War I, then nine hours a day until World War II, and only the most skilled employees earned more than a common laborer's pay. In many cases these poor conditions persisted until companies, following a "cut out and get out" policy and expecting the cleared land to become farms, began to exhaust their timber holdings and the industry declined in the 1920s.

Despite the status of agricultural and lumber workers, most people view the 1920s as good economic years. The average Texan's income was almost three-quarters that of the average American, and World War I had increased the demand for lumber (for wooden ships) and boosted the price of cotton to 20.9 cents per pound in 1919. But the relative economic position of the farmer slowly sank during that decade and many forests were decimated.

The Discovery of Oil

Like other places in the United States, Texas had been home to a modest oil industry for decades before the legendary discovery at Spindletop in 1901. The state's first producing field came in at Corsicana until 1894, and the real estate developers who owned it recruited several Pennsylvania oilmen—James M. Guffey, John H. Galey, and J. S. Cullinan—to help them develop the field, which, by 1900, was producing 836,000 barrels a year. Cullinan built the first refinery in the state there in 1898 to produce primarily kerosene. It was still generally true in 1900 that if a Texan drilled a well, he or she was looking for water, a far more precious substance than oil, especially in the western part of the state.

That began to change on January 10, 1901. The Gladys City Oil, Gas, and Manufacturing Company had been drilling for oil on Spindletop Hill near Beaumont ever since 1893, but they had been foiled by their out-of-date cable-tool drilling rig and the tricky sands of the salt dome formation and had run out of money. Anthony F. Lucas, the leading American expert on salt dome formations, leased the rights from the company and joined in the search in 1899. Initially, he suffered the same fate as the Gladys City company, but, convinced by his experience in Louisiana, he did not give up.

A new rotary drilling technique, combined with Lucas's experience in drilling in salt domes and money from the Mellon banking interests in Pittsburgh, brought success. On January 10, shortly after mud began bubbling from the well, the newly released pressure blew six tons of four-inch drilling pipe from the hole. Everyone watched, stunned, as the well seemed to settle down for a few minutes, then a geyser of mud, gas, and, finally, oil burst out of the hole. The oil spewed more than 100 feet into the air at an estimated rate of 100,000 barrels a day for

Burkburnett, near Wichita Falls, was one of the wildest of the early Texas oil boomtowns in 1918. Here, horse-drawn wagons loaded with tools and equipment jam the roads with a forest of oil derricks in the background. *(Archives Center, National Museum of American History, Smithsonian Institute)*

nine days—until the workers finally managed to cap it. By the time it was brought under control, a huge pool of oil surrounded the well, along with hundreds of oilmen, speculators, and onlookers. Inspired by the Spindletop discovery, wildcatters rushed into every part of the state looking for oil.

The first genuine oil boom in the state greatly expanded the regional economies.

Early Texas oil centers.

Texas had produced approximately 1,000 barrels of oil in 1896; that figure jumped to 21 million in 1902. Thousands of people moved into the area from Houston to Beaumont to Port Arthur, and real estate became more expensive—prohibitively so in some cases. Related manufacturing companies such as machine shops and distribution facilities relocated to the gulf coast. Augmenting the facilities at Galveston, the Houston Ship Channel opened in 1914, the same year that the Panama Canal opened, and Texas began to attract shipping from around the world.

The industry produced new terms and personalities to take their place alongside the cowboy in the pantheon of Texas characters: the "go-for-broke" wildcatter, the hard-working, hard-playing roughneck, and the "get-rich-quick" oilman. These characters were firmly established by the 1920s, but Edna Ferber gave them stereotypical expression in the fictional persona of Jett Rink, a merging of the cowboy and the get-rich-quick oilman, in her popular novel (which became a motion picture) *Giant* (1952).

Wildcatters drilled cheek by jowl with other rigs in boomtowns because there were no laws preventing it; more than 200 derricks rose within the city limits of Breckenridge, with several thousand more in the immediate area. Oil overflowed storage tanks and spilled into streams and polluted the air. There were shortages of food and fuel. Heavy rains and constant oilfield traffic turned dirt roads into mud bogs. When torrential rains fell in Desdemona in 1919, influenza and typhoid quickly reached epidemic proportions. Violent crime accompanied the gambling houses and brothels, and law enforcement officials chained prisoners to trees when jails became overcrowded. When the onslaught overwhelmed city and county services, the state intervened. The governor dispatched the Texas Rangers to Desdemona in 1920, Borger in 1927, and Wink in 1927 and again in 1928 and 1929, and the state militia to Mexia in 1922 and Borger in 1929.

Creation of the vast petrochemical complex on the gulf coast, today one of the world's largest, began soon after the discovery at Spindletop as dozens of small refineries located in the vicinity. In 1902, Guffey established a large refinery there (renamed Gulf Oil Corporation in 1907) to produce kerosene. That same year he and the Texas Company (later Texaco and now Shell) connected the pipelines between Spindletop and their Oklahoma field, and by 1916 Gulf's production capacity reached 50,000 barrels of crude oil per day. Sun Oil Company, Houston Oil Company, and Security Oil Company (a subsidiary of Standard Oil Company, later Magnolia Petroleum Company, one of the forebears of ExxonMobil Corporation) also established sizable installations on the gulf coast.

The state began taxing oil production at the rate of 1 percent of the value of the product in 1905, collecting $101,403 during the first full year of taxation. But by 1919 tax revenues from oil exceeded $1 million, and in 1929 they had reached almost $6 million. The state would become increasingly dependent upon this source of revenue.

The Climate for Reform

The second factor in building a modern Texas was the political and cultural climate that encouraged development and permitted various reforms to occur. Governor Hogg had introduced significant improvements during his two terms in office; the growing economy, one-party rule, with its inherent factions, and an emerging cultural transformation created an environment in which additional changes could be made; and the election of several progressively minded governors during these years encouraged reform. The major exceptions were two of the state's most famous governors, James E. Ferguson and his wife, Miriam Ferguson, the first woman to be elected governor of the state, and even they seem only mildly retrograde when compared with some of the governors of other southern states.

The cultural change that became apparent in Texas as the twentieth century dawned was important because it permitted Texans to throw off the emotional shackles of the "lost cause," provided them with a positive outlook, and encouraged them to accept modernity in the form of new ideas, including increased participation in and assistance from the federal government.

Historian Walter Buenger says that Texans shifted from an allegiance to the South to an allegiance to Texas itself, which he defines as resembling the American dream in that it contained neither the burden of slavery nor the defeat of the Civil War; the fact that Texans successfully resisted Union invasion during the Civil War enabled many to persist in the belief that they had not been conquered. The commemoration of Texas uniqueness had begun as early as 1886 when orators throughout the state celebrated the fiftieth anniversary of the state's independence, comparing Stephen F. Austin and Sam Houston to George Washington and Thomas Jefferson rather than Robert E. Lee and Jefferson Davis. By 1900 the state had acquired more than 330 acres of the San Jacinto battlefield as a memorial; by 1905 it had purchased additional parts of the Alamo and turned it over to the Daughters of the Republic of Texas to administer as a shrine. And in 1901 artist Henry McArdle loaned his two large paintings of significant moments in Texas history, *Dawn at the Alamo* (1905) and *Battle of San Jacinto* (1895), to the state for exhibition in the new capitol. Today they hang in the Senate chamber and have been reproduced in Texas history books for decades.

At the same time, the Texas State Historical Association, founded in 1897, had begun to publish heroic stories of early Texas in its journal. Later directors of the association, Eugene C. Barker and Walter Prescott Webb, would write great books—Barker's biography of Stephen F. Austin (1926) and Webb's *The Great Plains* (1931) and *The Texas Rangers* (1936)—that focused on the state's westernness rather than its southernness. In 1906, *Dallas Morning News* editorial cartoonist John Knott personified the state in a character that became famous as "Old Man Texas," known for his belief in fiscal responsibility, low taxes, and honesty in government, just as the character of Uncle Sam represents those values for the country as a whole. In addition, generations of schoolchildren learned the history of the state from an enormously popular comic strip, *Texas History Movies*, first published in the *Dallas Morning News* beginning in 1926, then distributed to the schools by Magnolia Petroleum Company for years.

The result, according to Buenger, is that Texans like novelist Walter Humphrey grew up reenacting the battle of the Alamo in their childhood games instead of the battles of Bull Run and Gettysburg. This developing "Texanness" led the state's residents to associate themselves with victory at San Jacinto rather than defeat at Appomattox. It culminated in the state's centennial celebration in Dallas in 1936, by which time cowboys, cowgirls, and the Big Bend mountains had officially replaced planters, southern belles, and East Texas cotton fields as the state's symbols, despite the fact that the state's two largest cities, Houston and Dallas, are in East Texas. By then one could hardly tell if Knott's "Old Man Texas" was an East Texas planter or a West Texas rancher. This does not mean that the cult of Texas exceptionalism had only positive effects, but it did provide the intellectual underpinning for a newer and more positive culture in Texas than in the other Southern states.

Nor did it mean that vestiges of the "bloody shirt," the Southern penchant for recalling Yankee horrors committed during the Civil War, no longer existed, for these years also saw the installation of dozens of Confederate monuments overlooking courthouse squares, parks, and cemeteries throughout the state. Sculptors such as Pompeo Coppini, an Italian who first moved to Texas in 1901, earned their living from commissions such as the Confederate monument on the capitol grounds (1901–03), the statues on the south mall of the University of Texas at Austin, the Confederate soldier in Victoria (1911), and the John H. Reagan Memorial in Palestine (1911), featuring a personification of the "lost cause," a Roman soldier sitting pensively at Reagan's feet, contemplating defeat. In most cases, it meant that Texans saw no conflict in thinking of themselves as both Texan and Southern.

The Conservatives Take Charge

With the breakup of the Populism movement, the last significant opposition to the Bourbon Democrats faded and the back-to-back elections of Joseph D. Sayers (1899–1903) and Samuel W. T. Lanham (1903–07) as governor and Culberson as senator (1899–1923) confirmed their hold on power. Supported by House and "our crowd," Sayers and Lanham were both former members of the U.S. Congress and were the last two Confederate veterans to serve as governor. Neither Sayers nor Lanham (1903–07) was as reform-minded as Hogg. They were sophisticated men but lacked his transforming zeal and realized that the modernization of Texas depended on the vast oil reserves at Spindletop and the continued exploitation of the East Texas timberlands. In a political party divided by factions, House had virtually negotiated their nominations, almost arguing that their administrations would be "caretaker" administrations rather than proactive ones. As House bluntly put it, "the people wanted no disturbance" in 1902 and Lanham "managed to say nothing in a most convincing and masterly way." The resulting friendly business climate was reflected in a decline in the proportion of farmers in the legislature; both Sayers and Lanham, however, continued to prosecute antitrust violations and, together, brought more cases in Texas than the federal government prosecuted in the entire nation during the same period. Lanham was the last governor that House actively supported before turning his attention to national politics, and, House left behind no real machine or organization because his power was based on personal contacts and influence.

It was also during their administrations that the Bourbon Democrats, with traditional motives as well as a desire for genuine reform, overhauled the state's election laws, which admittedly were a confusing mélange of local laws. Block voting and ballot stuffing were endemic, and the state needed a good system of voter registration. But, disturbed by the fact that the combination of African American Republicans and Populists almost brought victory in 1896, the Democratic legislature moved in 1902 to institutionalize the one-party rule as well as solve the registration problem. The legislature first recommended a constitutional amendment that would permit a poll tax (which passed with a 65 percent majority), then in 1903 enacted a series of "reforms" that encouraged the counties to continue the all-white primaries (which, in this case, was interpreted to include Mexicans as well, to accommodate the South Texas political bosses), made third-party competition more difficult, and established a poll tax that had to be paid six months before the primaries and nine months before the general election.

A majority of middle- and upper-class whites favored the poll tax, as did reformers who reasoned that it would be an efficient way of registering voters and discouraging block voting and manipulation of voters. Former legislator Alexander Watkins Terrell was one of those who had advocated a poll tax for years, and he made clear his intention to prevent "the thriftless, idle and semi-vagrant element of *both races*" from voting. The poll tax did make the job of ward politicians and brewing interests more expensive, but they continued to buy the votes of large blocks of workers, tenant farmers, railroad employees, and opponents of prohibition. And, it was effective in reducing the number of people who voted. Political scientists estimate that at the high tide of Populism, 1896, more than 80 percent of those eligible to vote actually participated in the election. That figure dropped to approximately 35 percent in 1904, the first year the poll tax was enforced, and to less than 25 percent in 1906.

Terrell returned to the legislature in 1903 to offer further reforms that would, at the same time, make it even more difficult for minorities to vote. The stated intent of the laws that bear his name was to standardize voting across the state and eliminate fraud. They required, for example, that all counties hold their conventions on the same day, preventing manipulators such as Colonel House from scheduling early conventions in favorable counties. An even more pervasive law enacted in 1905 required primary elections for those parties that had received at least 100,000 votes in the previous general election (later raised to 200,000, then to 20 percent of the vote) and defined the process by which candidates would be nominated for office as well as who would be permitted to vote. Known collectively as the Terrell election laws, these statutes culminated the Bourbon Democrat effort to institutionalize one-party rule. A disgruntled Republican realized as early as 1912 that "the primary election law . . . [is] so effectual . . . that today, a nomination in the Democratic primaries is tantamount to election."

This revamping of the election law, however, did not include women. The Texas Woman Suffrage Association organized in Houston with the intent of establishing chapters throughout the state, but the group's activities stopped when one of its main leaders, Annette Finnegan, left the state in 1905. A small group in Austin carried on the fight until the movement gained greater public support a few years later. In the meantime, women took pride in the fact that the concerted action of many groups, including the Texas chapter of the Woman's Christian Temperance Union, the Grange, the Texas Federation of Women's Clubs, and the Texas Woman's Press Association, led to the establishment of Texas Woman's University in Denton in 1903.

Half a Dozen Fights

With its newfound dominance, the Democratic Party became the only serious venue for discussion of the state's social and economic problems. It also became home to a number of factions, that, although based on such strong characteristics as class, race, and ideology, moved in and out of the party from time to time and followed one or another of the charismatic leaders who vied for center stage. Powerful orators such as Senator Joseph W. Bailey and Governor Oscar B. Colquitt attempted to persuade the faithful with regard to issues such as voting, workers' and women's rights, tenancy and land ownership, political corruption, railroad law, regulation of insurance companies, penal and tax reform, antitrust legislation, education, conservation, and creation of a highway system, with no one faction gaining dominance. The astute Jim Hogg had helped the party find a middle ground between the conservative, prorailroad wing and the more radical Populist demands, and Colonel House had negotiated between various factions of the party for another decade. But no such passionate and domineering a figure as Hogg appeared again until an unknown forty-three-year-old independent-minded Temple banker-turned-politician, James E. Ferguson, announced for governor in 1913, and he did so by casting aside the overriding political and cultural issue of the day—prohibition.

Others were not as bold. To Thomas B. Love of Dallas, speaker of the Texas House of Representatives in 1907, and Thomas H. Ball of Houston, who ran against Ferguson for the Democratic gubernatorial nomination, prohibition was a sincere motive, but they also recognized it as an issue that motivated voters. The railroads had submitted to the regulating authority of the Railroad Commission, and other "foreign" corporations had either fled the state or reconciled themselves to Texas's parochial commercial interests. Lacking a genuine corporate bully, urban abuses, or corrupt political bosses (outside of South Texas) to rally against, Texas reformers soon united around the prohibition question. Most, like Love and Ball, were fervent in their conviction, but it was also good politics. The typical Texas resident was white, ethnocentric, conservative, and had roots in the South. He or she also lived in a rural area, farmed, and espoused traditional values, as opposed to the sinful vices associated with the growing cities. That also made them naturally suspicious of racial and ethnic minorities who, it seemed, consistently opposed prohibition.

With no threat to their power, the Democrats could afford these intraparty struggles, but the overriding issue that seemed to cut across all the others was prohibition, which inspired endless debate, with Bible-quoting evangelists such as J. B. Cranfill of Dallas and J. Frank Norris of Fort Worth on one side and on the other the majority of Roman Catholics, members of less evangelical Protestant sects, African Americans, Mexicans, urban dwellers, and Democratic conservatives. "We have only one political party in Texas," Governor Colquitt told a Dallas audience in 1911, "but there are enough political fights in that one for half a dozen."

Texas and the Federal Government

Even as the Democratic party in Texas reorganized and strengthened itself it was on the verge of bringing Texas to national political prominence. The presidential election of 1912 ushered the Democrats back into the White House and a number of Texans into significant positions in the federal government. Part of this resurgence was due to Colonel House's personal friendship with the new president, Woodrow Wilson of New Jersey, but an equal part of it was the team of talented officeholders that the state sent to Washington. Even before Wilson began his run for the presidency, Texans had elected Morris Sheppard of Pittsburg, in northeast Texas, to the Congress in 1902; he would become a member of the U.S. Senate in 1913. John Nance Garner of Uvalde joined Sheppard in the House in 1903, and he would later become Speaker of the House and vice president under President Franklin D. Roosevelt. Sam Rayburn of Bonham, who would also serve as speaker, joined this distinguished company as a member of Congress in 1912.

Although House played no role in Wilson's nomination—indeed, he had concluded that the governor could not be nominated and suggested to his friend Senator Culberson that he support someone else—the Texas delegation to the Democratic convention in Baltimore did. In a close ballot—and through forty-six roll calls—the Texas delegation, or the "immortal forty," as they became known, remained loyal to Wilson and lobbied others to join them, and Wilson did not forget the Texans. With Colonel House as one of the president's closest advisors, the state found itself in an ideal position to play a major role in the new government.

While he took a much-needed vacation, Wilson left Colonel House to come up with nominations for his cabinet and other appointments. After House recommended a number of Texans, the Lone Star State also found itself in an excellent position to influence federal legislation and programs at the same time as the growing political changes within the state had led Texans to expect more of their government. Texans were pleased to see a Treasury Department that took more interest in the South, and they welcomed the Federal Reserve Act (1913), the Federal Farm Loan Act (1916), aid to agricultural education, lower tariffs, and increased military appropriations in the state as World War I loomed. These federal programs and the largess made the social reforms that often accompanied them a bit more palatable to the conservative state; the coming war in Europe provided the ideal opportunity for Texas to exercise its influence, as army bases were established throughout the state, and Texas oil began to play an important role in the national economy. The state Democratic Party platform of 1920 endorsed the actions of the Wilson administration in direct contradiction to Senator Bailey's lament of the "growing tendency to regulate everything by law."

Pressure for Reform

Aware of the national campaign to reform government and industry, widely publicized by muckraking journalists such as Lincoln Steffens, Ida M. Tarbell, and

Ray Stannard Baker, Texas reformers, lacking a political base during the years between governors Hogg and Campbell, began at the grass-roots level. A new labor group, the State Federation of Labor, organized in 1898, joined with the even newer Farmers' Union to develop a legislative program and to lobby for its implementation. The Texas Federation of Women's Clubs, founded in 1897 and with more than 230 clubs and more than 5,000 members by 1903, took on other aspects of the Progressive agenda, such as better schools and libraries. The Texas Local Option Association organized in 1903 to defend the state's local option laws, but its members also concerned themselves with moral issues of the day as well as labor and agriculture reforms.

Although different groups focused on different issues, the causes seemed to fall in three areas: monopolistic business practices, individualistic excesses, and social engineering and increasing efficiency. Among the goals on the various reformers' agendas were improving government; ending political corruption; curtailing the influence of large, particularly out-of-state, corporations; and improving all aspects of life, from the farm to the city and from schools to prisons and charitable institutions. The reformers believed that such social goals could be achieved through efficient bureaucracies, the application of scientific research and training, and public education.

But prohibition was, in fact, the dominant issue in Texas politics for much of this period. It cut across political factions and classes and gained additional support when women won the right to vote. Progressives believed that "demon rum" would corrupt a democratic society and the fact that most Germans, Mexicans, and other ethnic groups opposed prohibition only seemed to reinforce the point that it would benefit the Anglo-Saxon society. Having failed in previous attempts at statewide prohibition in 1887 and 1911, antiliquor forces concentrated on local-option laws, vowing to dry up the state one precinct at a time.

The "wets," as those who were against prohibition were called, responded with similar propaganda and organization. Although the wets had prevailed, 237,393 to 231,096, in a statewide election in 1911, they now faced an aroused nation and state. On February 28, 1918, the legislature ratified the Eighteenth Amendment, a prohibition amendment to the U.S. Constitution that outlawed the sale of alcoholic beverages, and immediately enacted a statewide prohibition law.

Government Reform

One of the first reforms to sweep the state in the twentieth century was a new form of municipal government. Although it was not a result of the devastating hurricane that struck Galveston Island on September 8, 1900, that tragic event, the greatest natural disaster to strike North America, hastened its implementation.

Galveston had been engaged in an all-out civic struggle with Houston for dominance in gulf shipping, but the hurricane tipped the balance decisively in Houston's favor. Nevertheless, the people of Galveston struggled back heroically. Under the leadership of a group of wealthy businessmen, who feared that the city

Walking along the Galveston beach after the storm, with some of the devastation apparent in the background. *(Courtesy of the Rosenberg Library, Galveston, Texas)*

would never recover its prosperity with the current city council, the city changed its governmental structure. The oligarchy devised a plan to elect commissioners at large, rather than from specific wards or precincts. The commissioners would then elect the mayor from among their number, and the commission would be both a policy-making and administrative body: Individual commissioners would also serve as heads of specific departments. The intent of the plan was to bring increased expertise and efficiency to the rebuilding of the city. Progressives did not object to the elite running the city as long as they made the correct decisions.

The effective and businesslike manner in which Galveston recovered from the storm—including building a seventeen-foot seawall on the gulf side of the island, raising the grade level of the city, and building an all-weather bridge to the mainland—caught Governor Campbell's attention, and he encouraged other cities to implement the commission form of government. Houston adopted it in 1905. Dallas, Fort Worth, Denison, Greenville, and El Paso followed in 1907, and by 1920 seventy other Texas cities had implemented the plan along with more than 400 cities nationwide. The Galveston Plan, or the "Texas Idea" as it was known outside the state, continued to spread across the country, but it further eroded minority representation. The at-large elections meant that a majority population could determine the makeup of the entire commission.

Educational Reforms

One of the most important Progressive goals, second in importance only because of the tragedy at Galveston, was educational reform. In general, there were two types of schools at the turn of the century: common schools, which were usually rural and independently governed by trustees who organized for the purpose of hiring a teacher and operating and maintaining the school, and independent districts that usually resembled the present-day school system. Critics of the common schools usually argued that the one-teacher, one-room rural schools offered an inferior education and proposed consolidating these schools and transporting students to the regional schools at no charge. Progressives, further, insisted upon compulsory attendance, an increase in the tax base, increased teacher qualifications, and free textbooks. They wanted all school districts to use the same books, offer similar courses, and have the same requirements for graduation and teacher certification. They created the new State Board of Education to oversee the curriculum and textbooks.

Because of the state's relative poverty, only a few of the changes could be implemented. A newly created Normal School Board of Regents began oversight of the teacher-training schools. Perhaps the Progressives' major impact on education in the state, however, was a change in philosophy. Progressives advocated practical training, but they also thought education should be more relevant to students' lives and supported curriculum changes that introduced the new social sciences of psychology and sociology. Schools took on additional duties, including supervised recess periods, supervised athletic and academic competitions (under the University Interscholastic League at the University of Texas, 1910), and improved health care. The goal of public schools significantly changed from imparting technical skills to improving the social order. By 1930, white Texans had a wide range of choices for higher education at a relatively low cost, and student enrollment increased more than tenfold from 2,148 in 1900 to 23,134 in 1929.

Social Reforms

The initial success of the Galveston Plan seemed to indicate that Progressives were right in their contention that science and training could lead to efficiency. They sought further governmental reforms in the areas of prisons, where they hoped to end inhumane treatment, improve health and sanitation, and regularize paroles. They favored segregated facilities so that women would not be housed with men, juvenile offenders with adults, those who had committed minor violations with murderers. The legislature addressed the problem in 1911, ending contract leasing of prisoners in 1912. It established the Gainesville School for Girls in 1917, and transferred the Gatesville School for Boys to the State Board of Control in 1919, with instructions that the school emphasize reform and education. It replaced hanging as the preferred method of execution with the electric chair, thought to be more humane, in 1923, and established the Texas Prison Board in

Minnie Fisher Cunningham (right) became the first woman from Texas to campaign for the U.S. Senate when she ran for the office in 1928. *(PICA 16817 Austin History Center, Austin Public Library)*

1927 to reorganize the system. But Progressives and most Texas citizens wanted the prison system to be self-supporting, so further solutions had to be found.

Because the federal Social Security program had not yet been enacted, other Progressive efforts focused on establishing county poorhouses and hospitals for the indigent and improving conditions in state asylums, and all such organizations were placed under the State Board of Control. Not all the reforms were carried out, because most citizens felt that the state was too poor to support such programs, while other reforms, such as women's suffrage, continued to be defeated at the ballot box. Minnie Fisher Cunningham, Jane Y. McCallum, Annie Webb Blanton, Jessie Daniel Ames, and others worked hard for the cause, unsuccessfully seeking legislative approval of suffrage amendments in 1915 and 1917.

Good Roads

Although many national issues, such as urban political machines, did not really apply to Texas, others did. In addition to prohibition and women's suffrage, Progressives in Texas also campaigned for good roads and conservation of timber. The demand for good roads emerged around 1910 as the number of automobiles

increased. Because the Texas constitution relegated road upkeep and maintenance to the counties, the state had no network of roads and those that did exist
were in appalling condition, often being little more than rocky trails that followed
along old Indian routes, circled around hills, large trees, and boulders, forded
creeks, and zigzagged in right-angle turns along fence-lines. Some stretches of flat
road developed a ripple pattern known as the "washboard" and there were no
barriers to keep motorists from skidding into ditches along the road or signs to
warn of upcoming hazards such as a dip. During the seasonal torrential rains, dirt
roads became quagmires and often held water or flowed like a creek on the rise.
A publicity-shrouded trans-continental drive sponsored by five Southern newspapers, including the *Dallas Times Herald* and the *Houston Post,* almost came to a
halt in 1913 when the automobile became mired in the impassable black gumbo
soil of Hill County, en route from Waco to Dallas. The first modern road from
Austin to San Antonio was built only when Travis, Hays, Comal, and Béxar counties each agreed in 1914 to pay their share of the $140,000 required to convert the
old wagon road to a sixteen-foot wide roadway covered with a foot of gravel.
Governor Colquitt "plowed the first furrow for the great highway" behind a "big
road plow drawn by six restless mules," according to a reporter for the *New
Braunfels Herald,* and the Austin–San Antonio Post Road was completed a year
and one-half later.

Advocates of good roads began working in various parts of the state as early as
1903. They organized auto tours, encouraged volunteer road work and posted di-
rectional signs for travelers. In 1910 they met at the state fair to promote the idea
of a central authority to oversee and maintain a statewide network of roads. Hoping to overcome the traditional objection to centralization of power and to educate both the legislature and citizens of the growing need, they organized the Texas
Good Roads Association in 1911. In 1916, the first year of automobile registration,
194,720 Texans registered cars and trucks. But the good road enthusiasts faced formidable opposition, because the county commissioners courts did not have the
money to finance the roads and did not want to give up their authority.

The national Progressive agenda came to their rescue, however, as Congress
enacted the Federal Aid Road Act in 1916, offering matching funds to all states
that created a central planning authority and joined the national highway network. The following year the legislature created the Texas Highway Department
(THD), now the Texas Department of Transportation, overseen by a three-member
commission appointed by the governor.

Conservation

The Progressives were not as successful with conservation. Their primary focus
was East Texas, where the timber industry had enjoyed outstanding years during
the first decade of the century with an average cut of more than 2 billion board
feet a year. As World War I came on, lumbering grew to the point that it threatened the very existence of the vast pine forests. W. Goodrich Jones, a Temple

banker, led the effort to regulate the timber industry and implement a program of reforestation.

After attending President Theodore Roosevelt's White House Conference of Governors on Conservation in 1908, Jones returned to Texas and organized the Texas Forestry Association, which espoused a statewide program of forest conservation that called for prevention of fire, selective cutting, sustained yield, and reforestation. Because of the Association's encouragement—and Jones's lobbying of fellow Temple resident Governor Jim Ferguson—the legislature established the Texas Department of Forestry as a part of the Agricultural and Mechanical College. Despite much good work on the part of the agency, however, the legislature failed to follow through in other ways. By the 1920s, the intensive lumbering had virtually destroyed the great virgin forests of East Texas, and the boom came to an end. The Progressives got their agency, but it had little power, and by 1932 Texas timber production had decreased to its lowest point since 1880.

Reformers in Charge

Despite the factionalism, all of the candidates in the 1906 gubernatorial campaign identified themselves as reformers who called for antilobby, antitrust, and protax legislation and support for the state's educational and charitable institutions. With no Colonel House to orchestrate the results, Palestine lawyer Thomas M. Campbell returned to the fray and swept his three primary opponents aside. Although the electorate remained divided on key issues, Campbell's administration, along with the Thirtieth Legislature, became the most reform-oriented government in the state's history. Together, they enacted a number of laws characteristic of reforms throughout the South such as several antirailroad laws that former Governor Hogg supported, an antinepotism law, prolabor laws, antitrust laws, and insurance regulations. During his four years in office, Campbell created a department of agriculture and a library and historical commission and encouraged prison and public school reforms. The Robertson Insurance Law (1907) required insurance companies to invest their policy reserves in the state. Campbell's administration also stopped the contract lease system for prisoners and implemented more humane treatment. Under his administration the legislature even passed a law taxing the intangible assets of corporations, thereby doubling the value of assets on the tax roll. Although he failed in his effort to enact an income tax, Governor Campbell's efforts led to the only major increase in state revenue before oil began to play a major role in the state's economy.

The more conservative Oscar Branch Colquitt (1911–15) continued some of the progressive reforms, such as regulation of child labor, factory safety standards, women's work hours, and the state's first workers' compensation law, when he was elected in 1910. But, unlike Campbell, he was against prohibition and that, along with his pro-German sentiments as World War I approached, alienated many Democrats. Ultimately, Governor Colquitt had to spend most of his time dealing with two problems. One, the tax system, was chronic. As the progressive governors increased spending on the state's institutions, it became apparent that the Texas did not have a broad enough tax base. Colquitt had inherited a $1 million debt from Campbell and, although he had campaigned on the basis of lowering taxes, he soon had to increase them to pay for growth in public education, prisons, and bureaucracies.

The second problem related to the disturbances along the Rio Grande border resulting from economic chaos and revolution in Mexico. Increased numbers of Mexican refugees had been arriving for some time, and events such as the so-called Garza War of 1891, in which journalist Catarino E. Garza became a folk hero by using a base in Texas to launch a rebellion against Mexican President Porfirio Díaz, did nothing to calm the furor. Governor Hogg had called for assistance from the U.S. Army and had sent a small Texas Ranger force to deal with the matter. Garza finally slipped away into exile in Central America, leaving his followers to return to their South Texas and northern Mexican *ranchos*.

Colquitt never felt that the federal government did enough to protect Texas citizens or to keep Mexican insurgents from using Texas as a safe haven to arm themselves and plan their assaults. He sent the Texas National Guard to join the small Ranger force in an effort to maintain control, but the problem flared into open warfare when U.S. troops invaded northern Mexico on at least two different occasions. These incidents resulted in long-standing disputes and hard feelings between the Anglos and Mexicans in South Texas.

Fergusonism and Texas on the World Stage

The "farmer's friend," James "Pa" Ferguson was a self-made man who aimed his message at the long-suffering rural population of the state. Having been born to a central Texas farm family and found his early employment in the fields and work gangs of backcountry Texas, he understood the problems of country folk. Having moved up in life by combining a law practice with real estate and banking, he understood the needs of an evolving economy. Ferguson and his wife Miriam ("Ma"), who became the first woman governor of the state, despite their shortcomings tended to represent the modern ideals of fair government and greater economic opportunity for most Texans.

Ferguson's Rise to Power

In shunning prohibition as a rallying cry, James E. Ferguson did not give up the ability to excite voters, for he focused on what he considered to be a greater societal ill and, at the same time, a greater source of support in a state where the political system was still dominated by rural voters. Farm tenancy had occupied the attention of academics and agricultural journals for a number of years, but it had been ignored by state and national governments, despite the organization of the Land Renters' Union of North America in Waco in 1911. Rising land prices and high interest rates made it difficult for tenants to become landowners and move up the economic ladder, and their children toiled in the fields rather than attend school, dooming them to the same fate. "There is something rotten in Texas when over 50 per cent of our farm families are homeless renters," the *Houston Chronicle* editorialized in 1912. The number was 10 percent higher in the state's richest cotton growing area, the Blackland Prairie, where Ferguson grew up. "One of these days" the editor continued, "this issue is going to fly up and hit our lawmakers slap in the face; they'll know they have met it."

The Temple banker would ensure that they would meet it. Ferguson knew the plight of the tenant farmers, although his bank was apparently no more forgiving of their debts than his competition; as one who had worked in the fields himself as a young boy, he understood the hardships and despair of such a life. Although he had studied for a time at Salado College and later passed the bar, his campaign persona belied that heritage, especially when he lapsed into the dialect that his wife, Miriam, the daughter of a well-to-do Bell County farmer, called "country talk."

And he was good at it, an orator who purposely maligned his opponents with a unique mix of bad grammar, acerbity, libel, and wit: "He spoke the language of the corn rows and the vernacular of the country stores," a veteran Austin newspaper editor recalled. He called himself "Farmer Jim" and said he spoke for the "boys at the forks of the creek." His record of opposing local option prohibition in Bell County quickly brought him to the attention of the brewing interests. Like Jim Hogg before him, he co-opted some radical proposals, such as limiting the amount of rent that a landowner could charge a tenant.

Ferguson's second major campaign issue targeted what he considered to be the next most difficult problem that the state faced: a poor educational system that ranked thirty-eighth nationally and lagged in such categories as teacher salaries, spending per student, length of school year, and percentage of school-age children in school. His desire to improve the schools stemmed, again, from his own rural heritage as well as an understanding of his constituency and a conviction that education was one of the skills that could most quickly improve people's lives. In his campaign announcement, he declared that Texans should "buy all the education that we can pay for," beginning with "the little schoolhouse on the country road." Although he also talked about running a "business administration" in Austin, he spent most of his time campaigning in poorer agricultural districts, where he made more than 90 percent of his speeches.

Ferguson used homey props like a gourd and a wooden water bucket in his appearances, and relentlessly attacked the prohibitionist candidate, Thomas H. Ball. Ball was an experienced candidate. He had served in Congress, practiced law in Houston, and seemed the early favorite to win the race. Even veteran observers such as Colonel House felt that he would be the next governor. He fought back as best he could, but his schedule was leisurely compared to Ferguson's, and he could not excite a crowd as "Farmer Jim" could. He accused Ferguson of being under the influence of the Catholic church because he had received the endorsement of a priest in Temple. He quoted the banker as saying that "My pocket book is my principles" and suggested that his dealings with farm clients then belied his campaign on behalf of tenants now. But after hearing Ferguson at a campaign stop in Denton, one observer warned, "his cunning and knowledge of the class to which he is appealing will render him a formidable opponent for Col. Ball."

Even the endorsement of President Wilson and Secretary of State William Jennings Bryan could not save Ball. He did not speak the language of the majority of rural voters who cared more about their economic situation than about prohibition. Also, the brewing interests backed Ferguson with a well-financed campaign to reach voters in urban areas, South Texas, and the German district of Central Texas, claiming that prohibition diverted attention from the state's real problems. Ferguson handily defeated Ball with more than 55 percent of the vote, and his charismatic personality and his "vest-pocket vote" of thousands of tenants, small farmers, and laborers would flavor Texas politics for the next two and a half decades.

Ferguson's first term was relatively harmonious. He fulfilled his campaign pledge by getting a farm tenant bill through the legislature, but it was soon declared unconstitutional. He also followed up on his other main platform pledge with continued educational reform, increased appropriations for higher education, and the creation of a State Department of Forestry.

Trouble on the Border

There were early rumors of malfeasance on Ferguson's part, but they took a back seat to the continuing disturbances on the border. Reports from South Texas noted an increase in raiding as early as January 1915, but local authorities continued to see the raids as nothing more than "bandit activity" until officials arrested one of the insurrection organizers and discovered the *Plan de San Diego,* a revolutionary charter that called for Hispanics on both sides of the border to rally in a combined revolution and race war. Their goal was to seize the territory that Mexico had lost to the United States in 1848 and to establish an independent republic. The South Texas area was fertile ground for such a movement because it had absorbed literally thousands of Mexican immigrants in the preceding decade as well as an influx of Midwesterners who engaged in citrus farming, bringing about a wrenching transition from a pastoral, ranching economy to commercial agriculture. A way of life had changed, and many Tejanos were displaced in the process, sometimes now working for wages on property that they or their family had once owned. This tragedy was complicated by the revolution in Mexico and World War I, which had begun in Europe in August 1914, and included the threat of German activity in a disrupted Mexico.

The sporadic raids increased in July, and a number of Americans were killed in both Texas and Mexico. Ferguson sent the entire Texas Ranger force to the valley and called for additional U.S. troops. There were probably no more than fifteen or twenty Regular Rangers on the border, but they served as leaders, role models, and participants in the events that followed, supplemented by Ferguson's patronage appointment of many "Special" Rangers, probably including most of the local law enforcement officers. The raids peaked on August 8 when sixty Mexicans carrying a red flag emblazoned with the slogan *"Igualdad e Independencia"* ("Equality and Independence") attacked Las Norias Division of the King Ranch. The Rangers and local law enforcement officials immediately retaliated with a "systematic manhunt," brutally killing more than 100 Mexicans and perhaps as many as 300 in the process. Ferguson called out the Texas National Guard the following year to supplement federal forces under General John J. Pershing, who ultimately invaded Mexico in an effort to capture Pancho Villa, the Mexican rebel leader who had raided Columbus, New Mexico, on March 9, 1916. Virtually the entire combat-ready American army, almost 50,000 troops, was assigned to the border. As the Mexican Revolution drew to a close, and the United States recognized the Carranza government, the raids came to an end. This suggests, of course, that the raiding was directly related to the situation in Mexico, but the raiders would not have been as successful if conditions in South Texas had not been ripe.

These were tragic years on the border, with much of the Angelo community traumatized by the raiders and the Mexican American community brutalized by the lawless Rangers, Special Rangers, local officials, and vigilante groups who were ill prepared for the overwhelming situation they faced. This reign of terror on the Rio Grande came to an end in 1919, when both a U.S. Senate investigating committee and a legislative committee led by Brownsville representative J. T. Canales documented so many atrocities committed by the Rangers—some sources claim that as many as 5,000 Mexicans had been murdered—that the force was reorganized, or "purified," to use Canales's word, and reduced to four regular companies of seventeen men each.

Ferguson's Downfall

By contrast, Ferguson's escalating conflict with the University of Texas during his second term might seem trivial, but surprisingly, it, rather than the bloodbath in the valley, led to his impeachment and conviction. As early as 1915 Ferguson had disagreed with acting university president William J. Battle over the university's budget and had accused the startled scholar of duplicity. Battle, of course, was appalled by the governor's charges and resented his micromanagement. When the university's board of regents selected Robert E. Vinson, president of the Austin Presbyterian Theological Seminary, as the new president of the university without consulting the governor, who was courting his own candidate, Ferguson was further angered and determined to oust the university "clique." That summer he inserted a clause in the Democratic Party platform calling for each item in the university budget to be listed separately.

The evolving conflict probably could have been prevented had Ferguson and Battle managed to overcome the initial problem, but it would have been difficult to find two more opposite personalities. Battle was a slender, balding professor of Greek, Ferguson a rough-and-tumble politician who had far more in common with the masses who had elected him than he did with a Harvard-educated classicist. Perhaps Ferguson even harbored an inferiority complex similar to the one President Lyndon Johnson felt regarding the Ivy League graduates in the Kennedy administration. "I knew Battle for perhaps fifteen of his latter years," historian Joe B. Frantz later recalled, "and he was the essence of politeness. But I could never feel quite comfortable in his presence, as if he were measuring me. Jim Ferguson must have felt the same way."

Despite the increasing suspicions of his own financial malfeasance, Ferguson won reelection in 1916 over a lackluster but surprisingly strong candidate, Charles H. Morris of Winnsboro, and then stepped up his charges against the university, demanding the immediate dismissal of six professors whom he accused of forming an "oligarchy." To the board of regents he described the faculty as "tenants at will," and, in answer to a question about why the president of the university and the designated faculty members should be fired, he replied, "I don't have to give any reasons, I am Governor of the State of Texas."

The university was ably defended by a group of ex-students led by forty-three-year-old Will C. Hogg of Houston, son of the former governor and a member of the board of regents. Calling Ferguson a "pothouse politician," he and other ex-students began to gather information about the governor's finances and conduct in office. Others, whom Ferguson had spurned, ignored, or defeated, joined in the fight. The prohibitionists had not forgotten about the way he had embarrassed Colonel Ball, and the Texas Equal Suffrage Association, led by Minnie Fisher Cunningham, and women's clubs all over the state joined in because Ferguson was a staunch opponent of women's suffrage.

But the governor was a formidable opponent. He knew that a legislative committee was looking into his financial affairs, so he began to put them in order. Needing more than $150,000 to repay overdrafts to his old Temple bank, he approached friends in the brewing industry and asked for a loan. Then he launched his attack, calling the university's board of regents to his office on May 28, 1917, to inform them that he was going to veto the university's entire appropriation.

Then, on July 27, the Travis County grand jury indicted Ferguson and some of his aides on charges of embezzlement and misuse of public funds. The Speaker of the House issued what was surely an illegal call for a special session of the legislature to consider charges against the governor, but Ferguson legitimized it by issuing a call himself the day before the legislators got to Austin. Using information gathered by a special committee during the regular session and the grand jury, former attorney general Crane, as special counsel, led the legislature in listing twenty-one charges against Ferguson. Ferguson defended himself for more than two hours before the Senate and wrote an open letter to the public, but the Senate convicted him on ten of the charges, seven of which dealt with his finances. Ferguson resigned rather than submit to impeachment, but the Senate rendered its decision anyway, removing him from office and banning him from holding any future state offices. Ferguson's arrogance in office thoroughly provoked the growing urban, industrial, educated, and more progressive segment of the population. The trends that would shift the residual political power of agrarians to the urban dwellers were already in evidence by 1917. Thus did thirty-nine-year-old William P. Hobby, former journalist and editor from Houston, become governor of Texas on August 25.

"Before the time of Ferguson," wrote the political scientist V. O. Key, Jr., in *Southern Politics*, "elections were contested on issues that held deep meaning for the people of Texas. How the state was to protect its citizens from organizations of wealth, what the state was to undertake by way of public services for its citizens, for what citizens these services were intended, and who should pay the tax bill—these are ultimately the great concerns of democratic government, second only to maintenance of the democratic processes themselves in their importance to the citizenry." After Ferguson, and continuing into the late 1930s, the issue changed to "Fergusonism."

World War I Brings Change and Reform

Although Europe had gone to war in the summer of 1914, Texans initially saw no reason for the United States to get involved. The state was divided over President Wilson's initial efforts to prepare the nation for possible entry into the war, and many Texans agreed with the *Dallas Morning News* that the state's large German population bore at least a portion of the blame. That conviction intensified in March 1917 with the revelations in the infamous Zimmerman telegram. Alfred Zimmerman, the German foreign secretary, had instructed the German minister in Mexico City that, in the event of war with the United States, the minister should propose an alliance between Germany and Mexico that, if successful, would regain for Mexico all its lost territory in Texas and the Southwest. The British had intercepted the message and given it to Wilson. Coming, as it did, on the heels of the *San Diego* insurrection in South Texas, many Texans interpreted the telegram as confirmation that Mexico had inspired the raids, and it solidified the president's support across the country. Less than a month later, President Wilson called on the United States to enter the war to make the world "safe for democracy."

Almost a million Texans registered for the draft, including 449 women who served as nurses; 197,789 men actually served, and approximately 25 percent of these were African American. More than 5,000 Texans died in the conflict, many as the result of the Spanish influenza epidemic in 1918, and many more were injured. Most of the Texas troops trained at four large camps that the federal government established at Fort Worth, Houston, Waco, and San Antonio. But there were many other training sites in the state as well, such as a basic flight instruction school at the University of Texas. The mild climate and vast amounts of open space also led the government to establish other training facilities for fledgling aviators, the primary one at Kelly Field in San Antonio. Randolph Field, constructed in San Antonio in 1928, became "The West Point of the Air."

On the home front, the legislature acted to help those in the service by compensating them for economic losses while on active duty and forbidding the sale of a serviceman's property until one year after he had been discharged. Another act eliminated the poll tax for servicemen, and the Texas Council of Defense was organized to oversee the efforts of the more than 15,000 county and community defense councils. Unfortunately, some of them also became vigilante groups, harassing people with German names, especially if they refused to purchase war bonds or displayed pictures of the Kaiser in their home. The Socialist newspaper, *The Rebel*, which had attained a circulation of 23,000, was also shut down by government order. Using authority granted by the Hobby Loyalty Law of May 1917, Governor Hobby appointed almost 1,000 Special Rangers, whose primary duty, it seemed, was to insure Hobby's election in 1918.

Although welcome for many reasons, the vast infusion of federal resources also had an adverse effect in that it set off an inflationary spiral that greatly outpaced incomes and more than doubled the cost of some of the new state programs, such as the improved school system. The legislature also acted to limit the negative effects of the large military installations on communities—bars and prostitution—but did nothing to stem the racial tensions that existed. In Huntsville a white mob killed an African American man and six members of his family when he was accused of evading the draft, but an even worse incident occurred in Houston in 1917. The federal government had brought in the Third Battalion of the African American Twenty-fourth U.S. Infantry to guard two military installations that had been established near the newly opened Houston Ship Channel. On August 23, following a summer of growing tensions, a riot broke out with more than 100 armed and mutinous African American soldiers marching on the Fourth Ward police station. Fifteen whites, including five policemen, died, and eleven others were seriously wounded. Four African American soldiers also died, two accidentally shot by their own men. The army quickly removed the troopers to New Mexico, where, under wartime conditions, the military courts handed down harsh punishments: Nineteen soldiers were hanged and sixty-three sentenced to life in prison.

The war revived prohibition efforts in Texas. Prohibitionists called for a ban on alcohol within ten miles of military bases or schools and attacked its manufacture as wasteful in a time of war, its brewers as agents of the German Kaiser, and its effect on military personnel as unhealthy. When Secretary of War Newton D. Baker let it be known that the government would continue to send large numbers of soldiers to Texas bases if they insured "conditions of cleanliness and wholesomeness" nearby, Hobby submitted these new rules to a special session of the legislature in February 1918. With a majority in both houses of the legislature, the drys first approved a bill relating to military bases, then ratified the prohibition amendment (the Eighteenth Amendment) to the U.S. Constitution, which went into effect in 1919. From the depths of disappointment over the Ferguson victory in 1914, the drys had now put the finishing touches on nationwide prohibition.

Finally, the legislature amended the election law to require a runoff in primaries if no candidate received a majority and to extend the right to vote in primaries to women. The drafting of large numbers of men for World War I helped the women's suffrage movement nationwide. With so many men in the military, numerous home-front jobs opened up for women, and their new wartime responsibilities gave the movement impetus, even eliciting President Wilson's less than ardent support. After the legislature extended women the right to vote in primaries, Annie Webb Blanton was elected state superintendent of education, but women would have to wait until the Nineteenth Amendment to the Constitution was ratified, in 1920, before they could vote in the general election.

The enthusiasm from that special session carried Hobby through the 1918 gubernatorial election. Despite his impeachment and conviction, "Farmer Jim" Ferguson was on the ballot. His allies on the party's executive committee allowed him to run and he was still able to inspire an audience of farmers. After a slow start, however, Hobby proved to be an able campaigner, and his run took on the aspects of a patriotic rally. With prohibitionists and suffragists strongly behind him, he received a total of 461,479 votes to Ferguson's 217,012. No runoff was necessary.

The war came to a close a couple of months later, on November 11, when the Allies and the Germans signed the armistice. It had brought a measure of prosperity to Texas, as cotton production soared, but it had also brought a growing cultural conformity as the drive to unite a heterogeneous population for war continued long after the peace. The legislature made it a crime to criticize the U.S. government, the flag, the war effort, or soldiers' uniforms, and required that schools teach patriotism, fly the American flag, and teach all classes except foreign language classes in English. In 1919 Hobby vetoed the appropriation for the German department at the University of Texas, and most high schools dropped the language from their curriculum. The 1917 Russian Revolution had called the public's attention to what many perceived as a growing Bolshevik threat, and many Texans believed that union and civil rights activists were evidence of the menace at home. Oil producers rumored that a 1917–18 oilfield workers strike in Louisiana and Texas was inspired by the Industrial Workers of the World, and a violent and prolonged dock strike in Galveston led Governor Hobby to place the city under martial law. Lynchings and intimidation of African Americans continued as well; there was a race riot in Longview and an official of the National Association for the Advancement of Colored People (NAACP) was beaten by a white mob in Austin during what became known nationwide as the "red summer" of 1919.

By 1920, the population shift from rural to urban areas was becoming apparent. Meanwhile, the economic difficulties of farmers were temporarily obscured by two years of abundant crops that helped make up for the falling postwar prices. Governor Hobby would have encouraged the urban growth and economy but declined to do so in the face of a reluctant legislature and a "leave well enough alone" public attitude.

But that was not because the state did not have problems. Lynching was on the decline but still occurring from time to time, and economic refugees were arriving from Mexico in ever-increasing numbers, with perhaps as many as 126,811 settling in Texas between 1910 and 1920. The burgeoning oil and gas industry had spawned some swindlers and the usual lawlessness that, on occasion, required the intervention of the Texas Rangers and, on at least one occasion, the Texas National Guard; the cause of most of the crime, however, was undoubtedly the Volstead Act of 1919, which implemented the new prohibition amendment.

The decade of the 1920s soon became known throughout the nation as the Jazz Age, which was defined by the rise of cities, the decline of religion (coupled with the teaching of evolution), bootleggers and speakeasies, the growth of the Socialist Party and the "red scare," increased European immigration, and the advent of the "New Woman." And perhaps the prototypical Jazz Age flapper was Gordon Conway, born in Cleburne and reared in Dallas. An extremely productive commercial graphic artist and costume designer for stage and film in New York, London, and Paris, Conway produced paintings and drawings of the New Woman for *Vogue, Vanity Fair, Harper's Bazaar,* and many other publications, including her hometown newspapers, from World War I into the Depression. Conway's New Woman was, in many ways, a parody of New York society women involved in charity work, but the new type caught on. The New Woman and the flapper became icons of the 1920s.

The Elements of Jazz

From the hard-scrabble cultures of the cotton farms and lumber mills of East and Central Texas came one of the truly American forms of music, jazz, which, because of its varied folk roots, has been called a true expression of democracy. One strand of jazz can be traced to Texarkana in the 1880s, when Scott Joplin, a young son of a former slave, learned music from a German teacher and began to perform in medicine shows and vaudeville. Joplin, composer and pianist, known as the "father of ragtime," developed his musical talent in the saloons and brothels of Saint Louis, Missouri, and named his best-known composition, the "Maple Leaf Rag," after an employer, the Maple Leaf Club in Sedalia, Missouri. "Maple Leaf Rag" included some of the syncopated rhythms and structure that would later be incorporated into jazz. Joplin's music was featured in the soundtrack of the 1973 Hollywood movie *The Sting,* and he was posthumously awarded a Pulitzer Prize in 1976 for *Treemonisha,* the first grand opera by an African American. Another ragtime composer from Texas, Euday L. Bowman of Fort Worth, composed "Twelfth Street Rag" sometime around 1915, which trumpeter Louis Armstrong made famous with his 1927 recording. And Eddie Durham of San Marcos, who played in a number of regional bands during the 1920s before moving on to Kansas City and New York City, perhaps contributed as much to jazz history as any other Texas musician.

A second strand of jazz is the blues, which can be traced to East Texas as early as 1890 and is represented by two of its most famous practitioners, Blind Lemon

Jefferson (1897–1929) and Huddie "Leadbelly" Ledbetter (1888–1949), who were active in the 1920s and actually played together for a while in the Deep Ellum district of Dallas. A third strand was "barrelhouse-style piano," perhaps better known as boogie-woogie, which probably came out of the lumber camps of East Texas. Itinerant musicians and traveling bands spread these various musical styles along the railroad tracks, in the prisons, and in the communities. Because of the rural nature of the state, many of these performers and composers moved to Kansas City, where they were among the first generation to compose, perform, and record jazz.

Another icon of the Jazz Age was the lawlessness accompanying the oil boom that gained nationwide publicity as the veterans returned from World War I. The oil boom only hastened the migration from rural to urban areas, and Texans were quick to display the decline of moral values that was supposedly going on throughout the nation. Less than a year after passage of prohibition, bootlegging was so widespread in Texas that a still with a 130-gallon capacity was found on the Austin-area farm of U.S. Senator Morris Sheppard, the author of the Eighteenth Amendment.

Reaction to Reform: The Ku Klux Klan

The Achilles' heel of the Progressive movement—indeed, of virtually all political movements of the day—was racism. During the early part of the twentieth century the rights that African Americans had gained after the Civil War were systematically taken away. Shocked by the near-success of the Populist Party coalition of poor African American and white farmers, the Bourbon Democrats had embarked upon a campaign to divide the poor by claiming that African Americans were inherently inferior and a threat to society. Their goal was to segregate African Americans into a separate society, divided by law and custom and governed by leaders for whom they could not vote. They largely succeeded.

There were 670,722 African Americans in Texas by 1900, 854,964 by 1930, most of them living in rural areas and working as tenants and farm laborers. But others had attempted to escape the racial and economic conditions of rural life by moving out of the state—to northern cities and to Louisiana and Oklahoma—or to Texas cities such as Houston and Dallas. The urban African American population increased from 19 percent in 1900 to 32 percent in 1930; the number of African American males employed in nonagricultural jobs increased from 57,000 to almost 115,000 during that same period, most still in manual labor or servant jobs. Ministers and teachers made up most of a small African American bourgeoisie that also consisted of doctors, dentists, lawyers, and undertakers. There were more than 1,700 African American–owned retail stores in the state in 1929, most of them mom-and-pop operations such as grocery stores, drugstores, and restaurants. Hobart Taylor, Sr., of Houston, who invested in insurance and taxicabs, may have been the first African American millionaire in the state. Prairie View A&M offered courses for African Americans at both the high school and college level, with emphasis on technical, agricultural, and educational training.

The Ku Klux Klan reached a membership of approximately 90,000 in Texas during the 1920s. Here, the Klan is shown parading in Beaumont on November 10, 1922. (*Tyrrell Historical Library, Beaumont, Texas*)

The first step toward racial segregation had occurred when the Redeemers won control of the state government in 1876. The second step was African American disenfranchisement, accomplished by the Terrell election laws. When the Supreme Court, in *Nixon v. Herndon* (1927), agreed that all-white primaries violated the Fourteenth Amendment, Texas responded by defining political parties as private organizations that could select their own qualified voters. The court agreed, and African Americans remained effectively shut out of the electoral process.

Next came the segregation of public facilities. Passenger trains had been segregated by race as early as 1891. In 1910 and 1911 the legislature required the establishment of separate waiting rooms in railroad stations and separate drinking fountains and restrooms in public facilities. Several cities adopted residential segregation laws after 1910, but the U.S. Supreme Court invalidated them. Cities got around the Court by resorting to zoning regulations. That led to a degradation of health and recreational services and city services such as utilities, paving, and police protection in the African American areas. By the 1930s, African Americans could no longer attend sports or cultural events, eat at restaurants, or stay in hotels unless those facilities provided separate accommodations. Although these laws were not passed with the Mexican population in mind, community cultural mores often denied Mexicans many services and opportunities.

Where laws did not sufficiently enforce segregation, vigilante action often did. The Ku Klux Klan of the 1920s was a relic of Reconstruction. William Joseph Simmons, an ex-Methodist minister near Atlanta, Georgia, reorganized the Klan in 1915 as an antidote to what he perceived as moral deterioration and a lack of patriotism. He sent field representatives (kleagles) to organize new chapters (klaverns) throughout the nation and by 1922 the Klan had more than 700,000 members, by 1925 perhaps as many as 5 million. Its militant fundamentalism and anti-Catholicism appealed to many in the South and the Midwest, including progressive reformers in the urban areas, where the new middle class, usually with rural values still intact, identified with the Klan's goals. With issues such as prohibition foremost in society, the Klan attracted progressive reformers who did not object to enforcing a moral code so long as it was theirs. Thomas B. Love of Dallas, who had supported Wilson for the presidency, characterized the Klan as "made up almost wholly of misled and misguided good people who are on the moral side of moral questions and on the progressive side of economic questions" who would quickly grow tired of the effort. The Klan moved into Texas in 1920.

The Klan gained many adherents in North, East, and Central Texas. Membership was not nearly so high in heavily Catholic South Texas. Despite the fact that the Klan resorted to such extralegal practices as flogging, tar-and-feathering, and branding to enforce its will (there were more than fifty cases of Klan violence during 1921 alone), many prominent citizens, including Governor Neff, refused to speak out against it. With oil boomtowns bursting out of control on occasion and the Mexican Revolution troubles on the border, the Klan claimed that unparalleled lawlessness forced it to act, and Governor Neff seemed to agree. By playing on fears aroused by race riots, labor disruptions, and rumors of Bolshevik influence, the "invisible empire" gained many members; by 1922 these members included a sympathetic U.S. Senator, Earle B. Mayfield, who triumphed over "Farmer Jim" Ferguson in a bitter contest.

With prohibition now law, the Klan itself became the main issue in Texas politics during the early 1920s, as major newspapers in Dallas, Houston, and El Paso attacked it. As Imperial Wizard of the Klan, Hiram W. Evans of Dallas instituted a policy of political action rather than violence and intimidation. The Klan denied responsibility for any of the lynchings that took place during these years, but it is likely that the emotionalism and moral passion of its rallies incited them, at the very least. Miriam Ferguson's victory in the 1924 governor's race over the Klan-backed candidate for governor, Felix D. Robertson of Dallas—the choice between "a bonnet or a hood"—marked the end of significant Klan influence in Texas politics.

The Fergusons Return

The "business progressivism" of Governors Hobby and Neff had provided Texans with a respite from "Fergusonism," but Miriam Ferguson signaled a return to the populism of her husband. Miriam Ferguson won the election because the cult of personality continued to dominate the Democratic Party in 1924, and the dominant personality of the last decade had been her husband, "Farmer Jim" Ferguson. Ferguson had continued to publish his newspaper, *Ferguson's Forum,* ever

Miriam Ferguson, the first woman to be elected governor of Texas, delivering her inaugural address in the House chamber on January 20, 1925. *(The Institute of Texan Cultures at University of Texas, San Antonio)*

since his impeachment, claiming that the major newspapers had "submarined the truth." Still able to energize a rural audience, he had run for president on the American Party ticket in 1920 and for senator in 1922. Although he clearly disagreed with the Klan on the issue of prohibition, the 1922 election may have been the first time that he ran afoul of the organization. Unable to get his name on the Democratic primary ballot in 1924, he came up with the ruse of running his wife, Miriam, and the main issues of the campaign became prohibition and the Klan itself in another insulting, mud-slinging contest. He stumped the state on behalf of his wife, proclaiming "two governors for the price of one" and referring to Imperial Wizard Evans as the "Grand Gizzard." Again, the prohibition candidate was no match for the crafty veteran, and Miriam Ferguson won the primary runoff by almost 100,000 votes.

Once in office, and with her husband at her side, Mrs. Ferguson struck back at the Klan, securing passage of a law that prohibited the wearing of masks in public. She vetoed a number of line items in the University of Texas appropriation and granted more than 2,000 paroles, pardons, and extensions, many of which went to prohibition violators. She lamented the fact that most of those convicted of such violations were poor whereas the wealthy continued to have access to drink in their private clubs and she offered a $500 reward for the arrest and conviction of any liquor-law violator who had property worth more than $5,000. But her term was also tainted by charges of graft and scandal. "Pa," it seems, acted as attorney for many of the successful pardons that she granted and saw to it that state contracts for school textbooks and highway construction were awarded to those who bought ads in the *Ferguson Forum*. A final irony may have been the fact that most people who supported the vote for women expected them to clean up corruption in politics, but Miriam Ferguson's election put her cunning and scandal-plagued husband back in power. Attorney General Dan Moody successfully brought suit to cancel a number of highway contracts that had been awarded to Ferguson friends and allies.

Those charges proved to be the basis of Moody's successful campaign against Miriam Ferguson in 1926. The main issue was "Fergusonism" and corruption, and the self-styled liberals in the Democratic Party rallied to Moody's reform banner. Moody was a personable, thirty-two-year-old who had successively been elected to office as the Williamson County attorney, district attorney of the Twenty-sixth Judicial District, and attorney general. With his business-progressive point of view, he set about reorganizing several government departments. He led an ostensibly prosperous and increasingly urban state for four years as it sank, along with the nation, into the worst depression that the country has ever known. Few noticed that 1929, the same year that the New York stock market crashed, was also the first year in which the value of crude oil production in Texas ($322,520,000) exceeded the value of the cotton crop ($315,200,000).

Conclusion

In 1929, Texans seemed about to enjoy the rewards of more than two decades of reform and progress. Farming and ranching had certainly suffered during the 1920s, but that was largely disguised by the booming economy nationwide and the growing influence of oil on the state's economy. Prohibition was now a national law, thanks, in part, to platoons of righteous women voters. The "business progressives" had apparently beaten back the Fergusons, and the state seemed to be coming of age in other ways. Progressive historians at the University of Texas led the way in investigating the state's past with the founding of the *Southwestern Historical Quarterly* in 1897. George Pierce Garrison began teaching the first course in Texas history that year, and two and a half decades later his protégé, Eugene C. Barker, published his classic biography of Stephen F. Austin. At the same time, Paris-trained Dallas artist Frank Reaugh was leading his students on summer expeditions into West Texas and extolling the virtues of interpreting the Texas landscape. Most Texans were outraged at the publication of Dorothy Scarborough's novel, *The Wind* (1925), because of its haunting and inhospitable portrait of West Texas. They took pride, however, in the work of one of the state's most distinguished writers of fiction, Katherine Anne Porter, who grew up in Kyle and San Antonio, but whose Texas-based short stories gained her international fame.

SUGGESTED READINGS

Useful general studies of the first three decades of the century include Lewis L. Gould, *Progressives and Prohibitionists: Texas Democrats in the Wilson Era* (1992); Walter L. Buenger's *The Path to a Modern South: Northeast Texas Between Reconstruction and the Great Depression* (2001); and Seth S. McKay and Odie B. Faulk, *Texas After Spindletop* (1965).

The Texas Economy
Works on economic history include Donald E. Green, *Land of the Underground Rain: Irrigation on the Texas High Plains, 1910–1970* (1973), and Diana Davids Olien and Roger M. Olien, *Oil in Texas: The Gusher Age, 1895–1945* (2002).

The Climate for Reform
A useful work on politics and reform is Evan Anders, *Boss Rule in South Texas: The Progressive Era* (1982). The best work on the Galveston storm of 1900 is Erik Larson, *Isaac's Storm: A Man, a Time, and the Deadliest Hurricane in History* (2000). Excellent works on urban history include David G. McComb, *Galveston, A History* (1986); McComb, *Houston: A History* (1986); David C. Humphrey, *Austin, an Illustrated History* (1985); and Patricia Everidge Hill, *Dallas: The Making of a Modern City* (1996).

Ferguson and Texas on the World Stage
Norman D. Brown, *Hood, Bonnet, and Little Brown Jug: Texas Politics, 1921–1928* (1984) contains an excellent discussion of much of the Ferguson era. For information on the border troubles, see Don M. Coerver and Linda B. Hall, *Texas and the Mexican Revolution: A Study in State and National Border Policy, 1910–1920* (1984), and David Montejano, *Anglos and Mexicans in the Making of Texas, 1836–1986* (1987). Works on women and minorities include Judith N. McArthur, *Creating the New Woman: The Rise of Southern Women's Progressive Culture in Texas, 1893–1918* (1998); Alwyn Barr, *Black Texans: A History of African Americans in Texas, 1528–1995* (1996); and Arnoldo De León, *Mexican Americans in Texas: A Brief History,* 2nd ed. (1999). For information on the Texas Rangers, see Robert M. Utley, *Lone Star Justice: The First Century of the Texas Rangers* (2002). Biographical essays on Edward M. House, Morris Sheppard, John Nance Garner, Tom Connally, and Sam Rayburn are included in Kenneth E. Hendrickson, Jr. and Micael L. Collins, Eds., *Profiles in Power: Twentieth-Century Texans in Washington* (1993).

12

Depression and War, 1929–1945

Ⅰn 1929, my father was employed as a locomotive engineer," recalled Robert Ozment of the years just before the Great Depression struck. Ozment and his family lived in Temple, a Central Texas farming and railroad center. "We had a new Overland Whippet auto, were buying a home, had money in the bank, and plenty of food and clothing. By 1933 all this was gone except the Whippet. We were living in a rent-free house which bordered the Negro section of Temple. We often had little to eat but oatmeal, we were without electricity, and had few clothes. I remember this house well because it had no coverings on the splintery old floors. My one pair of shoes had to be saved for winter use, and during the summer my feet were constantly bandaged from the . . . splinters.

"I also remember the Whippet. We had no money for either gas or tires so it just sat in the shed. It became a kind of physical symbol of the times to me because, like some of the humans, it was waiting [for] a chance to go to work and did not understand why it could not. All it could do was to waste away its productive years waiting and hoping until the inexorable end should arrive. We sold it for five dollars in 1939 . . .

"I once asked my mother what had caused the depression they talked about so much. Considering the fact that neither we nor any of our family were farmers, her answer may seem a bit peculiar. She said: 'The bottom fell out of the cotton market.' To a person living in Bell County, it was just that simple: the bottom fell out of the cotton market. I was just old enough to remember the physical deprivations which my family suffered," he concluded, "but none of the psychological trauma."

1929	New York stock market crashes; LULAC founded
1930	East Texas oil field discovered; price of oil falls to 8 cents per barrel
1931	Price of cotton falls to 5 cents per pound
1933	Eighteenth Amendment is repealed
1935	Texas repeals its prohibition law
1936	Texas Centennial
1937	Soil Conservation Service recorded 72 dust storms on the plains
1938	U.S. Congressman Martin Dies becomes the first chair of the House Un-American Activities Committee
1941	Japanese attack Pearl Harbor, U.S. enters World War II
1942	Bracero program adopted
1943	"Big Inch" pipeline completed
1944	"Little Inch" pipeline completed; Texas's all-white primary held to be unconstitutional by the U.S. Supreme Court

In 1945, Texas emerged from World War II fully industrialized and one of the most rapidly growing urban areas in the nation. The two economic dynamos—oil and agriculture—continued to propel the state forward, and the federal government became even more important during the turbulent years from 1930 to 1945. During these years, Texas and the nation faced two of their greatest challenges—the Great Depression and World War II—and the state's inability to act forcefully to combat the ravages of the depression required the federal government to play an even more significant role than it had. But another force, almost as powerful as the economy, according to some, was the sense of Texas chauvinism and modernism that emerged in the midst of the Great Depression of the 1930s and was celebrated at the centennial of Texas independence in 1936. It was a chauvinism based on the state's colorful history and honed in the hard work on a thousand cotton fields, ranches, and oil fields.

As the presidential election of 1928 approached, many Texans reflected on the good economic times of the Roaring Twenties, when the state's population had increased by almost 25 percent, to more than 5.8 million and cotton, lumber, truck and citrus farming, livestock, and oil and gas fueled the economy, apparently more efficiently than ever. By 1929 the state was the world's leading supplier of crude oil, having produced more than 2 billion barrels, and the development of the Houston Ship Channel had made that city the state's busiest port. Electrical appliances, lights, radios, telephones, and plumbing facilities had greatly improved urban life, and several Texas cities—Dallas, Houston, and San Antonio—were among the most rapidly growing in the country. The number of automobiles, which facilitated the move to urban areas, increased to the point that Texans owned one car for every 4.3 residents. Such affluence led to talk of "Coolidge prosperity," after President Calvin Coolidge (1925–29), and the general feeling that the nation had created a permanent cornucopia.

The Great Depression

But the economy had a soft underbelly. Texas farmers, like those of other states, had suffered hard times throughout the seemingly prosperous decade. Farmers had not adjusted their production at the end of World War I and quickly accumulated surpluses that brought a sharp decline in prices in 1920–21. Instead of reducing production, they increased it. The number of Texas farms increased from 436,038 to 495,489, and the amount of cultivated land grew by 3.5 million acres, while at the same time, printed notices of sheriff's sales, business failures, and bankruptcies became characteristic of the farm country, and newspaper editors resorted to homilies—"many a family that has lost its car has found its soul. . . ."

Few people were aware of the nation's deeper economic problems. Inequitable distribution of wealth, with a mere 2 percent of the population controlling 28 percent of the wealth whereas the bottom 60 percent controlled only about 24 percent, was only one of the harbingers of the coming difficulties. But economic crisis was hardly on the minds of Texans as they went to the polls in 1928 to vote against a wet Catholic and for a continuation of the good times. The Democrats had nominated Governor Alfred E. Smith of New York, a Catholic and an antiprohibitionist, at their Houston convention, but Texans voted *en masse* for Herbert Hoover, the first Republican presidential candidate to carry the state.

The Stock Market Crash

Before Hoover had completed his first year in office, however, the failing economy grabbed the nation's attention in a spectacular way: The New York Stock Exchange crashed. The steady advance of the market, which had begun in the mid-1920s and encouraged many investors to speculate by purchasing stocks on margin (with borrowed money), came to an end in September, 1929, and only got worse throughout October. "Black Thursday," October 24, was bad, but the worst occurred on October 29, when 16 million shares of stock, more than ever before, changed hands and the *New York Times* industrial average dropped nearly forty

San Antonio bank depositors wait for access to their safety-deposit boxes at City-Central Bank and Trust on October 1, 1931, the first day they were allowed access to their boxes after the bank failed to open on September 28. The City-Central Bank and Trust was one of 298 U.S. banks that failed that month. (*The Institute of Texan Cultures at University of Texas, San Antonio*)

points. A coalition of New York bankers tried but could not stem the tide, and by November exchange listings had declined an average of 37.5 percent. Because relatively few of them owned stock, Texans felt insulated from the troubles of the market. They seemed to agree with the editor of the *Taylor Daily Press,* who said that his concern was "Jim Rural" and "Joe Normal," whom he expected would continue to do business as usual, and with the editor of the *Houston Post-Dispatch,* who suggested that "the changes in stock prices are purely an affair of and for stock speculators." Governor Moody finished his term in office without feeling the full force of the coming depression or taking any action to prepare for it.

Nor was the economy the chief concern of voters in the gubernatorial election of 1930. Citing his need to enter the private practice of law to pay his debts, Governor Moody declined to run for a third term, and Ross S. Sterling, a founder and former president of Humble Oil and Refining Company, carried the business-progressive mantel in the campaign. His primary opponent was former governor Miriam Ferguson, who filed after the state Supreme Court had refused to let her husband put his name on the ballot.

Sterling called for prison reform, better roads and labor conditions, and more support for education. His service as Moody's able chair of the State Highway Commission led him to champion a $300–$350 million bond issue for state highways. James Ferguson, who did most of the campaigning for his wife, initially did not take seriously the heavy-set Sterling, who had once been introduced to an audience as "your fat boy from Houston," and Miriam Ferguson led Sterling in the primary by more than 70,000 votes. But personalities came to the fore as she and Sterling met in the runoff. The added influence of former Governor Moody and other officials, who announced for Sterling and began making speeches on his behalf, pushed him to victory, and he won by almost 90,000 votes.

The Depression Deepens

The election was, however, a sideshow to the main event, as cotton prices continued to fall and unemployment soared. The Hoover administration offered little more than the appearance of action—an endless series of meetings, each of which seemed to culminate with hollow statements of confidence that "prosperity is just around the corner." The optimism continued into 1931, with the *Fort Worth Star-Telegram,* for example, claiming that Texans did not "know what hard times are," and pointing to increased construction, railroad traffic, and oil production, and stable cattle and poultry sales. Even as late as 1933, Jesse H. Jones, the Houston banker whom President Hoover had appointed to the board of the Reconstruction Finance Corporation, told a Dallas audience that, "The most important thing before the nation today is to balance the budget."

In Temple, meanwhile, the impact of the Wall Street crash came in 1930—sooner than anyone had expected—when the local banks began to lay off experienced employees. As early as January, 1930, labor union officers asked San Antonio officials to vote bonds to provide work for the growing number of unemployed construction workers, and in Houston a local news vendor reported that his business was up because people who "don't look like they have much more than the price of a newspaper in their pockets . . . are buying them now to read the want ads." New oil softened the blow in a few places such as Taylor and Kilgore, but in Midland oil prices crashed because of overproduction in the East Texas field, which led to declining leases and drilling and more unemployment. The population of Midland dropped by perhaps 1,000 between 1930 and 1932. Between Black Thursday and 1932, more than 5,000 banks failed and 100,000 businesses closed nationwide, and the national income was halved—from $80 billion to $40 billion.

By 1933 more than 7 percent of Texas families were on relief, compared to 10 percent nationally. The number in Texas increased to about 13 percent the following year. Some historians have suggested that rural Texans did not suffer as much as city dwellers because they had gardens and continued to raise much of their food. But, as the economy faltered, the average wage paid for the backbreaking labor of picking cotton dropped from $1.21 per 100 pounds in 1928 to 44 cents in 1931. By then farmers had other concerns as well. "I did not go to . . . [church tonight]," William G. DeLoach of Crosby County in the Texas Panhandle recorded in his diary in 1931. "I am afraid to go. That is[,] all of us go away at night. Some people are losing their canned goods. We have quite a lot of foods of different kinds canned up, can't afford to take a chance on some road tramp coming here and getting it, so I stayed home."

Family and friends initially rallied to help those who fell victim to unemployment, and when their resources were expended, private charities helped out. When charitable funds were depleted, only the local and state governments remained to help. Some cities established public works programs to offer temporary aid to the unemployed, but usually tried to limit it to local residents. Midland and other cities sent police officers to train stations to make sure that transients got back on the train. Houston, meanwhile, reserved relief for whites, denying it to African Americans and Mexican Americans. A typical "buy at home" campaign urged Austinites to "talk Austin, write about Austin, work for Austin, and live for Austin." School districts and retail merchant associations issued scrip when they ran out of money. Some school districts refused to employ single women and, on the assumption of only one breadwinner per family, fired married women if their spouse had a job. Finally, the depression became so severe that only the federal government stood between the country and complete collapse.

The Dust Bowl

Even if the depression did take longer to arrive in Texas than in other parts of the country, it was no less devastating. Conditions on the farm got even worse as a combination of poor land maintenance and a devastating drought created what became known as the Dust Bowl on the Great Plains. Growing numbers of enthusiastic young farmers had moved onto the plains since the turn of the century,

Dust storm rolls into Spearman, Hansford County, in April 1935. (*The Texas Collection, Baylor University, Waco, Texas*)

and in just a few years, through cattle raising and row-crop agriculture, they had destroyed most of the native grasses that held the dirt in place. Between 1925 and 1930, with the new gasoline tractors, entrepreneurs like the movie mogul Hickman Price, who in 1929 established a fifty-four-square-mile factory farm in Swisher County, plowed up the vegetation on millions of acres of the Southern Plains in what one writer has called "the great plow-up."

The rain stopped abruptly in late 1931, and one of the periodic droughts that plague the semiarid region set in and lasted through 1934. But this was not an ordinary drought. With almost 33 million acres of plains land bare and open to the characteristically high winds, the phenomenon known as the Dust Bowl began. The onset of a polar air mass that might, in an ordinary year, have produced common "sand blows" now incited "black blizzards" that were sometimes accompanied by fantastic displays of lightning. Atmospheric electricity lifted the windblown dirt as high as 7,000–8,000 feet—until it looked like a winter blizzard or a huge thunderstorm. In 1932 the Soil Conservation Service counted fourteen dust storms on the plains. That number increased to thirty-eight in 1933, twenty-two in 1934, forty in 1935, sixty-eight in 1936, and seventy-two in 1937, the worst year on record.

The storm of April 1935 was the worst. As it blew in on April 9, William De-Loach recorded that visibility fell to 200–300 yards. His family remained in the house for several days. On Sunday, while the rest of the family was at church and he sat reading, the worst of the storm hit: "One could hardly get breath," he wrote.

The well-known photographer Dorothea Lange made this photograph of a young cotton picker in South Texas in August 1936. *(Library of Congress, Prints & Photographs Division, FSA/OWI Collection, LC-USF34-009828-E)*

"I thought I would choke when I went to bed." Even in Austin, legislators and staff wore gauze face masks in the capital.

Thousands of tenants and sharecroppers, and even some landowners, gave up and left. Many joined the exodus to California, a trek that John Steinbeck made famous in his novel *The Grapes of Wrath* (1939). But a large number of the Dust Bowl migrants were not victims of drought, windstorm, and grasshoppers. A number of them were tenants who had been forced off the land by tractors and wage laborers; others had been replaced by Mexican laborers who had been immigrating northward in increasing numbers since the turn of the century and were willing to work for less. The net result was a reduction of almost 200,000 in the number of people living on farms in Texas between 1930 and 1940.

Even in the face of such tragedies, Governor Sterling apparently agreed with the Hoover administration that his first responsibility as governor was to reduce the state's expenses. He vetoed a number of bills passed by the forty-second legislature, usually because they did not provide taxes to cover their costs. Despite the fact that the legislature met for 131 days, little was done to assist in the state's crisis during what was characterized as a "do-nothing session." This pay-as-you-go approach was traditional in Texas, and the state constitution required it.

Chaos in the East Texas Oil Field

Sterling's greatest concerns were the state's two largest economic engines—oil and agriculture—and, ironically, overproduction was the problem in both cases. Overproduction of oil was a problem even before Sterling took office. By 1930, oil had been discovered all over Texas, and the new wells in the Yates field in West Texas were so productive that many industry experts began to warn of overproduction. Then, in October 1930, Columbus Marion (Dad) Joiner brought in the Daisy Bradford No. 3 near Kilgore and the boom was on. The East Texas field was even bigger than Spindletop. Within two years it boasted more than 10,000 producing wells, and the price of oil fell from a little over a dollar a barrel in 1930 to eight cents a barrel in 1931. In the peak year of 1933 the East Texas production reached 204,954,000 barrels of oil, more than the rest of the state combined.

The East Texas field was an anomaly for at least two reasons. The first was its sheer size. Within a few months of Joiner's discovery, successful wells had been drilled into this huge reservoir in five counties spread over 140,000 acres. Experts estimated that it contained about 5.5 billion barrels of oil, approximately one-third of the nation's then-known oil reserves.

The second anomaly—the absence of major oil companies—brought a new element into the industry. This field became known as "the promised land of independent producers and small royalty owners," and they, along with entrepreneurs, swindlers, prostitutes, hustlers of all kinds, gathered around the oil field workers in Kilgore, the center of most of the activity. When the wildcatters realized that they were not drilling in separate fields, as they had thought, but into one giant pool, the frenzy began in earnest. The rule of capture—the law governing the development of oil fields ever since a Pennsylvania Supreme Court decision in 1889—meant that the person who pumped the oil owned it, even if it had migrated from an adjoining lease. Landowners began to sell leases that were measured in feet rather than acres, and, ultimately, one city block in Kilgore contained forty-four wells. The massive overproduction soon forced the price of oil down, and kept it down, as the unusual circumstances of this particular field ensured that everyone would continue to drill and pump as fast as they could. No one would agree to limit production unless they all did.

Governor Sterling first suggested that the Railroad Commission act, under the authority granted by the legislature in 1917. But the problem was not easily resolved. Conservationists and the major oil companies were concerned that unrestrained production not only wasted natural resources but also threatened the very existence of the East Texas field by reducing the internal pressure that made the oil flow. The independent producers refused to stop pumping, because their survival was at stake. Most of them were operating on a shoestring or on borrowed money, and slowing down or stopping would have meant bankruptcy. Second, they suspected the motives of the major producers, whose reserves would diminish significantly in value if the price of oil remained low. The independents argued that such restrictions were not for the sake of conservation, but were, in fact, illegal price fixing.

The Railroad Commission initially ordered production limited to about 1,000 barrels per day at each well, but a federal court struck down the order on the grounds that it was price fixing. Through three special sessions in the summer of 1931 the legislature was unable to reach a solution. In the meantime, the major producers, who owned the refineries, stopped buying East Texas oil, claiming that they did not need it. The independents established "teakettle" refineries and their own gasoline stations. Finally, with more than a million barrels of oil a day pouring from the East Texas field, and agreement among the operators apparently not possible, Governor Sterling declared martial law in four counties and sent in the National Guard. The fact that he was a former president of Humble Oil and that the National Guard commander in the field, General Jacob F. Walters, was an attorney for the Texas Company gave the independents grounds to doubt the state's objectivity in the matter.

The "hot" oil, that is, oil produced in violation of the Railroad Commission's orders, continued to flow, and the secrecy required to circumvent the National Guard also made it extremely difficult to determine the amount of oil produced, who owned it, and whether correct royalties were being paid. In another special session, in the fall of 1932, the legislature authorized the Railroad Commission to prorate production according to market demands and in 1932, at the request of Ernest O. Thompson, chair of the Railroad Commission, the governor sent a force of Texas Rangers to stop the flow of hot oil.

The chaos in the East Texas field was the immediate impetus for Roosevelt's secretary of the interior, Harold Ickes, to propose federal control of the oil industry. As he saw it, the price of oil needed to be higher in the interest of the country's financial recovery, so the unchecked flow of hot oil constituted a problem for the country as well as the industry. His efforts at federal control met fierce resistance, particularly among the independent oil producers whose point of view was well represented by the Texas congressional delegation. By 1933 the Rangers had restored some measure of order to the East Texas field, and in January 1934 a federal court upheld the Railroad Commission's right to prorate oil production. But it was not until later that year, with the establishment of the Federal Tender Board and the threat of prison, that the flow of hot oil declined sharply. When the Supreme Court declared unconstitutional the National Recovery Administration, under whose auspices the federal government had acted, Texas Senator Tom Connally sponsored the Connally Hot Oil Act of 1935 specifically to make interstate transportation of hot oil illegal.

Within a few years, most of the small independents had sold out to the stronger, better-capitalized major producers, who owned 80 percent of the East

Texas field by the time World War II broke out. Later in the century, when the Organization of Petroleum Exporting Countries (OPEC) nations were struggling to control their own overproduction, they found their model for stabilizing the international price of oil in the Texas Railroad Commission. Sterling had dealt successfully with the East Texas oil crisis, but in doing so he had alienated large numbers of East Texas voters.

Agricultural Overproduction

Sterling's other problem grew out of the continuing agricultural depression. The price of cotton, already low at 9–10 cents per pound in 1930, fell drastically in 1931, bottoming out at around 5 cents per pound that fall. The prices of other commodities fell as well, but not as much. The net result was that farmers' purchasing power was about one-third of what it had been before World War I.

The problem would not have been as severe if Texas farmers had been more diversified or had voluntarily limited production. They had tried several different marketing cooperatives, including the Federal Farm Board and the Texas Marketing Association, both of which failed in the face of the 1931 crop of more than 17 million bales of cotton nationally (5.32 million in Texas), the second largest in history.

Any action to limit Texas cotton producers would have failed without the cooperation of the other cotton-producing states, so, in response to a joint resolution of the legislature, Sterling called a governor's conference for the summer of 1931 to try to come up with a plan for unified action. Five states sent representatives, who agreed to limit cotton production if Texas would. During one of the special sessions of 1931, the legislature passed a law limiting the 1932 cotton acreage to 30 percent of the 1931 crop. Most farmers simply ignored the law, and a few days later the courts held it to be unconstitutional. The 1932 yield in Texas alone was 4.5 million bales.

Fergusonism Revived

James Ferguson, an astute and veteran observer of the political scene, concluded that 1932 could be a good "Ferguson year," and Miriam Ferguson filed to run against Sterling, along with seven other candidates. As always with the Fergusons, personalities rather than issues seemed to inspire the voters. The Fergusons accused the wealthy Sterling of trying to buy the election, of misusing the highway fund, and employing political allies in the highway department. Sterling accused them of voter fraud, and probably with reason. The Ferguson strongholds of East Texas issued only 359,667 poll tax receipts, but reported that 397,386 votes were cast in the July primary. Sterling lost the runoff by fewer than 4,000 votes out of almost 1 million cast, but was unable to get the fourth special session of the legislature to investigate the election or to get the Supreme Court to keep Miriam Ferguson's name off the general election ballot.

Miriam Ferguson accomplished little during her second term because the legislature was wary of all proposals that she presented, and because the early efforts of newly elected President Franklin D. Roosevelt to deal with the depression overshadowed and preempted state actions. She resumed her policy of liberally pardoning prisoners and turned the Texas Rangers into a form of political patronage by appointing 2,344 "Special Rangers." Plans to consolidate state agencies and reorganize the state's higher education system failed. The Twenty-first Amendment to the U.S. Constitution, which repealed the Eighteenth Amendment and once again left the management of alcoholic beverages up to state and local officials, was ratified in December 1933, but Texas did not repeal its prohibition amendment until August 1935. Essentially, the depression had overwhelmed local, state, and private efforts, and, with the election of Franklin D. Roosevelt in 1932, Texas, along with the rest of the nation pinned its hopes for recovery on the federal government.

The New Deal

We know in hindsight that no president could have prevented the depression or quickly returned the nation to prosperity, but President Hoover's lackluster personality and political ineptness made him a ready scapegoat, and Texans were ready to return to the Democratic fold in 1932. "Truly, I have been hit hard," one penitent voter wrote, "but I deserve no sympathy, I voted for Hoover." When Speaker of the U.S. House of Representatives John Nance Garner of Uvalde accepted second place on the ticket with Roosevelt, that sealed the deal as far as Texans were concerned: More than 88 percent of the state's voters supported Roosevelt and Garner in their call for a "New Deal for the American people."

With Garner as vice president and de facto head of the Texas delegation, the state was well positioned within the federal government. Some historians consider Garner to have been the most powerful vice president in history, because, as a former Speaker of the House who knew virtually every legislator personally, he wielded enormous influence. Sam Rayburn, the congressman from Bonham and Garner's long-time associate and protégé, headed the Interstate and Foreign Commerce Committee. Six other Texans chaired House committees, and in the Senate Tom Connally chaired Public Buildings and Grounds and Morris Sheppard headed Military Affairs. In addition, Roosevelt elevated Hoover-appointee Jesse Jones to the chair of the Reconstruction Finance Corporation (RFC), which soon became one of the most powerful agencies in Washington.

Congress structured the RFC as an independent agency, but in reality it was a government bank that made loans, received repayment of loans, and earned interest, and, from time to time, added to its capital. The RFC funded some of the most significant New Deal agencies, but perhaps the most important thing it did was save the banking system itself by purchasing preferred stock in threatened banks. Of course, Jones gained support in Congress by funding a pet project on occasion, but his real source of power was Garner and the Texas delegation, who usually stood united on the important issues. By January 1936 the RFC had disbursed more than $8 billion, received $3.2 billion, and earned $294 million in interest.

All of these federal programs had an impact on Texas. The Federal Emergency Relief Administration provided funds for direct relief as well as work relief. RFC money went to banks and to state and local bodies for relief efforts; because of the requirement that the state governments share the burden, Texans had to amend the 1876 Constitution so that the state could provide $20 million in matching "bread bonds" to feed the hungry. Other programs provided jobs: The Civilian Conservation Corps; the National Youth Administration, directed for awhile by the young Lyndon B. Johnson; the Federal Emergency Administration for Public Works; and the Works Progress Administration employed thousands of Texans. The federal dollars went for relief, for civic construction projects, and for culture. Interviewers paid by the federal government documented the lives of literally thousands of Texans—former slaves, old cowboys, Indians, and pioneer residents in all parts of the state—and federally funded artists painted and sculpted historically based public art works for courthouses and post offices throughout the state. All told, the federal government, through public works and relief programs, invested some $351,023,546 in Texas between 1933 and 1936. State and local funds provided another $80,268,595 in assistance.

Unfortunately, many of the poor received little help. Programs that encouraged lower production in an effort to forestall sinking prices for the farmer drove up the price of food for the consumer, making it difficult for those below the poverty line to maintain an adequate diet; Mexican American and African American families were among those who suffered the most. Programs that rewarded owners for taking land out of production and mechanizing their farms drove tenants off the land. Meanwhile, although there was a higher percentage of African American workers on relief than white workers, African American workers in Houston received 25 percent less per month than whites. Some relief agencies placed African American workers only in unskilled jobs, and others would not hire them at all. These agencies also denied Mexicans work on the grounds that they were not citizens. At the same time, because of large-scale unemployment, the federal government undertook a deportation campaign. All told, perhaps as many as half a million Mexicans were deported from the United States during the 1930s, with almost half of that number coming from Texas. Despite widespread discrimination, some agencies had a better record than others—the National Youth Administration under Lyndon Johnson, for example—and the New Deal caught the attention of Texas African Americans, who realized that the Democratic Party of Franklin Roosevelt, despite the wage differentials and hiring discrimination, would offer them more opportunity for economic relief than the Republicans.

In 1934, Texas Attorney General James V. Allred campaigned for governor by identifying with Roosevelt and the New Deal. Although conservative criticism of the president and his programs had begun to surface, Roosevelt still had the support of a huge majority of Texans. And Allred, who had come to public attention as an opponent of out-of-state monopolies and political lobbies, probably had better name recognition than any of his opponents after Miriam Ferguson declined to run, as she said, because of the two-term tradition. The evangelical Allred attracted attention, one Houston reporter likening him to an actor with expert political and oratorical skills. Nevertheless, his call for a Public Utilities Commission, restrictions on lobbies, and a modest tax on chain stores to limit out-of-state competition did not arouse large numbers of voters. A reporter for the *Austin Statesman* claimed that most voters had responded with a "wide yawn." A *New York Times* correspondent called the response "apathetic." Allred led the first primary over five other candidates, but he knew that he had a fight on his hands against Tom Hunter, an independent oil man who was the runner-up.

Allred had been emphasizing his opposition to federal control of the oil industry with the slogan that "Texans should rule Texas." In an effort to increase voter interest in the runoff, he decided to make Jim Ferguson an issue. Although "Ma" Ferguson did not run, "Pa" had actively supported Charles C. McDonald, a former Texas secretary of state, and switched his support to Hunter for the runoff. Allred began to interest the voters when he charged that Hunter had made a corrupt bargain to gain the former governor's support. In the two weeks before the runoff, Allred managed to associate Hunter with a sales tax proposal and edged him out by only about 40,000 votes out of more than 950,000 cast.

A New Image for Texas

One of Allred's more enjoyable duties as governor was to preside over the Texas Centennial in 1936. The main celebration took place in Dallas, but the Centennial was acclaimed all over the state as a watershed event for a society on the cusp of a modernized economy as well as a mature concept of itself. The voters approved a constitutional amendment to establish the Texas Centennial Commission in 1932, and Governor Ferguson appointed the first commission in June 1934. Because it presented the best-funded and best-organized proposal, Dallas was chosen as the site of the official celebration over what many people considered the more historically interesting cities of Houston, near the site of the battle of San Jacinto, and San Antonio, home of the Alamo.

The primary goals of the Centennial, to introduce Texas to the world and to bring out-of-state tourists to Texas, suggested to the committee that the state needed a public relations makeover. Believing that most people thought of Texas as a primitive, frontier area, or as an extension of the culturally and economically backward South, the committee decided to take advantage of the state's romantic history and myth. It was then that, in the words of Centennial historian Kenneth B. Ragsdale, "ten-gallon hats, six-shooters, high-heeled boots, Texas Rangers, bluebonnets, and sex" became the icons of the celebration. The committee's success was assured when Texan Janice Jarratt, the model regularly seen throughout the nation in newspaper and magazine ads as the Chesterfield cigarettes girl, agreed

Governor James Allred tries on a new pair of cowboy boots in preparation for the Texas Centennial in 1936. *(Austin History Center, Austin Public Library)*

to be the "Sweetheart of the Texas Centennial." A picture of her dressed in western style and waving the official Centennial hat on the patio of the spanish Governor's palace in San Antonio was displayed all over the state.

The Centennial itself opened on June 6 and carried out this theme in its most popular attraction, *The Cavalcade of Texas,* a historical pageant depicting four centuries of Texas history. The *Cavalcade* was an instant hit, selling out two performances a day and playing before 60,000–70,000 people a week. Children who had grown up playing the battles of the Alamo and San Jacinto and cowboys and Indians now had a fully articulated historical myth of their own to celebrate. That image was further popularized in what was probably the best-attended attraction outside the main Centennial celebration, the Billy Rose–produced extravaganza in Fort Worth, featuring the "Frontier Follies," the "Winning of the West," and the stripper Sally Rand. "Let Dallas . . . educate the people," the always-quotable Rose told reporters. "We'll entertain them in Fort Worth."

Nor did the focus on Texas history and legend fade away with the passing of the Centennial: The Texas Centennial Commission placed a marker in every county indicating the date of its establishment and the source of its name. Historical buildings and museums received assistance, and new ones were established,

Janice Jarrett was the poster girl for the Texas Centennial celebrations of 1936. Cover of "Pictorial Parade of Texas," published by the Texas Centennial Committee. *(From the Gov. James V. Allred Papers Courtesy of Special Collections & Archives, University of Houston Libraries)*

including the Texas Memorial Museum at Austin, the Sam Houston Memorial Museum at Huntsville, the Corpus Christi Centennial Museum, the El Paso Centennial Museum, the West Texas Museum at Lubbock, the Big Bend Historical Museum at Alpine, and the San Jacinto Monument near Houston. In many ways, the Centennial personified the new Texas identity as a part of the West, and scholarly publications such as Walter Prescott Webb's *The Great Plains* and *The Texas Rangers,* lent academic credibility to it, and the Texan producer/director King Vidor made a popular movie of *The Texas Rangers* in 1936.

Recovery from the Depression

On the political front, Allred had to face the grim realities of the depression. He fulfilled one of his campaign promises when the legislature approved the chain store tax in 1935 during the first of three special sessions, but the primary problem with his initiatives was that the state lacked sufficient money to fund them. Another problem was that many of the New Deal programs that offered assistance—such as the Social Security Act of 1935—required matching state funds, which meant that the federal government dictated much of the governor's tax agenda. The act established the Social Security program that we know today, funded by both the employee and the employer, as well as federal-state programs to cover unemployment insurance, care of dependent mothers, children, disabled and blind persons, public health services, and a pension to assist destitute persons over age sixty-five.

Another problem was the violence that sprang from a society in turmoil. It seems to have begun with the agricultural slump of the 1920s, prohibition, the revival of the Klan, labor and industrial conflict, and the wild and lawless oil boom towns like Kilgore, Desdemona, Mexia, Wink, and Borger, followed by a nationwide depression. There were bootleggers in every county, gambling in most Texas cities, and a series of bank robberies and other crimes throughout the state. At the same time, Miriam Ferguson's election in 1924 and again in 1932 brought a return of her husband's practice of appointing Special Rangers—"a contemptible lot by any standard," according to one historian—who soon became more a part of the problem than the solution.

With the exploits of John Dillinger, Pretty Boy Floyd, and others making headlines throughout the Midwest, Texas too seemed plagued by an epidemic of such infamous criminals as George "Machine-Gun" Kelly, Raymond Hamilton (who made two successful prison breaks), and Clyde Barrow and Bonnie Parker in the Dallas–Fort Worth area, and the Whitey Walker gang in Central Texas, who robbed and murdered apparently at will. State and local authorities seemed outwitted and outgunned, and most Texans were aware of the problem: "A Ranger commission and a nickel can get you a cup of coffee anywhere in Texas," one newspaper editor sardonically remarked. The situation was so bad that in May 1934 Governor Ferguson was forced to go outside the Texas Rangers, to Senior Captain Frank Hamer, who had resigned in protest when she was elected, to find a man to track down Bonnie and Clyde.

The Texas Centennial did not aid law enforcement officials either. As Dallas geared up for the celebration, newspaper publisher and civic leader Amon Carter, Sr. of Fort Worth allegedly reached an accommodation with the liquor control board that would permit the open sale of liquor at the well-publicized "Frontier Follies," which he and others in Fort Worth had organized to compete with the official centennial in Dallas. Not wanting to be upstaged, Dallas officials decided to "open up" their city so they could compete with "Cow Town."

When Allred took office in early 1935, he understood that reorganization of the state's law enforcement agency was one of his most urgent tasks. He immediately proposed a bill creating the Texas Department of Public Safety, which would consist of a new three-person Public Safety Commission to oversee the Texas Rangers, the Highway Patrol, and the Headquarters Division in Austin, which was to be a new, modern scientific crime laboratory. The Fergusons had left the Rangers in complete disarray, and one of the first acts of the new commission was to rehire the Rangers who had been fired and give them tenure. The commissioners also established standards for the operation of the agency.

Recovery from the depression continued to dominate Allred's agenda after he was reelected in 1936. An Allred-backed state constitutional amendment permitting establishment of an old-age pension passed handily that fall, so one of his first goals was to get the pensions funded. The state had estimated that there might be about 63,000 people eligible for pensions, but by the fall of 1936, 81,000 applications had already been filed, and the commission administering the program estimated that number might go as high as 125,000. The state tightened the eligibility requirements, but still lacked funding for such a large program, so Allred opted for a middle course, advocating pensions only for the needy elderly. Most of the money for his plan came from increased taxes on liquor. When Allred proposed new taxes on oil, gas, carbon black, and sulfur to cover other needed programs, the legislature balked. He had to call two special sessions of the legislature in 1936 to work out the details of the program. Even so, when Allred declined to run for another term in 1938 and accepted appointment as a federal judge, the state was $19 million in debt.

The Impact of Radio and Old-Age Pensions

As the 1938 gubernatorial race got underway, thirteen candidates announced for the office. Attorney General William McCraw was the early favorite in what appeared to be a routine race, but the political establishment had no idea that the state's politics were about to be turned upside down. In May of that year, a Fort Worth flour salesman, Wilbert Lee O'Daniel, who had been advertising and performing for several years on a radio program that featured country-and-western music, told his audience that several listeners had written him suggesting that he run for governor. He feigned lack of interest in the idea, but asked members of the audience to write him if they thought he should run. After receiving more than 54,000 letters in one week, O'Daniel announced that he was a candidate for governor. In keeping with the homilies that he delivered on his program, he claimed that his motto would be the Golden Rule and his platform the Ten Commandments.

O'Daniel was not the hillbilly that he portrayed on his radio program. An Ohio native, he had moved to Fort Worth in 1925 to become general manager of a milling company. He discovered the potential of the relatively new medium of radio when he fired the "hillbilly" band, the Light Crust Doughboys—including the creator of "western swing," Bob Wills—that performed on a program his company sponsored. Thousands of fans wrote requesting that the show be put back on the air. O'Daniel did not like the band's music, but he recognized the opportunity. He rehired the Light Crust Doughboys, took over as master of ceremonies for the program, moved it to the strongest radio station in the area, WBAP in Fort Worth, and put it on the Texas Quality Network during the prime-time noon hour each day. After being fired from his general manager job, O'Daniel organized his own band, the Hillbilly Boys, and was soon selling "Hillbilly Flour" under his own label. His program began with a woman's voice asking, "Please, pass the biscuits, Pappy," and O'Daniel was soon known throughout the state as "Pappy."

Texas politicians underestimated W. Lee O'Daniel's bid for governorship because they did not realize how popular he was because of the radio. The placement of this huge, cabinet-model radio in the middle of this Hidalgo County couple's living room in 1939 suggests its importance. Photograph by Russell Lee. *(Library of Congress, Prints & Photographs Division, FSA/ OWI Collection, LC-USF34-TO1-032010-D)*

O'Daniel would not have been such a political surprise if politicians had taken note of the impact of the new medium of radio. President Roosevelt had proved its power while he was still governor of New York, and his fireside chats as president had become legendary throughout the 1930s. But commercial radio had only come to Texas in the early 1920s and had spread slowly because of the rural nature of the state; even by 1940 some sections of Texas still had no broadcasting stations, and fewer than 1 percent of the residents of the Hill Country, for example, had radios in their homes. Politicians had begun to use radio in their campaigns—Allred had made liberal use of it in his 1934 campaign—but apparently it had no demonstrable impact on elections.

O'Daniel's program, on the other hand, consisted of hillbilly music, homely stories, advice on family life, and maudlin poems such as "The Boy Who Never Got Too Old to Comb His Mother's Hair," and became one of the most popular programs on the air. Although he was a bit aloof, even austere, in person, O'Daniel affected a folksy voice that worked on the radio; he even composed and sang his own songs, such as "Beautiful Texas" and "Put Me in Your Pocket." O'Daniel had

O'Daniel campaigning for governor in 1938. (*Jimmie A. Dodd Photograph Collection, 1937–1966, CN 08129, The Center for American History, The University of Texas at Austin*)

never thought seriously about politics and probably considered himself a performer rather than anything else but by the time he ran for governor he may have been, according to some political observers, the best-known personality in Texas because of the popularity of radio. Roy Bedichek, who traveled frequently in his job as head of the University Interscholastic League at the University of Texas, recalled seeing men all over the state "slapping their thighs with delight around filling station radios" as they listened to O'Daniel.

Once in the race, O'Daniel employed the same showmanship in his political campaign that he had in his flour business. He fitted out an old bus with a loudspeaker and, with his hillbilly band, traveled from town to town, drawing thousands of people at every stop. After entertaining the crowd with music, he would launch into his stump speech, proclaiming that he was for "less Johnson grass and politicians; more smokestacks and businessmen." Then he would ask for contributions to his campaign, and his daughter would walk through the crowd with collection plates that had been made in the form of barrels labeled "Flour—Not Pork." Some doubted that he was serious about the race—at one point he told a reporter, "I don't know whether or not I'll get elected, but boy! It sure is good for the flour business"—and few realized that it was all an act, that some of his most unpretentious comments and much of the campaign itself was the product of the fertile and expert mind of Dallas public relations executive Phil Fox.

The other candidates initially underestimated the attraction the voters had for "Pappy." When it became clear that he was a serious candidate, the opposition began to ridicule him as "the big town hillbilly candidate" and "the banjo man from Fort Worth." But he handled the attacks with aplomb. When a reporter asked how he would govern under his platform of the Ten Commandments, O'Daniel smiled and said, "Well, take the fourth commandment, Honor Thy Father and Thy Mother: Doesn't that mean old-age pensions just as plain as day?" The increasingly large crowds loved it. Former chair of the Railroad Commission, Ernest O. Thompson, who had been one of the favorites in the race, confessed that he "didn't even see O'Daniel. The first thing I knew he passed all of us and left me with a cloud of flour dust in my eyes."

Even an old pro like "Farmer Jim" Ferguson, who sat out this race, had to be impressed. O'Daniel conducted his campaign like an old-time religious revival, holding the rallies outside, "basking in God's sunlight." And he presented the issues in the same way as the camp meeting preacher: They were black or white, you were for him or against him, good for Texas or bad for Texas. Having never paid a poll tax or voted, O'Daniel called for abolition of the poll tax and capital punishment. Novelist George Sessions Perry of Rockdale aptly remarked that had O'Daniel "been even slightly less astute, had he made a slightly less careful analysis of his own talents and the emotional requirements of his constituents, he might very well have gone on the road with a medicine show." O'Daniel won without a runoff in one of the biggest upsets in state history, with his largest majorities coming from the WBAP listening area around Fort Worth.

The Conservative Backlash

Although O'Daniel appeared to some to be little more than a popular personality, his homilies cloaked his conservative agenda. He invoked President Roosevelt's name on the campaign trail, but in reality was more representative of the remnants of the Jeffersonian Democrats, a conservative group that had organized in an almost fatalistic attempt to defeat Roosevelt in 1936. The Jeffersonian Democrats adamantly opposed the "court packing" plan and saw the attempted purge of anti-Roosevelt Democratic members of Congress in 1938 as un-American. As some measure of prosperity returned to the middle class, their message of limited government, lower taxes, and individual freedom gained adherents. Knowing that they had no chance as a third party, however, they worked against New Deal programs and candidates from within the Democratic Party; they undoubtedly played a role in the 1938 defeat of liberal congressman Maury Maverick of San Antonio and in the return to Congress of Martin Dies of Orange, initially a Roosevelt supporter but now chair of the House Un-American Activities Committee (HUAC), an ardent anti–New Dealer. Men of such stripe were O'Daniel's friends, advisors, and supporters.

Congressman Martin Dies, speaking perhaps in San Antonio in 1940, established and chaired the House Un-American Activities Committee (HUAC) until 1945. *(Courtesy of Sam Houston Regional Library and Research Center)*

Because of the deficit that O'Daniel had inherited from the Allred administration, everyone realized that taxation would be the dominant issue of his term. The state was still trying to catch up with its side of the funding under the Social Security Act, which had grown to $48–$60 million, but was so poor that members of the House had sat through the last legislative session with umbrellas when it rained because there was no money to repair the capitol roof. It was clear that the governor and the legislature would have to work together to come up with that much new money.

O'Daniel had denounced a sales tax during the campaign but had not revealed where he would find the money to cover the deficit or the pensions that he had promised, and speculation began to spread that he would endorse an income tax. He waited until his inaugural, which attracted a crowd of approximately 60,000 to the University of Texas Memorial Stadium in January 1939, to unveil his plans for a "transactions tax" of 1.6 percent. It was a thinly disguised and regressive sales tax, of course, something that he had condemned during the campaign. He also scaled back on his primary campaign platform of universal old-age pensions to assistance for those over age sixty-five who did not have an income of at least $30 per month. Unable to get even these modest measures through the legislature, he identified those who opposed him in his folksy Sunday morning radio addresses from the porch of the governor's mansion, and the legislature soon was inundated with warnings from voters that the lawmakers should quit playing politics and support the governor. His tax plan had no chance of passing, but many of those who opposed him either did not run in the next election or were defeated.

Meanwhile, claiming lack of funds, he vetoed money for new buildings at state hospitals and cut more than 50 percent from the state Highway Department's budget. He slashed the Texas Rangers' budget to the point that they had to borrow bullets from Highway Patrol officers. O'Daniel began appointing ultra-conservative businesspeople to the University of Texas Board of Regents with the intent of gaining control of the university without enduring the public drubbing that Ferguson had suffered. The plan would come to fruition under his successor, Coke Stevenson, when the conservatives took over the board and fired several professors before dismissing President Homer P. Rainey himself. The legislative session ended with no tax bill and an increase of some $10 million in the state's deficit.

World War II

War came to Europe in the fall of 1939 with a suddenness that few in Texas anticipated. There had been adequate warnings: Japan had invaded Manchuria in 1931 and China in 1937 and had gradually expanded its influence over the western Pacific. In the meantime, Germany, bristling under the onus of its World War I defeat and subsequent treaties, began its regeneration under Chancellor Adolf Hitler, while Benito Mussolini took power in Italy. Italy attacked Ethiopia in 1936, and the following year Germany successively occupied Austria, the Sudentenland (German-speaking Czechoslovakia), and Czechoslovakia itself. But it was the German invasion of Poland in 1939 that began the European phase of the war, and in April 1940, the German blitzkrieg overcame Denmark, Holland, and Belgium. France fell only a few weeks later. Then Hitler turned his bombers toward Britain.

Texans and National Politics

As President Roosevelt struggled with the delicate task of helping Britain while at the same time preparing a reluctant nation for war, he also had to decide whether he would seek a third term. O'Daniel faced a similar decision about his own political future in Texas. But, unlike Roosevelt, whose sense of duty called, O'Daniel's failure to accomplish even the more modest of his platform goals seemed to diminish his interest in reelection. Indeed, his poor performance inspired several challengers. The old veteran, "Pa" Ferguson, believed that the governor had made such a mess of things that "Ma," now almost sixty-five years old, would be a shoo-in to retake the mansion. Highway Commissioner Harry Hines announced. Jerry Sadler, a member of the Railroad Commission, joined the fray. Political observers anticipated the moment when "Pa" and "Pappy" would square off, but it did not happen. Ferguson tried. Still wearing his trademark black hat and string tie, he baited O'Daniel, calling him a "slickhaired banjo player who crooned his way into the governor's office" and "has been giving the people of Texas a song and dance ever since."

O'Daniel stuck to what he did best. He began his campaign on the radio, wondering aloud whether he should run for reelection. A few weeks later he announced that "thousands of my friends" had beseeched him to run and that he would honor their request. Despite the fact that Europe was engulfed in war, he offered the same clichés as his platform, decried that state agencies were nothing more than "juicy play-pretties for professional politicians," and denounced the "powerful oligarchies" in Austin. In his few campaign appearances he took little notice of the fact that the Nazis had occupied Paris and the Luftwaffe was bombing London, except to claim that he had sent President Roosevelt a telegram detailing the activities of fifth columnists in Texas, which, needless to say, he did not follow up on after the election. He won again without a runoff, and Miriam Ferguson's poor fourth-place finish finally retired the duo that had dominated Texas politics for more than two decades.

Vice President Garner momentarily diverted attention from the statehouse when he allowed his name to be put forward for the presidency in 1940 in an effort to keep Roosevelt from winning a third term. Garner had been a conservative influence on Roosevelt from the beginning, warning him to slow down in the spring of 1934 and calling some of the New Deal program just "plain damn foolishness" in 1935. But the greatest rift occurred when, in his second inaugural address in 1937, Roosevelt shocked the political establishment by calling for expansion of the U.S. Supreme Court. The conservatives on the Court had declared both the National Recovery Act and the Agricultural Adjustment Act, as well as several other pieces of legislation, unconstitutional in a series of five-to-four decisions in the spring of 1936. Roosevelt felt that adding a few friendly justices to the Court might solve the problem. Garner was only one of many who fiercely opposed this proposal, and he became the silent leader of the Democratic opposition. Another Texan, Hatton Sumners, chair of the House Judicial Committee, blocked the "court packing" plan in the House, and the conservatives ultimately defeated it in the Senate. The difficulty passed when vacancies enabled Roosevelt to make several new appointments to the Court, but the split with Garner was irreparable. After the 1940 election, the seventy-one-year-old vice president joined the Fergusons in retirement.

O'Daniel began 1941 with a renewed mandate, but he still had to face the need for a tax bill, and he again submitted his plan for a 1.6 percent transactions tax and a tax on natural resources and public utilities. The legislature virtually ignored him, and his bills died one by one in various committees. Eventually, the legislature put together its own plan, which became known as the Morris omnibus tax bill, and it passed both houses overwhelmingly. O'Daniel salvaged an anti-labor bill but the session was an open rebuke of the governor, and the state seemed on the verge of another political crisis.

A solution of sorts appeared when U.S. Senator Morris Sheppard, who had served the state in the Senate since 1913, died on April 9, 1941. O'Daniel saw an opportunity to take his antilabor campaign national, and many of his detractors saw an opportunity to get him out of the governor's mansion. The legislature even passed a resolution requesting that he appoint himself to the Senate. Instead, O'Daniel selected the ailing, eighty-seven-year-old son of Sam Houston, Andrew Jackson Houston, to replace Sheppard and announced it in his typically heavy-handed and ostentatious manner: He elbowed aside University of Texas folklorist and author J. Frank Dobie, the guest speaker at the San Jacinto Day ceremonies at the monument, to present Houston as the new senator, then led the crowd in singing "Beautiful Texas." It was only a ploy to reserve the position for himself in the upcoming election, of course, and Houston managed to attend only one committee meeting before he died.

O'Daniel then filed as a candidate in the 1941 special election to fill the seat, facing the young New Deal congressman from Johnson City, Lyndon Baines Johnson, who had the support of President Roosevelt; East Texas Congressman Martin Dies; and Attorney General Gerald Mann. Johnson ran a modern, well-financed campaign focusing on the president's support. To counter O'Daniel, he, too, hired a hillbilly band, staged "patriotic rallies," and allowed the entertainment to take precedence over his carefully written and rather pompous speeches. He also bought time on the radio, but his stilted performance was no match for Pappy. O'Daniel stepped up his radio messages, broadcasting from the governor's mansion every day at noon and at 6:00 A.M. on Sundays. He declared that his platform remained "one hundred percent approval of the Lord God Jehovah, widows, orphans, low taxes, the Ten Commandments, and the Golden Rule." If the United States had to get involved in the war, he mused, then perhaps Texas should have its own army and navy, and he emphasized his one legislative accomplishment, the passage of the antistrike law, which he said had driven labor organizers out of the state.

"Pa" Ferguson was able to play his last political trick in this election. Ferguson protégé Lieutenant Governor Coke Stevenson would advance to the governor's office should O'Daniel be elected to the Senate. Ferguson also had reasons to dislike O'Daniel, aside from "Ma's" 1940 defeat. O'Daniel was a staunch prohibitionist who had tried unsuccessfully to appoint three prohibitionists to the Texas Liquor Control Board and complained when the Senate turned down these "good clean honest Christian dry citizens." With a few well-placed telephone calls to old friends in East Texas, "Pa" set in motion the process by which O'Daniel was elevated to the U.S. Senate and Coke Stevenson into the governor's office.

According to Jake Pickle, one of Johnson's young staff members who later represented Austin in the U.S. Congress, the election process was imperfect in Texas in 1941, and a shrewd candidate would have his supporters withhold a final count of their votes until the situation became clear. If the vote were close, the candidate would know how many votes were needed to win, and the candidate's friends around the state who had not yet certified their results would then discover "uncounted" ballots in their precincts. This was how Miriam Ferguson had defeated Sterling in 1932. But Johnson and his twenty-four-year-old campaign manager, John B. Connally, were novices, and, because Johnson wanted to appear to be winning early on, Connally instructed George Parr, the self-styled political boss of Duval County and one of Johnson's good friends, to report his votes as soon as the polls closed. With 96 percent of the vote counted the morning after, Johnson led by approximately 5,000 votes. But as the Ferguson strongholds in East Texas began to report their official tallies, the gap between Johnson and O'Daniel began to close.

Connally pleaded with Parr to report more votes, but the "Duke of Duval County" had already served one jail term, and he refused, saying he would not risk prison again. The young congressman had made a rookie's mistake: He had let the opposition know how many votes they needed, and now with outright fraud, and in some cases the actual switching of votes from Martin Dies to O'Daniel, they were harvesting them from the same fertile East Texas fields that had been so good to the Fergusons over the years. Johnson might have filed a protest but for the glaring irregularities and clear violations of election law in his own campaign. Lyndon Johnson had learned a hard lesson that he would never forget.

Texas in the War

Many Texans had continued to feel that a European war did not concern them, but on Sunday, December 7, 1941, a ham radio operator in South America picked up the news from Hawaii of the Japanese attack on the American naval base at Pearl Harbor and relayed it to amateur radio operators in Texas. The worst was soon confirmed: Nineteen ships had been sunk—most of the U.S. Pacific fleet—hundreds of men killed, and the harbor badly damaged. Before U.S. Senator Tom Connally could get to the capitol the next morning to introduce the resolution declaring war against Japan, young Texans had already lined up in front of recruiting offices. Germany and Italy declared war on the United States three days later.

O'Daniel's departure for Washington did nothing to calm state politics, because he had to run again in the regular election in 1942 to hold onto his seat. He prepared for the campaign by introducing several antilabor, antistrike bills in the Senate, never gathering more than a handful of supportive votes, yet he later had the audacity to claim that he had enabled the United States to win World War II because his antilabor efforts had prevented strikes.

Two former governors—James Allred and Dan Moody—opposed him this time, and he ridiculed them as the "gold dust twins," charging that "Communistic labor leader racketeers" and professional politicians were financing their campaigns. He wondered aloud why Allred would leave his "$10,000-a-year job" as a federal judge to run for the Senate unless he were being paid off by the Communists. Allred and Moody attacked O'Daniel for opposing the draft, but O'Daniel countered by talking about his son, who was now serving in the armed forces. They hired private investigators who uncovered damaging information about the senator—he was single during World War I yet failed to serve in the military; his flour-milling business in Kansas had gone bankrupt and some alleged fraud; and he had not paid all of his property taxes in Tarrant County—but the magic had not entirely faded. With Moody falling by the wayside in the primary, O'Daniel defeated Allred in the runoff by almost 20,000 votes. Despite his poor record in office, O'Daniel had done a remarkable thing: He had won four contested, statewide elections in five years. His proposed transactions tax foreshadowed the sales tax that is today by far the state's largest revenue generator, and his suggestion that the state find a way to import water from the spring floods in the Rocky Mountains would be much more welcome today that it was in 1941 when he introduced it.

O'Daniel's return to Washington did bring a period of relative political calm to the state, as Texans pitched into the war effort. For one thing, Coke R. Stevenson from Junction, the new governor, was a much quieter person, a man of few words. He smoked a pipe and had a habit of drawing on it several times before responding to a question, which led the capitol press corps to nickname him "Calculating Coke." Even then, his response was usually brief and uninformative. He was a seasoned official, having served as speaker of the House of Representatives before being elected lieutenant governor, and he managed to establish a cordial relationship with the capitol press corps by visiting with them frequently on an informal basis and inviting them to his ranch in the summers. Probably seeing himself as the guardian of the state's financial stability rather than as a politician, Stevenson espoused the simple life and conservative politics, meaning that he opposed expansion of federal powers. Expansion of the state's economy during the war enabled him to balance the budget without excessively cutting services, and he oversaw several improvements in the highway and educational systems. He faced no serious opposition and was easily reelected to the office in 1942 and 1944.

Ever since World War I, Texas had been a military training center, with the Third Army headquartered at Fort Sam Houston, and aviators stationed at Randolph, Brooks, and Kelly airfields, all in San Antonio. That infrastructure expanded during World War II. Fifteen major army camps in Texas trained more than 1.2 million troops between 1940 and 1945, and several prisoner-of-war camps were built in the state, ultimately housing almost 80,000 German, Italian, and Japanese prisoners of war by June 1944.

Approximately 750,000 Texans served in the armed forces, including 12,000 women, more than any other state. Two of the war's greatest military commanders were born in Texas—General Dwight D. Eisenhower at Denison and Fleet Admiral Chester W. Nimitz at Fredericksburg—and Audie Murphy of Farmersville became the war's most decorated hero before coming home to pursue a career in the movies. Texas A&M University alone, which at the time was a male-only, military-

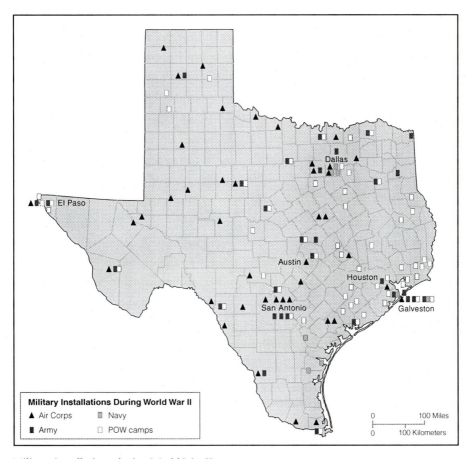

Military installations during World War II.

oriented institution, provided some 14,000 officers during the war, more than both the U.S. Military Academy and the U.S. Naval Academy combined.

The war finally brought an end to the depression. As the federal payroll stimulated local businesses, Texans sacrificed for "our boys overseas" and bought war bonds and planted "victory gardens," as they had during World War I. Rationing of sugar, coffee, meat, shoes, rubber, automobile parts, and gas became a way of life. Governor Stevenson accepted the rationing of everything except gasoline because, he said, Texas had plenty of it and with such vast distances to cover, it was as necessary as "the saddle, the rifle, the ax, and the Bible." Farmers now put all their land back in cultivation, got high prices for their crops, and helped feed the Allies.

With the assistance of the federal government, the largest petrochemical complex in the world developed along the gulf coast. Crucial to its growth was the construction of two pipelines from Texas to the Midwest and the East Coast. As

J. R. Parten, director of the Transportation Division of the Petroleum Administration, in-spects construction of the "Big Inch" pipeline that would carry Texas oil to the East Coast. June 1943. *(Jubal R. Parten Papers, CN 09603, The Center for American History, The University of Texas at Austin)*

early as 1940, Interior Secretary Ickes realized that German submarines might in-terfere with tanker ships along the coastline and urged the construction of the pipelines. It was not until the attack on Pearl Harbor, however, that he persuaded independent oilman J. R. Parten to head the Petroleum Administration for War and to undertake the construction of the pipelines. With financing from the RFC, construction was completed on the "Big Inch" (24 inches in diameter), to deliver Texas crude from East Texas to Illinois and then on to the East Coast, in August 1943; the "Little Inch" (20 inches in diameter), from the Houston-Beaumont area to New Jersey, was completed in 1944. After the war the pipelines were acquired by Texas Eastern Transmission Corporation, formed by George and Herman Brown and their partners.

Other wartime industries were established all over the state: steel mills in Houston and Daingerfield; the largest tin smelter in the world at Texas City; air-craft factories at Garland, Grand Prairie, and Fort Worth; huge shipyards at Beaumont, Port Arthur, Houston, Galveston, and Corpus Christi. The war rein-vigorated the paper and wood-pulp industries in East Texas and supported syn-thetic rubber and munitions plants in other parts of the state. The number of

The Standard Oil (New Jersey) Refinery in Baytown, 1946. *(Standard Oil Collection, Photographic Archives, University of Louisville)*

wage earners tripled, with opportunities now available in the work force for minorities and women, including positions that had formerly been reserved for men. The popular song "Rosie the Riveter" heralded the accomplishments of women in new roles such as pipe fitter, lathe operator, and assembly-line worker. All told, manufacturing increased fourfold between 1939 and 1944, from $453 million to $1.9 billion. This newfound prosperity enabled Governor Stevenson to sweep away the $42 million debt that the state had accumulated and, at the same time, improve state highways, raise teaching salaries, and undertake a building program at the University of Texas. Still, one of his most important contributions was the adoption, early in his term, of the constitutional amendment (Article III, Section 49a) that put the state on a "pay-as-you-go" basis; it prohibits the legislature from spending more than the State Comptroller (tax collector) certifies will be on hand when the bills come due.

Minorities and the War

African Americans from all over the country trained in and staffed Texas camps, and they were expected to conform to the local customs regarding segregation. They lived separately from white troops, trained separately, and were not welcome in the white service clubs or movie theaters or had separate seating. Almost

258,000 African American Texans registered for the selective service, and about one-third of them were assigned to segregated units, usually commanded by white officers. As would be expected, there were racial incidents under such circumstances, and African American leaders protested the discrimination. The Fair Employment Practices Commission conducted investigations in some fifty cities, which in some cases heightened the existing tensions.

The urban areas were even more volatile because of the wartime growth. African Americans already made up one-third of the population in the Beaumont-Port Arthur area, but that number increased by 20 percent in the three years after 1940. On a hot summer night in 1943, the city erupted into racial violence as 2,000 white shipyard workers rioted in the African American section of Beaumont because it had been rumored (falsely) that an African American man had raped a white woman. Two people were killed and more than seventy injured before the local authorities, the Texas Rangers, and the National Guard restored order.

President Roosevelt acted preemptively to maintain good relations with Mexico and the other Latin American countries by establishing the Office of Inter-American Affairs (OIAA). When Mexico banned laborers from coming into Texas under the 1942 Bracero program, which had been negotiated to ensure a supply of wartime field hands and other laborers, the OIAA brought the matter to Governor Stevenson's attention, and the following year he appointed a Good Neighbor Commission, funded by the OIAA. The commission worked to improve the treatment and living conditions of Mexicans in Texas, and became a state agency in 1945.

Although many minorities, both African Americans and Mexican Americans, fell between the cracks during the New Deal, the government programs and the war created an increased political awareness among them that enabled them to improve their situations. African American businesspeople and civil rights leaders such as Maceo Smith and Juanita Craft in Dallas and Hobart T. Taylor, Sr., Carter W. Wesley, and Lulu B. White in Houston took leadership roles in the local chapters of the NAACP. The NAACP's challenge to the state's white primary law led to the 1944 Supreme Court decision, *Smith v. Allwright*, in which the Court held that the white primary was unconstitutional. Mexican Americans, meanwhile, had formed the League of United Latin American Citizens (LULAC) in an effort to eliminate racial prejudice and win equal rights. LULAC was largely a middle-class organization that opposed strikes, demonstrations, boycotts, and other acts that might be interpreted as disloyal. It encouraged Mexican Americans to vote and sent delegations to protest inequity and police brutality. In El Paso, Mexican American women protested their low wages, and in San Antonio 12,000 pecan shellers, mostly Hispanic women, walked off the job in protest of low wages. In 1942 the United States and Mexico signed the Mexican Farm Labor Program Agreement, known as the Bracero program, to permit much-needed Mexican laborers to come into the United States to help alleviate the labor shortage. The agreement guaranteed the workers a minimum wage of 30 cents an hour and humane treatment. Because of the record of discrimination and mistreatment of Mexicans in Texas, however, the Mexican government—despite the legislature's passage of the Caucasian Race Resolution in 1943, which guaranteed Mexicans equal rights in public places—refused to let Mexican laborers come into Texas under the program until 1947.

Conclusion

The labor shortage was only one indication of the major changes that had taken place in agriculture during the war. The diversification of crops continued, with increases across the board in the production of grain sorghums, cattle, sheep, goats, horses, turkeys, tomatoes, onions, spinach, pecans, and roses, in addition to cotton. The number of farms decreased during the war, but the average size of farms grew and total production increased by as much as 30 percent because of the increased use of machinery.

By 1945, Texas industry, fueled by the needs generated by the war, had greatly outstripped agriculture in production. The state once again had a financial surplus, for which Governor Stevenson claimed credit, but which, in fact, was due more to the federal expenditures that poured into the state during and after the war. In addition to the federal payroll—perhaps one out of every ten members of the armed services trained in Texas—private industry expanded at an unprecedented rate. Fort Worth, Garland, and Grand Prairie boasted aircraft factories; Houston, Port Arthur, Orange, and Beaumont had new shipyards; and the huge petrochemical industry was firmly established on the coast. In addition, munitions plants, steel mills, and the world's largest tin smelter (at Texas City) added to the state's industrial muscle. Needless to say, the older, established industries, such as the oil and lumber industries, did equally well, and by 1945 Texas had replaced California as the leading petroleum producer in the nation.

Although Governor Stevenson was reelected in 1942 and 1944 virtually without opposition, the war years saw the beginning of a liberal-conservative rift in the Democratic Party that became even more pronounced after the war. The party remained united behind Vice President Garner as the U.S. presidential election approached in 1940, but when Roosevelt decided to run for a third term, Texas conservatives, who called themselves the Texas Regulars, split from the New Deal faction of the party. Two episodes, in particular, ignited their fury. The first was the supposed infiltration of the University of Texas by Communists and other subversives, which led to the ultraconservative board of regents firing the president, Homer P. Rainey, an ordained Baptist minister, in November 1944. The second was the U.S. Supreme Court's *Smith v. Allwright* decision in April 1944, which brought an end to the all-white primaries. Within a few decades, this liberal-conservative split would evolve into the two-party system that characterized the state's politics at the close of the twentieth century.

SUGGESTED READINGS

Overviews of this period include Donald W. Wisenhunt, *The Depression in Texas: The Hoover Years* (1983); Lionel V. Patenaude, *Texas Politics and the New Deal* (1983); and James Smallwood, *The Great Recovery: The New Deal in Texas* (1983).

The Great Depression

For information on the Great Depression in Texas, see Robert C. Cotner et al., *Texas Cities and the Great Depression* (1973) and Kenneth B. Ragsdale, *Centennial '36: The Year America Discovered Texas* (1987). Robert S. Maxwell, *Texas Economic Growth, 1890 to World War II: From Frontier to Industrial Giant* (1981), is also helpful. For information on agriculture, see Donald E. Green, *Land of the Underground Rain: Irrigation on the Texas High Plains, 1910–1970* (1973).

The New Deal

George Norris Green, *The Establishment in Texas Politics: The Primitive Years, 1938–1957* (reprint, 1984) is the best treatment of politics during this period. Robert Dalleck, *Lone Star Rising: Lyndon Johnson and His Times, 1908–1960* (1991), and Robert A. Caro's *The Years of Lyndon Johnson: Means of Ascent* (1990) and *The Path to Power* (1982) are the best treatments of Lyndon B. Johnson. See also Seth S. McKay, *W. Lee O'Daniel and Texas Politics* (1944), and biographical essays of Morris Sheppard, John Nance Garner, Jesse Jones, Tom Connally, Sam Rayburn, and Johnson in Kenneth E. Henderickson, Jr., and Michael L. Collins, eds., *Profiles in Power: Twentieth-Century Texans in Washington* (1993).

Information on minorities and women may be found in Alwyn Barr, *Black Texans: A History of African Americans in Texas, 1528–1995* (1996); Julia Kirk Blackwelder, *Women of the Depression: Caste and Culture in San Antonio, 1929–1939* (1984); and Rebecca Sharpless, *Fertile Ground, Narrow Choices: Women on Texas Cotton Farms, 1900–1940* (1999).

Texas in World War II

The best information on Texas in World War II is found in *The Handbook of Texas* and the *Southwestern Historical Quarterly.*

13

A "Confluence of Anxieties": Texas from 1946 to 1972

In 1949 a forty-one-year-old Texan named V. O. Key, Jr., who was then a professor at Johns Hopkins University in Baltimore, published the results of his seminal study of the electoral process in the South, Southern Politics in State and Nation. The South had long been recognized as the most depressed part of the nation, especially after President Roosevelt identified it as such in 1938. The question was how it would prevail over its problems to participate in the prosperity that the rest of the nation enjoyed. Many people assumed that the most difficult problem the South had to overcome was racism and segregation; Key agreed that years of race baiting on the part of the ruling oligarchy to maintain the loyalty of poor whites had worsened the situation. Although Key was not a Marxist, he concluded that the lack of class conflict in the South prevented economic and electoral progress. In Texas, however, Key saw a glimmer of hope, suggesting that the beginnings of a class conflict had erupted there in the liberal-conservative split in the Democratic Party. He predicted that the one-party system, by which the ruling elite held power, would gradually succumb to the forces of urbanism, industrialism, and organized labor and would transform into a two-party system, with one liberal party and the other conservative. Because "politics generally comes down, over the long run, to a conflict between those who have and those who have less," he argued, the issues in most disputes are taxation and expenditure: who pays the taxes, and how the money is used. It was almost as if he had written a script for the postwar decades in Texas.

1949	Gilmer-Aiken laws passed; fifty-first legislature adopts the state's first billion-dollar budget
1950	U.S. Supreme Court decides *Sweatt v. Painter* and Heman Sweatt admitted to University of Texas Law School; 59.8 % of the state's population live in cities and towns; Korean War begins
1953	U.S. Congress enacts legislation confirming Texas ownership of its tidelands out to three leagues
1954	Texas Instruments produces first silicon transistor and first portable radio
1956	U.S. Congress approves national system of interstate highways
1957	Senator Lyndon B. Johnson is instrumental in the U.S. Congress's passage of the first civil rights act in more than eighty years; Soviet satellite Sputnik launches space race
1958	Texas pianist Van Cliburn wins the prestigious Tchaikovsky Piano Competition in Moscow
1960	John Tower becomes the first Republican U.S. senator from Texas since Reconstruction
1961	Legislature passes 2 % general sales tax, and Governor Daniel permits it to become law without his signature
1963	President Kennedy assassinated in Dallas
1964	President Johnson's Great Society program, including the Civil Rights Act of 1964 and the Voting Rights Act of 1965; the Twenty-fourth Amendment to the U.S. Constitution declares poll taxes illegal in federal elections; Southwest Airlines founded; Dr. Michael DeBakey of Methodist Hospital in Houston performs the first successful coronary artery bypass graft procedure
1965	The Astrodome, the world's first enclosed, domed, multipurpose sports stadium, opens in Houston
1965	First U.S. combat troops sent to Vietnam
1966	Rio Grande valley farm workers march on the state capitol
1967	Governor Connally leads in reorganizing higher education, including establishment of the University of Texas system
1968	Dr. Denton Cooley performs the first heart transplant in the U.S. at St. Luke's Hospital in Houston
1969	Neil Armstrong speaks first words from the lunar surface, "Houston, the Eagle has landed."
1971	Sharpstown scandal
1972	Equal Rights Amendment to the Texas constitution adopted

As World War II ended, Texan veterans came home to a changed state. Industrialization and a large population increase brought on by the war effort had transformed the economic, social, and political fabric of the state, and it would take some time before most people understood the ramifications. Opportunities in Texas, including the huge growth of the oil industry, even attracted out-of-state veterans, such as the future president George Herbert Walker Bush, who came to Midland with his growing family after graduating from Yale in 1948. The "modified class politics" that Key had documented in Texas was not the product of a plantation oligarchy, as in other Southern states, or of an "upthrust of the masses" that had forced the upper class to defend itself, but the result "of the personal insecurity of men suddenly made rich who are fearful lest they lost their wealth." And it quickly became apparent during the biennial gubernatorial races and subsequent sessions of the legislature as various constituencies fought over the commonly accepted solution: tax revenue—where to get it and how to use it. Rapid urbanization and increased population forced the state to expand its educational institutions, social services, and bureaucracy, which, of course, required additional taxes. But increased taxation challenged the traditional agrarian-inspired approach to Texas government—that low taxation would attract new industry, and the only relatively new source of money in the state, the oil industry, had accumulated enough political and economic clout to ensure that it would not have to bear the brunt of these new initiatives.

Stressing the One-Party System

The party harmony that had prevailed during World War II, which saw Coke Stevenson virtually unopposed as governor, dissolved after the war, as liberal and conservative factions renewed their battles. As the first postwar gubernatorial campaign began in 1946, the favorite seemed to be Homer P. Rainey, the former president of the University of Texas who was searching for vindication for his firing by the board of regents. Hosting a radio show in which he defended his official behavior, Rainey drew increasing support from liberals and newly-enfranchised African Americans. He espoused, to one degree or another, academic freedom, civil rights, labor union rights, and taxes on natural resources; his opponents suspected him of, and accused him of, supporting integration—the kind of race-baiting that Key described—although he was on record against it. Rainey's opponents included three conservative officeholders who attacked him either on personal issues or for permitting Communist infiltration of labor unions and the University of Texas and for supporting integration of public facilities. Rainey's proposed tax on natural resources was anathema to the oil industry, and, with the exception of a few liberal stalwarts such as independent oilman J. R. Parten of Madisonville, the industry unified behind the more moderate Beauford H. Jester, a member of the Railroad Commission, who positioned himself between the conservative trio and the liberal Rainey.

Rapid wartime industrialization had led to increased union membership in Texas. By 1946 approximately 350,000 Texans had joined unions, some 225,000 of them in unions affiliated with the American Federation of Labor (AFL), the largest labor group in the country. Another 60,000 belonged to unions associated with the Congress of Industrial Organizations (CIO), the second largest labor group, which had its state headquarters in Dallas and was making significant gains in East Texas. The largest numbers of union members were located in the heavily industrialized areas of Houston-Beaumont and Dallas–Fort Worth, although many unions were located in areas of specific industry, such as Daingerfield (steelworkers), Greenville (auto workers), and Tyler (oil field workers). At the same time, the state CIO became active in politics in 1944 and in 1946 supported Rainey for governor, which further tainted the former university president in the eyes of the conservative businesspeople. As election day neared, and the nation endured hundreds of strikes by union laborers trying to keep up with postwar inflation, including work stoppages at the General Tire and Rubber Plant in Waco and Consolidated Vultee Aircraft in Fort Worth, the electorate began to see Rainey in a new and, to them, more dangerous, light.

Modified Class Politics

The more conservative Jester ran a well-financed campaign, positioning himself as a moderate, whereas Rainey had to spend most of his time refuting charges of being a political and personal extremist. Jester portrayed Rainey as a super-liberal, when, in fact, the scholar was a New Deal Democrat. Jester campaigned on the basis of no new taxes, states' rights, and opposition to labor unions. The Rainey campaign was the first in the state to profit from the emerging urban coalition of labor, minorities, and independent progressives that would ultimately challenge the state's Democratic establishment for control of the party itself, and it was here that Key had seen a flash of what he perceived as a budding "modified class politics." Although Rainey led in the polls right up to election day, Jester took a small lead in the first primary and concluded with a resounding victory in the runoff.

Candidate Jester had urged enactment of several labor laws in his 1946 campaign, such as voluntary mediation and arbitration in contract disputes and binding arbitration in public and quasi-public utility disputes; with conservative business support, however, the legislature went even further in 1947, passing laws requiring an "open shop," forbidding strikes by public employees, severely limiting picketing, and prohibiting picketing of utilities. Meanwhile, Jester's own proposals died for lack of support. Jester did not really agree with the antiunion laws, but he did not fight them, and an expanding, postwar economy enabled him to keep his promise of no new taxes. He swept into office a second time in 1948 without really having to campaign.

Other Texans had the reform spirit as well. Several of the state's cities were still plagued by organized crime. Gambling, bootlegging, and various kinds of rackets were prosperous endeavors for a number of notorious characters, including Lester "Benny" Binion of Dallas, who had become the local kingpin as the war

Governor Beauford Jester delivering his inaugural address, January 22, 1947. (*The Institute of Texan Cultures at University of Texas, San Antonio*)

ended. The Maceo brothers still ruled Galveston, where the local police commissioner bragged to an attorney that he was on the payroll of almost fifty brothels. A number of veterans, just home from making the world safe for democracy, felt that the gangsters threatened democracy at home and embarked on reform. In 1946 a crusading district attorney, Will Wilson, chased Binion out of Dallas to Las Vegas, where he became a fixture of the gambling establishment in that city. In 1949 Attorney General Marion Price Daniel, Jr. sent investigators into cities across the state to look into rumors of bookies and gambling and, on August 15, sent Texas Rangers on successful raids in Fort Worth, Odessa, and Beaumont. Advance warning permitted operators in Galveston, perhaps the most wide-open town in the state, to hide their equipment and escape prosecution, but in 1957 they fell victim to newly-elected Attorney General Will Wilson, who closed them down.

The 1948 Elections

The 1948 elections sharply delineated the kind of liberal-conservative conflict that Key described, both on the national and state levels. The presidential race pitted President Harry S. Truman against New York's Republican Governor

Thomas E. Dewey, and the U.S. Senate race featured former governor Coke Stevenson and Congressman Lyndon B. Johnson. By comparison, the gubernatorial contest between Jester and seven other candidates was a mere sideshow, with Jester winning without a runoff.

Truman inherited all the anti–New Deal sentiment that had built up in Texas when he succeeded Roosevelt in 1945. Many of the conservatives who had called themselves the Texas Regulars and organized around Senator O'Daniel and Congressman Martin Dies and campaigned against Roosevelt now joined with the Dixiecrats and nominated Strom Thurmond of South Carolina to challenge Truman. They opposed Truman on the basis of his continuation of New Deal policies, his foreign policy, and, specifically, his civil rights initiatives of 1947 and 1948. Truman won the nomination, however, carrying Texas by more than a million votes, his largest majority of any state, and upset Dewey. Governor Jester maintained control of the Democratic Party and helped Truman to his huge majority.

The senatorial primary was equally dramatic. Coke Stevenson represented the Texas establishment and was heavily favored over Lyndon Johnson, but the contest turned out to be one of the closest elections in the state's history. Stevenson had served as wartime governor for almost three terms (finishing O'Daniel's second term, then being elected twice on his own). Lyndon Johnson, his more liberal opponent, had gone into the campaign believing that he had been cheated out of victory in the 1941 special election against O'Daniel and determined not to let it happen again.

Johnson had continued to serve as a member of Congress from the Hill Country and had earned a reputation as a New Dealer. He was only forty years old in 1948 and tried to depict himself as a modern politician, relying heavily on radio commercials and crisscrossing the state in a helicopter named the "Johnson City Windmill." Johnson also worked twenty hours a day and ran a well-organized campaign, whereas Stevenson's campaign was poorly organized and haphazard. Johnson contrasted what he depicted as Stevenson's old-fashioned conservative, antigovernment views with his own stance as a responsible official who was attentive to his constituents. Campaign manager John Connally, a future Texas governor, had his advance team in each town ahead of Johnson to prepare for the brief visit. The helicopter brought out the crowds, enabling the candidate to talk to more voters, and during June and July Johnson visited 118 cities in seventeen days. He portrayed the sixty-year-old Stevenson as old, old-fashioned, and out of touch. He expected to win in the first primary, but finished more than 71,000 votes behind the better-known Stevenson. Only the fact that the third candidate in the race, Houston attorney George Peddy, got enough votes to force a runoff saved Johnson from defeat.

Stevenson's runoff campaign was even more disorganized than the primary, and he soon made his biggest blunder of the election. A special session of Congress provided the occasion. The governor had announced that he would visit Washington to talk with federal officials and foreign policy experts, undoubtedly an attempt to discount any advantage that Johnson might have in the runoff

Senatorial candidate Lyndon Baines Johnson campaigning in 1948 with a thunderstorm behind him. The first candidate to use a helicopter in his campaign, Johnson made 370 stops in five weeks, including several "flyovers" of his opponent Coke Stevenson's rallies. *(LBJ Library Photo)*

because of his experience and wide acquaintance in the capital. When Stevenson looked at possible office space in the Senate Office Building and met with real estate agents about purchasing a home, it appeared to many that he was taking the election for granted. But Stevenson's real difficulty occurred at a press conference. In what many considered an effort to appear more conservative than Stevenson, Johnson had supported the Taft-Hartley Act, which reaffirmed workers' rights to join unions, bargain collectively, and strike, but prohibited closed shops, permitted states to pass "right-to-work" laws, and enabled the president to get a court-ordered injunction for an eighty-day "cooling off" period before unions could close down an entire industry. As a result, the Texas AFL had endorsed Stevenson, despite his antiunion record, and Stevenson had refused to take a position on Taft-Hartley during the primary. If he had opposed it he would have lost his conservative backers, and if he had favored it he would have lost the support of the AFL. So Johnson suggested that one of the reporters ask Stevenson to explain his position on the Taft-Hartley Act. At first Stevenson refused to answer, saying that his comments had already been published. When the reporter persisted, Stevenson lamely replied, "All my notes and papers are back in Texas. I am facing these questions without any material." The syndicated columnist Drew Pearson, a friend of Johnson's, was unmerciful the next day, writing that Stevenson "evaded more issues and dodged more questions than any recent performer in a city noted for question dodging." The Johnson team spread thousands of copies of the column across the state as the runoff approached, and "Silent Coke's" refusal to take a stand became the theme of the Johnson runoff campaign.

Johnson returned to Texas and continued to work until the last votes were in. His final strategy was to use the same tactic in 1948 that he was convinced had defeated him in 1941: He had his supporters hold their vote totals in the precincts where he was strongest, in South Texas, until he knew how many votes he needed. Everyone knew that the election would be close. The day after the runoff, with Stevenson leading by only a few hundred votes, the *Dallas Morning News* declared, "Anything can happen." During a period of thirty-four hours, the Texas Election Bureau, a consortium of news organizations, unofficially reported that the lead changed almost every five hours as election officials all over the state filed and refiled their returns. Both Stevenson and Johnson knew what was going on. It was only a question of whose supporters would file last, and whether they could get away with it. Bob Murphey of Nacogdoches, Stevenson's nephew and driver throughout the campaign, later acknowledged that Stevenson was at a huge disadvantage at this stage because of Johnson's better organization. A week after election day, officials in Jim Wells County finally reported an additional 200 votes for Johnson, enough votes to give him the victory—by eighty-seven votes. (No one is certain how many extra votes were reported. Some sources say that it was 200, and others say that it was 201, with one vote for Stevenson. Still others report that it was 202 with two votes for Stevenson.)

Johnson had not contested O'Daniel's controversial victory in 1941 because he knew that his campaign could not withstand investigation itself, but Stevenson had no such qualms (despite knowledge that some of his supporters in East Texas had been equally devious) and immediately charged that Johnson had stolen the election. Rather than call for a statewide recount, which might have confirmed Johnson's victory, Stevenson felt that he could find evidence in the boss-ruled counties of South Texas that Johnson supporters had stuffed the ballot box and that he could have those votes disqualified. He went to Alice with long-time friend and ex-Texas Ranger Frank Hamer, who had tracked down Bonnie and Clyde, to investigate the matter of Box 13 in Jim Wells County, which had reported the additional 200 votes for Johnson a week after the election. They found their evidence: The last 200 names on the voting list were written in the same hand, but a different hand from the rest of the list, in a different color ink than the rest of the list, and in alphabetical order. Stevenson's attorneys even took depositions from several people whose names were on the list but who said that they had not voted.

Stevenson took his evidence directly to the state Democratic Election Committee, which upheld Johnson's victory by a vote of 29 to 28. Then, with fistfights punctuating the meeting and a delegate who suffered a heart attack in the hotel lobby assigning his proxy to a Johnson supporter before being taken to the hospital, the state convention confirmed the committee's decision. Stevenson challenged the election in U.S. District Court and got a temporary restraining order keeping Johnson's name off the general election ballot, but with Abe Fortas, whom Johnson later appointed to the Supreme Court, planning the strategy, the Johnson forces convinced Supreme Court Justice Hugo Black to set the order aside. The full Court later affirmed Black's ruling, and Johnson went on to win the general election. Stevenson, still unwilling to give up, contacted several Republican senators in an effort to have the Senate refuse to seat Johnson. But the Democrats won control of the Senate that fall, and Johnson had enough friends among them that no challenge would have been successful. Johnson realized that he entered the Senate with the reputation of a wheeler-dealer and a cloud of illegality hanging over his head, and he gave himself a nickname based on the event: In a radio speech, he jokingly referred to himself as "Landslide Lyndon" because of his eighty-seven-vote runoff victory, and it stuck.

Because the fight occurred in the Democratic Party primary, and because both sides were thought to have participated in the shenanigans, little in the way of election reform resulted. After confronting Johnson with rumors of illegalities in his 1941 campaign, reporter Jack Anderson summed up the matter in a memo to his boss, syndicated columnist Drew Pearson: "The circumstantial evidence, at least, is overwhelming against Lyndon. At the same time, he gave me such a sales talk that I can't help believing he is so much better than the crowd fighting him that I hate to play into their hands. . . . On the whole, Lyndon's record has been far better and more progressive than the average Texan."

Johnson's election would help the Texas delegation regain some of the power it had lost with the departure of Garner and others. Sam Rayburn had become Speaker of the U.S. House of Representatives in 1940 and served until the Republicans took over the House in 1947. He would return to the Speaker's chair in 1950, and two years later Johnson began his rapid ascent in the Senate, first with his election to minority whip (1952) and then to majority leader in 1955. Johnson's first committee assignments were Armed Services and Interstate and Foreign Commerce, which permitted him to push for more military bases in Texas, and to shape legislation that affected his friends in the oil and natural gas business. He soon had a hand in legislation that helped to build more houses around military bases, subsidized the tin smelting business in Texas City, loaned money to the Lone Star steel plant in northeast Texas, and sold surplus war equipment to the University of Texas for use in government-contracted research. Such results turned more than a few "recalcitrant and hardened Ag'inners" into "I told you so supporters," according to one business leader.

Jester's Reforms

With Jester's easy reelection, he unveiled an ambitious plan to deal with some of the state's increasingly serious problems. Unlike those who preceded and followed him, Jester was a moderate. Working with the legislature, he initiated an antilynching law and prison reforms and appropriated more money for the elderly and for the state's health services. They reformed the state's educational institutions, providing more money for higher education and establishing Lamar University in Beaumont. But the most important reforms they made were in the area of public education, where the Gilmer-Aikin laws brought about many changes: The laws consolidated 4,500 school districts into 2,900; instituted state equalization funding, based on attendance, which supplemented local taxes; required a minimum of 175 teaching days per year; and raised teacher salaries as well as educational requirements. Finally, the appointed nine-member State Board of Education and the elected state superintendent of public instruction became an elected twenty-one-member board with the power to appoint a commissioner of education, subject to confirmation by the Texas Senate, and a new agency, the State Department of Education (now the Texas Education Agency) was created to support the board and the commissioner.

Jester also supported the Colson-Briscoe Act of 1949, which appropriated $15 million a year from the Omnibus Tax Clearance Fund to be used in the construction of what became known as farm-to-market roads. The highway commission had authorized construction of 7,500 miles of rural roads funded equally by the state and federal government in 1945, immediately after the war. This proved to be a popular program, and the legislature increased the appropriation in 1962 so that a minimum of $23 million would be spent each year. By March 1989 the Texas farm-to-market system included almost 42,000 miles of paved roads, the most extensive network of secondary roads in the world.

Along with other Southern governors, Jester opposed President Truman's civil rights program, but he advised University of Texas officials in the spring of 1949 that they would have to admit qualified African American students to medical school at Galveston unless the legislature created a separate medical school at Texas State University for Negroes (now Texas Southern University) in Houston. An African American applicant to the law school, Heman Sweatt, had already filed suit against the university in 1946, claiming that he had been turned down for admission because of his race and challenging the segregation system itself. As that suit wound its way through the courts, two African Americans filed for application to the medical school in Galveston in 1949, and one of them was admitted that fall.

Although the fifty-first legislature passed the state's first billion-dollar budget in 1949, many of Jester's reforms needed additional funding, and he vetoed much of the second year of the biennial appropriation because the comptroller ruled that there was insufficient income. The state still needed other sources of revenue because, in addition to increased expenses, the growing competition from Middle Eastern crude had cut into the state's oil revenues. The Gilmer-Aikin law, for example, was financed by a selective consumer tax. Jester had also convinced the legislature to propose a series of constitutional amendments to repeal the poll tax, prohibit discrimination on juries, establish civil-service protections, and require the legislature to meet annually. But before he could pursue these proposals, he died of a heart attack on July 11, shortly after the session ended. Lieutenant

Governor Allan Shivers succeeded him, and that fall the voters rejected all of the proposed amendments.

The Conservatives Take Charge

Allan Shivers had begun his political career as a prolabor member of the legislature from Jefferson County. Like Jester, he graduated from the University of Texas, where he had been president of the student body. He earned the respect of his colleagues while in the legislature and emerged as a leader. In 1937 he married Marialice Shary, daughter of a wealthy Rio Grande valley land developer, John H. Shary, who was called the father of the Texas citrus industry. After service in the army during World War II, he returned to Texas in 1946 and was elected lieutenant governor (and reelected in 1948); he instituted changes that brought considerable power to the office, enabling him to become the first lieutenant governor to influence and shape the state's legislative agenda by controlling Senate committee appointments. Although he was considered a moderate, Shivers pursued a more conservative course on social and economic issues after election to statewide office.

Governor Allan Shivers campaigning for reelection in 1954. (*Russell Lee Photograph Collection, 1935–1977, CN 09623, The Center for American History, The University of Texas at Austin*)

Whether one agrees with Shivers or not, it is clear that he was one of the ablest chief executives in the state's history. In preparation for a special session of the legislature in 1950, Shivers called a number of lobbyists and business leaders to the governor's mansion to convince them of the need for new taxes, then called a special session of the legislature for January 1950 to address the matter. In his speech before that session he still exhibited some of his early liberal ideals. He also instituted administrative changes that, ironically, because he is generally known as one of the stronger chief executives, weakened the power of the governor but improved efficiency: He created the Legislative Council to research and draft bills and the Legislative Budget Board, with the lieutenant governor and Speaker of the House as chair and vice chair, to prepare the annual budget. Previously, each agency had submitted a memorandum to the governor, who determined what to recommend to the legislature.

The reforms continued during the 1951 legislative session. Shivers asked the legislature for more money for roads, prisons, schools, and the mentally ill. He supported safety inspections for automobiles and liability insurance for motorists, with the intent that motorists must prove that they had sufficient resources to cover any accident that they might cause. The legislature also passed the first redistricting bill in thirty years, which began a long process of transferring power from the rural areas with diminishing population to the growing urban areas.

As Shivers expanded his political power, he began to express his conservative views more clearly. Early in 1951 he supported a measure that permitted candidates for public office to cross-file—that is, they could file in both the Democratic and Republican primaries. Liberals objected to some of the more conservative, antilabor legislation that Shivers had supported during the last session, and they finally broke with him when, because of the tidelands issue, he decided to support the Republican candidate, Dwight D. Eisenhower, in the 1952 presidential election. In what V. O. Key would have considered a prime example of the rising class conflict, Shivers won control of the executive committee of the state Democratic Party that year and purged the more liberal members.

The Tidelands

Ownership of the tidelands, the submerged land from the point of low tide to three leagues (about ten and a half miles) out in the Gulf of Mexico, further split the Democratic Party and made Shivers a stronger states' rights advocate. After oil was discovered in the tidelands, federal officials claimed that the offshore lands belonged to the nation. California was the first state to press its claim to tidelands in 1945, but the Supreme Court decided against it. Congress even passed legislation guaranteeing California's ownership of the tidelands, but President Truman vetoed it, asserting national ownership. Texas pleaded that it was in a different situation than California, and President Truman seemed to agree, saying during a presidential campaign stop in Austin in 1948 that "Texas is in a class by itself; it entered the Union by Treaty." In the meantime, Texans had miffed Truman by awarding leases in the tidelands without consulting him, and after the election (in which he handily carried Texas) he instructed his attorney general to file suit against the state, claiming that these lands too belonged to the nation. The Supreme Court ruled against Texas by a vote of 4 to 3 (with two abstentions). In 1952 Rayburn pushed another bill through Congress that would have given Texas possession of its tidelands, but Truman vetoed that one too. With Texas Attorney General Price Daniel leading the fight, the tidelands became the foremost issue during the upcoming presidential election and one of the most serious conflicts between states and the federal government during the twentieth century.

The tidelands dispute split the state Democratic Party. Adlai Stevenson of Illinois, the Democratic presidential candidate, supported the Truman administration's position but native Texan Dwight D. Eisenhower, the Republican presidential candidate and revered commander of Allied forces in Europe during the war, supported the Texas claim. Maintaining control of the party machinery, Governor Shivers led a Democrats for Eisenhower campaign. Liberal Democrats, including the state's two most important national leaders, Sam Rayburn and Lyndon Johnson, remained loyal to Stevenson, but Texas voted Republican for only the second time in the twentieth century. In the governor's race Shivers defeated Ralph Yarborough, a liberal attorney and former judge, by more than 400,000 votes. In 1953 the Congress passed and Eisenhower signed a quitclaim bill that recognized that the tidelands extended three leagues into the Gulf of Mexico along the coast of Texas and the west coast of Florida. The General Land Office reported that by 1987 the Texas public school fund had received nearly $2 billion from leases, rentals, and royalties on this property.

In retrospect, the 1952 election marked the beginning of an increasingly harsh rhetoric between liberal and conservative forces that signified deeper change in the state's politics—change that V. O. Key had predicted and that would continue until most of the conservatives had joined the Republican Party. The demographics of Texas had changed as a result of the war. Increasing numbers of immigrants from the North and the Midwest fueled the state's move toward urbanization, then suburbanization. As racial and ethnic minorities—African Americans and Mexican Americans—began to exercise political power, old political allegiances faltered. The Democratic Party was splitting into liberal and conservative factions, but the conservative faction maintained control of the party apparatus.

The Cold War and Class Politics

Shivers drifted toward conservatism on the tidelands issue as well as the wave of anti-Communism in America. The "red scare" or McCarthyism of the 1950s was partly a result of the undocumented charges by Wisconsin Senator Joseph McCarthy that Communist party members had infiltrated the government, especially the State Department. But Texas had its own brand of anti-Communism in

Martin Dies, who became the first chair of the U.S. House of Representatives Un-American Activities Committee in 1938, and in the Texas Senate committee, established in 1941 for the purpose of ferreting out Communists. Many political figures also mixed red-baiting with race-baiting. Key would have recognized it as a Cold War variation on a theme.

Many date the Cold War from the famous 1945 Yalta Conference between President Roosevelt, British Prime Minister Winston Churchill, and Soviet Premier Joseph Stalin—from the moment that Stalin asserted Russia's authority in Eastern Europe, dividing Europe along what Churchill dramatically called the "iron curtain" in a speech at Fulton, Missouri, the following year. By the end of 1949, the Soviet Union had detonated its first atomic bomb, ending the U.S. monopoly on atomic power, and the Communists had driven the nationalists out of China; in June 1950 North Korean troops crossed the 38th parallel that separated the Communist north from the western-oriented south, pushing the poorly-prepared defenders before them. President Truman responded quickly, committing U.S. troops under the United Nations banner. But as the war dragged on, and the Chinese entered the conflict on the side of the North Koreans, Americans became increasingly frustrated. Shivers was among those who called Truman soft on Communism and claimed that he was committed to a "no win" policy in Korea.

Such difficulties provided a following for Senator McCarthy, which included Houston oilman Hugh Roy Cullen and Jesse H. Jones, publisher of the *Houston Chronicle,* which supported the Wisconsin Senator through much of his career and publicized his 1950 speech in Houston. By the spring of 1951 chapters of the Minute Women of the U.S.A., whose goals were to fight Communism in government and education and ensure that schools and colleges taught American heritage, had formed in Houston, Dallas, San Antonio, and Wichita Falls. Among other things, the Minute Women forced the Houston school superintendent out of office. The legislature required loyalty oaths of all public employees, but the crusade to get Communists out of the public schools resulted in only one dismissal out of more than 65,000 employees. In Dallas, Jerry Bywaters, director of the city-supported Dallas Museum of Fine Art, came under attack from conservative citizens who claimed that the museum exhibited paintings by Communist artists. Although some citizens may have been concerned about Spanish artist Pablo Picasso's Communist sympathies, later research proved, ironically, that the accusations originated with a group of realist artists who probably felt threatened by the modernist and abstract works that the museum was exhibiting rather than by the artists' political sympathies. The real problem was that the "red scare" and the Cold War combined with social changes such as urbanization and the expansion of civil rights to threaten the status quo, causing many citizens to identify these needed changes as also un-American.

Civil Rights

Another issue that split the state Democratic Party was integration. Although the state had established Alta Vista Agricultural College (now Prairie View A&M University) in 1878, before Sweatt's lawsuit African Americans had to go outside the state to pursue a professional education as a lawyer, doctor, engineer, or architect. But civil rights litigants had been increasingly successful in the federal courts after World War II, and the Houston chapter of the NAACP, with the support of Thurgood Marshall, the well-known attorney and future Supreme Court justice, challenged segregation in Texas. Heman Sweatt, a graduate of Wiley College in Marshall and a former medical student at the University of Michigan and now a postal employee and civil rights advocate in Houston, had become interested in law and applied to the University of Texas law school in 1946. Marshall successfully sued the university in the U.S. Supreme Court (*Sweatt v. Painter*), winning a major decision in 1950. Shivers led the segregationist forces, and the state attempted to resolve the dilemma by creating a law school for African Americans as part of the newly created Texas State College for Negroes (now Texas Southern University), but the Court held that the new school did not meet the "separate but equal" provision required by the 1896 *Plessey v. Ferguson* case and ruled that the university had to admit him. This decision, however, did not apply to undergraduate education.

The decision that made racial separation illegal was *Brown v. Board of Education* in 1954, which was far more sweeping in its effect. In that decision the court brushed aside the "separate but equal" argument and held that segregation of the public schools was unlawful because to separate children "from others of similar age and qualifications solely because of their race generates a feeling of inferiority . . . that may affect their hearts and minds in a way unlikely ever to be undone."

The majority of Texas voters opposed racial integration, and it became one of the central issues of the 1954 gubernatorial race, pitting Governor Shivers, seeking an unprecedented third term, against the garrulous and liberal Ralph W. Yarborough, an Austin attorney and former judge whom Shivers had defeated in 1952. The election confirmed several of Key's conclusions: that the poll tax and other repressive measures kept poor citizens from voting, that the coalition of organized labor and poor rural folk was developing, and that the liberal-conservative class conflict, represented by Yarborough and Shivers, was at hand. As the race grew closer, and after the Supreme Court had handed down the *Brown v. Board of Education* decision, Shivers charged not only that "Communist labor racketeers" supported Yarborough but that Yarborough also advocated full integration. Yarborough forced Shivers into a runoff, but Shivers won by fewer than 100,000 votes.

Integration continued to be an issue after the election. Conservative Attorney General and fierce state's rights advocate John Ben Shepperd contended that the Supreme Court decisions did not apply to Texas. But the University of Texas and Texas Western College did admit their first African American undergraduate students in 1955. The San Antonio and El Paso school districts began integrating their schools in 1956. But when three African American students attempted that same year to enroll in the Mansfield school, near Fort Worth, members of the local community resisted federal court orders, and Shivers, by then a lame-duck governor, sent Texas Rangers to preserve the status quo.

Scandal Hurts Shivers

Shivers's historical reputation probably would have been better served if he had not run for a third term. The school crisis was an ugly affair, and he was beset with charges of corruption as insurance scandals eroded public confidence in his administration. Reporters exposed illegal operations in the Veterans' Land Board that resulted in the sentencing of General Land Office Commissioner James Bascom Giles to six years in the penitentiary. Even worse were the insurance scandals. The state's regulation of the insurance industry was so lax that more insurance companies called Texas home than any other state. So many had failed that Yarborough made it an issue during the 1954 campaign. One of the largest failures was U.S. Trust and Guaranty, which had grown quickly into a large company that controlled seventy-four other insurance companies in twenty-two states, but more troubling politically was the failure of the Insurance Company of Texas. Its founder, Ben Jack Cage, was indicted for bribery and embezzlement and fled to Brazil, where he lived for the rest of his life.

Shivers again led Eisenhower's campaign in Texas in 1956, but the state Republican Party nominated only a few candidates for office, preferring to vote for the conservative Democrats who had cross-filed as Republicans as well. The liberal Yarborough made his third run for the governor's office, but lost to the moderate Price Daniel, who had the support of Johnson and Rayburn and who resigned his U.S. Senate seat to become governor. Johnson, Rayburn, and Daniel formed a coalition with liberals to wrest control of the party machinery away from Shivers and the conservative establishment, and, in the major liberal victory of the decade, Yarborough won the open senatorial seat with only 38 percent of the vote in a winner-take-all special election over twenty-one other candidates.

President Eisenhower had taken no action in the school integration crisis because he was in the midst of a reelection campaign and Texas was a crucial state. But the following year, when Governor Orville Faubus of Arkansas attempted to keep nine African American students from enrolling in Little Rock's Central High School, Eisenhower sent federal marshals to enforce the Court's ruling. Shivers, meanwhile, appointed an Advisory Committee on Segregation in the Public Schools with the specific instructions that they prevent "forced integration." The committee presented a number of racist proposals to the legislature. In the debate, state senator Henry B. González of San Antonio, the lone Mexican American in the legislature, became a hero to liberals when he filibustered against the proposals. He had many supporters, but two of the bills eventually became law: 1) Local voters had to approve integration before state funds could be used for an

When African Americans, led by NAACP attorney Thurgood Marshall (second from left), prepared to sue to integrate the Dallas independent school district in 1956, the school board voted to integrate. With Marshall are (left to right): U. S. Tate, C. B. Bunkley, and W. J. Durham. *(R. C. Hickman Photographic Archive, 1949–1961, 1969, CN 08028, The Center for American History, The University of Texas at Austin)*

integrated school, and 2) Any reason on a list of approved reasons could be legally used to prevent integration. Price Daniel, who succeeded Shivers as governor, signed the bills into law but made no effort to enforce them. Daniel had pledged to support local boards of trustees in their decisions, implying his support of segregation, but the new attorney general, Will Wilson, recognized that federal laws and Supreme Court decisions did apply to Texas, and segregation gradually came to an end in Texas over the next two decades.

Mexican Americans also defended their rights in several notable federal court cases. *Delgado v. Bastrop ISD* (1948), prosecuted by the League of United Latin American Citizens and the American G.I. Forum of Texas, forced local school districts to cease de facto segregation; in 1954 they won the *Hernández v. State of Texas* case, which prohibited discrimination based on class. World War II veteran Dr. Hector García had organized the forum in 1948 to help Mexican American veterans get the benefits due them under the G.I. Bill of Rights of 1944, but quickly began to address other concerns. One such concern was the refusal of a Three Rivers funeral home director to permit the use of his chapel for the funeral of Félix Longoria, an American soldier who was killed in the Philippines during the last days of World War II but whose body had just been recovered. García wrote to a number of Texas senators and members of Congress, and Senator Lyndon Johnson was the only one to respond. He arranged for Longoria to be buried in Arlington National Cemetery in 1949.

Better Roads

The press of urbanization threatened to leave agricultural and rural areas of the state behind because Texas was, until the admission of Alaska in 1959, the largest state in the nation. Throughout the 1930s, rural Texans felt isolated from their neighbors and often had to drive for hours over unpaved roads to reach the nearest market community. The state tackled the problem in 1949 with the passage of the Colson-Briscoe Act (Dolph Briscoe would later be elected governor) for construction of farm-to-market roads. The real push came during the decade of the 1950s, however, when the federal government took the lead in the construction of superhighways as a part of national interstate highway construction.

A new road system was high on President Eisenhower's agenda when he took office. Ever since he had made a cross-country trip with an Army convoy in 1919, he had realized how badly the nation needed good roads. The trip from Washington, D.C. to San Francisco had taken sixty-two days, and the soldiers had encountered all kinds of difficulties caused by poor roads and extreme temperatures. Like most Americans, Eisenhower was impressed with the German *autobahns* and noted how much more rapidly American forces moved once they reached the good German roads. President Roosevelt and Congress had made several false starts on improving the roads during the 1930s, then postponed everything as the war effort consumed the country's attention and economic resources. Eisenhower began to work on the National System of Interstate and Defense Highway Act as early as 1954, and Congress approved it in 1956. The goal was to link every major population center with a modern, high-speed expressway. The states had to finance the expensive roads, but the federal government reimbursed them for 90 percent of the cost. Texas was a major beneficiary of the system because of its size and geographical location. By 1989, the state had 3,234 miles of superhighway, more than any other state.

Better highways combined with war-related industrialization and the large number of military bases across the state greatly accelerated urbanization. In 1940, 45.4 percent of the population lived in cities; that figure increased to 59.8 percent by 1950, slightly higher than the percentage for the country as a whole (58.6 percent). There were more than 34,000 miles of highway in the state that year; increased construction of farm-to-market roads, the interstate highway system, and freeways such as North Central Expressway in Dallas (1954) accelerated the process during the next decades until, by 1995, Texas had 183,150 miles of improved roads. This led to the development of the suburbs, as mobility permitted workers to live outside the city centers. And that, in turn, led to the development of what one author has termed "edge cities"—suburban business districts, minicities, or service cities—smaller city cores outside the central business district of the larger cities, the Galleria areas in Houston and Dallas, for example, and Las Colinas in Irving. Today these edge cities are marked by the presence of office towers and hotels and are usually located near interstate highway junctions.

Growing cities, and the long distances between them, also fostered the development of commuting by air. Texas cities had long been served by Braniff Airways (founded in 1928) and Texas International Airways (founded in 1947 as Trans-Texas Airways), but their flights served primarily as one leg of a longer, out-of-state flight. Meanwhile, Rollin King's small air-taxi service gave him the idea of establishing a commuter service between the state's three major cities: Houston, Dallas, and San Antonio. King joined with his attorney, Herb Kelleher, to create Southwest Airlines, which, by the turn of the century, had become one of the leading airlines in the nation.

Governor Price Daniel

The most important issues facing Texas as Price Daniel took the governor's office were taxation and expansion of state services such as water (the worst drought in the history of the state occurred from 1949 to 1956), schools, highways, care of the elderly, law enforcement, and prison reform. But the state's antiquated tax system creaked and groaned under the pressure, and little could be done without increased revenue. Daniel favored "sin" taxes (for example, on tobacco and liquor) and business taxes, but, after two special sessions in 1961, and despite his public objections, the legislature presented him with a 2 percent general sales tax, which he permitted to become law without his signature. The regressive nature of the tax was somewhat tempered by the exemption of food, drugs, clothing, farm supplies, and some other items, but the subsequent need for additional funds has since caused some of those items to be added to the tax list. Daniel ran for an unprecedented fourth term in 1962 but was defeated because much of the electorate blamed him for the new sales tax.

Although Daniel would not be called a champion of civil rights, he clearly stood to the left of Shivers, and neither he nor Attorney General Wilson agreed with the positions taken by Shivers and Shepperd. On the national scene, meanwhile, Johnson took a leading role in passing the 1957 Civil Rights Act, while Rayburn supported it behind the scenes so as not to offend voters in his home district. The act provided for a civil rights commission, a civil rights division within the Justice Department, and a compromised voter rights section.

The Lyndon Johnson Era

Johnson's support of the 1957 Civil Rights Act was based on his personal convictions as well as his belief that he needed a dramatic achievement to advance his national political aspirations. Johnson had grown up in the Hill Country and

Speaker of the U.S. House of Representatives Sam Rayburn, John B. Connally, and Vice President Lyndon Johnson on the occasion of Connally's appointment as secretary of the navy. *(LBJ Library Photo by DOD Signal Corps)*

graduated from Southwest Texas State Teachers College (now Texas State University) in San Marcos, where he earned his elementary teacher's certificate in 1928. He spent a year as principal and teacher at Cotulla, in South Texas, where the poverty of his students and their families deeply impressed him. His first important political job in 1935 was as director of the National Youth Administration in Texas, a job that he left in 1937 to run for Congress, and then for the Senate in 1948. Johnson apparently had his eyes on the presidency all along and viewed the Civil Rights Act as necessary both for racial harmony in the South and for his political career. But racial harmony was immediately disrupted by Arkansas Governor Faubus's stand against integration of Central High School in Little Rock; polls showed that Johnson's popularity suffered as a result, because people in Texas linked him with Eisenhower's program. Johnson was able to regain significant ground when the Soviets launched *Sputnik I*, the first artificial earth satellite, later that year, and he seized the moment to convene hearings on its impact and the American response. He received a large part of the credit when the Democrats gained twenty-eight seats in the Senate in the 1958 midterm elections.

Rather than immediately announce for the presidency in 1960, Johnson remained in Washington, presenting the image of a hard-working senator doing his job. Rayburn and others portrayed him as a seasoned leader whose accomplishments and wisdom made him a far better choice than the young and inexperienced

Gubernatorial candidate Paul Eggers, senatorial candidate George H. W. Bush, Senator John Tower, and President Richard Nixon, campaigning in Texas. When Tower won election to the U.S. Senate and Bush to the U.S. House of Representatives, it was apparent that Texas was becoming a two-party state. *(From* Two Party Texas, *by John Knaggs, Eakin Press)*

John F. Kennedy of Massachusetts, who was already campaigning hard around the country. Johnson felt that Kennedy's weaknesses would become apparent during the campaign and that a deadlocked convention would then turn to him as the only truly qualified candidate to lead the party. He had protected his Senate seat, however, by getting the Texas legislature to move the state's primary to May so that he could be a candidate for both the Senate and the presidency.

Nominated on the first ballot at the Los Angeles convention, Kennedy was shrewd enough to realize that he needed Johnson's help to carry Texas and other crucial Southern states. He offered Johnson the vice presidential slot, and, against the advice of Rayburn and his closest advisors, Johnson accepted. The Republicans nominated Vice President Richard Nixon for president and Henry Cabot Lodge III for vice president. The 1960 campaign featured the first televised debates between presidential candidates.

Everyone had predicted a close vote in Texas, and an incident in Dallas may have swung it toward the Kennedy-Johnson ticket. Campaigning with his wife, Lady Bird, in downtown Dallas, Johnson encountered some aggressive supporters of Dallas

Republican congressman Bruce Alger, who cursed them, one of them hitting Lady Bird with a campaign sign, probably by accident. But the news media covered the event, and when the Alger camp showed little or no remorse, a number of voters probably expressed their disapproval at the ballot box. Another event that surely helped the Kennedy-Johnson ticket was Henry B. González's gubernatorial campaign of 1958. Although González had finished a poor second to Daniel, his political organization was still intact in 1960 and delivered a large percentage of the Hispanic vote to the Democrats; reversing the trend of the last two presidential elections, the Democrats carried Texas (by fewer than 50,000 votes out of the almost 2.3 million cast). Nationwide the margin was only 118,574 votes out of the more than 68 million cast. Kennedy was actually a minority president, garnering only 49.7 percent of the vote. Johnson had literally made it possible for him to become president.

Although their party had lost the presidency, Texas Republicans saw the 1960 election as something of a turning point. Despite their loss, Nixon and Lodge had captured more votes in Texas than any Republican candidate ever had. John Tower, an unknown assistant professor from Midwestern University (now Midwestern State University) in Wichita Falls, had polled more than 900,000 votes against Johnson for the Senate seat; he then won the special election over conservative Democrat William Blakely and dozens of other candidates in a runoff to fill Johnson's vacant seat and became the first Texas Republican senator since Reconstruction.

John Connally

As the Republicans grew to become a mature political party, the Democrats engaged in a divisive ideological battle that at times became quite personal. In 1962 John B. Connally, Jr. challenged five other candidates, including the incumbent, Price Daniel, for the governorship. Connally had long been a friend of Johnson's and had served as manager for all of Johnson's major campaigns so he had the makings of a statewide network in place.

Many noticed a big difference between Connally's campaign and previous Democratic establishment efforts. Johnson's election to the vice presidency as well as the newly found potency of the liberal wing of the party, evidenced by Yarborough's election to the Senate, influenced Connally to openly court the votes of labor, African Americans, and Hispanics. After a close election, Connally took office saying that he wanted to be the "education governor" because he believed that education was the key to addressing the pressing social problems of race relations and poverty.

In hindsight, many have suggested that the incident in which Johnson and his wife were jostled—particularly when coupled with a later incident in which UN Ambassador Adlai Stevenson was heckled and hit with a placard—was illustrative of the sentiment in Dallas in the early 1960s. Dallas was home to retired general Edwin A. Walker, who had resigned from the army when he was reprimanded for distributing right-wing propaganda to his troops and had recently taken to flying the American flag upside down at his residence as a distress sign because of the federal government's integration policy. It was also home to others of similar sentiment, such as H. L. Hunt, the wealthy oilman who financed extremely conservative causes.

It was in that setting, on November 22, 1963, that President Kennedy was assassinated as he rode in a motorcade through downtown Dallas. He had come to Texas primarily in an attempt to heal the liberal-conservative rift in the state Democratic Party and to raise funds for his coming reelection campaign in 1964. Riding in the same car with the president, Governor Connally was seriously wounded, apparently by the same sniper, Lee Harvey Oswald, shooting from the Texas Schoolbook Depository. Many blamed the city's conservatism for Kennedy's death, but the Warren Commission, established immediately after the assassination, concluded in 1964 that Oswald acted alone. In 1979, after reviewing the Warren Commission findings and gathering new information, the House Select Committee on Assassinations concluded that Kennedy "was probably killed as the result of a conspiracy," but was unable to identify any participants other than Oswald or the person or persons who planned the assassination. Despite passage of the President John F. Kennedy Assassination Records Collection Act in 1992, which unsealed all of the federal records pertaining to Kennedy's assassination, conspiracy theories continue to abound.

Kennedy's assassination changed the course of both national and state politics. Lyndon Johnson became president, and John Connally, who had narrowly defeated a political unknown in 1962, now became virtually unbeatable as governor. He won reelection in 1964 by a 3–1 margin and in 1966 with 72 percent of the vote. At the same time, Johnson's ascendance was a setback to state Republicans, and he momentarily stymied their surge in Texas and quieted the battle within the state Democratic Party. Johnson led the Democratic ticket in 1964 against Republican Barry Goldwater of Arizona, defeating him by more than 700,000 votes. The future Republican president, George H. W. Bush, who had represented a Houston district in Congress for two terms, failed in his bid to unseat Yarborough in the Senate race, and the Republicans lost both of their congressional seats and all but one of their legislative offices.

Safely elected on his own, President Johnson embarked upon an ambitious program. He had already signed the Civil Rights Act of 1964, the most far-reaching civil rights act in the nation's history, which addressed voting rights, public accommodations, and discrimination both in education and on the job, and had begun to talk about the Great Society program, which would include a "war on poverty" as well as other social programs like health care for the elderly (Medicare) and the Neighborhood Youth Corps. Along with more than 200 other bills passed during Johnson's first two years, Congress passed the Voting Rights Act of 1965. The other bills included the National Museum Act, the Public Broadcasting Act, and the national endowments for the arts and humanities. At the same time, Lady Bird Johnson called attention to the environment with her well-received beautification program. Unfortunately, Johnson also prosecuted the growing war in

Vietnam, which ultimately divided the country and eroded his political base to the point that he declined to run for reelection in 1968.

The Great Society had an immediate impact on Texas. Governor Connally had opposed the public accommodations section of the 1964 Civil Rights Act but endorsed the Head Start program, thinking that Johnson might have taken the idea from a language program for Mexican American children that he had begun in Texas. In other areas of the domestic legislative package, however, Connally feuded with Johnson, because, in Connally's view, they reduced the power of the state too much and actually vetoed an eleven-county Neighborhood Youth Corps project.

Higher Education

With his new popularity and the political assistance of a new Speaker of the House, his protégé Ben Barnes, Connally began to push his programs in higher education, increased tourism, and recruitment of out-of-state industry, and he proved himself to be one of the ablest and most powerful of the state's twentieth-century governors. Connally looked like most people thought a Texas governor should, tall in his elegant boots, with distinguished wavy gray hair frequently hidden under his white Stetson. He was articulate and, on occasion, rose to the level of oratory. *Dallas Morning News* political reporter Richard Morehead claimed that Connally was the only governor in the nation who could hold his own with California Republican governor Ronald Reagan at the annual governors conferences, where he frequently found himself defending Johnson's policies against Reagan's charges. Now he applied that power of persuasion and salesmanship to implementing his campaign promises. Early in his term, Connally had described his goal to State Department counselor and later Johnson aide Walt W. Rostow: He wanted to unify Texas, and in his opinion the best way to do that was to focus on higher education. There was plenty of room for improvement. Eighty-six percent of the graduates of the University of Texas at Austin who pursued graduate studies did so elsewhere; faculty salaries were forty-sixth in the nation; and New York produced five times more Ph.D.s annually than did Texas. Connally believed that education would be the engine that drove his other two goals.

Connally's record of achievement is impressive. He established a coordinating board for higher education and raised taxes so that he could increase faculty salaries, enlarge campuses, and create the University of Texas system in 1967. Under the leadership of his close friend, Frank C. Erwin, whom he appointed to the board of regents, appropriations for the flagship campus in Austin increased in little more than a decade from $40.4 million to $349.7 million. The system's enrollment also increased rapidly, from 29,940 to 77,437 during the same period.

Connally's programs, plus a large infusion of federal grants from the Great Society program, also led to a major increase in medical research and the number of medical schools in the state. As World War II ended, the state had only three medical schools—the University of Texas Medical Branch at Galveston, Baylor College of Medicine in Houston, and Southwestern Medical College in Dallas— that graduated about 200 doctors per year, not enough to care for the state's growing population. With the availability of federal funding, however, Texas established four new schools during the 1960s and 1970s. Although it was a private institution, Baylor would begin to receive some state funds during the 1980s.

With increased federal financing for medical research as well as the Lyndon B. Johnson Space Center (originally known as the Manned Spacecraft Center), which the National Aeronautics and Space Administration (NASA) had located near Houston, doctors at several of the Texas medical schools produced distinguished treatments and research. Perhaps the best known are Michael E. DeBakey of Methodist Hospital and Denton Cooley of St. Luke's Hospital in Houston, who have been in the forefront of heart surgery and transplants since the 1960s. DeBakey performed the first successful coronary artery bypass graft procedure in 1964, and Cooley performed the first heart transplant in the United States in 1968. Both have continued their research by working on mechanical hearts. In Dallas, meanwhile, Joseph L. Goldstein and Michael S. Brown of the University of Texas Health Science Center performed research in physiology and medicine that would be recognized with the Nobel Prize in 1985.

The Arts

Connally's establishment of the Texas Fine Arts Commission (now the Texas Commission on the Arts) in 1965, which also receives funds through the National Endowment for the Arts, called attention to the state's growing cultural facilities. Long famous for its philanthropists, Texas is fortunate that a number of them chose to establish museums. One of the first to do so was Jessie Marion Koogler McNay of San Antonio, who left her Mexican-Mediterranean style mansion and art collection as a private museum, which opened in 1954. The Amon Carter Museum, designed by New York architect Philip Johnson, followed in 1961. Five years later the Museum of Fine Arts in Houston opened Bayou Bend, the mansion that architect John F. Staub had designed for Ima Hogg and her brothers, as a decorative arts center. Perhaps the best known of the Texas museums is the Kimbell Art Museum in Fort Worth, which opened in 1972 but one of the most eclectic, which opened to the public in 1978, is the Stark Museum of Art in Orange, containing H. J. Lutcher Stark's vast collections of Americana.

Museums also seemed to lead the way for modern architecture in the state. In 1950 John and Dominique de Menil hired architect Philip Johnson to design an International Style house for them in Houston. He went on to design the campus plan and several of the buildings for the University of St. Thomas in Houston in 1958, the same year that Ludwig Mies van der Rohe, one of the pioneers of the International Style, designed Cullinan Hall as an addition to the Museum of Fine Arts. At the same time, San Antonio architect O'Neil Ford was designing the campus of Trinity University with the revolutionary lift-slab construction technique that cut building costs considerably. Other distinguished architecture can be seen in the San Antonio Art Museum, which moved into the spectacularly renovated Lone Star Brewery in 1981; the new (1984) Dallas Museum of Art designed by Edward Larrabee Barnes; the Louis Kahn–designed Kimbell Art Museum in Fort Worth; and the new Museum of Fine Arts and the Menil Collection in Houston.

Perhaps the most recognizable building in the state after the Alamo is the Astrodome, the world's first fully air-conditioned, enclosed, domed, multipurpose sports stadium, which opened as the home of the Houston Astros baseball team in 1965. When it was determined that baseball players could not see fly balls against the bright glare of the plastic roof and crisscrossed girders during daylight, Judge Roy M. Hofheinz, head of the Houston Sports Association, ordered the roof painted. The lack of sunlight meant that natural grass could not grow in the stadium, so in a well-publicized event, Hofheinz obtained an artificial grass called Astroturf®. The Houston Oilers football team played there until moving to Nashville in 1997, and the domed stadium has hosted dozens of other sporting events as well as concerts, conventions, and religious meetings. Today the Astrodome is a relic, with both the Astros and the Houston Texans football team playing in other stadiums, but it continues to be popular with tourists, averaging approximately 4 million visitors a year since it opened.

Music in Texas still reflects the state's heterogeneous character. For years German music could be heard in the beer halls and gardens of San Antonio, while just a few streets over, in La Plaza del Zacate or Haymarket Square, Tejanos played Mexican folk and popular music. Adopting the accordion from German musicians, Tejanos created the *conjunto* style, now popular through Texas and Mexico. Meanwhile, the folk music of the South combined with the cowboy style of Texas to create what became known as "hillbilly" music, which later evolved into the upscale country-and-western tunes that most of the state's radio stations now play. The first national country-and-western star may have been the singer Jimmy Rogers, who moved to Kerrville in 1929. A few years later, Bob Wills borrowed from such great jazzmen as Benny Goodman to create "western swing" and became popular as part of the band on W. Lee O'Daniel's radio program. Maurice Woodward "Tex" Ritter carved a niche for himself and other singing cowboys in what became known as "western music" and smoothed the way for the stars of the B-grade western movies of the 1950s. One such star was Gene Autry (from Tioga), who parlayed his matinee stardom into a chain of radio stations and, ultimately, ownership of the California Angels major league baseball team and the establishment of the Autry Museum of Western Heritage in Los Angeles. Ernest Tubb took country music in another direction and pioneered what was widely known as "honky-tonk" music, whereas performers like George Jones retained his "country" style but moved more toward the popular genre. Meanwhile, Willie Nelson and a few others who had become disaffected with the growing mainstream of country music moved to Central Texas, where they developed the "Austin sound." Tejanos have contributed to country-and-western music, too, with singers like Trini López, Freddy Fender, Johnny Rodríguez, and Selena.

African Americans have also added much to the Texas arts mix. Ornette Coleman of Fort Worth has revolutionized the way the saxophone is used in what has been called "free jazz." Weldon Leo "Jack" Teagarden of Vernon became a famous jazz trombonist and orchestra leader and played with Benny Goodman, Louis Armstrong, and Paul Whiteman, among others. Perhaps the most famous African American Texan artist, however, is Alvin Ailey of Rogers, who debuted on Broadway in 1954 and stayed on in New York to study ballet and modern dance, founding the Alvin Ailey American Dance Theater in 1958. Drawing upon his "blood memories" of Central Texas, the blues, spirituals, and gospel music, he choreographed his masterpiece, *Revelations,* in 1960, and the company remains popular today with its unique blend of modern and African American expression.

Classical music in Texas also boomed in postwar Texas. Although the state had three major symphony orchestras during the 1950s (in Dallas, Houston, and San Antonio), it was pianist Van Cliburn's triumph at the prestigious Tchaikovsky Piano Competition in Moscow in 1958 that really attracted the public's attention. Van Cliburn was born in Shreveport, Louisiana, but grew up in Kilgore. After winning international fame, in 1962 he helped establish the Van Cliburn International Piano Competition in Fort Worth. Meanwhile, smaller orchestras gained prominence and proficiency in Amarillo, Fort Worth, Austin, Wichita Falls, Corpus Christi, Beaumont, and Lubbock, and other cities. Opera companies perform throughout the state, but there are professional companies in San Antonio, Fort Worth, Houston, Dallas, and Austin. In addition, pianist James Dick performs and administers the International Festival-Institute at Round Top, established in 1971 to provide advanced musical instruction to gifted young musicians.

After Johnson and Connally

Both Johnson and Connally announced that they would not run again in 1968. Johnson was driven from office by the social unrest and urban riots accompanying the war in Vietnam. He returned to the Hill Country, where he wrote his memoirs and supervised construction of the Lyndon Baines Johnson Library and Museum on the campus of the University of Texas at Austin.

When Connally stepped down after three terms, Preston Smith of Lubbock, who had served the same length of time as lieutenant governor, was elected governor in 1968. Having grown up on a West Texas farm and worked his way through high school and college, Smith was a plainspoken, uncharismatic but sensitive person who suffered by comparison with Connally and was offended by suggestions that he lacked a vivid or humorous personality. His trademark polka-dot tie (Governor Price Daniel had advised him to wear something distinctive) seemed only to call attention to his bland personality. "He doesn't look very good," an editorial writer once said in comparing him to the former University of Texas All-American quarterback, Bobby Layne, also from Lubbock, "all he can do is beat you. . . ."

Smith was an informal governor, who often answered his own telephone and placed calls himself, but Smith seemed to have an inherent mistrust of city dwellers, and the feeling was mutual. He immediately set the tone for his administration when he was called to Washington in the spring of 1969 to learn the details of a federal plan designed to ease slum housing problems. He opposed the plan, he told reporters, because "some people just like to live in slums." Elected at the same time as Smith was Lieutenant Governor Ben Barnes, almost Smith's polar opposite and the apparent heir of the Johnson/Connally mantle. He had been the youngest person to serve as Speaker of the Texas House when he was elected in 1965 at age twenty-six and polled more votes than any other Texas politician—more than 2 million—to win the lieutenant governor's office.

The third member of the leadership was House Speaker Gus Mutscher, who assumed the office with the opening of the legislative session in 1969. A conservative from rural Washington County, Mutscher soon exercised surprising control over the House (even more than Barnes had exercised) by sticking to his motto, "never quit politicking and never underestimate your opponent." With Mutscher as Speaker and Barnes as lieutenant governor, Smith proposed a program that met with only limited success. He got a pay raise for schoolteachers, but his water plan, which proposed transferring water from East Texas or from outside the state to needy areas like West Texas, went down to defeat at the hands of East Texas legislators. He supported the establishment of two new medical schools, one in Houston and the other in Lubbock, and got funding for a minimum wage and for vocational education. In the face of a "housewives' revolt," he was embarrassed to have to back away from a Barnes/Mutscher proposal to add food to the list of items subject to a sales tax.

The State and the Federal Government

Federal interventions during the 1960s and early 1970s continued to alter the social and political fabric of Texas, much as Key had anticipated. First, U.S. Supreme Court decisions continued to have an impact: *Baker v. Carr* (1962) and *Reynolds v. Sims* (1964) brought about what became known as "one-man, one-vote," which meant that both houses of a state legislature had to be reapportioned regularly so that each representative and each senator would represent approximately the same number of citizens. Subsequent decisions affecting Texas held that a county could have more than one member of the Senate and more than seven members of the House. These were important legal victories for urban areas, for the first time permitting neighborhoods such as Houston's largely African American fifth ward to have its own representation.

Federal actions also continued to broaden the electorate. The Twenty-fourth Amendment to the U.S. Constitution in 1964 made it illegal to require a poll tax to vote in federal elections. The big change, however, came with the Voting Rights Act of 1965, which outlawed state and local restrictions on voters as being prejudiced against minorities and provided federal officials to monitor elections. Even after adoption of the Twenty-fourth Amendment, Texas had kept the poll tax for state elections, but it succumbed to the Voting Rights Act in 1966 when Judge Homer Thornberry, a Johnson protégé on the U.S. Court of Appeals of the Fifth Judicial Circuit, ruled it to be a violation of the Fourteenth Amendment. Subsequent to these reforms, Barbara Jordan from Houston's fifth ward became the first African American to be elected to the Texas Senate since Reconstruction, and Curtis Graves and J. E. Lockridge were elected to the House. In 1971, the Twenty-sixth Amendment to the U.S. Constitution gave eighteen-year-olds the right to vote.

These changes also opened up local elections and changed the face of governing bodies in Texas. The political complexion of the Senate changed overnight, for example, as moderates or liberals gained office. The impact of these changes also reached the local level, and organizations such as the Citizen's Charter Association in Dallas and the Good Government League in San Antonio, which had dominated local politics for years, lost their control.

Coupled with these federal acts, African Americans and Hispanics continued to campaign for their rights. Nonviolent protests that began in Greensboro, North Carolina in 1960 spread to Texas. Students at two historically African American colleges, Wiley and Bishop, staged nonviolent demonstrations that year, and the following year students at Texas Southern, the University of Texas, North Texas State, and other colleges protested against segregated theaters and restaurants. James Farmer, a native Texan, headed the Congress of Racial Equality (CORE). Fear of bad publicity and federal laws gradually brought segregation to an end. In Houston, for example, local businesspeople quietly reached an agreement with a group of college students and community leaders that if they would not demonstrate, public facilities would be integrated. While cities throughout the nation dissolved into confrontations and riots, for the most part Texas cities remained calm.

Meanwhile, the Hispanic takeover of the city council of Crystal City, the G.I. Forum, Henry González's losing gubernatorial campaign, and the 1960 presidential race had all encouraged Mexican Americans to participate in the political process. The result was the Political Association of Spanish-speaking Organizations (PASO), which, assisted by Teamsters officials, helped organize the Hispanic voters in Crystal City in 1963. Their new majorities on both the city council and school board sent a message to the white minority population throughout South Texas that their rule would no longer go unchallenged, and there were subsequent victories in Carrizo Springs and Cotulla.

This new-found Hispanic activism resulted in one of Governor Connally's most embarrassing moments in the summer of 1966. In an effort to get the legislature to adopt a minimum wage of $1.25 per hour, organizers in South Texas decided to march the almost 500 miles from Rio Grande City to the capital to focus publicity on the effort.

Although he had planned to be out of the capitol building on Labor Day, when the marchers were scheduled to arrive, Connally told Speaker of the House Ben Barnes, "I don't think it's right for them to just march up here and nobody be here." With Barnes and Attorney General Waggoner Carr in tow, he headed to New Braunfels, where he found the bedraggled little band. Shaking hands all around, Connally urged them to call off their march because "things can get out of hand in marches," a veiled reference to the riots, violence, and bloodshed that had occurred throughout the nation, and said that he would not receive them in Austin because he did not want to "lend the dignity" of his office to any such demonstration. When state labor leaders arrived at the scene, the mood turned more confrontational and developed into a standoff, and Connally, Barnes, and Carr departed in their executive limousine.

The marchers rallied and continued gathering supporters as they neared Austin and as word of Connally's rather highhanded attempt to stop them spread. Senator Yarborough met the marchers at the capitol on Labor Day along with a number of supporters, including labor leader Cesar Chavez of the United Farm Workers and Connally's brother, Golfrey, an economics professor at San Antonio College. The minimum wage law did not pass that year, but historian Arnoldo de León considers this incident one of the formative events of the Chicano movement.

Some of the most dramatic changes during this time gave women many rights that they had been long denied. One woman who epitomized women's rights was Oveta Culp Hobby, wife of the former governor, who had been the head of the Women's Interest Section in the army during the war and then became the first commander of the Women's Army Corps. She supported Eisenhower for president in 1952 and was named to his cabinet as the first secretary of health, education, and welfare in 1953. When she returned to Houston in 1955, she resumed her position as president and editor of the *Houston Post* and, in 1956, became chair of the board of directors of the newly organized Bank of Texas. Another prominent woman in Texas at this time was Dallas attorney Hermine D. Tobolowsky, president of the Texas Federation of Business and Professional Women. Tobolowsky had been active in women's rights issues since the 1940s and had identified a number of laws that she considered discriminatory, such as the denial of women's right to control property they owned at marriage or had inherited. Tobolowsky testified before a state Senate committee hearing in support of a bill that would have changed a number of these laws. The bill failed, and her treatment before the committee caused her to resolve instead to support an equal rights amendment to the Texas Constitution. She traveled around the state speaking to women and civic groups, rallying support for the amendment. It was introduced at each session of the legislature from 1959 until it was finally passed in 1972, after the introduction of the federal Equal Rights Amendment in Congress provided greater credibility for the effort. Tobolowsky became known as the mother of the Texas Equal Rights Amendment.

As the feminist movement gained strength nationally, many Texas women began to pay attention. The National Organization for Women (NOW) established chapters in Texas, and the Texas Women's Political Caucus encouraged women to get involved in the political process. New methods of birth control (such as the birth control pill) influenced many women to delay marriage and family while pursuing an education or a career. Again, actions of the federal government had an impact. Title VII of the 1964 Civil Rights Act (upheld by later court decisions) gave women control of their property and prohibited discrimination in the workplace. Title IX of the 1972 Education Amendments required universities receiving federal funds to allow women to participate in many activities that had been closed to them. In sports, for example, universities organized a number of teams for women athletes that had not existed before Title IX. That same year Texan attorney Sarah Weddington argued and won the case of *Roe v. Wade* in the U.S. Supreme Court, which struck down many state laws forbidding abortion.

The Sharpstown Scandal

Another federal intervention in Texas helped bring down the curtain on an era. In 1971 the Securities and Exchange Commission (SEC) charged several state officials and others with illegally profiting from a quick-turnover stock deal. According to the SEC, Houston businessman Frank Sharp wanted a banking bill passed that would provide state-backed depositor's insurance to exempt his bank, Sharpstown State Bank, from regulation by the Federal Deposit Insurance Corporation; he bribed several current and former state officials by loaning them money from his bank to purchase stock in one of his companies, the National Bankers Life Insurance Company, with the understanding that once the bill had passed, they could sell their stock at a handsome profit. Governor Smith included the bank bill in the agenda for the second special legislative session in 1971, and Speaker of the House Gus Mutscher, Jr. and his allies pushed it through. Smith later vetoed the bill on the advice of the state's banking law experts, but not until he and several others had sold their stock at a profit. A Travis County grand jury indicted Mutscher, Representative Tommy Shannon, and Rush McGinty (an aide to Mutscher) for bribery and conspiracy, and in March 1972 they were convicted by an Abilene jury and given a sentence of five years' probation. The SEC alleged that Governor Smith, state Democratic chair and state banking board member Elmer Baum and others had been bribed, but did not charge them.

The result was a political house-cleaning and modest shift to the left in the state's politics. Conservative rancher Dolph Briscoe of Uvalde, who had run in 1968, swept the gubernatorial primary with a "Mr. Clean" image. This election ended the political career of Lieutenant Governor Barnes, who had also borrowed money from Sharp's bank, even though he was not named in the scandal, and was, therefore, connected to it in the minds of most voters. The same fate awaited Governor Smith, who ran a poor fourth.

The vengeful voters elected moderate Houston newspaper executive William P. Hobby, Jr., son of Governor Hobby, as lieutenant governor over seven other Democratic candidates, and reform-minded moderate Democrat John L. Hill of Houston, a former secretary of state, defeated the popular three-term attorney general, Crawford C. Martin, who had been criticized for his handling of the stock fraud scandal and for his own relationship with Frank Sharp. The makeup of the legislature also changed significantly, with many newcomers winning election to both the House and the Senate. Virtually all of these newly elected officials were committed to reform of some kind, and Briscoe did not try to control the party machinery in the same way that his predecessors had.

The Sharpstown scandal proved a boon to Republicans. Coupled with it was former Governor John Connally's service as secretary of the treasury in Republican President Richard Nixon's administration and his support of Nixon against Democrat George McGovern in the 1972 presidential election.

Conclusion

Although by 1972 the state was not engaged in the kind of class conflict that Key had foreseen, there was no denying that Texas had changed. The post-war growth of the oil and gas industry (including the state's acquisition of the Tidelands) had major impact on the economy, but not sufficient to offset the dramatic growth in population. The percentage of population growth in Texas outpaced that of the nation throughout the twentieth century. In 1962 the state passed the 10-million mark in population, reaching 11,197,730 in 1970, and most Texans lived in the cities. Rather than being restructured, however, the state's antiquated tax system was merely amended, primarily by the 1961 sales tax, which by 2000 supplied 55 percent of the state's revenue. By the election of 1972, economic and political power had shifted to the cities, raising the issues of urban poverty, crime, and pollution for Texas that had long plagued eastern urban centers. The state's cultural institutions flourished after the war, with new museums, orchestras, and educational facilities being established, but, again, these improvements hardly kept pace with the needs that an increased population demanded.

Major changes in governing procedures opened up the Democratic Party, tilting it toward the liberals, despite Governor Shivers' conservative influence. Lyndon Johnson's long career had a great impact on the state, but with his departure from office, the move back to the right, and to the Republican Party, resumed and included even his long-time friend and campaign manager, John Connally. These issues, along with the perennial problem of water, would dominate political dialogue during the last quarter of the twentieth century.

SUGGESTED READINGS

Stressing the One-Party System
The best overview for these years is George Norris Green, *The Establishment in Texas Politics: The Primitive Years, 1938–1957* (1984).

Conservatives Take Charge
One of the key books of the era is V. O. Key, Jr., *Southern Politics in State and Nation* (1949). Chandler Davidson, *Race and Class in Texas Politics* (1990) provides a

thoughtful update and analysis of Key's theories. See also Paul Casdorf, *A History of the Republican Party in Texas, 1865–1965* (1965); Roger M. Olien, *From Token to Triumph: The Texas Republicans Since 1920* (1982); and Don E. Carleton, *Red Scare: Right-Wing Hysteria, Fifties Fanaticism, and Their Legacy in Texas* (1985).

For agriculture, see Donald E. Green, *Land of the Underground Rain: Irrigation on the Texas High Plains, 1910–1970* (1973).

Lyndon Baines Johnson Era

Among the more useful and readable biographies of Lyndon Johnson are Robert A. Caro, *The Years of Lyndon Johnson: Means of Ascent* (1990) and *Master of the Senate* (2002); Robert Dalleck, *Lone Star Rising: Lyndon Johnson and His Times, 1908–1960* (1991); also see Dorsey B. Hardeman and Donald C. Bacon, *Rayburn: A Biography* (1987); Sam Kinch, Jr. and Stuart Long's *Allan Shivers: The Pied Piper of Texas Politics* (1974); James Reston, Jr.'s *The Lone Star: The Life of John Connally* (1989); Don E. Carleton's *A Breed So Rare: The Life of J. R. Parten, Liberal Texas Oilman, 1896–1992* (1999); and Patrick Cox's *Ralph Yarborough: The People's Senator* (2001).

For information on African Americans, see Alwyn Barr, *Black Texans: A History of African Americans in Texas, 1528–1995* (1996); Robert D. Bullard, *Invisible Houston: The Black Experience in Boom and Bust* (1987); Merline Pitre, *In Struggle Against Jim Crow: Lulu B. White and the NAACP, 1900–1957* (1999). For material on women, see Ruthe Winegarten, *Black Texas Women: A Sourcebook* (1996). Good studies relating to the history of Mexican Americans include Carl Allsup, *The American G.I. Forum: Origins and Evolution* (1982), and Guadalupe San Miguel, Jr., *Let All of Them Take Heed: Mexican Americans and the Campaign for Educational Equality in Texas, 1910–1981* (1987).

14

Recognizing Old and New Realities

"Don't go for it unless it's already in your pocket," Lyndon Johnson had advised Texas state senator Barbara Jordan when she contemplated running for a seat in the U.S. Congress. Having the seat in her pocket must have been hard to imagine in her first two attempts to gain election to a Texas legislative seat in the early 1960s. Then, the African American attorney from Houston's fifth district had campaigned hard as part of a liberal Democratic coalition, only to see many of the white males in the coalition get elected while she did not. At the time, her family—loving and supportive but reflecting the traditional values of the era—had encouraged her to curtail her political activity and think about getting married.

The political picture for Jordan and other minority candidates had begun to change with the federal actions of the mid-1960s: The Voting Rights Act had struck down some of the barriers to voting African Americans had experienced, the "poll tax" that had kept many poor people and minorities from exercising their franchise had been abolished, and the Supreme Court had mandated redistricting efforts, giving urban areas with larger populations more representatives than rural areas and moving from at-large legislative seats to officeholders representing specific areas.

All of this meant that Jordan could run again in a new Houston eleventh district with a significant percentage of African American voters. In 1966, she won a state senate seat and by 1972 had proven herself a skilled team player, enjoyed the support of former president Johnson, and served as vice chair of the newest senate redistricting panel, allowing her to help control the shape her district would take. Running for the U.S. Congress seat from herdistrict, she was opposed by another African American legislator, Curtis

1972	Women and minorities gain greater visibility in Texas political elections
1974	State legislators reject new state constitution
1975	State legislators approve revised new constitution, but voters reject it
1978	William Clements, Jr. becomes the first Republican governor of Texas since Reconstruction
1979	Juneteenth is made an official state holiday
Mid-80s	The oil business in Texas goes from boom to bust; Michael Dell begins his successful personal computer business
1985	Joseph L. Goldstein and Michael S. Brown of the University of Texas Health Science Center in Dallas win Nobel Prize in medicine for their research on cholesterol
1989	Southwest Airline revenues top $1 billion
1992	U.S., Canada, and Mexico enter into North American Free Trade Agreement (NAFTA)
1997	Senate Bill 1 creates a new state water-planning system
1998	After two decades of alternating Democratic and Republican administrations, Republicans consolidate control of state offices
2000	George W. Bush wins U.S. presidency; Hispanics are largest ethnic group in four major Texas cities
2001	Enron Corporation declares bankruptcy in Houston
2002	Rio Grande runs dry

Graves. She had such solid support, how-ever, both within the Texas political power structure and within her home district, that she became the "first black woman from a southern state to serve in Congress," the first African American elected to Congress from Texas, and one of only two African American represen-tatives elected from the South, which had not sent an African American to Con-gress since 1900. Chosen to speak before the Democratic National Convention in 1976, she would tell delegates, "[M]y presence here is one additional bit of ev-idence that the American Dream need not forever be deferred." Jordan's politi-cal success symbolized some of the changes that were taking place in Texas and the nation.

As Texans moved through the final decades of the twentieth century and into the twenty-first, their actions and attitudes as individuals and groups, along with broader economic and political trends, were redefining Texas identity. The state continued to have a significantly diverse population, but now that diversity was increasingly acknowledged and reflected in the political structures and culture of Texas. The state continued to be a land of economic opportunity, but this oppor-tunity increasingly took new forms—or new variations on old forms. Texans continued to value independence and limited government, but now these values had to be balanced even more than before with the challenges of dynamic urban growth, rural decline, and federal-state relations. Finally, the state continued to be defined in large part by the scope and character of its land, but Texans continued to be drawn to the cities; the remaining farmers and ranchers found the chal-lenges of working and managing the land more and more daunting; and Texans, in general, faced the challenges of preserving natural features and natural re-sources that they had previously taken for granted.

Diversity in Texas Politics and Culture

The entrance of women and minorities into the political arena reflected a new di-versity in Texas politics, due in part, to the rise of the liberal coalition in the Dem-ocratic party anticipated by Keys. This new political diversity also came from Republican inroads into, and eventual dominance of, state political power struc-tures as Texans reacted to the shift in the Democratic Party by choosing more conservative candidates.

Women Entering Texas Politics

Women—Mexican American, African American, and Anglo—began setting po-litical agendas and winning local elections. In the late 1960s, Anita Martinez of Dallas had already become the first Mexican American woman to win a city council seat in Texas, and Wilhemina Delco had become the first African Ameri-can, male or female, to be elected to the Austin school board. But the year 1972 proved to be a watershed for Texas women in politics. Other women saw Barbara

Jordan campaigning for the U.S. Congress and Sissy Farenthold for the governor-ship and began to see opportunities for themselves. Farenthold had directly chal-lenged the power structure in her three years in the House. She would recall, "I went there knowing blacks weren't represented, knowing Mexican Americans weren't represented. I found that Texans weren't even represented." She and Jor-dan cosponsored the Equal Legal Rights amendment to the Texas constitution.

Sefronia Thompson, a former junior- and senior-high-school teacher, would recall being galvanized by Jordan's and Farenthold's campaigns: "I just wanted to be part of this big harvest, so I ran. And I won." Thompson was one of a record half-dozen women elected to the Texas legislature, along with a young lawyer named Sarah Weddington, who was about to win a landmark Supreme Court case, *Roe v. Wade,* that legalized abortion in the United States. Among the other five were two African American women, Thompson and Eddie Bernice Johnson, and two Republican women, Betty Andujar and Kay Bailey.

Farenthold, perceived to be too liberal by many, lost to Dolph Briscoe in the 1972 runoff, but at the Democratic National Convention that year, she finished second in the voting for the vice presidential slot on the Democratic presidential ticket. Forty percent of the delegates were women—compared to a mere 13 per-cent only four years before. At the Republican convention as well, a previously unheard-of 30 percent of the delegates were women.

Throughout the 1970s women would continue to emerge in positions of local and regional political power. In 1973 Lucy Patterson became the first African American woman elected to the Dallas city council. In 1975 Lila Cockrell became the first female mayor of a major Texas city, in this case, San Antonio. The next year, Irma Rangel, a former teacher and lawyer from Kingsville, became the first Mexican American woman to take a seat in the Texas House of Representatives, and Ann Richards, on her way to the governor's mansion, became a Travis County commissioner.

After election, these women found themselves facing an entrenched power structure. "There was a great deal of questioning and suspicion and challenge we could see on the faces of those who had been there longer, because this was a new crop of people for a new era," Eddie Bernice Johnson would recall, "and we ush-ered in that era, and we made a lot of changes."

Johnson worked on bills to eliminate credit discrimination against women and housing and home loan discrimination against minorities. She also labored to see that poor children got school breakfasts and pregnant teachers got benefits and job security. She and most of the other women in these new roles supported the federal Equal Rights Amendment (ERA), first introduced in 1923 to promote gender equality and resurrected in the fertile activist climate of the late 1960s. The U.S. House and Senate had passed the measure. Now enough states needed to ratify the ERA to make it law, and the Texas legislature was among the first in the southern states to do so, having recently also ratified the Equal Legal Rights amendment to the state constitution sponsored by Jordan and Farenthold.

By the late 1970s, the national mood had become more conservative and national ERA ratification failed. Nonetheless, many of the 2,000 delegates to the 1977 International Women's Year National Conference in Houston remained energized by the possibilities of addressing social, legal, and economic ills and inequities in government. Charged by the federal government with preparing a national plan, they produced a host of resolutions dealing with women's rights and general societal improvements.

Minorities Entering Texas Politics

Even as women focused on bringing gender issues into the public forum, members of ethnic minorities—male and female—continued to fight for their own distinctive identities as Texans and for inclusion in the political power structure. African Americans were building on the civil rights movement of the 1950s and the activism of the 1960s. So were Texas Hispanics, primarily Mexican Americans and Mexicans but also those with roots in other Central and South American countries.

In 1970, the census showed 2 million Mexican Americans in the state—about one in every five Texans. They were concentrated in the major cities, but also spread through the agricultural and cattle-raising towns of South and West Texas. Although many were laborers, an increasing number—some 40 percent—constituted a Mexican American middle class. Activism was growing among young urban Hispanics, particularly with the rise of the Mexican American Youth Organization (MAYO) after a 1967 activist meeting in El Paso and 1968 meetings in San Antonio and Laredo. MAYO leaders felt that institutional racism in the United States was so entrenched that only an alternate educational system delivered by Mexican Americans for Mexican Americans and through a separate political party could address their concerns. Their activism led to another political coup in Crystal City—and to a serious run by candidates of a Mexican American party for the offices of Texas governor and lieutenant governor.

The earlier Crystal City "electoral revolt" had come to naught by 1965, leaving many of the town's Mexican Americans wary when José Angel Gutiérrez returned to the town as a MAYO organizer in 1969. Gutiérrez, who had participated in the 1963 revolt as a college student, found that despite the wariness, many in the community were upset over the stipulation that candidates for the Crystal City High School homecoming queen and court must have a parent who had graduated from the school. In this era of limited schooling for most Mexican Americans, this requirement eliminated most Hispanic students. Now Gutiérrez, his wife Luz, activist Virginia Músquiz, and others organized a response that put pressure on the school board and mounted a student boycott that emptied the high school of almost 65 percent of its students.

By spring, a new political party was coalescing across South Texas—*La Raza Unida* (United Race or United People), which would come to be known as RUP (*Raza Unida* Party). In Crystal City, Gutiérrez and other RUP candidates captured school board and city council seats. Gutiérrez would explain, "We were chicanos [a

1970s term for activist Mexican Americans] who were starved for any kind of meaningful participation in decision making, policy making and leadership positions."

Similar victories occurred in other South Texas towns, with RUP leaders pushing an agenda of Chicano power and pride, although the results were not as dramatic as in Crystal City, where Gutiérrez became school board chair. Here Anglo teachers uneasy with the new regime were replaced with RUP supporters; much of the curriculum centered on Mexican American experience; and militant stances became the norm—for example, the boycott of lettuce picked by exploited migrant workers.

On the heels of the RUP victories came a barrage of legal challenges to the party's place on the ballot and, in the next local South Texas elections, significant vote fraud against the activists. Gutiérrez, anticipating opposition from Mexican American Democrats, among others, felt that the party was not ready for statewide races in 1972; other activists overruled him, however, and Gutiérrez assisted in selecting an RUP candidate for governor, a twenty-nine-year-old attorney from Waco and MAYO member named Ramsey Muñiz.

Muñiz, a former lineman on the Baylor University football team, traveled the state in a red 1962 Plymouth announcing that "the days of being led to the polls to vote straight ticket for these two other parties are over." He was personable and energetic, militant without being overbearing, and his campaign gained momentum when Dolph Briscoe beat Farenthold for the Democratic nomination, for Briscoe, to many, was an old-style Democrat unfriendly to minorities.

Muñiz's running mate for the lieutenant governor slot, Alma Canales, was only twenty-four years old, more radical, and less able or less inclined to court the middle class, whether Mexican American or Anglo. Her presence on the ticket signaled the depth of Tejana activism. In fact, in 1971 in Houston, Mexican American women had put together "the first national conference ever organized to deal specifically with Mexican-American women's concerns." Even the relatively conservative LULAC Women's Affairs Committee in this election year had a Texas convention at which they urged LULAC to work for women in important governmental positions.

With Muñiz officially a candidate, Gutiérrez became his campaign manager, and they drew an array of not only militant but moderate Mexican Americans and liberal Anglos to consider voting for the third party. At the same time, they drew the ire of liberal Democrats unhappy with Briscoe but unwilling to desert the party. Lawyer Mark Smith warned ominously, "A vote for La Raza Unida . . . is nothing more than a vote for destruction of the liberal wing of the Democratic Party in Texas. It can only result in destroying any hope for a two-party state in which the Democratic Party is representative of the voice of the people and their aspirations for justice."

On election day, Muñiz's 6.28 percent of the vote may have looked negligible to some, but it was sufficient to worry the leaders of the Texas Democratic Party, for Muñiz almost became the spoiler in a race in which Briscoe could have expected the RUP votes.

La Raza Unida continued to challenge the traditional political power structure. Gutiérrez, who would go on to become judge for Zavala County, called for education and urban renewal that would take into account Mexican American claims, plans, and dreams for their city communities. Many of the activists advocated a brand of cultural nationalism that seemed as exclusive in its way as that of the Anglo-dominated institutional structures; these activists split off both from other Mexican American groups and from the RUP, with different ideologies and political plans. But they stimulated older organizations, such as the G.I. Forum and LULAC, to address issues of equality more boldly, and they demonstrated that Tejanos and Tejanas could and would participate in defining local and state government issues. Another organization, the Mexican American Legal Defense and Education Fund (MALDEF) led the way in creating court challenges to the imbalances in power.

The Rise of the Republican Party

For more than a century, the traditional power structure in Texas had been strongly, consistently based in the Democratic Party. But with the changes of the 1960s and 1970s, liberals had gained power within the party and had drawn activist reformers and minority voters in to it. Most of the women and minorities entering politics in the 1970s did so as Democrats. More conservative Texans— including many concerned with the rapid rate of societal and political change they saw the activists advocating—switched to the Republican Party. This was already evident in 1972, when white middle-class voters uneasy with Lyndon Johnson's Great Society and affirmative action elected seventeen Republicans to the House and three to the Senate. Among these new legislators were the two Republican women mentioned earlier, Betty Andujar and Kay Bailey. In the state elections of 1978, for the first time since Reconstruction, a Republican—Dallas oilman William Clements, Jr.—was elected governor of the state. His victory, albeit by a narrow margin, surprised his opponent, Attorney General John Hill, and was attributed in part to Democratic president Jimmy Carter's declining popularity.

In the 1980s, Texas was clearly a two-party state. Democrat Mark White defeated Clements in the election of 1982, but four years later, their positions were reversed, with Clements defeating the incumbent White.

Minorities and women continued to make inroads. In 1981, Democrat Henry Cisneros was elected mayor of San Antonio; not since the administration of Juan Seguín 140 years earlier had a Hispanic headed the city government. That same year, El Paso native Sandra Day O'Connor was appointed to the U.S. Supreme Court by the Republican administration of Ronald Reagan, and became the first woman on the Court. In 1982, Democrat Ann Richards won election as Texas state treasurer; not since the second election of Ma Ferguson in 1932 had a woman achieved election to statewide office.

In 1986, Democrat Judith Zaffirini of Laredo joined the Texas state senate as its first Mexican American woman. A former volunteer lobbyist for the mentally ill and mentally retarded, Zaffirini set out to effect what she termed a "momma agenda," advocating legislation that reflected her concerns as a mother, such as requiring immunizations for Texas children. She playfully reminded a fellow legislator, "[Y]ou study legislation from the perspective of Bubba. I study legislation from the perspective of Momma."

Zaffirini entered the senate as conservatism continued to grow nationally. The American South as a whole shifted heavily from Democratic to Republican, the majority voting in national elections for Ronald Reagan for president, then for his former vice president and former Texas congressman George H. W. Bush, who was elected president in 1988. In Texas, Clements could enjoy a "veto-proof" second term, as the 1986 elections had given Republicans more than one-third of the House votes. Then in 1990 former Travis County commissioner and state treasurer Ann Richards outpolled Republican oilman and rancher Clayton Williams in the governor's race. At the same time, Republican Kay Bailey, now Kay Bailey Hutchinson, won election as state treasurer, earning recognition as the first Republican woman to secure a statewide elective position, and Democrat Dan Morales became the first Hispanic attorney general. Two years later, Morris Overstreet became the first African American to gain statewide office with his election as a judge on the Texas Court of Criminal Appeals.

Despite these gains—and Richards's appointments of women, Hispanics, and African Americans to various boards and commissions—the percentages of women and minority officeholders remained low. For example, in the early 1990s, city councils in Texas, on average, had one Hispanic for every twenty members, even though the Hispanic population statewide was one in five. In 1997, the Texas House and Senate had thirty-three women members, but this constituted less than 20 percent of the total membership.

The biggest political story of the 1990s was the consolidation of Republican power in the state. George W. Bush, son of the former president, won the governorship in 1994 and again in 1998, making Republican inroads even in heavily Hispanic counties identified with the liberal Democrats. In 1998 Republicans also won the offices of lieutenant governor, attorney general, comptroller, land commissioner, and agriculture commissioner. Republicans were a majority in the Texas state senate and close to a majority in the House. Among these numbers were women and minorities; for example, Susan Combs served as the first female agriculture commissioner, and Michael Williams, an African American, became a railroad commissioner.

The growing power of the Texas Republican Party in the 1990s reflected national events, including a "Republican revolution" in 1994 during the administration of Democratic president Bill Clinton. The Republican Party vowed to regain the control it had lost when incumbent George H. W. Bush lost the presidency to Clinton in 1992, and it did so in large part by propelling Texas governor George W. Bush into the White House in the election of 2000. Governor Bush ran against Democrat Al Gore, Clinton's vice president, for the presidency. Vote-count problems, particularly in Florida, delayed election results, but a Supreme Court ruling on the returns confirmed totals that led to Bush's victory in the electoral college.

Cultural Diversity

The political ferment of the 1960s and 1970s had made clear that Texans were not homogenous. It gave rise to a new or more widely shared appreciation for different cultural roots and ways of life. The Institute of Texas Cultures, first opened in 1968 as part of the San Antonio World's Fair at Hemisfair Plaza, began producing exhibits and information on Texans of various ethnic origins, its mission statement to "enhanc[e] the understanding of the history and diverse cultures of Texas." In 1973 San Antonio students and community members of Mexican heritage staged an original play, *El Alamo: Our Version of What Happened.* Visitors flocked to celebrations of traditional German holidays such as Oktoberfest and those adapted from their experiences in Texas, such as the Easter Fires pageant in Fredericksburg, which combines ancient custom with Texas frontier legend. Texans of African American descent reinvigorated the celebration of "Juneteenth," a holiday originally established to mark the public recognition of Texas slaves' freedom—the reading of the Emancipation Proclamation in Galveston with the arrival of federal troops after the Civil War. In 1979, the legislature voted to make the date, June 19, a state holiday.

The Hispanic population of Texas, primarily Mexican and Mexican American, continued to grow, with census figures doubling between 1970 and 1990. Holidays such as Cinco de Mayo and Mexican Independence Day were more widely celebrated. In many parts of the state, Hispanic families staged elaborate *quinceaneras* (fifteenth-birthday parties) for their daughters, complete with formal dresses and tuxedos for the honoree and attendants, with dances and dinners. In this era, Tejano music became more widespread and prevalent. The biggest Tejana sensation in this period was a young woman from South Texas, Selena Quintanilla Perez, who became the "queen of Tejano music." Known only as Selena, she achieved national prominence in the early 1990s, before her untimely death in 1995.

By the time of Selena's death, Texas's cultural diversity was apparent to the most casual observer, much of it of a strong ethnic character and much of it simply reflecting a range of cultural expression. New immigrants to Texas, most of them urban, added to the mix of perspectives and experiences. They joined long-term residents in both challenging and celebrating the stereotypes of Texans as oil-rich ranchers, as "urban cowboys" and rural ones, as "outlaws" in keeping with the country music scene of the 1970s, when Willie Nelson, Waylon Jennings, and others brought a fresh Texas-based perspective to the genre. Texans could navigate the steps of the cotton-eye Joe in country dance halls and attend local opera productions in Houston, Dallas, Fort Worth, San Antonio, Austin, and Beaumont. They could visit exhibits of art produced in the state and also study the paintings of the old masters at the Kimbell Art Museum in Fort Worth; they could camp out at the Kerrville Folk Festival and attend the symphony orchestra productions in Texas's major cities.

The new acknowledgment of cultural and ethnic diversity did not come without some friction. Prominent Hispanic author Sandra Cisneros sparked controversy by painting her house a vivid shade of purple in the King William district of San Antonio, a historic area in which homeowners agreed to restrictive codes to maintain nineteenth-century appearances. When some neighbors and other city residents complained, Cisneros argued before the San Antonio Historic Review Board that the color was historically accurate for the population of Mexican heritage. The new exterior paint stayed.

There were larger issues based on ethnic identity, such as historic claims to land ownership, with Hispanics descended from pre-Revolution Spanish and Mexican families fighting in court for title to lands taken over years before by Anglos. Prominent in this regard was the Balli family, which included hundreds of descendants of a Spanish priest who had received an eighteenth-century grant to what is now Padre Island. The Ballis had arrived in Spanish Texas in 1749 and had amassed "more than a million acres of ranchland by 1800." By 1938, however, the family was struggling economically, and eleven family members sold their portions of the island to a New York lawyer named Gilbert Kerlin.

Family members contended in subsequent lawsuits that Kerlin had cheated them out of agreed-upon mineral rights and had failed to return a portion of the island to them in a 1942 settlement of competing claims. Generations of the Balli family vowed to carry on the fight as Kerlin's wealth, in part from oil and gas royalties from Padre Island, soared. In late 2000, a Brownsville jury sided with them, granting almost 300 family members a judgment of $2.7 million.

Another issue was the rights of the three remaining Native American tribes in Texas. The Alabama-Coushattas of East Texas, a small group with long ties of loyalty and friendship to the state, had been recognized by the state as a tribe in the nineteenth century. The Kickapoos, who in the nineteenth century had sought refuge from land and cultural pressures by moving through Texas to Mexico, had established enough of a presence on the Rio Grande border that in 1983 they were granted recognition from the U.S. government and land in Texas near El Indio. The Tiguas of Ysleta had been considered virtually extinct and had received no state or federal recognition, and therefore had no official tribal identity or claim to government benefits. The Tiguas' quest for federal recognition and the introduction of gambling operations by the three tribes reminded other Texans of the continued presence of Native American groups and of the challenges posed by the new awareness of diversity.

In the 1960s, El Paso city officials contacted the Bureau of Indian Affairs to report that the Tiguas, descendants of Pueblo Indians who had settled near El Paso after the 1680 Pueblo revolt against the Spanish, were living in the expanding city on land tribal members had occupied "for centuries" and were unable to pay their property taxes.

The Tiguas had never been under the jurisdiction of the Bureau of Indian Affairs, but the federal government rather grudgingly acknowledged the Tiguas as a tribe, leading the way to tax exemption. It insisted, however, that the state rather than the federal government act as their trustee. State funds proved inadequate and uneven, and the Tiguas continued a marginal existence, relying in large part on the development and management of a restaurant and tourist center.

Then, in 1984, state attorney general Jim Mattox ruled that it was against the state constitution for Native American tribes to have "special rights." This meant that the Tiguas would lose both the limited state funds and their tax exemption. Tribal members responded by petitioning for federal trust status, along with the Alabama-Coushatta tribe, which was seeking a restoration of this status.

In August 1987, the Tiguas—1,124 individuals—won federal trust status, thereby protecting their land claims and securing federal funds and services. Some tribes nationally were turning to gaming operations to improve employment rates and living conditions the federal government had not effectively addressed. As part of the trust agreement, however, the Tiguas acknowledged that gambling would not occur "where gambling is not permitted in Texas." The state government did not want to open the door to Native American gaming, and the Tiguas were expected not to maneuver around this stipulation by claiming federal reservation rights.

But when the state entered the lottery business in 1992, the Tiguas argued that gambling was now permitted across Texas, and they opened a bingo hall, then a high-stakes gambling casino. By 1999 the casino was pulling in almost $60 million a year in profits and had become a major economic force in the El Paso area, employing 800 people, less than half of whom were tribal members.

In 1999 Texas attorney general John Cornyn filed suit against the Tiguas, arguing that they had violated the 1987 trust status provision against gambling where gambling was not permitted in the state. In September 2001 he won against the Tiguas in district court, and in early 2002, having lost an appeal, they closed the casino. The ruling also affected the Alabama-Coushattas, who only briefly opened a casino in 2002, but despite the judgment, the state was unable to stop a Kickapoo gaming operaion at Eagle Pass on the Mexican border.

In the 2000 census, Native Americans added up to .5 percent of all Texans; the African American population continued to hover at about 12 percent of the state total; and the Hispanic population was growing rapidly, at 32 percent constituting almost one-third of the census total. Although a little over half of the population was categorized as "white," by 2000, in El Paso and San Antonio as well as Houston and Dallas, Hispanics were the largest ethnic group, outnumbering African Americans and Anglos. The effect of such shifts was dramatically demonstrated in the Democratic primary runoff for the governorship in 2001, when for the first time the two contenders, Dan Morales and Tony Sanchez, publicly debated in both English and Spanish.

The changes in public perceptions could be profound. After winning her seat in the U.S. Congress, Barbara Jordan had gone on to become a national figure: a

Barbara Jordan built upon her experience as a Texas legislator to mount a winning run for the U.S. Congress in 1972; as "the first black woman from a southern state" in Congress, she became a powerful national political figure. *(© Bettmann/CORBIS)*

formidable member of the House Judiciary Committee during the 1974 Watergate hearings, keynote speaker at the 1976 and 1992 Democratic National Conventions, professor at the Lyndon Baines Johnson School of Public Affairs in Austin, and ethics advisor to Governor Ann Richards. Jordan had traveled a long way from her modest beginnings in Houston's Fifth Ward and from the double challenge of growing up black and female in an era when African Americans did not share in the power structure and women were expected to focus on being wives and homemakers. After Jordan's death in 1996, Texas playwright Larry King's play *The Dead President's Club* included an appearance by God in the form of a strong, articulate black woman. No one could miss the resemblance to Jordan.

Developing Economic Opportunity

As new faces and agendas appeared on the Texas political scene, the economic landscape of the state was changing as well. One then-unheralded sign of these changes was Michael Dell's arrival at the University of Texas in fall 1983 to begin his freshman year. He was starting college as a premed student, but had brought three computers with him and a lot of ideas about making and selling them. Dell's future, like the Texas economy, was about to take some interesting turns.

The Oil Industry

During the 1970s and early 1980s, economic opportunity in Texas remained largely defined by the state's status as the chief oil-producing state in the nation. The 1974 Arab embargo on oil to the United States led to higher prices for Texas oil, and the oil and gas industry continued to fuel the Texas economy to the extent that the state gained a great degree of economic independence. Nationally, worries over the availability of foreign oil proliferated as high oil prices prevailed, taking another spike upward as a result of the Iranian revolution and reductions in Saudi Arabian oil production. By 1981, the industry generated more than one-fourth of the state's economic revenues and provided a bonanza of funds both for the state and for private enterprise. These funds gave the state legislature a surplus and stimulated prolific business growth and real estate speculation.

Then, when the Middle Eastern Organization of Petroleum Exporting Countries dropped its prices, Texas oil revenues stopped climbing and soon began to drop. In the mid-1980s, the economy built on oil teetered and crashed. Rigs closed down; large numbers of oil workers lost jobs. Even more ominous for the state as a whole, the state government lost revenues from oil and property taxes from oil producers and was forced to cut back services. At the same time, the spiraling real estate market that had been tied to oil prosperity took a nosedive; people were suddenly stuck with mortgages that far exceeded the new value of their property, and new office space now sat empty.

Then, to make things worse,, the savings and loan industry in Texas blew apart. With recent federal deregulation by the Reagan administration, savings and loan institutions had been operating with little restraint and foresight, offering generous interest rates to depositors, generous loans to the real estate speculators and energy developers, and—in many cases—generous payouts to their top personnel. As an economic recession took hold, the savings and loans failed at a rate not seen since the Great Depression of the 1930s, and out-of-state investors claimed them, again undercutting an independent Texas economic base. The whole banking industry in Texas was affected, the ten largest banking operations passing out of the control of state corporations by 1990.

By 1993, money generated by the oil and gas industry had dropped to 7 percent of total state revenues, and one-third of the jobs in the petroleum industry from the early 1980s had vanished. This trend continued as oil prices remained low— at $10 a barrel in 1999, less than a third of what the prices had been in the early 1980s. The same year, 6,658 wells were drilled, less than a quarter of the number drilled in the peak year of 1984.

Although oil prices started rising in 2000, even the most optimistic observers no longer saw the petroleum industry as a viable foundation for the Texas economy. The lesson of the mid-1980s was to diversify, and Texans had done so, reviving the economy with a variety of enterprises by the mid-1990s.

Private and Public Enterprise

Perhaps the most prominent success stories were in the field of electronics and computer technology. Texas businessman H. Ross Perot had already become a billionaire in the 1960s with his Electronic Data Systems (EDS) in Dallas, which supplied software and services for the fledgling computer industry. Dallas-based Texas Instruments, which had introduced "the first portable hand-held calculator" in 1971, struggled in the 1970s and early 1980s. But it rebounded, continuing to provide electronics and electronic research for the military and for commercial use, extending its research and development into computer graphics and related areas. Microelectronics and Computer Technology Corporation (MCC), begun by people in computer and semiconductor manufacturing in Austin in 1982, became one of the biggest research and development consortia for the U.S. electronics industry; it drew together government and university researchers, high-tech companies, and users of their technologies.

Another significant research and development venture got underway in Texas in the early 1990s. The U.S. Department of Energy had selected the state as the location for a superconducting super collider, a huge particle accelerator that would serve as a research tool for particle physicists studying the dynamics of matter by accelerating the subatomic particles in an extended tunnel. With congressional funding, more than 2,000 employees were brought together at a site outside Waxahachie, where a laboratory and tunnel were under construction. As the cost of the project climbed, however, a nervous Congress withdrew funding, halting progress on the project in 1993.

In the midst of all of these scientific and technological ups and downs, Michael Dell became a phenomenal success story. In his one year at the University of Texas, he had registered his own company, PC's Limited, with the state of Texas, and by the end of that school year had incorporated the company under the name Dell Computer Corporation. On the proceeds of his direct sales of "upgraded PCs, upgrade kits, and add-on components to people in the Austin area," he rented office space in North Austin and hired an engineer to use the newly available chip sets (streamlined versions of the chips necessary to put together a PC) to create Dell's first computer. Dell developed a business model that allowed the company to avoid the costs of high levels of inventory by building the computers according to customer specifications.

By 2002 Dell Computer Corp. claimed 14 percent of the global market in computers and appeared poised to continue increasing its share. "If you want to be in the PC business, you have to compete against Dell," noted the chief executive officer (CEO) of another company, "and that is very, very difficult." Dell Computer Corp. became the largest employer in Austin and Michael Dell became the richest individual under the age of 40 in the world.

Other innovative, entrepreneurial growth appeared as solid but proved chimerical. In 1986, Enron Corporation, an energy-trading firm that had grown out of a small gas-pipeline operation, moved its headquarters to Houston and in an

When energy-trading giant Enron Corporation crashed in late 2001, workers at its headquarters facility and individual stockholders were not the only Texans affected; Houston lost a major source of philanthropic funding, and state teacher and employee retirement systems suffered heavy stock and bond losses. *(© Reuters NewMedia Inc./CORBIS)*

age of energy deregulation proceeded to become "the world's largest energy-trading company"; by 2000 Enron reported over $100 billion in annual revenues and mounted what was touted as "the most successful Internet effort of any firm in any business." The company built a handsome forty-story headquarters, with a million-dollar hand-etched glass relief map of the world suspended in the atrium. It subsidized the arts in Houston and the Astros baseball stadium, putting its distinctive "E" logo on the facility, and even sponsored a venture capital initiative to aid and nurture minority businesses in Houston's Fifth Ward.

In late fall 2001, however, it became clear that Enron's reported revenues had little basis in fact. Not only did thousands of Enron employees and individual investors lose their substantial investments in the company, but Texas's teacher retirement system and employee retirement system together lost almost $60 million in stocks and bonds. In the litigious aftermath of Enron's fall, Houston itself felt the pinch as not only jobs but a variety of vital community funding disappeared.

More stable economic activity in this period centered on other enterprises. The timbering industry employed almost 100,000 people in 1999. Tourism drew more than 1 million international visitors in 1999; the overall tourist rate was second only to California's, and the Sea World Amusement Park in San Antonio rivaled—but did not surpass—the Alamo as the top tourist attraction. The construction industry was robust, and exports in 2001 made up more than 13 percent of all U.S. exports. Most of these exports fell into four categories: "electronics, industrial machinery (including computers), chemicals and petrochemicals, and transportation equipment." Also significant were retail trade, health services, and some manufacturing.

The aerospace industry continued to develop. In the 1990s NASA partnered with other agencies, private firms, and Texas universities to develop new methods of exploring outer space. The airline industry in Texas continued to grow as well. American Airlines, which had relocated its headquarters from the New York area to the Dallas–Fort Worth area, set up the first of a series of hubs at Dallas–Fort Worth airport in 1981. Meanwhile, entrepreneur Herb Kelleher persevered in his vision of a "no-frills" airline based in Texas to create Southwest Airlines with the aid of Rollin King, owner of a small Texas flying service, and former Universal Airline president Marion Lamar Muse. The first in-state flight took off from Love Field in 1971, and by 1973, the airline had become profitable, despite fares as low as $10. In 1989, Southwest's annual revenues topped $1 billion, and it would go on to become the United States's "most consistently profitable airline" in the 1990s.

Other Texans with a vision made their fortunes in a wide variety of ways. Houston native Mary Kay Ash started a modest beauty business in the 1960s with a formula for face cream and parlayed it into an industry bringing in $2 billion annually.

As some Texans parlayed their visions into corporate enterprises, others found employment in the major cities. By 2000, eighty-four out of every 100 Texans lived in urban areas, and eight out of every ten new jobs were located in only five "magnet" cities: Dallas, Fort Worth, Austin, San Antonio, and Houston. In these cities, the average wage was about $40,000 a year, whereas in the rest of Texas it remained about $29,000 a year. The latter figure seemed large in many rural counties; in the four counties at the bottom of the personal-income scale, all located along the Rio Grande, average annual income ranged from $8,588 to $10,826.

Organized labor had been in a decline since the 1970s, as workers increasingly entered fields without strong unionizing traditions—fields such as retail trade and government—and as employment shrank in jobs associated with unions, such as oil and manufacturing. From the early 1970s to the early 1990s, the percentage of the labor force employed in "highly unionized industries" dropped by more than half, from 47 percent to 21 percent. Other factors were involved as well, including a political climate less receptive to unionizing, corporate practices such as contracting with outside firms and individuals, and development of the computer and other industries in which management proved resistant and workers unresponsive to labor organizing.

One controversial economic measure in this era was a national free trade agreement that promised to impact Texas more than it would other states. In 1992, President George H. W. Bush joined Canadian and Mexican leaders in signing the North American Free Trade Agreement (NAFTA). This agreement promised a gradual reduction of trade barriers throughout North America, making it easier and more economical for the three nations to move their goods across the borders. It greatly altered U.S.-Mexican trade, and most of that trade centered in or moved through Texas. Critics feared that the increased Mexican truck traffic would strain the state's highways and that there would be environmental costs, especially along the border where Mexico's *maquiladoras* (industrial plants) multiplied under the new agreement. But the pact did significantly increase commerce between Texas and Mexico, infusing money and thousands of jobs into the state economy. One study by the Texas Public Policy Foundation showed that trade with both Mexico and Canada had increased Texas exports to these countries by $16 billion between 1993 and 1999. Further, 70 percent of all American exports to Mexico moved through Texas.

Ranching and Farming in Texas

The three components of an earlier state economy—farming, ranching, and oil—seemed far removed from the lives of most Texans. Large operations and small remained, however. The fabled King Ranch, invigorated by oil and gas royalties totaling more than $1 billion between 1945 and 1994, had become a corporation with its own exploratory oil and gas division and international cattle operation. Most Texas ranches were far more modest in scope, even economically marginal, but the flush oil years of the 1970s and early 1980s had stimulated the ranching business in some areas of the state. A study of Washington County, a portion of Stephen F. Austin's old colonies, showed oilmen and other wealthy investors buying up ranches after World War II and making improvements to the land and to the breeding of the cattle. This "rural gentrification" became more pronounced in the 1970s, as wealthy Houston residents continued to buy Washington County farms and ranches and raise cattle, often consulting with local agricultural extension agents. There was a certain extravagance and simple hobbyist mentality to much of the activity in the late 1970s and early 1980s, as the "mink and manure set" gave lavish parties to show off their pricey purebred cattle. The phenomenon was fueled primarily by their ability to sink large amounts of money into ranching. But many of them did preserve and improve the ranch lands and participate in the modernization of ranching practices.

By the 1990s, only about 1 percent of Texas workers were "directly engaged in agriculture," and the number of people in the ranching industry had dwindled as well. Nevertheless, Texas continues to claim an important role nationally in farming and ranching. In 1999, even though the number of Texas farms had dropped by more than 40 percent since 1940, the 227,000 remaining constituted the largest number of farms in any American state, as did the land they covered—131 million acres. They also were valued at more than 18 times their 1950 prices. Texas continued to lead all states in cotton production in most annual tallies, producing one-fourth of all cotton grown in the United States and exporting large amounts to Mexico, Japan, and South Korea. In the meantime, ranchers were contributing almost 65 percent of the agricultural revenues in Texas, with almost

Despite the economic challenges, many Texans continue to be drawn to ranching. Sandy Faison is representative of those who made a shift to part- or full-time ranching after years of employment in urban areas. *(© Robert Burns, Texas Cooperative Extension)*

all of the 254 counties ranking cattle first among their agricultural revenues. The state was also unmatched in the United States not only in beef cattle but also in cattle "on feed," wool, mohair, goats, sheep, and lambs.

These achievements required great diligence and modern approaches. Many people were surprised to learn that more cattle were being raised in East Texas and more cotton grown in West Texas, the latter thanks to extensive irrigation. But heat and drought, frigid and changeable winters, rains at the wrong time, the heavy expenses of maintaining a farm or a ranch—all conspired to keep farmers and ranchers sweating out their profit margins. Those ranchers who could do so depended on oil production on their ranch land to help finance their livestock and other agricultural losses.

Most farmers and ranchers continued in these occupations because of a deep attachment to the work, to the land and the cattle. In a 1998 interview on his ranching operation, famed baseball pitcher Nolan Ryan explained, "It's an emotional attachment you have. . . . Those cows, they live with you day in and day out, and you have raised them from the first day they hit the ground to the day they become a producing cow in your herd."

With all the challenges of raising crops and cattle, however, farmers and ranchers knew to use the technology at their disposal. They employed computers to maintain business records, information, and projections on crop treatments and yields and cattle development. "There's a record that follows the calf all the way to the end product," ranch manager Tom Woodward of the Broseco Ranch would explain, with computer files showing "everything that was done to that calf from the day he was born, even before he was born," including his diet and vaccines. Ranchers even used technological imaging to determine the state of a live animal's hide.

Farmers and ranchers employed a range of scientific management techniques, including pest- and disease-control, efficient irrigation, improved breeding and crossbreeding of plants and animals, improved medical treatment for the cattle, and wildlife management. Ranchers used improved grazing systems, such as "time controlled grazing."

With a continued increase in mechanization and improved equipment, many of the old jobs of farm and ranch were completed more efficiently. With state-of-the-art working pens, Woodward noted, "our guys can put a herd of 300 cows and 300 calves in the pens and have them worked before lunch."

Innovations were fueled in part by the work in research facilities, such as the Institute of Biosciences and Technology at the Houston Medical Center and the Crop Biotechnology Center at Texas A&M, both established in the 1990s. Research goals included the strengthening and diversifying of crops and cattle breeds to avoid such situations as a disease wiping out one's whole crop or herd.

In many ways, farmers and ranchers simply learned to work smarter—for example, videotaping cattle for sale rather than taking them to market (cattle often lose valuable weight in the process), and purchasing already trained horses rather than using ranch resources to raise them.

These people still intimately tied to the land, however, also faced the vagaries of the weather in ways the majority of Texans could no longer fully appreciate. In the extended drought of 1994–96, farmers lost their crops and ranchers sold off their cattle, but the cattle market then became saturated and prices fell. In the meantime, the feed on which ranchers depended in dry times for their remaining herds grew more expensive. A frigid winter in 1996–97 compounded problems for many, and when it was followed by more drought conditions in 1998, 1999, and 2000, farmers and ranchers faced billions of dollars of agricultural losses, including an estimated $515 million in 2000 alone. Some gave up on staple crops; even though cotton remained big business in Texas in 2002, farmers could not sell it for even half of what it cost many of them to grow it.

In the Rio Grande valley, continuing drought combined with the Mexican government's failure to deliver on a shared water treaty to turn the Rio Grande into a trickle and leave farmers' fields high and dry. Third-generation farmers converted citrus groves to goat pastures and cotton, vegetable, and sugar cane fields into grain sorghum fields, the latter a good dry-weather crop but one that produces little profit. Almost half of the valley's irrigated cropland had become dry farmland in only six years. Bud Wentz, a long-term farmer outside Brownsville, told a reporter, "I used to want to keep the farm for the next generation. Now, I could care less." He expressed an eagerness to walk away "if I could sell every acre for a decent price."

Most held on, however, and the overall productivity remained impressive, with agriculture generating almost $28 billion of business in the state in 2000. The Texas economy itself performed well that year, given a boost by improved export markets and by a new upturn in oil and gas activity. Unemployment rates were lower than they had been in more than twenty years. Texans continued to look for ways to innovate and diversify in a new world in which "knowledge work" and service work predominated, the former based on the use, manipulation, interpretation, and transmission of information. The economic growth of the cities, however, generated new problems, including how the cities could absorb the new immigrants and continue to provide jobs. Further, the social and economic disparities between the vital cities and the rest of the state became more pronounced, leading Pampa representative Warren Chisum to note that "rural Texas is in real trouble." In the meantime, Texas government officials sought to address the shifting contours of Texans' lives and work.

Governing a Changing State

Through this period, Texas government had to adapt to the needs and pressures of a burgeoning citizenry, to continued movement of Texans and out-of-state immigrants to key cities, to the changes in the state economy, and to increasingly complex relations with the federal government. And it had to do so with a constitution that was already dated when it was first adopted in 1876, with its emphasis on agrarian interests and a limited state government. Further, while redistricting in the 1970s had "broken the conservative male domination of the legislature," the legislature continued to operate with traditional and limited responses to many pressing modern problems.

Government in the 1970s and 1980s

In the early 1970s, reformers began pushing to rewrite the state constitution rather than continue the unwieldy system of multiple amendments. It took a constitutional convention amendment to start the process, which voters approved in 1972. Legislators were to meet for this purpose in January 1974. In the meantime, a commission appointed by state officials prepared a new constitution for their consideration. Among its changes: convening the legislature every year rather than every other year and granting the governor more power.

When the legislature met as a convention, it rejected the document; the measure failed by three votes to gain the necessary two-thirds majority approval. Some had argued that the changes did not go far enough, others that they went too far. The governor at the time, Dolph Briscoe, had appeared indifferent to the initiative, and ultimately came out against it. The next legislature, in 1975, tried a different tack: Members put together eight amendments to the old constitution that resembled the one rejected the previous year. They won passage of the amendments in the legislature, but not among the voters. Texas would continue into the twenty-first century with the 1876 Constitution and its elaborate set of amendments—ninety-one were approved in the decade of the 1980s alone, a total of more than 350 passed into law by the mid-1990s. It would also continue under this constitution with a chief executive with very limited powers and a legislature that shut down for long periods.

Governors of the 1970s and 1980s provided uneven and generally uninspired leadership as they continued to grapple with where to get and how to use tax money, most of them focusing on educational initiatives and budget matters. Briscoe's predecessor, former legislator and lieutenant governor Preston Smith, demonstrated an impressive insider's knowledge of state government. His emphasis on school funding did yield a number of new colleges, professional schools, and branches of technological institutes, including some in his native West Texas, which had had few higher education options. But overall, as his comment on people "lik[ing] to live in slums" indicates, his administration largely maintained the status quo.

Briscoe focused primarily on his pledge of "no new taxes," in part by transferring much school funding from the state to local school districts. Republican governor Clements also focused on cost-cutting measures, in part by requiring state agencies to justify their existence and their work forces.

After the gubernatorial election of 1982, when attorney general and Democrat Mark White defeated Clements, White put much emphasis on education. Students continued to swell the state's college population, particularly at its two flagship public universities, the University of Texas and Texas A&M University, as well as at other state schools funded and regulated by a legislatively-approved coordinating board. White led in the legislature's passing of House Bill 72, or the Educational Reform Act, a weighty and far-reaching education law that reconfigured the state board of education. The bill instituted a "no pass, no play" requirement for students in public schools—barring students who had failed a class from participating in extracurricular activities in the next grading period—and tried to balance the state funding allocated to poor and wealthy districts. Many saw the "no pass, no play" law as aimed at student athletes and feared it would undermine high school sports programs in a state where high school football has often been a focal point for whole communities. After a legal challenge in which a Texas court upheld the rule, the U.S. Supreme Court refused to consider the issue. The law stood, although it was modified in the mid-1990s, shortening the suspension period and allowing the suspended student to practice or rehearse with the extracurricular group.

School Funding

Although the "no pass, no play" rule was controversial, most problematic was the attempt to balance the funding allocated to Texas K-12 school districts. Because most of the money for schools came from property taxes in the areas served by the schools, wealthier communities received more money per student than poorer communities. Thus, in the late 1980s the Alamo Heights independent school district had more than fourteen times the property value per student of the Edgewood independent school district, also in Béxar County.

Unsatisfied with White's attempts at reform, the Edgewood independent school district pursued a lawsuit asserting that the state's reliance on local property taxes made its educational system imbalanced and unconstitutional.

Clements returned and defeated White in 1986, as White struggled with the education issues and as the state experienced the economic downturn brought on by falling oil prices. Facing loss of one-fourth of the state's revenue as a result, Clements, too, struggled to keep the state government functioning, reluctantly abandoning his own "no new taxes" stance and dealing with a new state court ruling that indicated the need for more taxes to maintain the public schools. Under his administration, the legislature continued to work to equalize school expenditures per student across the state, as poorer districts still had less than half of what the richer districts had to spend per student. In the meantime, as a result of the Edgewood lawsuit the Texas Supreme Court in 1989 instructed the legislature to put into place an equitable system before school started in the fall of 1990.

A series of legislative initiatives resulted, each deemed unacceptable by the courts. Finally, in 1993, the legislature offered a plan whereby each school in the wealthy districts would aid redistribution in one of five ways: by combining its tax base with that of a poorer district, by giving the state money "to help pay for students in poorer districts," by "contracting to educate students in other districts," by simply consolidating with another district or other districts, or by "transferring some of its commercial taxable property to another district's tax roles."

By the end of the twentieth century, this new refinement of a so-called Robin Hood law had led to much dissatisfaction. The limited but important state funding for schools declined and districts judged "wealthy" fought to hang onto their resources, many of them in the midst of major spurts in enrollment. In 2001, a number of these school districts sued to get "Robin Hood" overturned, but a district judge affirmed its legality.

Other Governing Challenges

The governors of this era also contended with federal government involvement in Texas affairs. Federal courts enforced integration plans for public schools in the early 1970s. Federal agencies such as the U.S. Justice Department, the Occupational Safety and Health Administration, and the Environmental Protection Agency required compliance with federal regulations. The federal government at varying rates supplemented state coffers for public schools, for cities, for highways and transportation, and for welfare costs, but Texas continued to rank low in federal grants awarded to states.

In the 1980s prison reform became an issue illustrating the tensions and complexities of federal-state relations. Texas had been convicting and incarcerating

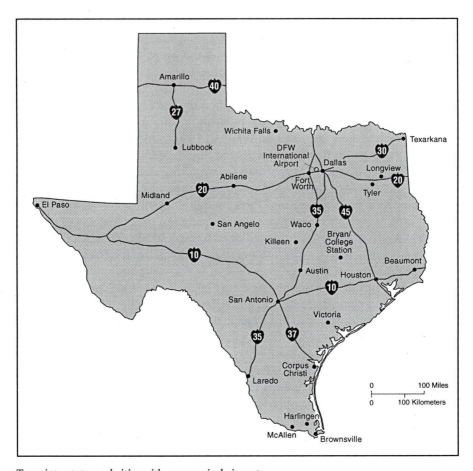

Texas interstates and cities with commerical airports.

convicts at a rate far exceeding the national average, and although the state population had grown 19 percent between 1968 and 1978, the prison population had doubled. David Ruiz, an inmate who had been convicted of armed robbery, led other Texas inmates in filing suit against prison system director W. James Estelle in 1972, citing overcrowding and other substandard prison conditions. In 1980 federal judge William Wayne Justice agreed that the conditions constituted "cruel and unusual punishment," outlawed by the U.S. Constitution. He ordered the state to make major penal changes. Officials scrambled to comply, in part by establishing new prison facilities. But the prison population continued to swell disproportionately to the general population.

Texas also became a lightning rod for national and international debate in its use of the death penalty. The death penalty had been reinstated by the state legislature during the Briscoe administration, reflecting a national trend in which most Americans polled favored it. But Texas became far more rigorous than other states in employing capital punishment. By 2002, Texas's thirty-three executions for the year made up almost half of the U.S. total for the year.

The governors of the 1990s continued to struggle with such issues, but in an improving economy. Texas was changing rapidly in this decade. Not only was the minority population becoming the majority in many cities, but key cities and out-lying areas were experiencing staggering population growth. In the oil boom of the 1970s and early 1980s, Texas had attracted 2.5 million immigrants, making it the third most populated state. Now, in the 1990s, as more people were drawn to business opportunities or high-tech jobs and the warm climate, it shot to second place, behind California. By 2002, despite some slowdown in growth and employment, three of the fastest-growing counties in the nation were located in Texas.

In El Paso and other urban areas outside the five magnet cities, rapid growth was the rule, but not prosperity. City governments faced infrastructure problems, including clogged highways, urban sprawl, crowded new schools, and a general drain on city services. Even in the magnet cities—primarily Dallas, Houston, and Austin—unemployment sometimes jumped dramatically, as more hopefuls poured in and the economy shifted.

In the midst of such urban challenges, there remained among much of the populace a resistance to local, state, and federal government regulation. At its most pronounced, this resistance was manifested in the separation of the Branch

Traffic jams, urban sprawl, and other growth issues kept local, county, regional, and state officials busy as Texas in the 1990s became the second most populous state in the nation, with some of the fastest-growing counties in the United States. (© *Ralph Krabner/Index Stock Imagery, Inc.*)

Davidians under David Koresh until their final fatal encounter with federal agents at the Branch Davidian compound outside Waco in 1993, and in the 1990s activities of a group in West Texas calling itself the "Republic of Texas" and asserting that Texas remains independent of the United States. On a milder level, Texans have repeatedly rejected the idea of a state income tax, including a brief attempt by officials to introduce one in the late 1980s. Residents of Houston in the 1980s also resisted attempts to institute standard zoning measures that would regulate the city's growth; in doing so, they maintained Houston's record as "the largest unzoned city in the United States." Smaller communities wrangled over the rules and regulations that would come with incorporation, particularly those involving land use.

At the state level, although the economy was strong during the administrations of Ann Richards and her successor, George W. Bush, many problems remained. For example, in 1998, Texas ranked first among the states in people without health insurance, second in the number of people in state prisons, and third in the number of people living below the poverty level. There also remained a violent strain of racism, as evidenced that year by the dragging death of African American James Byrd, Jr., by three white men in East Texas. The men were captured and tried, and hate-crime legislation was developed to address such crimes of racism and prejudice. With Bush vacating the governorship for the presidency, the post passed to Lieutenant Governor Rick Perry, who signed this legislation and identified transportation and higher education as his priorities.

As Texas moved into the twenty-first century, government officials grappled with urban and suburban growth and rural decline, lack of a state income tax, and Texas's low ranking in a number of health-and-welfare areas, including welfare payments, mental health care, and immunizations. They also faced the knowledge that Texas ranked first among the states in releases of toxic chemicals into the air and was developing serious problems in meeting the water needs of communities, farms, ranches, and industries. Although conservation efforts were underway, much of the Texas landscape had been polluted, depleted, and scarred.

Tending the Land

In the last few decades of the twentieth century, the federal and state governments passed legislation reflecting a new awareness of the need to preserve and protect the land and its resources. In this they were aided or spurred by national environmental organizations such as the Sierra Club and Audubon Society and also by local Texas grass-roots organizations concerned about vanishing species, an altered landscape, and air, ground, and water pollution. In particular, water pollution, shortages, and anticipated shortages began to come to the fore as a major issue for twenty-first-century Texas.

The Environment

Most of the Big Thicket, a biological treasure trove in East Texas, gained federal protection as the first national biological preserve in 1974. Here were found "relict" plants, located nowhere else and nurtured by the unique combination of soil and humidity. In the late 1990s the preserve provided sustenance for hundreds of bird and plant species, as well as fifty kinds of reptiles and sixty mammal species.

Yet the Texas environment was much altered and diminished from the days when the Spanish explored its grasslands and flowing rivers. Texas in the 1700s had over 12 million acres of Blackland Prairie, over 16 million acres of bottomland hardwood forests, and over 12 million acres of coastal wetlands. By the late 1990s all of these had been reduced by more than half, endangering a range of plants and animals—from ocelots to brown pelicans, from red-cockaded woodpeckers to Kemp's ridley sea turtles.

Texas had boasted the largest expanses of prairies in the United States, with as many as 300 native plant species and with great stands of Indian grass, switchgrass, big bluestem, and little bluestem predominating. Yet even on the remaining prairie acreage, plowing had destroyed the native grasses.

The picture was far from uniformly grim. Environmental organizations were seeking to preserve and expand the pockets of native grasses, rich in nutrients and part of a healthy ecosystem. The East Texas forests had benefited from efforts by the U.S. Forest Service and the Civilian Conservation Corps of the 1930s, as well as improved timbering practices by companies in the late twentieth century, so significant reforestation occurred in some of the areas already stripped or "farmed out."

In addition, farmers, ranchers, and even suburbanites had worked with biologists, game wardens, and other state and federal officials on stewardship of their land and its resources. The federal Endangered Species Act of 1973 with its rules for habitat protection had not always been popular in the state, as landowners struggled with requirements that sometimes seemed harsh and unreasonable. Many landowners were deeply committed to caring for their property but felt constrained by government regulations made at a distance. Yet good land-use and wildlife management practices, whether imposed by law or sought out and adopted, had yielded thriving wild turkey and deer populations and made Texas the premier bird-watching area in the world.

The government and citizens' groups tried to stop or reduce industry pollution in Texas as aging smokestacks continued to belch out sulfur dioxide and nitrogen oxide compounds. For example, in late 2001, the Central Texas environmental group Neighbors for Neighbors spurred the state to investigate Alcoa, Inc.'s Rockdale plant by charging that it was releasing unsafe amounts of these chemicals into the air, then in 2002 joined a lawsuit to force the plant to spend hundreds of millions of dollars to clean up emissions.

Even relatively benign development, such as light, "clean" industry or housing, put a strain on those cities and counties that were burgeoning; officials and neighbors of the new development struggled with everything from traffic problems and school overcrowding to loss of natural habitat for animals and plants. But increasingly, the greatest strain became how to ensure enough clean water.

Water Challenges

Water quality and availability in the late twentieth century became a chief concern for Texans, from the wetlands of the coast to the *playas* (shallow rainwater pools of the High Plains far to the northwest), from the state's many southward flowing rivers to its aquifers, the ancient, shallow underground seas fed by rainwater. The legislature, prodded by Lieutenant Governor Bob Bullock, slowly awoke to the issue, in 1997 passing Senate Bill 1, which split the state into sixteen water-planning areas. In each area, a regional water-planning group would project water needs and strategies for the next fifty years; all of these plans would be consolidated in 2002 and updated every five years.

The coastal wetlands, in particular, had suffered from the industrial development of the twentieth century. The Texas gulf coast shared with the Louisiana coast a distinction as "the petrochemical center of the nation," the Texas portion claiming almost 60 percent of American petrochemical capacity. Galveston Bay, the seventh largest estuary in the United States, remained a busy port and the site of extensive petroleum refining and chemical production. Although the Texas Solid Waste Disposal Act of 1969 helped protect Galveston and other gulf bays from direct discharge of industrial waste, this estuary, also the location of a vital fisheries industry, continued to absorb pollution from the Houston Ship Channel, which connects it to the city of Houston. The channel, still narrow and shallow despite mid-twentieth-century attempts to improve it, continued to be the site of oil spills and other freighter, barge, and tanker accidents and collisions, many of the damaged ships carrying poisonous cargo.

Far away on Texas's High Plains the *playas* hosted more than a hundred species of migrant waterfowl, such as lesser Canada geese and mallards, and were home to sandhill cranes and other bird species. Almost half of the *playa* region was in Texas; beginning in the 1980s, the United States, Mexico, and Canada shared an agreement to protect these sites.

Major concern centered on Texas rivers. By 2002 some had appeared on lists of the most endangered U.S. rivers, among them the Clear Creek, the Trinity, the San Jacinto, the Concho, and the Guadalupe and its tributaries. In the last case, the environmental group American Rivers charged, the state was allowing too much of the Guadalupe's water to be used by urban areas, industries, and farmers, thereby adding to the ravages of drought and not only affecting water quality and flow but also doing damage to the coastal estuaries that normally received that flow. In 1993 the Rio Grande, a vital water source for Mexico, New Mexico, and Texas and the second longest river in the nation, was named one of the top ten endangered rivers in the United States and came to be known as the "Sewer Grande." In its more than 40,000 square miles of drainage in Texas, it provided irrigation for the cotton, pecan, and vegetable crops of West Texas and the citrus fruits, cotton, and vegetables of the lower Rio Grande valley in South Texas. But dams, drought, and too many people relying on what water existed took their toll. In addition, the proliferation of *maquiladoras* along the river border meant more human crowding, with inadequate sanitary conditions, and more industrial water and air pollution, with associated hazardous waste disposal issues.

These water woes were exacerbated by the treaty struggle between the United States and Mexico that had Rio Grande valley farmers worried and incensed. A 1944 agreement specified that Mexico would "provide the U.S. with one-third of all water that flows from six Rio Grande tributaries, or a minimum of . . . about 114 billion gallons." In exchange, the United States would provide Mexico "at least 1.5 million acre-feet of water per year from the Colorado River," with an acre-foot being the amount of water it takes to inundate an acre to the depth of a foot. By 1950, the United States was fulfilling its part of the agreement. But over the years between 1944 and 2002, Mexico built up a huge water debt while increasing irrigated acreage and claiming deferments based on drought conditions. In September 2001, the debt stood at 350,000 acre-feet.

With recurring droughts, water-sharing troubles with Mexico, and aquifers being pumped at a rapid rate, water issues in Texas have become critical. Various state and private organizations now seek to preserve and conserve Texas's water resources. (© *Bob Boerner, Texas Water Quality Association*)

In the meantime, the Rio Grande shrank dramatically in just twenty years (1982–2002), its flow at El Paso reduced from 33.39 cubic meters per second to 11.79 cubic meters. In spring 2002, the river simply ran dry before reaching its gulf outlet near Brownsville.

Aquifers presented an equally troubling picture. Texas was blessed with an abundance of these underground water sources—nine major ones (including the Edwards Aquifer) and twenty smaller ones spreading under four-fifths of the state. The problems with their depletion were illustrated when businessman Ron Pucek tapped the Edwards Aquifer, which spread through a maze of channels, fractures and limestone formations underlying nine central Texas counties. In 1991, Pucek spent $1 million drilling "the world's largest water well" into the aquifer to create the 85-acre Living Waters Artesian Springs Catfish Farm, confident that he could do this under the "right of capture" on which Texas water law is based: the idea that a landowner can draw as much water as he can pump from underneath his land.

In the same year, a scientific study showed that the Edwards Aquifer was being rapidly depleted and warned what would happen if a drought of the severity of the 1950s struck central Texas again. San Antonio alone made heavy demands upon the aquifer for its municipal water supply, being "one of the largest cities in the world that relies solely on a single ground-water source" for this purpose. Yet by some estimates Pucek, whose well could pump 40,000 gallons a minute, was using as much water as the city of San Antonio needed for a quarter million people, or one-fourth the population of the city.

In part, this meant that Pucek had a viable operation; the heavy flow of water helped ensure that the fish would be healthy, and the Medina River, into which his operation discharged, would remain unpolluted by the enterprise. In fact, the water discharge from the farm, although not usable as drinking water, promised to help "the downstream environment and the bays and estuaries of the Gulf Coast." Of course, the question arose as to whether Pucek should have the right to such vast amounts of a resource that could renew only slowly. Although the right of capture had made some sense in an earlier era when untapped ground water could not be accurately mapped or measured, most states had adopted more cautious approaches to groundwater supplies. Pucek's defenders argued that the water was available for reuse and that farming operations should take precedence over watering lawns in urban and suburban areas.

After just one season of operation, a series of challenges stopped the catfish farm operation. Finally, in 2000, after almost a decade of legal wrangling, Pucek sold the catfish farm and most of his water rights for $9 million to the trustees of the San Antonio water system. Legally, he had retained the right of capture, and he walked away a financial winner by selling the water rights. In the meantime, the city struggled with whether to allow new ventures that would impact its water supply. In 2002 some city officials endorsed a proposed Professional Golf Association resort with three planned golf courses to be perched over the Edwards Aquifer. Critics pointed out that one golf course normally used hundreds of thousands of gallons of water a day, as well as draining fertilizers and pesticides into the ground.

As Texas entered the new century, the tapping of groundwater, primarily for farmer's irrigation and use by cities but also for ranching, mining, and manufacturing, was still depleting the aquifers faster than they could refill through the natural slow percolation of rainwater. The largest aquifer, the Ogallala Aquifer underpinning the Texas High Plains, had been pierced by more than 50,000 irrigation wells. It is estimated that the natural refilling of the Ogallala would take 6,000 years. Yet the Department of Commerce warned in the 1990s that by 2020, if groundwater use continued at the same rate, two-thirds of this aquifer would be empty.

Water projections were grim in many areas of the state. In Williamson County, one of the three Texas counties among the ten fastest-growing in the United States, it was estimated that by 2050, the county "would face a shortfall of as much water as it takes to fill Lake Georgetown." Planners were considering a variety of costly options, including piping water from the Carrizo-Wilcox Aquifer. But this would require landowners in nearby counties to grant pumping rights, a risky proposition for the grantees.

More troubling for many was the state water plan compiled from the regional water-planning groups established by Senate Bill 1 in 1997. Houston *Chronicle* editorial writer Ken Kramer noted in May 2001 that in an era of water conservation, too many of the plans depended on "major new dams and pipelines" costing almost $17 billion. Dallas had actually projected an increase in per-capita water use to be supported by a costly dam when, Kramer contended, the dam "would be unnecessary if the per capita water use in Dallas is kept in line with more conservation-minded cities." Kramer and others made it clear that water issues would only grow more pressing.

Conclusion

In the last three decades of the twentieth century, recognition of old realities and new shaped a Texas for the twenty-first century. The historical experience of all who called Texas home took on greater meaning, diversity was acknowledged, and members of groups formerly excluded from political power began to share in that power. New ways of making a living and a fortune developed to reshape the Texas economy, but the old economic staples of oil, ranching, and farming remained integral to the economy through ups and downs and to Texans' sense of identity. An old independent spirit wary of government had to be balanced with challenges born of rapid, shifting population growth and the intricacies of state-federal relations. The land and its resources no longer seemed endless and therefore needed renewed care and communal effort.

All of these changes brought to the fore issues of Texas identity, and Texas myth: the stories about Texas identity that Texans—and non-Texans—have created or absorbed as part of their understanding of the world. Of course, these stories had been shaped through the region's history in a number of ways, from "Texians" embracing images of their land as a cradle of liberty in the Revolutionary era to the conscious adoption of western images by framers of the Texas Centennial. Key stereotypes ranged from stalwart pioneers, Texas Rangers, ranchers, and cowboys to larger-than-life businessmen engaged in boom-and-bust enterprise. Key elements included an emphasis on rugged individuality and a rather testy and exploitative frontier mentality. As Professor Betty Sue Flowers of the University of Texas has noted, "Texas stayed in a kind of perpetual state of primal, rural independence of mind."

But myths evolve. By the twenty-first century, some of the old myths have been exposed as skewed in favor of the group getting to tell the story; for example, many Anglos over the course of the nineteenth and twentieth centuries accepted and transmitted negative characterizations of Mexicans and Tejanos. Some myths can be seen to lack the basis in truth they may have had in an earlier era—for example, the images of Texas as having limitless land and resources. Some can be affirmed and adapted: If Texas is distinctive as a place, then its environment is worth protecting and preserving.

Many of the changes described in this chapter, then, are attempts to rewrite the myth, to address old ways of thinking that turned out to be wrong, no longer viable, or true in a different, more complex sense. In the process, Texas has retained a distinctive dynamic. In December 2002, *The Economist* published an article arguing that Texas had emerged as the most influential state in the American union, one leading the way into an American future, in part through its "sheer size and dynamism," in part through its citizens' "entrepreneurship" and cultural and ethnic diversity.

The Texas entering the twenty-first century, then, was poised to further sharpen and enhance its identity as a distinctive land of opportunity and diversity. It remained immense with possibilities for new economic, social, and political visions, new forms of innovation, new community configurations. Possessed of a rich, checkered, and complex history, it remained a place to, in the words of republic president Anson Jones, "commence the world anew."

SUGGESTED READINGS

Information on this era comes largely from the *Texas Almanac* (2001) and from newspaper articles listed in the bibliography; much of the history of Texas in the late twentieth century remains to be written. For discussions of Texas myth, see "Texas Values/Texas Future," in the Philosophical Society of Texas *Proceedings of the Annual Meeting at Austin, Dec. 3–5, 1999,* and Robert F. O'Connor, ed., *Texas Myths* (1986).

Diversity in Texas Politics and Culture

For information on the life of Barbara Jordan, consult Barbara Jordan and Shelby Hearon, *Barbara Jordan: A Self-Portrait* (1979) and Mary Beth Rogers, *Barbara*

Jordan, American Hero (1998). Other useful works that deal with Texas women in politics during this era include *Capitol Women,* by Nancy Baker Jones and Ruthe Winegarten (2000); *Texas Women Frontier to Future* (1998), by Ann Fears Crawford and Crystal Sasse Ragsdale; and *Claytie and the Lady: Ann Richards, Gender, and Politics in Texas* (1994), by Sue Tollison-Rinehart and Jeanie R. Stanley. For information on Mexican American activism in the 1970s, see Ignacio M. Garcia's *United We Win: The Rise and Fall of La Raza Unida Party* (1989) and Arnoldo DeLeon's *Mexican Americans in Texas: A Brief History* (1993). For one account of Mexican family land claims, see Abel Rubio's *Stolen Heritage: A Mexican-American's Rediscovery of His Family's Lost Land Grant* (1998). Information on the Tiguas appears in Jeffrey M. Schulze's "The Rediscovery of the Tiguas: Federal Recognition and Indianness in the Twentieth Century" in *Southwestern Historical Quarterly* (2001).

Developing Economic Opportunity

In addition to the *Texas Almanac* and newspapers, the *New Handbook of Texas* contains numerous helpful entries on public and private enterprises in Texas—see, for example, "AMR Corporation" and "Southwest Airlines." Michael Dell's story can be found in his *Direct from Dell: Strategies that Revolutionized an Industry* (1999).

Newspaper articles chronicle the challenges of farming, but ranching continues to draw loving book-length appraisals; see, for example, Lawrence Clayton's *Contemporary Ranches of Texas* (2001) and Kathleen Jo Ryan's *Deep in the Heart of Texas: Texas Ranchers in Their Own Words* (1999), from which some of the quotes in this section were drawn. Also useful is Mark Friedberger's "'Mink and Manure': Rural Gentrification and Cattle Raising in Southeast Texas, 1945–1992" in *Southwestern Historical Quarterly* (1999).

Governing a Changing State

Although it provides only a brief overview of the governors since 1969, a good reference work is Kenneth E. Hendrickson, Jr.'s *The Chief Executives of Texas from Stephen F. Austin to John B. Connally, Jr.* (1995). Donald Walker provides a positive assessment of Governor Smith in "Governor Preston E. Smith," *West Texas Historical Yearbook* (1999). The *New Handbook of Texas* includes useful information on this period on such topics as education and the prison system.

Tending the Land

A good general source is Richard C. Bartlett's *Saving the Best of Texas* (1995). Information on Ron Pucek's catfish farm and other environmental matters can be found on the Internet at the Edwards Aquifer home page, *www.edwardsaquifer. net.* Consult the *New Handbook of Texas* for a variety of related articles—see, for example, "Environmental Health."

A

Texas Governors

Governors of Spanish Texas

Domingo Terán de los Ríos	1691–92
Gregorio de Salinas Varona	1692–97
Francisco Cuerbo y Valdez	1698–1702
Mathías de Aguirre	1703–5
Martín de Alarcón	1705–8
Simón Padilla y Córdova	1708–12
Pedro Fermín de Echevérs y Subisa	1712–14
Juan Valdez	1714–16
Martín de Alarcón	1716–19
Joseph de Azlor, Marqués de Aguayo	1719–22
Fernando Pérez de Almazán	1722–27
Melchor de Media Villa y Azcona	1727–30
Juan Antonio Bustillos y Ceballos	1730–34
Manuel de Sandoval	1734–36
Carlos Benites Franquis de Lugo	1736–37
Prudencio de Orobio y Basterra	1737–41
Tomás Felipe Wintuisen	1741–43
Justo Boneo y Morales	1743–44
Francisco García Larios	1744–48
Pedro del Barrio Junco y Espriella	1748–51
Jacinto de Barrios y Jáuregui	1751–59
Angel Martos y Navarrete	1759–66
Hugo Oconor	1767–70
Barón de Ripperdá	1770–78
Domingo Cabello	1778–86
Bernardo Bonavía	1786 (appointed, but did not serve)
Rafael Martínez Pacheco	1786–90

Manuel Muñoz	1790–99
José Irigoyen	1798–1800 (appointed, but never served)
Juan Bautista de Elguézabal	1799–1805
Antonio Cordero y Bustamante	1805–8
Manuel María de Salcedo	1808–13
Juan Bautista Casas	Jan.–Mar., 1811 (insurgent governor)
Cristóbal Domínguez	1813–14
Ignacio Pérez	1816–17
Manuel Pardo	May–Oct., 1817
Antonio Martínez	1817–22 (continued to serve after Mexican independence)

Governors of Provincial Texas

José Félix Trespalacios	1822–23
Luciano García	1823

Governors of Coahuila y Texas

Rafael Gonzales	1824–26
José Ignacio de Arizpe	1826
Victor Blanco	1826–27
José Ignacio de Arizpe	1827
José María Viesca y Montes	1827–31
José María Letona	1831–32 (died in office)
Rafael Eca y Músquiz	1832–33
Juan Martín de Veramendi	1833 (died in office)
Francisco Vidaurri y Villaseñor	1833–34
Juan José Elguézabal	1834–35
José María Cantú	1835
Marciel Borrego	1835
Agustín Viesca	1835
Miguel Falcón	1835
Bartolomé de Cárdenas	1835
Rafael Eca y Músquiz	1835

Provisional Governor of Texas During Texas Revolution

Henry Smith	Nov. 1835–Mar. 1836

Presidents of the Republic of Texas, 1836–1846

David G. Burnet	Mar.–Oct., 1836 (interim)
Sam Houston	Oct. 1836–Dec. 1838
Mirabeau B. Lamar	Dec. 1838–Dec. 1841
Sam Houston	Dec. 1841–Dec. 1844
Anson Jones	Dec. 1844–Feb. 1846

Governors of the State of Texas

J. Pinckney Henderson	Feb. 1846–Dec. 1847
George T. Wood	Dec. 1847–Dec. 1849
Peter Hansborough Bell	Dec. 1849–Nov. 1853
J. W. Henderson	Nov. 1853–Dec. 1853
Elisha M. Pease	Dec. 1853–Dec. 1857
Hardin R. Runnels	Dec. 1857–Dec. 1859
Sam Houston	Dec. 21, 1859–Mar. 1861 (removed from office by Secession Convention)
Edward Clark	Mar. 1861–Nov. 1861 (appointed to office by Secession Convention)
Francis R. Lubbock	Nov. 1861–Nov. 1863
Pendleton Murrah	Nov. 1863–June 1865
Andrew J. Hamilton	June 1865–Aug. 1866 (appointed by President Andrew Johnson)
James W. Throckmorton	Aug. 1866–Aug. 1867 (removed from office by Gen. Philip H. Sheridan during Reconstruction)
Elisha M. Pease	Aug. 1867–Sept. 1869 (appointed by Gen. Philip H. Sheridan but resigned in protest of radical Reconstruction policies)
Edmund J. Davis	Jan. 1870–Jan. 1874
Richard Coke	Jan. 1874–Dec. 1876
Richard B. Hubbard	Dec. 1876–Jan. 1879
Oran M. Roberts	Jan. 1879–Jan. 1883
John Ireland	Jan. 1883–Jan. 1887
Lawrence Sullivan Ross	Jan. 1887–Jan. 1891
James Stephen Hogg	Jan. 1891–Jan. 1895
Charles A. Culberson	Jan. 1895–Jan. 1899
Joseph D. Sayers	Jan. 1899–Jan. 1903
S. W. T. Lanham	Jan. 1903–Jan. 1907
Thomas Mitchell Campbell	Jan. 1907–Jan. 1911
Oscar Branch Colquitt	Jan. 1911–Jan. 1915

James E. Ferguson	Jan. 1915–Aug. 1917
William Pettus Hobby	Aug. 1917–Jan. 1921
Pat Morris Neff	Jan. 1921–Jan. 1925
Miriam A. Ferguson	Jan. 1925–Jan. 1927
Dan Moody	Jan. 1927–Jan. 1931
Ross S. Sterling	Jan. 1931–Jan. 1933
Miriam A. Ferguson	Jan. 1933–Jan. 1935
James V. Allred	Jan. 1935–Jan. 1939
W. Lee O'Daniel	Jan. 1939–Aug. 1941
Coke R. Stevenson	Aug. 1941–Jan. 1947
Beauford H. Jester	Jan. 1947–July 1949
Allan Shivers	July 1949–Jan. 1957
Price Daniel	Jan. 1957–Jan. 1963
John Connally	Jan. 1963–Jan. 1969
Preston Smith	Jan. 1969–Jan. 1973
Dolph Briscoe	Jan. 1973–Jan. 1979
William P. Clements	Jan. 1979–Jan. 1983
Mark White	Jan. 1983–Jan. 1987
William P. Clements	Jan. 1987–Jan. 1991
Ann W. Richards	Jan. 1991–Jan. 1995
George W. Bush	Jan. 1995–Dec. 2000
James Richard Perry	Dec. 2000 to present

Sources: Vito Alessio Robles, *Coahuila y Texas desde la consumación de la Independencia hasta el Tratado de Paz de Guadalupe Hidalgo,* 2 vols. (1945, reprint, Mexico: Editorial Porrua, 1979); Arturo Berrueto González, comp., *Diccionario biográfico de Coahuila* (Saltillo: Gobierno del Estado, 1999); H. P. N. Gammel, comp., *The Laws of Texas, 1822–1897,* vol. 1 (Austin: Gammel Book Co., 1898); "About Texas," Texas State Library Website <http://www.tsl.state.tx.us/ref/abouttx/prerepub.html>; *Handbook of Texas Online* <http://www.tsha.utexas.edu/handbook/online/index.html>.

B

Comparative Population Statistics

Year	Province of Texas[1]	New Spain[1]
1731–39	1,499	
1740–49	3,203	
1750–59	3,683	
1760–69	3,436	
1770–74	3,076	
1780–89	2,919	
1790		4,636,074
1790–99	3,316	
1803		5,764,731
1805–9	4,329	
1810		6,122,354
1815–19	3,778	
1820		6,204,000

	Department of Texas[1]	Mexico[2]
1834–35	23,621	6,854,193

	Republic of Texas[3]	
1845	125,000	7,263,246

	State of Texas[4]	United States[4]
1850	212,592	23,191,876
1860	604,215	31,443,321
1870	818,579	38,558,371
1880	1,591,749	50,189,209
1890	2,235,527	62,979,766
1900	3,048,710	76,212,168
1910	3,896,542	92,228,496
1920	4,663,228	106,021,537
1930	5,824,715	123,202,624
1940	6,414,824	132,164,569
1950	7,711,194	151,325,798
1960	9,579,677	179,323,175
1970	11,196,730	203,211,926
1980	14,229,191	226,545,805
1990	16,986,335	248,765,170
2000	20,851,820	281,421,906

Sources: [1]Colonial-period estimates exclude independent Indian groups, which Meacham estimates to have declined in population from 35,600 in the seventeenth century to 20,100 early in the nineteenth century. Movement of Indians in and out of missions, the opening and closing of new mission fields, and the transfer of troops all kept the colonial-period population in flux. Estimates based on the work of Tina Laurel Meacham, "The Population of Spanish and Mexican Texas, 1716–1836" (Ph.D. diss., The University of Texas at Austin, 2000).

[2]"Population: 1821–1910," *Encyclopedia of Mexico: History, Society & Culture* (Chicago: Fitzroy Dearborn, 1997).

[3]"Census and Census Records," *Handbook of Texas OnLine,* www.tsha.utexas.edu/handbook/online/articles/view/CC/ulc1.html

[4]http://www.tsl.state.tx.us/ref/abouttx/census.html

Glossary of Spanish Terms

acequia: irrigation ditch

adelantado: governor with broad powers; usually reserved for the leader of a royally chartered expedition

agregado: additional or secondary settler

alcalde mayor: district magistrate

alcalde ordinario: municipal magistrate

alguacil mayor: constable, sheriff, jailer

ayuntamiento: town government

bracero: from *brazo,* arm; one who works with his hands; term applied to field laborers, particularly those who came to the United States during and after World War II

capitulación: royal charter

casas reales: town hall

castas: general term for mixed-bloods

compadrazgo: ritual kinship, godparenthood

corregidor: district magistrate

criado: reared or raised; a servant who is part of the household

criollo: American-born Spaniard

dictamen: official opinion

diezmero: a tithe collector

empresario: colonization agent; one who contracts with the government to introduce families into Texas

encomienda: grant of Indian tributaries to a Spaniard as a reward for services in an *entrada*

entrada: conquest, colonization, or settlement expedition

escribano: public scribe, notary

gachupín: derogatory term for European Spaniards, particularly popular at the end of the colonial period

genízaro: New Mexican term for a detribalized Indian incorporated into Spanish society

gente de razón: people of reason; term applied to all members of colonial society excepting Indians

grito: yell, scream, cry; a political declaration

hacendado: the owner of a *hacienda*

hacienda: large landed estate producing both livestock and crops for market

hidalgo: literally, "son of something"; lowest rung of Spanish nobility

intendencia: late colonial administrative unit based on French model intended to replace the old Hapsburg colonial structure

intendente: administrative head of an *intendencia*

junta: committee, governing directorate

justicia mayor: district magistrate

labor: tilling or plowing; an agricultural field; a Mexican era unit of land measure of approximately 177.1 acres.

mayordomo: overseer

mesteña or *mesteño:* unbranded stock

mestizaje: term applied to the process of race mixing among the European, African, and Indian populations of Spanish America

mestizo: offspring of a Spaniard and an Indian

patrón: master

peninsular: European-born Spaniard

peón: lowest category of permanent *hacienda* employee

porción: portion or allotment; long lot along the Rio Grande originally surveyed in 1767

primeros pobladores: first or original settlers

procurador: municipal attorney

pueblo: village, settlement, people; in New Mexico and Arizona, term applied to the various town-dwelling Indian tribes

quinto real: royal fifth; Spanish Crown's portion of treasure taken in an expedition or precious metals mined

rancho: term for a mixed-use, small-to-medium rural property that in Texas referred to a large livestock estate

reducción: gathering of nonsedentary Indians into a mission community

regidor: alderman, town councilman

regimiento: town council

república de españoles: one of two major divisions of Spanish colonial society composed of all non-Indians covered by a separate code of law

república de indios: one of two major divisions of Spanish colonial society composed of all Indians under Spanish rule covered by a separate code of law

requerimiento: summons, demand; formal statement of Spanish right to dominion in the New World, required to be read to Indians before war could be made on them

sistema de castas: ordering of Spanish American society according to racial-ethnic characteristics

sitio: place; a unit of land equivalent to approximately 4,500 acres of grazing land

subdelegado: district magistrate under the *intendencia* system

Tejano: a Texan of Mexican heritage

vaquero: cowboy

vecino: citizen

visitador: inspector general

Bibliography

Abbott, E. C., and Helena Huntington Smith. *We Pointed Them North: Recollections of a Cowpuncher.* Norman: University of Oklahoma Press, 1955.

Alessio Robles, Vito. *Coahuila y Texas desde la consumación de la Independencia hasta el Tratado de Paz de Guadalupe Hidalgo.* 1945. Reprint, Mexico City: Editorial Porrúa, 1979.

———. *Coahuila y Tejas en la época colonial.* Mexico City: Editorial Cultura, 1938.

Allen, Henry E. "The Parrilla Expedition to the Red River in 1759." *Southwestern Historical Quarterly* 43 (July 1939): 53–71.

Allen, Ruth A. *East Texas Lumber Workers.* Austin: University of Texas Press, 1961.

———. *The Great Southwest Strike.* Austin: The University of Texas Bulletin No. 4214, 1942.

Allsup, Carl. *The American G.I. Forum: Origins and Evolution.* Austin: University of Texas Press, 1982.

Almaráz, Félix D., Jr. *Governor Antonio Martínez and Mexican Independence in Texas: An Orderly Transition.* 1975. Reprint, San Antonio: Bexar County Historical Commission, 1979.

———. "The Legacy of Columbus: Spanish Mission Policy in Texas." *Journal of Texas Catholic History and Culture* 3 (1992): 17–36.

———. "San Antonio's Old Franciscan Missions: Material Decline and Secular Avarice in the Transition from Hispanic to Mexican Control." *Americas* 44 (July 1987): 1–22.

———. *Tragic Cavalier: Governor Manuel Salcedo of Texas, 1808–1813.* Austin: University of Texas Press, 1971.

Alonzo, Armando. *Tejano Legacy: Rancheros and Settlers in South Texas, 1734–1900.* Albuquerque: University of New Mexico Press, 1998.

Ambrose, Stephen E. *Eisenhower: Soldier and President.* Rev. ed. New York: Simon & Schuster, 1990.

Anders, Evan. *Boss Rule in South Texas: The Progressive Era.* Austin: University of Texas Press, 1982.

Anderson, Gary Clayton. *The Indian Southwest, 1580–1830: Ethnogenesis and Reinvention.* Norman: University of Oklahoma Press, 1999.

Anderson, H. Allen. "The Delaware and Shawnee Indians and the Republic of Texas, 1820–1845." *Southwestern Historical Quarterly* 94 (October 1990): 231–260.

Aten, Lawrence E. *Indians of the Upper Texas Coast.* New York: Academic Press, 1983.

Bacarisse, Charles A. "Baron de Bastrop." *Southwestern Historical Quarterly* 58 (January 1955): 319–330.

Bagur, Jacques D. *A History of Navigation on Cypress Bayou and the Lakes.* Denton: University of North Texas Press, 2001.

Bainbridge, John. *Super-Americans.* Garden City, NY: Doubleday, 1961.

Banks, Jimmy. *Money, Marbles, and Chalk.* Austin: Texas Publishing Co., 1971.

Barksdale, E. C. *The Meat Packers Come to Texas.* Austin: Bureau of Business Research, 1959.

Barnes, Donna A. *Farmers in Rebellion: The Rise and Fall of the Southern Farmers Alliance and People's Party in Texas.* Austin: University of Texas Press, 1984.

Barr, Alwyn. *Black Texans: A History of African-Americans in Texas, 1528–1995.* Norman: University of Oklahoma Press, 1996.

———. *Reconstruction to Reform: Texas Politics, 1876–1906.* Austin: University of Texas Press, 1971.

————. *Texans in Revolt: The Battle for San Antonio, 1835.* Austin: University of Texas Press, 1990.

Barr, Alwyn, and Robert A. Calvert, eds. *Black Leaders: Texans for Their Times.* Austin: Texas State Historical Association, 1981.

Barta, Carolyn. *Bill Clements: Texian to His Toenails.* Austin: Eakin Press, 1996.

Bartlett, Richard C. *Saving the Best of Texas.* Austin: University of Texas Press, 1995.

Bartley, Earnest R. *The Texas Tidelands Controversy: A Legal and Historical Analysis.* Austin: University of Texas Press, 1953.

Benavides, Adán, Jr., comp. and ed. *The Béxar Archives (1717–1836): A Name Guide.* Austin: University of Texas Press, 1989.

Benson, Nettie L. "A Governor's Report on Texas in 1809." *Southwestern Historical Quarterly* 71 (April 1968): 603–615.

————. "Bishop Marín de Porras and Texas." *Southwestern Historical Quarterly* 51 (July 1947): 16–40.

————. "Texas Failure to Send a Deputy to the Spanish Cortes, 1810–1812." *Southwestern Historical Quarterly* 64 (July 1960): 14–35.

Berrueto González, Arturo. *Diccionario biográfico de Coahuila.* Saltillo: Gobierno del Estado de Coahuila, 1999.

Bethell, Leslie, ed. *The Independence of Latin America.* Cambridge, UK: Cambridge University Press, 1987.

Biles, Roger. *The South and the New Deal.* Lexington: University of Kentucky Press, 1991.

Bishop, Bill. "Major Urban Areas See Most of Texas' Growth: As Cities' Amenities Attract Talented Workers—Companies, Jobs Follow." *Austin American Statesman* 3 March 2002—A1. <http://archives.statesman.com>.

Bixel, Patricia Bellis, and Elizabeth Hayes Turner. *Galveston and the 1900 Storm.* Austin: University of Texas Press, 2000.

Blackwelder, Julia Kirk. *Women of the Depression: Caste and Culture in San Antonio, 1929–1939.* College Station: Texas A&M University Press, 1984.

Blodgett, Jan. *Land of Bright Promise: Advertising and the Texas Panhandle and South Plains, 1870–1917.* Austin: University of Texas Press, 1988.

Bolton, Herbert E. *Coronado: Knight of Pueblos and Plains.* 1949. Reprint, Albuquerque: University of New Mexico Press, 1964.

————. *The Hasinais: Southern Caddoans as Seen by the Earliest Europeans.* 1987. Reprint, Norman: University of Oklahoma Press, 2002.

————. *Texas in the Middle Eighteenth Century: Studies in Spanish Colonial Administration.* 1915. Reprint, Austin: University of Texas Press, 1970.

Bolton, Herbert E., ed. and trans. *Athanase de Mézières and the Louisiana-Texas Frontier, 1768–1780.* 2 vols. Cleveland: Arthur H. Clark, 1914.

Boswell, Evault. *Texas Boys in Gray.* Plano: Republic of Texas Press, 2000.

Brading, David A. *Miners and Merchants in Bourbon Mexico, 1763–1810.* Cambridge, UK: Cambridge University Press, 1971.

Bradley, Ed. "Fighting for Texas: Filibuster James Long, the Adams-Onís Treaty, and the Monroe Administration." *Southwestern Historical Quarterly* 102 (January 1999): 323–342.

Bricker, Richard W. *Wooden Ships from Texas: A World War I Saga.* College Station: Texas A&M University Press, 1998.

Brown, Norman D. "Garnering Votes for 'Cactus Jack': John Nance Garner, Franklin D. Roosevelt, and the 1932 Democratic Nomination for President." *Southwestern Historical Quarterly* 104 (October 2000): 148–188.

————. *Hood, Bonnet, and Little Brown Jug: Texas Politics, 1921–1928.* College Station: Texas A&M University Press, 1984.

Bruseth, James E., and Nancy A. Kenmotsu. "From Naguatex to the River Daycao: The Route of the Hernando de Soto Expedition Through Texas." *North American Archaeologist* 14 (1993): 199–225.

Bryant, Keith L., Jr. *Arthur Stillwell: Promoter with a Hunch.* Nashville: Vanderbilt University Press, 1971.

———. *History of the Atchison, Topeka and Santa Fe Railway.* New York: Macmillan, 1974.

Buckley, Eleanor C. "The Aguayo Expedition into Texas and Louisiana, 1719–1722." *Quarterly of the Texas State Historical Association* 15 (July 1911): 1–65.

Buenger, Walter L. *The Path to a Modern South: Northeast Texas Between Reconstruction and the Great Depression.* Austin: University of Texas Press, 2001.

Buenger, Walter L., and Robert A. Calvert, *Texas Through Time: Evolving Interpretations.* College Station: Texas A&M University Press, 1991.

Bullard, Robert D. *Invisible Houston: The Black Experience in Boom and Bust.* College Station: Texas A&M University Press, 1987.

Calvert, Robert A., and Arnoldo De León. *The History of Texas.* 3d ed. Wheeling, Ill.: Harlan Davidson, Inc., 2002.

Campbell, Randolph B. *An Empire for Slavery: The Peculiar Institution in Texas, 1821–1865.* Baton Rouge: Louisiana State University Press, 1989.

———. *Sam Houston and the American Southwest.* New York: HarperCollins, 1993.

Cantrell, Gregg. *Kenneth and John B. Rayner and the Limits of Southern Dissent.* Urbana: University of Illinois Press, 1993.

———. "Racial Violence and Reconstruction Politics in Texas, 1867–1868." *Southwestern Historical Quarterly* 93 (January 1990): 333–356.

———. *Stephen F. Austin: Empresario of Texas.* New Haven: Yale University Press, 1999.

Carleton, Don E. *A Breed So Rare: The Life of J. R. Parten, Liberal Texas Oilman, 1896–1992.* Austin: Texas State Historical Association, 1999.

———. *Red Scare: Right-Wing Hysteria, Fifties Fanaticism, and Their Legacy in Texas.* Austin: Texas Monthly Press, 1985.

Carlson, Paul H. *The Plains Indians.* College Station: Texas A&M University Press, 1998.

———. *Texas Woollybacks: The Texas Sheep and Goat Industry.* College Station: Texas A&M University Press, 1982.

Carmody, Kevin. "Guadalupe Is in Jeopardy, Group Warns: Water Rights Issue Puts River System on Conservationists' List." *Austin American Statesman* 2 April 2002—B1. <http://archives.statesman.com>.

Caro, Robert A. *The Years of Lyndon Johnson: Master of the Senate.* New York: Alfred A. Knopf, 2002.

———. *The Years of Lyndon Johnson: Means of Ascent.* New York: Alfred A. Knopf, 1990.

———. *The Years of Lyndon Johnson: The Path to Power.* New York: Alfred A. Knopf, 1982.

Carraro, Francine. *Jerry Bywaters, A Life in Art.* Austin: University of Texas Press, 1994.

Carroll, John M., ed. *The Black Military Experience in the American West.* New York: Liverwright, 1971.

Carroll, Mark M. *Homesteads Ungovernable: Families, Sex, Race, and the Law in Frontier Texas, 1826–1860.* Austin: University of Texas Press, 2001.

Carter, Cecile Elkins. *Caddo Indians: Where We Come From.* Norman: University of Oklahoma Press, 1995.

Casdorf, Paul. *A History of the Republican Party in Texas, 1865–1965.* Austin: Pemberton Press, 1965.

Cashion, Ty, and Jesús F. de la Teja, eds. *The Human Tradition in Texas.* Wilmington, Del.: SR Books, 2001.

Castañeda, Carlos E. *Our Catholic Heritage in Texas.* 7 vols. Austin: Von Boeckmann-Jones, 1936–1958.

Chabot, Frederick C., ed. *Texas in 1811: The Las Casas and Sambrano Revolutions.* San Antonio: Yanaguana Society, 1941.

Champagne, Anthony. *Congressman Sam Rayburn.* New Brunswick, N.J.: Rutgers University Press, 1984.

Chapa, Juan Bautista. *Texas & Northeastern Mexico, 1630–1690.* Austin: University of Texas Press, 1997.

Chávez, Thomas E. *Spain and the Independence of the United States: An Intrinsic Gift.* Albuquerque: University of New Mexico Press, 2002.

Chipman, Donald E. "In Search of Cabeza de Vaca's Route Across Texas: An Historiographical Survey." *Southwestern Historical Quarterly* 91 (October 1987): 127–148.

———. *Spanish Texas, 1519–1821.* Austin: University of Texas Press, 1992.

Chipman, Donald, and Harriett Denise Joseph. *Notable Men and Women of Spanish Texas.* Austin: University of Texas Press, 1999.

Christian, Garna L. *Black Soldiers in Jim Crow Texas, 1899–1917.* College Station: Texas A&M University Press, 1995.

Clark, L. D., ed. *Civil War Recollections of James Lemuel Clark and the Great Hanging at Gainesville, Texas in October 1862.* Plano: Republic of Texas Press, 1997.

Clayton, Lawrence. *Contemporary Ranches of Texas.* Austin: University of Texas Press, 2001.

Coerver, Don M., and Linda B. Hall. *Texas and the Mexican Revolution: A Study in State and National Border Policy, 1910–1920.* San Antonio: Trinity University Press, 1984.

Conkin, Paul. *Big Daddy from the Pedernales: Lyndon Baines Johnson.* Boston: Twain, 1986.

Connor, Seymour V. *Texas: A History.* New York: Thomas Y. Crowell Co., 1971.

Cook, John R. *The Border and the Buffalo: An Untold Story of the Southwest Plains.* 1907. Reprint, Austin: State House Press, 1989.

Copelin, Laylan. "As Enron Sank, State Pension Funds Invested, Lost." *Austin American Statesman* 26 December 2001—A1. <http://archives.statesman.com>.

Cordell, Linda. *Archaeology of the Southwest.* 2d ed. San Diego: Academic Press, 1997.

Cotner, Robert C. *James Stephen Hogg.* Austin: University of Texas Press, 1951.

Cotner, Robert C., et. al. *Texas Cities and the Great Depression.* Austin: Texas Memorial Museum, 1973.

Cox, Patrick. *Ralph Yarborough: The People's Senator.* Austin: University of Texas Press, 2001.

Crawford, Ann Fears, and Crystal Sasse Ragsdale. *Texas Women Frontier to Future.* Austin: State House Press, 1998.

Crawford, Ann Fears, and Jack Keever. *John B. Connally: Portrait in Power.* Austin: Jenkins Co., 1973.

Crouch, Barry. *The Freedman's Bureau and Black Texans.* Austin: University of Texas Press, 1992.

Cruz, Gilbert R. *Let There Be Towns: Spanish Municipal Origins in the American Southwest, 1610–1810.* College Station: Texas A&M University Press, 1988.

Cummins, Light T. "Church Courts, Marriage Breakdown, and Separation in Spanish Louisiana, West Florida, and Texas." *Journal of Texas Catholic History and Culture* 4 (1993): 97–114.

Cutrer, Emily F. *The Art of the Woman: The Life and Work of Elisabet Ney.* Lincoln: University of Nebraska Press, 1988.

Dabbs, J. Autrey. "The Texas Missions in 1789." In *Preparing the Way: Preliminary Studies of the Texas Catholic Historical Society III.* Austin: Texas Catholic Historical Society, 2000.

Dallas Morning News. *Texas Almanac 2002–2003.* Dallas Morning News, 2001.

Dalleck, Robert. *Lone Star Rising: Lyndon Johnson and His Times, 1908–1960.* New York: Oxford University Press, 1991.

Dary, David. *Cowboy Culture: A Saga of Five Centuries.* Lawrence: University Press of Kansas, 1989.

Davidson, Chandler. *Race and Class in Texas Politics.* Princeton: Princeton University Press, 1990.

Davis, Graham. "Models of Migration: The Historiography of the Irish Pioneers in South Texas." *Southwestern Historical Quarterly* 99 (January 1996): 326–348.

Davis, William C. *Three Roads to the Alamo: The Lives and Fortunes of David Crockett, James Bowie, and William Barret Travis.* New York: HarperCollins, 1998.

Dawson, Sr., John C. *High Plains Yesterdays: From XIT Days Through Drouth* [sic] *and Depression.* Austin: Eakin Press, 1985.

De León, Arnoldo. *Mexican Americans in Texas: A Brief History.* 2d ed. Wheeling, Ill.: Harlan Davidson, Inc., 1999.

———. *They Called Them Greasers: Anglo Attitudes Toward Mexicans in Texas, 1821–1900.* Austin: University of Texas Press, 1983.

De Zavala, Adina. *History and Legends of the Alamo and Other Missions in and Around San Antonio.* 1917. Reprint, Houston: Arte Publico Press, 1996.

Deaton, Charles. *The Year They Threw the Rascals Out.* Austin: Shoal Creek Publishers, 1973.

Dell, Michael. *Direct from Dell: Strategies That Revolutionized an Industry.* New York: HarperBusiness, 1999.

Din, Gilbert C. "Spain's Immigration Policy in Louisiana and the American Penetration, 1792–1803." *Southwestern Historical Quarterly* 76 (January 1973): 255–276.

Dixon, Olive K. *Life of "Billy" Dixon.* Austin: State House Press reprint, 1987.

Doughty, Robin W. *At Home in Texas: Early Views of the Land.* College Station: Texas A&M University Press, 1987.

Downs, Fane. "Governor Antonio Martínez and the Defense of Texas from Foreign Invasion, 1817–1822," *Texas Military History* 7 (spring 1968): 27–43.

———. "'Tryels and Trubbles': Women in Early Nineteenth Century Texas." *Southwestern Historical Quarterly* 90 (April 1987): 35–56.

Dugas, Vera Lee. "Texas Industry, 1860–1880." *Southwestern Historical Quarterly* 59 (October 1955): 151–183.

Dugger, Ronnie. *Our Invaded Universities: Form, Reform and New Starts: A Nonfiction Play for Five Stages.* New York: W. W. Norton, 1974.

———. *The Politician: The Life and Times of Lyndon B. Johnson.* New York: W. W. Norton, 1982.

———. *Three Men in Texas: Bedicheck, Webb, and Dobie.* Austin: University of Texas Press, 1967.

Dunn, William E. "Apache Relations in Texas, 1718–1750." *Quarterly of the Texas State Historical Association* 14 (January 1911): 198–274.

Eckhardt, Gregg A. "Ron Pucek's Living Waters Catfish Farm." *The Edwards Aquifer Home Page.* 28 June 2002. <http://www.edwardsaquifer.net/pucek.html>.

Elliot, J. H. *Imperial Spain, 1469–1716.* New York: St. Martin's Press, 1964.

Everett, Dianna. *The Texas Cherokees: A People Between Two Fires, 1819–1840.* Norman: University of Oklahoma Press, 1990.

Exley, Jo Ella Powell. *Texas Tears and Texas Sunshine: Voices of Frontier Women.* College Station: Texas A&M University Press, 1985.

Faulk, Odie B. *The Last Years of Spanish Texas, 1778–1821.* The Hague: Mouton, 1964.

———. "The Penetration of Foreigners and Foreign Ideas into Spanish East Texas, 1793–1810." *East Texas Historical Journal* 2 (October 1964): 87–98.

———. "Ranching in Spanish Texas." *Hispanic American Historical Review* 45 (May 1965): 257–266.

Faulk, Odie B., and Laura E. Faulk. *Defenders of the Interior Provinces: Presidial Soldiers on the Northern Frontier of New Spain.* Albuquerque: Albuquerque Museum, 1988.

Flannery, Tim. *The Eternal Frontier: An Ecological History of North America and Its People.* New York: Atlantic Monthly Press, 2001.

Flint, Richard. *Great Cruelties Have Been Reported: The 1544 Investigation of the Coronado Expedition.* Dallas: Southern Methodist University Press, 2002.

Flint, Richard, and Shirley Cushing Flint, eds. *The Coronado Expedition to Tierra Nueva: The 1540–1542 Route Across the Southwest.* Niwot: University Press of Colorado, 1997.

Flores, Dan L. *Jefferson and Southwestern Exploration: The Freeman and Custis Accounts of the Red River Expedition of 1806.* Norman: University of Oklahoma Press, 1984.

Foik, Paul J. "Captain Don Domingo Ramón's Diary of His Expedition into Texas in 1716." In *Wilderness Mission: Preliminary Studies of the Texas Catholic Historical Society II.* Austin: Texas Catholic Historical Society, 1999.

Foley, Neil. *The White Scourge: Mexicans, Blacks, and Poor Whites in Texas Cotton Culture.* Berkeley: University of California Press, 1997.

Forman, Maury, and Robert A. Calvert, *Cartooning Texas: One Hundred Years of Cartoon Art in the Lone Star State.* College Station: Texas A&M University Press, 1993.

Forrestal, Peter J., trans. "The Solís Diary of 1767." In *Preparing the Way: Preliminary Studies of the Texas Catholic Historical Society I.* Austin: Texas Catholic Historical Society, 1997.

Foster, William C. *Spanish Expeditions into Texas, 1689–1768.* Austin: University of Texas Press, 1995.

Frantz, Joe B. *Texas: A Bicentennial History.* New York: W. W. Norton, 1976.

Frantz, Joe B., and Julian Ernest Choate. *The American Cowboy: The Myth and the Reality.* Norman: University of Oklahoma Press, 1955.

Frazier, Donald S. *Blood & Treasure: Confederate Empire in the Southwest.* College Station: Texas A&M University Press, 1995.

Freehling, William W. *The Road to Disunion: Secessionists at Bay, 1776–1854.* New York: Oxford University Press, 1990.

Friedberger, Mark. " 'Mink and Manure': Rural Gentrification and Cattle Raising in Southeast Texas, 1945–1992." *Southwestern Historical Quarterly* 102 (January 1999): 269–293.

"The Future Is Texas." Reprinted from *The Economist. Austin American Statesman* (5 January 2003): H1+.

Galbraith, John Kenneth. *The Great Crash, 1929.* Boston: Houghton Mifflin, 1955.

García, Ignacio M. *United We Win: The Rise and Fall of La Raza Unida Party.* Tucson: University of Arizona Press, 1989.

García, Mario T. *Desert Immigrants: The Mexicans of El Paso, 1880–1920.* New Haven: Yale University Press, 1981.

Gard, Wayne. *Frontier Justice.* Norman: University of Oklahoma Press, 1949.

Gardien, Kent. "Take Pity on Our Glory: Men of Champ d'Asile." *Southwestern Historical Quarterly* 87 (January 1984): 241–268.

Garrett, Julia K. *Green Flag Over Texas: A Story of the Last Years of Spain in Texas.* New York: Cordova Press, 1939.

Gee, Robert W. "Dry Fields Threaten Way of Life for Valley Farmers." *Austin American Statesman* 17 March 2002—A1. <http://archives.statesman.com>.

Gerhard, Peter. *The Northern Frontier of New Spain.* Princeton: Princeton University Press, 1982.

Goodwyn, Lawrence. *Democratic Promise: The Populist Movement in America.* New York: Oxford University Press, 1976.

Gould, Lewis L. *Progressives and Prohibitionists: Texas Democrats in the Wilson Era.* Austin: Texas State Historical Association, 1992.

Graham, Joe S. *El Rancho in South Texas: Continuity and Change from 1750.* Denton: University of North Texas Press, 1994.

Green, Donald E. *Land of the Underground Rain: Irrigation on the Texas High Plains, 1910–1970.* Austin: University of Texas Press, 1973.

Green, George Norris. *The Establishment in Texas Politics: The Primitive Years, 1938–1957.* 1979. Reprint, Norman: University of Oklahoma Press, 1984.

Green, James R. *Grass-Roots Socialism: Radical Movements in the Southwest, 1895–1943.* Baton Rouge: Louisiana State University Press, 1978.

———. "Tenant Farmer Discontent and Socialist Protest in Texas, 1901–1917." *Southwestern Historical Quarterly* 81 (October 1977): 133–154.

Groneman, Bill. *Eyewitness to the Alamo.* Plano: Republic of Texas Press, 1996.

Habig, Marion A. *The Alamo Chain of Missions: A History of San Antonio's Five Old Missions.* Chicago: Franciscan Herald Press, 1969.

Hackett, Charles W. "The Neutral Ground Between Louisiana and Texas, 1806–1821." *Louisiana Historical Quarterly* 28 (October 1945): 1001–1128.

Hackett, Charles W., ed. and trans. *Pichardo's Treatise on the Limits of Louisiana and Texas.* 4 vols. Austin: University of Texas Press, 1931–1946.

Haggard, J. Villasana. "The Counter-Revolution of Béxar, 1811." *Southwestern Historical Quarterly* 43 (October 1939): 222–235.

Haley, J. Evetts. *Charles Goodnight, Cowman and Plainsman.* Norman: University of Oklahoma Press, 1949.

———. *George W. Littlefield, Texan.* Norman: University of Oklahoma Press, 1943.

Hardeman, Dorsey B., and Donald C. Bacon. *Rayburn: A Biography.* Austin: Texas Monthly Press, 1987.

Hardin, Stephen L. *Texian Iliad: A Military History of the Texas Revolution.* Austin: University of Texas Press, 1994.

Harmon, Dave. "The Fight for a Historic Birthright: Padre Island Ruling Gives Hope to Latino Families." *Austin American Statesman* 10 January 2000—A1. <http://archives.statesman.com>.

Hatcher, Mattie Austin. "The Expedition of Don Domingo Terán de los Ríos into Texas." In *Wilderness Mission: Preliminary Studies of the Texas Catholic Historical Society II.* Austin: Texas Catholic Historical Society, 1999.

———. *The Opening of Texas to Foreign Settlement, 1801–1821.* 1927. Reprint, Philadelphia: Porcupine Press, 1976.

Haynes, Sam W. "Anglophobia and the Annexation of Texas: The Quest for National Security." In Sam W. Haynes and Christopher Morris, eds. *Manifest Destiny and Empire: American Antebellum Expansionism.* College Station: Texas A&M University Press, 1997.

———. *Soldiers of Misfortune: The Somervell and Mier Expeditions.* Austin: University of Texas Press, 1990.

Haynes, Sam W., and Cary D. Wintz, eds. *Major Problems in Texas History: Documents and Essays.* Boston: Houghton Mifflin, 2002.

Henderson, Richard B. *Maury Maverick, A Political Biography.* Austin: University of Texas Press, 1970.

Hendrickson, Jr., Kenneth B. *The Chief Executives of Texas: From Stephen F. Austin to John B. Connally, Jr.* College Station: Texas A&M University Press, 1995.

Hendrickson, Jr., Kenneth E., and Michael L. Collins, eds. *Profiles in Power: Twentieth-Century Texans in Washington.* Arlington Heights, Ill.: Harlan Davidson, Inc., 1993.

Henson, Margaret Swett, and Deolece Parmalee. *The Cartwrights of San Augustine: Three Generations of Agricultural Entrepreneurs in Nineteenth-Century Texas.* Austin: Texas State Historical Association, 1993.

Hester, Thomas R. *Digging into South Texas Prehistory: A Guide for Amateur Archaeologists.* San Antonio: Corona Publishing, 1980.

Hickerson, Nancy P. "How Cabeza de Vaca Lived with, Worked Among, and Finally Left the Indians of Texas." *Journal of Anthropological Research* 54 (summer 1998): 199–218.

———. *The Jumanos: Hunters and Traders of the South Plains.* Austin: University of Texas Press, 1994.

Hight, Bruce. "Tiguas Roll Snake Eyes in Court Fight; El Paso Tribe Must Close Casino after Nine Years but Can Continue Appeal." *Austin American Statesman* 12 February 2002—A1. <http://archives.statesman.com>.

Hill, Patricia Everidge. *Dallas: The Making of a Modern City.* Austin: University of Texas Press, 1996.

Hinojosa, Gilberto M. *A Borderlands Town in Transition: Laredo, 1755–1870.* College Station: Texas A&M University Press, 1983.

Hodge, Frederick W., and Theodore H. Lewis, eds. *Spanish Explorers in the Southern United States, 1528–1543.* 1907. Reprint, Austin: Texas State Historical Association, 1990.

Hogan, William Ransom. *The Texas Republic: A Social and Economic History.* 1946. Reprint, Austin: University of Texas Press, 1969.

Holden, William C. *Alkali Trails, or, Social and Economic Movements of the Texas Frontier, 1846–1900.* Dallas: Southwest Press, 1930.

Holmes, Jack D. L. "Showdown on the Sabine: General James Wilkinson vs. Lieutenant-Colonel Simon de Herrera." *Louisiana Studies* 3 (1964): 46–76.

Hudson, Linda S. *Mistress of Manifest Destiny: A Biography of Jane McManus Storm Cazneau, 1807–1878.* Austin: Texas State Historical Association, 2001.

Humphrey, David C. *Austin, an Illustrated History.* Northridge, Calif.: Windsor Publications, 1985.

Hyman, Harold. *Oleander Odyssey: The Kempners of Galveston, Ca. 1850–1987.* College Station: Texas A&M University Press, 1990.

Iber, Jorge. "Bridal Aguero and *El Editor* Newspaper: The Varied Roles of a Spanish Surnamed Entrepreneur in a Lubbock, Texas Barrio, 1977–1999." *West Texas Historical Association Yearbook* 75 (1999): 54–61.

Jackson, Jack. *Los Mesteños: Spanish Ranching in Texas, 1721–1821.* College Station: Texas A&M University Press, 1986.

Jackson, Jack, ed., William C. Foster, annot. *Imaginary Kingdom: Texas as Seen by the Rivera and Rubí Military Expeditions, 1727 and 1767.* Austin: Texas State Historical Association, 1995.

Jackson, Ron. *Alamo Legacy: Alamo Descendants Remember the Alamo.* Austin: Eakin Press, 1997.

Jacobs, Louis. *Lone Star Dinosaurs.* College Station: Texas A&M University Press, 1995.

Jasinski, Laurie. *Hill Country Backroads: Showing the Way in Comal County.* Fort Worth: Texas Christian University Press, 2001.

John, Elizabeth A. H. *Storms Brewed in Other Men's Worlds: The Confrontation of Indians, Spanish, and French in the Southwest, 1540–1795.* College Station: Texas A&M University Press, 1975.

John, Elizabeth A. H., ed., John Wheat, trans. "Inside the Comanchería, 1785: The Diary of Pedro Vial and Francisco Xavier Chaves." *Southwestern Historical Quarterly* 98 (July 1994): 27–56.

Jones, Billy Mac. *Health Seekers in the Southwest, 1817–1900.* Norman: University of Oklahoma Press, 1967.

Jones, Billy Mac. *The Search for Maturity.* Austin: Steck-Vaughn Co., 1965.

Jones, Nancy Baker and Ruthe Winegarten. *Capitol Women.* Austin: University of Texas Press, 2000.

Jones, Oakah L., Jr. *Los Paisanos: Spanish Settlers on the Northern Frontier of New Spain.* Norman: University of Oklahoma Press, 1979.

Jordan, Barbara, and Shelby Hearon. *Barbara Jordan: A Self Portrait.* Garden City, NY: Doubleday, 1979.

Jordan, Terry G. "A Century and a Half of Ethnic Change in Texas, 1836–1986." *Southwestern Historical Quarterly* 89 (April 1986): 385–422.

———. *German Seed in Texas Soil: Immigrant Farmers in Nineteenth-Century Texas.* Austin: University of Texas Press, 1966.

———. *North American Cattle-Ranching Frontiers: Origins, Diffusion, and Differentiation.* Albuquerque: University of New Mexico Press, 1993.

———. *Texas: A Geography.* Boulder, Colo.: Westview Press, 1984.

———. *Trails to Texas: Southern Roots of Western Cattle Ranching.* Lincoln: University of Nebraska Press, 1981.

Kearns, Doris. *Lyndon Baines Johnson and the American Dream.* New York: Harper & Row, 1976.

Kessell, John L. *Spain in the Southwest: A Narrative History of Colonial New Mexico, Arizona, Texas, and California.* Norman: University of Oklahoma Press, 2002.

Key, Jr., V. O. *Southern Politics in State and Nation.* New York: Alfred A. Knopf, 1949.

Kinch, Jr., Sam, and Ben Procter. *Texas Under a Cloud.* Austin: Jenkins Publishing Co., 1972.

Kinch, Jr., Sam, and Stuart Long. *Allan Shivers: The Pied Piper of Texas Politics.* Austin: Shoal Creek Publishers, 1974.

King, Larry L. *Confessions of a White Racist.* New York: Viking Press, 1971.

Kinnaird, Lawrence, ed. *The Frontiers of New Spain: Nicolás de Lafora's Description, 1766–1768.* Berkeley, Calif.: Quivira Society, 1958.

Knaggs, John R. *Two Party Texas: The John Tower Era, 1961–1984.* Austin: Eakin Press, 1986.

Knaut, Andrew L. *The Pueblo Revolt of 1680: Conquest and Resistance in Seventeenth-Century New Mexico.* Norman: University of Oklahoma Press, 1995.

La Vere, David. "Between Kinship and Capitalism: French and Spanish Rivalry in the Colonial Louisiana-Texas Indian Trade." *Journal of Southern History* 64 (May 1998): 197–218.

———. *The Caddo Chiefdoms: Caddo Economics and Politics, 700–1835.* Lincoln: University of Nebraska Press, 1998.

La Vere, David, and Katia Campbell, eds. and trans. "An Expedition to the Kichai: The Journal of François Grappe, September 24, 1783." *Southwestern Historical Quarterly* 98 (July 1994): 59–78.

Lack, Paul D. *The Texas Revolutionary Experience, A Political and Social History 1835–1836.* College Station: Texas A&M University Press, 1992.

Lack, Paul D., ed. *The Diary of William Fairfax Gray from Virginia to Texas, 1835–1837.* Dallas: De Golyer Library and William P. Clements Center for Southwest Studies, Southern Methodist University, 1997.

Larson, Erik. *Isaac's Storm: A Man, a Time, and the Deadliest Hurricane in History.* New York: Vintage Books, 2000.

Lemée, Patricia R. "Tios and Tantes: Familial and Political Relationships of Natchitoches and the Spanish Colonial Frontier." *Southwestern Historical Quarterly* 101 (January 1998): 341–358.

Leutenegger, Benedict, ed., and Marion A. Habig. "Report on the San Antonio Missions in 1792." *Southwestern Historical Quarterly* 77 (April 1974): 487–498.

Lindell, Chuck. "Texans Take Mexico Water Fight to D.C.; Growers Want U.S. to Push Mexico on Releasing Water to Rio Grande." *Austin American Statesman* 25 April 2002—B1. <http://archives.statesman.com>.

Linsley, Judith Walker, Ellen Walker Rienstra, and Jo Ann Stiles. *Giant Under the Hill: A History of the Spindletop Oil Discovery at Beaumont, Texas, in 1901.* Austin: Texas State Historical Association, 2002.

Little, Carol Morris. *A Comprehensive Guide to Outdoor Sculpture in Texas.* Austin: University of Texas Press, 1996.

Malone, Ann Patton. *Women on the Texas Frontier.* El Paso: Texas Western Press, 1985.

Marks, Paula Mitchell. *Hands to the Spindle: Texas Women and Home Textile Production, 1822–1880.* College Station: Texas A&M University Press, 1998.

———. *Turn Your Eyes Toward Texas: Pioneers Sam and Mary Maverick.* College Station: Texas A&M University Press, 1989.

Martin, Robert L. *The City Moves West: Economic and Industrial Growth in Central West Texas.* Austin: University of Texas Press, 1969.

Martin, Roscoe. *The People's Party in Texas: A Study in Third-Party Politics.* 1933. Reprint, Austin: University of Texas Press, 1970.

Matovina, Timothy. *Tejano Religion and Ethnicity in San Antonio, 1821–1860.* Austin: University of Texas Press, 1995.

———. *The Alamo Remembered: Tejano Accounts and Perspectives.* Austin: University of Texas Press, 1995.

Maxwell, Robert S. *Sawdust Empire: The Texas Lumber Industry, 1830–1940.* College Station: Texas A&M University Press, 1983.

McArthur, Judith N. *Creating the New Woman: The Rise of Southern Women's Progressive Culture in Texas, 1893–1918.* Urbana, Ill.: University of Illinois Press, 1998.

McCarty, Kieran. "Before They Crossed the Great River: Cultural Background of the Spanish Franciscans in Texas." *Journal of Texas Catholic History and Culture* 3 (1992): 37–44.

McCaslin, Richard B. "Wheat Growers in the Cotton Confederacy: The Suppression of Dissent in Collin County, Texas, During the Civil War." *Southwestern Historical Quarterly* 96 (April 1993): 527–539.

McComb, David G. *Galveston, A History.* Austin: University of Texas Press, 1986.

———. *Houston: A History.* Austin: University of Texas Press, 1986.

———. *Texas: A Modern History.* Austin: University of Texas Press, 1989.

McConal, Patrick M. *Over the Wall: The Men Behind the 1934 Death House Escape.* Austin: Eakin Press, 2000.

McKay, Seth S. *Texas and the Fair Deal.* San Antonio: Naylor Press, 1954.

———. *Texas Politics, 1906–1944.* Lubbock: Texas Tech University Press, 1952.

———. *W. Lee O'Daniel and Texas Politics.* Lubbock: Texas Tech University Press, 1944.

McKay, Seth S., and Odie B. Faulk. *Texas After Spindletop.* Austin: Steck-Vaughn Co., 1965.

McMath, Robert C., Jr. *American Populism: A Social History, 1877–1898.* New York: Hill and Wang, 1993.

———. *Populist Vanguard: A History of the Southern Farmer's Alliance.* Chapel Hill: University of North Carolina Press, 1975.

Meinig, D. W. *Imperial Texas: An Interpretive Essay in Cultural Geography.* Austin: University of Texas Press, 1969.

Meyer, Michael C. *Water in the Hispanic Southwest: A Social and Legal History, 1550–1850.* Tucson: University of Arizona Press, 1984.

Meyer, Michael C., William L. Sherman, and Susan M. Deeds. *The Course of Mexican History.* 6th ed. New York: Oxford University Press, 1999.

Miller, Thomas L. *The Public Lands of Texas, 1519–1970*. Norman: University of Oklahoma Press, 1972.

Moneyhon, Carl. "Edmund J. Davis in the Coke-Davis Election Dispute of 1874: A Reassessment of Character." *Southwestern Historical Quarterly* 100 (October 1996): 131–151.

Montejano, David. *Anglos and Mexicans in the Making of Texas, 1836–1986*. Austin: University of Texas Press, 1987.

Moorhead, Max L. *The Presidio: Bastion of the Spanish Borderlands*. Norman: University of Oklahoma Press, 1975.

Morehead, Richard. *Fifty Years in Texas Politics*. Burnett: Eakin Press, 1982.

Morfi, Juan Agustín. *History of Texas, 1673–1779*. Trans. and ed. Carlos E. Castañeda. 2 vols. Albuquerque: Quivira Society, 1935.

Morris, John Miller. *El Llano Estacado: Exploration and Imagination on the High Plains of Texas and New Mexico, 1536–1860*. Austin: Texas State Historical Association, 1997.

Murph, Dan. *Texas Giant: The Life of Price Daniel*. Austin: Eakin Press, 2002.

Myers, Sandra L. *The Ranch in Spanish Texas*. El Paso: Texas Western Press, 1969.

Nackman, Mark E. *A Nation Within a Nation: The Rise of Texas Nationalism*. Port Washington, N.Y.: Kennikat Press, 1975.

Navarro García, Luis. *Don José de Gálvez y la Comandancia General de las Provincias Internas del Norte de Nueva España*. Seville: Escuela de Estudios Hispano-Americanos de Sevilla, 1964.

Neu, Charles E. "In Search of Colonel Edward M. House: The Texas Years, 1858–1912." *Southwestern Historical Quarterly* 93 (July 1989): 25–44.

Neugebauer, Janet M., ed. *Plains Farmer: The Diary of William G. DeLoach, 1914–1964*. College Station: Texas A&M University Press, 1991.

Newcomb, W. W., Jr. *The Indians of Texas: From Prehistoric to Modern Times*. Austin: University of Texas Press, 1961.

——. *The Rock Art of Texas Indians*. Paintings by Forrest Kirkland. Austin: University of Texas Press, 1967.

Nunley, Parker. *A Field Guide to Archeological Sites in Texas*. Austin: Texas Monthly Press, 1989.

O'Connor, Kathryn Stoner. *Presidio La Bahia del Espiritu Santo de Zuniga, 1721–1846*. Austin: Von Boeckmann-Jones, 1966.

Oates, Stephen B., ed. *Rip Ford's Texas*. Austin: University of Texas Press, 1963.

Olien, Diana Davids, and Roger M. Olien. *Oil in Texas: The Gusher Age, 1895–1945*. Austin: University of Texas Press, 2002.

Olien, Roger M. *From Token to Triumph: The Texas Republicans Since 1920*. Dallas: Southern Methodist University Press, 1982.

Oliphant, Dave. *Texas Jazz*. Austin: University of Texas Press, 1996.

Olmsted, Frederick Law. *A Journey Through Texas, Or, A Saddle-Trip on the Southwestern Frontier*. 1857. Reprint, Austin: University of Texas Press, 1978.

Olson, Donald W., et al. "Piñon Pines and the Route of Cabeza de Vaca." *Southwestern Historical Quarterly* 101 (October 1997): 174–186.

Ornish, Natalie. *Ehrenberg: Goliad Survivor, Old West Explorer*. Dallas: Texas Heritage Press, 1997.

Osante, Patricia. *Orígenes del Nuevo Santander (1748–1772)*. Mexico: Universidad Nacional Autónoma de México, Instituto de Investigaciones Históricas, 1997.

Owens, William A. *A Season of Weathering*. New York: Scribner, 1973.

Pate, J'Nell L. *Livestock Legacy: The Fort Worth Stockyards, 1887–1987*. College Station: Texas A&M University Press, 1988.

Patenaude, Lionel V. *Texas Politics and the New Deal.* New York: Garland Publishing, 1983.

Paulissen, May Nelson, and Carl McQueary. *Miriam: The Southern Belle Who Became the First Woman Governor of Texas.* Austin: Eakin Press, 1995.

Pérez de Villagrá, Gaspar. *Historia de la Nueva México, 1610.* Albuquerque: University of New Mexico Press, 1992.

Perttula, Timothy K. *"The Caddo Nation": Archaeological and Ethnohistoric Perspectives.* Austin: University of Texas Press, 1992.

Pickering, David, and Judy Falls. *Brush Men and Vigilantes: Civil War Dissent in Texas.* College Station: Texas A&M University Press, 2000.

Pitre, Merline. *In Struggle Against Jim Crow: Lulu B. White and the NAACP, 1900–1957.* College Station: Texas A&M University Press, 1999.

———. *Through Many Dangers, Toils and Snares: The Black Leadership of Texas, 1868–1900.* Austin: Eakin Press, 1985.

Platt, Harold L. *City Building in the New South: The Growth of Public Services in Houston, Texas, 1830–1915.* Philadelphia: Temple University Press, 1983.

Powers, John, and Deborah Powers. *Texas Painters, Sculptors and Graphic Artists: A Biographical Dictionary of Artists in Texas before 1942.* Austin: Woodmont Books, 2000.

Poyo, Gerald E., ed. *Tejano Journey, 1770–1850.* Austin: University of Texas Press, 1996.

Poyo, Gerald E., and Gilberto M. Hinojosa, eds. *Tejano Origins in Eighteenth-Century San Antonio.* Austin: University of Texas Press, 1991.

Priestley, Herbert I. *José de Gálvez, Visitor General of New Spain, 1765–1771.* 1916. Reprint, Philadelphia: Porcupine Press, 1980.

Prindle, David F. *Petroleum Politics and the Texas Railroad Commission.* Austin: University of Texas Press, 1981.

Procter, Ben H. *Just One Riot: Episodes of Texas Rangers in the Twentieth Century.* Austin: Eakin Press, 1991.

———. *Not Without Honor: The Life of John H. Reagan.* Austin: University of Texas Press, 1962.

Pupo-Walker, Enrique, ed., and Frances M. López-Morillas, trans. *Castaways: The Narrative of Alvar Núñez Cabeza de Vaca.* Berkeley: University of California Press, 1993.

Ragsdale, Crystal Sasse. *The Golden Free Land: The Reminiscences and Letters of Women on an American Frontier.* Austin: Landmark Press, 1976.

Ragsdale, Kenneth B. *Centennial '36: The Year America Discovered Texas.* College Station: Texas A&M University Press, 1987.

Ramsay, Jack C., Jr. *Jean Laffite, Prince of Pirates.* Austin: Eakin Press, 1996.

Ratcliffe, Sam D. "'Escenas de Martirio': Notes on *The Destruction of Mission San Sabá.*" *Southwestern Historical Quarterly* 94 (April 1991): 507–534.

Reed, S. G. *A History of the Texas Railroads.* Houston: St. Clair Pub. Co., 1941.

Reichstein, Andreas, ed. "The Austin-Leaming Correspondence, 1828–1836." *Southwestern Historical Quarterly* 88 (January 1985): 247–282.

Reindorp, Reginald C. "The Founding of Missions at La Junta de los Ríos." In *Preparing the Way: Preliminary Studies of the Texas Catholic Historical Society III.* Austin: Texas Catholic Historical Society, 2000.

"Republican Party of Texas." <www.txgop.org/library/history.asp>.

Reston, James, Jr. *The Lone Star: The Life of John Connally.* New York: Harper & Row, 1989.

Reston, Maeve. "Growth Drains Williamson Water Supplies." *Austin American Statesman* 18 August 2000—B10. <http://archives.statesman.com>.

Rhinehart, Marilyn D. *A Way of Work and a Way of Life: Coal Mining in Thurber, Texas, 1888–1926.* College Station: Texas A&M University Press, 1992.

Rice, Lawrence D. *The Negro in Texas, 1874–1900.* Baton Rouge: Louisiana State University Press, 1971.

Richards, David. *Once Upon a Time in Texas: A Liberal in the Lone Star State.* Austin: University of Texas Press, 2002.

Richardson, Rupert N. *Colonel Edward M. House: The Texas Years, 1858–1912.* Abilene: Hardin-Simmons University Publications in History, 1964.

Richardson, Rupert N., Adrian Anderson, and Ernest Wallace. *Texas: The Lone Star State.* 8th ed. Englewood Cliffs, N.J.: Prentice-Hall, 2001.

Ricklis, Robert A. *The Karankawa Indians of Texas: An Ecological Study of Cultural Traditions and Change.* Austin: University of Texas Press, 1996.

Rister, Carl Coke. *Comanche Bondage.* 1955. Reprint, Lincoln: University of Nebraska Press, 1989.

Roberts, Randy, and James S. Olson. *A Line in the Sand: The Alamo in Blood and Memory.* New York: The Free Press, 2001.

Robertson, Robert J. *Her Majesty's Texans: Two English Immigrants in Reconstruction Texas.* College Station: Texas A&M University Press, 1998.

Rodnitzky, Jerry L., and Shirley R. Rodnitzky. *Jazz Age Boomtown.* College Station: Texas A&M University Press, 1997.

Roell, Craig H. *Remember Goliad! A History of La Bahía.* Austin: Texas State Historical Association, 1994.

Rogers, Mary Beth. *Barbara Jordan, American Hero.* New York: Bantam Books, 1998.

Rosenbaum, Robert J. *Mexicano Resistance in the Southwest: The Sacred Right of Self Preservation.* Austin: University of Texas Press, 1981.

Rubio, Abel. *Stolen Heritage: A Mexican-American's Rediscovery of His Family's Lost Land Grant.* 1986. Austin: Eakin Press, 1998.

Rundell, Walter, Jr. *Early Texas Oil: Photographic History, 1866–1936.* College Station: Texas A&M University Press, 1977.

Ryan, Kathleen Jo. *Deep in the Heart of Texas: Texas Ranchers in Their Own Words.* Berkeley, Calif.: Ten Speed Press, 1999.

Salinas, Martín. *Indians of the Rio Grande Delta: Their Role in the History of Southern Texas and Northeastern Mexico.* Austin: University of Texas Press, 1990.

Sanders, Leonard. *How Fort Worth Became the Texasmost City.* Fort Worth: Amon Carter Museum, 1973.

San Miguel, Guadalupe, Jr. *Let All of Them Take Heed: Mexican Americans and the Campaign for Educational Equality in Texas, 1910–1981.* Austin: University of Texas Press, 1987.

Santos, Richard G. *Aguayo Expedition into Texas, 1721: An Annotated Translation of the Five Versions of the Diary Kept by Br. Juan Antonio de la Peña.* Austin: Jenkins Publishing, 1981.

Schmelzer, Janet L. *Where the West Begins: Fort Worth and Tarrant County.* Northridge, Calif.: Windsor Publications, 1985.

Schulman, Bruce J. *From Cotton Belt to Sunbelt: Federal Policy, Economic Development, and the Transformation of the South, 1938–1980.* New York: Oxford University Press, 1991.

Schulze, Jeffrey M. "The Rediscovery of the Tiguas: Federal Recognition and Indianness in the Twentieth Century." *Southwestern Historical Quarterly* 105 (July 2001): 15–39.

Schwartz, Jeremy. "Wimberley Seeks to Restore Harmony After Bitter Campaign." *Austin American Statesman* 12 May 2002—B1. <http://archives.statesman.com>.

Schwartz, Ted. *Forgotten Battlefield of the First Texas Revolution: The Battle of the Medina, August 18, 1813.* Ed. Robert H. Thonhoff. Austin: Eakin Press, 1985.

Serwer, Andy, and Julia Boorstin. "Dell Does Domination." *Fortune* (Asia) 145, 2 (21 January 2002): 43.

Sharpless, Rebecca. *Fertile Ground, Narrow Choices: Women on Texas Cotton Farms, 1900–1940.* Chapel Hill: University of North Carolina Press, 1999.

Shockley, John S. *Chicano Revolt in a Texas Town.* Notre Dame: University of Notre Dame Press, 1974.

Sibley, Marilyn. *The Port of Houston.* Austin: University of Texas Press, 1968.

Silverthorne, Elizabeth. *Plantation Life in Texas.* College Station: Texas A&M Press, 1986.

Simmons, Marc. *The Last Conquistador: Juan de Oñate and the Settling of the Far Southwest.* Norman: University of Oklahoma Press, 1991.

Skaggs, Jimmy M. *The Cattle-Trailing Industry: Between Supply and Demand, 1866–1890.* Lawrence: University Press of Kansas, 1973.

Smallwood, James. *The Great Recovery: The New Deal in Texas.* Boston: American Press, 1983.

Smith, F. Todd. *The Wichita Indians: Traders of Texas and the Southern Plains, 1540–1845.* College Station: Texas A&M University Press, 2000.

Smithwick, Noah. *The Evolution of a State, or Recollections of Old Texas Days.* 1900. Reprint, Austin: University of Texas Press, 1983.

Soukup, James R., et al. *Party and Factional Division in Texas.* Austin: University of Texas Press, 1964.

Spearing, Darwin. *Roadside Geology of Texas.* Rev. ed. Missoula, Mont.: Mountain Press, 1991.

Spellman, Paul N. *Forgotten Texas Leader: Hugh McLeod and the Texan Santa Fe Expedition.* College Station: Texas A&M University Press, 1999.

———. *Spindletop Boom Days.* College Station: Texas A&M University Press, 2001.

Spratt, John S. *The Road to Spindletop: Economic Change in Texas, 1875–1901.* Dallas: Southern Methodist University Press, 1955.

Spratt, John S. *Thurber, Texas: The Life and Death of a Company Coal Town.* Austin: University of Texas Press, 1986.

Stewart, Kenneth L., and Arnoldo De León. *Not Room Enough: Mexicans, Anglos, and Socioeconomic Change in Texas, 1850–1900.* Albuquerque: University of New Mexico Press, 1993.

———. *Tejanos and the Numbers Game: A Socio-Historical Interpretation from the Federal Censuses, 1850–1900.* Albuquerque: University of New Mexico Press, 1993.

Struve, Walter. *Germans and Texans: Commerce, Migration, and Culture in the Days of the Lone Star Republic.* Austin: University of Texas Press, 1996.

Sweet, David. "The Ibero-American Frontier Mission in Native American History." In Erick Langer and Robert H. Jackson, eds., *The New Latin American Mission History.* Lincoln: University of Nebraska Press, 1995.

Taylor, Alex. "Little Divides Manor Hopefuls: Schools Candidates Unified in Opposition to Wealth-Sharing Laws." *Austin American Statesman* 26 April 2002—B7.

Taylor, Virginia H., trans. and ed. *The Letters of Antonio Martínez, Last Governor of Texas, 1817–1822.* Austin: Texas State Library, 1957.

Teja, Jesús F. de la. "'A Fine Country with Broad Plains—the Most Beautiful in New Spain': Colonial Views of Land and Nature." In *On the Border: An Environmental History of San Antonio,* ed. Char Miller. Pittsburgh: University of Pittsburgh Press, 2001.

———. "'Only Fit for Raising Stock': Spanish and Mexican Land and Water Rights in the Tamaulipan Cession." In *Fluid Arguments: Five Centuries of Western Water Conflict,* ed. Char Miller. Tucson: University of Arizona Press, 2001.

———. *San Antonio de Béxar: A Community on New Spain's Northern Frontier.* Albuquerque: University of New Mexico Press, 1995.

———. "Spanish Colonial Texas." In *New Views of Borderlands History,* ed. Robert H. Jackson. Albuquerque: University of New Mexico Press, 1998.

Teja, Jesús F. de la, ed. *A Revolution Remembered: The Memoirs and Selected Correspondence of Juan N. Seguín.* 2d ed. Austin: Texas State Historical Association, 2002.

Teja, Jesús F. de la, and John Wheat. "Béxar: Profile of a Tejano Community, 1820–1832." *Southwestern Historical Quarterly* 89 (July 1983): 7–34.

"Texas Values/Texas Future." *Proceedings of the Annual Meeting at Austin, December 3–5, 1999.* Austin: The Philosophical Society of Texas, 2002.

Thomas, Alfred B. *Teodoro de Croix and the Northern Frontier of New Spain, 1776–1783.* Norman: University of Oklahoma Press, 1941.

Thompson, Jerry. *Mexican Texans in the Union Army.* El Paso: Texas Western Press, 1986.

———. *Vaqueros in Blue and Gray.* Austin: Presidial, 1976.

Thompson, Jerry, ed. *Civil War in the Southwest: Recollections of the Sibley Brigade.* College Station: Texas A&M University Press, 2001.

Thonhoff, Robert H. *El Fuerte del Cíbolo: Sentinel of the Béxar-La Bahía Ranches.* Austin: Eakin Press, 1992.

Tijerina, Andrés. *Tejano Empire: Life on the South Texas Ranchos.* College Station: Texas A&M Press, 1998.

———. *Tejanos and Texas Under the Mexican Flag, 1821–1836.* College Station: Texas A&M University Press, 1994.

Timmons, W. H. *El Paso: A Borderlands History.* El Paso: Texas Western Press, 1990.

———. "The El Paso Area in the Mexican Period, 1821–1848." *Southwestern Historical Quarterly* 84 (July 1980): 1–28.

Tjarks, Alicia V. "Comparative Demographic Analysis of Texas, 1777–1793." *Southwestern Historical Quarterly* 77 (January 1974): 291–338.

Tolleson-Rinehart, Sue, and Jeanie R. Stanley. *Claytie and the Lady: Ann Richards, Gender, and Politics in Texas.* Austin: University of Texas Press, 1994.

Tous, Gabriel, trans. "The Espinosa-Olivares-Aguirre Expedition of 1709." In *Preparing the Way: Preliminary Studies of the Texas Catholic Historical Society I.* Austin: Texas Catholic Historical Society, 1997.

———. "Ramón Expedition: Espinosa's Diary of 1716." In *Preparing the Way: Preliminary Studies of the Texas Catholic Historical Society I.* Austin: Texas Catholic Historical Society, 1997.

Turner, Elizabeth Hayes. *Women, Culture and Community: Religion and Reform in Galveston, 1880–1920.* New York: Oxford University Press, 1997.

Turner, Ellen Sue, and Thomas R. Hester. *A Field Guide to Stone Artifacts of Texas Indians.* Austin: Texas Monthly Press, 1985.

Utley, Robert M. *Lone Star Justice: The First Century of the Texas Rangers.* New York: Oxford University Press, 2002.

Vega, Garcilaso de la. *The Florida of the Inca.* Trans. and eds. John Grier Varner and Jeannette Johnson Varner. Austin: University of Texas Press, 1980.

Vigness, David M. *Spanish Texas, 1519–1810.* Boston: American Press, 1983.

Vincent, V. A. "The Frontier Soldier: Life in the *Provincias Internas* and the Royal Regulations of 1772, 1766–1787," *Military History of the Southwest* 22 (spring 1992): 1–14.

Walker, Donald. "Governor Preston E. Smith." *West Texas Historical Association Yearbook* 75 (1999): 6–17.

Wallace, Ernest, and E. Adamson Hoebel. *The Comanches: Lords of the South Plains.* Norman: University of Oklahoma Press, 1952.

Wallace, Ernest, David M. Vigness, and George B. Ward. *Documents of Texas History.* 1963. Reprint, Austin: State House Press, 1994.

Walsh, Patrick J. "Living on the Edge of the Neutral Zone: Varieties of Identity in Nacogdoches, Texas, 1773–1810." *East Texas Historical Journal* 37 (1999): 3–24.

Warren, Harris G. *The Sword Was Their Passport: A History of American Filibustering in the Mexican Revolution.* Baton Rouge: Louisiana State University Press, 1943.

Weaver, John D. *Brownsville Raid.* 1973. Reprint, College Station: Texas A&M University Press, 1992.

Weber, David J. *The Spanish Frontier in North America.* New Haven: Yale University Press, 1992.

Weddle, Robert S. *The French Thorn: Rival Explorers in the Spanish Sea, 1682–1762.* College Station: Texas A&M University Press, 1991.

———. *San Juan Bautista: Gateway to Spanish Texas.* Austin: University of Texas Press, 1968.

———. *The San Saba Mission: Spanish Pivot in Texas.* Austin: University of Texas Press, 1964.

———. *Spanish Sea: The Gulf of Mexico in North American Discovery, 1500–1685.* College Station: Texas A&M University Press, 1985.

———. *Wilderness Manhunt: The Spanish Search for La Salle.* Austin: University of Texas Press, 1973.

———. *The Wreck of the* Belle, *the Ruin of La Salle.* College Station: Texas A&M University Press, 2001.

Weems, John Edward. *Dream of Empire: A Human History of the Republic of Texas, 1836–1846.* New York: Simon & Schuster, 1976.

Whisenhunt, Donald W. *The Depression in Texas: The Hoover Years.* New York: Garland Publishing Co., 1983.

Whisenhunt, Donald W., ed. *Texas: A Sesquicentennial Celebration.* Austin: Eakin Press, 1984.

Willoughby, Larry. *Texas, Our Texas.* Austin: Holt, Rinehart and Winston, 1993.

Wilson, Maurine T., and Jack Jackson. *Philip Nolan and Texas: Expeditions to the Unknown Land.* Waco: Texian Press, 1987.

Winders, Richard Bruce. *Crisis in the Southwest: The United States, Mexico, and the Struggle Over Texas.* Wilmington, Del.: SR Books, 2002.

Winegarten, Ruthe. *Black Texas Women: A Sourcebook.* Austin: University of Texas Press, 1996.

———. *Texas Women: A Pictorial History, from Indians to Astronauts.* Austin: University of Texas Press, 1986.

Winegarten, Ruthe, and Sharon Kahn. *Brave Black Women: From Slavery to the Space Shuttle.* Austin: University of Texas Press, 1997.

Wooster, Ralph A. *Lone Star Generals in Gray.* Austin: Eakin Press, 2000.

———. *Texas and Texans in the Civil War.* Austin: Eakin Press, 1996.

Wooster, Ralph A., and Robert A. Calvert. *Texas Vistas: Selections from the Southwestern Historical Quarterly.* Austin: Texas State Historical Association, 1980.

Wooster, Robert. *Soldiers, Suttlers, and Settlers: Garrison Life on the Texas Frontier.* College Station: Texas A&M University Press, 1987.

Zamora, Emilio. *World of the Mexican Worker in Texas.* College Station: Texas A&M University Press, 1993.

Index